Antonio's Grace

Book 2 of The Antonio's Series

Yasmin Tirado-Chiodini

Antonio's Grace

Book 2 of The Antonio's Series

Yasmin Tirado-Chiodini

Black Hammock Books
Black Hammock Enterprises, LLC
Oviedo, Florida, U.S.A.
www.blackhammockbooks.com

ANTONIO'S GRACE is Book 2 of The Antonio's Series. It is a work of non-fiction containing enhanced photos of selected unpublished historical documents, document transcriptions and translations, factual information, newspaper clips, and author commentary and analysis that supplement the historical fiction novel ANTONIO's WILL by Yasmin Tirado-Chiodini. The commentary and analysis in ANTONIO'S GRACE represent the opinion of the author. ANTONIO'S GRACE is written as an independent book that is part of a series. As such, the reader will benefit from reading ANTONIO'S WILL before reading ANTONIO'S GRACE.

For permission requests, please address the Publisher at:

Black Hammock Enterprises, LLC
P.O. Box 622249
Oviedo, FL 32762
e-mail: info@blackhammockbooks.com
www.blackhammockbooks.com
Book's website: www.antoniosgrace.com

Published in 2015 by Black Hammock Enterprises, LLC
Paperback ISBN: 978-0-9817307-9-0
e-book ISBN: 978-0-9817307-8-3

12 11 10 9 8 7 6 5 4 3 2 1

Dedication

To What is Right

Author's translation of letter from citizens of Ponce, Puerto Rico (in back cover):

Nov[ember] 20 of 1915

Mr. Charles S. Whitman
Albany - New York
U.S.A.

The signatories, neighbors of the City of Ponce, P[uerto] Rico, and moved by the feeling of mercy, come before [Your Honor], imploring the pardon for the disgraced young man, Antonio Pontón.

We do not doubt that [Your Honor] would concede our request, and with the pardon of our compatriot, [Your Honor] will give an example of love and charity, akin to George Washington, who was never deaf before those who prayed for his clemency in a matter such as the one before us.

Sincerely,

José Barroas, Luis Valeón, A. Meléndez, Cantalicio Polanco, Zoilo Brita, J. Vázquez ...

Contents

List of Figures

"The death penalty is wrong because it lowers us all; it is a surrender to the worst that is in us; it uses ... official power to kill by execution–that has never elevated a society, never brought back a life, never inspired anything but hate.

There is absolutely no good reason to believe that using death as a punishment today is any better an answer now than it was in the past–when New York State had it, used it, regretted it and discarded it.

Because death penalty proponents have no other way to defend this policy, they cling unabashedly to the blunt simplicity of the ancient impulse that has always spurred the call for death: the desire for revenge."

- *Mario Cuomo, Governor of New York from 1983 to 1994,*
(Cuomo, 2011)

Prologue

How relevant are the voices of the past? Many refuse to listen. *"Why look back? Why not just focus on the present, or the future? ... Leave the past alone!"* Historical deafness comes at a great cost. Too often, it is the deciding factor between life and death.

How relevant? The U.S. Justice System relies on historical precedent. At its core is the U.S. Constitution, originally drafted in 1787. Its artisans are long gone, but the essence of their intent endures through the ages. In the course of adopting every constitutional amendment, legislators time-travel to interpret the drafters' thoughts, their *original intent*. Courts are bound to safeguard the rights afforded by this historical document. Yet, this pillar of justice has been fractured more than once.

Some people have more equal rights than others.

On January 7, 1916 José Antonio Pontón Santiago (Antonio Pontón), a Puerto Rican student at Albany Law School who suffered from mental illness, was executed in the electric chair at the Sing Sing Prison in Ossining, New York. His story of injustice is detailed in the historical novel *Antonio's Will* (Tirado-Chiodini, 2014). He is not the only human being who has been executed wrongfully. Over 600 men and women have succeeded him in this dreadful fate of execution, in the state of New York alone. There is no certainty of how many of them were innocent or suffered from mental illness. However, a study of modern-day wrongful convictions suggests 4.1 percent of those sentenced to death are innocent. (Gross, O'Brien, & Huc, 2014). In addition, Dr. Amos O. Squire, Sing Sing Chief Physician at the time of Pontón's execution, stated that during his tenure there, "I saw men executed who were certainly mentally unbalanced ... and who ... should not have been electrocuted" (Squire, 1935, p. 160).

The case of Antonio Pontón, along with the history surrounding it,

3

is as relevant today as it was in 1915. If we dared to look back, we would learn a shocking truth: The same factors of injustice that robbed Antonio Pontón of his constitutional rights a century ago are still extant in our society.

The death penalty was an abomination then, and it is so now. When comparing the past failures in Pontón's murder case with today's capital punishment system, its inherent bias, and its recurrent errors, a vivid image emerges. It shows us that–as a nation–the United States remains behind the rest of the civilized world in this medieval practice.

The historical novel *Antonio's Will* and this book, *Antonio's Grace*, unearth the pain and suffering of a century-old tragedy in an attempt to not only right a past wrong, but also to raise awareness and condemn the atrocity of the death penalty. *Antonio's Will* tells the story of those affected by the tragedy in a historical background spanning three countries and over one hundred years. *Antonio's Grace* embraces the cries of an entire island for a native son. It gives a forum to the voices of those who joined together to save a man carrying the burden of mental illness from being electrocuted. These voices of history return after a century to plead grace once again.

Antonio's Grace presents a selection of the thousands of documents found by this author, containing the clemency writings endorsed by over 21,000 people who prayed in vain for grace for Pontón. Among these are Pontón's own children, relatives, government officials, doctors, lawyers, prison wardens, community and religious organizations and leaders, university students, women, men, and school children. As with the U.S. Constitution, these historical documents cradle the original intent of drafters who are no longer with us. It is embedded in their words and signatures. Their feelings of sorrow, desperation and unfounded faith in justice lay dormant in boxes for a century. They all converge in their messages: *Spare the life of a sick man. ... Society does not attain justice by executing a human being. ... Revenge is not the answer. ... The death penalty is uncivilized and barbaric.*

How relevant are the voices of the past? They are crucial. They deliver fundamental checks and balances that calibrate our thoughts and actions. We must listen to the voices of history, so we can evolve and correct course. Ignoring them has a high price: A society that will replay history at its worst and will continue to be haunted by injustice.

4

One

Flashback of a Tragedy

O n October 2, 1914, Antonio Pontón, a former Albany Law School student, stabbed Bessie S. Kromer to death and then attempted suicide. She was his girlfriend of over three years, a grade school teacher of Dutch ancestry born in the town of Schoharie, Schenectady County, New York. He was the son of a prominent tobacco planter from the town of Comerío, Puerto Rico, and the first in his family to attend a university in the United States. **Figure 1** shows a photo of the couple in Coney Island.

Figure 1. Antonio Pontón and his girlfriend Bessie S. Kromer in Coney Island. Enhanced image from source. (Schenectady Gazette, 1914a).

In 1912, Antonio Pontón entered Albany Law School in New York, set to graduate with the Class of 1915, depicted in **Figure 2.**

Figure 2. Albany Law School Class of 1915. It is uncertain whether Antonio Pontón is in this photograph, as student names were unavailable from the source for this photo. However, he may be the man identified within the circle. Enhanced photo from original courtesy of Albany Law School. (Albany Law School, 1915).

Pontón fell in love with his English tutor Bessie S. Kromer while boarding at her house in Schoharie a year before entering law school. A serious relationship ensued. The couple had been together for over three years, appeared to have secured an apartment to move in together, and were planning to marry. Evidence presented at the murder trial revealed that Antonio Pontón's and Bessie Kromer's relationship had turned into a rollercoaster, leading to his attempting suicide some time before the incident. This was due in part to Mrs. Nora Kromer's pressures on her daughter Bessie to leave "The Spaniard," as she called Pontón. The situation worsened with Pontón's progressive mental illness, the stress of law school, and Mrs. Kromer's unsuccessful attempts to sever the relationship. **Figure 3** shows Bessie Kromer with her mother and grandmother.

Figure 3. From left to right, Bessie S. Kromer, her grandmother, and her mother, Nora Kromer. Enhanced image from source. (Schenectady Gazette, 1915a).

On September of 1914, Mrs. Kromer filed for a protective order and had Pontón arrested for allegedly carrying a revolver, which was never found in his possession or home. A search of his apartment revealed he had brass knuckles stored in a locked trunk, and this was basis for a discretionary police arrest under the 1911 *Sullivan Law* of New York. This new law was criticized for being discriminatory against immigrants. (Carter, 2012). Pontón was jailed, and his bail was set at $500, a very high amount for the time. The arrest resulted in Pontón being expelled from Albany Law School. Embarrassed at having lost it all, and highly depressed, Pontón purchased a knife, wrote suicide letters to friends and family, and took the train to see

Bessie Kromer. Their encounter resulted in her murder and his suicide attempt.

Figure 4 shows a composite of some of the sensational murder newspaper headlines that immediately followed. This was one of the most gruesome crimes committed in Schenectady County in 24 years.

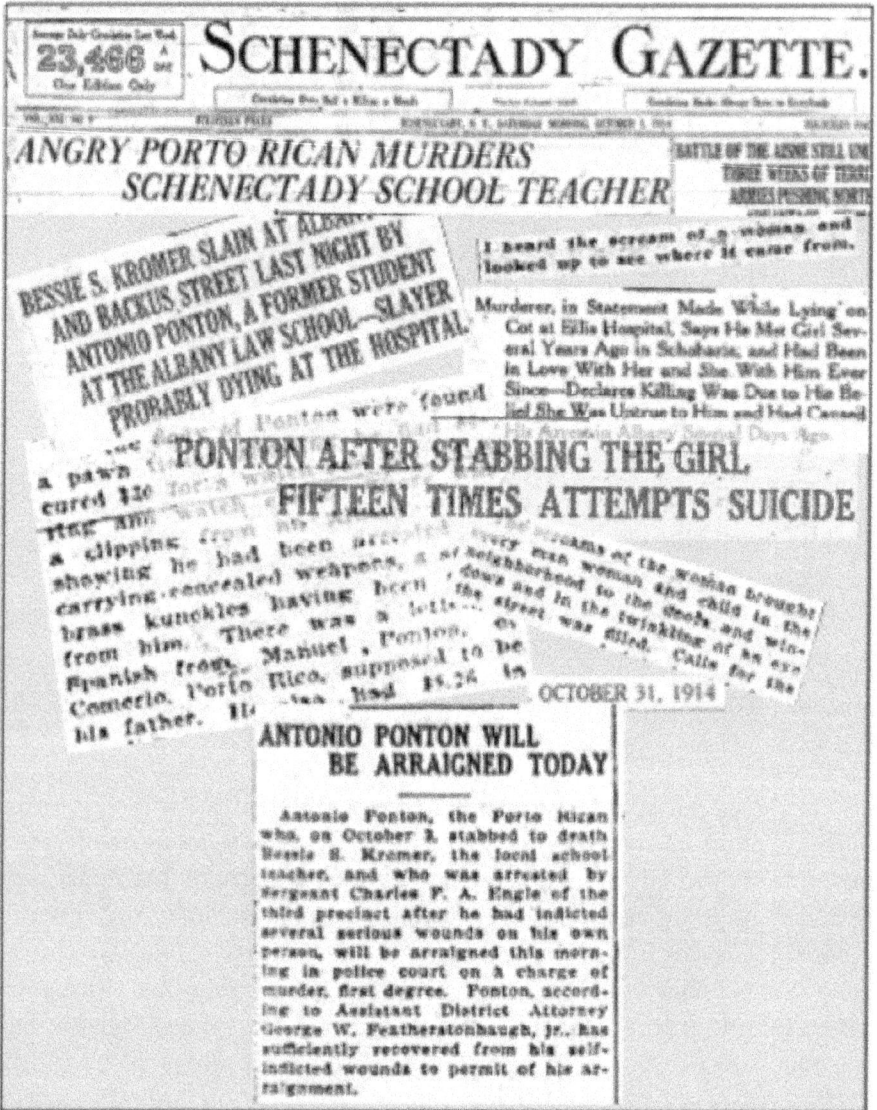

Figure 4. Composite image from selected newspaper headlines. (Schenectady Gazette, 1914a, 1914b).

Pontón surprisingly recovered from three stab wounds he inflicted on himself after slaying Bessie Kromer. One missed his heart by an inch. **Figure 5** shows the cover of Pontón's Grand Jury Indictment filed by Schenectady District Attorney Alexander T. Blessing on December 14, 1914. The trial date was set for April 19, 1915.

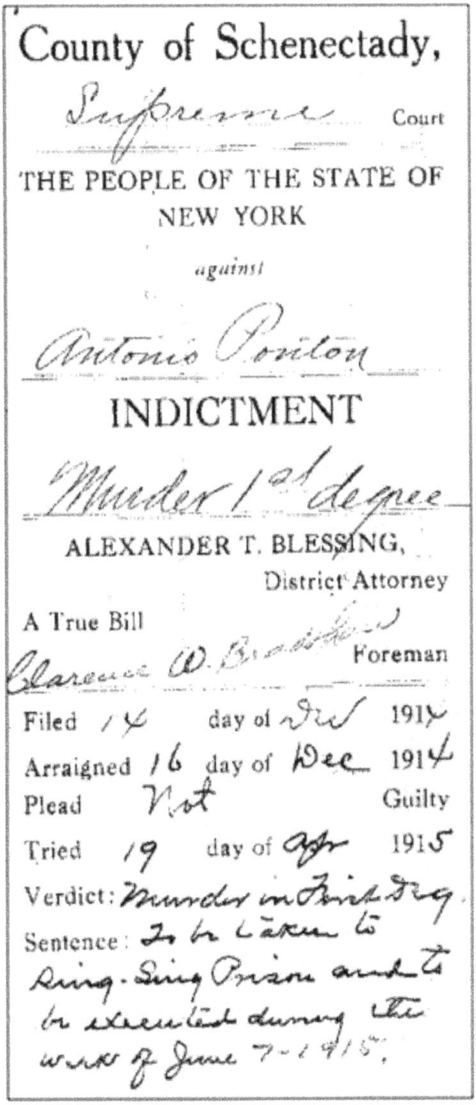

County of Schenectady,

Supreme Court

THE PEOPLE OF THE STATE OF NEW YORK

against

Antonio Ponton

INDICTMENT

Murder 1st degree

ALEXANDER T. BLESSING,
District Attorney

A True Bill

Clarence W. B[illegible] Foreman

Filed 14 day of Dec 1914

Arraigned 16 day of Dec 1914

Plead Not Guilty

Tried 19 day of Apr 1915

Verdict: Murder in First Deg.

Sentence: To be taken to Sing-Sing Prison and to be executed during the week of June 7-1915.

Figure 5. Cover of Indictment filed by Schenectady District Attorney Alexander T. Blessing. Enhanced image from copy of original. (Schenectady District Attorney, 1914).

Unable to afford private counsel for his murder trial, Pontón was assigned two young public defenders with no experience in capital murder, Homer J. Borst and George B. Smith of the Borst & Smith law firm in Schenectady, New York. Andrew J. Nellis, a former judge from Albany with previous experience in defending capital murder cases, later joined as "Of Counsel" to the defense to assist the young lawyers with their legal representation.

The defense's theory was insanity: Pontón was insane at the time he committed the crime and did not know what he was doing, or that what he was doing was wrong. They sustained that he wanted to kill himself, but he killed Bessie S. Kromer in a momentary frenzy. In support of this theory, two defense medical expert witnesses testified that Pontón was insane when he committed murder. They declared that in addition to having a family history of mental illness, Pontón's blood test showed that he suffered from *neurosyphilis*, an incurable disease that had invaded his brain and rendered him insane.

In addition, the trial court granted the defense's request to authorize a *Puerto Rico Lunacy Commission* to gather evidence of insanity on Pontón's maternal family in Puerto Rico. The Government of Puerto Rico, Reverend Andrés Echevarría (the Pontón family priest), and Antonio Pontón's brother Sixto worked diligently to gather the necessary evidence. However, the information was delayed, and the trial court did not wait for its arrival to start the trial. The jury never saw the Commission's evidence of the family history of mental illness, although the defense presented some evidence to that effect via witness testimony. In addition, the prosecution introduced testimony about declarations made by Pontón to state doctors during state medical examinations, where Pontón made mention of his family history of mental illness.

While acknowledging that it was a fact that Pontón had *neurosyphilis*, Judge Charles C. Van Kirk mistakenly stated to the jury that the defense had advanced *no evidence of insanity*. This prevented the jurors from deciding the issue of insanity, which was an *issue of fact* for the jury to decide, not an *issue of law* for the judge to determine. This material court error, along with other critical mistakes, constitutional violations and factors of injustice during trial (discussed in detail in **Chapter Three**, ahead), sealed the fate of Pontón.

After dramatic scenes at the Schenectady Courthouse, on April

23, 1915, Antonio Pontón was convicted of murder in the first degree and sentenced to die by electrocution at the Sing Sing Prison in Ossining, New York. The execution was scheduled for the week of June 7, 1915. **Figure 6** presents a composite image of some of the newspaper headlines reporting on Pontón's trial and outcome.

The largest crowd and the most disgraceful scenes ever witnessed in the Schenectady county court house marked the yesterday afternoon session of the trial of Antonio Ponton for the alleged murder of Bessie S. Kromer. With every inch of seating space in the court room, both inside and outside the rail, filled with a crowd in which women formed at least half, another crowd of 300 or more surged about in the corridor. The stairway was packed, man...

Unruly Crowd, Unable to Secure Admittance, Creates Disturbance—Defense Swears Many Witnesses to Show Peculiarities of Defendant—Inherited Insanity, Aggravated by Disease, the Defense—May Seek Delay to Await Depositions—Expert Testimony Will Be Heard Today.

SCHENECTADY GAZETTE.

PONTON DOOMED TO DEATH IN CHAIR; GUILTY OF MURDER IN FIRST DEGREE; SCREAMS AT VERDICT, THEN IS CALM

PONTON MEANT TO MARRY KROMER GIRL

"Guilty of murder in the first degree, as charged," was the verdict returned at 6:36 o'clock last night in Supreme Court against Jose Antonio Ponton for slaying Bessie Kromer, the young Schenectady school teacher October 2. Justice Charles C. Van Kirk at once pronounced sentence of death in the electric chair at Sing Sing in the week beginning June 7. Aside from a scream when the verdict was announced and an excited statement to the court before sentence was passed, Ponton received his doom with self possession which was remarkable after the lack of control he has displayed during the week of the trial.

Figure 6. Composite image of selected newspaper headlines and coverage of Antonio Pontón's murder trial. (Schenectady Gazette, 1915b, 1915d).

Shortly after his sentence was entered, Pontón was transferred from the Schenectady Jail to the Sing Sing Prison in Ossining, New York, and was admitted on death row. **Figure 7** shows his Sing Sing Prison "Receiving Blotter."

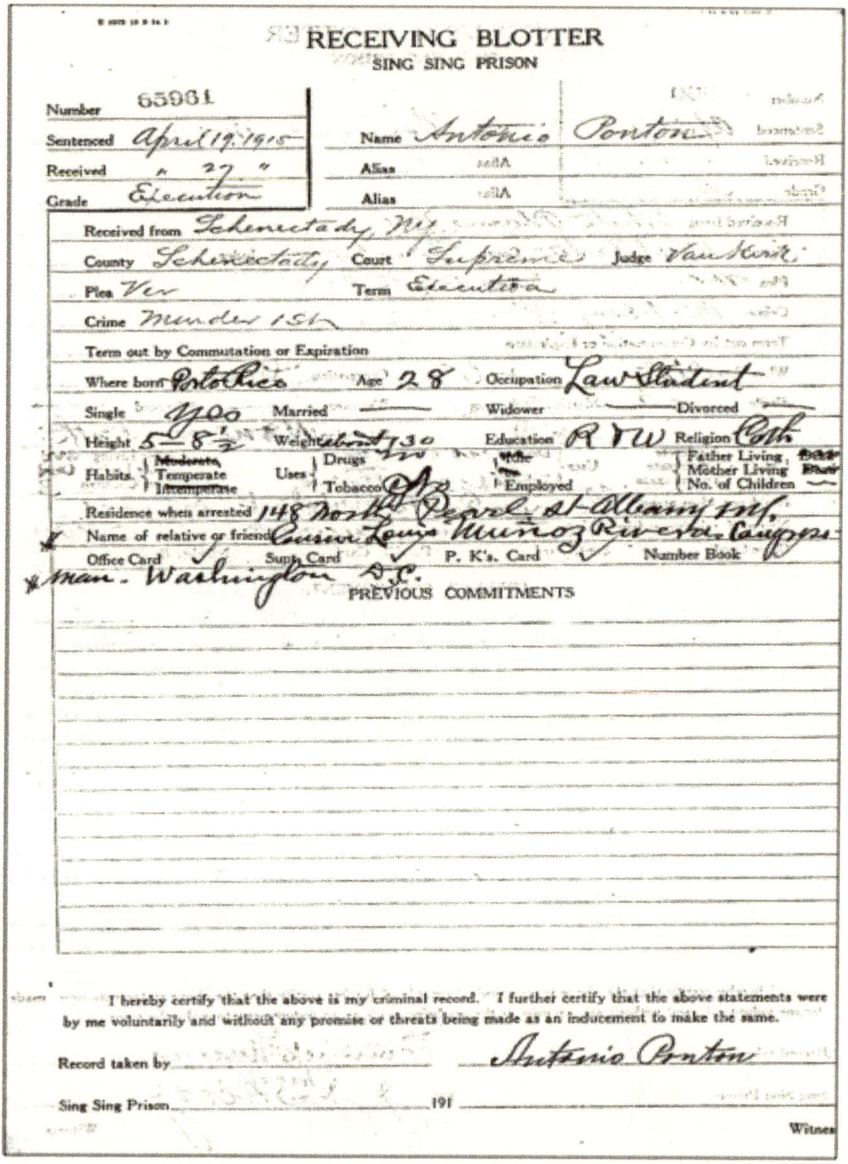

RECEIVING BLOTTER
SING SING PRISON

Number 65961
Sentenced April 19. 1915
Received " 27 "
Grade Execution
Name Antonio Ponton
Alias
Alias
Received from Schenectady, N.Y.
County Schenectady Court Supreme Judge Van Kirk
Plea Not
Term Execution
Crime Murder 1st
Term out by Commutation or Expiration
Where born Porto Rico Age 28 Occupation Law Student
Single Yes Married — Widower — Divorced —
Height 5-8½ Weight about 130 Education R W Religion Cath
Habits: Moderate, Temperate, Intemperate Uses: Drugs, Tobacco Employed Father Living, Mother Living, No. of Children
Residence when arrested 148 North Pearl St. Albany N.Y.
Name of relative or friend Cousin Louis Muñoz Rivera, Congressman, Washington D.C.
Office Card ✓ Supt. Card ✓ P. K's. Card ✓ Number Book

PREVIOUS COMMITMENTS

I hereby certify that the above is my criminal record. I further certify that the above statements were by me voluntarily and without any promise or threats being made as an inducement to make the same.

Record taken by ______ Antonio Ponton

Sing Sing Prison ______ 191 ______

Witness

Figure 7. Sing Sing Prison Receiving Blotter for Antonio Pontón. Enhanced photo of original document. (New York State, Dept. of Correctional Svcs., 1915).

In his "Receiving Blotter," under "Relative or Friend," Pontón listed the name of Puerto Rico's Resident Commissioner in U.S. Congress, Luis Muñoz Rivera, as his cousin. Indeed, as described in the novel *Antonio's Will*, Muñoz Rivera was Pontón's mother's cousin. **Figure 8** shows an aerial view of the Sing Sing Prison, where Pontón would live for eight months and nine days.

Figure 8. Aerial view of the Sing Sing Prison in Ossining, New York. Enhanced photo from source. (Library of Congress, George Grantham Bain Collection, 1920).

After Judge Van Kirk denied the defense's motions for a new trial, the next step for the defense was to file an appeal to the New York Court of Appeals. Pontón's appeal would include the Puerto Rico Lunacy Commission's new evidence of insanity that the trial jury never saw, as it had arrived and was now in the hands of the defense. The appeal postponed the initial date of execution set for June 7, 1915.

On October 29, 1915 the New York Court of Appeals affirmed the trial court without an opinion (People v. Ponton, 1915), despite the clear trial errors and the new evidence of mental illness that had been unavailable for consideration by the trial jury. The execution was now set for the week of December 20, 1915.

Grace appeared to be the only recourse left for Antonio Pontón.

$\mathcal{T}wo$

A Timeline for Antonio's Grace

On November 1, 1915, with the help of his lawyers and supporters, Antonio Pontón drafted a long and detailed letter to the Puerto Rican people, pouring out his heart. In his letter, Pontón begged his people to help him overcome a horrendous and inevitable fate in the electric chair, asked them to write to New York's Governor Charles S. Whitman, and requested they form a commission to secure grace on his behalf. He mailed the letter to Puerto Rico newspapers for publication, including the newspaper "La Democracia."

Figure 9 presents a copy of Antonio Pontón's letter in Spanish. The author's translation of Pontón's letter into English follows.

```
V O Z   D E   U N   C O N D E N A D O   A   M U E R T E

        C A R T A   D E   A N T O N I O   C O R T O N
PIDE A SUS COMPATRIOTAS Y HERMANOS PUERTORRIQUEÑOS QUE
        LE  S A L V E N   L A   V I D A

                        Correspondence Department.
                        Sin Sing Prison-

                        354 Hunter St.
                        Ossining St.

                                    N.Y.
```

(Continued)

Yasmin Tirado-Chiodini

Señor DIRECTOR DE "LA DEMOCRACIA"

San Juan, Puerto Rico.

Con el dolor más grande de mi alma dirijo a usted estas
lineas esperando de su amabilidad se sirva publicarlas
en su ilustrado periódico, dando a usted las gracias por
este favor.
El que esta lineas escribe es el desgraciado
puertorriqueño que hoy se encuentra en la Carcel de Sin
Sing Estado de Nueva York, sentenciado a muerte. El día
29 del pasado octubre según periodico del que le remito
a usted recorte e información de los abogados que actua
ron en mi defensa, dicha sentencia de muerte ha sido con
firmada por la Corte de Apelaciones de este Estado y el
proximo mes de diciembre a mediados de mes la vida me
será arrebatada. Si no obtengo misericordia del Gobernador de este Estado tendré que morir en la silla electrica, tendré que morir como un criminal, cuando solo soy
un desgraciado incapaz de contener los pensamientos que
a mi mente vienen porque algo en mi interior me impulsa
o me lanza a realizarlo.
Hasta el año 1911 permanecí en ese mi querido
Puerto Rico y mi vida fué una vida de amargura y sufri-
mientos, ninguna harmonia existió entre mis padres, hermanos y yo; ninguna existió entre la que fué mi buena es-
posa y yo, ninguna harmonia tuve con mis amigos. Todo
cuanto emprendía en busca de bienestar, fracasaba. Un
pensamiento ligero vino a mi mente de venir a este pais
a estudiar leyes. Ingresé en el Colegio "Albany Law
School" en la capital de este estado. En dicho colegio
tuve el honor de conocer a mis queridos compatriotas se
ñor Pedro Baiges, de Añasco; Vera y López de San German.
Creo que hoy se encuentran en esa despues de haber obte
nido cada uno de ellos el título de abogado. Ellos son
testigos de si obtuve tienfos o fracasos en mis estudios
Todo fué un fracaso para mí en el Colegio. Tampoco tuve
harmonia con ellos que podrá decir si es verdad o menti-
ra esto que escribo.
Un año antes de ingresar en el Colegio, estu-
ve en un pueblo pequeño, Schoharie, tomando clases de in-
gles. En este pueblo conocí la muger que robó el cariño
de mi corazon. Me sedujo de tal manera que solo era feliz cuando me encontraba a su lado. Varias veces intenté
cometer suicidio por ella. No puede explicar los pensamientos que a cada momento venian a mi mente, hasta el
extremo que hoy sabeis que me encuentro sentenciado a
muerte, esperando el momento fatal en que me quiten mi
vida en el proximo mes de diciembre, sí mi querido Puer-

(Continued)

16

(2)

Rico no es por mí, por-que me encuentro solo en este país.

Creeis vosotros puertorriqueños y damas puerto-rriqueñas que intencionalmente he manchado el buen - nombre de mi querido Puerto Rico? Creeis vosotros y vosotras que merezco morir en este país por medio de la silla alectrica? Si así lo creeis no hagais nada en absoluto por mí,dejadme morir, pero si creeis que no soy un criminal,sino un desgraciado, miembro de una familia desgraciada en la cual veinte y cinco han sufrido de enagenacion mental según datos adquiridos por el Reverendo Padre Andrés Echevarría,de Cayey, por favor os suplico que hagais algo por este desgraciado puertorriqueño y no me dejeis morir en este pais de - una manera tan cruel.Por favor hermanos puertorrique-ños, nombrad una comisión, como tambien para el gasto de abogado, para que venga aquí a trabajar con el Go-bernador del Estado la conmutación de mi sentencia,re-colectad por medio de subcriciones los gastos de un abogado para investigar los principales puntos de ena-genacion mental que yo he sufrido, los cuales no han sido presentados a la Corte y al Jurado que actuó en mi juicio.

Desde luego estos hechos deben ser llevados al Gobernador para que así vea si ha habido error y no justicia en mi causa. Me encuentro solo aquí y a uste-des queridos puertorriqueños y puertorriqueñas acudo en ruego para que se dirijan al Gobernador suplicando misericordia para mí/

Vosotras hermanas puertorriqueñas,acudid todas como si fueseis una sola enviada al Gobernador de este estado Mr. Charles S. Whitman,peticiones firmadas por el mayor número posible pidiendo la conmutación de mi sentencia,vosotras podeis hacer mucho por mí,porque vuestra voz es siempre oida,vosotras podeis tocar el corazón del Gobernador para que así extiendasu mano mi sericordiosa sobre mí,vosótras sois mi mayor esperanza y a vosotras os suplico como hermano desgraciado que hagan este acto humanitario,tenedme como si fuera uno de vuestros propios hermanos y luchad por mi vida,no me dejeis morir de una manera tan cruel, acordaos voso-tras de que teneis hermanos,sed por mí.

(Continued)

En vosotros y vosotras hermanas puertorriquenas
yo grabo todas mis esperanzas y confió que no me dejeis solo en estos dias de tristeza para mí y mi familia, en vosotros y vosotras confió que obtengais la -
commutación de la sentencia,porque no soy digno de mo-
riri de esa manera tan cruel;no soy culpable; si fuese
merecedor de ese castigo no os molestaría; nada os di-
ría, no elevaría a ustedes mi suplica de que seais por
mí y salveis mi vida, moriria como un hombre sin decir
una palabra, pero a ustedes acudo porque Dios solo sa-
be que no merezco morir en una silla electrica, por lo
tanto os ruego de todo corazón que me salveis la vida.

Todo cuanto hagais por mí tiene que ser de un
modo urgentísimo,porque solo seis semanas desde hoy no
viembre primera tengo de vida y todos los trabajos de
peticiones firmada por el mayor número posible de da-
más de cada pueblo y peticiones firmadas por el mayor
número de vosotros de toda la isla,tienen que estar he
chas antes de estas seis semanas. Deseo que nombreis
en la Comisión que venga al Reverendo Padre Andres -
Echevarría, de Cayey, y que esta comisión que vosotros
nombreis sea una al Señor Luis Muños Rivera,Residente
en Washinton, para que todos unidos trabajen y luchen
la conmutación de mi sentencia. No les mencioné mi familia porque desde luego espero y confió que mi querido hermano Sixto venga para que represente a la fami-

(3)

lia ante el Gobernador. Sed por mi queridos hermanos
puertorriqueños y luchad por este desgraciado,que se
encuentra solo en este país, sin que nadie sea por él.

En vosotros yo deposito todas mis esperanzas.
No me dejen solo, no me dejen solo/

ANTONIO PONTON

Figure 9. Antonio Pontón's Letter to Puerto Rico. (Tirado-Chiodini Collection, 1914-1916).

English translation of Antonio Pontón's letter:[1]

"THE VOICE OF A MAN CONDEMNED TO DIE
LETTER FROM ANTONIO CORTON (SIC)
ASKS HIS PUERTO RICAN COMPATRIOTS AND BROTHERS
[AND SISTERS] TO SAVE HIS LIFE

Correspondence Department
Sing Sing Prison
354 Hunter St.
Ossining, NY

Mr. Director of "La Democracia"
San Juan, Puerto Rico

With the greatest pain in my soul I direct these lines, hoping that out of kindness you would publish them in your illustrious newspaper, giving you thanks for this favor.

The one who writes these lines is the disgraced Puerto Rican who today finds himself at the Sing Sing Prison in the state of New York, sentenced to die. The 29th day of this past October, according to the newspaper clips that I remit to you here and the information from the lawyers who acted in my defense, said death sentence was confirmed by the Court of Appeals of this state, and the next month of December, in the middle of the month, my life will be raptured from me. If I do not obtain clemency from the Governor of the state, I will have to die in the electric chair. I will have to die like a criminal, when I am only a disgraced man incapable of containing my thoughts and the thoughts that come to my mind because something inside of me impulses me or thrusts me into acting.

I lived in my dear Puerto Rico until the year 1911, and my life was a life of bitterness and suffering. There was no harmony between my parents, brothers and I. None existed between the one who was my good wife and I, and no harmony did I have with my friends. Anything I undertook in a quest for success failed. A thought came in haste to my mind to come to this country to study law. I enrolled in the school "Albany Law School" in the capital of the state. And there I had the honor of knowing my compatriots, Mr. Pedro Beiges from the town of Añasco, Vera and López from San German. I believe that today they find themselves [in Puerto Rico], after having obtained each one of them the title of lawyer. They are witnesses to whether I obtained successes or failures in my studies. All was failure for me in the school. I also did not have harmony with them, who can say if it is true or a lie, this I write.

A year before enrolling in the school, I lived in a small town, Schoharie, taking English lessons. In this town I knew the woman who stole the love from my heart. She seduced me in such a way that I was only happy when I was by her side. Many times I tried to commit suicide because of her. I could not explain the thoughts that each moment would come to my mind, to the extreme that today you all know that I am sentenced to death, waiting for the fatal moment in which they steal the life away from me the next month of December, if my dear Puerto

[2]

Rico is not there for me, because I find myself alone in this country.

Do you believe Puerto Rican gentlemen and ladies that I intentionally tainted the good name of my dear Puerto Rico? Do you believe that I deserved to die in this country in the electric chair? If you so believe, do not do absolutely anything for me. Let me die. But if you believe that I am not a criminal, but a disgraced man, a member of a disgraced family in which twenty five have suffered of mental illness, according to data acquired by the Reverend Father Andrés Echevarría of Cayey, please, I beg you, that you do something for this disgraced Puerto Rican, and not let me die in this country in such a cruel manner. Please, Puerto Rican sisters and brothers, name a commission, also to afford legal expenses, to come here to work with the Governor of the State in the commutation of my sentence. Collect by means of subscriptions the [funds to pay for the] expense of an attorney to investigate the main points of my mental alienation, which have not been presented in the court or [to] the jury that served in my case.

Of course, these facts must be brought before the Governor so that he can see if there has been an error, and not justice, in my cause. I find myself alone here, and I come to you Puerto Rican men and women, begging you to address the Governor and plead for mercy for me/

You, Puerto Rican sisters, join together as one to send petitions to the Governor of this state, Mr. Charles S. Whitman, signed by the greatest number possible, asking for the commutation of my sentence. You can do much for me, because your voices are always heard. You can touch the heart of the Governor, so that he can extend his hand of mercy over me. You are my greatest hope, and to you I plead as a disgraced brother that you perform this humanitarian act, have me as one of your own brothers and fight for my life. Don't let me die in such a cruel manner, remember you have brothers, be there for me.

In you, Puerto Rican brothers and sisters, I engrave all my hopes and trust that you will not leave me alone in these days of sorrow for me and for my family. In you I trust to obtain the commutation of the sentence because I don't deserve to die in this manner, so cruel; I am not guilty. If I deserved this punishment, I would not bother you. I would not say anything. I would not raise to you my prayer to ask you to be there for me and save my life. I would die like a man, without uttering a word, but I come to you because God only knows that I do not deserve to die in an electric chair. Thus, I beg you with all my heart to save my life.

All that you do for me must be in the most urgent manner, because starting today, November first, I only have six weeks of life left and all the work towards petitions signed by the greatest amount of people throughout the island have to be submitted before these six weeks. I wish that Father Echevarría, of Cayey, be named as a member of the commission that comes, and that the commission join Mr. Luis Muñoz Rivera, Commissioner Resident in New York, so that all together, they work and fight for the commutation of my sentence. I have not mentioned my family because I, of course, hope and trust that my dear brother, Sixto, comes to represent my fami-

[3]

ly before the Governor. Be there for me my dear Puerto Rican brothers and sisters and fight for this disgraced man, who finds himself alone in this country, without anyone.

I deposit all my hopes with you. Don't leave me alone, don't leave me alone/

ANTONIO PONTÓN
/s/"

As a result of Pontón's letter, as depicted in **Figure 10**, Puerto Ricans promptly organized in every island town and in the United States to plead Governor Whitman for grace. The governor received thousands of prayers on behalf of the condemned man.

Figure 10. Image composite of selected Puerto Rico newspaper clippings documenting the island-wide efforts for Antonio Pontón. (Tirado-Chiodini Collection, 1914-1916).

The "Mothers and Ladies of Comerío," from Pontón's hometown, appealed to Governor Whitman in a letter dated November 12, 1915. Dozens of signatures accompanied the petition (**Figure 11**).

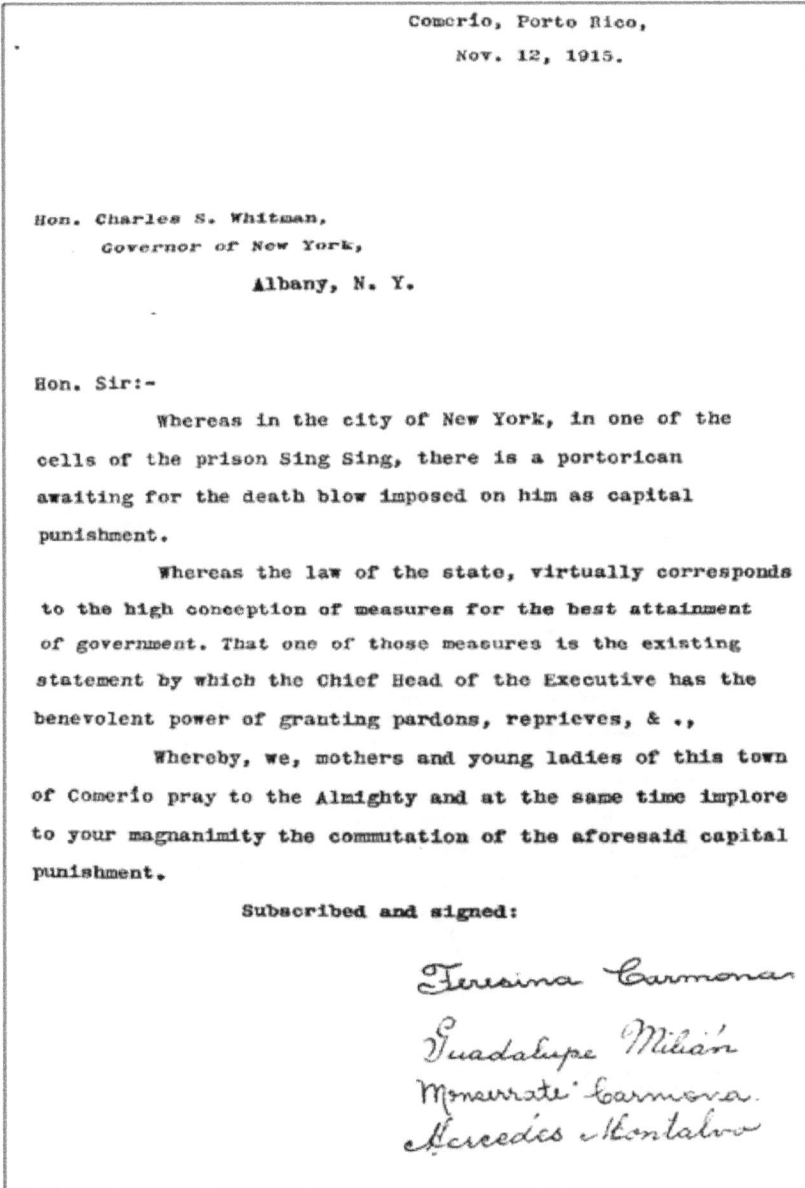

Comerío, Porto Rico,
Nov. 12, 1915.

Hon. Charles S. Whitman,
Governor of New York,
Albany, N. Y.

Hon. Sir:-

Whereas in the city of New York, in one of the cells of the prison Sing Sing, there is a portorican awaiting for the death blow imposed on him as capital punishment.

Whereas the law of the state, virtually corresponds to the high conception of measures for the best attainment of government. That one of those measures is the existing statement by which the Chief Head of the Executive has the benevolent power of granting pardons, reprieves, & .,

Whereby, we, mothers and young ladies of this town of Comerío pray to the Almighty and at the same time implore to your magnanimity the commutation of the aforesaid capital punishment.

Subscribed and signed:

Teresina Carmona
Guadalupe Milián
Monserrate Carmona
Mercedes Montalvo

Figure 11. Letter from the "Mothers and Ladies of Comerío," from Pontón's hometown. (Tirado-Chiodini Collection, 1914-1916).

The "Ladies of Puerto Rico" wrote to Governor Whitman on November 15, 1915, highlighting that Antonio Pontón was the first Puerto Rican to ever be executed in the electric chair. Over 3,000 signatures supported the letter (**Figure 12**).

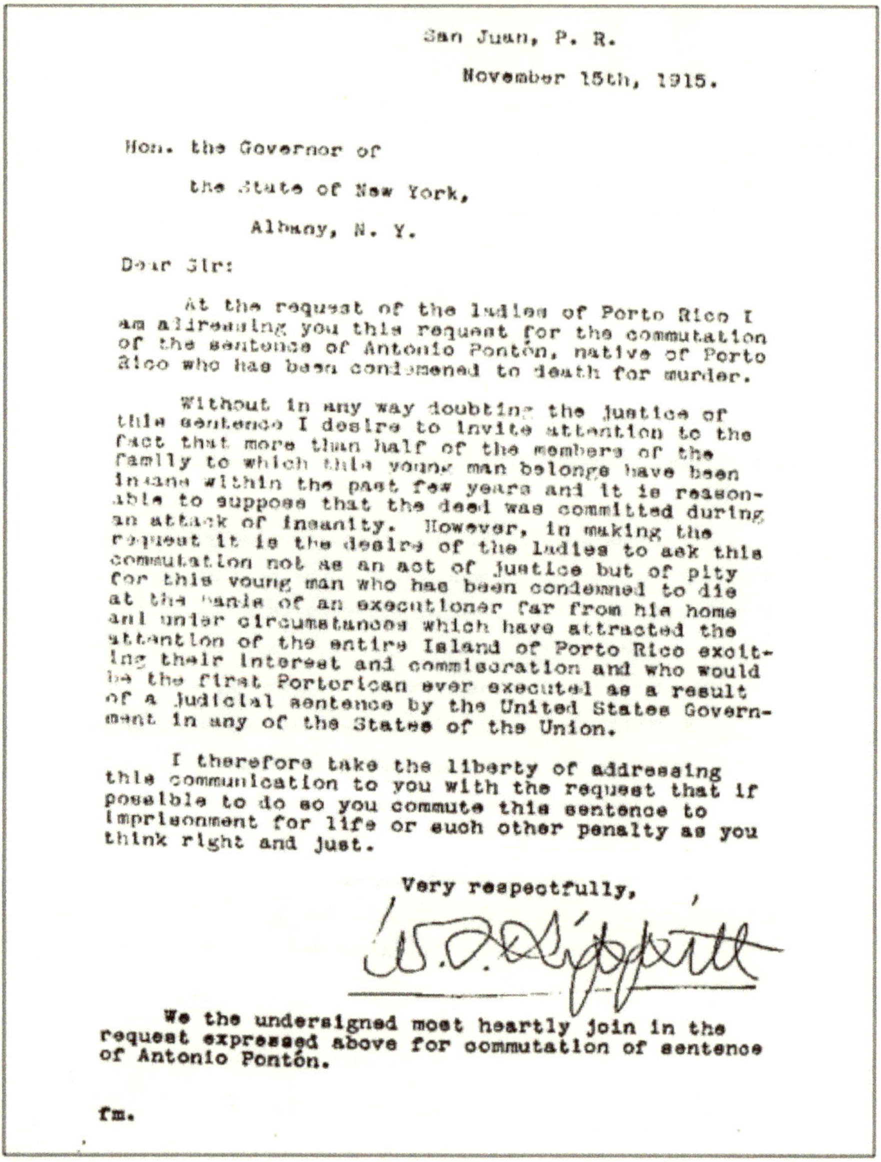

San Juan, P. R.

November 15th, 1915.

Hon. the Governor of

the State of New York,

Albany, N. Y.

Dear Sir:

At the request of the ladies of Porto Rico I am addressing you this request for the commutation of the sentence of Antonio Pontón, native of Porto Rico who has been condemned to death for murder.

Without in any way doubting the justice of this sentence I desire to invite attention to the fact that more than half of the members of the family to which this young man belongs have been insane within the past few years and it is reasonable to suppose that the deed was committed during an attack of insanity. However, in making the request it is the desire of the ladies to ask this commutation not as an act of justice but of pity for this young man who has been condemned to die at the hands of an executioner far from his home and under circumstances which have attracted the attention of the entire Island of Porto Rico exciting their interest and commiseration and who would be the first Portorican ever executed as a result of a judicial sentence by the United States Government in any of the States of the Union.

I therefore take the liberty of addressing this communication to you with the request that if possible to do so you commute this sentence to imprisonment for life or such other penalty as you think right and just.

Very respectfully,

We the undersigned most heartily join in the request expressed above for commutation of sentence of Antonio Pontón.

fm.

Figure 12. Clemency letter by "The Ladies of Puerto Rico," supported by over 3,000 signatures. (Tirado-Chiodini Collection, 1914-1916).

In their November 19, 1915 letter to Governor Whitman, the student group "Eco Estudiantil" from the town of Río Grande, Puerto Rico posed sound arguments against the death penalty, supported by hundreds of signatures (**Figure 13**).

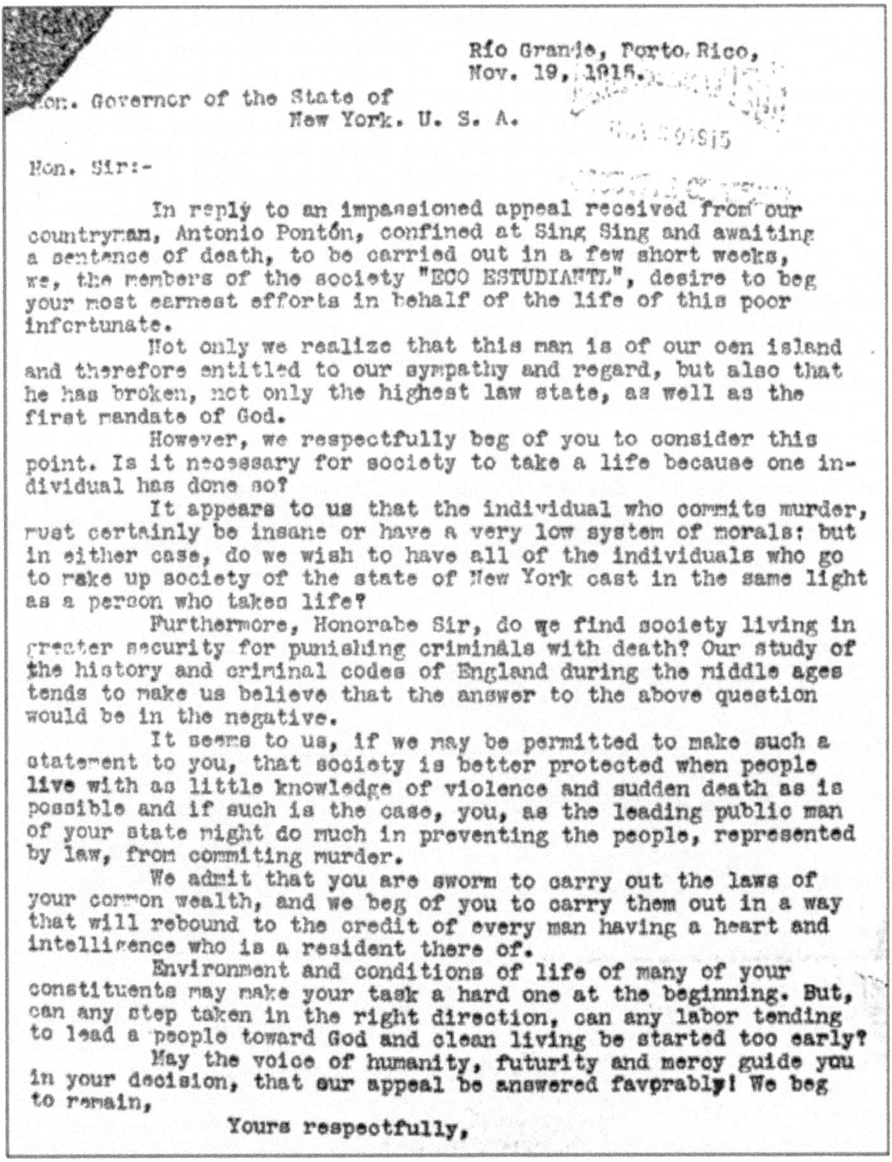

Río Grande, Porto. Rico,
Nov. 19, 1915.

Hon. Governor of the State of
New York. U. S. A.

Hon. Sir:-

      In reply to an impassioned appeal received from our countryman, Antonio Pontón, confined at Sing Sing and awaiting a sentence of death, to be carried out in a few short weeks, we, the members of the society "ECO ESTUDIANTIL", desire to beg your most earnest efforts in behalf of the life of this poor infortunate.
      Not only we realize that this man is of our own island and therefore entitled to our sympathy and regard, but also that he has broken, not only the highest law state, as well as the first mandate of God.
      However, we respectfully beg of you to consider this point. Is it necessary for society to take a life because one individual has done so?
      It appears to us that the individual who commits murder, must certainly be insane or have a very low system of morals; but in either case, do we wish to have all of the individuals who go to make up society of the state of New York cast in the same light as a person who takes life?
      Furthermore, Honorabe Sir, do we find society living in greater security for punishing criminals with death? Our study of the history and criminal codes of England during the middle ages tends to make us believe that the answer to the above question would be in the negative.
      It seems to us, if we may be permitted to make such a statement to you, that society is better protected when people live with as little knowledge of violence and sudden death as is possible and if such is the case, you, as the leading public man of your state might do much in preventing the people, represented by law, from commiting murder.
      We admit that you are sworn to carry out the laws of your common wealth, and we beg of you to carry them out in a way that will rebound to the credit of every man having a heart and intelligence who is a resident there of.
      Environment and conditions of life of many of your constituents may make your task a hard one at the beginning. But, can any step taken in the right direction, can any labor tending to lead a people toward God and clean living be started too early?
      May the voice of humanity, futurity and mercy guide you in your decision, that our appeal be answered favorably! We beg to remain,

          Yours respectfully,

Figure 13. Letter to Governor Whitman from the student group "Eco Estudiantil." (Tirado-Chiodini Collection, 1914-1916).

On November 23, 1915, various grade schools from San Juan directed a letter to Whitman, appealing to the humanity of former U.S. Presidents Abraham Lincoln and George Washington. Hundreds of students signed the petition (**Figure 14**).

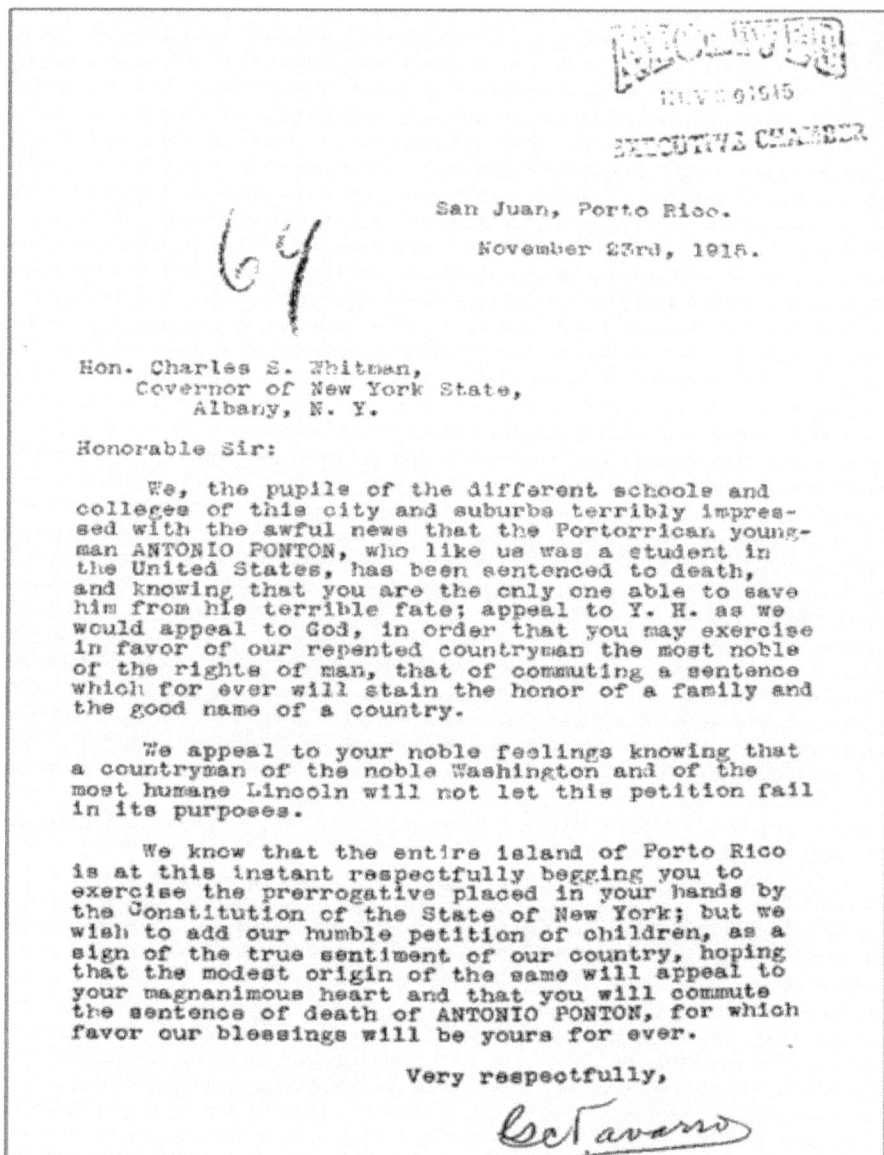

San Juan, Porto Rico.
November 23rd, 1915.

Hon. Charles S. Whitman,
    Governor of New York State,
        Albany, N. Y.

Honorable Sir:

    We, the pupils of the different schools and colleges of this city and suburbs terribly impressed with the awful news that the Portorrican youngman ANTONIO PONTON, who like us was a student in the United States, has been sentenced to death, and knowing that you are the only one able to save him from his terrible fate; appeal to Y. H. as we would appeal to God, in order that you may exercise in favor of our repented countryman the most noble of the rights of man, that of commuting a sentence which for ever will stain the honor of a family and the good name of a country.

    We appeal to your noble feelings knowing that a countryman of the noble Washington and of the most humane Lincoln will not let this petition fail in its purposes.

    We know that the entire island of Porto Rico is at this instant respectfully begging you to exercise the prerrogative placed in your hands by the Constitution of the State of New York; but we wish to add our humble petition of children, as a sign of the true sentiment of our country, hoping that the modest origin of the same will appeal to your magnanimous heart and that you will commute the sentence of death of ANTONIO PONTON, for which favor our blessings will be yours for ever.

            Very respectfully,

Figure 14. San Juan school students address Governor Whitman on behalf of Pontón. (Tirado-Chiodini Collection, 1914-1916).

Students from Fajardo High School compiled almost 3,000 signatures supporting their clemency petition, dated November 24, 1915 (**Figure 15**).

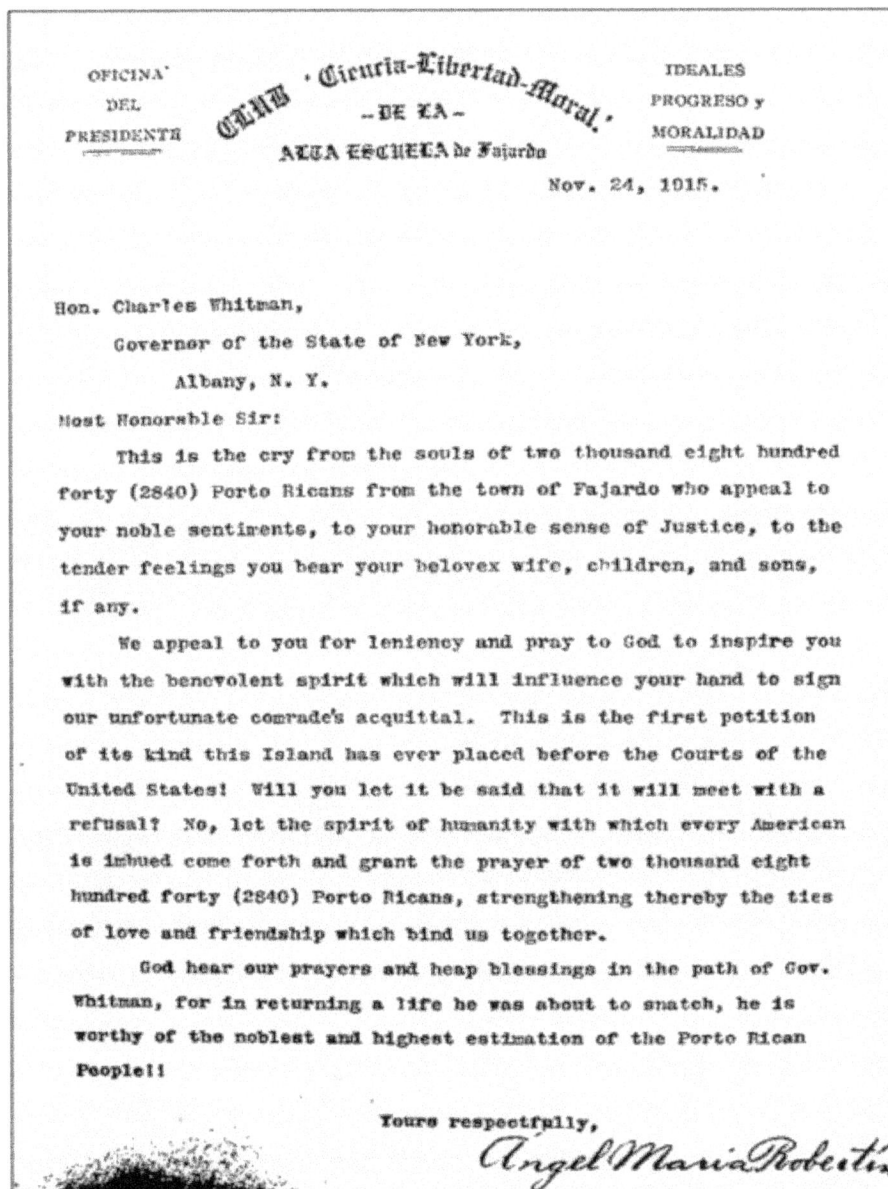

OFICINA
DEL
PRESIDENTE

· Ciencia-Libertad-Moral ·
-- DE LA --
ALTA ESCUELA De Fajardo

IDEALES
PROGRESO y
MORALIDAD

Nov. 24, 1915.

Hon. Charles Whitman,

    Governor of the State of New York,

      Albany, N. Y.

Most Honorable Sir:

    This is the cry from the souls of two thousand eight hundred forty (2840) Porto Ricans from the town of Fajardo who appeal to your noble sentiments, to your honorable sense of Justice, to the tender feelings you bear your belovex wife, children, and sons, if any.

    We appeal to you for leniency and pray to God to inspire you with the benevolent spirit which will influence your hand to sign our unfortunate comrade's acquittal. This is the first petition of its kind this Island has ever placed before the Courts of the United States! Will you let it be said that it will meet with a refusal? No, let the spirit of humanity with which every American is imbued come forth and grant the prayer of two thousand eight hundred forty (2840) Porto Ricans, strengthening thereby the ties of love and friendship which bind us together.

    God hear our prayers and heap blessings in the path of Gov. Whitman, for in returning a life he was about to snatch, he is worthy of the noblest and highest estimation of the Porto Rican People!!

          Yours respectfully,

          Angel Maria Robertí

Figure 15. Letter supported by almost 3,000 signatures from Fajardo High School students. (Tirado-Chiodini Collection, 1914-1916).

The "Porto Rico" Temperance League of the Church of Disciples of Christ appealed to the governor on the basis of Pontón's hereditary insanity, in their letter dated November 24, 1915 (**Figure 16**).

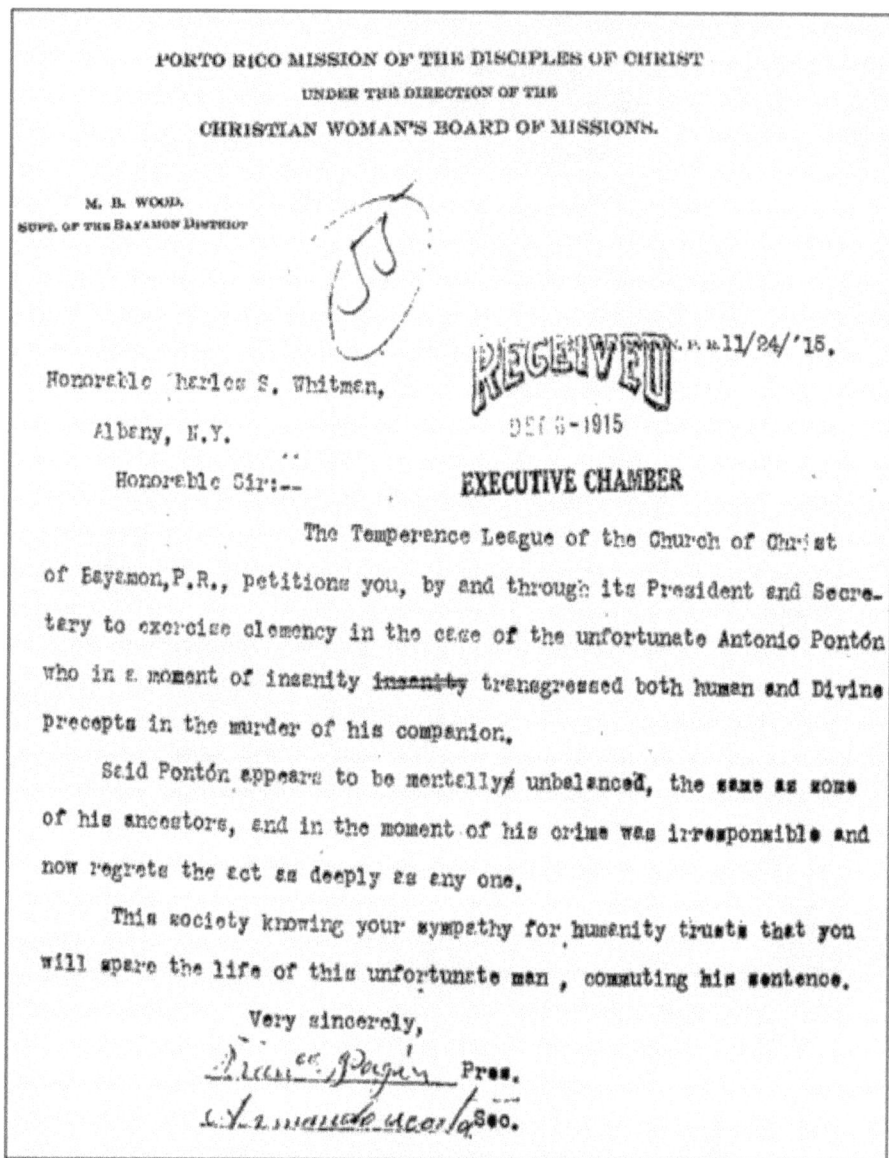

PORTO RICO MISSION OF THE DISCIPLES OF CHRIST

UNDER THE DIRECTION OF THE

CHRISTIAN WOMAN'S BOARD OF MISSIONS.

M. B. WOOD,
SUPT. OF THE BAYAMON DISTRICT

Honorable Charles S. Whitman,

Albany, N.Y.

Honorable Sir:—

RECEIVED P. R. 11/24/'15.

DEC 3 - 1915

EXECUTIVE CHAMBER

    The Temperance League of the Church of Christ of Bayamon, P.R., petitions you, by and through its President and Secretary to exercise clemency in the case of the unfortunate Antonio Pontón who in a moment of insanity ~~insanity~~ transgressed both human and Divine precepts in the murder of his companion.

    Said Pontón appears to be mentally unbalanced, the same as some of his ancestors, and in the moment of his crime was irresponsible and now regrets the act as deeply as any one.

    This society knowing your sympathy for humanity trusts that you will spare the life of this unfortunate man , commuting his sentence.

    Very sincerely,

Pres.

Sec.

Figure 16. Clemency letter from the "Porto Rico" Temperance League, Church of Disciples of Christ. (Tirado-Chiodini Collection, 1914-1916).

The entire family of Ulpiano Crespo, Pontón's Albany Law School classmate and friend, addressed Governor Whitman on Thanksgiving Day (**Figure 17**).

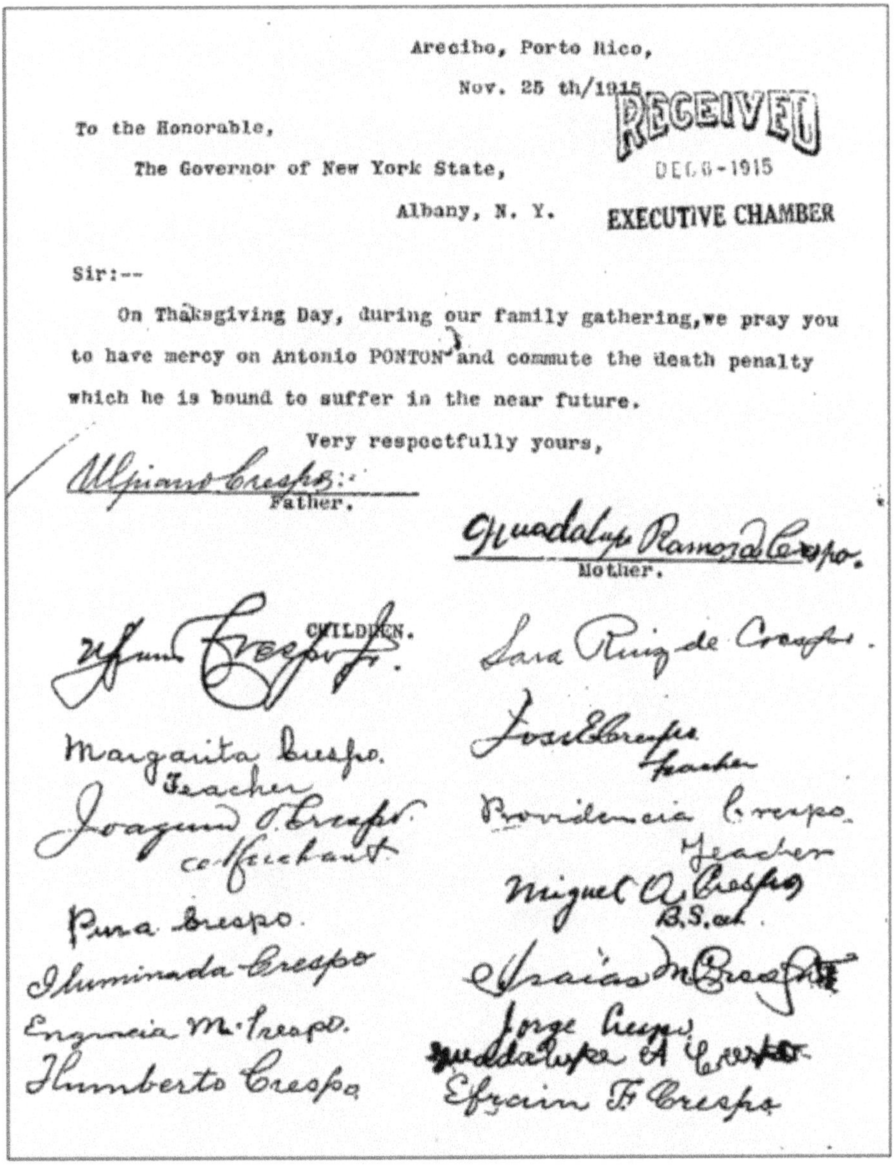

Arecibo, Porto Rico,

Nov. 25 th/1915

RECEIVED
DEC 6 - 1915
EXECUTIVE CHAMBER

To the Honorable,

The Governor of New York State,

Albany, N. Y.

Sir:--

On Thaksgiving Day, during our family gathering, we pray you to have mercy on Antonio PONTON and commute the death penalty which he is bound to suffer in the near future.

Very respectfully yours,

Ulpiano Crespo
Father.

Guadalupe Ramos de Crespo.
Mother.

CHILDREN.

Ulpiano Crespo Jr.

Sara Ruiz de Crespo.

Margarita Crespo.
Teacher

José E. Crespo
Teacher

Joaquín O. Crespo
Commerchant

Providencia Crespo.
Teacher

Miguel A. Crespo
B.S.

Pura Crespo.

Iluminada Crespo

Isaías M. Crespo

Engracia M. Crespo.

Jorge Crespo

Guadalupe A. Crespo

Humberto Crespo

Efraín F. Crespo

Figure 17. Ulpiano Crespo and his family request clemency for Antonio Pontón. (Tirado-Chiodini Collection, 1914-1916).

On November 26, 1915 Antonio Pontón's children, Antonio and Manolo, addressed Governor Whitman in an effort to save the life of their fallen father. A photograph of the children (**Figure 18**) accompanied the letter (**Figure 19**).

Figure 18. Photo of Antonio Pontón's children, Antonio and Manolo. (Tirado-Chiodini Collection, 1914-1916).

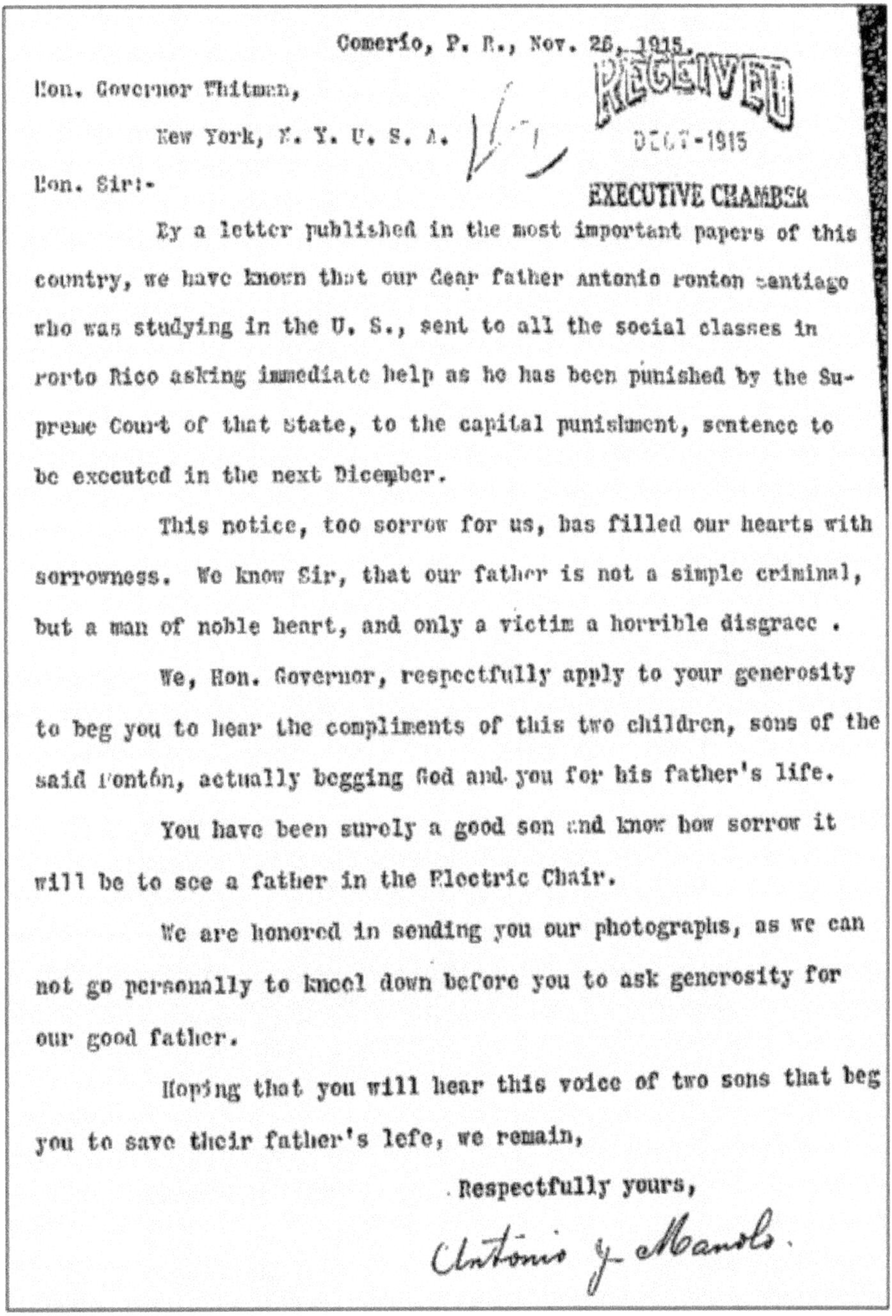

Comerío, P. R., Nov. 25, 1915.

Hon. Governor Whitman,

New York, N. Y. U. S. A.

Hon. Sir:-

RECEIVED

DEC 7-1915

EXECUTIVE CHAMBER

By a letter published in the most important papers of this country, we have known that our dear father Antonio Pontón Santiago who was studying in the U. S., sent to all the social classes in Porto Rico asking immediate help as he has been punished by the Supreme Court of that state, to the capital punishment, sentence to be executed in the next Dicember.

This notice, too sorrow for us, has filled our hearts with sorrowness. We know Sir, that our father is not a simple criminal, but a man of noble heart, and only a victim a horrible disgrace .

We, Hon. Governor, respectfully apply to your generosity to beg you to hear the compliments of this two children, sons of the said Pontón, actually begging God and you for his father's life.

You have been surely a good son and know how sorrow it will be to see a father in the Electric Chair.

We are honored in sending you our photographs, as we can not go personally to kneel down before you to ask generosity for our good father.

Hoping that you will hear this voice of two sons that beg you to save their father's lefe, we remain,

Respectfully yours,

Antonio y Manolo.

Figure 19. Clemency letter from Antonio Pontón's children to Governor Whitman. (Tirado-Chiodini Collection, 1914-1916).

Throughout Puerto Rico, town councils held meetings to secure formal resolutions to support their official petitions for clemency before Governor Whitman. The resolution in **Figure 20** is for the town of Yauco, signed by Mayor Domingo Antommattei and Secretary Manuel Troche on December 4, 1915. (A translation follows.)

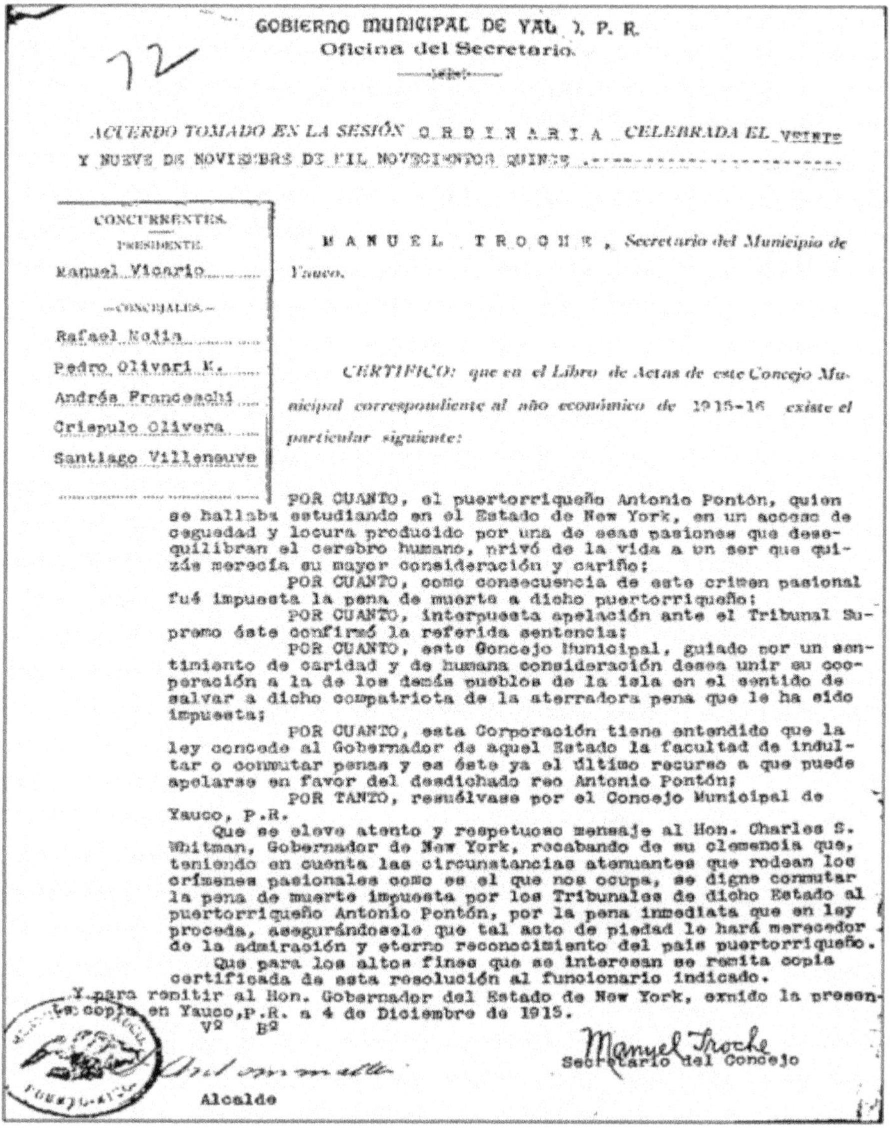

GOBIERNO MUNICIPAL DE YAU[C]O, P. R.
Oficina del Secretario.

72

ACUERDO TOMADO EN LA SESIÓN ORDINARIA CELEBRADA EL VEINTE Y NUEVE DE NOVIEMBRE DE MIL NOVECIENTOS QUINCE.

CONCURRENTES.
PRESIDENTE:
Manuel Vicario
—CONCEJALES.—
Rafael Mejía
Pedro Olivari M.
Andrés Franceschi
Crispulo Olivera
Santiago Villeneuve

MANUEL TROCHE, Secretario del Municipio de Yauco.

CERTIFICO: que en el Libro de Actas de este Concejo Municipal correspondiente al año económico de 1915-16 existe el particular siguiente:

POR CUANTO, el puertorriqueño Antonio Pontón, quien se hallaba estudiando en el Estado de New York, en un acceso de ceguedad y locura producido por una de esas pasiones que desequilibran el cerebro humano, privó de la vida a un ser que quizás merecía su mayor consideración y cariño;

POR CUANTO, como consecuencia de este crimen pasional fué impuesta la pena de muerte a dicho puertorriqueño;

POR CUANTO, interpuesta apelación ante el Tribunal Supremo éste confirmó la referida sentencia;

POR CUANTO, este Concejo Municipal, guiado por un sentimiento de caridad y de humana consideración desea unir su cooperación a la de los demás pueblos de la isla en el sentido de salvar a dicho compatriota de la aterradora pena que le ha sido impuesta;

POR CUANTO, esta Corporación tiene entendido que la ley concede al Gobernador de aquel Estado la facultad de indultar o conmutar penas y es éste ya el último recurso a que puede apelarse en favor del desdichado reo Antonio Pontón;

POR TANTO, resuélvase por el Concejo Municipal de Yauco, P.R.

Que se eleve atento y respetuoso mensaje al Hon. Charles S. Whitman, Gobernador de New York, recabando de su clemencia que, teniendo en cuenta las circunstancias atenuantes que rodean los crímenes pasionales como es el que nos ocupa, se digne conmutar la pena de muerte impuesta por los Tribunales de dicho Estado al puertorriqueño Antonio Pontón, por la pena inmediata que en ley proceda, asegurándosele que tal acto de piedad lo hará merecedor de la admiración y eterno reconocimiento del país puertorriqueño.

Que para los altos fines que se interesan se remita copia certificada de esta resolución al funcionario indicado.

Y para remitir al Hon. Gobernador del Estado de New York, expido la presente copia en Yauco, P.R. a 4 de Diciembre de 1915.

Vº Bº

Antommattei
Alcalde

Manuel Troche
Secretario del Concejo

Figure 20. Town of Yauco Resolution to petition clemency on behalf of Pontón. (Tirado-Chiodini Collection, 1914-1916).

Translation of Yauco municipal resolution into English:[2]

"MUNICIPAL GOVERNMENT, YAUCO, P.R.
Office of the Secretary

Agreement reached in the ordinary session celebrated on the twenty ninth of November of [the year] one thousand nine hundred and fifteen. ------------

[Left Box] Attendees: President: Manuel Vicario; Council Members: Rafael Mejía, Pedro Olivari M., Andrés Franceschi, Críspulo Olivera, Santiago Villeneuve

Manuel Troche, Secretary of the Municipality of Yauco,

I CERTIFY that in the Book of Proceedings of this Municipal Council corresponding to Fiscal Year 1915-16, the following particular exists:

WHEREAS, the Puerto Rican Antonio Pontón, who was studying in the State of New York, in a bout of blindness and madness produced by one of those passions that cause imbalance in the human brain, took the life of a being that may have deserved his utmost consideration and love;

WHEREAS, as a result of this crime of passion the death penalty was imposed on said Puerto Rican;

WHEREAS, an appeal was submitted before the Supreme Tribunal, and it confirmed said sentence;

WHEREAS, this Municipal Council, guided by a sentiment of charity and humane consideration, wishes to join in cooperation with the other towns of the island with the hopes of saving the life of said compatriot from the terrifying penalty imposed onto him;

WHEREAS, this Corporation understands that the law affords the Governor of said state the faculty to pardon or commute the penalty, and this is the last resort that can be had in favor of the *unfortunate Antonio Pontón;*

WHEREAS, it shall be resolved by the Municipal Council of Yauco, P.R.

That an attentive and respectful message be elevated before Hon. Charles S. Whitman, Governor of New York, to gather his clemency that—taking into account the mitigating circumstances surrounding crimes of passion like the one at hand—he may commute the death penalty imposed by the Tribunals of said State on the Puerto Rican Antonio Pontón, for the [lower] immediate penalty provided under the law, assuring him that said act of mercy will make him deserving of the admiration and eternal recognition of the country of Puerto Rico;

That for the high goals and interests at hand, a certified copy of this resolution be sent to the proper functionary.

And for submittal to the Hon. Governor of the State of New York, I create the present copy in Yauco, P.R. on December 4, 1915.

Approved by,

/s/Domingo Antommattei
Mayor

/s/Manuel Troche
Council Secretary"

Among the government and official requests for commutation sent to Governor Whitman was a letter dated December 10, 1915, from U.S. Representative James S. Davenport (D-Okla.) (**Figure 21**).

COMMITTEE ON THE TERRITORIES.

HOUSE OF REPRESENTATIVES, UNITED STATES.

WASHINGTON, D. C.

December 10th,

1915.

Hon. Charles S. Whitman,

Governor of the State of New York,

Albany, N. Y.

My dear Governor:-

You will please pardon this communication but, knowing the conditions and being familiar to some extent with the people of the Island of Porto Rico, I am appealing to you in behalf of an unfortunate Porto Rican, who is to be electrocuted, as I understand, either the 15th or 18th of this month. The Porto Rican to whom I refer is Antonio Pon Tón. He was charged and has been convicted, so I am advised, of the killing of Bessie Kramer, an American. I am not writing to justify the crime of Pon Ton but, as he is a Porto Rican and as I am advised by my friends who reside in Porto Rico and those who have visited there quite often, he is an unfortunate young man. I am advised also that several members of his immediate family have been insane, and it is probable that he, too, became insane and committed the unfortunate crime of which he has been convicted and for which he will be executed unless Executive clemency should be extended to him. I do not appeal for a pardon but I do at this time appeal for a

(Continued)

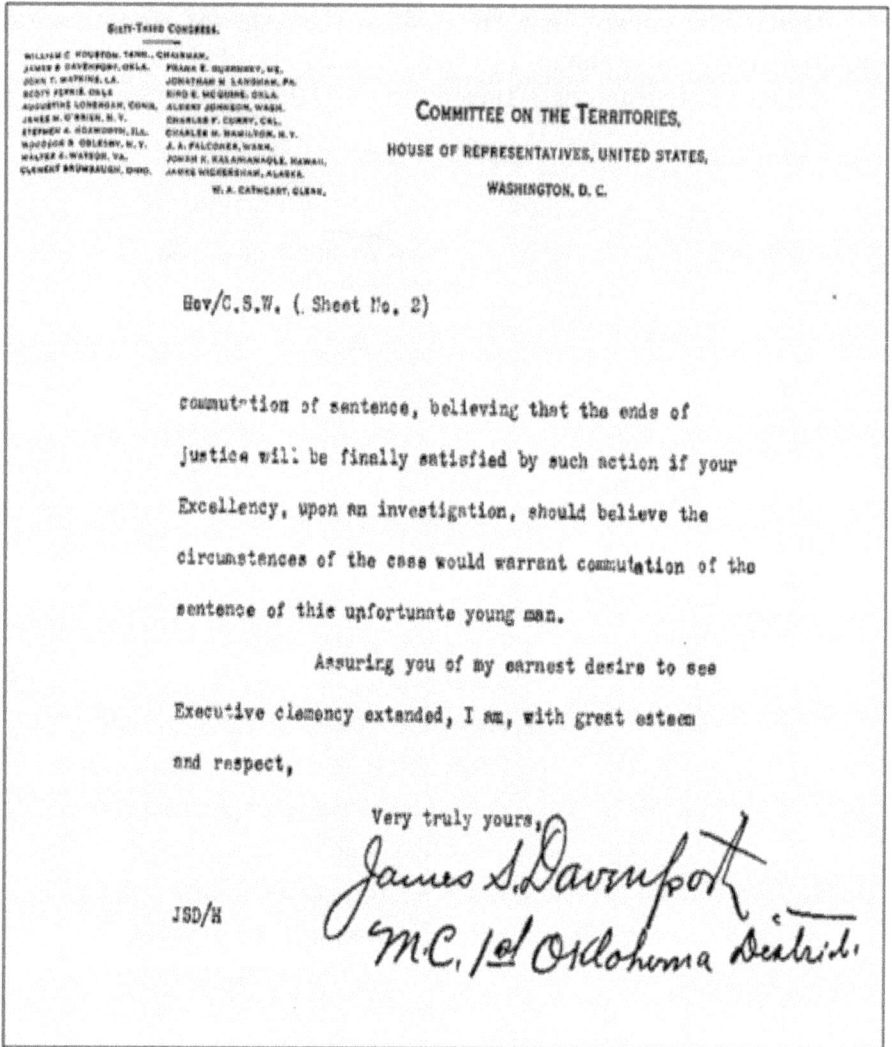

Figure 21. Clemency letter from U.S. Representative James S. Davenport (D-Okla.) to Governor Whitman. (Tirado-Chiodini Collection, 1914-1916).

Representative Davenport was a member of the U.S. Congress, House of Representatives Committee on the Territories. He had been one of the attorneys for the Cherokee Nation from 1901 to 1907 and went on to become a judge for the Oklahoma Court of Criminal Appeals in 1926. (Oklahoma Historical Society, 2015a).

U.S. Senator Thomas P. Gore (D-Okla.), Chairman of the U.S. Congress Committee on Agriculture and Forestry, addressed Governor

Whitman on December 15, 1915, drawing attention to the evidence of insanity in Antonio Pontón's family (**Figure 22**). The senator, who was also a lawyer and had become blind as a child, was an avid human rights advocate. (Oklahoma Historical Society, 2015b).

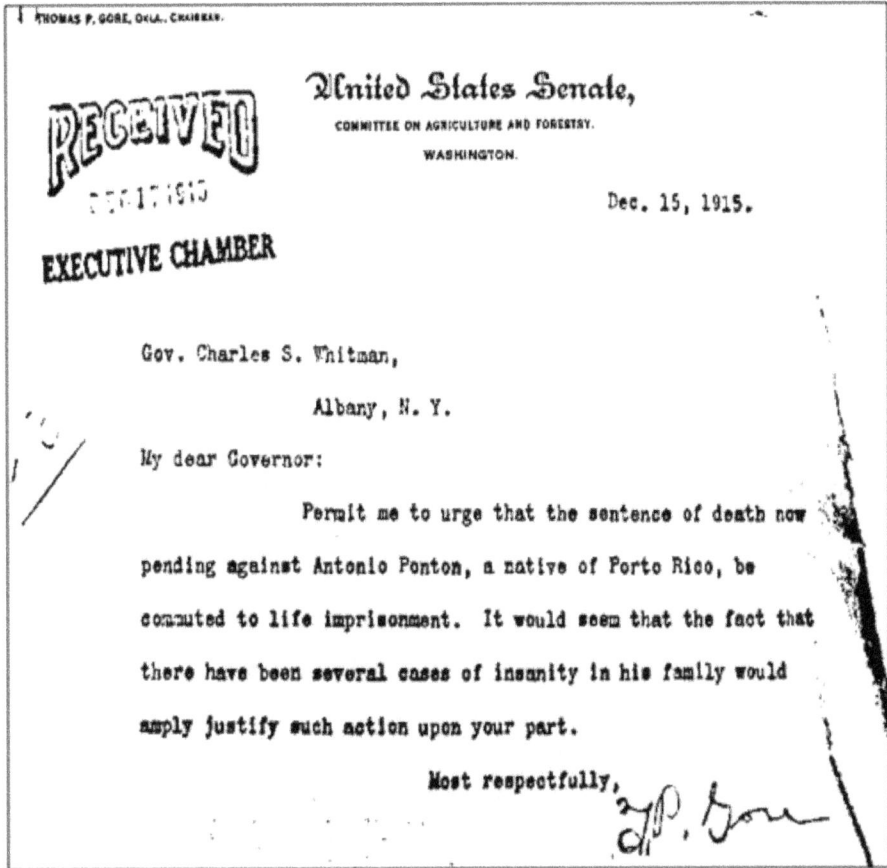

Figure 22. Letter from U.S. Senator Thomas P. Gore (D-Okla.) to Governor Whitman requesting grace for Antonio Pontón. (Tirado-Chiodini Collection, 1914-1916).

Pennsylvania Governor, Dr. Martin G. Brumbaugh, former Puerto Rico Commissioner of Education from 1900-1902, wrote a supportive letter to Governor Whitman on December 3, 1915 (**Figure 23**), attaching an appeal by University of Pennsylvania students written on November 27, 1915 (**Figure 24**). The students stressed that Pontón's insanity evidence had not been presented in its totality before the jury.

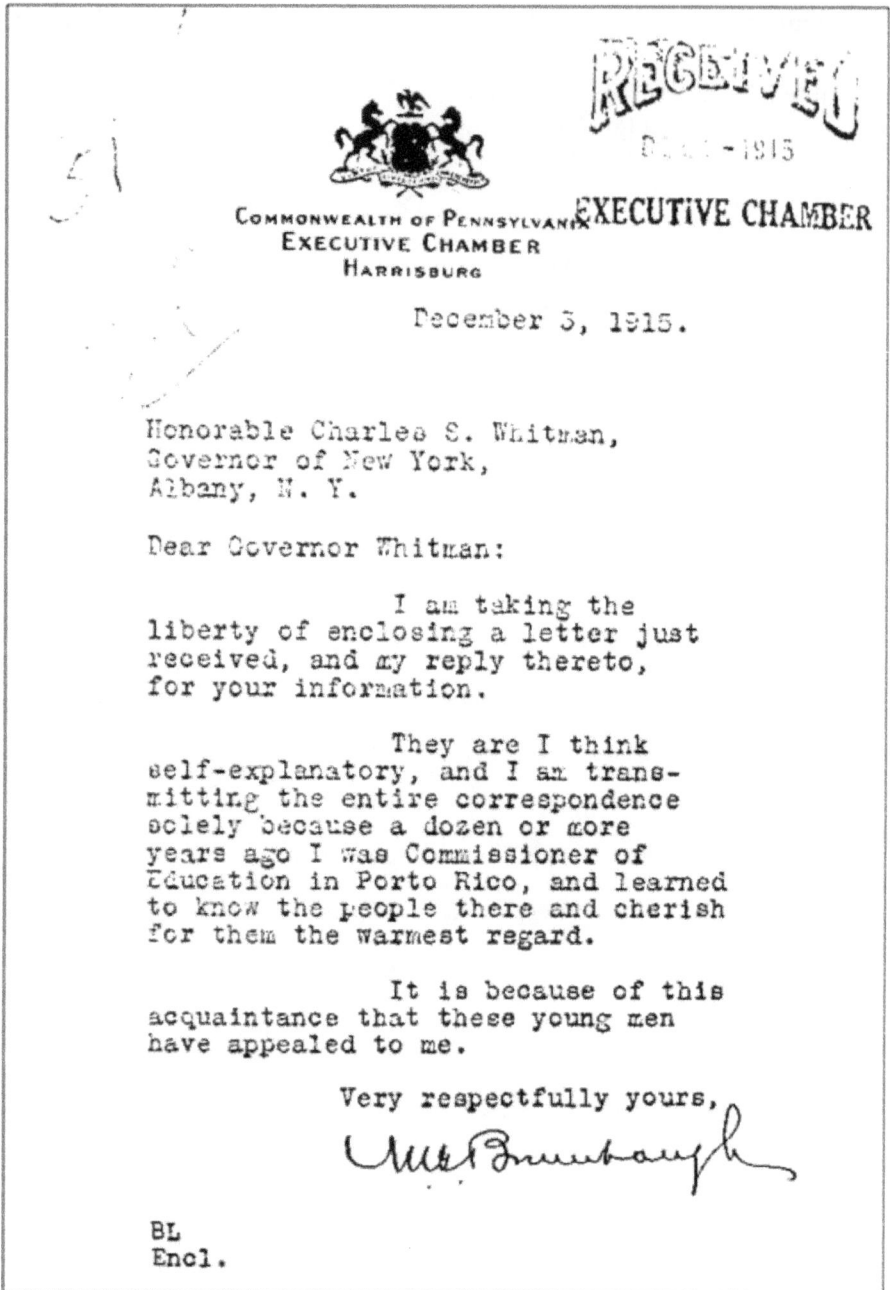

COMMONWEALTH OF PENNSYLVANIA
EXECUTIVE CHAMBER
HARRISBURG

EXECUTIVE CHAMBER

RECEIVED
D... -1915

December 3, 1915.

Honorable Charles S. Whitman,
Governor of New York,
Albany, N. Y.

Dear Governor Whitman:

I am taking the
liberty of enclosing a letter just
received, and my reply thereto,
for your information.

They are I think
self-explanatory, and I am trans-
mitting the entire correspondence
solely because a dozen or more
years ago I was Commissioner of
Education in Porto Rico, and learned
to know the people there and cherish
for them the warmest regard.

It is because of this
acquaintance that these young men
have appealed to me.

Very respectfully yours,

BL
Encl.

Figure 23. Letter to Governor Whitman from Governor of Pennsylvania, Dr. Martin G. Brumbaugh, enclosing clemency appeal by University of Pennsylvania students. (Tirado-Chiodini Collection, 1914-1916).

38

3236 Chestnut St.,
Phila. Pa.
Nov. 27, 1915.

Hon. Martin G Brumbaugh, Governor of
Pennsylvania.
Harrisburg, Pa.

Our dear Governor:-

Confident that you
know our beautiful beautiful island,
Porto Rico, and knowing that you are
interested in anything that pertains
to her and her people, we, the undersigned, in the name of the fifteen
Porto Rican students in the University
of Pennsylvania, who cherish your
name with grateful remembrances,
wish you, first of all, personal happiness and prosperity, and, in the second
place appeal to you on a matter
which goes deeply into our hearts as
true Porto Ricans.

The matter exceedingly interests
us. It is as follows: a Porto Rican student
Antonio Pontón, of a good family, is
sentenced to death in New York. No

(Continued)

utation of Pontón's sentence,
for they know that Pontón is not
responsible for his act. Almost
all the Porto Rican students in uni-
versities and colleges of this country
will send petitions to Governor Whitman
imploring clemency from him. Moreover, we are helping Pontón in
a generous pecuniary way. Our
strong conviction is that our
fellow-student is not a criminal.

The students of the primary and
secondary schools of Porto Rico will also
send petitions to the Governor of New York
and pecuniary help to Pontón. Respectable
ladies of Port Rico are sending cable-
grams and letters to President Wilson
to obtain aid from him.

We write all this, our dear
Governor Brumbaugh, in order that
you be able to see that our object
is a worthy one, and would
appreciate greatly and forever
any personal help which you
may render Antonio Pontón in

(Continued)

doubt, he was insane when he committed the alleged murder. We expected his acquittal by the Court of Appeals of New York; however, we have been disappointed. It has been proved that many members of his family have suffered from insanity. He himself has suffered attacks of insanity, which fact was not brought before the jury in his trial. The date for his electrocution is fixed for the 20th of December, 1918.

Now we have been working diligently during the last three weeks for the commutation of his death sentence. Many people in Porto Rico are working for the same object. A commission of Porto Ricans will come to New York to present new facts to the Governor for his consideration and, at the same time, to beg clemency from him.

Undoubtedly Archbishop Jones and Governor Yager of Porto Rico as well as many prominent Porto Ricans will recommend the commu-

(Continued)

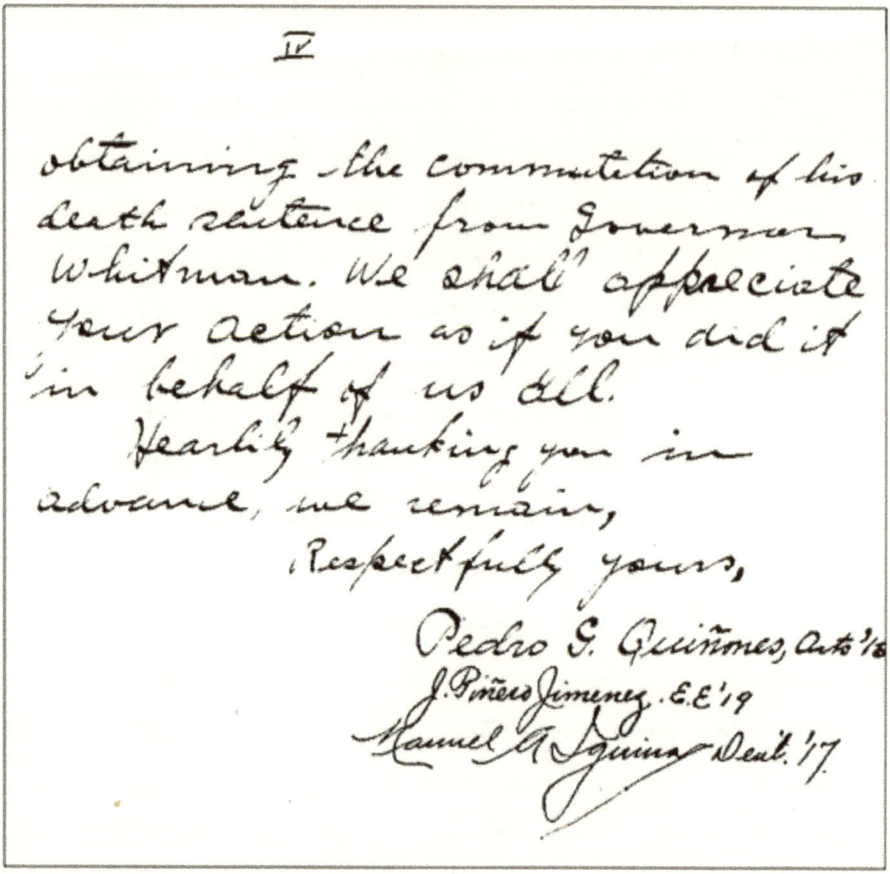

IV

obtaining the commutation of his death sentence from Governor Whitman. We shall appreciate your action as if you did it in behalf of us all.

Heartily thanking you in advance, we remain,

Respectfully yours,

Pedro G. Quiñones, Arts '16
J. Piñero Jiménez, E.E. '19
Manuel A. Iguina, Dent. '17

Figure 24. Pennsylvania University students' letter to Governor Dr. Martin G. Brumbaugh appealing for the life of Antonio Pontón. (Tirado-Chiodini Collection, 1914-1916).

Other university students addressed the governor, among them students from Syracuse University in New York, Loyola University Medical School in Chicago, University of Puerto Rico Law School and Engineering School. University groups, such as the PHI CHI DELTA Fraternity in various states, also raised their voices seeking clemency for Pontón. They all prayed for compassion for their compatriot, who suffered from mental illness.

A letter from Puerto Rican students in Philadelphia respectfully addressed Whitman on December 4, 1915 (**Figure 25**). The students asked the governor to consider Pontón's illness and the fact that he was in a foreign land, far away from friends and family.

PHILADELPHIA, PA.

RECEIVED

DEC 13 1915

December 4, 1915

EXECUTIVE CHAMBER

To His Excellency, Hon. Charles S. Whitman, Governor of New York:

Dear Sir: We, the undersigned, residents of Porto Rico now sojourning in the United States, most of us being students, have followed closely the trial and conviction of Antonio Ponton, a former student at law in Albany, who is now a prisoner at Sing Sing prison under sentence of death for the crime of murder.

We anxiously awaited the decision of the Court of Appeals of your State trusting that the conviction and sentence of our fellow countryman would be reversed, but in this we have been greatly disappointed. You can naturally understand, Sir, our interest in anything pertaining to our countrymen and our solicitation for one whom your Courts have sentenced to death.

Upon learning of the charge against Ponton, we made careful investigations concerning his antecedents and his own prior life; among other things, we discovered the fact that in his immediate family there have been frequently recurring cases of insanity; and Ponton himself has always impressed people with whom he came in contact, both in his own land and since he came to America, as being very peculiar and subject to attacks of mild insanity. It is true, unfortunately, that we are not prepared to present to you conclusive evidence to prove that Ponton was

(Continued)

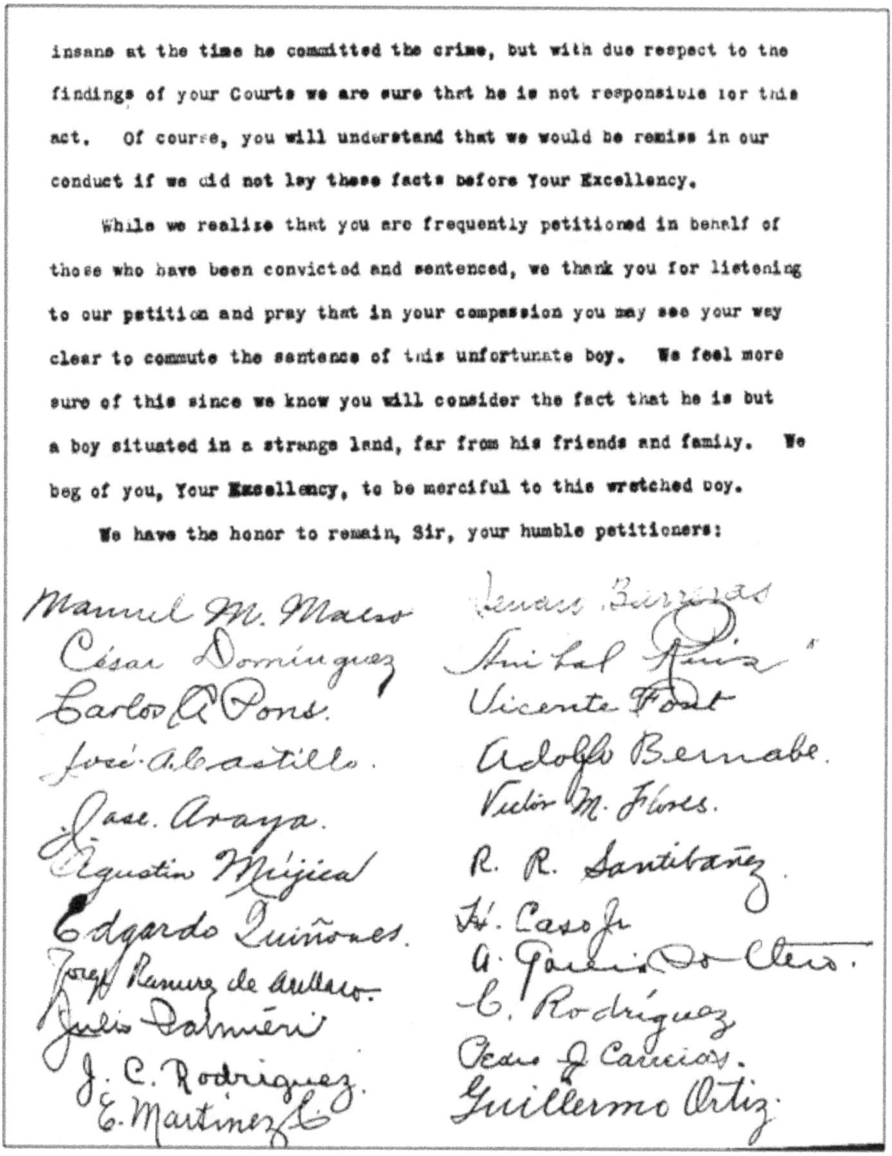

insane at the time he committed the crime, but with due respect to the findings of your Courts we are sure that he is not responsible for this act. Of course, you will understand that we would be remiss in our conduct if we did not lay these facts before Your Excellency.

While we realize that you are frequently petitioned in behalf of those who have been convicted and sentenced, we thank you for listening to our petition and pray that in your compassion you may see your way clear to commute the sentence of this unfortunate boy. We feel more sure of this since we know you will consider the fact that he is but a boy situated in a strange land, far from his friends and family. We beg of you, Your Excellency, to be merciful to this wretched boy.

We have the honor to remain, Sir, your humble petitioners:

Manuel M. Matso
César Domínguez
Carlos A. Pons.
José A. Castillo.
José. Araya.
Agustín Mújica
Edgardo Quiñones.
Jorge Ramírez de Arellano.
Julio Palmieri
J. C. Rodriguez.
E. Martínez C.

Tenaso Barreras
Aníbal Ruiz
Vicente Font
Adolfo Bernabe.
Víctor M. Flores.
R. R. Santibañez.
H. Caso Jr.
A. García Otero.
C. Rodríguez
Oscar J. Carrión.
Guillermo Ortiz.

Figure 25. Puerto Rican Students in Pennsylvania write to Governor Whitman. (Tirado-Chiodini Collection, 1914-1916).

Whitman also received a letter dated December 9, 1915 from Harvard University students, acknowledging the gravity of Pontón's crime, but begging for grace, as Pontón did not have a criminal history and his execution would add to the tragedy (**Figure 26**). They appealed for a penalty commutation. Pedro Albízu y Campos and Manuel Matienzo, who would later become avid supporters of Puerto Rico's national autonomy, were among the students signing the letter.

RECEIVED

DEC 14 1915

EXECUTIVE CHAMBER

Harvard University,

Cambridge, Mass.,

December 9, 1915.

Petition:

To His Excellency,

Charles E. Whitman,

Governor of New York

Albany, New York.

Excellency:

We, the undersigned, Porto Rican members of Harvard University beg to request Your Excellency the commutation of the capital sentence decreed by the Courts of the State of New York in the case of Antonio Ponton, a Porto Rican, who was a student in the Albany Law School. The justice of the decision, in view of the evidence, is unquestionable. However, we appeal to Your Excellency's clemency to commutate the sentence, because it is impossible to think that a man in whose family no criminals have been found, could be an individual incapable of repentance and reform. and be submitted to the treatment becoming to an habitual criminal.

(Continued)

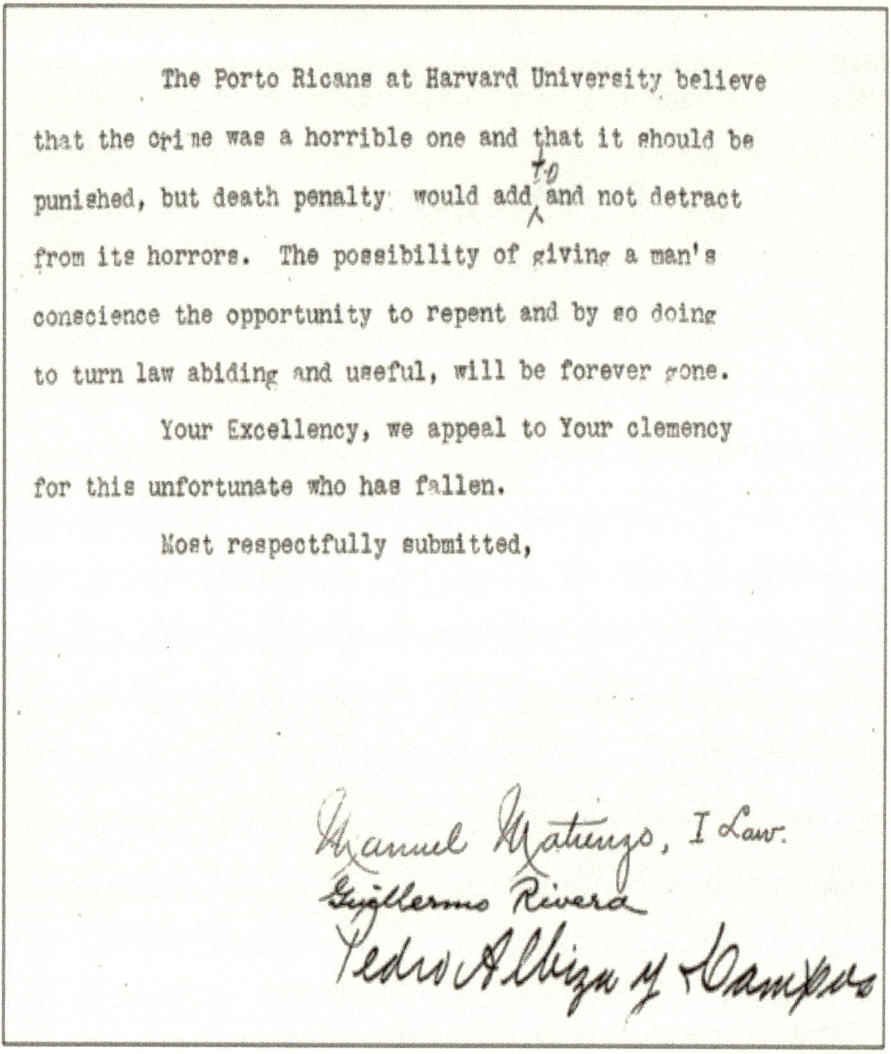

The Porto Ricans at Harvard University believe that the crime was a horrible one and that it should be punished, but death penalty would add to and not detract from its horrors. The possibility of giving a man's conscience the opportunity to repent and by so doing to turn law abiding and useful, will be forever gone.

Your Excellency, we appeal to Your clemency for this unfortunate who has fallen.

Most respectfully submitted,

Manuel Matienzo, I Law.
Guillermo Rivera
Pedro Albizu y Campos

Figure 26. Letter from Harvard University students to Governor Whitman, requesting Pontón's death penalty be commuted to life. (Tirado-Chiodini Collection, 1914-1916).

On December 13, 1915 the members of the Latin American Association of students in the State College of Pennsylvania wrote to Governor Whitman (**Figure 27**). They requested that he allow Pontón to remedy his sentence by continuing his journey of penance in this world, attributing his criminal conduct to his mental illness. The students also called for compassion for Pontón's mother.

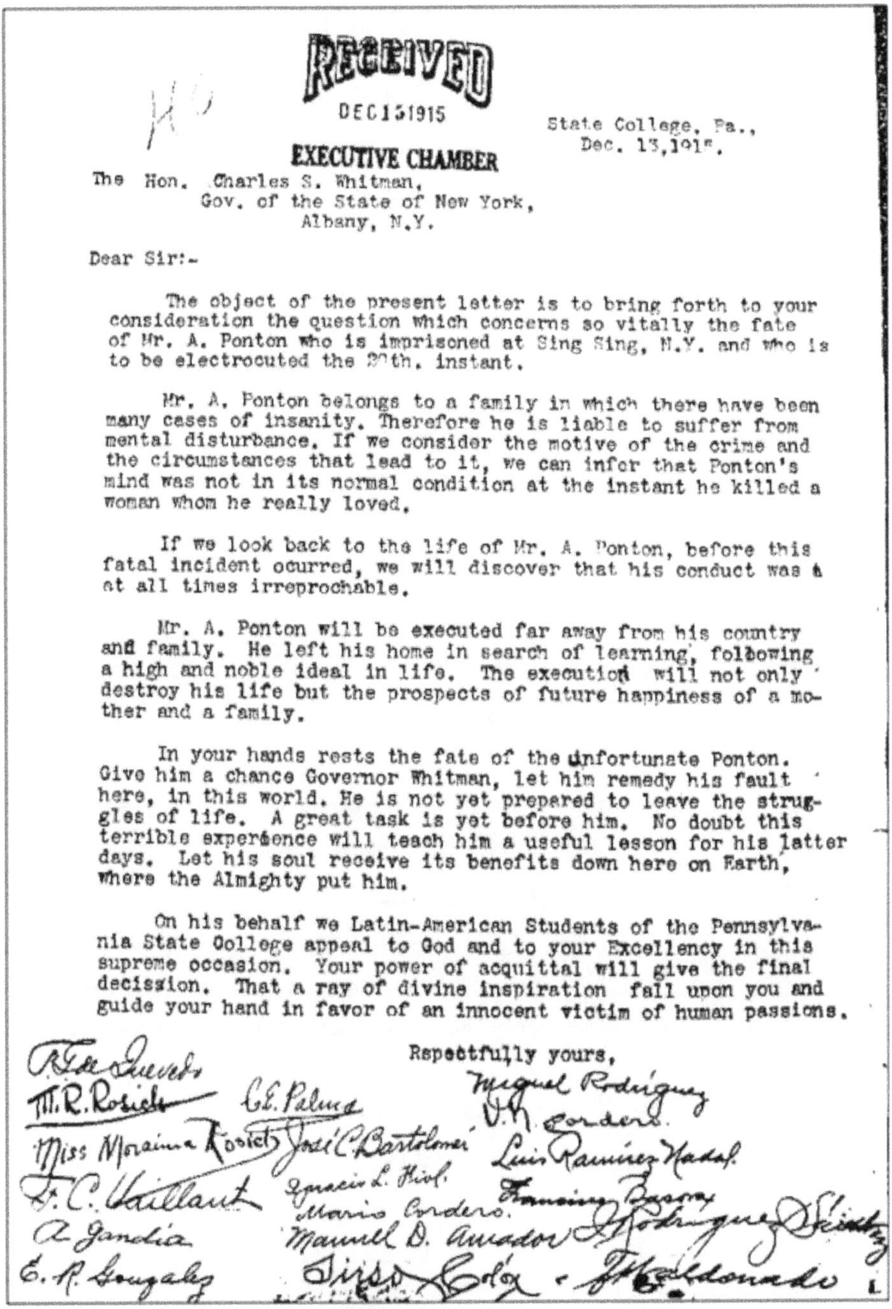

RECEIVED
DEC 15 1915
EXECUTIVE CHAMBER

State College, Pa.,
Dec. 13,191.

The Hon. Charles S. Whitman,
Gov. of the State of New York,
Albany, N.Y.

Dear Sir:-

The object of the present letter is to bring forth to your consideration the question which concerns so vitally the fate of Mr. A. Ponton who is imprisoned at Sing Sing, N.Y. and who is to be electrocuted the 20th. instant.

Mr. A. Ponton belongs to a family in which there have been many cases of insanity. Therefore he is liable to suffer from mental disturbance. If we consider the motive of the crime and the circumstances that lead to it, we can infer that Ponton's mind was not in its normal condition at the instant he killed a woman whom he really loved.

If we look back to the life of Mr. A. Ponton, before this fatal incident ocurred, we will discover that his conduct was at all times irreprochable.

Mr. A. Ponton will be executed far away from his country and family. He left his home in search of learning, following a high and noble ideal in life. The execution will not only destroy his life but the prospects of future happiness of a mother and a family.

In your hands rests the fate of the unfortunate Ponton. Give him a chance Governor Whitman, let him remedy his fault here, in this world. He is not yet prepared to leave the struggles of life. A great task is yet before him. No doubt this terrible experience will teach him a useful lesson for his latter days. Let his soul receive its benefits down here on Earth, where the Almighty put him.

On his behalf we Latin-American Students of the Pennsylvania State College appeal to God and to your Excellency in this supreme occasion. Your power of acquittal will give the final decission. That a ray of divine inspiration fall upon you and guide your hand in favor of an innocent victim of human passions.

Respectfully yours,

[signatures]

Figure 27. Letter from Latin American Association students at Pennsylvania State College requesting clemency for Antonio Pontón. (Tirado-Chiodini Collection, 1914-1916).

47

The Spanish Embassy in Washington, DC wrote to the governor on December 10, 1915 (**Figure 28**). Consul Juan Riaño y Gayangos signed the letter supporting Antonio Pontón, the son of a Spaniard.

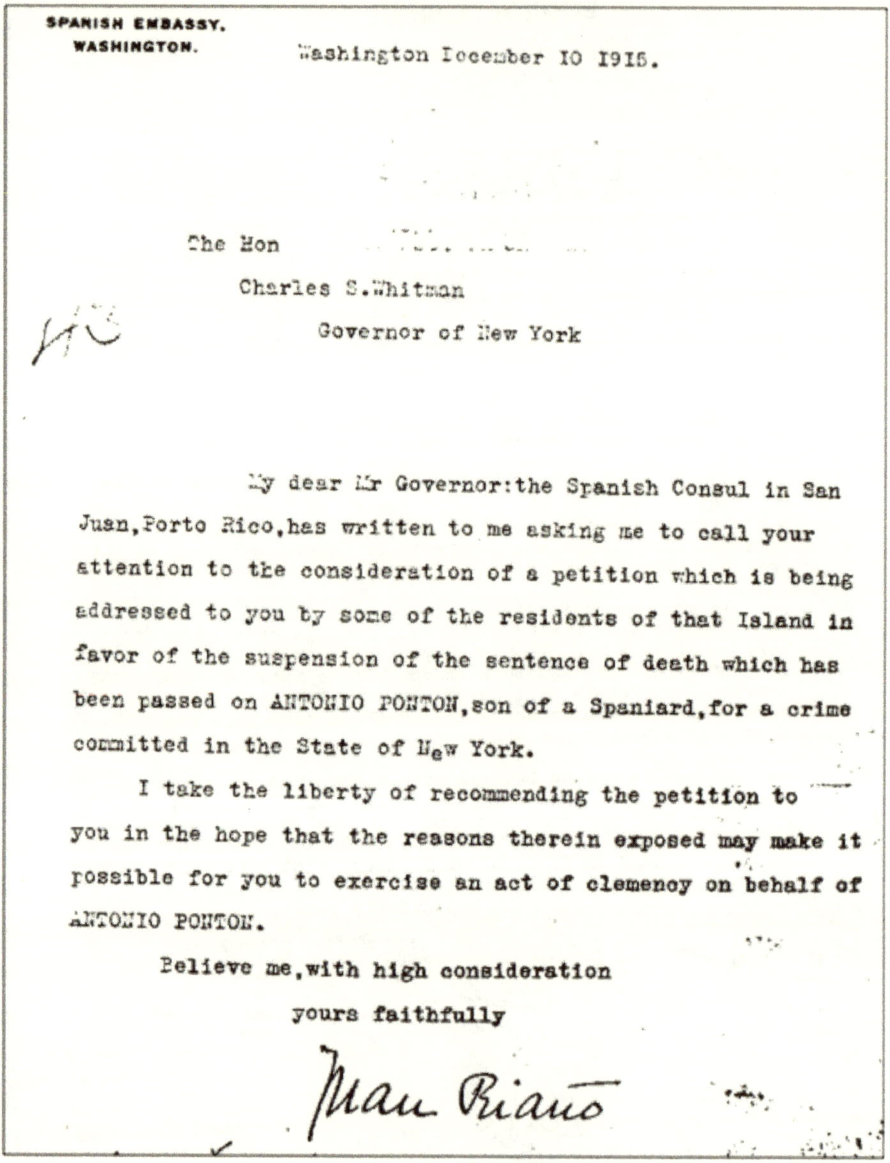

**SPANISH EMBASSY,
WASHINGTON.**

Washington December 10 1915.

The Hon

Charles S.Whitman

Governor of New York

My dear Mr Governor:the Spanish Consul in San Juan,Porto Rico,has written to me asking me to call your attention to the consideration of a petition which is being addressed to you by some of the residents of that Island in favor of the suspension of the sentence of death which has been passed on ANTONIO PONTON,son of a Spaniard,for a crime committed in the State of New York.

I take the liberty of recommending the petition to you in the hope that the reasons therein exposed may make it possible for you to exercise an act of clemency on behalf of ANTONIO PONTON.

Believe me,with high consideration

yours faithfully

Juan Riaño

Figure 28. Letter by Spain's Consul Juan Riaño to Governor Whitman, pleading that Pontón's sentence be commuted. (Tirado-Chiodini Collection, 1914-1916).

On December 11, 1915, the U.S. Attorney General forwarded correspondence to Governor Whitman (**Figure 29**). The enclosed letter, dated November 30, 1915, was signed by Angelina Balseiro de Feliú representing the ladies from the town of Bayamón and was addressed to U.S. President Woodrow Wilson (**Figure 30**). Supported by about 600 signatures, the letter requested a pardon and clemency for Antonio Pontón and described the deep suffering of his mother. It also implored grace on religious grounds. The President and fiancée Edith Bolling Galt–scheduled to marry on December 18, 1915–would return to the White House from their honeymoon on January 3, 1916. (New York Press, 1916). It is unlikely that any Pontón appeal reached them.

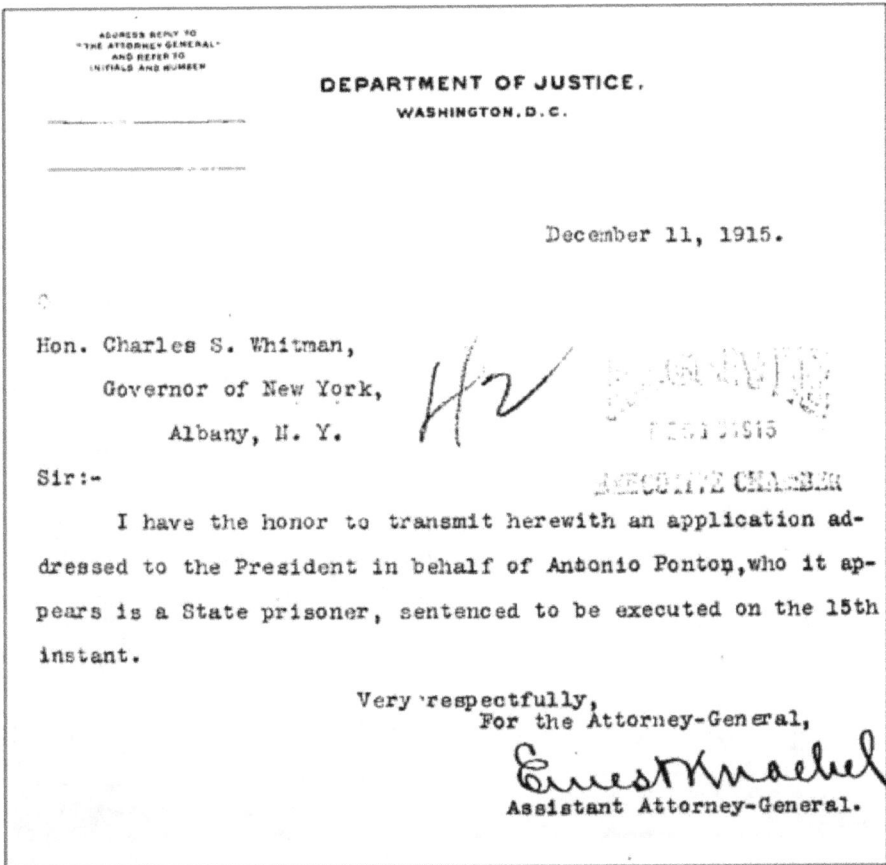

DEPARTMENT OF JUSTICE,
WASHINGTON, D.C.

December 11, 1915.

Hon. Charles S. Whitman,

Governor of New York,

Albany, N. Y.

Sir:-

I have the honor to transmit herewith an application addressed to the President in behalf of Antonio Pontón, who it appears is a State prisoner, sentenced to be executed on the 15th instant.

Very respectfully,
For the Attorney-General,

Assistant Attorney-General.

Figure 29. U.S. Attorney General's letter to Governor Whitman, enclosing letter from the "Ladies of Bayamón." (Tirado-Chiodini Collection, 1914-1916).

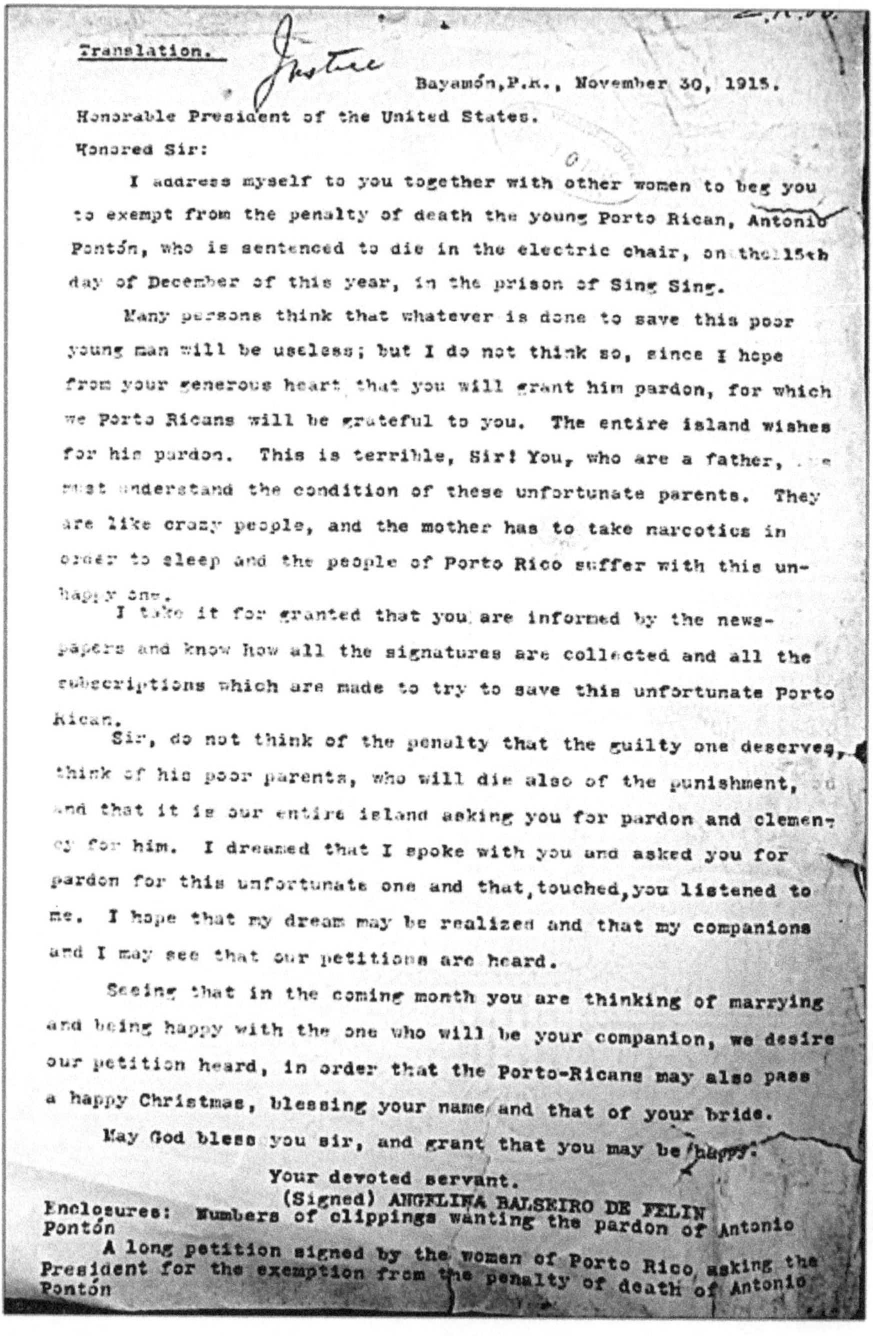

Translation.

Justice

Bayamón, P.R., November 30, 1915.

Honorable President of the United States.

Honored Sir:

I address myself to you together with other women to beg you to exempt from the penalty of death the young Porto Rican, Antonio Pontón, who is sentenced to die in the electric chair, on the 15th day of December of this year, in the prison of Sing Sing.

Many persons think that whatever is done to save this poor young man will be useless; but I do not think so, since I hope from your generous heart that you will grant him pardon, for which we Porto Ricans will be grateful to you. The entire island wishes for his pardon. This is terrible, Sir! You, who are a father, ... must understand the condition of these unfortunate parents. They are like crazy people, and the mother has to take narcotics in order to sleep and the people of Porto Rico suffer with this unhappy one.

I take it for granted that you are informed by the newspapers and know how all the signatures are collected and all the subscriptions which are made to try to save this unfortunate Porto Rican.

Sir, do not think of the penalty that the guilty one deserves, think of his poor parents, who will die also of the punishment, and that it is our entire island asking you for pardon and clemency for him. I dreamed that I spoke with you and asked you for pardon for this unfortunate one and that, touched, you listened to me. I hope that my dream may be realized and that my companions and I may see that our petitions are heard.

Seeing that in the coming month you are thinking of marrying and being happy with the one who will be your companion, we desire our petition heard, in order that the Porto-Ricans may also pass a happy Christmas, blessing your name, and that of your bride.

May God bless you sir, and grant that you may be happy.

Your devoted servant.
(Signed) ANGELINA BALSEIRO DE FELIN

Enclosures: Numbers of clippings wanting the pardon of Antonio Pontón

A long petition signed by the women of Porto Rico asking the President for the exemption from the penalty of death of Antonio Pontón

Figure 30. Clemency letter from the "Ladies of Bayamón" to U.S. President Wilson, signed by Angelina Balseiro de Feliú. (Tirado-Chiodini Collection, 1914-1916).

As the December 20th date of execution approached, an increasing number of telegrams arrived at the desk of Governor Whitman, appealing for Pontón's life. **Figure 31** depicts a composite of some of the telegrams sent to the New York governor.

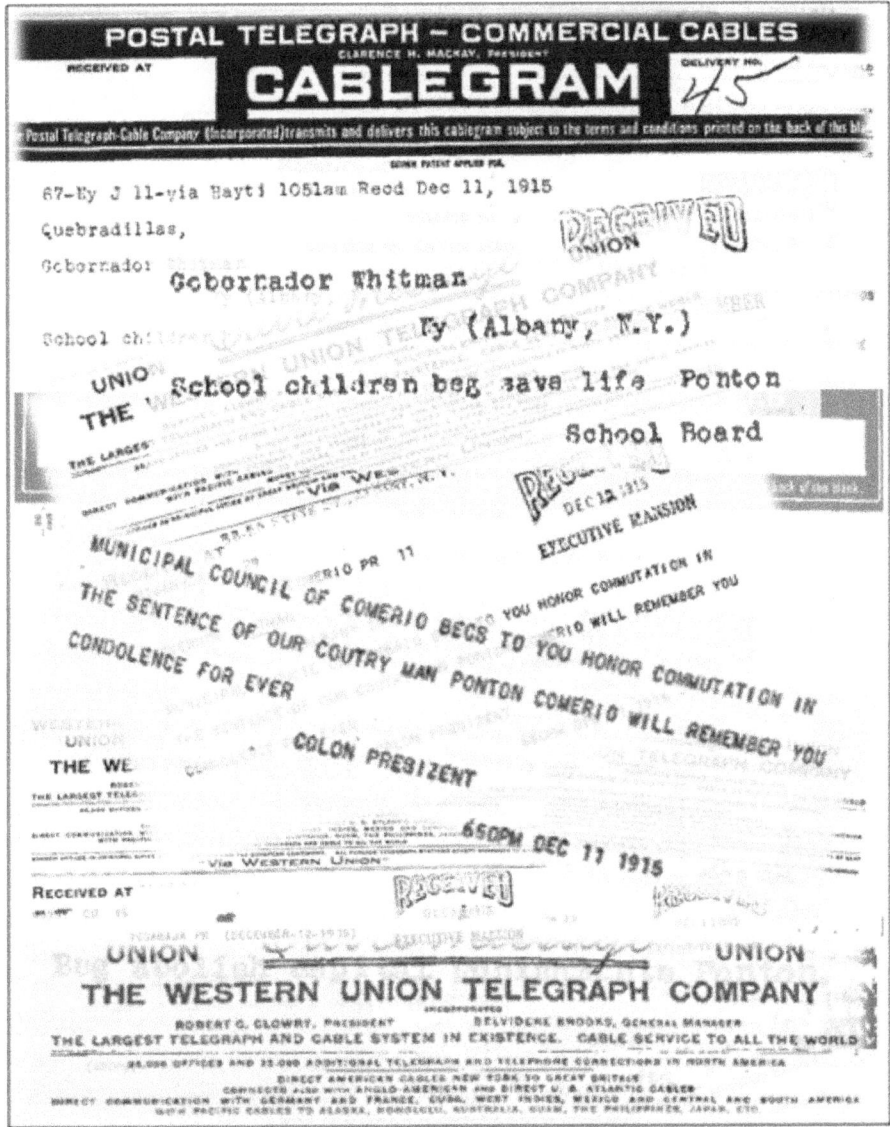

Figure 31. Image composite of selected telegrams sent to Governor Whitman as Pontón's execution date of December 20, 1915 neared. (Tirado-Chiodini Collection, 1914-1916).

The clemency effort extended beyond the Caribbean island to Puerto Ricans in the U.S. mainland. On December 5, 1915, Dr. Julio J. Henna, a physician and respected Puerto Rican leader residing in New York, called a meeting at the Ansonia Hotel in New York City. His objective was to organize a committee to offer grassroots support and collect signatures for the cause of Pontón. **Figure 32** shows a newspaper clip reporting on the meeting.

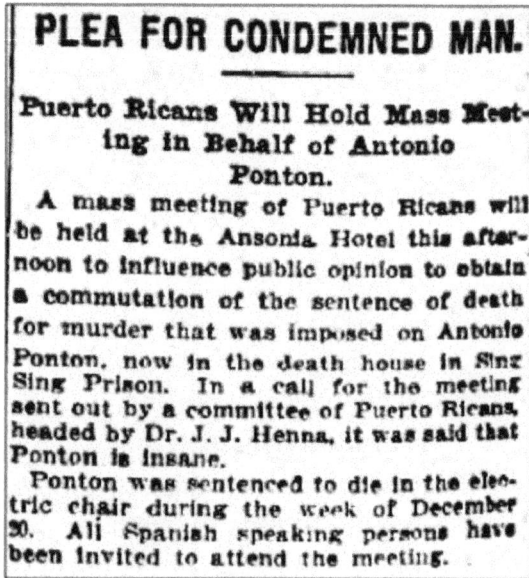

PLEA FOR CONDEMNED MAN.

Puerto Ricans Will Hold Mass Meeting in Behalf of Antonio Ponton.

A mass meeting of Puerto Ricans will be held at the Ansonia Hotel this afternoon to influence public opinion to obtain a commutation of the sentence of death for murder that was imposed on Antonio Ponton, now in the death house in Sing Sing Prison. In a call for the meeting sent out by a committee of Puerto Ricans, headed by Dr. J. J. Henna, it was said that Ponton is insane.

Ponton was sentenced to die in the electric chair during the week of December 30. All Spanish speaking persons have been invited to attend the meeting.

Figure 32. Puerto Ricans organize a Pontón support committee at the Ansonia Hotel in New York City. (New York Herald, 1915).

Father Andrés Echevarría, a prominent Catholic priest from the town of Cayey, led the Puerto Rico Commission's meeting with Governor Whitman on December 14, 1915. The Commission directed a written clemency petition to Whitman (**Figure 33**), which the press reported to include 15,000 signatures. (New York Herald, 1916). However, research by this author revealed this figure to be much greater. Hundreds of additional letters, telegrams, and documents with thousands of signatures arrived at Governor Whitman's Executive Chambers from Puerto Rico and the U.S. mainland. Some of the organizations represented are listed in **Chapter Four** and in the **Appendix** of this book, along with the names transcribed by this author of over 21,000 people who signed the clemency petitions, also endorsed by respected P.R. and U.S. leaders.

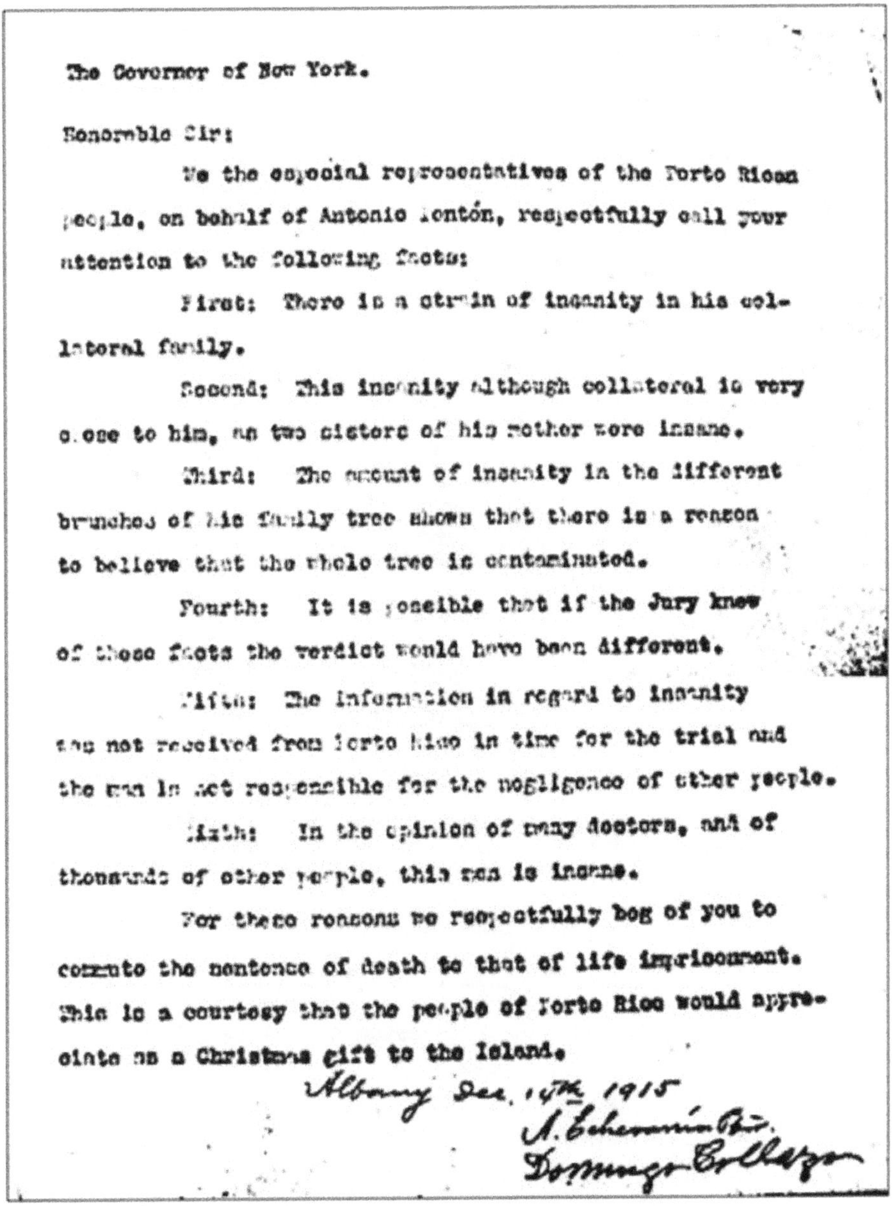

The Governor of New York.

Honorable Sir:

We the especial representatives of the Porto Rican people, on behalf of Antonio Lentón, respectfully call your attention to the following facts:

First: There is a strain of insanity in his collateral family.

Second: This insanity although collateral is very close to him, as two sisters of his mother were insane.

Third: The amount of insanity in the different branches of his family tree shows that there is a reason to believe that the whole tree is contaminated.

Fourth: It is possible that if the Jury knew of these facts the verdict would have been different.

Fifth: The information in regard to insanity was not received from Porto Rico in time for the trial and the man is not responsible for the negligence of other people.

Sixth: In the opinion of many doctors, and of thousands of other people, this man is insane.

For these reasons we respectfully beg of you to commute the sentence of death to that of life imprisonment. This is a courtesy that the people of Porto Rico would appreciate as a Christmas gift to the Island.

Albany Dec. 19th 1915

A. Echevarría Pbo.

Domingo Collazo

Figure 33. Letter from the Puerto Rico Commission, signed by Rev. Andrés Echevarría. (Tirado-Chiodini Collection, 1914-1916).

53

As depicted in **Figure 34**, despite the overwhelming amount of letters, telegrams, signatures, and his meeting with the Puerto Rico Commission, Governor Whitman adhered to his position. He denied the requested grace and declared that Pontón's electrocution go on as scheduled on December 20, 1915.

MATTER OF APPLICATION FOR EXECUTIVE CLEMENCY
IN BEHALF OF ANTONIO PONTON.

Ponton was convicted in the county of Schenectady in April 1915, of the crime of Murder 1st degree and sentenced to be electrocuted during the week beginning June 7th, 1915. The case was appealed to the Court of Appeals and that Court on October 29th, 1915, unanimously affirmed the decision of the trial court, and thereafter fixed the week beginning December 20th, 1915, as the date for the execution of Ponton.

The question as to whether Ponton was sane or insane was before the Jury which convicted him and by their verdict they found him to be sane. The same question was in the case before the Court of Appeals which affirmed the conviction.

On December 14th, 1915, I gave a hearing in this case and nothing was developed at such hearing which would justify me in interfering with the execution of the judgment of the court.

The application is therefore denied.

Figure 34. Governor Whitman's notice denying clemency after the December 14, 1915 hearing with the Puerto Rico Commission. (Tirado-Chiodini Collection, 1914-1916).

However, on December 18, 1915, the governor received a letter from New York City Attorney Charles E. Le Barbier, a former District Attorney in New York City, who had been retained as private counsel to represent Pontón (**Figure 35**).

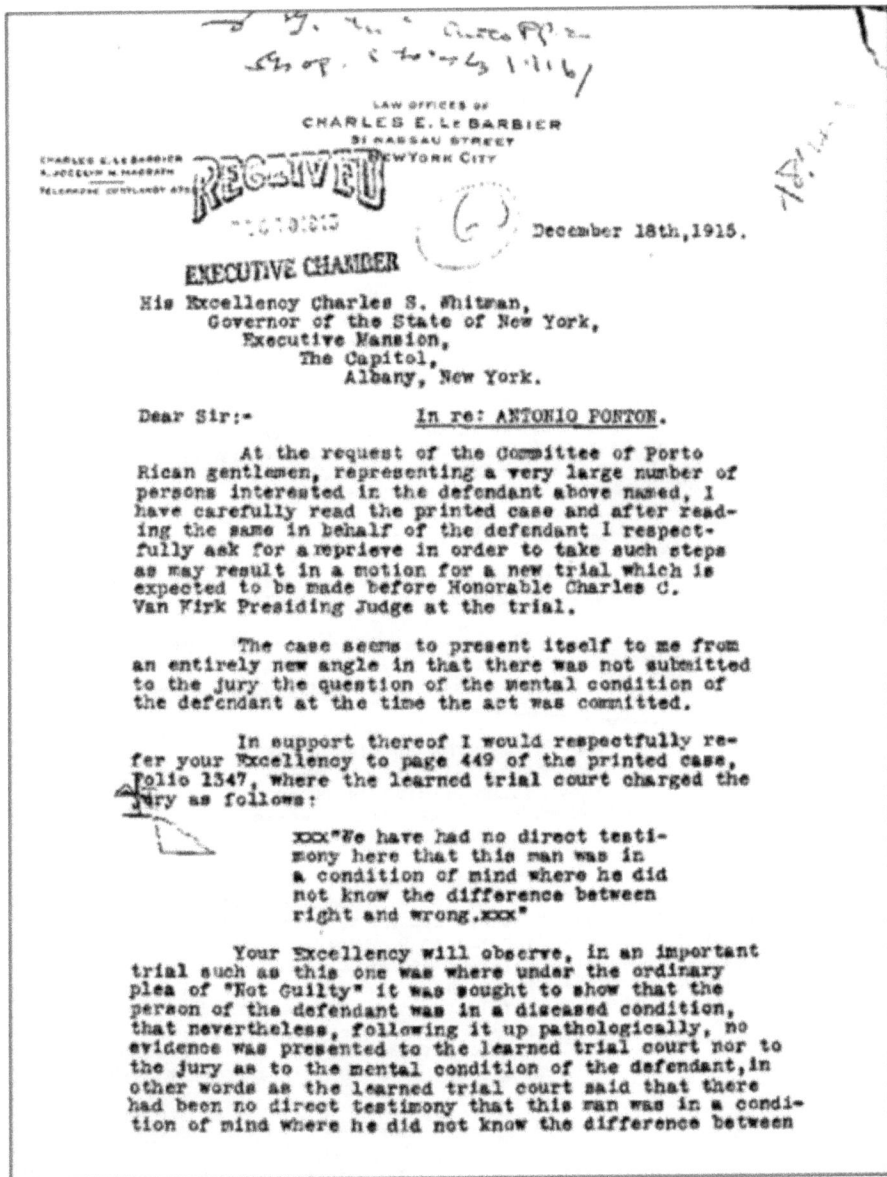

LAW OFFICES OF
CHARLES E. Le BARBIER
31 NASSAU STREET
NEW YORK CITY

December 18th, 1915.

EXECUTIVE CHAMBER

His Excellency Charles S. Whitman,
Governor of the State of New York,
Executive Mansion,
The Capitol,
Albany, New York.

Dear Sir:-   In re: ANTONIO PONTON.

At the request of the Committee of Porto Rican gentlemen, representing a very large number of persons interested in the defendant above named, I have carefully read the printed case and after reading the same in behalf of the defendant I respectfully ask for a reprieve in order to take such steps as may result in a motion for a new trial which is expected to be made before Honorable Charles C. Van Kirk Presiding Judge at the trial.

The case seems to present itself to me from an entirely new angle in that there was not submitted to the jury the question of the mental condition of the defendant at the time the act was committed.

In support thereof I would respectfully refer your Excellency to page 449 of the printed case, folio 1347, where the learned trial court charged the jury as follows:

xxx"We have had no direct testimony here that this man was in a condition of mind where he did not know the difference between right and wrong.xxx"

Your Excellency will observe, in an important trial such as this one was where under the ordinary plea of "Not Guilty" it was sought to show that the person of the defendant was in a diseased condition, that nevertheless, following it up pathologically, no evidence was presented to the learned trial court nor to the jury as to the mental condition of the defendant, in other words as the learned trial court said that there had been no direct testimony that this man was in a condition of mind where he did not know the difference between

(Continued)

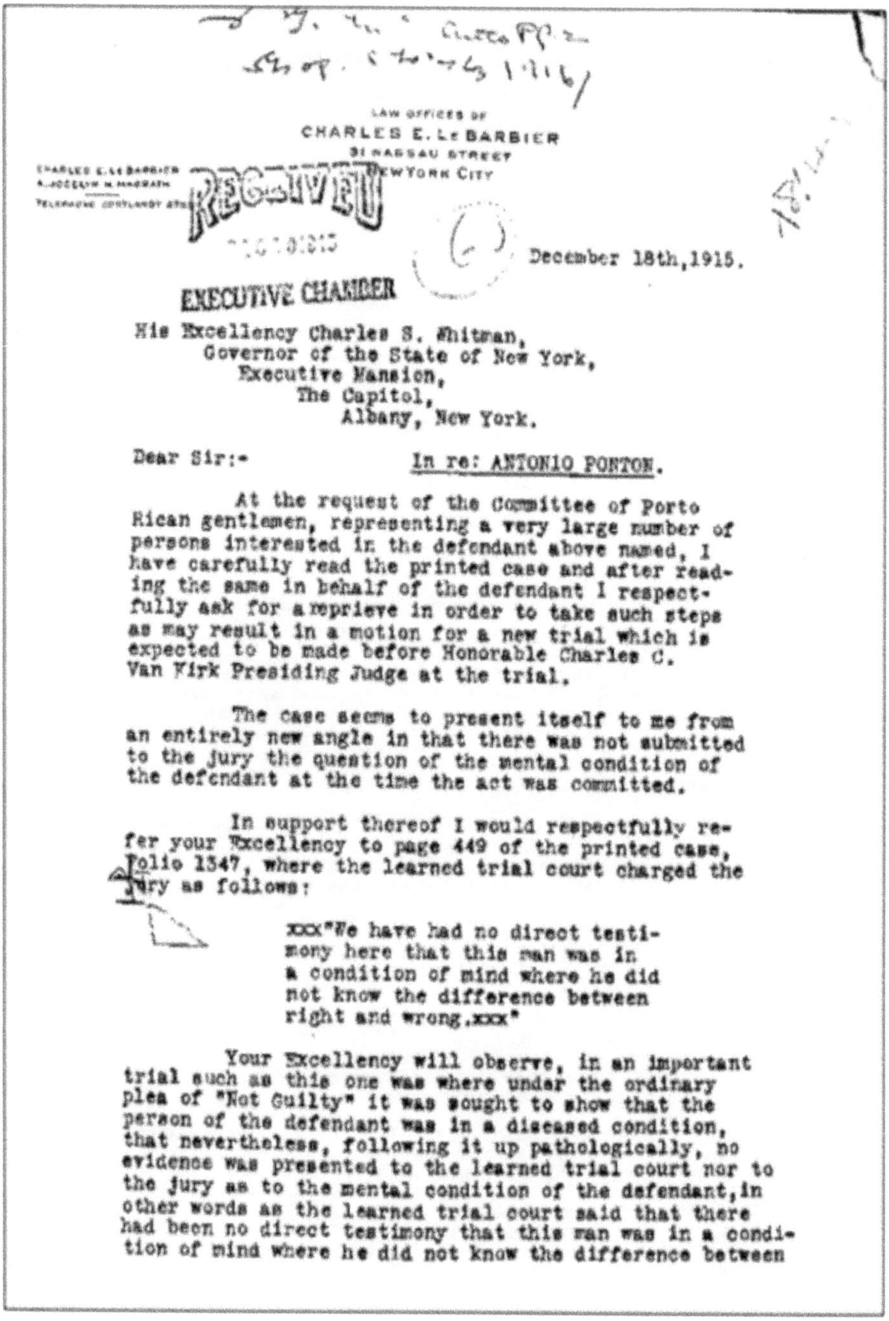

Figure 35. Letter from attorney Charles E. Le Barbier to Governor Whitman pointing out trial error. (Tirado-Chiodini Collection, 1914-1916).

In his letter to Whitman, Le Barbier cited the murder trial's transcript[3] section revealing the grave error committed by Judge Van Kirk when instructing the jury on the issue of insanity.

Le Barbier's argument–and the continued outpour of letters–persuaded Whitman to grant a respite until the week of January 3, 1916. The Sing Sing Prison Warden at the time, Thomas Mott Osborne, acknowledged the respite in a letter dated December 20, 1915 (**Figure 36**).

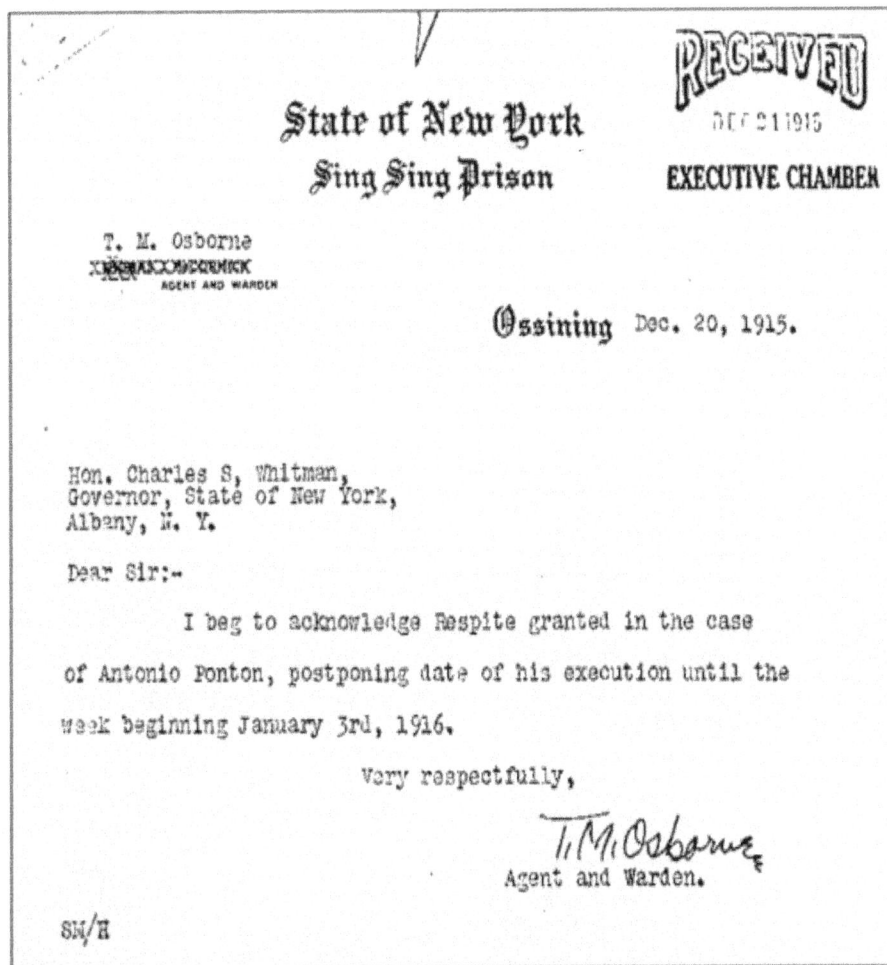

State of New York

Sing Sing Prison

RECEIVED
DEC 21 1915

EXECUTIVE CHAMBER

T. M. Osborne
XXXXXXXXXXMCCORMICK
AGENT AND WARDEN

Ossining Dec. 20, 1915.

Hon. Charles S, Whitman,
Governor, State of New York,
Albany, N. Y.

Dear Sir:-

I beg to acknowledge Respite granted in the case

of Antonio Ponton, postponing date of his execution until the

week beginning January 3rd, 1916.

Very respectfully,

T. M. Osborne
Agent and Warden.

SM/B

Figure 36. Letter from Sing Sing Prison Warden Thomas M. Osborne to Governor Whitman, acknowledging respite for Antonio Pontón until the week of January 3, 1916. (Tirado-Chiodini Collection, 1914-1916).

Meanwhile, other clemency petitions poured onto Whitman's desk, including letters from U.S. businesses and individuals opposing Pontón's execution. **Figure 37** shows a letter from E. Ferrett, agent of *Wright's Indian Vegetable Pills Co., Inc.*, sent on December 7, 1915. As **Chapter Three** explains, this letter could have been key in Pontón's defense, but the underlying reason why likely eluded defense counsel.

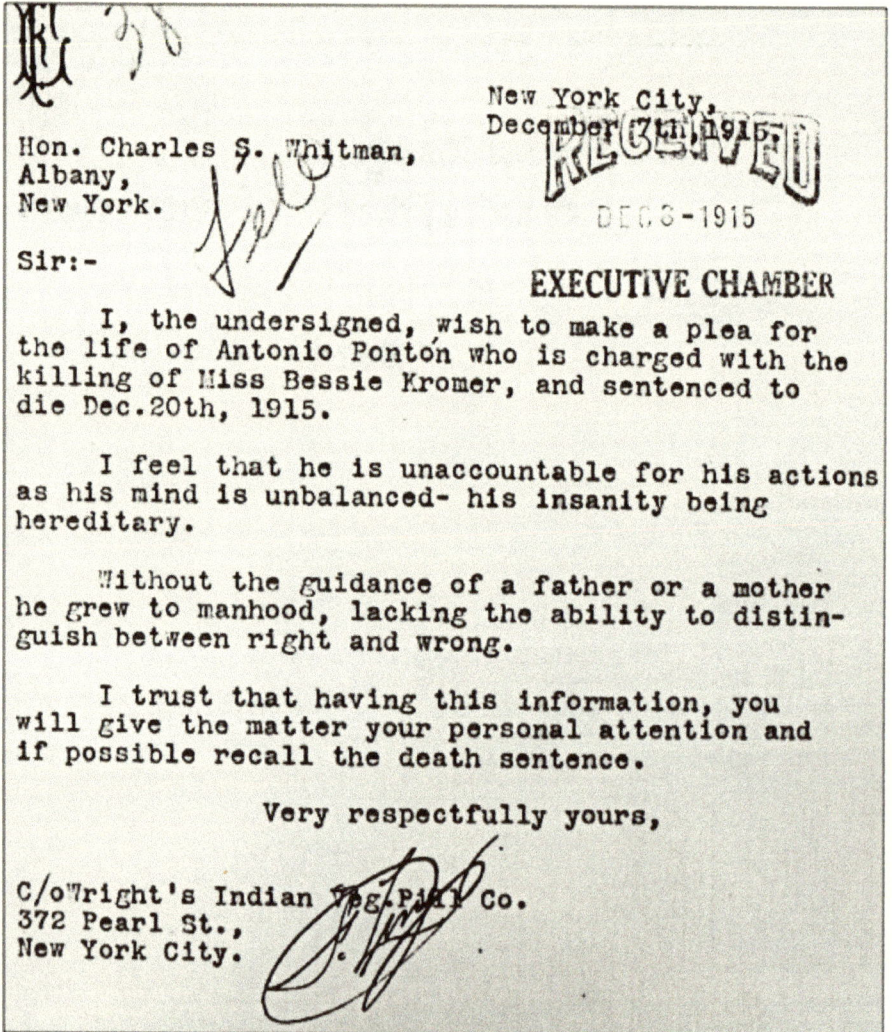

Figure 37. Clemency letter from E. Ferrett, agent for Wright's Indian Vegetable Pills Co., Inc. (Tirado-Chiodini Collection, 1914-1916).

Angelina Perrotta, an Italian immigrant from Schenectady, New York, wrote an emotional letter on December 18, 1915 (**Figure 38**).

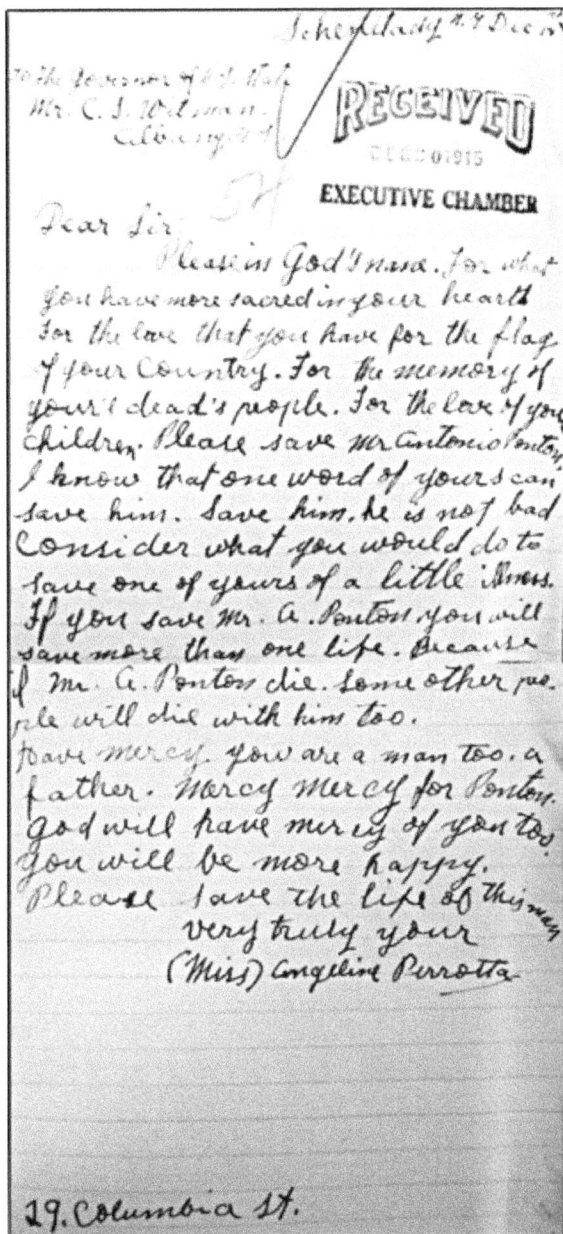

Figure 38. Letter from Angelina Perrotta to Governor Whitman. (Tirado-Chiodini Collection, 1914-1916).

Mrs. Anna Warner of Schenectady, New York, addressed Whitman on December 23, 1915 on behalf of Pontón (**Figure 39**).

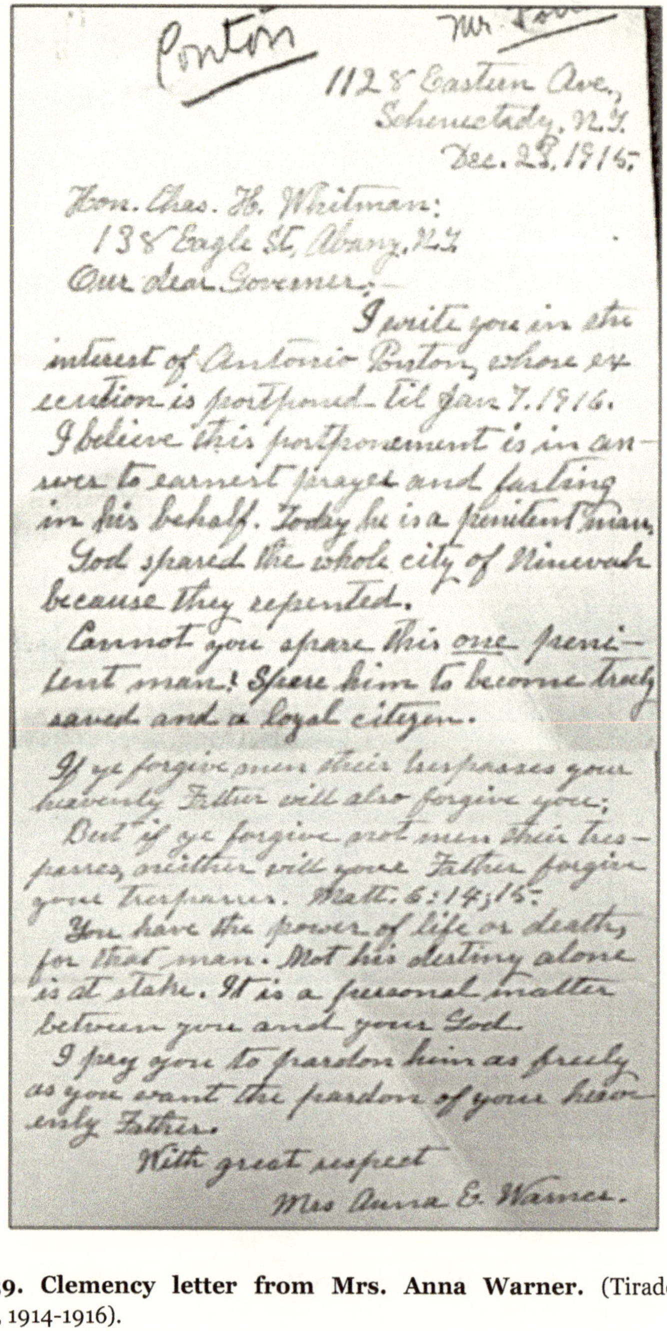

Pontón

Mr.

1128 Eastern Ave,
Schenectady, N.Y.
Dec. 23, 1915.

Hon. Chas. H. Whitman:
138 Eagle St, Albany, N.Y.

Our dear Governor;—

I write you in the interest of Antonio Ponton, whose execution is postponed til Jan 7. 1916.

I believe this postponement is in answer to earnest prayer and fasting in his behalf. Today he is a penitent man.

God spared the whole city of Nineveh because they repented.

Cannot you spare this one penitent man! Spare him to become truly saved and a loyal citizen.

If ye forgive men their trespasses your heavenly Father will also forgive you;

But if ye forgive not men their trespasses, neither will your Father forgive your trespasses. Matt. 6:14;15.

You have the power of life or death, for that man. Not his destiny alone is at stake. It is a personal matter between you and your God.

I pray you to pardon him as freely as you want the pardon of your heavenly Father.

With great respect

Mrs Anna E. Warner.

Figure 39. Clemency letter from Mrs. Anna Warner. (Tirado-Chiodini Collection, 1914-1916).

Among the thousands of petitions for clemency received by Whitman stood a single letter, written by Jack Hunter from Schenectady, New York, urging the governor that the death penalty for Pontón could not arrive soon enough (**Figure 40**).

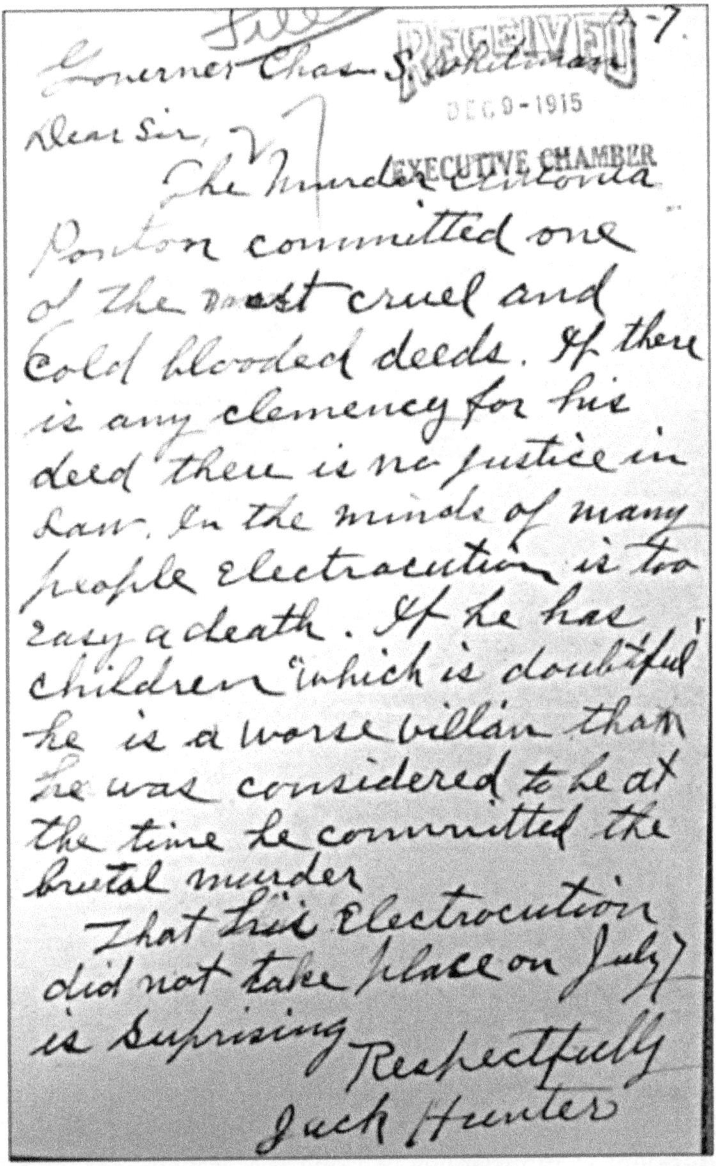

File 7.
RECEIVED
DEC 9-1915
EXECUTIVE CHAMBER

Governer Chas. S. Whitman

Dear Sir,

The murder Antonio Ponton committed one of the most cruel and cold blooded deeds. If there is any clemency for his deed there is no justice in law. In the minds of many people electracution is too easy a death. If he has children which is doubtful he is a worse villian than he was considered to be at the time he committed the brutal murder

That his Electrocution did not take place on July 7 is suprising

Respectfully
Jack Hunter

Figure 40. Letter from Jack Hunter requesting the death penalty for Antonio Pontón. (Tirado-Chiodini Collection, 1914-1916).

Attorney Le Barbier motioned to the trial court and requested it appoint independent medical experts to evaluate Antonio Pontón's mental state. Judge Alden Chester appointed two renowned physicians as medical experts to examine Pontón, Dr. Harold Lyons Hunt and Dr. Edward Anthony Spitzka.

On December 30, 1915, the doctors conveyed the results of their examination to Governor Whitman via telegram: Pontón suffered from delusional insanity, was profoundly insane, and did not know the difference between right and wrong–at present and at the time he committed the crime. Pontón's illness was progressive and incurable. His execution would amount to a miscarriage of justice (**Figure 41**).

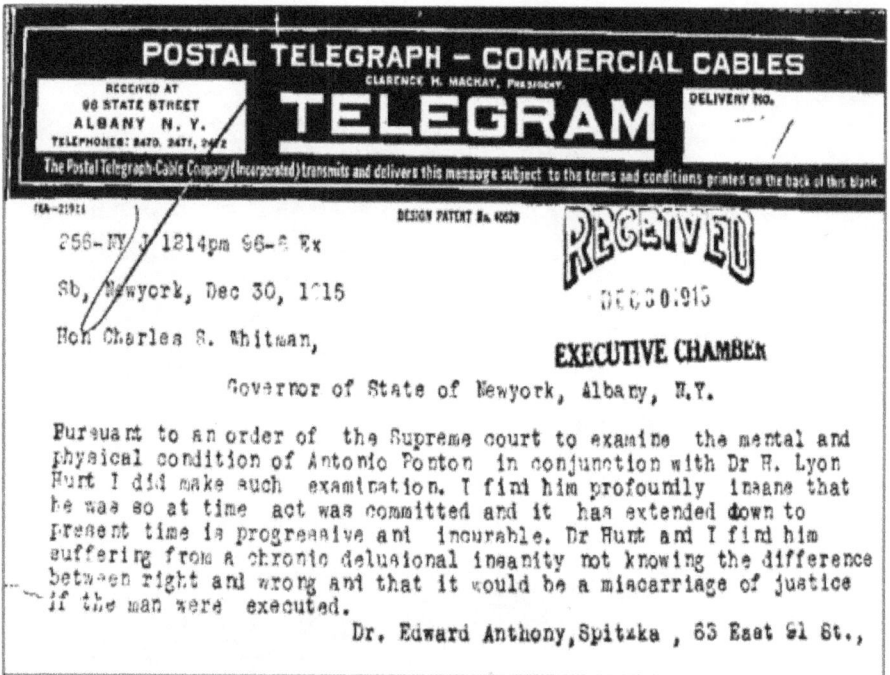

Figure 41. Telegram from Dr. Edward A. Spitzka to Governor Whitman. (Tirado-Chiodini Collection, 1914-1916).

On December 31, 1915, being privy to the information transmitted by Le Barbier and Drs. Spitzka and Hunt, Luis Muñoz Rivera, Puerto Rico's Resident Commissioner in Congress, issued another telegram to Governor Whitman, stating the clear grounds for commutation and seeking grace for Pontón (**Figure 42**).

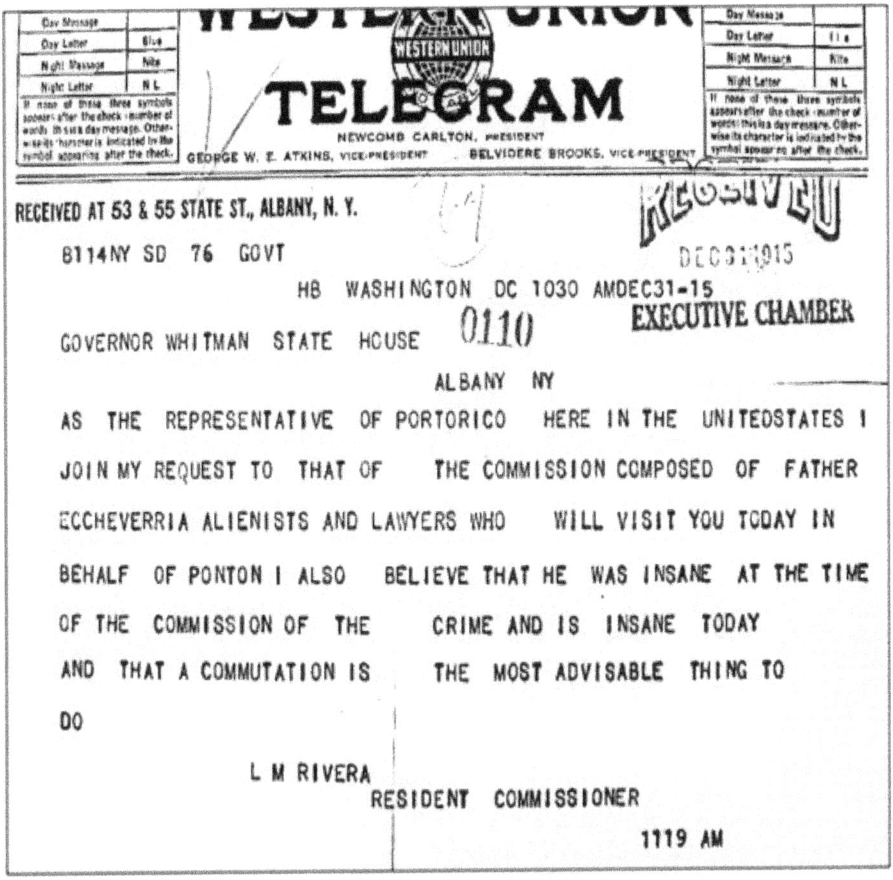

WESTERN UNION TELEGRAM

NEWCOMB CARLTON, PRESIDENT
GEORGE W. E. ATKINS, VICE-PRESIDENT
BELVIDERE BROOKS, VICE-PRESIDENT

RECEIVED AT 53 & 55 STATE ST., ALBANY, N. Y.

RECEIVED DEC 31 1915
EXECUTIVE CHAMBER

B114NY SD 76 GOVT

HB WASHINGTON DC 1030 AMDEC31-15

GOVERNOR WHITMAN STATE HOUSE 0110

ALBANY NY

AS THE REPRESENTATIVE OF PORTORICO HERE IN THE UNITEDSTATES I JOIN MY REQUEST TO THAT OF THE COMMISSION COMPOSED OF FATHER ECCHEVERRIA ALIENISTS AND LAWYERS WHO WILL VISIT YOU TODAY IN BEHALF OF PONTON I ALSO BELIEVE THAT HE WAS INSANE AT THE TIME OF THE COMMISSION OF THE CRIME AND IS INSANE TODAY AND THAT A COMMUTATION IS THE MOST ADVISABLE THING TO DO

L M RIVERA
RESIDENT COMMISSIONER

1119 AM

Figure 42. Telegram from Puerto Rico's Resident Commissioner in U.S. Congress, Luis Muñoz Rivera, petitioning for a sentence commutation for Antonio Pontón, based on clear evidence of insanity. (Tirado-Chiodini Collection, 1914-1916).

Despite Le Barbier's letter, the doctors' assertions, and Representative Muñoz Rivera's request, Governor Whitman refused to commute Pontón's sentence. However, on January 1, 1916, he granted another respite, so that Le Barbier could motion to the trial court with the doctors' examination. As shown in **Figure 43**, the press reported on Whitman's respite, the efforts of the Puerto Rican leaders to save Pontón, and the declarations of Drs. Spitzka and Hunt. The renowned New York doctors concurred that Pontón was profoundly insane, was so at the time he committed the crime, and it would be an injustice to execute him. (New York Herald, 1916).

NEW YORK HERALD, SATURDAY, JANUARY 1, 1916.

NEW RESPITE FOR SLAYER SENTENCED TO DIE ON MONDAY

Governor Whitman Grants Another Delay in the Case of Antonio Ponton.

Responding to the petition of 15,000 Puerto Rican residents of this country, Governor Whitman yesterday granted another reprieve to Antonio Ponton, sentenced to die on Monday in the electric chair at Sing Sing. The Governor's action followed an appeal by Ponton's attorney, which was supported by what the condemned man's friends assert to be incontrovertible proof that Ponton, wealthy and member of one of the most prominent families of the West Indies, is insane, and was at the time he stabbed his sweetheart to death in Schenectady, N. Y., and then tried to take his own life.

Agitation to save the life of Ponton was begun by his countrymen almost immediately after the sentence of death was made. Several days ago two hundred and fifty prominent Puerto Ricans met at the Ansonia Hotel and formed a committee, which was instructed to formulate the petition which with the statement was laid before the Governor. The petition finally bore fifteen thousand names.

"There can be no doubt but Ponton is insane and that his legal execution would be a miscarriage of justice," said Dr. Hunt last night. "The proof of his mental irresponsibility I believe is absolute. He is suffering now from chronic delusional insanity and was suffering in the same manner at the time he committed the crime.

"Even now, Ponton does not realize that Miss Kromer is dead and in his cell in the Sing Sing death house constantly calls for her, and refers to her as the sweetheart with whom he soon will be reunited. He is insensitive to pain and many other tests which we have made convinces us that he should not suffer the death penalty, but that he should be transferred to a hospital for the criminal insane.

"In taking the testimony we have been able to gather proofs that Ponton's only two living cousins on his mother's side are in asylums and that thirteen out of fifteen of his relatives either are, or have been adjudged insane. We have learned that he drove a horse off the edge of a high cliff in Puerto Rico for the single purpose of seeing what would happen to the animal, and that on another occasion he drove an automobile with passengers at high speed backward for twenty miles."

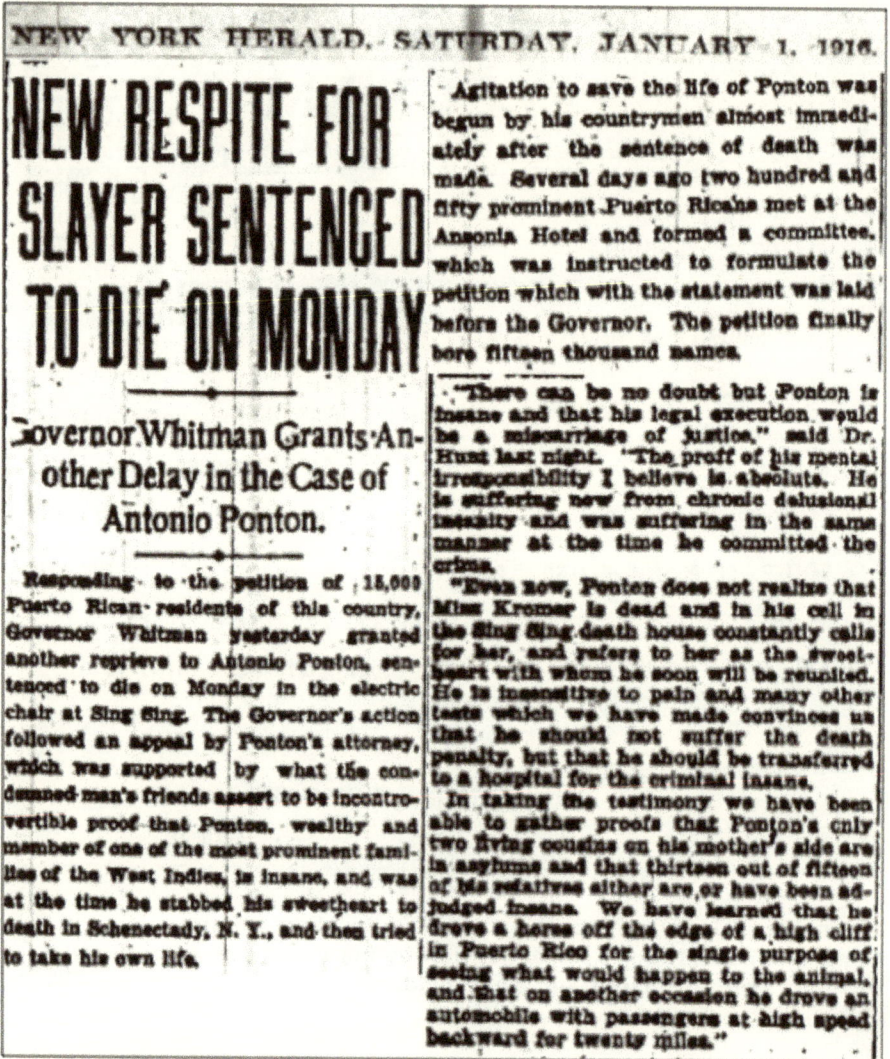

Figure 43. Excerpts from press coverage of the last respite granted by Governor Whitman, the Puerto Rico Committee efforts, and the doctors' declarations on the clear insanity of Pontón. Image composite from source. (New York Herald, 1916).

Neither the strong evidence before the court nor the material trial errors moved the judge. Judge Van Kirk denied Le Barbier's motion and ordered Pontón's execution to proceed on January 7, 1916. Desperate requests from top Puerto Rican leaders would soon follow (**Figure 44** and **Figure 45**).

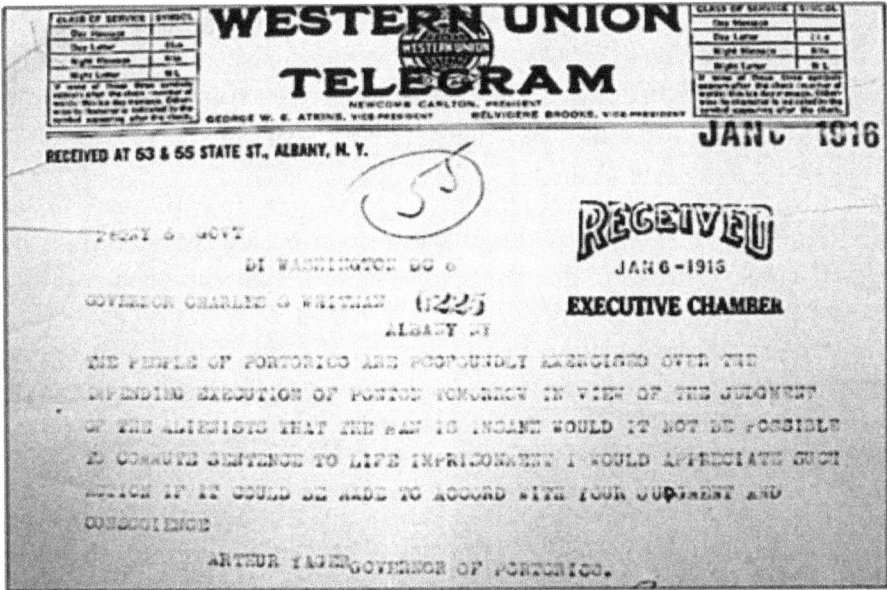

Figure 44. Telegram from Governor of Puerto Rico, Arthur Yager, to Governor Whitman pleading commutation of Pontón's death sentence. (Tirado-Chiodini Collection, 1914-1916).

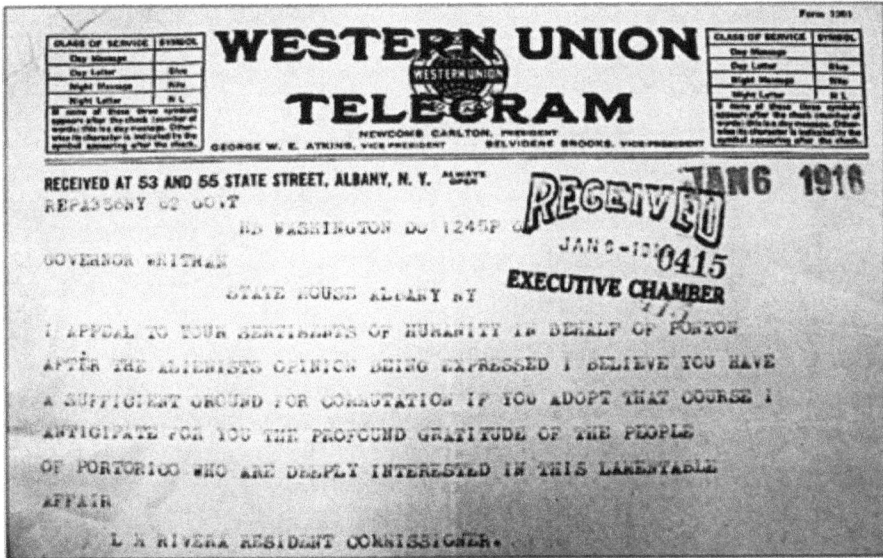

Figure 45. Telegram from Luis Muñoz Rivera, Puerto Rico's Resident Commissioner in U.S. Congress, once again urging Governor Whitman to grant Pontón clemency. (Tirado-Chiodini Collection, 1914-1916).

On January 6, 1916, the last requests from the highest leaders in Puerto Rico arrived at Governor Whitman's Executive Chambers, begging the governor's grace. Representative Muñoz Rivera and Arthur Yager, Governor of Puerto Rico, desperately appealed to Whitman's senses to exercise his clemency powers.

Also on that date, Antonio Vélez Alvarado, a Puerto Rican leader and member of the Puerto Rico Committee in New York chaired by Dr. Henna, addressed the governor via telegram on behalf of the committee (**Figure 46**). Vélez Alvarado urged Whitman to convene a *Governor's Lunacy Commission* prior to the execution. This was a discretionary option under Section 408-a of the New York Code of Criminal Procedure (Fitzpatrick, 1915, p. 206) that the governor had not yet exercised.

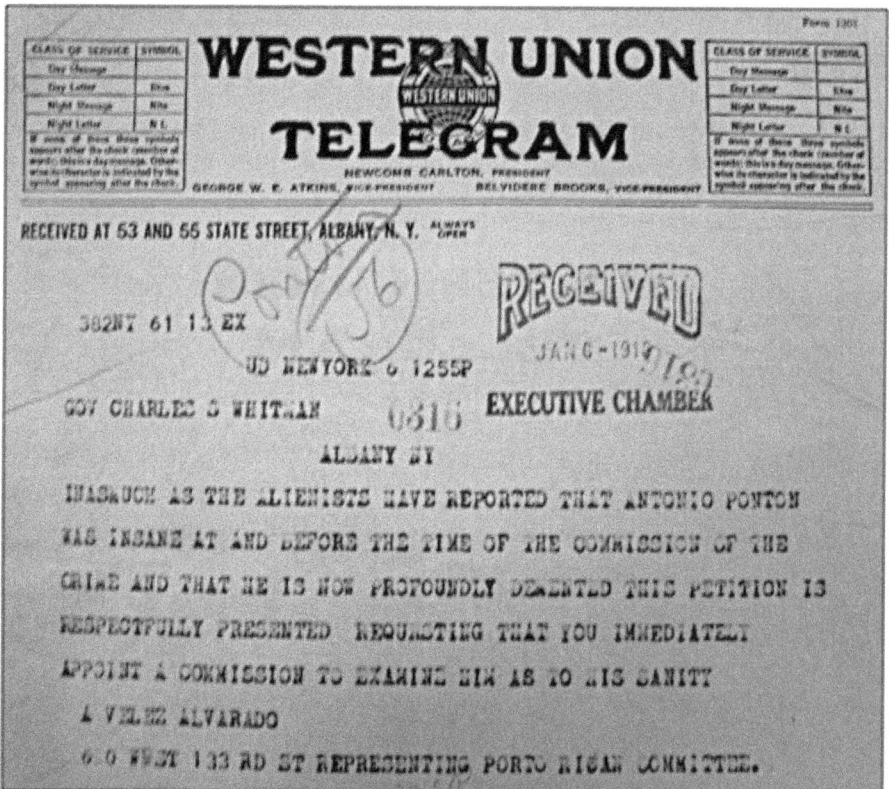

Figure 46. Telegram from Puerto Rican leader Antonio Vélez Alvarado to Governor Whitman. (Tirado-Chiodini Collection, 1914-1916).

The same day, Sing Sing Prison Deputy Warden Spencer Miller also sent a telegram to Governor Whitman requesting that he confer with new warden George W. Kirchwey regarding the appointment of a Governor's Lunacy Commission (**Figure 47**). Warden Kirchwey had voiced to the press his opposition to capital murder soon after he assumed his responsibilities as Sing Sing warden earlier that week.

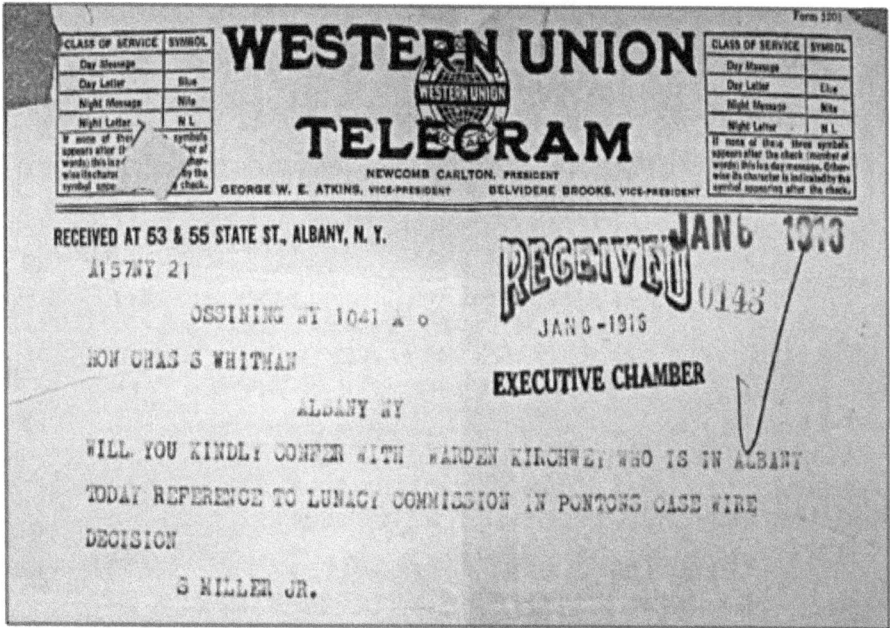

Figure 47. Telegram from Sing Sing Prison Deputy Warden Spencer Miller to Governor Whitman requesting he urgently confer with Warden George W. Kirchwey on the appointment of a Governor's Lunacy Commission to examine Pontón. (Tirado-Chiodini Collection, 1914-1916).

Despite the overwhelming evidence of insanity confirmed by renowned doctors, the clear trial errors, the many requests for grace, and the court's blatant refusal to award the motion for a new trial, Governor Whitman, who was running for reelection in 1916, disregarded the great miscarriage of justice about to occur and turned away from exercising his clemency powers. After conferring with Judge Van Kirk via telephone the night of January 6, 1916, Whitman would not interfere with the court. He ordered that Pontón's execution be carried out the next morning.

PONTON MET DEATH WHILE OFFICIAL CONDEMNED LAW

"Blot on Civilization," Declared Assistant Warden Miller as State's Witnesses Went to See Slayer of Bessie A. Kromer Punished

Father Echevarria and other Porto Rican friends of Ponton left no stone unturned to save him from the chair but Governor Whitman, after a long conference with Justice Charles C. Van Kirk the other day, refused absolutely to interfere—and so notified Mr. Miller over the telephone that night.

"What you are about to witness," said Assistant Warden Miller to the witnesses, "is a blot upon the civilization of the twentieth century. I know that you .... him.

... see t ...

"God, my Lord; God, my Lord" were the last words the witnesses heard as the mask was put over his face, but ...

bring about the ... punishment on that ... have a second chair which the new Sin cased."

and Dr. H. L. Mereness of Albany, assistant prison physician, and Dr. A. O. Squires of Ossining, applied their stethoscopes to the man's heart. Twice the doctors shook their heads quietly and twice more the current was sent into Ponton's body, making three contacts in all. The third time his right leg was burned and smoke arose from where the electrode was fastened. Exactly at 6:24 Dr. Mereness pronounced Ponton dead and prison officials declared the execution had been without a hitch. Immediately after the

Figure 48. Image composite of selected press coverage of Antonio Pontón's execution. (Albany Evening Journal, 1916).

On January 7, 1916, Antonio Pontón became the first Puerto Rican and the first Hispanic[4] person convicted of murder in the first degree and executed by electricity in the United States. As shown in the newspaper headlines composite on **Figure 48,** the press reported on Pontón's last moments of life, including his last words. It took three shocks to electrocute him. A weeping Deputy Warden Spencer Miller referred to Pontón's execution and the death penalty as "a blot upon the civilization of the 20th century" (Albany Evening Journal, 1916).

As **Chapter Three** explains, an environment filled with bias, ignorance and taboo against immigrants and those suffering from mental illness, the flawed laws of the times, political agendas, weak defense counsel, and the courts' failure to properly apply the law and constitutional protections overcame justice and due process in Antonio Pontón's case.

Three

The Case of Antonio Pontón,
One Hundred Years Later

The case of Antonio Pontón was buried with him. Until the publication of the historical novel *Antonio's Will* (Tirado-Chiodini, 2014), mention of this tragedy in the annals of history during the last century was virtually nonexistent, despite its historical, social and legal significance. There has been some progress in the adjudication and eradication of capital punishment in the United States since 1915, but not enough. Today, the country seems to be "back to square one" regarding the constitutionality of the death penalty.

In 1965, five decades after Antonio Pontón's death sentence, the New York Legislature amended the death penalty law, recognizing its flaws and the wrongs perpetrated against mentally ill defendants. The revised law afforded added protections for those suffering from mental illness under a more lenient standard, which would allow a reasonable jury more latitude to find someone like Pontón not guilty of murder in the first degree, by reason of insanity.

Is it possible that a reasonable jury could have found Pontón insane under the older and stricter law? We will never know for sure. The errors by the court and defense attorneys interfered with this process. But one thing is certain, Antonio Pontón, a mentally ill man of severely diminished capacity at the time he committed murder, should not have been executed. Instead, he should have been granted a new trial, where a jury could have rightfully considered the totality of the evidence to fairly decide on the issue of insanity. With a just trial, Pontón would have been found insane and sent to a mental institution, like Harry K. Thaw, the multimillionaire murderer and accused child molester described in *Antonio's Will*.[5] In the alternative, the jury should have found Pontón guilty of the lesser charge, and he should have been sentenced to spend life in prison.

As last resort, the law empowered Governor Charles S. Whitman to grant clemency. The governor had sufficient evidence in his hands to right the wrongs of the trial court and the court of appeals. The comments and evidence submitted by U.S. congressmen and other U.S. and Puerto Rico government officials, doctors, and advocates consistently drew attention to Pontón's mental illness, calling for a penalty commutation. The entire weight of the evidence supported an insanity defense: Antonio Pontón's maternal insanity history, his blood test revealing *neurosyphilis* (an insanity-causing disease), Pontón's medical examinations, and the medical expert testimony offered by four of the most renowned physicians in New York at the time. The defense met its "preponderance of the evidence" burden of proof, their required standard of proof at trial.

In a letter to Governor Whitman citing the court transcript, Charles E. Le Barbier, new defense counsel and former New York City District Attorney, clearly pointed out one of the trial court's material errors. Yet the governor opted to ignore the damaging error, the strong insanity evidence, the expert medical opinions, and the thousands of petitions. He refused to exercise his power under the law to commute Pontón's death sentence.

The justice system murdered Antonio Pontón. This murder, unlike Pontón's crime, was intentionally orchestrated by the "sane minds" of society. His electrocution was premeditated, horrific, and with malice aforethought, yet society and its leaders escaped accountability for the wrongful killing committed in the name of revenge.

Under modern New York law, even if found guilty of murder in the first degree, Pontón would not suffer the ultimate penalty of death. The last electrocution in New York occurred in 1963. The New York Court of Appeals abolished the death penalty in 2007, and the Sing Sing Prison death house was eliminated in 2008 by Executive Order.

But the nationwide debate on capital murder continues. As of this writing, the United States stands side-by-side with retentionist third-world countries and dictatorships, consuming invaluable time and resources in the "legalized killing" of human beings and in trying to devise ways to justify this barbaric policy, even when the most advanced nations in the world have risen above the medieval practice.

The U.S. Federal Government and many states still endorse capital punishment, when it clearly violates the constitutional and human rights of those condemned.

Aside from moral and human rights factors, other reasons trump the validity and effectiveness of capital punishment. These include the complexity of the criminal mind, the variables affecting free will, the lingering stigma regarding mental illness, the role of society in the creation of criminals, and a flawed justice system. The death penalty system is cursed by inherent bias, has failed in its implementation, and is economically prohibitive. But it is still living in the United States. A century after Antonio Pontón's execution, the blot upon civilization remains.

1. Issues and Errors in Antonio Pontón's Trial

As depicted in the historical novel *Antonio's Will*, there were considerable errors with Antonio Pontón's murder trial.[6] The most salient issues emerged from violations of the Fifth[7] and Sixth[8] amendments of the U.S. Constitution and were influenced by politically driven decision-making and the legal and social environment of the time. The injustice stands, even after applying the filter of *presentism*[9] to this case.

The most salient issues affecting Pontón's trial are discussed below. These are: (a) The inconsistent scientific knowledge and understanding of the connection between mental illness, free will, and the criminal mind; (b) The defects in the death penalty law; (c) Barriers set by the lack of financial resources and the adverse location of the trial; (d) The composition of the jury; (e) The admission of unreliable testimony; (f) The admission of the extrajudicial statement (hearsay) Pontón made to a reporter at Ellis Hospital, without counsel present; (g) Bias; (h) The evidence of family history of insanity and aggravating factors that the jury never evaluated; and (i) The flawed jury instructions.

(a) Mental Illness, Free Will, and the Criminal Mind

What made Antonio Pontón become a murderer? Was he a victim of his culture, his upbringing, his heredity, his illness, or a combination of all of these factors? Raised in a privileged family, he appeared to have it all: money, family love, and a promising future as a lawyer. Despite these favorable factors, he was unable to find harmony within his own mind.

Notwithstanding all the advances throughout the years in the field of psychology, psychiatry and social and behavioral sciences, it seems that modern society still cannot grasp a full understanding of the inner workings of the human mind. Psychiatry, also known as mental hygiene, was an emerging field during the time of Pontón's trial. However, top practitioners of the time had already acknowledged the tangible nexus between mental illness and criminal behavior. In his 1935 book *Sing Sing Doctor* (Squire, 1935), Dr. Amos O. Squire, Sing Sing's Chief Physician at the time of Pontón's execution, stated: "Anyone can be a criminal [and] none of us need to congratulate ourselves any too much on our success in keeping out of prison" (p.31). The doctor thought the main reason why people stay away from incarceration, aside from not being caught, is that they have been able to attain a balance between the expression and the restraint of their normal impulses. Dr. Squire maintained that this balance depends on complex factors inherent in each individual, which are influenced by environment, upbringing and disease. He believed that every human being possesses the egoistic traits that brought about the Sing Sing prisoners' fate, such as hate, anger, jealousy, passion, aggressiveness, possessiveness, greed and ruthlessness. The way humans balance these elements influences their criminal fate.

The Sing Sing Doctor felt that consideration for the rights of others is a major element in keeping people balanced, but he proposed that "just as some people are born stone deaf, some people are born ethically or morally deaf" (Squire, 1935, p. 32). He thought that most people have at least a rudimentary sense of honesty. The environment and upbringing at home and in school are heavy influencers. And then, there are some people who are robbed of their free will by disease.

Squire (1935) believed that the human body requires "certain chemicals in the right amount" (p. 46) in order to function properly. For the human mind to be sound, especially during its formative years, it requires proper nourishment. A person's behavioral upbringing must also be balanced. Too much love can be detrimental and create "a hopeless, helpless parasite," and too little love and attention can drive a child into "premature and ruthless self-assurance" (p. 47). No responsibility in a child's early life can produce a "functionally inadequate individual, incapable of coping with the world" (p. 46). Similarly, too much responsibility while young could rob a child from his childhood and an opportunity for the child to adequately mature. Dr. Squire observed that regardless of the situation, "parents must share largely in the blame" (p. 47). He also strongly believed that criminal conduct could be traced to early home environment that was "negligent, faulty, improper or evil" (p. 51).

The Sing Sing Doctor's forward-thinking observations were likely ahead of his time. While he had a tangible following as a frequent lecturer on the criminal mind, the law had not caught up with his observations. Can an individual fully control how he or she attains the necessary balance to stay away from crime? This early 20th century doctor did not think so, and modern scientists agree.

The science to understand the cause and effect of biological and chemical imbalances was in diapers at the dawn of the 20th century, even though visionary scientists such as Dr. Squire clearly acknowledged this key influence on human behavior. To date, the brain has been increasingly studied, but its functionality is not yet totally unveiled. The field of medicine has only learned to "calibrate" some disorders recently, with the help of medications nonexistent in the early 20th century. It is likely that with modern medicine and pharmacology, Pontón's mental state could have been stabilized. Certainly, antibiotics (unavailable until the 1940's) would have prevented him from developing syphilitic insanity. (American Chemical Society, 1999). Societal understanding of Pontón's disorders would have provided additional options to manage his behavior and might have helped in preventing his criminal conduct. While modern medications were unavailable, *there was* sufficient knowledge in 1915 to realize that Pontón could not control his will at the time he committed murder. This knowledge should have been applied to help Pontón, and perhaps could have even prevented his crime. In the end, those driving the hand of justice did not care to evaluate all the information available. The decision to execute Pontón seemed to reside not on facts or the law, but on an "arbitrary and subjective elsewhere."

Attorney Kevin M. Doyle founded New York State's Capital Defender Office in 1995 and served as Capital Defender until the spring of 2008. His essay *Lethal Crapshoot: The Fatal Unreliability of the Penalty Phase* (Doyle, 2008) is a revised section of the brief he used to successfully argue the abolition of the death penalty in New York in the case of *People v. Taylor* (People v. Taylor, 2007). In his essay, Doyle confirmed the observations made by Dr. Amos O. Squire many years earlier. Doyle (2008) stated that "human action and character emerge from personal choice but also from circumstances not chosen ... [and] ... while we should hold the individual to account for how he has played his cards, neither justice nor honesty allows us to pretend we are all dealt the same hand or even draw from the same deck. The relevance of life-history evidence is a given" (p. 291). And so, each case has its own set of circumstances, and it should be weighed as such.

Consistent with Dr. Squire's early observations, Doyle (2008) also touched on the strong established consensus in modern law as to very specific early risk factors for violent adult criminality. These include poverty, abuse (direct or indirect), neglect, noxious moral example, and brain defect or damage. In addition, he cited genetic research revealing that some people are born with a particular vulnerability to depression, violence, or addiction that can lead to criminal behavior. He also referenced environmental experiments that have uncovered compelling links between certain forms of pollution (i.e., metal, lead, pesticide) and a heightened incidence of violence. Further, he addressed experimental data relating maternal prenatal nutrition and drug addiction with a child's incidence of violence as an adult. Moreover, Doyle cited nutrition studies pointing to dietary risk factors for violence. These hard findings thwart both old and current theories of free will and culpability, nullifying the basis for the death penalty.

To date, the brain–particularly the aspect of free will or volition with regards to moral and legal responsibility–remains a focus for research and debate by psychologists, psychiatrists, philosophers, behaviorists, criminal lawyers and the courts, requiring much further exploration (Meynen, 2010; Baer, Kaufman, & Baumeister, 2008). As Doyle (2008) well stated, "mental-health experts then are guides not gods, even if some jurors will mistake them for the latter when presented by the defense or the prosecution" (p. 320). We cannot expect juries to make an accurate decision when the experts cannot make one, but even if we had the workings of the human mind conquered by hard science, Doyle (2008) asserts that "mass culture virtually inoculates against genuine consideration of mitigation evidence born of highly specialized knowledge" (p. 311). In other words, even if society had a strong grasp of the science behind the human mind, the bias inherent in jurors would override it.

Given our lack of understanding of the human mind and the reluctance of jurors to process highly specialized knowledge when considering mitigating factors in a capital murder case, how can a moral society justify the death penalty?

The Stigma of Mental Health

The manner in which Antonio Pontón's mental health was handled at home, in the community, and at Albany Law School shows the absence of popular knowledge of this subject at the turn of the century. It also reveals the profound stigma attached to mental health back then. Any issues Pontón might have suffered were diluted, disregarded, or deflected by his social status, denial, ignorance, taboo, and shame.

In hindsight, answers to many questions could help decipher whether Pontón's crime could have been prevented, or whether it was even triggered or exacerbated by the behavior of those surrounding him. At home, why was he not placed in an institution like some of his relatives were? Were there any signals when he was in grade school that could have prompted early treatment? Once in New York, some people around him looked the other way, even though they knew there was "something wrong" with Pontón, while others rightfully tried to help as best the knew how. Could his landlady, who evicted him after his first suicide attempt, have done something more for him to help change the course of events? When they saw his desperation, Pontón's law school friends rushed to his aid and urged him to return to Puerto Rico. Even his girlfriend Bessie Kromer and her spiritual counselor Reverend Charles M. Karg tried to help, but they simply did not know how. Could the Albany Law School Registrar Charles Watson have better assisted Pontón? Could Albany Law School's Dean J. Newton Fiero, a champion of ethics, have come to the rescue of his ill student before it was too late? Was the humiliation of expelling him necessary? What would have happened if Mrs. Nora Kromer had not fabricated the story of the revolver and had Pontón arrested on false pretenses, causing him to be expelled from Albany Law School, and pushing him to his limits? Was Mrs. Kromer justified in her behavior, even though she acted to protect her daughter, Bessie Kromer? Was having Pontón arrested effective to protect Bessie Kromer? What other options existed? In situations like these, where do society's responsibilities begin and where do they end?

Answering all these questions does not come without challenge. Hindsight is indeed 20-20, and there are critical lessons to be learned from this tragic story. Undoubtedly, the ignorance and stigma accompanying mental illness largely contributed in setting off the course of unfortunate events in Pontón's case. The fact that taboo and bias against those suffering from mental illness still inhabits modern society is distressing.

(b) The Defects in the Law: The Insanity Defense Law in New York

The Insanity Defense in New York During 1914-1916

Prior to 1965, New York Courts applied the "the right-wrong test" of the M'Naghten Rule,[10] which declared that an accused was "legally sane" if he had knowledge of right and wrong in relation to his act (Gluece, 1925). Under the New York codified M'Naghten Rule, then codified as § 1120 of the New York Penal Law (St. John's Law Review, 1965), the defendant would not be excused "except upon proof that, at the time of committing the alleged criminal act, he was laboring under such a defect of reason as: 1. Not to know the nature and quality of the act he was doing; or 2. Not to know that the act was wrong" (St. John's Law Review, 1958; St. John's Law Review, 1965). Under this standard, defendants like Pontón, while medically insane, could *subjectively* be denied the protection of the legal insanity defense. This decision *solely* relied on the jury. In turn, much like today, the jury relied on the judge's instructions and the evidence presented in court, largely influenced by their believability of the expert witnesses and the effectiveness of the "smoke and mirror" theatrics of counsel.

To save Pontón from electrocution, his lawyers had to proffer evidence at trial to show *by a preponderance of the evidence* that *at the time he committed the crime, he did not know the nature and quality of the act* he was undertaking, or he did not know that *the act* he was committing *was wrong*. The prosecution then had the burden of proving their case, including proving sanity, *beyond a reasonable doubt*. So, to defeat the defense's evidence of insanity caused by *neurosyphilis* in Pontón's trial, the prosecution had to show *beyond a reasonable doubt* that when Pontón was committing the act, he knew the nature of what he was doing or knew that what he was doing was wrong.

The ultimate decision on insanity was an *issue of fact for the jury* to decide, not an *issue of law* corresponding to the court. However, as described in Section (i) ahead, the court in Pontón's case never gave the jury the opportunity to properly decide this issue of fact. Mistakenly, *the judge decided this issue*, aiding the prosecution in meeting their burden. The judge stepped out of bounds when he stated to the jury that the defense had not presented evidence of insanity. He also failed to instruct the jury properly on the issue of *premeditation*.

Therefore, the jury based its decision on a subjective law, partial evidence of insanity and flawed court instructions, among other factors, fatally prejudicing Pontón.

Modern Insanity Defense in New York

Through the years, it became evident that the New York law addressing the insanity defense in capital murder cases was defective, and mentally ill inmates were being unjustly executed under the strict standard of *M'Naghten*.[11] In 1965, the New York statute was replaced to excuse criminal responsibility if the accused lacked the *substantial capacity* to know the nature or consequences of such conduct or that such conduct was wrong, as a result of a mental disease or defect. In addition, a psychiatrist who has examined the defendant could testify to the defendant's knowledge of the nature of his conduct or its wrongfulness.[12]

The current insanity defense is codified in New York Penal Law § 40.15, and it has substantially expanded on the M'Naghten Rule. The current law states (emphasis added): "In any prosecution for an offense, it is an affirmative defense that when the defendant engaged in the proscribed conduct, he lacked criminal responsibility by reason of mental disease or defect. Such lack of criminal responsibility means that at the time of such conduct, as a result of mental disease or defect, he lacked *substantial capacity* to know or appreciate either: 1.

79

The nature and consequences of such conduct; or 2. That such conduct was wrong" (Donnino, 1987, pp. 297-299).

So, unlike the *total impairment* required by the M'Naghten Rule when Pontón was tried (requiring that the defendant be *totally impaired* in order to be excused), today the defendant's lawyers must prove by a *preponderance of the evidence* that at the time of his conduct, the defendant lacked *substantial capacity* to know or appreciate either the nature and consequences of his conduct, or that his conduct was wrong. Proof of either one by the defendant is sufficient.

Under the revised law (absent the flawed court instruction at Pontón's trial) it would have been much easier for the defense to prove that Pontón was both medically and legally insane at the time he committed the crime. The defense would have likely prevailed with the insanity defense by proving that even if Pontón knew what he had done, he nevertheless did not appreciate it or did not understand the legal and moral implications of his conduct. In addition to the blood test evidence showing Pontón had a disease that rendered him insane, doctors who examined Pontón testified at his murder trial that Pontón did not know Bessie Kromer was dead, and he did not even remember killing her. He certainly lacked the substantial capacity to appreciate his conduct. The defense expert witness testimony by Drs. Charles L. Bailey, Ellis Kellert and subsequently, Drs. Harold L. Hunt and Edward A. Spitzka, converged in that Pontón, at the time he committed the crime, lacked the capacity, required knowledge, or appreciation of his egregious conduct, or that his conduct was wrong. Arguably, this testimony would have been strong enough–even under M'Naghten–to excuse Pontón from the death penalty.

If found insane under New York law at the time, Antonio Pontón would have been sent to a mental institution.[13]

(c) Barriers Set by Lack of Financial Resources and the Adverse Location of the Trial

Financing the Best Defense

Often, justice belongs to those who can afford it. This contravenes the Magna Carta fundamental mandate "to no one will we sell, to no one deny or delay right or justice" (National Endowment for the

Humanities, 2015). Interestingly, while Antonio Pontón's insanity defense did not stand a chance, highly paid defense lawyers eventually secured the insanity defense in favor of multi-millionaire railroad heir Harry K. Thaw, who murdered his wife's former lover in 1906. (New York American, 1906).[14] Thaw's artful lawyers succeeded under the same legal standards applicable during Pontón's trial. The defense's cost in Thaw's first murder trial alone (which ended in a hung jury) was reported to total $225,000, of which $100,000 went to defense lawyers. (Chicago's Daily Tribune, 1907). This was an exorbitant amount for the time. Thaw was able to buy justice, while Pontón could not afford it.

As relayed in *Antonio's Will*, Antonio Pontón's self-made father Manuel Pontón was considered wealthy in Puerto Rico, due to the assets he secured from his work as a prominent tobacco planter. However, all the pre-trial legal battles he fought on behalf of his son divested Manuel Pontón of the cash flow to afford private counsel for his son's murder trial. This placed Antonio Pontón at the mercy of inexperienced public defenders. He simply did not have the financial means or the clout that Harry K. Thaw had.

How can two murder cases with similar facts and tried under the same law result in such inconsistent outcomes? Money was a great differentiator.

The Adverse Location of the Trial

The New York law in 1915 directed that the place where the offense was charged determined the location or *venue* of the trial (Beavers v. Henkel, 1904). However, to safeguard against local prejudice, the law also allowed a defendant to change or remove the venue from one county to another, when a fair trial could not be had where the indictment was pending. This right existed in common law and was later codified in the laws of New York by 1915.[15] Changing the location of the trial was deemed a substantial right necessary to protect the rights of a defendant.

The gruesome murder of Bessie Kromer, a young local elementary school teacher, opened the floodgates to insurmountable press attention and drama. No similar crime had occurred in Schenectady County in 24 years. The outpour of press coverage–including the publication of the statement Pontón allegedly made from his Ellis Hospital bed to the *Schenectady Gazette* reporter the night of his crime and failed suicide–had an extraordinary emotional impact on the community. (Schenectady Gazette, 1914a, p. 8). As discussed ahead in Section (f), the court admitted Pontón's statement into the record even when it was likely that prior to the trial, everyone–including judges, witnesses, and potential jurors–became tainted against Pontón as a cold-blooded *Porto Rican* murderer. Pontón's fate was sealed in Schenectady, yet no evidence was found of any effort made by defense counsel to remove the trial elsewhere.

The trial may have had a different outcome if Pontón's lawyers had requested a change in venue. However, as Pontón's lawyers were new public defenders, factors such as lack of experience and politics might have come into play. Then again, the young attorneys may not have wished to request this right for their client. After all, Pontón's was a high-visibility case, and the fees paid by the court were attractive for a young attorney.[16]

If Pontón had access to the funds necessary to retain private attorneys through the entire trial, as Harry K. Thaw did, perhaps a change in venue would have been pursued. Even if the court did not grant a change in venue, Pontón's trial outcome might have taken a different turn if financed in the same manner as Thaw's murder trial, as previously discussed.

(d) The Composition of the Jury

The composition of the jury violated Antonio Pontón's Sixth Amendment constitutional right to due process and his Fourteenth Amendment constitutional right to the equal protection of the law.[17] Well before Pontón's trial, Art. I, § 2 of the New York Constitution incorporated the right to a jury trial. (New York Constitution, 1894). States that adopted trial by jury were subject to the jury impartiality requirement of the U.S. Constitution, which dictated that the jury be *drawn from a cross-section of the community* and that *race could not be used to disqualify jurors from serving.* (U.S. Const. amend. VI). In addition, Art. I, § 1 of the New York Constitution stated that "no member of this State shall be disfranchised, or deprived of any of the rights or privileges secured to any citizen thereof, unless by the law of the land, or the judgment of his peers" (New York Constitution, 1894).

"The requirement of impartiality stands as one of the few and one of the prime safeguards insuring that a jury will reach a fair and just result" (Gobert, 1988). The right to have a "jury of peers" does not require that the jury itself include members of the defendant's own race, gender, or ethnicity. However, courts have strongly upheld a defendant's right to an *impartial jury*, drawn from a pool containing a cross-section of the community. Even as early as 1879, the U.S. Supreme Court in *Strauder v. West Virginia* ruled that it violates the Equal Protection Clause to exclude African Americans [non-whites] from juries. (Strauder v. West Virginia, 1879). [18] This precedent applied during Pontón's trial, and subsequent cases shed light as to the scope of protection of the *cross-section* standard.[19]

Despite the safeguards afforded Pontón under the U.S. Constitution, reaffirmed under the applicable *Strauder* precedent, there was no Hispanic representation in Pontón's jury. All jurors were Caucasian Anglo men, most were of a particular social class, and a large number of them were General Electric workers. (Schenectady Gazette, 1915a; New York State Archives, 1910, 1915, 1920).

It defies reason that Pontón's defense lawyers would have passed up an opportunity to include a Hispanic juror in the jury. But there were likely no such candidates in the jury pool, despite the presence of Hispanics in Schenectady, New York. Although some area Hispanics may have met the U.S. citizenship requirement to serve as jurors,[20] it is unknown whether they met the remaining juror qualifications of property ownership, literacy, and dominion of the English language required under N.Y. Jud. Law § 598. (State of New York, 1917). Not only did this law divest Hispanic jurors (and likely other minorities and the poor), *in effect* the law also divested Hispanic defendants of their constitutional right to an impartial jury.

Even though the New York census reflects that Puerto Rican persons lived in Schenectady, New York on and around the time of Pontón's trial (New York State Archives, 1910, 1915, 1920), finding a Puerto Rican juror who was also a U.S. citizen in 1915 was near to impossible. Congressional discussions about U.S. citizenship for Puerto Ricans and Puerto Rico's statehood were actively ongoing since the occupation of the island by the United States in 1898. In 1900, racial discrimination discourse by even the highest of legal scholars helped defeat the existing presidential and congressional support for Puerto Rico's statehood and the granting of U.S. citizenship for its people. This racial bias delayed the arrival of U.S. citizenship for

Puerto Ricans for almost two decades, with dire consequences for Puerto Ricans in the island, as well as in the mainland.[21]

In 1915, due to the racial prejudice deeply rooted in the U.S. social fabric, Puerto Ricans were deemed non-aliens while still being deemed non-U.S. citizens (Gonzales v. Williams, 1904).[22] This *non-citizen national* status caused Puerto Ricans to be systematically excluded from jury service in the United States, even when Puerto Rico had been a U.S. territory since 1898.[23] U.S. citizenship was not granted to Puerto Ricans until 1917, under the Jones-Shafroth Act (The Jones-Shafroth Act, 1917), a year and two months too late for Antonio Pontón. Statehood has not arrived to the date of this writing, and this fact continues to be subject of heightened controversy.

The withholding of U.S. citizenship from Puerto Ricans in *Gonzales v. Williams* created a "constitutional loophole" that was particularly egregious to both prospective Puerto Rican *defendants* and prospective Puerto Rican *jurors*. The Puerto Rico political limbo, nurtured by bias, divested Pontón of his equal protection rights *and* of his right to an impartial jury. It also trumped the *Strauder* precedent in his case.

Ironically, although Puerto Rican men living in New York at the time of Pontón's trial could not exercise their right to participate as jurors, they were required to register with the New York National Guard, as Pontón did.[24] If they were considered qualified to serve in the *militia* or military, Puerto Rican men should have also been considered qualified to serve as jurors.

The constitutional inequities Pontón suffered as the first Puerto Rican defendant tried for capital murder in the United States raise important due process and fairness flags. Pontón's public defenders overlooked this key constitutional rights issue.[25] Judicial review of this case at a Federal level may have been appropriate, as this was a *case of first impression*. This was the first death penalty case involving a Puerto Rican whose constitutional rights were eroded by the "non-alien, non-U.S. citizen" *constitutional rights limbo* the U.S. Supreme Court had established in *Gonzales v. Williams*.

Curiously, Charles E. Le Barbier, Antonio Pontón's last attorney, was one of the attorneys in the *Gonzales v. Williams* defense team years earlier. (Erman, 2008). He was responsible for filing the appeal in the case before the U.S. Supreme Court in 1904. Given this prior experience, why would Le Barbier not follow a similar strategy with the Pontón matter? Financial and political reasons might have been key factors in this decision. First, Le Barbier was a private attorney for hire (not a public defender), and as previously discussed, the financial resources available to Pontón had been depleted. Second, the *Gonzales* matter received the support of the Puerto Rico Commissioner Resident to U.S. Congress in 1903, Federico Degetau, an advocate for U.S. citizenship who also argued the *Amicus Curiae Brief* in the *Gonzales* case. (Erman, 2008). Third, in 1915, concurrent with Pontón's battle against time, Puerto Rico was again undergoing discussions with legislators in U.S. Congress on the issue of U.S. citizenship. This environment may not have favored an appeal to the U.S. Supreme Court by a "mentally ill Puerto Rican murderer" who happened to be related to Puerto Rico's Resident Commissioner at that time, Luis Muñoz Rivera. Still, the Pontón matter presented an *issue of first impression*. This was a critical issue affecting the constitutional rights of Puerto Rican (and other Hispanic and Latino) criminal defendants in the United States, deserving of higher judicial scrutiny. Time would bring this deserving issue before the highest court decades later.

Almost 40 years after the Pontón case, the U.S. Supreme Court evaluated this issue in a Texas murder case involving a Mexican defendant. The court in *Hernandez v. Texas* ruled that the systematic exclusion of persons of Mexican descent from jury service–in the Texas county in which petitioner was indicted and tried for murder–deprived the petitioner of the equal protection of the laws guaranteed by the Fourteenth Amendment. On this basis, the court reversed the defendant's conviction in a state court. (Hernandez v. Texas, 1954).

Based on the above, consistent with the *Strauder* precedent, and in the spirit of the *Hernandez v. Texas* ruling, Pontón should have been afforded the right to have a jury pool with a fair cross-representation of the community. Since it was nearly impossible for Pontón to secure an impartial jury, this violation was a basis for reversal. Without a fair cross-representation in the jury pool, the death penalty was unconstitutionally imposed in Pontón's case.

(e) The Admission of Unreliable Expert Testimony

As described in *Antonio's Will*, defense attorney Andrew J. Nellis argued during Pontón's trial that admitting into evidence unreliable testimony would violate Pontón's constitutional rights. Specifically, the prosecution's expert testimony by Drs. Nishan Pashayan and Dr. William Scott was founded on the long-term memory recollection of the state-paid physicians (taken up to five months prior to their testimony); the doctors admitted to taking no notes whatsoever of their medical examinations of Pontón, which in itself places further doubt on the accuracy of their testimony; and they conducted their medical examinations of Pontón without defense counsel present, in violation of Pontón's Fifth and Sixth Amendment rights.

The doctors likely examined hundreds of other patients throughout the elapsed timeframe between the first examination of Pontón in December of 1914 and the date of their trial testimony in late April of 1915. Without any notes or medical records, how could their memory reliably recall the details of their examination of Pontón? How could they accurately remember what Pontón said to them? In addition, the doctors did not take any blood tests and did not care to document the advanced state of illness of Pontón. However, the illness was documented by the defense, supported by the blood test taken by the defense doctors, and undisputed at trial.

Further, the Fifth Amendment provides protection against self-incrimination by stating, in part, that a defendant "shall [not] be compelled in any criminal case to be a witness against himself" (U.S. Const. amend. V). The defense maintained that the prosecution's doctors violated Pontón's right against self-incrimination by not informing Pontón that anything he said or did during the examination could be used against him in a court of law.

For the above reasons, any evidence of the prosecution's expert examinations should have been discarded as unreliable and in violation of Pontón's Fifth Amendment rights against self-incrimination, as well as his Sixth Amendment right to counsel. Yet the court admitted the unreliable and infringing expert testimony, which became the basis for Pontón's death sentence.

(f) The Admission of the Extrajudicial Statement (Hearsay) Made by Antonio Pontón at Ellis Hospital, without Counsel Present

Hearsay consists of extrajudicial statements offered to prove the truth of the matter asserted (5 J. Wigmore, Evidence § 1361,

Chadbourn 1974). This type of testimony was freely admissible in court at early English common law, but as the judicial process changed from being a general "inquest" to an "adversarial" process, hearsay was regarded as a threat to justice for a defendant because of the intrinsic unreliability of the extrajudicial statements made. Even as early as 1690, lawyers were overtly cognizant of the impropriety of using hearsay testimony in court, to the point in which, on at least one occasion, an ethical prosecutor halted the declarations on his very own witness, "for example's sake" (Wigmore, 1904). Therefore, well before Pontón's trial, there was already an implicit understanding in the legal profession of the impropriety of hearsay and the potential erosion of the defendant's constitutional rights as a result of admitting such evidence.

Yet, even though keeping hearsay out of the courtroom was the ethical measure and a professional standard at the time of Pontón's trial, Judge Charles C. Van Kirk permitted the introduction of hearsay by allowing witnesses to testify about their personal knowledge and about what they heard others say outside of court. As described in *Antonio's Will* and mentioned earlier, the court even admitted the statement made by Pontón to a *Schenectady Gazette* reporter from his Ellis Hospital bed the night of the murder. This statement was unreliable, as it was made under duress, while Pontón was disoriented, ill and sedated, and without the benefit of counsel present, also raising grave Fifth and Sixth Amendment constitutional issues.

Today, state and federal courts in the United States have established "hearsay rules" to compel court officers to keep hearsay out of the courtroom. Jurors can only rely on testimony directly presented in court, unless there is an exception to the applicable hearsay rule. (Wigmore, 1904; Fordham University School of Law, 1972).

To avoid a violation of Pontón's constitutional rights, what the prosecution's experts, Drs. Pashayan and Scott, heard Pontón declare while examining him could have been rightfully suppressed from the trial under Fifth and Sixth Amendment grounds, as Pontón had a constitutional right to counsel and had a right against self-incrimination. He had these rights, even though the *Miranda Rule* did not exist yet to guard constitutional protections. The U.S. Supreme Court established this rule in 1966 in the case of *Miranda v. Arizona*.

(Miranda v. Arizona, 1966). The rule levies a requirement on the State to provide a warning to criminal suspects in police custody (or in a custodial interrogation) before they are questioned, advising them of their rights to remain silent, that anything they say can be used against them in a court of law, that they have the right to consult with and have an attorney present during the interrogation, and that they can be assigned an attorney free of cost if they cannot afford retaining counsel. In *Miranda*, the court held that the admission of an elicited incriminating statement by a suspect not informed of his or her constitutional rights violates the Fifth Amendment right against self-incrimination and the Sixth Amendment right to counsel. (Miranda v. Arizona, 1966). Providing a *Miranda* warning prior to securing a statement would help preserve its admissibility in criminal proceedings for use against the defendant. Thus, the warning is intended to protect such important defendant's rights that had been historically violated—as in Pontón's case—when their protection was left at the discretion of police, prosecutors and the courts.

Back in 1915, without the *Miranda Rule* in place, whatever Pontón said and any information gathered from him during the State's medical examination became admissible in the record and could be used against him during trial, *unless* Judge Van Kirk refused to admit the information, in protection of Pontón's constitutional rights. The judge chose not to protect these rights, allowing the unreliable and damaging evidence in the record, key in Pontón's death penalty conviction.

(g) Bias

As described in *Antonio's Will*, prejudice of a diverse nature influenced the environment surrounding Antonio Pontón's trial. This included racial, national origin, cultural, religious, and social bias. Copious statements of bias paraded before the jury during trial, where counselors and witnesses alike addressed Pontón as "The Spaniard" and "The Porto Rican" before the jury; in numerous occasions witness testimony referenced Pontón being Catholic, and the court even asked Pontón what faith he professed, prior to sentencing him. In addition, Pontón's mental illness and "loathsome disease" prejudiced the jury more so against him. Although medical professionals of the times acknowledged the social stigma inherent in these two key factors, the

Pontón court did not weigh the great influence any of the above factors had in tipping the scales of justice. As discussed below, modern courts recognize all of these elements of bias as highly discriminatory and a basis for a mistrial.

Race

The negative impact that racial bias plays in death penalty sentences has been clearly acknowledged. (New York State Assembly, Standing Committee on Codes, Judiciary and Correction, 2005). In his 2008 paper, New York capital defender Kevin M. Doyle stated that race strains "every crack in the machinery of death," and it is a "barrier to empathy" that regularly clouds judgment and erodes fairness. (Doyle, 2008, p. 275).

In addition, prominent concerns about the criminality of the foreign-born around 1915 were baseless, as incarceration rates for violent crimes committed by immigrants to the United States in the early 20th century have been found to be very similar to those of non-immigrants, for all ages (Moehling & Morrison Piehl, 2009). Even back then, Sing Sing Doctor Amos O. Squire flat out rejected popular theories that immigrants have a higher incidence of criminality. He wrote: "[W]hatever antisocial tendencies they may have are not to blame, as much as the failure of the 'melting pot' to properly adjust to diversity and change" (Squire, 1935, p. 50). Today, as the United States continues to struggle with the stereotypes and challenges presented by immigration, courts have acknowledged that "signals scramble" in cross-cultural settings and this poses lethal dangers for a defendant. (Doyle, 2008, p. 288). For example, in the 1992 case of *Mak v. Blodgettj* the 9th circuit court affirmed relief from a death sentence and faulted trial counsel for failing to present an expert witness to educate the jury on issues of cultural differences. The defendant was Chinese, and his demeanor could be misunderstood as cold and unremorseful. (Mak v. Blodgettj, 1992).

Even though Puerto Rico had become a U.S. territory 17 years before Pontón's trial, in New York he was still considered "a Spaniard" or "Porto Rican." As such, he was regarded as an immigrant "of a different race," with all the negative connotations and discrimination given to this class during that time. Undoubtedly, a court approach similar to the 9th circuit court in *Mak v. Blodgettj* would have mitigated racial and cultural bias in the Pontón case. However, this precedent was not available in 1915. Surprisingly damaging, as depicted in *Antonio's Will*, defense counsel Nellis referred to his own client during closing statement as "a member of a race which is, historically, ... unmoral" (Schenectady Gazette, 1915d), suggesting that Pontón would not know right from wrong because of his "unmoral" race, and this "fact" could excuse Pontón's criminal behavior. This statement, while perhaps intended to release this defendant from a charge of murder in the first degree and free him from a death sentence, surely backfired with a jury seeking rightful justice for the victim. Certainly, defense attorney Nellis was no cultural or race expert. His statement to the jury placed a blot on Pontón's character based on bias, and it deprived Pontón of proper counsel representation, a right afforded under the Sixth Amendment of the U.S. Constitution. Having no proper representation, Pontón's case should have been thrown out solely on this basis. However, as discussed in Section (h) ahead, all defense motions appear to have been limited to motions for a new trial founded on the lack of jury exposure to the full weight of the insanity evidence.

Doyle (2008) said it best: "Maintaining a death penalty in a society with America's racial history is like building a munitions depot on a volcano" (p. 323). It not only invites, but it also nurtures, danger and injustice, as it did the case of Antonio Pontón.

The "White Victim Effect"

Today it is widely accepted that minorities convicted of killing white non-minorities are more prone to receiving the death penalty. According to *Race and the Death Penalty*, a report by the *American Civil Liberties Union (ACLU)*, a University of Maryland study commissioned by the Maryland Governor concluded that defendants are much more likely to be sentenced to death if they have killed a white person. Similar studies have reached consistent conclusions. (ACLU, 2003). The ACLU report references other studies that converge in their finding that the likelihood of being sentenced to death increases when the victim is white. For example, a North Carolina study found that the odds of a death sentence increased three and a half times if the victim was white rather than black; a California study found that Latino defendants tried for murder of a white (non-

Latino) victim are 11 times more likely to receive the death penalty than if they had killed a Latino victim; a Philadelphia 1997 study found that the rate of death penalty sentencing increased 38 percent when the defendant was black. In addition, the ACLU report states that research from nationwide studies conducted by government and private institutions have produced similar findings. (ACLU, 2003). Undoubtedly, this evidence points to a systemic failure in the consistent administration of the death penalty at state and federal levels in the United States.

Bessie Kromer was a white victim. Antonio Pontón was regarded as non-white due to his Puerto Rican national origin. His own lawyer sustained in his closing statement before the jury that Pontón was of a different race. These and the above factors likely heightened the odds of Pontón being condemned to death by electrocution.

Religious Bias

In 1915, in addition to racial, cultural and national origin bias, there was also great prejudice against those who professed the Catholic religion. (Bilhartz, 1986; Billington, 1938). Puritans and Congregational English immigrants brought anti-Catholic fears into America. The fear reached a peak in the 19th century when Protestants became distressed by the increased number of Catholic immigrants. They claimed that Catholics were destroying the culture of the United States. This sentiment was still prevalent in U.S. society at the time of Pontón's trial. The fact that Pontón was Catholic was repeatedly represented during his trial, forming part of the record. The court also asked Pontón to state his religion when he made his pre-sentence statement. Religion was a factor weighing on the jury's and the court's death penalty decision.

Social Prejudice

Social prejudice towards Antonio Pontón for having contracted a loathsome disease and for suffering of mental illness invited a death penalty sentence. A thriving *Eugenics* movement promoted the elimination of the sick and weak and of those with "poor genetics," particularly those of a "lesser race," and those with hereditary insanity and "loathsome" diseases like syphilis. (Wilson, 2003; Black, 2012).

The pronounced social stigma levied by syphilis was unwarranted, particularly because the then incurable disease was so prevalent at the turn of the century in the United States. (Jabbour, 2000). Largely unreported due to its stigma, well over 15 percent of the population suffered it. The incidence of syphilis was much higher in the military. Enlisted men in Puerto Rico reported almost a 40 percent incidence in 1915. (Costa Mandry, 1943) citing (Vedder, 1915).

Based on the above, Pontón's race, culture, national origin, religion, his mental illness, and a "loathsome disease" were cumulative factors for considerable prejudice, skewing justice in his murder trial.

(h) Evidence not Before the Jury: Entire Family History of Mental Illness and Aggravating Factors

As described in *Antonio's Will*, on the date of Antonio Pontón's trial, the evidence from the court-authorized *Puerto Rico Lunacy Commission* had not yet arrived. The Lunacy Commission was to gather evidence of the history of insanity on Pontón's maternal family. The evidence, documenting the incidence of mental illness in Pontón's relatives, was geared to strengthen the mental illness nexus for the defense. Even though there was direct court testimony as to the frequency of mental illness in Pontón's maternal family, the trial went on without the Lunacy Commission's evidence, and the jury was unable to evaluate it. The evidence arrived after the trial had concluded. The court denied motions for a new trial based on the new evidence, and the New York Court of Appeals affirmed the lower court, without considering the evidence. (People v. Ponton, 1915).

In addition to the incomplete evidence at trial, there is material information pointing to evidence that was never considered by the defense. Of particular interest is the clemency letter written by E. Ferrett, agent for *Wright's Indian Vegetable Pills Co., Inc.* in New York City (**Figure 37**). This communication does more than document a pleading for Pontón's cause. As discussed ahead, this letter actually brings forward a key piece of information: Antonio Pontón was likely a regular customer of Ferrett's, and Pontón–as did many people at the turn of the century–consumed Wright's pills to treat his health ailments. This discovery introduces the likelihood that the Wright's pills potentiated Pontón's violent behavior. Thus, not only did Pontón act under the influence of a mental illness, chemicals in his medication also affected his conduct.

During the 1800s and 1900s, the Wright's pills were among the many unregulated medications advertised and sold directly to consumers under the claim that they possessed cure-all properties due to their powerful ingredients, purportedly based on American Indian herb recipes. Wright's marketed these "miracle pills" in the United States and Puerto Rico for the treatment of dozens of illnesses and discomforts. Sold for consumption by adults and children alike, Wright's represented that besides curing depression and venereal disease, its pills would heal ailments arising from indigestion, menstrual cramps, pregnancy discomfort, labor, headaches, eye inflammation, nervousness, jaundice, fever, hemorrhoids, and anemia, among a multitude of other health issues (United States Food and Drug Administration, 1918, pp. 130-131, 661). Wright's marketed via newspaper ads, scenic and themed postcards, and almanacs. For example, **Figure 49** shows a photograph of an ad taken from an original "Wright's Pictorial Family Almanac" the author acquired from an antiques and collectibles dealer, listing the purported miraculous curative powers of the pills. (Wright's Indian Vegetable Pills, 1889). As shown in **Figure 50,** the agent listed on the cover was E. Ferrett, in all likelihood (based on the letter's monogram, signature, and address) the same person who authored the clemency letter on **Figure 37.**

The alleged healing properties of the Wright's popular remedies proved to be false, and today Wright's pills have joined the annals of "quack" medicine. In 1915, when confronted in Federal Court by the Puerto Rico Attorney General, Wright's admitted to mislabeling pills that the company had introduced in Puerto Rico. In fining Wright's for its violation of the *Food and Drugs Act*, the court stated that the pills were "entirely worthless" for the purposes stated. (United States Food and Drug Administration, 1918, p. 132).

In addition, U.S. government chemical analysis performed on the Wright's pills revealed opium and morphine as active ingredients in the pills. (United States Food and Drug Administration, 1918, p. 661). These were common ingredients in many products freely accessible commercially since before the U.S. Civil War, as the U.S. government did not regulate their distribution until after 1914.[26]

Figure 49. Photo of an ad of "Wright's Indian Vegetable Pills" taken from an original "Wright's Pictorial Family Almanac" listing E. Ferrett as agent. (Wright's Indian Vegetable Pills, 1889).

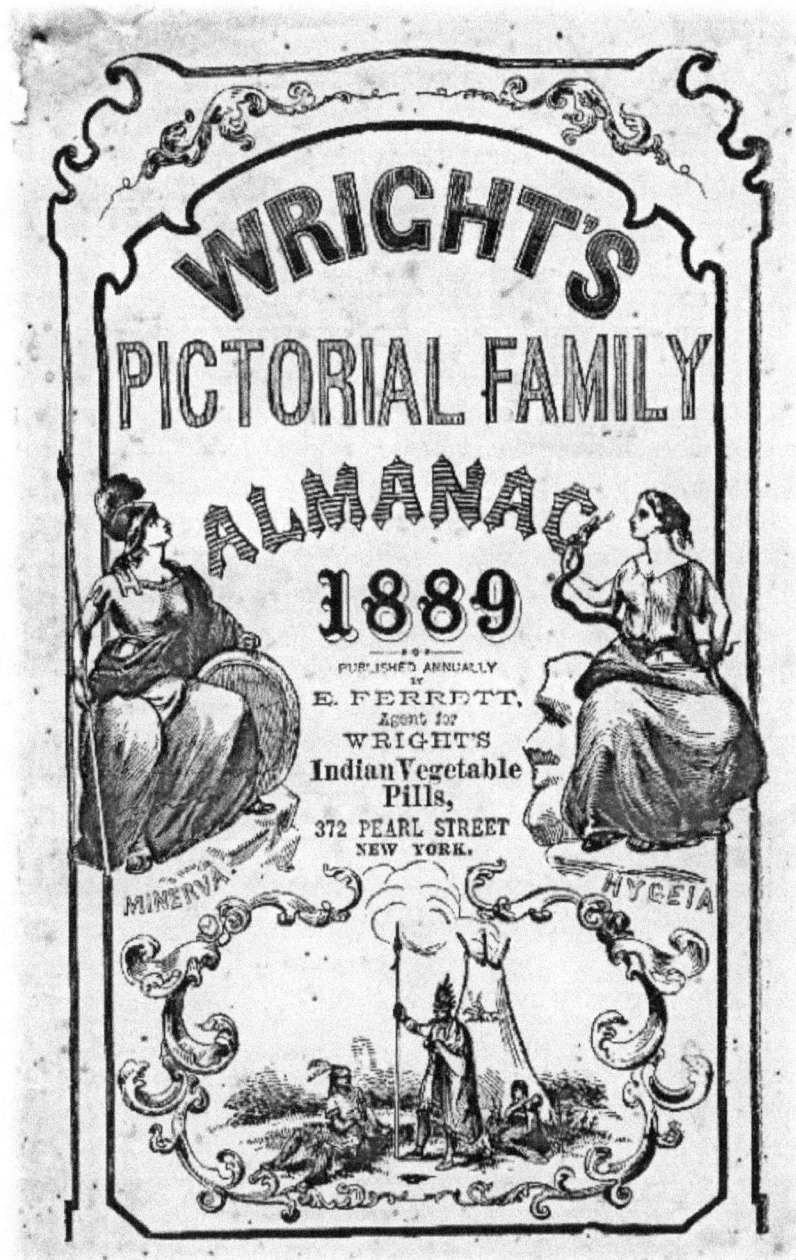

**Figure 50. Photo of cover of a 1889 "Wright's Pictorial Family Almanac,"
listing E. Ferrett as Agent for "Wright's Indian Vegetable Pills" in New
York.** (Wright's Indian Vegetable Pills, 1889).

Today, drugs containing opium and morphine are highly regulated by the *Federal Drug Administration*, as they can create a strong addiction and severely affect mental illness. "People with mental illness who abuse opiates are at increased risk of impulsive and potentially violent acts, and they are more likely to both attempt suicide and to die from their suicide attempts" (National Alliance on Mental Illness, 2013). In addition to prompting self-harm, the use of drugs containing these chemicals is known to trigger the commission of criminal acts against others. (National Institute of Justice, 2012).

Although the use of medications containing chemicals like opium and morphine was widespread (and even encouraged by the medical and pharmaceutical community), by 1915 the nexus between these substances and criminal behavior was evident to health professionals and government officials, but not to the general consumer. (Kleiman & Hawdon, 2011, p. 96). It follows–from information available then and now–that if Pontón consumed the Wright's pills, the opiates in these pills likely affected his behavior. Yet, even with the existing knowledge about the impact of these chemicals on human behavior, defense attorneys did not address the potential aggravating effect of opiates on Pontón's conduct, a factor that could have swayed the jury against the death penalty.[27]

If a medication could trigger the onset of criminal behavior, forcing a person's criminal intent, then this is enough justification to discard the death penalty on its face. This tangible possibility in Pontón's situation adds to the many reasons making his death conviction and execution a grave error.

(i) The Flawed Jury Instructions

Today, jury instructions in death penalty cases that do not address mitigating factors regarding the defendant's mental health are deemed to violate the defendant's Eighth Amendment rights against cruel and unusual punishment. (Penry v. Lynaugh, 1989; Bigby v. Dretke, 2005; U.S. Const. amend. VIII). At the time of Pontón's trial, this instruction was not a requirement. Under modern standards, Judge Van Kirk would have been required to emphasize in his instructions to the jury that Pontón's mental health was a mitigating factor for the jury to consider in determining capital punishment.

However, as described in *Antonio's Will*, although the judge did acknowledge that the presence of syphilis in Pontón's blood was an *undisputed fact*, he stated, as a matter of opinion–and against testimony to the contrary–that *the defense had advanced no evidence* that Pontón's illness had caused him dementia. The judge did this, even though the issue of insanity was an *issue of fact* for the jury to decide, not the court.[28] This was a material error.

In addition, Judge Van Kirk's instruction to the jury regarding premeditation was incomplete. When Charles B. Cox, the jury foreman, asked the judge about the time needed for premeditation, the judge did not tell him that premeditation *cannot* take a fraction of a second or occur *at the moment of striking the fatal blow*, the applicable standards under *People v. Conroy*. (People v. Conroy, 1897). Certainly, this would have made a difference to jurors who were clearly considering the lesser charge and sought guidance from the court.

The jury did not have all the facts; it did not have reliable–or even complete–evidence to make a life or death decision *beyond a reasonable doubt,* and now it had flawed instructions from the court. In an environment affected by subjective information, flawed laws, prejudice and court errors, the jury wrongfully chose death for Antonio Pontón.

3. The Death Penalty in Modern Times: Important Considerations

The topic of death penalty continues to be a controversial issue in the United States. (New York State Assembly, Standing Committee on Codes, Judiciary and Correction, 2005). The U.S. capital punishment system is flawed, unevenly applied and arbitrary, greatly disfavoring defendants who suffer from mental illness and those who are minorities. (Dieter, 2011). Yet the United States remains engaged in the use of this medieval practice when the more evolved countries in the world have abolished it.

In the United States, many states placed a death penalty moratorium–or have abolished the penalty altogether–since the 1972 landmark case of *Furman v. Georgia,* where the U.S. Supreme Court struck down Georgia's death penalty law. In *Furman,* the court held that the death penalty constituted cruel and unusual punishment in violation of the U.S. Constitution. Justices William J. Brennan and

Thurgood Marshall concurred, stating that the death penalty was unconstitutional in all instances. Other justices concurred, highlighting the arbitrary nature with which death sentences had been imposed and acknowledging the finding that the death penalty had been administered with unlawful racial bias. (Furman v. Georgia, 1972).

However, this decision was short-lived. In 1976, the U.S. Supreme Court in *Gregg v. Georgia* declared the death penalty constitutional, so long as properly administered, because it furthered the rationale of retribution and deterrence. (Gregg v. Georgia, 1976). As a result, the death penalty was reinstated in some states, and it was adopted again in New York in 1995, promoted by Governor George Pataki. In 1997, the American Bar Association called for a moratorium on capital punishment, and in 2004 in *People v. LaValle* the New York Court of Appeals found the New York death penalty statute unconstitutional. (People v. LaValle, 2004). In 2007, in *People v. Taylor,* the New York Court of Appeals commuted the last New York death row inmate's death penalty to life imprisonment. (People v. Taylor, 2007; DPIC, 2015c).

As of this writing, capital punishment seems to be in decline in the United States, but it is far from being extinguished: 19 states[29] have abolished the death penalty and 31 retain death penalty laws. The U.S. Federal Government and the U.S. military[30] have also continued to uphold the death penalty (New York State Assembly, Standing Committee on Codes, Judiciary and Correction, 2005), which still applies to states that have abolished it, and to U.S. territories where there is no death penalty, like Puerto Rico.

No Deterrent Effect

According to the *Death Penalty Information Center*, in U.S. states that abolished the death penalty the crime is actually lower than in states that have upheld it. (DPIC, 2011). The finding is consistent at an international level, as well. (United Nations, Office of the High Commissioner for Human Rights, 2014). This indicates that capital punishment *does not have the intended deterrent effects*. This position has been advocated by many scholars and others, including former U.S. President Jimmy Carter, who observed in 2012 that "the homicide rate is at least five times greater in the United States than in any Western European country, all without the death penalty" (Death Penalty Pro's and Con's, 2015). This same perspective was highlighted a century ago and brought to light in the clemency letters that Puerto Rican groups like *Eco Estudiantil* and *University of Pennsylvania* students addressed to Governor Whitman as part of their prayers for grace in the case of Antonio Pontón (See **Chapter One**.) Most dissenters, including former U.S. President George W. Bush and former New York Governor George Pataki, have based their arguments in favor of the death penalty largely on retribution or victims' rights, and there is no real consensus among them on the statistical effectiveness of capital punishment in deterring crime. (Death Penalty Pro's and Con's, 2015).

Time on Death Row

Currently, in the states that sponsor capital punishment, the defendant will not likely be put to death within the first year-and-a-half of his indictment, as was the case with Pontón. The modern appeal process is much more extensive and affords greater opportunity for reconsideration of the ultimate decision to execute a condemned defendant. (Capital Punishment in Context, 2015; GRIP and NDTRAN, 2015). In fact, there are prisoners who have been on death row for *decades*. This raises in itself a constitutional issue of cruel and unusual punishment due to the time and poor conditions of long-term imprisonment on a death row environment.

Cost of the Death Penalty

In the United States, the cost to carry out the death penalty for one person is massive, and for some jurisdictions it is cost-prohibitive and akin to financing a natural disaster. *Amnesty International USA* has reported on the exorbitant costs of capital punishment, citing a number of state reports. (Amnesty International, 2015). For example:

• A December 2003 survey by the *Kansas Legislative Post* found that the estimated cost of a death penalty case there was 70 percent more than the cost of a comparable non-death penalty case. Death penalty case costs were counted through to execution (median cost $1.26 million). Non-death penalty case costs were counted through to the end of incarceration (median cost $740,000).

• A 2004 Report from the *Tennessee Comptroller of the Treasury Office of Research* shows that death penalty trials there cost an average of 48 percent more than the average cost of trials in which prosecutors seek life imprisonment.

• The March 2008 Urban Institute report, *The Cost of the Death Penalty in Maryland,* showed that death penalty cases there cost three times more than non-death penalty cases, or $3 million for a single case.

• The July 2008 study by *The California Commission for the Fair Administration of Justice* reported that in California the current death penalty system costs $137 million per year, when it would cost $11.5 million for a system without the death penalty.

Executing the Mentally Ill, A View from the Inside

In his book *Sing Sing Doctor,* Dr. Amos O. Squire (1935) chastised the laws of the times for ignoring the impact of mental illness on crime. He stated: "Under strict application of [the law], few men that are not positive imbeciles or maniacs can be held legally insane" (Squire, 1935, pp. 79-80). Regarding the prisoners in Sing Sing Prison during his 1914-1925 tenure there, the doctor observed that about 75 percent of the cases of "feeble-mindedness" that he encountered could be attributed to heredity. Other causes Dr. Squire highlighted included scarlet fever, meningitis, syphilis, alcohol or narcotics use by the parents, an injury to the mother during pregnancy or to the child at birth, or an injury during childhood. Dr. Squire observed that there was an inherent flaw in the way society dealt with crime and punishment, as the required criminal intent was certainly influenced by the hereditary conditions of the condemned. (p. 80). This is consistent with today's research, as former New York Capital Defender Kevin Doyle explained in his paper. (Doyle, 2008, p. 275). It also concurs with the *National Alliance for the Mentally Ill (NAMI)* observations regarding the mental state of those incarcerated, as discussed ahead.

In describing the different types of insanity observed in the Sing Sing prisoners, Squire (1935) addressed the manic-depressive as the type of person who alternates between "vigorous and violent activity" and complete docility and apathy. When suffering a tantrum, the manic-depressive is capable of attacking "anyone who gets in his way, with disastrous results" (Squire, 1935, pp. 82-83). He added that marital offenses are often the result of insanity, such as the murder of a spouse resulting from paranoid delusions. The doctor's observations correlate with the advanced state of Pontón's illness that defense counsel and expert physicians tried to convey in court, unsuccessfully.

Squire (1935) stressed that in the old days the distinction between being medically insane and being a criminal was seldom drawn, if ever, and these were treated as one and the same. He shared that by applying the same testing used by the U.S. Army during World War I, he was able to determine that the effective mental age of many Sing Sing inmates was similar to that of new military recruits, thirteen and one-half years old. (Squire, 1935, p. 85). If this testing was accurate, this is a grave cause for concern when assessing the intent and knowledge elements required for a capital murder conviction, particularly with modern studies and legal precedent against executing those with a diminished capacity, or those younger than 18 years old.

To date, the U.S. judicial system has made some progress in the area of mental health, but our society is just beginning to appreciate the substantial role of mental health on crime and how to address it. Although the U.S. Supreme Court has ruled that executing the mentally ill is unconstitutional, much remains to be accomplished in this realm. (Capital Punishment in Context, 2015). In 1986, the U.S. Supreme Court held in *Ford v. Wainwright* that executing the insane is unconstitutional because this type of inmate does not understand the purpose of his or her punishment, and executing them has no retributive or deterrent effect. However, if the prisoner's mental competency has been restored, he or she can then be executed. (Ford v. Wainwright, 1986).[31] More recently, in 2002 the U.S. Supreme Court ruled in *Atkins v. Virginia* that executing convicts with mental retardation was unconstitutional. (Atkins v. Virginia, 2002). Further, in the 2005 case of *Roper v. Simmons*, the U.S. Supreme Court ruled that death penalty should not attach to persons 18 years of age or younger, due to their diminished capacity. (Roper v. Simmons, 2005).

In 1998, the *Bureau of Justice Statistics* estimated that an average of 283,000 persons with mental illness are incarcerated in the United States. The *National Alliance for the Mentally Ill (NAMI)* assessed that 20 percent of those sentenced to death in the United States suffer of a serious mental illness. Ron Honberg of NAMI stated:

"[O]nly ... after [these] crimes were committed, was treatment provided, usually for the purpose of achieving competence to stand trial. Frequently, more money is spent executing people with severe mental illness than was [spent] on providing treatment" (New York State Assembly, Standing Committee on Codes, Judiciary and Correction, 2005, pp. 35-37).

In addition, research shows that jurors' perceptions concerning a mentally ill defendant's remorse (or apparent lack of remorse) can be a significant factor in the choice between life and death, as severe mental illness can make a defendant appear more dangerous. Consequently, jurors are more prone to decide in favor of the death penalty in cases where the defendant is severely mentally ill (New York State Assembly, Standing Committee on Codes, Judiciary and Correction, 2005, p. 36), as it was in the case of Antonio Pontón.

The above findings present a sad irony: Antonio Pontón's insanity, while a valid excuse to his death penalty sentence, could have been a key deciding factor for the jury towards his execution.

The Many Victims

Murder victims and their families deserve justice. But, does the death penalty provide justice, or does it simply provide a means for vengeance? Are justice and vengeance one and the same? With profound deference and respect for the loss and pain suffered by all murder victims, the impact an execution has on the rest of the victims, including society, also merits significant consideration.

The proponents of the death penalty must balance the mythical deterrence and perceived retribution benefits of the death penalty against the detrimental impact executions have on *all victims*. There are many victims to consider: the murder victim, the individuals closest to the victim and the executed, those who have to support the death penalty system (such as the jurors, the executioners, the prison officers, lawyers, and judges, among others), and society as a whole.

The existence of this broader set of victims has been widely acknowledged. (New York State Assembly, Standing Committee on Codes, Judiciary and Correction, 2005, p. 55). Recognizing a nexus of suffering, groups of the murder victims' families have joined with the family of the executed to fight against the death penalty. For example, in partnership with NAMI, *Murder Victims' Families for Human*

Rights *(MVFHR)* is a U.S.-based international non-profit organization of relatives of homicide victims and relatives of those who have been executed, all who oppose the death penalty in all cases. (MVFHR, 2015). They challenge the idea that all victims' families want and need the death penalty, and they oppose the death penalty from a *victim perspective* (asserting that executions do not help victims achieve justice or closure) and from a *human rights perspective* (asserting that executions violate the most basic of human rights.) In 2004, they launched "Prevention, Not Execution," a collaborative project geared to opposing the death penalty for persons with severe mental illness, whose culpability is perceived as less than the average person. (Sheffer, 2009).

Certainly, from the thousands of clemency letters written in Pontón's case, it is clear that the nexus of suffering extended well beyond Pontón's parents and family members. The citizens of the island of Puerto Rico repeatedly showed blatant opposition to the death penalty and to Pontón's execution. They opposed capital punishment under ethical, medical, legal, humanitarian, religious and societal reasons.

And then there are those who have to administer the penalty as part of their job. The novel *Antonio's Will* addressed the horrific impact the ultimate penalty had on those implementing *justice by execution*: The Sing Sing Prison executioner, John Hulbert, who killed himself after expressing he was tired of killing people (New York Times, 1929); Sing Sing Prison Warden George W. Kirchwey, who stated that he rather be electrocuted himself than be present at Pontón's execution (New York Sun, 1916); Deputy Warden Spencer Miller, who wept at Pontón's execution (Syracuse Journal, 1916); other employees, who opposed and were stressed by the practice; on execution witnesses, who became physically ill and described the experience as subhuman; and Sing Sing Prison Chief Physician, Dr. Amos O. Squire, who developed a psychosis to touch the inmate while being electrocuted, which eventually forced him to resign from his post. (Squire, 1935).

Not only did Dr. Squire oppose the death penalty and grew averse to participating in executions, he had become frustrated by witnessing the grave injustice of executing mentally ill inmates. Squire (1935) described his agony in his book:

I did not realize the trend of my subconscious thoughts until duty took me to the death chamber again, and I stood on the edge of the rubber mat, within reach of the chair. On that occasion, just after I had given the signal for the current to be turned on—while the man on the chair was straining against the straps as the load of 2,200 volts shot through his body—I felt for the first time a wild desire to extend my hand and touch him. Afterwards I subjected myself to severe self analysis ... At each subsequent execution the impulse became stronger. It finally got so compelling that I was forced to grip my fingernails into my palms in order to control it. Each time I had to stand farther and farther from the chair. But even then I would feel a sudden, terrifying urge to rush forward and take hold of the man in the chair while the current was on. (Squire, 1935, pp. 220-221).

Squire resigned from his job as Sing Sing Prison Chief Physician in 1925, after his daughter, who had learned of his anxiety through a confident of Squire's, begged her father to quit. He admitted had he not done so, he would not have been able to cope with the anxiety of executing human beings, levied on his job by society and the justice system.

The impact of the death penalty on jurors has also been documented. A study initiated in 1991 by the *Capital Jury Project, School of Criminal Justice at Albany University*, interviewed 1,198 jurors from 353 capital trials across multiple states in the United States, revealing that 62.5 percent of female jurors and 37.5 percent of male jurors sought counseling after sitting on a capital trial, and 81 percent of female jurors and 18 percent of male jurors regretted the decisions made in their cases. (School of Criminal Justice, SUNY at Albany, 2015).

Today, in some states like Oklahoma, Missouri and Texas, the identity of those who participate in administering the death penalty is concealed for their protection, as well as the identity of the companies that provide the lethal chemicals to terminate the life of the condemned. Legal challenges to disclose this information have been unsuccessfully advanced. [32] However, jurors' identities after the sentence are not kept secret.

In February of 2013, Frank Thompson, a retired prison superintendent for the Oregon State Penitentiary, stated in a commentary to *The Oregonian* newspaper: "Asking decent men and women to participate in the name of a failed public policy that takes human life is indefensible and rises to a level of immorality" (Thompson, 2015). In February of 2015, Thompson wrote to Oregon's Governor John A. Kitzhaber a day before the governor left office, urging him to convert 35 death sentences to life without the possibility of release, stating:

> *Based on my experiences as a correctional professional, capital punishment is a failed public policy. ... I know firsthand that the death penalty is not applied fairly or equally in Oregon. I have known hundreds of inmates who are guilty of similar crimes yet did not get the death penalty because they reached a plea bargain of life without parole simply because they had the means for professional legal assistance. ... I also understand, from my experiences in corrections, the potential awful and lifelong repercussions that can come from participating in the execution of prisoners. Living with the nightmares is something that some of us experience. This is particularly the case with those of us who have had more hands-on experience with the flawed capital punishment process, and/or where an execution under our supervision did not go smoothly. (Thompson, 2015).*

On November 22, 2014, Oregon's Governor Kitzhaber had already halted all executions during his term in office, stating: "I refuse to be a part of this compromised and inequitable system any longer; and I will not allow further executions while I am Governor" (DPIC, 2014). As a physician sworn to the Hippocratic Oath, his personal conflict with capital punishment must have been heartfelt. However, he left his office on February 17, 2015 without commuting the death sentences of 34 other inmates in Oregon's death row, as requested by Thompson and many others. (Green, 2015). The request had precedent, as other governors have issued blanket commutations of death sentences before. In 2003, former Illinois Governor George Ryan commuted the sentences of more than 150 death row inmates just before leaving office. Earlier in 2015, one day before the end of his term, former Maryland Governor Martin O'Malley granted clemency to the last four inmates on death row. He had previously persuaded lawmakers to abolish Maryland's death penalty law. On February 20,

2015 new Oregon Governor Kate Brown stated that she would keep the former governor's moratorium in place while needed discussions on the subject develop. (Benham, 2015).

When the Innocent is Falsely Convicted or Executed

Capital punishment fails on its face when it falsely convicts and–even worse–when it executes the innocent. In the United States alone, the first country to use post-conviction genetic testing on a large scale, 151 death convictions were thrown out between January 1, 1973 and March 23, 2015. (DPIC, 2015e). The figures speak for themselves. Any irreversible system that allows for such a high risk to take the life of an innocent human being should be revoked.

As depicted in *Antonio's Will*, Charles Stielow was a death row inmate at the Sing Sing Prison when Antonio Pontón was executed. Stielow's execution was stayed minutes before the switch was drawn, based on the last minute confession of the true perpetrators of the crime for which Stielow had been convicted. Governor Whitman subsequently commuted Stielow's sentence to life and appointed a special investigator to the case. The governor finally commuted Stielow's life sentence in 1918, after the special investigation uncovered Stielow was not guilty of the crime charged, and there had been prosecutorial misconduct. Whitman and the public, who initially supported Stielow's guilt, were astonished at the turn of events and the flawed inner-workings of the prosecution attorneys, who had based their case on a false confession and fabricated evidence. The governor had stated that he supported the justice system and the nine judges who had reviewed the case, and he thought Stielow was guilty, but explained he had to commute Stielow's death sentence to life upon credible evidence suggesting the possibility that he was not guilty. After the special investigation cleared Stielow, Whitman expressed concern regarding the wrongful conviction and the terrible mistake it would have been to execute an innocent man. The governor stated: "No other criminal case, where clemency has been asked, has perplexed and distressed me, as has this" (New York State, 1919).

A century after Stielow's near miss, we still face the same issues of wrongful convictions. On March 11, 2014, Glenn Ford was released from Louisiana's death row after 30 years there, when the state admitted new evidence proving Ford was not the killer and should not have been convicted for the 1983 death of a Shreveport jeweler. In a letter to *The Shreveport Times* in response to an editorial highlighting the errors committed in Ford's 1984 first-degree murder trial, attorney A. M. "Marty" Stroud III, the lead prosecutor in the case, stated:

> *Facts are stubborn things, they do not go away. ... As a prosecutor and officer of the court, I had the duty to prosecute fairly. While I could properly strike hard blows, ethically I could not strike foul ones. ... I did not hide evidence, I simply did not seriously consider that sufficient information may have been out there that could have led to a different conclusion. ... I was arrogant, judgmental, narcissistic and very full of myself. I was not as interested in justice as I was in winning. ... Mr. Ford spent 30 years of his life in a small, dingy cell. His surroundings were dire. Lighting was poor, heating and cooling were almost non-existent, food bordered on the uneatable. Nobody wanted to be accused of 'coddling' a death row inmate. ... [I]nvestigators uncovered evidence that exonerated Mr. Ford. Indeed, this evidence was so strong that had it been disclosed during [the course] of the investigation there would not have been sufficient evidence to even arrest Mr. Ford! ... I was too passive. ... I did not question the unfairness of Mr. Ford having appointed counsel who had never tried a criminal jury case much less a capital one. It never concerned me that the defense had insufficient funds ... The jury was all white, Mr. Ford was African-American. ... After the death verdict in the Ford trial, I went out with others and celebrated with a few rounds of drinks. That's sick. I had been entrusted with the duty to seek the death of a fellow human being, a very solemn task that certainly did not warrant any "celebration." ... [A]s a young 33-year-old prosecutor, I was not capable of making a decision that could have led to the killing of another human being. ... No one should be given the ability to impose a sentence of death in any criminal proceeding. We are simply incapable of devising a system that can fairly and impartially impose a sentence of death because we are all fallible human beings. ... The clear reality is that the death penalty is an anathema to any society that purports to call itself civilized. It is an abomination that continues to scar the*

fibers of this society, and it will continue to do so until this barbaric penalty is outlawed. Until then, we will live in a land that condones state assisted revenge and that is not justice in any form or fashion. (Stroud III, 2015).

Shortly after his release, Ford was diagnosed with lung cancer that was untreated while he was in solitary confinement. He died on June 29, 2015, less than a year after his release. Other than giving him $20 for a bus ticket home, the state refused to compensate Ford for the court's grave error. (USA Today, 2015a).

There are hundreds of cases similar to the above (Radelet, Bedau, & Putnam, 1994) that draw attention to the weakness and inhumanity of the U.S. Justice System and its high propensity for error: a sword to any pro-death penalty shield.

Clemency Boards and Posthumous Pardons

In the United States, the governor, a clemency board, or both, may grant clemency in the form of reprieves, commutations, or pardons for almost all convictions. To date, 13 states limit this power to the governor, five limit it to a clemency board, in 9 states the governor *may* consider the recommendation of a board, and in eight states the governor *must* have the recommendation of a board (in Florida, the governor is part of such board.) For Federal Death Row inmates, the President of the United States has the sole pardon power. (DPIC, 2011; DPIC, 2015a; DPIC, 2015b).

In New York, there is currently no death penalty. However, the New York State Constitution and the Executive Law give the governor the power to grant clemency for other offenses with the assistance of a clemency board known as *The Executive Clemency Bureau,* a unit within the New York State Department of Corrections and Community Supervision. (New York State Services, 2015). This bureau evaluates petitions on humanitarian grounds, and assists by compiling information to help the governor determine whether clemency is warranted. At the time of Pontón's trial, clemency power resided solely with the governor.

To date, in addition to the 151 death convictions thrown out since 1973, posthumous pardons have been granted on at least 20 occasions in U.S. history involving 107 individuals, 12 of them wrongfully executed. (Greenspan, 2011). These were mostly based on proven innocence, biased and unfair trial or post-trial proceeding, changed political, moral or legal climate, reward for exemplary character, and excessive sentence.

Posthumous pardons for cases more than a century old have been granted in the United States at federal and state levels to repair injustice and in the name of public policy. (Jackson, Smith, Sisson, & Krassnoff, 1999). Most recently, at an international level, the *Irish Innocence Project* secured a pardon for Harry Gleeson, who was hanged 74 years ago for a crime he did not commit. (Hertz, 2015).

Based on the above, there is precedent for granting posthumous clemency to Antonio Pontón.

Sing Sing Prison Today

Prior to the abolition of the death penalty in New York, death row had been relocated away from Sing Sing. It was no longer referred to as "death row," but as the "Unit for Condemned Persons (UCP)." There were two facilities, one for men and one for women. Men were housed at the Clinton Correctional Facility in Dannemora, New York, located 15 miles south of the Canadian border. A facility in the Bedford Hills Correctional Facility in Westchester County was designed to house women on death row.

Critics of the conditions at UCP stated the restrictive solitary confinement was unduly harsh. The cells were lit 24 hours a day, and human contact between inmates was severely limited. Exercise periods and visits were restricted. This environment would likely lead to cognitive, emotional, and behavioral deterioration, and result in other forms of potentially disabling psychological harm. It also had the effect of discouraging inmates from continuing to appeal or fight their convictions. Advocates for the restrictions imposed stated that the lives of criminals on death row should be greatly altered as part of the punishment received, and even if they were sentenced to life without possibility of parole, life's comforts and privileges should be totally removed, as these were lost upon conviction. They argued the measure would serve retribution and deterrent goals resulting in less crime. (New York State Assembly, Standing Committee on Codes, Judiciary and Correction, 2005, p. 54). Yet, practices such as solitary confinement and the removal of all prisoner privileges have been proven to deteriorate the minds of prisoners, doubling and tripling the expense of maintaining such punitive systems, which are often deemed cruel and unusual. (ACLU, 2015).

The Sing Sing Prison currently houses about 2,000 prisoners, and there are ongoing plans to convert the original 1825 cellblock into a museum. Since the first execution of William Kemmler on August 8, 1890, there have been a total of 694 men and women executed in the Sing Sing Prison *death house* in the electric chair, which people had nicknamed "Old Sparky." Eddie Lee Mays, convicted of murder and executed on August 15, 1963, was the last prisoner executed in the electric chair there. (Death Penalty USA, 2015). After the 1972 U.S. Supreme Court decision in *Furman v. Georgia* declared the death penalty unconstitutional, the Sing Sing electric chair was removed to the Greenhaven Prison. (DeChillo, 1991). It was in working condition, but it was never used since. After being on loan to an Alexandria, Virginia museum and the Newseum in Washington, DC, (Newseum, 2015), it is now in Sing Sing Prison storage, although an exact replica is on display at the Sing Sing Prison Museum in Ossining, New York. The *death house* is now a vocational education center. (Historic Hudson River Tours, Ossining, 2015).

"Modern?" Methods of Execution

After reinstating the death penalty in 1976, New York law provided that death would be administered by *lethal injection*, defined as "the intravenous injection of a substance or substances in a lethal quantity into the body of a person convicted until such person is dead" (New York State Assembly, Standing Committee on Codes, Judiciary and Correction, 2005, p. 54).[33] The majority of the states upholding the death penalty use lethal injection. Some would still use electrocution if lethal injection were not available. A few use the gas chamber. As of this writing, Utah just reinstated execution by firing squad as a backup to lethal injection. Some states allow the condemned to choose their preferred method of execution. There are claims and evidence that the lethal injection, like its predecessors, also amounts to cruel and unusual punishment, violating the defendant's Eighth Amendment's rights. The drugs used in the executions are said to cause extreme and unnecessary pain, which is sometimes masked from the sight of those administering the death penalty by the combination of chemicals used. The "cruel and unusual" debate seems a never-ending vicious and wasteful circle.

Federal District Courts in California and Missouri have issued initial rulings on the use of lethal injection, holding that the execution procedures in those states are unconstitutional due to the lack of safeguards and oversight of the proper application of the procedure. In addition, in Arizona (among other states) the method of asphyxiation with cyanide or *gas chamber* is currently used with reportedly extensive pain and suffering. (DPIC, 2015a).

As with the electric chair, witnesses to the arguably "more humane" lethal injection and gas executions have likewise fainted and suffered emotional injuries after witnessing the inmate be killed, sometimes the administration of death lasting for over an hour while the inmate moans and twists in pain and gasps for air. (DPIC, 2015a).

Despite the controversy, in the 2008 case of *Baze v. Rees*, the U.S. Supreme Court ruled that Kentucky's three-drug protocol for execution by lethal injection did not amount to cruel and unusual punishment under the Eighth Amendment. (Baze v. Rees, 2008). Justice John Paul Stevens concurred with the decision, but stated, in part: "I am now convinced that this case will generate debate not only about the constitutionality of the three-drug protocol, and specifically about the justification for the use of the paralytic agent, *pancuronium bromide,* but also about the justification for the death penalty itself" (Baze v. Rees, 2008; Greenhouse, 2008). Justice Stevens was one of the co-authors of the U.S. Supreme Court's 1976 decision reinstating the death penalty, but shortly after the *Baze v Rees* case in 2008, the 88-year-old judge announced to the *Washington Post* that he evolved his position in the matter and had changed his mind, that he believed capital punishment is unconstitutional. He further stated that decisions made by judges and legislators in favor of capital punishment are based on "habit and inattention," instead than on an "acceptable deliberative process" (Barnes, 2008).

More recently, on April 29, 2014, Oklahoma's governor issued a two-week stay in executions after the execution of Clayton Lockett was halted when his vein exploded during the injection of lethal drugs. He was seen writhing and clenching his teeth after receiving the lethal injection. It took 43 minutes for him to die of a heart attack. (McBride, 2014). On July 23, 2014, to the horror of witnesses, Joseph Wood gasped for air for close to two hours during his botched Arizona lethal injection execution. The witnesses compared his struggle to breath as that of a "fish out of water" (Ford, Watts, & Hanna, 2014).

European drug manufacturers that oppose the death penalty are halting their sales to U.S. governments that intend to apply the drugs for executions. For this reason, some states are returning to earlier execution measures. (McBride, 2014). In 2014, the Virginia legislature considered a bill to bring back the electric chair, but the bill was shelved for the year. (Weiner, 2014). In February 2015, the state's legislature introduced a broad secrecy bill to dangerously exclude inquiry into the execution process. (Lithwick, 2015). On February 13, 2015, Utah's legislature reinstated the method of execution by firing squad as backup for lethal injection. The last execution by firing squad there was in 2010. (Associated Press, 2015). In March of 2015, Alabama's legislature approved the use of the electric chair as a backup measure if lethal injection becomes unavailable. (Ollstein, 2015).

While some states seem to be reverting into the dark ages, the death penalty continues to be questioned at the highest judicial levels. On June 29, 2015, the same day Glenn Ford (the wrongfully convicted man who was held in death row for 30 years) died, the U.S. Supreme Court rendered an opinion on the constitutionality of the "drug cocktail" used to administer lethal injection. The "fiercely divided court," as described by the press, ruled 5-4 that the plaintiffs failed to prove that the drugs cannot mask excessive pain, and that they did not identify a better alternative. The dissent, written by Justice Sonia Sotomayor, stated that the court's decision "leaves petitioners exposed to what may well be the chemical equivalent of being burned at the stake" (USA Today, 2015b). Justice Stephen Breyer, in a separate dissent, invited a broader challenge to the constitutionality of the death penalty, citing four reasons: the potential for error, its arbitrary application, great delays, and increasing abandonment of its use. (USA Today, 2015b). The issue was raised before the court in the case of *Glossip v. Gross*, brought by Oklahoma death row inmates on Eight Amendment grounds. (Glossip v. Gross, cert. granted Jan. 23, 2015). This case came after the botched execution of inmate Clayton Lockett in 2014. The U.S. Supreme Court had agreed to hear the case, but it was too late for Charles Wagner, one of the plaintiffs, who was executed on January 15, 2015.

In addition, in the case of *Hurst v. Florida,* the U.S. Supreme

Court is expected to rule before October 2015 on the constitutionality of Florida's system for imposing the death penalty, where the law allows a judge to make the ultimate death decision, instead of a jury, contrary to the Sixth Amendment of the U.S. Constitution. (Hurst v. Florida, Case No. 14-7505). In this case, lawyers for defendant Timothy Lee Hurst argue that a jury, not a judge, should have decided whether he was mentally disabled and therefore ineligible for the death penalty. The outcome of this case may affect more than 20 states that have similar systems. (Bloomberg, 2015). Various organizations have filed *Amicus Curiae Briefs* in support of Hurst, including the American Civil Liberties Union (ACLU) (ACLU et al., 2015) and the American Bar Association (ABA) (American Bar Association, 2015).

The constitutionality of the death penalty at a federal level is also questionable as it applies to the residents of Puerto Rico as a territory of the United States. Puerto Rico abolished the death penalty in 1929 and prohibits it in its constitution since 1952. (Puerto Rican Coalition Against the Death Penalty, 2012). However, its residents can still be subject to the death penalty at the U.S. federal level (Federal Death Penalty Act, 1994), despite the fact that they are not allowed to vote in U.S. elections or influence federal law, as U.S. states do. This is a key issue for controversy, and it is also a human rights red flag. According to the *World Coalition Against the Death Penalty*, all Latin American and Caribbean countries have abolished capital executions (by law or *de facto*) but for the U.S. territories. The last known execution in the region was in Cuba in 2003 by firing squad. (World Coalition Against the Death Penalty, 2015).

In the United States, amid the debate, the death penalty continues its walk of destruction, an aimless monster. Much like it was a century ago, when legislatures debated the use of the electric chair as a novel and "more humane" method of execution, modern "more humane" killing methods will be proposed and subsequently ruled out as "cruel and unusual." Nevertheless, despite its obvious inhumane, flawed and arbitrary application, proponents of the death penalty insist on demanding the measure, and with this, the development of new killing machines, or in the alternative, the reversion to old barbaric methods to administer death.

At an international level, the death penalty is disfavored as a human rights violation, and democratic and evolved countries have abolished it. (United Nations, Office of the High Commissioner for Human Rights, 2014). Of all known executions that took place in 2013, most were carried out in six countries: China, Iran, Iraq, Saudi Arabia, United States and Somalia. (DPIC, 2015f). It is disturbing that a nation like the United States, which was founded on the noblest of ideals of human rights and liberties, is listed in this group.

3. The Ghost of Mental Health: Modern Working Solutions

After examining the flawed policies and crime statistics over the course of a century, it becomes clear that the area of mental health has been devoid of much-needed attention, even when tending to this area will undoubtedly reduce crime. Prisons continue to be repositories for mentally ill human beings who perhaps would not have ended up in the system if sound community policies and infrastructure were in place to prevent and manage mental health. Although some pilot programs are emerging to manage mentally ill offenders at the court level, earlier preventative measures must be employed.

Mental Health in the Community and Mental Health Courts

During the 1960s and early 1970s there was a shift in public policy producing a massive deinstitutionalization of persons with mental illness. States closed or reduced their psychiatric hospitals without adequately funding community-based treatment. This released many people with mental illness into the community, where they were (and remain) unable to access adequate support services or medication. This issue was exacerbated by the stigmatization of persons with mental illness and by their own improper behavior, creating a vicious circle. The stigma marginalizes the mentally ill, who find it difficult to integrate into the community and find employment. They end up living in isolation, depressed, and hopeless. Nearly two-thirds of all people with diagnosable mental disorders do not seek treatment, largely due to the stigma of receiving such treatment. Alcohol and drugs aggravate this situation, resulting in homelessness and behavior that can extend to the commission of criminal offenses. (National Institute of Justice, 2012).

The criminal justice system was a substitute for asylums a century ago, and it continues to perform this function today, as prisons are increasingly inundated with individuals suffering from mental illness. The *National Institute of Justice* reports that those with serious mental health issues are three times more likely to be housed in jails and prisons than in hospitals. (National Institute of Justice, 2012). Modern research has repeatedly shown that prison populations have higher rates of mental illness than the general population, often revealing up to 65 percent of the total prison population in some cases (vs. 11 percent in the general population.) This finding is consistent with the early 1900s observations by Squire (1935) pointing to the great incidence of Sing Sing Prison inmates suffering from mental illness. Not much has changed in a hundred years in this realm.

Around the year 2000, Kings County, New York and Pinellas County, Florida introduced the concept of the mental health court to manage the mental health element in crime. (National Institute of Justice, 2012). These courts are specialized court dockets created for certain defendants with mental illness, geared to substitute a mental illness problem-solving model in place of the traditional court model. The program identifies participants through mental health screening and assessments, and they voluntarily participate in a court-supervised treatment plan developed by court staff and mental health professionals. The participants "graduate" from the program when they complete it successfully. This program has shown some positive results, although affected individuals would benefit from attention well before they reach this court stage.

Education and Community Initiatives

Mental health education is absent from the grade school curriculum, missing a golden opportunity to remove the stigma of mental illness from society, teach students about mental health and anger management, about acceptance, and possibly help mitigate violence, bullying and crime. This is a long-lasting gap, unattended for years. Squire (1935) also identified this void in his writings. He believed schools were largely failing at educating individuals in life management skills. He stated that an education that teaches only facts and leaves out values is only going halfway. (Squire, 1935, p. 51). Today, it seems that the U.S. education system continues to miss some critical areas of opportunity.

Although the incarceration rates of young Americans have greatly decreased since 1975, this is the result of a fusion of various factors. There are lower rates of juvenile crime in some states, but there is also a shift away from interventions focused on long-term incarceration, motivated by fiscal pressures. The yearly cost of incarcerating a juvenile person amounts to $88,000. (Paulson, 2013). The yearly cost of educating one student in public school is about $12,000. (National Center for Education Statistics, U.S. Dept. Ed., 2011).

While some would rightfully advocate that progress has been made, the United States has a much higher youth incarceration rate than Western European countries. For example, the incarceration rate for juveniles is 18 times greater in the United States than that of France, and more than seven times greater than that of Britain. In Finland or Sweden young offenders are seldom imprisoned. (Paulson, 2013). The prevalent school violence, the bullying, killings, drugs, and even instances of human trafficking in the United States demand proactive attention to these issues, now magnified by technological advances and social media (Center for Disease Control and Prevention, 2015). The level of violence among young children 10 to 14 years old remains alarming. (Kellerman, 2003). The need to intervene is not limited to decreasing violence in the schools themselves with passive solutions (e.g., a hotline, limited community programs for elite students), but it also extends to actively mitigating mental health and anger management issues that will likely lead to crime in school and out of school; issues that will follow the students everywhere they go in their adult life. Such active solutions should focus on the inclusion of mental health and anger management subjects in the grade school class curriculum. Certainly, history has made it clear by now that this is not a task that must be levied exclusively on the children's households, or on religious and social organizations. Our children spend a massive portion of their lives at school, and this is a venue where a tangible impact can be made.

Therefore, in addition to the call for a heightened focus on values, as timelessly pointed out by Squire (1935), there is an opportunity and need to address mental health directly in our schools. Attention to both, values and mental health, must take precedence over all investment made in implementing a death penalty system that is obviously not the right path.

4. Conclusion

One hundred years of history have shown that the New York death penalty law during 1914-1916 and thereafter was defective, and that the method of electric execution selected a century ago as "most humane" amounts to cruel and unusual punishment, violating the executed defendant's constitutional rights. Likewise, capital punishment laws and practices are frowned upon as unjust and backwards, whether modern or ancient. Apparently frozen in time, the issue of the constitutionality of the death penalty is again about to be formally challenged in the highest court of the United States.

Those administering the prison system, those in closest contact with death row inmates—including wardens, officers and physicians—have historically opposed the death penalty as barbaric, atrocious and "a blot on human civilization." The most progressive governments in the world have embraced the abolition of capital punishment.

In Pontón's case, not only did the law and his lawyers fail him; the environment surrounding him created "The Perfect Storm" for judges, leaders and politicians to "look the other way" on a decision to commute his sentence, even though the weight of the evidence—his family history of insanity, qualified medical expert opinion of the most renowned physicians of the times, and the surrounding environment filled with errors and bias—warranted saving Pontón's life.

It was too much of a political risk to save Antonio Pontón, the mentally ill *Porto Rican* student, but the life of multi-millionaire murderer, purported sadist and child molester Harry K. Thaw was spared, and he was eventually released as "cured," under the same legal system and environment that killed Pontón. Their dissimilar verdicts were clearly arbitrary. In violation of the Magna Carta charter that justice cannot be sold, Thaw was able to purchase justice, while Pontón could not afford to do so. Justice was denied to Pontón.

The future of the death penalty is uncertain in the United States, but it has become increasingly clear that capital punishment has failed in its implementation. The demonstrated ineffectiveness in deterring crime by killing offenders, the cost of the death penalty, and the inherent flaws in administering the ultimate punishment—aside from the moral hypocrisy of a society that promotes the killing of a human being for mere vengeance—do not justify the measure.

It is too late to undo Antonio Pontón's fate, but others can be saved. Rather than continuing to support a capital punishment system that is morally wrong and undoubtedly broken, the United States must evolve, redirect the investment placed in barbaric executions, and focus these resources towards crime prevention, education, and mental health initiatives. This investment will yield higher tangible returns, not only morally and socially, but also economically.

Death penalty history must not repeat itself. The United States should take pause, listen to the voices of history and learn from the horrific mistakes made in Antonio Pontón's case and others. The voices of history are relevant. They can be the difference between life and death, not only for the human beings executed by their fellow humans, but also for the makeup and survivability of an entire nation.

Will you listen to the voices of history?

Four

The Voices

V oices of Clemency, the **Appendix** of this book, contains the names of all those who traced their signature on the many petitions for grace to prevent Antonio Pontón's electrocution. Their names lay dormant in documents found through research by this author, a referenced selection of which was presented in **Chapter Two**.

The prayers for grace consisted of letters and telegrams sent during the months of November 1915 through the first week of January 1916. Most petitions arrived at the New York governor's desk before December 20, 1915, the date set for Pontón's execution after his motions for a new trial and appeal failed. All but one of the petitions found were directed to Governor Charles S. Whitman as governor of New York. The *Ladies of Bayamón* addressed an emotional petition to U.S. President Woodrow Wilson, who was scheduled to marry on December 18. The U.S. Attorney General forwarded this correspondence to Governor Whitman without Presidential comment.

As described earlier in this book, while the press reported that 15,000 signatures supported the requests for Antonio's grace, the documents this author found and transcribed revealed that over 21,000 signatures accompanied the many petitions, and research suggests there were many other signed documents that were likely lost or destroyed. This figure is substantial, particularly considering the circumstances of collection: the year of the event, the communication and transportation barriers of the times, and the widespread efforts undertaken to secure resolutions, fundraise, write letters, send telegrams and gather thousands of signatures from all social and demographic spheres. The bulk of the massive effort was undertaken in just about a month, during the Christmas holiday season.

While traveling through the list of names, readers will encounter known historical figures. They will cross paths with activists, governors, mayors, statesmen, councilmen, politicians, poets, writers, journalists, doctors, lawyers, Masons, country officials, priests, spiritual guides, firemen, teachers, mothers, farmers, laborers, university and grade school students, among many others.

In addition to those described in **Chapter Two**, some of the Puerto Rican leaders signing the petitions include *José de Diego* (statesman, journalist, poet, lawyer, and advocate for Puerto Rico's independence), his wife *Georgina*, *Arturo Alfonso Schomburg* (historian, writer, and civil rights activist), *Roberto H. Todd* (Mayor of San Juan and founder of Puerto Rico's Republican Party), *Felisa Rincón* (who would become Mayor of San Juan in 1947), relatives of *Francisco Oller* (renowned impressionist painter and former teacher of Cézanne), the children of *Agustín Stahl* (medical doctor who also excelled in botany and zoology), *Teodoro Moscoso* (pharmacist, businessman and politician), and the children of *Luis Lloréns Torres* (poet and politician), among many others (**Figure 51**).

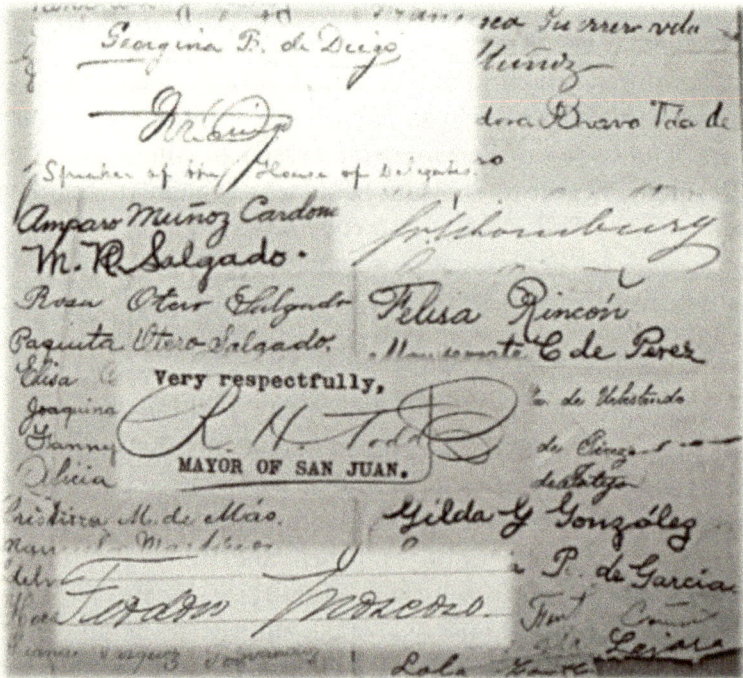

Figure 51. Signatures of various Puerto Rican leaders in clemency documents. (Tirado-Chiodini Collection, 1914-1916).

But perhaps more personal to readers of this list is that they may encounter the names of ancestors who participated in the unprecedented collective effort of compassion to save Antonio Pontón from the claws of the electric chair.

As described in the novel *Antonio's Will*, the clemency endeavor for Pontón united the entire island of Puerto Rico under the fundamental principle of human rights. Teachers leveraged the tragedy as an opportunity to teach a key lesson in their classrooms. The phrase *"Odia el delito y compadece al delincuente,"* towered over signatures inscribed in the petitions sent by school children (**Figure 52**). "Hate the crime and pity the criminal." The Golden Rule permeated through the words and the enormous outpour of compassion towards Pontón that emerged from Puerto Rico and mainland United States.

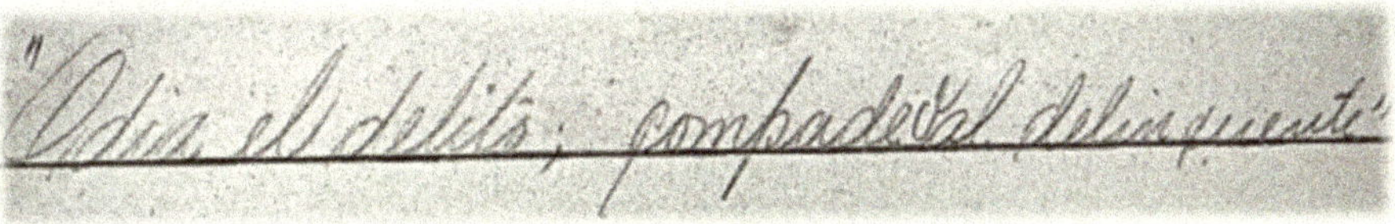

Figure 52. "Odia el delito y compadece al delincuente," (Hate the crime and pity the criminal), a headline over school children signatures in clemency petitions. (Tirado-Chiodini Collection, 1914-1916).

Personal notes like the one in **Figure 53** below (translated ahead) accompanied some of the signatures. Their authors were hopeful that the governor of New York would take the time to read their personal pleas.

Figure 53. A note accompanying one of the signatures in a clemency petition. (Tirado-Chiodini Collection, 1914-1916).

121

Translation of **Figure 53**:

"Asunción de la Cruz. If the governor of New York forgives the Puerto Rican brother, I will believe that he and all his countrymen are the most noble [people] in the globe."

For this author, the journey of transcribing the thousands of names was a personal pilgrimage to listen to the voices of the many who strived to save the life of a man suffering from mental illness; those who tried to shelter his family from the pain of his loss through a horrible execution. This profound gesture of humanity must not remain buried and forgotten in history, as it has been for the last century.

This list is not a mere litany of faceless names. These are the voices of history, an island's plea for a native son, still praying for Antonio's grace.

Epilogue

The morning of January 7, 1916, Warden George W. Kirchwey sent the last telegram to the New York governor, Charles S. Whitman. This time, it was not to pray for grace, but to inform the governor that Antonio Pontón had been executed that morning "in accordance with the law" (**Figure 54**).

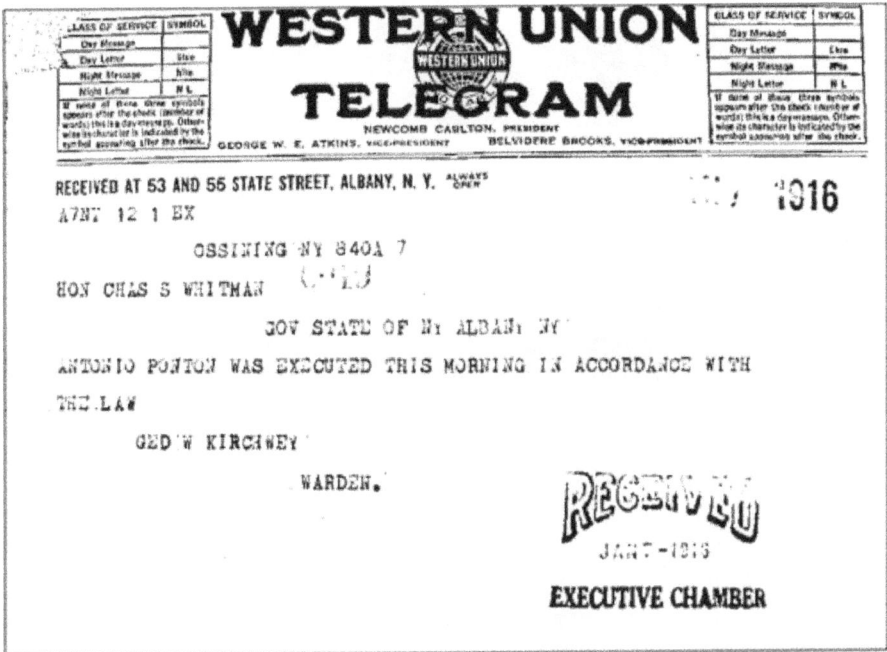

Figure 54. Telegram from Sing Sing Prison Warden George W. Kirchwey to Governor Charles S. Whitman informing him that Antonio Pontón had been executed. (Tirado-Chiodini Collection, 1914-1916).

The appropriate entries were made in the Sing Sing Prison log, the court's and the governor's records. Pontón's case was closed, and

123

it remained closed for 100 years after, as of this writing.

Yet, the facts of this case still yearn for grace today. They call for forgiveness, as did the spectator who took pen to paper in 1915 and wrote to a Puerto Rican newspaper in response to Pontón's desperate prayer to his Puerto Rican brothers and sisters. The spectator's note to the editor (**Figure 55**) is a photograph of a newspaper clip enclosed in one of the clemency letters addressed to Governor Whitman.

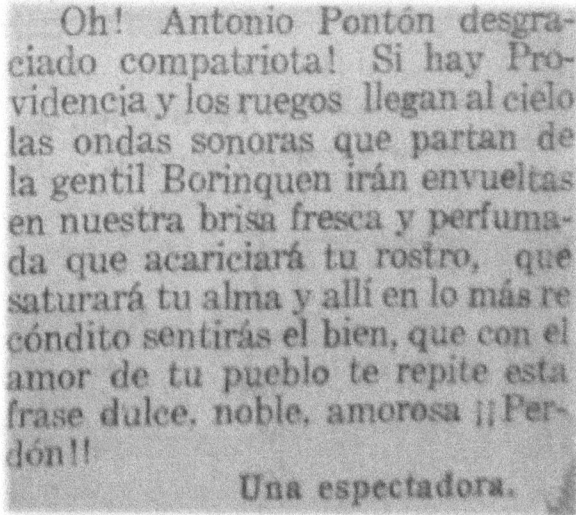

Figure 55. Puerto Rico newspaper clip with an anonymous message from "a spectator" from the town of Vega Baja, pleading forgiveness for Antonio Pontón. (Tirado-Chiodini Collection, 1914-1916).

Translation of the newspaper clip in **Figure 55**, above:[34]

"Oh! Antonio Pontón, disgraced compatriot! If there is Providence and our prayers reach Heaven, the sound waves departing from this gentle Borinquen will travel wrapped in our fresh and perfumed breeze to caress your face and saturate your soul. And there, amidst the most recondite place, you will feel the goodness that with the love of your people repeats this sweet, noble and loving phrase: Forgiveness!!

A Spectator."

The facts yearn for forgiveness, and they also call for justice.

Figure 56. Antonio Pontón's photograph. Enhanced image from source. (Schenectady Gazette, 1915d).

Antonio Pontón (above in **Figure 56**) tragically took the life of another human being. But all evidence shows that he suffered from mental illness and had no control over his will. His constitutional rights as a Puerto Rican criminal defendant were severely violated. He was executed, against the U.S. Constitution, the law, and the evidence; against the pleas of government officials, doctors, prison wardens, and thousands of others praying for his life; against the voices of grace.

In the bench of timeless justice lives a question: Should posthumous clemency be granted to Antonio Pontón?

Acknowledgements

I would like to acknowledge anti-death penalty national and international organizations for their advocacy and dedication to protecting the rights of those convicted, and for their commitment to abolishing the death penalty. Among them:

American Civil Liberties Union (Capital Punishment Project), https://www.aclu.org/capital-punishment

Amnesty International, USA (Abolish Capital Punishment Campaign), http://www.amnestyusa.org

Campaign to End the Death Penalty, http://www.nodeathpenalty.org

Equal Justice U.S.A., http://ejusa.org

Greater Caribbean for Life, http://gcforlife.org

Journey of Hope from Violence to Healing (Family of victims and death row inmates against the death penalty), http://www.journeyofhope.org

Murder Victims Families for Reconciliation (Victims' families against the death penalty), http://www.mvfr.org

National Coalition to Abolish the Death Penalty (Largest national abolition group with numerous state level and local chapters.), http://www.ncadp.org

National Coalition to Abolish the Death Penalty, http://www.ncadp.org

Students Against the Death Penalty, http://www.studentabolition.org

The Innocence Project, http://www.innocenceproject.org

Witness to Innocence (Innocent people freed from death row and their families working to abolish the death penalty), http://witnesstoinnocence.org

World Coalition Against the Death Penalty, http://www.worldcoalition.org

Notes

[1] English translation by Yasmin Tirado-Chiodini. (Some punctuation may have been modified for clarity.)

[2] English translation by Yasmin Tirado-Chiodini. (Some punctuation may have been modified for clarity.)

[3] Per exchanges with the staff of the New York Archives in Albany, New York, the Schenectady District Attorney's office, relevant courts, and historical societies, among other organizations consulted, the actual transcript records of Antonio Pontón's murder trial were destroyed. The author continues to research in the event a copy exists elsewhere.

[4] Today, the U.S. Census Bureau defines "Hispanic" or "Latino" as "a person of Cuban, Mexican, Puerto Rican, South or Central American (except for Brazil), or other Spanish culture or origin regardless of race" (U.S. Census Bureau, 2011). Hispanics or Latinos can be of any race, any ancestry, and any ethnicity. (Pew Research Center, 2009).

[5] See also (New York American, 1906).

[6] As trial transcripts and records were destroyed (See Note 3), the trial accounts discussed in *Antonio's Grace* rely on factual information collected from newspaper reports of the actual trial, referenced throughout this book, as well as the letter by Charles E. Le Barbier to Governor Charles S. Whitman (Tirado-Chiodini Collection, 1914-1916). These were also basis for plot development in the novel *Antonio's Will.*

[7] The Fifth Amendment to the U.S. Constitution provides protection against self-incrimination by stating: "No person shall be held to answer for a capital, or otherwise infamous crime, unless on a presentment or indictment of a grand jury, except in cases arising in the land or naval forces, or in the militia, when in actual service in time of war or public danger; nor shall any person be subject for the

same offense to be twice put in jeopardy of life or limb; nor shall be compelled in any criminal case to be a witness against himself, nor be deprived of life, liberty, or property, without due process of law; nor shall private property be taken for public use, without just compensation" (U.S. Const. amend. V).

[8] The Sixth Amendment to the U.S. Constitution sets forth rights related to criminal prosecutions. It reads: "In all criminal prosecutions, the accused shall enjoy the right to a speedy and public trial, by an impartial jury of the State and district wherein the crime shall have been committed, which district shall have been previously ascertained by law, and to be informed of the nature and cause of the accusation; to be confronted with the witnesses against him; to have compulsory process for obtaining witnesses in his favor, and to have the Assistance of Counsel for his defense" (U.S. Const. amend. VI).

[9] *Presentism* is an attitude toward the past dominated by present-day attitudes and experiences. (Merriam-Webster Dictionary Online, n.d.)

[10] Also referred to as "McNaughton Rule."

[11] In 1928, in *People v. Moran*, the young defendant was electrocuted, even when the court recognized that he was a "psychopathic inferior man of low and unstable mentality" (People v. Moran, 1928). In 1954, the dissenting opinion in *People v. Horton* stressed the failure of the law when evaluating the clearly insane defendant. The court focused on the defendant's conduct in planning and executing the crime, when it should have interpreted the defendant's knowledge of the wrong as being disturbed by the mental illness. (People v. Horton, 1954). See (St. John's Law Review, 1965, p. 76).

[12] N.Y. Code Crim. Proc. §398-b, as amended, N.Y. Sess. Laws 1965, cl. 593, § 2, 1965.

[13] On this issue, the New York Penal Code § 454 (1915) stated: "When defendant acquitted on the ground of insanity, the fact to be stated with the verdict; commitment of defendant to state asylum. When the defense is insanity of the defendant the jury must be instructed, if they acquit him on that ground, to state the fact with their verdict. The court must, thereupon, if the defendant is in custody, and they deem his discharge dangerous to the public peace or safety, order him to be committed to the state lunatic asylum, until he

becomes sane" (Fitzpatrick, 1915, p. 183).

[14] The murder, Thaw's subsequent stories of crime, and the reported Thaw history of purchasing people and justice are addressed in more detail in *Antonio's Will* (Tirado-Chiodini, 2014).

[15] *When and in what case indictment may be removed before trial.* (N.Y. Code Crim. Procedure § 344, 1915). *See* (Fitzpatrick, 1915).

[16] The New York Supreme Court, Judge Van Kirk presiding, allowed a payment of $562 to defense counsel in the trial of Antonio Pontón. (Schenectady County (NY) Board of Supervisors, 1915).

[17] The "Equal Protection Clause" of the Fourteenth Amendment to the U.S. Constitution took effect in 1868 and provides that "no state shall deny to any person within its jurisdiction the equal protection of the laws" (U.S. Const. amend. XIV).

[18] Women did not serve as jurors in the United States until well into the 20th century. In 1879, the Supreme Court in *Strauder v. West Virginia* continued to sanction this practice, stating that even though jury service could no longer be restricted to whites under the Fourteenth Amendment, it could continue to be restricted to males. In 1975, the Supreme Court in *Taylor v. Louisiana* stated that "the exclusion of women from jury venires deprives a criminal defendant of his Sixth Amendment right to trial by an impartial jury drawn from a fair cross-section of the community" (Taylor v. Louisiana, 1975).

[19] In 1946, the Supreme Court in *Ballard v. United States* acknowledged that by systematically excluding a class from jury service, the injury extends beyond the defendant to the community as a whole and to the democratic ideal that should be reflected by the courts. Exclusion creates stereotypes, fostering prejudice against the excluded class. (Ballard v. United States, 1946). In 1979, the Supreme Court in *Duren v. Missouri* stated that the impartial jury fair "cross-section" standard requires that a distinctive class of jurors not be systematically excluded from the jury pool. (Duren v. Missouri, 1979).

[20] In 1848, the *Treaty of Guadalupe Hidalgo* extended U.S. citizenship to about 80,000 Mexicans who lived in the Mexican territories acquired by the United States. With time, some moved away from these lands into other parts of the mainland. Between 1850 and 1920, the U.S. census counted most Mexicans as racially "white" (Latino Issues: A Reference Handbook, 2011, p. 149). By 1920, there were about 12,000 Puerto Ricans in New York City. (Chenault, 1938,

p. 57). Some of them lived in Schenectady and worked there as laborers. According to the New York census records for 1910, 1915 and 1920, there were men of Puerto Rican, Spanish, Mexican, Colombian, Argentinean, Cuban and other Hispanic ancestry living in Schenectady. (New York State Archives, 1910, 1915, 1920). Their U.S. citizenship status is unknown as of this writing.

[21] In 1900, President William McKinley supported U.S. citizenship and statehood for Puerto Ricans, and so did some members of the U.S. Congress. Speaking on behalf of a presidential commission assessing Puerto Rico, Chairman Rev. Henry Carroll stated that the island's people were moral, industrious, intellectually capable, obedient and respectful of the law. He relayed that he had "no hesitation in affirming that the people have good claims to be considered capable of self-government," and that he was convinced that they possessed the qualities to develop "a high type of citizenship" (Torruella, 1985, p. 32). Senator Jacob Bromwell, a Republican from Ohio, stated during congressional sessions: "They are orderly, law abiding, and anxious for development. If any people on earth deserve fair and considerate treatment, it is the people of Puerto Rico" (p. 34). New York's Representative, George B. McClellan, Jr., a Democrat, agreed. "[Puerto Rico] is part of the United States. The constitution extends over it; its territory is our territory; its people are our citizens" (p. 34).

These favorable sentiments were overcome by opposing scholars tainted by racial bias. For example, Simeon E. Baldwin, a Harvard University Law School scholar, wrote: "Our constitution was made by civilized and educated people. ... To give the ignorant and lawless brigands that infest Puerto Rico ... the benefit of such immunity from the sharp and sudden justice—or injustice—which they have hitherto being accustomed to expect, would of course be a serious obstacle to the maintenance there of an efficient government" (Baldwin, 1899). Talcott H. Russell, a Yale Law School scholar, wrote: "Its inhabitants are at such low stage of human development as to be beyond the pale of constitutional guarantees. ... [T]hey cannot be for a moment considered as citizens of the United States" (Russell, 1900). Opponents inflicted fear and persuaded the U.S. Congress and the courts over the impact that making Puerto Rico a state—and Puerto Ricans U.S. citizens—would have on the relationship between the U.S.

and the Philippines, whose people they addressed as "savages" (Torruella, 1985, p. 34).

[22] The matter of *Gonzales v. Williams*, 192 U.S. 1 (1904), arrived to the U.S. Supreme Court on appeal from the Circuit Court of the United States for the Southern District of New York, filed on February 27, 1903. Isabel González was a Puerto Rican woman who was detained at the Port of New York in 1903 by the U.S. Commissioner of Immigration under the charge that she was an alien "likely to become a public charge." González challenged the lower court's decision to deport her after having her Writ of Habeas Corpus dismissed. Her appeal argued in favor of U.S. citizenship for Puerto Ricans as inhabitants of a U.S. territory. The U.S. Supreme court ruled that González was not an alien but did not decide on the issue of U.S. citizenship for Puerto Ricans. (Erman, 2008). While the court responded in part to the appellant's prayer, its decision created an effective "constitutional rights limbo" for Puerto Ricans. Although Puerto Ricans were now free to travel to and from the U.S. mainland as "non-aliens," they were still regarded as "non-citizens" of the United States, devoid of the protection of key U.S. constitutional rights and privileges.

[23] Regarding the application of the U.S. Constitution in the territory of Puerto Rico, in 1898 the U.S. Supreme Court originally stood by the premise that U.S. citizenship and the Bill of Rights "followed the flag" (Thompson v. Utah, 1898). However, influenced by the existing undercurrent of racial discrimination and by the racist scholars opposing U.S. citizenship for Puerto Ricans, in 1901 the U.S. Supreme Court created the *Territorial Incorporation Doctrine*. The court crafted the doctrine after a series of cases called the *Insular Cases,* which stood for giving second-class citizen treatment to the residents of U.S. territories, including Puerto Rico. Under the doctrine, those residing in Puerto Rico would not be afforded full constitutional rights, such as trial by jury. (Torruella, 1985). Nevertheless, Puerto Ricans residing in the United States would be afforded full constitutional rights (at least in theory), including the right to be tried by an impartial jury.

[24] The New York Constitution, Art. XI § 1, required that "All able-bodied male citizens between the ages of eighteen and forty-five years, who are residents of the State, shall constitute the militia" (New York

Constitution, 1894). Consistent with this provision, Antonio Pontón registered in the Tenth Infantry of the New York National Guard. (New York Guard Service Cards and Enlistment Records, 1906-1918).

[25] The specific legal issue was: Whether Puerto Rican U.S. residents (non-citizen nationals residing in the United States) could qualify to serve as jurors in the United States, so that Puerto Rican defendants like Pontón could be afforded their constitutional right to an impartial jury drawn from a cross-section of the community. A broader issue would apply to all persons in a similar situation as in Pontón's case (not just Puerto Ricans), who would automatically be disqualified to serve as jurors under the discriminatory law.

[26] The *Pure Food and Drugs Act*, enacted in 1906, prohibited interstate commerce in adulterated and misbranded food and drugs. (Pure Food and Drugs Act, 34 Stat. 768, 1906). The law was later amended and eventually led to the creation of today's *Food and Drug Administration*. The *Harrison Narcotics Tax Act*, enacted in 1914, regulated and taxed the production, importation, and distribution of opiates and coca products. (Harrison Narcotics Tax Act, Ch. 1, 38 Stat. 785, 1914).

[27] As mentioned in Note 3, Ponton's trial transcript and case records were destroyed. However, the hundreds of newspaper articles covering Pontón's crime, murder trial, and execution provided copious detail of the trial testimony and defense legal theories. These made no mention of the potential effect of medications on Pontón's conduct, suggesting this subject was never addressed by the defense.

[28] As described in *Antonio's Will* and in **Chapter Two** of this book, in his letter to Governor Whitman, attorney Charles E. Le Barbier provided an excerpt of the trial transcript with the court's instruction to the jury, and he requested a respite to bring the new evidence before the court on a motion for a new trial.

[29] On May 27, 2015, Nebraska legislators, largely conservative and acting against their Republican governor Pete Ricketts, abolished the death penalty there in a bipartisan effort, citing that capital punishment is inefficient, expensive and inconsistent with their values. Lawmakers also cited religious and moral reasons for supporting the repeal. (New York Times, 2015).

[30] The U.S. military has its own death penalty statute using lethal injection to administer death, though no executions have been carried

out under the statute in over 30 years. (DPIC, 2015c; DPIC, 2015d).

[31] In 1915, this was also codified under Section 495-a of the New York Penal Law and Code of Criminal Procedure. (Fitzpatrick, 1915).

[32] On April 2014, the Oklahoma Supreme Court ruled against convicted murderers Clayton Lockett and Charles Warner in their challenge to the state's so-called secrecy provision, which forbids disclosing the identities of anyone involved in the execution process or suppliers of any drugs or medical equipment. Missouri and Texas have similar secrecy provisions. (McBride, 2014).

[33] Citing 66 N. Y. Correct. Law § 658.

[34] Translation by Yasmin Tirado-Chiodini. (Some punctuation may have been modified for clarity.)

Table of Cases

References

5 J. Wigmore, Evidence § 1361. (Chadbourn 1974).

ACLU et al. (2015, June 17). *Hurst v. Florida – Amicus Brief.* Retrieved from https://www.aclu.org/legal-document/hurst-v-florida-amicus-brief

ACLU. (2003). *Race and the Death Penalty.* Retrieved from American Civil Liberties Union. Aclu.org: https://www.aclu.org/capital-punishment/race-and-death-penalty

ACLU. (2015). *We Can Stop Solitary.* Retrieved from https://www.aclu.org/we-can-stop-solitary

Albany Evening Journal. (1916, January 7). Ponton Met Death While Official Condemned Law. *Albany Evening Journal,* p. 1.

Albany Law School. (1915). Albany Law School, Class of 1915 (Photograph). Albany, NY.

American Bar Association. (2015, June 4). *Brief of Amicus Curiae American Bar Association in Support of Petitioner.* Retrieved from http://www.americanbar.org/content/dam/aba/images/abanews/hurst_v_florida_amicus.pdf

American Chemical Society. (1999). *The Discovery and Development of Penicillin.* Retrieved from http://www.acs.org/content/dam/acsorg/education/whatischemistry/landmarks/flemingpenicillin/the-discovery-and-development-of-penicillin-commemorative-booklet.pdf

American Medical Association. (1921). *Nostrums and Quackery: Articles on the Nostrum Evil and Quackery, Reprinted from the Journal of the American Medical Association* (Vol. 2).

Amnesty International. (2015). *Death Penalty Cost.* Retrieved from AmnestyUSA.org: http://www.amnestyusa.org/our-work/issues/death-penalty/us-death-penalty-facts/death-penalty-cost

Associated Press. (2015, February 14). *In close vote, Utah*

House OKs firing-squad proposal. Retrieved from Foxnews.com Politics: http://www.foxnews.com/politics/2015/02/14/in-close-vote-utah-house-oks-firing-squad-proposal

Atkins v. Virginia, 536 U.S. 304 (2002).

Baer, J., Kaufman, J. C., & Baumeister, R. F. (2008). *Are We Free? Psychology and Free Will*. New York, NY: Oxford University Press.

Baldwin, S. E. (1899). The Constitutional Questions Incident to the Acquisition and Government by the United States of Island Territory. *Harv. L. Rev., 12*, 393, 415.

Ballard v. United States, 329 U.S. 187 (1946).

Barnes, R. (2008, April 17). *In Reversal, Stevens Says He Opposes Death Penalty*. Retrieved from The Washington Post: http://www.washingtonpost.com/wp-dyn/content/article/2008/04/16/AR2008041603073.html

Baze v. Rees, 553 U.S. 35 (2008).

Beavers v. Henkel, 194 U.S. 73 (1904).

Benham, S. (2015, February 20). *Gov. Brown says she'll keep Kitzhaber's death penalty moratorium*. Retrieved from Katu.com Politics: http://www.katu.com/politics/Gov-Brown-says-shell-keep-Kitzhabers-death-penalty-moratorium-in-place-293005101.html

Bigby v. Dretke, 402 F.3d 551 (5th Cir. 2005).

Bilhart, T. (1986). *Urban Religion and the Second Great Awakening: Church and Society in Early National Baltimore*. Cranbury, N.J.: Farleigh Dickinson University Press.

Billington, R. (1938). *The Protestant Crusade 1800-1860*. N.Y.: Macmillan.

Black, E. (2012). *War Against the Weak: Eugenics and America's Campaign to Create a Master Race*. Washington, DC: Dialog Press.

Bloomberg. (2015, March 9). *Florida's Death Penalty Rules Get Supreme Court Review*. Retrieved from Bloomberg.com Politics: http://www.bloomberg.com/politics/articles/2015-03-09/florida-s-death-penalty-rules-get-u-s-supreme-court-review

Burris, A. (2015, June 30). *Update: Glenn Ford dies*. Retrieved from The Shreveport Times (shreveporttimes.com): http://www.shreveporttimes.com/story/news/2015/06/29/exonerated-glenn-ford-dies/29457649

Capital Punishment in Context. (2015). *The Capital*

Punishment Appeals Process. Retrieved from The Capital Punishment Appeals Process: http://www.capitalpunishmentincontext.org/resources/dpappealspro cess

Carter, G. L. (2012). *Guns in American Society: An Encyclopedia of History, Politics, Culture, and the Law* (Vol. 3). Santa Barbara, CA: ABC-CLIO.

Center for Disease Control and Prevention. (2015). *School Violence: Data & Statistics*. Retrieved from http://www.cdc.gov/violenceprevention/youthviolence/schoolviolenc e/data_stats.html

Chenault, L. R. (1938). *The Puerto Rican Migrant in New York City*. New York, NY: Columbia University Press.

Chicago's Daily Tribune. (1907, April 13). New Thaw Trial; First is Fiasco. pp. 1-2.

Costa Mandry, O. (1943). Studies of Syphilis in Puerto Rico. 453. San Juan, PR: Department of Health of Puerto Rico, School of Medicine.

Cuomo, M. (2011, October 2). *Death penalty is dead wrong: It's time to outlaw capital punishment in America - completely*. (Op-Ed). Retrieved from New York Daily News: http://www.nydailynews.com/opinion/death-penalty-dead-wrong-time-outlaw-capital-punishment-america-completely-article-1.961087

Death Penalty Pro's and Con's. (2015). Retrieved from http://deathpenalty.procon.org/view.answers.php?questionID=0009 83

Death Penalty USA. (2015). *Executions in New York State 1890-1963*. Retrieved from http://www.DeathPenaltyUSA.org

DeChillo, S. (1991, June 6). *A Glimpse 'Up the River' in Ossining*. Retrieved from New York Times: http://www.nytimes.com/1991/06/09/nyregion/a-glimpse-up-the-river-in-ossining.html

Dieter, R. (2011). *Struck by Lightning: The Continuing Arbitrariness of the Death Penalty Thirty-Five Years After Its Re-instatement in 1976*. Death Penalty Information Center. Washington, DC: Death Penalty Information Center.

Donnino, W. C. (1987). N.Y. PEN. LAW § 40.15. *Penal Law § 40.15, Practice Commentary, Book 39*, 297-299. McKinney's Consolidated Laws of New York.

Doyle, K. M. (2008). Lethal Crapshoot: The Fatal Unreliability of the Penalty Phase. *U. Pa. J.L. & Soc. Change, 11* (2), 275.

DPIC. (2015a). *Botched Executions.* Retrieved from Death Penalty Information Center: http://www.deathpenaltyinfo.org/some-examples-post-furman-botched-executions

DPIC. (2015b). *Clemency Process.* Retrieved from Death Penalty Information Center:
http://www.deathpenaltyinfo.org/clemency#process

DPIC. (2015c). *Death Penalty in NY.* Retrieved from Death Penalty Information Center: http://www.deathpenaltyinfo.org/new-york-1

DPIC. (2011). *Deterrence.* Retrieved from Death Penalty Information Center: http://www.deathpenaltyinfo.org/deterrence-states-without-death-penalty-have-had-consistently-lower-murder-rates

DPIC. (2015d). *Federal Death Penalty.* Retrieved from Death Penalty Information Center:
http://www.deathpenaltyinfo.org/federal-death-penalty

DPIC. (2015e). *Innocence List.* Retrieved from Death Penalty Information Center: http://www.deathpenaltyinfo.org/innocence-list-those-freed-death-row?scid=6&did=110

DPIC. (2015f). *Nations with Death Penalty.* Retrieved from Death Penalty Information Center:
http://www.deathpenaltyinfo.org/article.php?did=127&scid=30#interexec

DPIC. (2014). *Oregon Governor Moratorium.* Retrieved from Death Penalty Information Center:
http://www.deathpenaltyinfo.org/oregon-governor-declares-moratorium-all-executions

Duren v. Missouri, 439 U.S. 357 (1979).

Erman, S. (2008). Meanings of Citizenship in the U.S. Empire: Puerto Rico, Isabel Gonzalez, and the Supreme Court, 1898 to 1905. *Journal of American Ethnic History, 27* (4).

Federal Death Penalty Act. (1994). *18 U.S.C.A. sec. 3591, et. Seq.*

Fitzpatrick, J. T. (1915). Penal Law and the Code of Criminal Procedure of the State of New York, with All Amendments Passed by the Legislature at the Session of 1915 (7th ed.). New York, NY: Matthew Bender & Co.

Ford v. Wainwright, 477 U.S. 399 (1986).

Ford, D., Watts, A., & Hanna, J. (2014, September 8). *Another botched execution? Inmate gasps during two-hour execution.* Retrieved from CNN News: http://www.cnn.com/2014/07/23/justice/arizona-execution-controversy/index.html?hpt=hp_t1

Fordham University School of Law. (1972). The Hearsay Rule and the Right to Confrontation: States' Leeway in Formulating Evidentiary Rules. *40 Fordham L. Rev. 595.*

Furman v. Georgia, 408 U.S. 238 (1972).

Glossip v. Gross, No. 14-7955 (cert. granted Jan. 23, 2015).

Gluece, S. (1925). *Mental Disorder and the Criminal Law.* Boston, MA, USA: Little, Brown & Co.

Gobert, J. J. (1988). In Search of the Impartial Jury. *The Journal of Criminal Law & Criminology, 79* (2), 273.

Gonzales v. Williams, 192 U.S. 1 (1904).

Green, A. (2015, February 18). *John Kitzhaber leaves governor's office without commuting any death-row sentences.* Retrieved from The Oregonian/Oregon Live: http://www.oregonlive.com/politics/index.ssf/2015/02/word_on_or egons_death_row_inma.html

Greenhouse, L. (2008, April 18). *Justices Uphold Lethal Injection in Kentucky Case.* Retrieved from The New York Times: http://www.nytimes.com/2008/04/17/washington/17scotus.html?pa gewanted=all&_r=0

Greenspan, S. (2011). *Posthumous Pardons Granted in American History.* Retrieved from Death Penalty Information Center: http://www.deathpenaltyinfo.org/documents/PosthumousPardons.p df

Gregg v. Georgia, 428 U.S. 153 (1976).

GRIP and NDTRAN. (2015). *Capital Defense Handbook for Defendants and their Families.* Retrieved from http://www.ndran.org/capital%20defense%20handbook.htm

Gross, S. R., O'Brien, B., & Huc, C. (2014). Rate of false conviction of criminal defendants who are sentenced to death. (L. D. Ross, Ed.) *Proceedings of the National Academy of Sciences of the United States of America, 111* (20), 7235.

Harrison Narcotics Tax Act, Ch. 1, 38 Stat. 785. (1914, December 17). Retrieved from http://legisworks.org/sal/38/stats/STATUTE-38-Pg785.pdf

Hernandez v. Texas, 347 U.S. 475 (1954).

Hertz, K. (2015, April 4). *Irishman hanged for murder 74 years ago posthumously pardoned*. Retrieved from Irish Central: http://www.irishcentral.com/news/Irishman-who-was-hanged-for-murder-74-years-ago-will-be-posthumously-pardoned.html

Historic Hudson River Tours, Ossining. (2015). Retrieved from http://www.hudsonriver.com/ossining

Hurst v. Florida, Case No. 14-7505, Case No. 14-7505.

Jabbour, N. (2000). Syphilis from 1890 to 1920, a Public Nightmare and the First Challenge to Medical Ethics. *Essays in History, 42.*

Jackson, D. W., Smith, J. H., Sisson, E. H., & Krassnoff, H. T. (1999). Bending Toward Justice: The Posthumous Pardon of Lieutenant Henry Ossian Flipper. *Indiana Law Journal, 74* (1251), 1251-1296.

Kellerman, J. (2003). *Savage Spawn: Reflections on Violent Children*. New York, NY: Ballantine Books.

Kleiman, M. A., & Hawdon, J. E. (2011). *Encyclopedia of Drug Policy*. SAGE Publications.

Latino Issues: A Reference Handbook. (2011). ABC-CLIO.

Library of Congress, George Grantham Bain Collection. (1920). Sing Sing Prison, Aerial View, LC-B2- 5299-12 [P&P]. (D. Library of Congress Prints and Photographs Division Washington, Compiler) Washington, DC: Library of Congress.

Lithwick, D. (2015, February 3). The Capital Punishment Cover-Up. *The Slate.*

Mak v. Blodgettj, 970 F.2d 614 (9th Cir. 1992).

McBride, B. (2014, April 29). *Oklahoma Botches Clayton Lockett's Execution*. Retrieved from The Huffington Post: http://www.huffingtonpost.com/2014/04/29/oklahoma-clayton-lockett-execution_n_5236297.html

Meynen, G. (2010). Free will and mental disorder: Exploring the relationship. *Theoretical Medicine and Bioethics, 31* (6), 429-443.

Miranda v. Arizona, 384 U.S. 436 (1966).

Moehling, C., & Morrison Piehl, A. (2009). Immigration, Crime, and Incarceration in Early Twentieth-Century America. *Demography, 46* (4), 739-763.

MVFHR. (2015). *Murder Victims' Families for Human Rights.*

Retrieved from http://www.mvfhr.org

National Alliance on Mental Illness. (2013, March). *Opiate Abuse and Mental Illness Fact Sheet*. Retrieved from http://www2.nami.org/factsheets/opiates_factsheet.pdf

National Center for Education Statistics, U.S. Dept. Ed. (2011). *Fast Facts*. Retrieved from National Center for Education Statistics: https://nces.ed.gov/fastfacts/display.asp?id=66

National Endowment for the Humanities. (2015). *Magna Carta: Cornerstone of the U.S. Constitution*. Retrieved from http://edsitement.neh.gov/lesson-plan/magna-carta-cornerstone-us-constitution

National Institute of Justice. (2012). *Criminal Justice Interventions for Offenders with Mental Illness: Evaluation of Mental Health Courts in Bronx and Brooklyn, New York. Final Report. Prepared under ASP BPA 2004BF022, Task Requirement T-014, Task Order 2006)*. National Institute of Justice, New York, NY.

New York American. (1906, June 26). Harry Thaw Kills Stanford White on Roof Garden. *New York American*, p. 1.

New York Constitution. (1894). Retrieved from https://www.nycourts.gov/history/legal-history-new-york/documents/Publications_1894-NY-Constitution.pdf

New York Guard Service Cards and Enlistment Records. (1906-1918). *Series: B2000, Film Number: 19*. Albany, New York: New York State Archives.

New York Herald. (1916, January 1). New Respite for Slayer Sentenced to Die on Monday: Governor Whitman Grants Another Delay in the Case of Antonio Ponton. p. 4.

New York Herald. (1915, December 5). Plea for Condemned Man. p. 4.

New York Press. (1916, January 1). Wilson To-Day Gives New Year Party. p. 3.

New York State Archives. (1910, 1915, 1920). State Population Census Schedules, 1910, 1915, 1920. *Election District: 03; Assembly District: 01; City: Schenectady Ward 09; County: Schenectady*. Albany, New York: Ancestry.com.

New York State Assembly, Standing Committee on Codes, Judiciary and Correction. (2005). *The Death Penalty in New York, A Report of Public Hearings on the Death Penalty in New York*. Retrieved from http://assembly.state.ny.us/comm/Codes/20050403/deathpenalty.pdf

New York State. (1919). *Public Papers of Charles Seymour Whitman: 1916.* New York, NY: J.B. Lyon & Co.

New York State Services. (2015). *Application for Clemency.* Retrieved from http://www.ny.gov/services/apply-clemency

New York State, Dept. of Correctional Services. (1915, April 27). Sing Sing Prison, Inmate admission register for Antonio Ponton. Ossining, NY: New York State Archives, Albany, New York.

New York Sun. (1916, January 5). Won't *See* Execution. p. 7.

New York Times. (1929, February 22). Hulbert, Former Executioner, Is a Suicide; Man Who Put 140 to Death Shoots Himself. p. 12.

New York Times. (2015, May 27). *Nebraska Bans Death Penalty, Defying a Veto.* Retrieved from nytimes.com: http://www.nytimes.com/2015/05/28/us/nebraska-abolishes-death-penalty.html

Newseum. (2015, March). Whereabouts of Sing Sing Electric Chair. (Y. Tirado-Chiodini, Interviewer)

Oklahoma Historical Society. (2015a). *Davenport, James Sanford.* Retrieved from OKHistory.org Publications: Retrieved from http://www.okhistory.org/publications/enc/entry.php?entry=DA013

Oklahoma Historical Society. (2015b). *Gore, Thomas Pryor.* Retrieved from OKHistory.org Publications: http://www.okhistory.org/publications/enc/entry.php?entry=GO013

Ollstein, A. (2015, March 12). *Alabama Lawmakers Vote To Bring Back the Electric Chair.* Retrieved from Think Progress: http://thinkprogress.org/justice/2015/03/12/3632826/alabama-lawmakers-vote-bring-back-electric-chair

Paulson, A. (2013, February 27). *Why juvenile incarceration reached its lowest rate in 38 years.* Retrieved from The Christian Science Monitor: http://www.csmonitor.com/USA/Justice/2013/0227/Why-juvenile-incarceration-reached-its-lowest-rate-in-38-years

Penry v. Lynaugh, 492 U.S. 302 (1989).

People v. Conroy, 153 N.Y. 174 (1897).

People v. Horton, 4 Ill. 2d 176 (1954).

People v. LaValle, 3 N.Y.3d 88 (2004).

People v. Moran, 249 N.Y. 179 (1928).

People v. Ponton, 110 N.E. 1046 (N.Y. 1915).

People v. Taylor, 9 N.Y.3d 129 (2007).

Pew Research Center. (2009, May 28). *Who is Hispanic?* Retrieved from Hispanic Trends: http://www.pewhispanic.org/2009/05/28/whos-hispanic

Puerto Rican Coalition Against the Death Penalty. (2012). *Annual Report*. Retrieved from WordCoalition.org: http://www.worldcoalition.org/media/resourcecenter/PRCADP-AnnualReport2012-EN.pdf

Pure Food and Drugs Act, 34 Stat. 768. (1906). Retrieved from FDA.gov: http://www.fda.gov/RegulatoryInformation/Legislation/ucm148690.htm

Radelet, M. L., Bedau, H. A., & Putnam, C. E. (1994). *In Spite of Innocence: Erroneous Convictions in Capital Cases*. Boston, MA: Northwestern University Press.

Roper v. Simmons, 543 U.S. 551 (2005).

Russell, T. J. (1900). Results of Expansion. *Yale L. J., 9*, 239, 240-42.

Schenectady County (N.Y.) Board of Supervisors. (1915). Schenectady County Board of Supervisors Proceedings, (p. 402). New York.

Schenectady District Attorney. (1914, December 14). Enhanced Photograph of Antonio Ponton's Indictment. Schenectady, NY: New York State Archives, Albany NY.

Schenectady Gazette. (1914a, October 3). Angry Porto Rican Murders Schenectady School Teacher. p. 1.

Schenectady Gazette. (1914b, October 31). Antonio Ponton Will be Arraigned Today. p. 1.

Schenectady Gazette. (1915b, April 21). Eye Witnesses Tell Harrowing Stories of Girl's Murder. p. 1.

Schenectady Gazette. (1915d, April 24). Ponton Doomed to Death in Chair; Guilty of Murder in First Degree; Screams at Verdict, Then is Calm. p. 1.

Schenectady Gazette. (1915c, April 23). Ponton's Fate will Rest with the Jury by Noon Recess Today. pp. 1-2.

Schenectady Gazette. (1915a, April 17). Trial of Ponton on the Charge of Committing One of the Most Startling Murders in History of County May be Featured with Night Sessions. p. 5.

School of Criminal Justice, SUNY at Albany. (2015). *What is the Capital Jury Project?* Retrieved from Albany.edu: http://www.albany.edu/scj/13189.php

Sheffer, S. (2009). *Double Tragedies.* National Alliance on Mental Illness. Arlington, VA: National Alliance on Mental Illness.

Squire, A. O. (1935). *Sing Sing Doctor.* Garden City, NY: Double Day, Doran & Company.

St. John's Law Review. (1958). Criminal Responsibility and Proposed Revisions of the M'Naghten Rule. *St. John's Law Review, 32* (2), 247.

St. John's Law Review. (1965). Legislative Changes in New York Criminal Insanity Statutes. *St. John's Law Review, 40* (1, Art. 5), 76.

State of New York. (1917). *McKinney's Consolidated Laws of New York Annotated* (Vol. 29). (W. M. McKinney, Ed.) New York, NY: West Publishing Company.

Strauder v. West Virginia, 100 U.S. 303 (1879).

Stroud III, A. M. (2015, March 15). *Lead prosecutor apologizes for role in sending man to death row [Letter to the Editor].* Retrieved from The Shreveport Times, ShreveportTimes.com Opinion: http://www.shreveporttimes.com/longform/opinion/readers/2015/0 3/20/lead-prosecutor-offers-apology-in-the-case-of-exonerated-death-row-inmate-glenn-ford/25049063

Syracuse Journal. (1916, January 7). Executioner Weeps Killing Girl's Slayer. p. 1.

Taylor v. Louisiana, 419 U.S. 522 (1975).

The Jones-Shafroth Act. (1917, March 2). *ch. 145, § 5, 39 Stat. 951 (codified as amended at 8 U.S.C. § 1402 (2006)) .*

Thompson v. Utah, 170 U.S. 343 (1898).

Thompson, F. (2015, February 7). *Commentary: Commute Oregon's death sentences to life imprisonment.* Retrieved from The Statesman Journal: http://www.statesmanjournal.com/story/opinion/readers/2015/02/1 7/commute-oregons-death-sentences-life-imprisonment/23565589

Tirado-Chiodini Collection. (1914-1916). Enhanced Photographs of Original Antonio Ponton Clemency Documents, Copyright 2014-2015 Yasmin Tirado-Chiodini. *New York State Archives; Albany, New York, Governor Whitman Pardons.* Oviedo, FL: Black Hammock Enterprises, LLC.

Tirado-Chiodini, Y. (2014). *Antonio's Will*. Oviedo, FL, USA: Black Hammock Enterprises, LLC.

Torruella, J. R. (1985). *The Supreme Court and Puerto Rico: The Doctrine of Separate and Unequal*. Rio Piedras, PR: University of Puerto Rico.

U.S. Census Bureau. (2011, May). *The Hispanic Population: 2010*. Retrieved from census.gov: http://www.census.gov/prod/cen2010/briefs/c2010br-04.pdf

U.S. Const. amend. V. (n.d.).

U.S. Const. amend. VI. (n.d.).

U.S. Const. amend. VIII. (n.d.).

U.S. Const. amend. XIV. (n.d.).

United Nations, Office of the High Commissioner for Human Rights. (2014). *Moving Away from the Death Penalty: Arguments, Trends and Perspectives*. New York, NY.

United States Food and Drug Administration. (1918). *Notices of Judgment Under the Food and Drugs Act, Issue 4001; Issue 5000*. U.S. Government Printing Office.

USA Today. (2015a, June 29). *Glenn Ford, exonerated death row inmate, dies*. Retrieved from USAToday.com: http://www.usatoday.com/story/news/nation/2015/06/29/glenn-ford-exonerated-death-row-inmate-dies/29489433

USA Today. (2015b, June 30). *Supreme Court refuses to ban controversial method of execution*. Retrieved from USAToday.com: http://www.usatoday.com/story/news/nation/2015/06/29/supreme-court-lethal-injection/28648145

Vedder, E. B. (1915). *The Problem of Syphilis in the Army*. Office of the Surgeon General, War Department. Washington, DC: Government Printing Office.

Weiner, R. (2014, February 10). *Virginia electric chair bill dies for the year in state Senate*. Retrieved from The Washington Post, Virginia Politics: http://www.washingtonpost.com/local/virginia-politics/virginia-electric-chair-bill-dies-for-the-year-in-state-senate/2014/02/10/ed6d1468-9260-11e3-b227-12a45d109e03_story.html

Wigmore, J. H. (1904). The History of the Hearsay Rule. *17 Harv. L. Rev. 437*, 443.

Wilson, P. K. (2003). Bad Habits and Bad Genes: Early 20th-Century Eugenic Attempts to Eliminate Syphilis and Associated

'Defects' from the United States. *Canadian Society for the History of Medicine (CBMH)*, *20* (1), 11-41.

World Coalition Against the Death Penalty. (2015). *Presentation*. Retrieved from http://www.worldcoalition.org/presentation

Wright's Indian Vegetable Pills. (1889). Photographs of Wright's Pictorial Family Almanac (Original Document). *1889 Wright's Pictorial Family Almanac*. New York, NY: Ferret, E. (Agent).

Appendix: The Voices of Clemency

C **hapter Four** provides background relevant to the collection of information in this **Appendix**. The author transcribed over 21,000 names from signatures appearing in documents and clemency letters found as part of the author's research referenced in (Tirado-Chiodini Collection, 1914-1916). The list does not include names from documents that may have been destroyed or may reside in other sources. The names are organized under various groups and organizations.

The author made a best effort to transcribe each individual name *as signed*. Therefore, some names may appear abbreviated or have an uncommon spelling. The words and names on the list are provided without Spanish tildes (accents) to facilitate electronic searching in the e-book version of this book. Some signatures were difficult, if not impossible, to transcribe. A few names included notes or titles next to them, which were also transcribed. Some towns may have joined efforts with other towns, and the signatures of residents may appear integrated, without reference to their town of residence. Some names appear to be in duplicate and have been so labeled, but each mention is representative of each signature found and may belong to family members or others with common names. Organizations appear alphabetically by town, when possible. The individual names in the **Appendix** appear in alphabetical order under each corresponding group or organization.

The groups and organizations represented with signatures on the clemency petitions found as of this writing are summarized in the list below.

I. SOCIETIES AND CIVIC ORGANIZATIONS

- Puerto Rico Commission to New York
- Asociación de Dependientes (Chamber of Commerce), Ponce
- Centro Español (Spanish Center), Ponce
- Centro Social (Social Center) Casino de Ponce
- Cuerpo Municipal de Bomberos (Municipal Firemen), Ponce
- Federación Libre de Trabajadores (American Assoc. of Labor Affiliate), Ponce
- Federación Regional de Trabajadores (Regional Federation of Laborers), Ponce
- Liga Progresista (Progressive League) Casino de Ponce

- Puerto Rico Benevolent Society, Ponce
- Sociedad FFF (FFF Society), Playa de Ponce
- Sociedad Teosófica Ananda (Ananda Theosophical Society), Ponce
- Agricultores (Farmers), Sabana Grande
- Liga Literaria (Literary League), San Juan

II. MASONIC LODGES

- Logia Sol Naciente (Rising Sun Lodge), Aguadilla
- Logia Obreros Unidos (United Workers Lodge), Grande Oriente Español, Arecibo
- Logia Tanamá (Tanama Lodge), Arecibo
- Logia Perla del Océano (Ocean Pearl Lodge), Arroyo
- Logia Amparo (Solace Lodge), Caguas
- Logia Almas Unidas (United Souls Lodge), Cidra
- Logia Verdaderos Hermanos (Odd Fellows Lodge), Coamo
- Logia Hijos de la Luz (Sons of the Light Lodge), Fajardo
- Logia La Unión (Union Lodge), Guayama
- Logia Regeneración (Regeneration Lodge) No. 9110, Guayama
- Logia Luz del Meridiano (Meridian Light Lodge), Juana Díaz
- Logia Fraternidad Española (Spanish Fraternity Lodge), Ponce
- Logia Luz de Borinquen (Light of Borinquen Lodge) No. 7990, Ponce
- Logia Luz de Oriente (Western Light Lodge), Yauco

III. RELIGIOUS ORGANIZATIONS

- Disciples of Christ, Christian Women's Board Mission, Bayamón
- Disciples of Christ, Temperance League, Bayamón
- Men's Methodist Brotherhood, Guayama
- Círculo Lúmen (Lumen Circle) Spiritual Society, Ponce
- Catholic Church, San Juan

IV. GOVERNMENT ORGANIZATIONS

- Congressmen, U.S. Congress
- Government of Puerto Rico
- Government of Pennsylvania
- Sing Sing Prison Officials
- Spanish Consulate

V. ATTORNEYS AND MEDICAL EXPERTS

VI. UNIVERSITY STUDENT ORGANIZATIONS

- PSI CHI DELTA Fraternity, Ch. EPSILON, Chicago, IL
- PSI CHI DELTA Fraternity, Ch. MU, University of PA

- PSI CHI DELTA Fraternity, Ch. IOTA, Washington, DC

VII. INDIVIDUALS AND BUSINESSES

VIII. SCHOOL TEACHERS AND STUDENTS

TEACHERS

- Departamento de Educación (Department of Education), Aguadilla
- Teachers Association, Añasco
- Asociación de Maestros (Teachers Association), Juncos
- Teachers and Students, Morovis
- Junta Escolar (School Board), Ponce
- School Board, Quebradillas
- Teachers Association, Rio Piedras
- Teachers, Salinas
- Teachers, Santa Isabel
- Asociación Local de Maestros (Teachers Association), Yauco

SCHOOLS

- Students, Añasco School
- Public School Students, Canóvanas
- School Students, Ciales
- Baldorioty Graded School, Gurabo
- Club Ciencia, Libertad y Moral, Fajardo High School
- Hatillo High School, Hatillo
- Almodóvar School, Juncos
- School Students and Teachers, Maricao
- Central Grammar, San Juan
- Central High School, San Juan
- Concordia School, Ponce
- Band of Mercy, Ponce
- Reina School, Ponce
- School Pupils, Ponce
- School Students, Ponce
- School Students, Liga de la Bondad ("Benevolence League"), Ponce
- Public School Children, Puerto Rico
- School Students, Rincón
- Bancroft School, Río Grande
- Eco Estudiantil, Río Grande
- Escuela Luchetti, San Juan
- School Students, Santa Isabel
- Labra School, Santurce

- School Students, Vega Baja
- High School Ladies, Yauco

IX. UNIVERSITY STUDENTS

- Loyola Medical School Students, Chicago, IL
- Harvard University Students, Cambridge, MA
- University of Syracuse Students, NY
- State College of PA Students, PA
- University of Pennsylvania Students, PA
- University of Puerto Rico, College of Agriculture and Mechanic Arts, Mayagüez, PR

X. MAYORS, TOWN MUNICIPAL COUNCILS AND CITIZENS

Aguada	Coamo	Loíza	Río Piedras
Barranquitas	Comerío	Mayagüez	San Juan
Bayamón	Fajardo	Morovis	San Sebastián
Cabo Rojo	Hatillo	Naguabo	Santa Isabel
Camuy	Humacao	Patillas	Toa Alta
Carolina	Isabela	Peñuelas	Trujillo Alto
Ciales	Juncos	Ponce	Vieques
Cidra	Lares	Rincón	Yauco

I.

SOCIETIES & CIVIC ORGS.

Puerto Rico Commission to New York

Collazo, Domingo
Echevarria, Andres
(Pbir.) (*Commission Chair and Catholic Priest*)

Asociacion de Dependientes (Chamber of Commerce), Ponce

---, Constantino
Alonso, A.
Alonso, Federico
Alvarez, Jose B.
Alvarez, R.
Anziaru, Francisco A.
Aparicio, Felix
Ascortes, L.
Barquet Hermanos
(Corporation)
Barral, Julio
Barue, Juan
Bas Saldaña, I.
Basch, Jesus M.
Benitez, Eduardo
Brau, Francisco
Campiano, Fusele S.
Cartagena & Co.
(Corporation)
Casiano and Sons Co.
(Corporation)
Cepeda Perez, M.
Coll, Dionicio
Corrales, Antonio
Covas, Pedro G.
Delucca, L. C.
Emanuelli, A. & Co.
(Corporation)

Escribano, Luis E.
Espinet, Busquet &
Sons (Corporation)
Espinet, Busquet &
Sons
(Corporation)(2nd
signature)
Fernandez, Guillermo
Figueroa Hermanos &
Co. (Corporation)
Figueroa, Jose
Figueroa, Sue B.
(Corporation)
Frau, Juan
Gandara, Generoso
Garcia, Francisco
Garcia, P.
Gauthier, Manuel S.
Gonzalez, Juan (Jr.)
Guegla, Francisco
Hamar, P.
Hems, Arbona
Hernandez, Carlos
Labra, Arias F.
Lombo, Antonio
Lopez, Oberto
Mas, Juan
Mattei, Miguel
Mattei, Miguel P.
Matute, Rafael
Medecina, Bernardo
Medecina, Ramon
Mirandez, Francisco
Monserrate,
Concepcion
Montañez, Antonio
Morey, Benito
Nazario, Miguel J.
Noriega Alvarado
Paredes, Victor
Perez Guerra,
Encarnacion
Pizarro, Juan P.
Pomar, Jose
Portela, D.
Pratt, Gaspar
Puig, R.
Quiñones, Cesar
R. Medecina & Hnos.
(Corporation)
Ramirez Prat, Tomas
Ramirez, A.
Raneu, Eduardo
Regau, Juan M.

Reyo, Francisco
Riga, Lope A.
Rivas, Candida
Robles, Domingo
Roig, Jose
Ruiz, Francisco
Schuck, E.
Schuck, Pedro
Serra, Salvador
Simonet, Miguel
Sobrino Gandara,
Claudino
Sobrino, Manuel
Sobrinos de Gandara
(Corporation)
Tormes, Maria Teresa
Torres, Gabriel
Torres, Manuel
Torres, Rafael
Usera, Remigio
Veloz, Jose
Vicente, A.
Vidal, Manuel

Centro Español (Spanish Center), Ponce

Aparicio, Jose
(Treasurer)
Arbona, Antonio
(Secretary)
Arbona, Bartolome
("Vocal")
Ballesteros, Francisco
("Vocal")
Bonnin Fuster, Pedro
Juan ("Vocal")
De la Pila, Manuel
Higueras, Fidel
("Vocal")
Morell, Damian
(President)
Otero, R. (Vice
President)
Ramery (de), E.
("Vocal")

...

Centro Social (Social Center) Casino de Ponce

Alietri, Hector
Bainsord, A.
Battistini, T.
Becerra, J.
Beunet, Efrain
Bosmin, R. J.
Bou, Jose
Braggi, Julio E.
Brau Gary, Fermin
Brau, M.
Brum, J.
Cabrera, A.
Casals, Luis F.
Catinchi, A. (Jr.)
Catinchi, M. A.
Cintron, R.
Clemente, T. A.
Colon Rosich, Ernesto
Colon Rosich,
Fernando
Colon Rosich, G. R.
Costas, A. L. (D.D.S.)
Cuevas, Paco
De Jesus, Jose
Descartes, Mauricio G.
Felici, Enrique
Feran, Lerida
Figueroa, Antonio
Figueroa, Manuel
Maria
Garriga, Juan Enrique
Ginart Garcia, E.
Hofgord, Thomas P.
Hys, O.
Julia, Jose
Laham, K.
Leix, Juan
Linstrong, Alberto
Loasado, J. E.
Mattei, Eduardo
Mila, J. E.
N., J.
Navas, M. B.
Oppenheimer, J.
Perez Guerra, H.
Perez Gual, R.
Quiacal, P.

155

Ramirez Pratt, Tomas
Romaguera, Jose
Romaguera, A.
Romaguera, Miguel
Salazar, C.
Salazar, Luis
Salazar, S. M.
Sanchez, Jose
Schuck, A.
Schuck, F. William
Scott, Rafael
Serbia, R.
Straundry, Salvador
Salichs, Jose
Taboada, T.
Torres, Acasio (Jr.)
Torres, Amador
Torres, Eduardo
Torres, M.
Torruella, N. Vidal
(P.J.)
Torruella, Sergio
Usera, J.
Velazquez, Luis G.
Velez, Antonio
Vive Ascoaga, Luis
Vives Bazan, S.

Cuerpo Municipal de Bomberos (Municipal Firemen), Ponce

B---, Ed (Lieutenant)
Biaggi, Julio E.
(Captain)
Bigas, Modesto
(Lieutenant)
Font, Ernesto
(Lieutenant)
Higueras, Fidel
(Captain)
Lastra, Cheeney (Asst.
Chief)
Marcano, L. (Captain)
Ramos, Joaquin
(Secretary)
Schuck, Pedro (2nd
Chief)
Seix, Juan (1st Chief)

Toro, E. (Lieutenant)
Usera, F. H.
(Lieutenant)

Federacion Libre de Trabajadores (American Association of Labor Affiliate), Ponce

Castillo Lozano, Rafael
(President)
Vargas, Guillermo
(Secretary)

Federacion Regional de Trabajadores (Regional Federation of Laborers), Ponce

Lamour Rivera, A.
(Vice President)
Pastor, Leocadio
(Secretary)
Ramos, Victor
(President)

Liga Progresista (Progressive League) Casino de Ponce

Colon Rosich, Ernesto
(Manager)

. . .

Puerto Rico Benevolent Society

Aguilo (de), Josefa F.
Almonte (de), Teresa
A.
Alonso (de), Nora M.
Alonso (Vda. de),
Senin
Alonso, Ramon
Amadeo, Jose H.
Annair, M. (M.D.)
Antonsanti, Jesus
(Mrs.)
Armstrong (de),
Dolores T.
Astol (de), Sisila A.
Astol, Adela
Biordia, Conchita
Biordia, Mariana
Bisconte (de), Isabel
M.
Cabrera (de),
Margarita B.
Casals (de), Ana B.
Casuela, Engracia Y.
Catoni, E. M. (Mrs.)
Chardon (de), Isabel
O.
Chaviez (de), Ines B.
Chuck, A. (Mrs.)
Citron, Zoilo (Mrs.)
Colon, Juan J. (Jr.)
Dapena (de), Maria L.
(T.T.O.)
De Celis Vda. de
Motta, Elena
De Jesus, Antonia C.
De la Pila, Asuncion I.
De Leon (Vda. de),
Teresa P.
Del V. de Armstrong,
Josefa
Donato (de), Teresa G.
Dorna (de), Rosa G.
Ferrer (de), Carolina
R.
Ferrer (de), Josefina
P.
Forteza, Dolores
Forteza, Herminia
Franceschi (de),

Margarita L.
Galicrup, P. J. (Mrs.)
Garafas (Vda. de),
Maria Sanchez
Garcia (de), Ynes N.
Garcia, Luis
Garcia, Maria
Gautier (de), E.D.
Girard, Jose R.
Gonzalez Ginorio (de),
Concepcion A.
Gonzalez, Julia Elena
Graham (de), S.S.S.
Guerra, Arturo,
Guerrero (de), Elena
G.
Guerrero (Vda. de),
Aurelia A.
Iglesia (de),
Concepcion O.
Lafaye, Julio
Laury (de), Ysabel F.
Lee, J. E. (Mrs.)
Llorens de Lausell, G.
Lomba, Betsabe
Lomba, Diego
Lomba, Jose
Lopez Landin, Juan
Lopez Padin, Ana
Mandry, M. M. (Mrs.)
Martin (de), Pilar C.
Martin, Isidoro
Mas, Enrique
Morales, J. M. (Mrs.)
Morales, M. R. Mrs
Morell (de), Aminda
P.
Morell, D. (Mrs.)
Nater Rivera, Jose
Otero (de), Emilia Y.
Otero (de), Paca R.
Otero, Ana Maria
Otero, Jose
Otero, Julia
Panso (de), Marcelina
R.
Parra (de), Elena V.
Pastor (de), Joaquina
P.
Perez (de), Antonia C.
Porrata, Francisco
(Mrs.)
Portela (de), Carmen
F.

156

Portela, Consuelo
Portela, Manuel R.
Poventud, J. A. (Mrs.)
Praly Vda. de Parra,
  Enriqueta O.
Puertas, Enrique
Quintero, Maria M.
Radon Vda. de
  Biordia, Ana
Ramery (de), Isabel de
  N.
Relaral, Maria Luisa
  M.
Reyes, Georgina
Rodriguez (de),
  Carmelita O.
Rodriguez (Vda. de),
  Monserrate
Rodriguez, Goyitra
Rodriguez, Mercedes
Romero, Rita
Salazar (de), Luisa F.
Salazar (de), Mercedes
  A.
Salazar, Dr. (Mrs.)
Sanchez (de), Rosenda
  M.
Sandin (de), Agripina
  M.
Sandin (de), Manuela
  M.
Sandoval (de), Vicenta
  F.
Sandoval, Rosalina
Sanjurjo (de), Josefa
  R.
Serralles (de), Rosa
  Maria S.
Silva, Flora
Silva, Margarita
Sobrino, Ramon
Toro (de), Carmen D.
Toro (de), Maria S.
Torruella (de), Rita F.
Torruella, J. H. (Mrs.)
Torruellas, G.
Tous Soto (de), Belen
  G.
Trapaga (de), Carmen
  O.
Valdecilla de la Pila,
  Marina
Van Leenhoff, Maria
Vega (de), Tomasa G.

Vela de Diego, Amelia
  N.
Vendrell (de), Isabel T.
Vilaro (de), Nisi A.
Wirsching (de), J. S.
  (Mrs.)
Zauronto, Fabian

Sociedad FFF, Playa de Ponce (FFF Society, Ponce Beach)

Abrahan, Hector
Abreu, Enrique
Acevedo, Vicente
Acosta, Alejo
Acosta, Carlos
Acosta, Claudino
Acosta, Domingo
Acosta, Jose
Agueria, Josefa (Srta.)
Alarcon, Rafael
Alcaide (de), Esther L.
Aleman, Arsenio S.
Aleman, Jose (II)
Aleman, Maria D.
Aleman, Modesto
Aleman, Victor
Alindato, Marco
Alvarado, Telesfora
Alvarez de Forquet,
  Natividad
Alvarez, Jose (I)
Alvarez, Jose (Jr.)
Alvarez, Alfonso
Alvarez, Feliciano
  (Sra.)
Alvarez, Felicita
Alvarez, Luis
Alvarez, Maria Luisa
Alvarez, Oliva
Alvarez, Pablo
Anabitarte, Fernando
Anavitarte, Dolores
Andrea, Ramon
Anton, Carlos C.
Antonsanti,
  Fabriciano
Aponte (de), Rufina T.
Aponte, Carlos
Arce, Arturo

Arjona, Fernando
Armar, Juana
Arroyo, Maria (Srta.)
Arroyo, Tulio
Aviles, Dionisio
Aviles, Fabian
Ayala, Julian
Baez, Gregorio
Barber, Francisco
Baro, Tomas
Batista, Juana
Batistine, Alfredo
Becerra y Toro, A.
Belmond, Guillermo
  (Jr.)
Belmont, Domingo
Beltran, Encarnacion
Berga, Ismael
Bernard, Maria
Bertran, Jose D.
Bibiloni, C.
Biermer, Otto
Biso, Juanita
Blanes, Camelia
Bombi, Jove
Bosch, Francisco
Burquet, Fernando
Burquet, Luis
C. J.
Cabanellas, Teresa
Cabassa, Eustaquia
Cabassa Gumbes,
  Antonia
Cabassa, Amelia
Cabassa, Araceli G.
Cabassa, Carmen
Cabassa, Juan
Cabrera (de),
  Concepcion R.
Cabrera, Carmen
Cabrera, Eugenia
Callard (de), Amena A.
  (Sra.)
Caquia, Luz Maria
Cardona, Carmen
Carras, Marina
Castellano, Damaso
Castello, Catalina
Castro, Arturo
Castro, Oscar
Caverira, Julio
Cintron, Josefina
Cobal, Francisco J.
Coll (de), Maria

Adriana R.
Coll de Costa, Jacinta
Coll, Antonia
Coll, Jose B.
Coll, Rafael Dario
Coll, Teresita
Collado de Morazzani,
  Isabel
Collazo, Alejandrina
Collazo, Luis
Collazo, Victoria
Collazo, Victoria (Sra.)
Colomer Aima,
  Alfonso
Colon (de), Filomena
  L.
Colon Montes, Alberto
Colon, Antonia
Colon, Isabel
Colon, Rita
Colon, Teresa
Colour, Antonio
Cordero (de), Angela
  B.
Cordero, Agustina
Cordero, Bernardino
Cordero, Catalina
Cordero, Francisco
Cordero, Francisco
Cordero, Patria L.
Cortes, Angela
Cortes, Candelaria
Cortes, Jose
Cortes, Panchito
Cortes, Pedro
Costa y Coll, Juanita
Costas, Francisca
  (Dña.)
Cruz Lara, Luis
Cruz, Angel
Cruz, Enrique
Cruz, Luis (Jr.)
Cruz, Manuel
Cruz, Maria L. (Srta.)
Cruz, Pedro
Cruz, Providencia
  (Sra.)
Cuadro, Maria
Cuestas, Amalia
  (Dña.)
Cummings Sallaberry,
  Guillermo
Cummings, Carmen
Curbelo, Eduardo

Dapena, Victoria
David, Peter
De Jesus, Vicente
De Leon, Esteban
Del Rio, Pedro A.
Del Valle (de),
 Robertina C.
Del Valle, Francisco
Dennisten, Leon
Diaz (de), Tomasa O.
Diaz, Antonio
Diaz, Ignacio
Diaz, Isidora
Diaz, Juan
Diaz, Marcela
Diaz, Ramon
Dijols, Justo
Dinoley, Ines
Dominguez, Ana
Echevarria, Eleuterio
Echevarria, Enrique
Echevarria, Juana
Echevarria, Manuela
Enamorado (de),
 Maria Luisa C.
Enamorado, J.
Enamorado, Julita
Enrique, Luca
Esquilin, Quintin V.
Fernandez, Eugenia
Fernandez, Ezequiela
Fernandez, Fernando
Fernandez, Julia
Fernandez, Santiago
Figueroa (de),
 Justiniana R.
Figueroa, Antonio
Figueroa, Francisca
Figueroa, Jose
Fontanillas, Rosendo
Forquet, Colita
Forquet, Jose
Forquet, Juan M.
Forquet, Rafael
Fourquet, Alfonso
Fourquet, Carmen M.
Fourquet, Joaquin
Fourquet, Juan J.
Fourquet, Leonor R.
Fourquet, Luis M.
Fur (Vda. de), Ana R.
Fur, Josefa G.
Galvan, Marvin
Gando, Martin

Garcia de Cummings,
 Manuela
Garcia Velez, Elisa
 (Sra.)
Garcia, Enrique
Garcia, Francisco
Garcia, Ramon
Garcias, Providencia
German, Francisco
Gimenes, Nicolas
Gonzalez (de),
 Concepcion H. (Sra.)
Gonzalez (de), Rafaela
 P.
Gonzalez (Vda. de),
 Dolores (Sra.)
Gonzalez Berga, Juan
Gonzalez, Andres
Gonzalez, Dolores
 (Srta.)
Gonzalez, Jose M.
Gonzalez, L. A.
Gonzalez, Maria Luisa
Gonzalez, Marta
Gonzalez, Pedro
Gonzalez, Ramon H.
Gonzalez, Santos
Gorbea, Carlos
Gorbea, Manolo
Gotay (de), Isabel G.
Gotay, Manuel
Grateron, Emilia
 (Sra.)
Grateron, Senovia
Guadalupe, Adelaida
 (Sra.)
Guerra, Carlota
Gutierrez, Natalio
Guzman, Gregoria
Guzman, Paquita
Hernandez (de), Rosa
 G.
Hernandez, Carmen
Hernandez, Catalina
Huertas (de), Ana M.
Irizarri, R.
Irizarry, Ramon
Jorge, Felicita (Sra.)
Julian (de), Mariana
 L. T.
Julian, Amalia
Julian, F.
Jusino, Ramona
Laboy, Alejita (Srta.)

Laboy, Gregoria
Laboy, Gregoria (Sra.)
Laboy, Luis M.
Laboy, Pascual
Laco de Rosario,
 Enriqueta
Lahoz, Angel
Lahoz, Francisco
Lantana, Angela
Laureano, Carmen
Laureano, Josefino
Leon de Quevedo,
 Crescencia
Lindato, Isabel A.
Llorens (de), Julia G.
Llorens, Alfredo
Llorens, Luis S.
Lopez, Pablo
Lopez, Petra
Lopez, Susana
Lugo de Santana,
 Vicenta
Lugo Hernandez, E.
Lugo, Antonia
Lugo, Carmen (Srta.)
Lugo, Ceferino A.
Lugo, Josefa (Srta.)
Lugo, Providencia
 (Srta.)
Lugo, Ramon
Lugo, Romualdo
Lugo, Yrenes
Luña (de), Cruz P.
Lundt (de), Mercedes
 M.
Lundt de Castro, Ana
Lundt, Maria L.
MacFee Diaz, T.
Macias, Sebastian
Maldonado, Pedro
Maldonado, Petra
 Maria (Srta.)
Manaton, Carmen
Manhattan, H.
Manich, Ernesto
Manich, R.
Marca, Francisco
Marrero (de),
 Marcelina H.
Marrero, Antonio
Marrero, Domingo
Marrero, J. A.
Marrero, Juan G.
Marrero, Rosa Maria

Martin de A., Catalina
Martinez de Alvares,
 Derfina
Martinez, Calisto
Martinez, Maria A.
Martinez, Meliton
Martinez, Petra
Martinez, Tira
Matos, Luis
Matos, Pepa
Matos, R.
Mayol, Miguel
Mayoral, Leonor
Medina, Javier
Medina, Masima
 (Sra.)
Mejias, Josefa (Sra.)
Mercado, America
Mercado, Antonia
Mercado, Carmen
 Maria
Mercado, Cruz (St.)
Mercado, Epifanio
Mercado, Gregoria
Mercado, Vicenta
 (Sra.)
Minnielle, Milita
Miranda, Geronimo
Morazzani Pietri, J.
Montero, Cristino
Morales, Agustina
Morales, Emilio
Morales, Emilio
Morales, Enriqueta
Morales, Pedro
Morales, Tito
Morera, Alejo
Morin, Jose
Navarro, Juan
Navarro, Luis
Navarro, Valero
Nazario, Luciano del
 O.
Negron, Agripina
Negron, Alabado
Negron, Justina
Negron, Luz Maria
Noguera, Sebastian
Oben, Rafael
Oliva, Enriqueta
Olivera, Gaspar
Olivera, Hermilio
Olivera, Isabel (Srta.)
Oliviery, Juanita

(Srta.)
Orbiztondo, Carmelina
Ortiz, Antonia
Ortiz, Antonia
Ortiz, Guillermina
Ortiz, Jose de la Cruz
Ortiz, Juanito N.
Ortiz, Justiniano
Ortiz, Ursula (Srta.)
Pagan, Paulina
Palmer, Gregorio
Pared, Catalina
Parra, Petra Maria
Parrondo, Isabel (Srta.)
Parsy, Julio
Pastor de Colomer, Concepcion
Pastor, Rosario
Pastor, Sofia
Paviras, Ines
Pedraja, Cecilia
Pedraja, Margarita
Pedrajas, Vicente
Pedrajo, Manuel
Pedraza, Sinforosa
Pedrazo (de), Rosa C.
Peña de Ribarte, Ernesto
Peña, Blas (Jr.)
Peña, Clemensia (Srta.)
Perez, Carmen
Perez, Crecensio
Perez, Juana
Perez, Margarita
Pietri, Domino
Pino, Carmen
Pino, Mercedes
Pino, Pilar
Porrata, Carlota (Sra.)
Porrata, Guillermina
Prieto de Gonzalez, Rosa
Pubill, Modesta
Puente, Carmen (Srta.)
Puig, Miguel A.
Quesada (de), Juana C.
Quesada Lugo, Eloy
Quesada, Eloisa
Quesada, Josefa

Questell, Antonio
Questell, Elisa
Questell, Maria D.
Quevedo, Domingo
Quevedo, Eduardo
Quevedo, Froilan
Quevedo, Julio
Quiles, Jose
Quiñones, Ramon
Quirindongo, Carmen
Ramirez, Tomas
Ramos, Aleja
Ramos, Ana M. (Srta.)
Ramos, Carmelo
Ramos, Josefa (Dña.)
Ranier, N.
Renta, Carlos
Renta, Dolores
Renta, Ramiro
Renta, Santiago
Rentas, Carmelo
Rentas, Jesus
Reyes Vda. de Dijols, Daria
Reyes, Carmen
Reyes, Rafaela
Ribarteh, Ines
Riera Sanchez, J.
Rios, Josefa
Rios, Luisa (Señora)
Rios, Reparada (Srta.)
Riso, Anastasio
Risonde (de), Maria P.
Rivarte, Maximina
Rivas, Edicta
Rivas, Francisco
Rivas, Vicente
Rivera, Carmen
Rivera, Catalina
Rivera, Cornelia
Rivera, Luis P.
Rivera, Natalio
Rivera, Pedro
Rivera, Simplicio
Roble, Galletano
Rodil, Jose
Rodriguez (de), Cirila C.
Rodriguez Garbes, Juana
Rodriguez, Alejo
Rodriguez, Angel
Rodriguez, Concepcion

Rodriguez, Consuelo
Rodriguez, Cruz
Rodriguez, Domingo
Rodriguez, E.
Rodriguez, Eugenio
Rodriguez, Isabel (Srta.)
Rodriguez, Josefina (Sra.)
Rodriguez, Juan
Rodriguez, Juana (1)
Rodriguez, Juana (2)
Rodriguez, Justo
Rodriguez, Lola
Rodriguez, Manuel (1)
Rodriguez, Manuel (2)
Rodriguez, Masimino
Rodriguez, Maximo
Rodriguez, Ramon
Rodriguez, S.
Roman, Juan
Romero, Carmen (Miss)
Rosa Perez, Maria
Rosa, Candida (Srta.)
Rosa, Francisco
Rosado de Jimenez, Juana
Rosado, Alejandro
Rosado, Gregorio
Rosado, Hipolito
Rosado, Rufino
Rosario, Pedro Juan
Rosso, Carolina
Rosso, Joaquina
Rosso, Luis
Rubio Quimes, Dolores
Ruiz, Antonia (Srta.)
Ruiz, Benito
Ruiz, Ernesto
Ruiz, Rafael Ana
Saehras, Angel
Salaberry, Julia
Salgado, Carmen
Salgado, Jose R.
Salvador, Francisca
Salvador, Pedro
Sambrano, Juana
Sanchez Gonzalez, Dolores
Sanchez Martin, Luis
Sanchez, Angelica (Srta.)

Sanchez, Antonia
Sanchez, Eleuteria
Sanchez, Juan
Sanchez, Julio
Sanchez, Rosa
Sanchez, Tomasa
Sancho, Rosa
Santana, Angela
Santana, Claudina
Santana, Luis
Santana, Manuel
Santana, Monserrate
Santana, Ysmael
Santiago de N., Ermelinda
Santiago, Altagracia
Santiago, Amparo
Santiago, Avelino
Santiago, Bartolo
Santiago, Ceferino
Santiago, Eduvije
Santiago, Eva
Santiago, Francisca (Srta.)
Santiago, Julia (Sra.)
Santiago, Leonardo
Santiago, Leonor
Santiago, Marcos
Santiago, Nemesio
Santiago, Pedro (Sr. Dn.)
Santiago, Ramona (Srta.)
Santiago, Valeriana
Santos, Rosa Martina
Serrano, Matilde (Sra.)
Sierra, Cristina
Sierra, Leonor
Sierra, Pachita
Sinte, Dolores (Sra. Dña.)
Sinte, Rafaela (Sra. Dña.)
Sivico, Adolfina (Srta.)
Solis, Clementina (Srta.)
Soriano, Gustavo
Soriano, Pablo
Soto, Susana
Stening, R. A.
Suarez, Altagracia (Srta.)
Suarez, Angela Rosa

(Sra.)
Suarez, Gabriel
Suarez, Probidencia
(Srta.)
Suarez, Sere (Sr.)
Suirbes, Ricardo
Tejas, Guillermo
Tejas, Petra Maria
Teresa Santana, Maria
Toro (de), Irene C.
Toro, Luisa (Sra.)
Toros, Jose
Torres, Carlos S.
Torres, Carolina
Torres, Isabel (Srta.)
Torres, Luis
Torres, Mario
Torres, Nicolas
Torres, Pedro
Torres, Segundo
Vargas, Ballazon
Vargas, Evarista
(Señora)
Vargas, Ramon
Vazquez, J. R
Vazquez, Ramon
Vega, Manuela
Velazco, Ramon
Velazquez, Elena
Velazquez, Rosita
Velez Cruz, Carlos
Velez, Carmen (Sra.)
Velez, Damaso
Velez, Erenda (Srta.)
Velez, Josefina (Srta.)
Velez, Ramon R.
Velez, Sebastian
Vera, Agueda
Vera, Rafael
Vergara, Angela (Srta.)
Verges, Eglantina (1)
Verges, Eglantina (2)
Vidal, Alberto (Jr.)
Vidal, Antonio
Villa, Francisco
Virella, Guillermo
Yalboz, Tomas
Ybio, Juan Ramon
Ybio, Panchita
Zambrana, Rosario

. . .

Sociedad Teosofica Ananda (Theosophical Society), Ponce

Alfonzo, Osvaldina V.
Arias, Maria E.
Canevaro, Esteban C.
(President)
Fleurian (Vda. de),
Condesa (Secretary)
Medero, Abelardo
Olivero, Agustin
Paoli Vda. de Braschi,
Olivia
Rivera, J. R.
Sapia, G.
Silva (de), Rosa B.

Agricultores (Farmers), Sabana Grande

Acevedo, Moncino
Acosta, Dolores
Alameda, Eugenio
Baez Nazario, Miguel
Baez, Jose D.
Baez, Nazario, Pablo
Bonilla, Angel
Busigo, Jose A.
Carlo, William
Carlos y Fleitas, Jose
Carrera, Calixto
Casta, Juan
Castillo, Jose
Falcon, Angel
Figueroa, Ramon
Fila, Juan
Flores, Emilio
Garcia Acosta,
Alejandro
Garcia Rodriguez, H.
Garcia, E. I.
Garcia, Hipolito
Garcia, Jacinto
Garcia, Juan
Gastombi E., Jose
Ramon
Gaztambides Bussigo,

Jose Ramon
Gaztambides, Alberto
Gaztambides, Carmen
Gonzalez, Jose L.
Guiany, Jose M.
Irizarry, Fani
Irizarry, H. R.
Lago, Manuel
Languido, Felipe
Medina, Antonio
Milan, Joaq
Mislan, Rafael
Montalvo, Hilario
Olmeda, Eugenio
Olmeda, Jose Angel (1)
Olmeda, Jose Angel (2)
Ortiz, Demetria
Ortiz, Manuel
Padra, Bernabe
Padra, Pascual
Pagan Sepulveda,
Pedro
Pagan, Andres
Pagan, Jose
Pagan, Ulises
Panaini, Francisco
Peralta, Jose R.
Peralta, Manuel
Quiñones, Feliciano
Quiñones, Pedro
Ramirez, Angelina Ma.
Rigau, Agustin
Rigau, R.
Rios, Francisco
Rios, Rafael
Rivera, Eugenio
Rivera, Rafael
Rodriguez, Juanito
Ruiz, Enrique
Schettini, Jose A.
Sepulveda, Genaro
Sepulveda, Manuel
Soto Almodovar, R.
Sultero, Vicente
Vaez, Avelino
Valentin, Miguel
Varquez, Clemente
Vazquez, Jesus M.
Vega, Armando
Vega, Francisco
Mariano
Vega, Jorge
Vega, Juan
Vega, Manuel

Velasco, Rodolfo
Velez, Amadea
Velez, Juan
Velez, Rafael
Velez, Sinforoso
Vidal, Juan
Vidal, Julio
Vlasco, Quiterio
Zaragoza, Jose

Liga Literaria (Literary League), San Juan

Cobian Cuevas, Sergio
("Vocal")
Cuervas, E. (Ministro)
(Hon. Pesident)
Froilan, Mercedes
("Vocal")
Gommy, C. (Secretary)
Miranda Bosque,
Pablo (President)
Noriega Carreras,
Carlos ("Vocal")
Ranero, Francisco
(Treasurer)
Reus Garcia, E. (Hon.
Vice-President)
Riveras, Jorge (Vice
President)

❧

II.

MASONIC LODGES

Logia Sol Naciente (Rising Sun Lodge), Aguadilla

De Cardona, F.
(Worshipful Master)

Echevarria, Jose R.
(Sr. Warden)
Trinidad, Luis
(Secretary)
Vadi, Emilio (Jr.
Warden)

Logia Obreros Unidos (United Workers Lodge), Grande Oriente Español, Arecibo

Cortes, Amelio
Serrano, Rufino
Suez, M.

Logia Tanama (Tanama Lodge), Arecibo

Aleman, Fernando
(Dr.)
Aparicio, V.
Benitez, F.
Breni, Heriberto
Can --, Felix
Cortes, Manuel D.
Crespo, Ulpiano
F---, Ramon
Figueroa, Jesus
Frese, Nicolas
Frey, Rufino
G---, Antonio
Gandia, Luis
Luigi, J. E. (Dr.)(M.
M.) (M.D.)
Montilla, Francisco
Mora Rosado, Ramon
Mora, Pedro
Muñoz, M.
Olmo, W.
Perez Aviles, Manuel
Rodriguez, Juan Z.
Rosado, M.
Ruiz, Eduvigis

Sobrinos, M.
Suliveses, A.
Valencia, M.
Vega, Vicente
Zeus Cuevas, Antonio

Logia Perla del Oceano (Ocean Pearl Lodge), Arroyo (Telegram)

Doelter, Jacinto G.
(Secretary)

Logia Amparo (Solace Lodge), Caguas

Albizu, Enrique
Caballero, Bonifacio
Caballero, Juan
Collazo, Vicente
Cruz, Geronimo
Diaz, Edelmiro
Diaz, Eduardo
Diez Ramos, Federico
Echevarria, B.
Gonzalez Quiñones,
Jose
Lizardi Lebron,
Ramon
Miranda, Ramon
Mitchell, James
Nazario, Manuel
Negron, Lorenzo
Ocasio, Jose
Ortiz, Julio
Puitril, Jose
Rivera, Placido
Roldan, Ramon
Saldaña, Cecilio
Sanchez Colon,
Alfredo
Santana, Vicente
Santiago Colon,
Manuel
Sotomayor, R.
Tantao, Manuel R.
Valdes, Domingo

Logia Almas Unidas (United Souls Lodge), Cidra

Cordero, Gumersindo
(Secretary)
Santiago, Praxedes
(Ven. Maestro)

Logia Verdaderos Hermanos (Odd Fellows Lodge), Coamo

Quesada, Rosendo
(Permanent
Secretary)

Logia Hijos de la Luz (Sons of the Light Lodge), Fajardo

Negroni, Santiago
("Maestro")
Ortiz, Manuel
(Secretary)

Logia La Union (Union Lodge), Guayama

Huselini, Pomp. ("2nd
Vigilante")
Martin, Ramon B.
("Ven. Maestro")
Moieres, Avelino ("1st
Vigilante")

. . .

Logia Regeneracion (Regeneration Lodge) No. 9110, Guayama

Blumm--, Pedro
Byrie, Santos
Capo, Rafael
Colm, Ramon C.
Corelli, Yui
Delvosantis, C.
Goico Morgueson, H.
Haddock, G.
Lebron, Jose L.
Medina, Pedro J.
Molina, Felix
Naveira, A.
Nieto, Luis
Pagan, J.
Preinola, A.
Rodriguez, P.
Rodriguez, Ramon
Rosario, R.
Soto, Alejandro
Texidor, D.

Logia Luz del Meridiano (Meridian Light Lodge), Juana Diaz

Alvarez, Lorenzo
Arroyo, Julio
Barcelo, Ramon
Bisbal, Juan
Brunet, Carlos
(A.D.V.)
Brunett (de), G. G.
Caballero, Bonifacio
Cabrera (de), Vicenta
Cabrera, Angel
Cabrera, Santiago
Cains y Fernandez,
Juan
Camacho, Luis
Cano, Enrique G.
Capo, Lorenzo A.
Carmen, Joaquin

Carreras, Juan
Cedeño, Cirilo
Cintron, Maria
Cintron, R. S. (P. Cr.)
Clon, Maria Cristina
Collazo, Victoria
Collores, G.
Colon, Arturo
Colon, Cesare
Colon, Claudia
Colon, Ines
Colon, Jose A.
Colon, Mercedes
Cruz (de la), Maria
Cruz, Maria
Dage, Carlos
Davila, Juan C.
De Pineda,
  Clementina M.
Deehe, Eleuterio
Delgado, Fidel
Diaz Barcelo, Catalina
Diaz, F.
Diaz, Jose
Diaz, Pedro
Dominguez, Ramon
Dones, Angel
Ech ----, A. B.
Escobal de
  Antonsanti, Teresa
Espada Avila, Jose
Faria, Rosa Maria (1)
Faria, Rosa Maria (2)
Fernandez (de),
  Eufemia R.
Fernandez (de), Rosa
Fernandez, Francisco
  (D.C.)
Fernandez, Miguel
  (P.Cr.P.)
Fournier Vda. de
  Rivera, Elisa
Fournier, Angel Rivera
Franco, J.
Garcia, Aurea
Garcia, Herminia
Garcia, Ulises
Questell de Aneriro,
  Maria
Grabiron, Juana
Haddock, Petronila
Haddock, Ana Maria
Hernandez, Dionisio
Hoyos, Heraclio

J ---, Carlos R.
Lanauze Rolon, Jose
Lanauze, Carlos R.
Laria, Maria L.
Leon, Argaro
Leon, Sergio
Lopez Vidal, Ramon
Lopez, Panchita
Maldonado Collazo,
  Manuel
Martinez, Miguel
Martinez, Rafael
Martino --, D.
Matos, Ramon
Mattei Rivera, Maz
Medina Davila, Josefa
Medina Davila,
  Primitivo
Melida Ortiz, Maria
Melos, Roberto M.
Millan, Pedro
Monclova, Leon
Monsanto, Trinidad
Mora, Eugenio
Morales, Silverio
Morel de Negron, Cruz
Moura, Juan A.
Muñoz de Ortiz,
  Secundina
Muñoz, Cristino
Natal, Priscila
Nazario, Benigno (VJ)
Ocacio, Salvador
Ocasio, Jose
Ocasio, Pedro A.
Ocasio, Ramon
Olivencia, Maria
Oquendo de Valedon,
  Jose
Ortiz Velez,
  Sebastiana
Ortiz, Catalina
Ortiz, Lola
Ortiz, Luisa
Ortiz, Manuel
Ortiz, Rosalia
Ortiz, Sebastian
  (R.N.P.)
Ougay, Tomas
Overet (de), Luz
Pacheco (de), Carmen
  Belen
Pacheco, J. B. (2)
Pacheco, Manuel

Pacheco, Marina F.
Paonessa, Fernando
Pasarell, Dario (Jr.)
Pasarell, Raquel
Pastor, Leocadio
Perez Acosta, Jose
Perez Garcia, J.
Perez, Pedro
Perez, S. (D.D.S.)
Prado (Vda. de),
  Cristina
Prado, Gloria
Primola, Antonio
Quiles, N.
Quiñones, Modesto
Quiñonez, Luis
Raffaelli, Antonio S.
Ramos, Armando
Renta, Dominga
Renta, Petra
Reyes de Roman,
  Micaela
Rivas, Felix
Rivera de Cintron,
  Providencia
Rivera, Dolores
Rivera, Eulogio
Rivera, Jose
Rivera, Juan F.
Rivera, Rosalia
Robert, Jose
Rodriguez Cruz,
  Miguel
Rodriguez, Amparo
Rodriguez, C.
Rodriguez, Consuelo
Rodriguez, Martin
Rodriguez, Oscar
Rodriguez, Rafael
  (A.G.V.G.)
Rodriguez, Rosa
Rosado, Juana
Rosali, Carlos J.
Rosario, Juan
Ruiz Ortiz, Rafael
Salich, Francisco
Santana (de), Lauria
Santiago Colon,
  Manuel
Santiago, Demetrio
Santiago, Erasmo
Santiago, Hortencia
Santiago, Pastora
Schmidt, Julia

Segui, Juan
Soldevila, Angel
Soldevila, Luis
Solevila, Conchita
Soto de Cruz,
  Mercedes
Soto, Alejandro
Toro, Jose
Torres (de), Epitacia
  R.
Torres Canovas, Maria
Torres, Alberto
Torres, Juan Pilar
Valedon, Acasio
Valedon, Rafael
Valenzuela, Juan
Vazquez de Martinez,
  Maria
Vazquez Zayas,
  Juanita
Vazquez, Carmen S.
Vazquez, Jose M.
Vazquez, Juan
Vazquez, Placido
Vega Norat, Felipe
Vega, Rosa
Veiga (Vda. de), Ana
Veiga, Rosa Maria
Velazquez Norat, Juan
Velazquez, Eugenia M.
Velazquez, Juan
Villanueva, Juan
Virella, Jose C.
Wage Droz, Pilar
Zaldo, Geronimo
Zambrana, America
Zayas, Victoria
Zurita, Juana

**Logia
Fraternidad
Española
(Spanish
Fraternity
Lodge), Ponce**

(2 letters)

Hedilla, Manuel
Pubill, Fr.

Logia Luz de Borinquen (Light of Borinquen Lodge) No. 7990, Ponce

Albizu, Juan G.
Daliot, Caco
Gutierrez, Juan
Hoyo, Heraclio
Melendez, Francisco
Moura, Juan A.
Nuratal, J.
Pilar, Juan
Quiñones, Jose G.
Rivera, Sandalio
Robles, Antonio
Roca, Jose Antonio
Rodriguez Colon, Jose
Rodriguez, Rosario
Torres, Julio
Vazquez, Rafael (1)
Vazquez, Rafael (2)
Vega, Ramon
Velez, Felipe

Logia Luz de Oriente (Western Light Lodge), Yauco

Ortiz, Manuel
(Secretary)
Torres, M. ("Noble Grande")

III.

RELIGIOUS ORGS.

Disciples of Christ, Christian Women's Board Mission, Bayamon

Letter 1

Gonzalez, Rafaela
Santiago, Lucas

Letter 2

Acosta, Armando
Pagan, Francisco

Disciples of Christ, Temperance League, Bayamon

Ortiz, Vicente
(Secretary)
Montañez, Jose
(President)

Men's Methodist Brotherhood, Guayama

Arroyo, Manuel N.
(Secretary)
Nifendini, Mateo N.
(President)

Circulo Lumen (Lumen Circle) Spiritual Society, Ponce

Abreu, Jose Hilario
Acosta Carbonell, F.
Acosta, Jose C.
Alano, Andres
Albarez, Eleuterio
Alcala, Tomas
Alfonso, Luis
Almodovar, Antonio
Almodovar, Felicita
Almodovar, Jose
  Florencio
Almodovar, Maria
Almodovar, Miguel
Almodovar, Vicenta
Alus Aiya, Julio
Alvarado, Armando
Alvarado, Felipe R.
Alvarado, Narciso
Alvarez, Eduardo
Argarin, Victor
Arjona (de), Mercedes
  S.
Arjona, Francisco I.
Arroyo, Encarnacion
Arroyo, Juan Rogelio
Baez, Eloy
Barbosa, Jose
Bauza, Francisco M.
Beauchamp (de),
  Americo Custodio
Berdeguez, Regino
Bijas, Juan (Jr.)
Bijas, Andres
Bijas, Genaro
Bocachica, Agapito
Boisseu, E. H.
Bonafon, Geno
Bonilla, J. Leopoldo
Bou (de), Angela B.
Braschi, Luis
Burgenos, Miguel
Bustamante, A. W.
Cabrera, Carmelo
Cajal, Rosendo
Calbo Vega, Ynocencio
Calucho, Armando G.
Campos, Manuel M.

Canahuelas, Ventura
Canijas, Alfredo
Capa, Ecolastico
Cardon, Julio M.
Cardona, Jose C.
Castillo, Miguel
Castro, Angel
Cintron, Eustaquia
Clarad, C.
Collazo, Enrique
Colon, Manuel
Coppin, Juan
Corazon (de), Rosa Ll.
Corazon, Andres
Costa, Felicita
Costas, Jose
Cuebus, Jose
Cumbre (Vda. de),
  Maria R.
Davila, Juan
Del Valle Campillo,
  Jose
Devis, Flora
Diaz Cordero, Pedro J.
Diaz, Agripino
Domenech, Jose R.
Dros, Sayrto
Ducos, Teofilo
Echevarria, Angel
Echevarria, Miguel
Espinet, Carlos
Fajardo, Carmelo
Ferrer, G. R.
Ferrer, Oscar F.
Figueroa, Domingo
Figueroa, Salvador
Font (de), Prudencia
  M.
Font DeLord, Federico
Font Tavarez, Alfredo
Font, Alejandro
Furjio, Joaquin
Garay, Manuel
Garcia (de),
  Candelaria R.
Garcia de R.,
  Providencia
Garcia, Alfredo
Garcia, Augusto
Garcia, Baudilia
Garcia, Domitila
Garcia, Jesus
Garcia, Vicente
Gazard, Achiles

Getry, Garciano
Gomez, Juan Bautista
Gomez, Tomas
Gonzalez Renta, Felix M.
Gonzalez, Antonio
Gonzalez, Cirino
Gonzalez, Natalio
Gonzalez, Octavio
Gutierrez, Juan
Hedilla, Teodoro
Howell, J.
Hull Foso, Maria M.
Hull, Tomas
Hurtado, Emilia
Irizarri, Ramon
Irizarry, Ramon Benigno
Jovet, Joaquin
Juarez, Juan
Laboy, Ramon C.
Lebron, Antonio A.
Lebron, Luis M.
Lopez Barros, Julio
Lopez, Jovino
Loubriel, Lorenzo
Lugo Arce, Eduardo
Luna, Sixto
Malavet, Manuel
Maldonado, Antonio J.
Mali, Juan
Marirtarra, Emilio
Marquez, Nicolas
Martinez, J. G.
Martinez, Juan
Martinez, Manuel R.
Martinez, Pedro
Maura, Candida
Maura, Maria L.
Mayoral, Rafael (Jr.)
Medina, Francisco
Mirabal, Perfecto
Mitchell, Louis
Molinarez, R.
Montalvo, Miguel
Mora, Lorenzo
Moreno, C. W.
Moreno, Juan
Negron, Adolfo
Negron, O.
Nieves, Isabel
Ojeas, Silvio
Oliver Campos, F.

Olivieri, Francisco A.
Ortiz, Americo
Ortiz, Ramon
Otero, Carlota
Ovando, Z.
Padilla, Juan
Pagan, Claudio
Pagan, Jose M.
Pagan, M. R.
Patterne, Carlos M. (Jr.)
Pedehidon, Carmen M.
Perez Brun, Jose Antonio
Perez, Benita
Perez, Carlos
Perez, Juan
Perlon, Miguel
Petrilli, Ulises
Pont Zayas, Juan
Pou Gomez, Manuel
Pujols, Jacobo
Pujols, Jaime
Quiñones, Aurelia
Ramirez, Jose
Ramos de Anaya, Joaquin
Ramos, Juan N.
Ramos, Pedro
Renta, Ramon
Ribies, --
Rios, Jose Bo.
Rios, Ramon R.
Rivera Casal, Ramon
Rivera, Aurelio
Rivera, Carmelo
Rivera, Cristobal
Rivera, Eduardo
Rivera, Felipe
Rivera, Jose
Rivera, Juan
Rivera, Trema.
Robles, Antonio
Robles, Aristide
Robles, Ildefonso
Robles, Pedro
Robles, Pedro J.
Roca, Francisco
Roca, Juan
Roche, Vicenta
Rodriguez Muñoz, Rafael
Rodriguez, B. Aniceto

Rodriguez, Celestina
Rodriguez, Emilio
Rodriguez, Encarnacion
Rodriguez, Jimmy
Rodriguez, Jorge
Rodriguez, Luis
Rodriguez, Luis Angel
Rodriguez, Manuela
Rodriguez, Maria (1)
Rodriguez, Maria (2)
Rodriguez, Nicanor
Rodriguez, Nicolas
Rodriguez, Pedro
Rodriguez, Pedro M.
Rodriguez, Simon
Rosado, Lorenzo
Rosenfeld, Santos
Ruiz, Remigio
Ruiz, Salvador
Sabater, Arturo
Sanchez, Eriveto
Sanchez, Francisco
Sanchez, Jacinto
Sanchez, Jose
Santana, Agapito
Santana, Avelino
Santiago, Claudino
Santiago, Francisco
Santiago, Jose
Santos, Balbino
Silva, Higinio
Suarez, Asuncion
Tapia Olivera, R.
Texidor, Atanasia
Texitor, Alturo
Tirado Rivera, Antonio
Toledo, Ramona
Toro, Jose Ma.
Torres, David
Torres, Dionisio
Torres, Juan (1)
Torres, Juan (2)
Torres, Juan E.
Torres, Julio
Torres, Julio (Jr.)
Torres, Nicolas
Torres, Pablo
Torres, Santiago
Torres, Saturnilo
Torruella, Pedro J.
Vacero, Rafael
Valdezate, Ismael

Valdezate, Zoraida M.
Valedon, Adolfo
Vazquez, Gilberto
Vega, Lorenzo
Velez, Eugenio
Ventura, Enrique
Ventura, Feliz
Vidarte Lopez, Andres
Vilella, Alberto
Westervan, Alejandro
Yglesia, Manuel
Zayas, Daniel

Catholic Church, San Juan

Echevarria, Andres (Rev.) (See Puerto Rico Commission)

⧜

IV.

GOVERNMENT ORGS.

Congressmen, U.S. Congress

Davenport, James S. (U.S. Congress, Repr. D-Okla., Committee on the Territories)
Gore, Thomas P. (U.S. Congress, Senator D-Okla., Commitee on Agriculture & Forestry)

Government of Puerto Rico

Muñoz Rivera, Luis (Puerto Rico's Resident Commissioner in

Washington, DC)
Yager, Arthur
(Governor of Puerto
Rico)

**Government of
Pennsylvania**

Brumbaugh, Martin G.
(Governor of PA)

**Sing Sing
Prison Officials**

Miller, Spencer
(Deputy Warden,
Sing Sing Prison, NY)
on behalf of
Kerchway, George W.
(Sing Sing Prison
Warden)

**Spanish
Consulate**

Riaño, Juan (Spanish
Consul)

V.

**ATTORNEYS &
MEDICAL
EXPERTS**

Hunt, Harold Lyons
(Medical Expert)
Le Barbier, Charles E.
(Attorney)
Spitzka, Edward A.
(Medical Expert)

VI.

**UNIVERSITY
STUDENT
ORGS.**

**PSI CHI DELTA
Fraternity, Ch.
EPSILON,
Chicago, IL**

Casanova, Antonio

**PSI CHI DELTA
Fraternity, Ch.
MU, University
of PA**

Coll, Luis F.
Igunaz, Manuel C.
Ortiz, F.
Sifre, Ramon J.
Vazquez, R. Alberto
Vicente, Jose

**PSI CHI DELTA
Fraternity, Ch.
IOTA,
Washington,
DC**

Cortes, N. (Jr.)
Garcia, Jose S.
Gutierrez, F. A. (Jr.)
Hernandez, J. P.
Herrera, Luis
Rivera Aponte, Pedro
Rivera, A. A.
Villareal, Jose R.

VII.

**INDIVIDUALS
AND
BUSINESSES**

Crespo Family,
Arecibo

Crespo, Efrain F.
Crespo, Guadalupe A.
Crespo, Humberto
Crespo, Iluminada M.
Crespo, Isaias M.
Crespo, Joaquin O.
(Merchant)
Crespo, Jose E.
(Teacher)
Crespo, Margarita
(Teacher)
Crespo, Miguel A.
(B.S.CeA.)
Crespo, Pura
Crespo, Ulpiano
Crespo, Ulpiano (Jr.)
Ramos de Crespo,
Guadalupe
Ruiz de Crespo (de),
Sara

Other Individuals

"Un Puertorriqueño"
(Anonymous),
Fajardo, PR
Anonymous Girl
(Bayamon, PR)
Besosa (Vda. de), Ana
Agripina P.
De Llovio, Lucila
(Bayamon, PR)
Perrotta, Angelina
(Schenectady, NY)
Ponton, Antonio (Jr.)
(Comerio, PR)
Ponton, Manolo
(Comerio, PR)
Rivera, Angela L.
(Teacher) (San
German, PR)
Rivera, Charles

(Schenectady, NY)
Velez Alvarado,
Antonio (NY)
Warner, Anna
(Schenectady, NY)

**Western Union
Telegraph
Workers, PA**

Figarella, F.
Guardia, M. R.
Higueras, Joaquin R.
Miret, F. V.
Montequin, A.
Velez, Jose Pascual

**Wright's
Indian
Vegetable Pills
Co., Inc., New
York**

Ferret, E. (Agent, NY)

VIII.

**SCHOOL
TEACHERS &
STUDENTS**

-TEACHERS-

**Departamento
de Educacion
(Department of
Education),
Aguadilla**

Cruz Vazquez, Benito
(President)

Teachers Assoc., Añasco

Diaz, J. (Secretary)
Gonzalez, Ernesto (President)

Asociacion de Maestros (Teachers Assoc.), Juncos

Acosta, Antonio
Andino, Angela
Aquino, Manuel
Arnal, Jose A
Belen Viñolo, Carmen
Betancourt, Genoveva
Brau, Rafael
Callander, John
Campoamor, Concepcion
Carrion, Mercedes
Cristy, Carmelo
De Armas, Jose
Diaz, Victoria
Farnhan, Fred
Felix, Sotero
Figueroa, Roberto
Figueroa, Santiago
Fisker, Jorge
Font S., Juan
Font, Alfredo
Friedheim, Maria
Garcia, Valentina
Gimenez, Alfonso
Gonzalez, Concepcion
Gonzalez, Ramon
Gorbea, Alfonso
Gruipen, Milagros
Hernandez, Isabel
Ibañez, Antonio
Lee, Consuelo
Louis, Dignina
Marquez, Petra
Martinez, Carmen
Mitchell, Roberto
Otero, Francisco
Perez, Agudea
Perez, Mercedes
Perez, Miguel

Piñero, Fulgencio (Jr.) (Rep. House of Delegates, PR)
Quevedeo (de), Carlos G.
Reinhardt, Maria
Rios, Beatriz
Rivera Jorge, Antonio (Secretary)
Rodriguez, Jesus
Rosa, Gloria
Rosario, Pedro
Ryan, Cristobal
Saudi, Isabel
Socorro, Joaquina
Viader, Adela
Vieras, Josefa
Villanueva, Julio
Wulf, Eleonora

Teachers & Students, Morovis

Teachers & Students
Morovis (Telegram)

Junta Escolar (School Board), Ponce

Costas Ferrer, J.

School Board, Quebradillas (Telegram)

Teachers Assoc., Rio Piedras

Bagne, Julio (President)
Garcia Sandoval, M. (Secretary)
. . .

Teachers, Salinas

Alvarez, Julia
Amadeo, Rafaela
Beniamino (de), Francisca F.
Cabello, Maria
Campos, Vicente A.
Cantres, Julia M.
Cartagena, Luis
Castillo, Juan E.
Castillo, Petronila M.
Cintron, Francisco Modesto
Cintron, Lina
Cruz, A. S.
Esteban, Celia
Garcia Reyes, Maria
Guzman, Edelmira
Mercado, Monserrate
Modesto, Rafael
Ocasio, Rafael
Ramirez, Herminia C.
Rivera, Julia J.
Rodriguez, Ermelinda
Sagudo, Margarita
Sallaberry, Ventura, J.
Serrant, Juan de D.
Vazquez, Casimiro
Vazquez, Feliz

Teachers, Santa Isabel

Blanco, Felicita
Cajigas, Victoria
Cordero, Ana Luisa R.
Fontanes, Josefina
Gonzalez, Rita
Matos (de), Palmira C.
Quiñones, Carmen R.
Rivera, Josefa
Suarez, Isabel
Suarez, Rafael
Torres Rivera, Jose

. . .

Asociacion Local de Maestros (Teachers Assoc.), Yauco

Morales Salgado, S.

- SCHOOLS - Students, Añasco School

6th Grade

Alvarez, Mariana (Teacher)
Baiges, Salvador
Barletta, Dolores
Caballero, Jose
Chapel, Jose
Charneco, Rafael
Comas, Beatriz
Cualio, Marcolina
De Choudens, Augusto
De Choudens, Carmen
Diez, Josefa L.
Dominguez, America
Duran, Luis
Figueroa, Ramon
Font, Octavio
Font, Providencia
Garcia, Manuel
Gonzalez, Quintin
Martiz, Lila
Mendez, Francisca
Mendez, Ramon
Montoya, Consuelo
Muñoz, Manuel
Olivencia, Ernesto
Paz, Gloria
Reyes, Juan
Rivera, Ramon
Romero, Marcolina
Rousset, Antonia
Ruiz de Porras, Carmen
Soto, Ramon
Tirado, Carmen
Urrutia, Dolores
Vazquez, Francisco

Vazquez, Ignacio
Vazquez, Rafael
Velez, Camelia
Velez, Maria

Public School Students, Canovanas

Aguayo, Pilar
Alonso, Francisco
Alonso, Juan
Alonso, Rosario
Ayala, Julia
Betancourt, Gumersinda
Betancourt, Isaura
Betancourt, Jaime
Betancourt, Naufraga
Betancourt, Pilar
Bonilla, Maria
Bonilla, Trinidad
Brown, Mabel
Calderon, Aureo
Calderon, Carmen Maria
Calderon, Luis
Calderon, Pedro
Calderon, Ricardo
Calzada, Adriana
Calzada, Angela
Calzada, Antonia
Calzada, Concha
Calzada, Francisco
Calzada, Juan
Calzada, Nemesia
Calzada, Rosa
Casado, Dolores
Casado, Sixta
Castro, Francisco
Castro, Luis
Cazada, Maria
Correa, Domingo
Cruz, Faustino
De Jesus, Pablo
Elisier, Carmen
Encarnacion, Casilda
Encarnacion, Gerardo
Escobar, Anita
Escobar, Lucia
Esquilin, Cristino
Esquilin, Juan

Esquilin, Juliana
Febres, Ernesto
Febrez, Isabel
Fernandez, Cristobal
Fernandez, Ernesto
Fernandez, Francisco
Fernandez, Maria
Fernandez, Pedro
Franco, Eugenia
Franco, Patricio
Franquez, Jose
Gambaro, Maria I.
Gambaro, Natalia
Garcia, Julia
Garcia, Rafael
Guzman, Luis
Guzman, Reparada
Hance, Marcial
Hance, Ramona
Hernandez, Juan C.
Horta, Julia M.
Latimer, Adela
Lynn, James
Mundo, Francisco
Mundo, Juan B.
Mundo, Maria Teresa
Mundo, Rafaela
Mundo, Serafino
Olivero, Angelina
Olivero, Antonio
Olivero, Herminio
Osorio, Domitila
Osorio, Lino
Osorio, Paula
Osorio, Roque
Pacheco, Tomas
Pagan, Carmen
Palma, Carmen
Pastrana, Juana
Perez, Amparo
Perez, Armindo
Perez, Consuelo
Perez, Isabel
Perez, Teodosia
Pimentel, Maria
Pla, Agustin
Prados, Juan C.
Prados, Rosa C.
Quigley, Felipa
Rios, Antonia
Rios, Cruz
Rios, Maria
Rios, Trinidad
Rivera, Otilia

Robles, Cosmelina
Rodriguez, Antonio
Salgado, Rufina
Salomon, Aniseto
Sanchez, Juan F.
Sanchez, Julia
Soguendo, Maria
Solis, Herminio
Taleco, Fernando
Talero, Juan
Torres, Patricio
Trenche, Adsalon
Trenche, Alipio
Velez, Ramona
Vilalobos, Belen
Wolker, Aurea
Wolker, Florentino
Wolker, Mercedes
Wolker, Teresa

School Students, Ciales

(Telegram)

Baldorioty Graded School, Gurabo

2nd Grade

Group 1
Carrasquillo, Margarita
Collazo, Antonia
Con, Angelina
Davila, Carolina
Diaz, Francisco
Fajardo, Jose
Gonzalez, Enrique
Gonzalez, Juan
Huertas, Celia
Martinez, Ana Maria
Melendez, Juan
Morales, Manuel
Perez, Paula
Rivera, Marta
Rodriguez, Gertrudis
Roman, Mercedes

Sanabria, Paula
Suma, Gloria Maria
Vazquez, Esperanza
Villanueva, Amalia

Group2
Arzuaga, Cecilia A.
Bernabe, Ana
Candelaria, Manuel
Candelaria, Paula
Candelario, Rafael
Carrion, Alfonso
Castro, Jose
Cedeño, Amelia
Davila, Dolores
Davila, Paco
Diaz, Antonio
Diaz, Cristino
Diaz, Josefina
Fernandez, Magdalena
Flores, Jose
Franquiz, Concha
Goitia, Ana L.
Gomes, David
Gonzalez, Dolores
Laureano, Blas
Milian, Cruz
Milian, Mariana
Morales, Lidia
Nieves, Ernesto
Nuñez, Ines
O'Neill, Natividad
Ortiz, Fernando
Quiñones, Gustavo
Rivera, Faustina
Rivera, Ignacio
Rivera, Juan
Rodriguez, Juana
Rosa, Elisita
Sala, Maria
Sanchia, Rafaela
Santana, Maria
Suarez, Manuela
Torres, Ramona
Vazquez, Carlos
Vazquez, Timoteo

3rd Grade

Group 1
Aponte, Bautista
C., Luis Angel
Carrasquillo, Cruz

167

Carrasquillo, Rafael
Carrion, Aturo
Carrion, Jose
Castro, Fulgencio
Castro, Ines
Costas, Alberto M.
Coto, Carmen
Cuadrado, Rosa
Davila, Carlos
Davila, Rafaela
Diaz, Asuncion
Diaz, Carlos
Diaz, Maria Luisa
Diaz, Rosaura
Esquillin, Vicente
Feliciano, Roque
Flores, Dolores
Flores, Victor
Garcia, Guillermina
Garcia, Perfecto
Garda, Jesus
Hernandez, Carmen
Jimenez, Pedro
Jimenez, Santiago
Landrau, Rafael
Leon, Maria Rita
Lloveras, Guillermina
Lopez, Cruz
Lozada, Victor
M., Maria Isabel
Manugal, Adelina
Martinez, Jesus
Morales, Carmen
Morales, Jorge Arturo
Morales, Paula
Pereira, Joaquin
Pereira, Jose
Ramirez, Luis R.
Ramos, Aurelio
Ramos, Ramon
Rivera, Agripina
Rivera, Modesta
Rivera, Rafael
Rodriguez, Juan
Rodriguez, Luis
Rosa, Delfina
Santaella, Maria
Torres, Cruz
Torres, Jose
Torres, Luis
Vasquez, Julia
Velez Lajara, Julio

Group 2

Alejandro, Santiago
Cedeño, Ramon
Diaz, Marta
Diaz, Pedro Jose
Hernandez, Juan
Laureano, Domitila
Lluveras, Enrique
Marquez, Natividad
Martinez, Justino
Morales, Nicolas
Nuñez, Petra
Reyes, Ramon
Rodriguez, Maria
Rosa, Ernesto
Sanabria, Francisca
Torrent, Eugenia
Torres, Feliciano

4th Grade

Group 1

Agrinsonis, Eufrasio A.
Aponte, Hermenegilda
Arzuaga, Catalino
Carreras, Jesus Maria
Cuadrado, Manuela
Diaz, Ernestina
Diaz, Monserrate
Goitia, Isabel
Govin, Dolores
Mangual, Julio
Morales, Jose
Morales, Pedro
Peña, Jacinta
Rivera, Paula
Rodriguez, Elena
Sala, Concepcion
Sanchez, Justa
Sanchez, Luciano
Sanchez, Ruperta
Valentin, Enrique
Vazquez, Belen

Group 2

Bernabe, Maria
Borges, Providencia
Caldero, Petra
Calderon, Filomena
Carrion, Petra
Carrion, Porfirio
Carrion, Ramon

Correa, Isabel
Diaz, Catalina
Diaz, Esther
Diaz, Ramon
Flores, Meliton
Garcia, Pedro
Gonzalez, Rufo
Hernandez, Francisco
Hernandez, Ursula
Hernay, Luis
Jimenez, Ezequiela
Mangual, Concepcion
Morales, Rosalia
Nieves, Venancia
O'Neill, Eustacio
Pacheco, Rosa
Perez, Juana
Pomales, Celestino
Quiñones, Arturo
Quiñones, Rosa
Reyes, Braulio
Rivera, Andres
Rivera, Justino
Rivera, Sandalio
Rodriguez, Antonio
Rodriguez, Maria
Rodriguez, Norberto
Rodriguez, Rafael
Roque, Antonio
Rosa Gonzalez, Juan
Sanchez, Bartolo
Severon, Tomas
Torres, Candida
Torres, Ramona
Villafañe, Juana

5th Grade

Group 1

Boria, Concepcion
Carrion, Dolores
Davila, Marcelo
Hernandez, Jose
Laureano, Braulio
Lopez, Francisco
Rivera, Maximino
Sloane, Jose David
Torres, Rafael

Group 2

Amador, Maria A.
Bernabe, Secundino
Carrasquillo,

Monserrate
Davila, Carmen
Davila, Conrada
Diaz, Camelia
Diaz, Daniel
Diaz, Emilio
Diaz, Rita
Flores, Justa
Gomez, Rafael
Guzman, Rosa
Jimenez, Marcla
Landrau, Saturnina
Mangual, Crescencio
Medina, Justino
Miranda, Epifania
Mont, Fundador
Morales, Ines
Morales, Juanita
Morales, Pedro Jose
Pizarro, Gregorio
Rivera, Manuela
Rodriguez, Emilia
Rosa, Carmen
Rosa, Dolores
Rosa, Mario
Santana, Virginio
Valedon, Jose
Velez, Concepcion

6th Grade

Agrinsonis, Rafael
Aponte, Bartolome
Aponte, Benigno
Arestigueta, Juana
Arzuaga, Pascual
Betancourt, Americo
Carrion, Providencia
Carrion, Rita
Colon, Felipe
Cuevas, Luisa
Diaz, Francisco
Diaz, Julio
Diaz, Nicomedes
Diaz, Teresa
Figueroa, Julian
Garcia, Agustin
Gonzalez, Alicia
Gonzalez, Manuela
Gonzalez, Ramona
Gorrin, Corina
Hernandez, Encarnacion

Landrau, Acacia
Laureano, Antonia
Laureano, Rafaela
Marcano, Felix
Martinez, Concepcion
Morales, Angel
Morales, Belen
Nuñez, Antonio
Nuñez, Susano
Pacheco, Juan
Pastor, Emiliio
Rivera, Cruz
Rosa, Ramona
Santana, Pedro
Santana, Rafael
Trinidad Morales, Matea

7th Grade

Alvarez, Maria
Carrion, Rafael
Diaz, Crispulo
Diaz, Enrique
Diaz, Natividad
Garcia, Maria
Hernandez, Eliseo
Hernandez, Ramona
Laureano, Gregorio
Loiz, Cecilio
Nieves, Pua
Nuñez, Vicente
Peña, Leandro
Gomz
Sanchez, Ana
Sanchez, Margarita
Santa, Esperanza

8th Grade

Barros, Fausto
Davila Diaz, Agripina
Davila, Bautista
Flores, Jesus M.
Gonzalez, Encarnacion
Hernandez, Genoveva M.
Miranda, Eufemio
Morales, Amelia
Nuñez, Eufemia
Nuñez, Juana
Rivera Morales,

Francisco
Torrent, Carmen
Torres, Agripina
Vazquez, Antonio

Club Ciencia, Libertad y Moral (Science, Liberty and Morals Club), Fajardo High School

Abrahim, Carmen
Acevedo, Adela
Acevedo, Norberto
Acosta, Ana M.
Acosta, Conchita
Acosta, Eduardo
Acosta, Emilia L.
Acosta, Emilio
Acosta, Eugenio
Acosta, Jeronimo
Acosta, Jose
Acosta, Luis
Acosta, Maria Teresa
Aguiar, Carmelo
Alejandro, Adela
Alejandro, David
Alejandro, Francisca
Alvarez, Ramon
Aneda, Ramon
Anglero, Felix A.
Aponte, Gloria
Aponte, Justa
Aponte, Manuel
Aponte, Mercedes
Arambuso, Emilia
Aramis, Ramon
Arel, Julio
Arieta, Tomas
Arome, Amparo
Atiles, Maria
Avila, Antonio
Avila, Catalino
Avila, Efigenia
Avila, Rafaela
Ayala, Aleja
Ayala, Alejandro
Ayala, Dolores
Ayala, Erin

Ayala, Fabian
Ayala, Josefina
Ayala, Miguel
Ayala, Natalia
Baez, Juana
Baralt, Jose Lopez
Barcelo, Jaime
Barreto, Carlos M.
Bayne H., Hugh
Becerril, Justino
Becerril, Benito
Becerril, Carmen
Becerril, Federico
Becerril, Ramon
Belaval, Emilio
Benitez, Ramona
Berillo, Juan
Bermudez, Hipolita
Bermudez, Margarita
Bird Gonzalez, Modesto
Bird Lopez, Carlos
Bird, Coelo
Bird, Eloisa
Blanco Cestano, Juan
Blanco, Felicia
Blanco, Florinda
Blanco, Rosario
Bloise, Maria
Bloise, Deodalo
Bloise, Nunciata
Borras, Adolfo
Borras, Julia
Borras, Ramona
Buitrago, Josefa M.
Burgos, Manuela
Cahola, Eladia
Calderon, Angelica
Calderon, Arcadi
Calderon, Benita
Calderon, Candida
Calderon, Francisca
Calderon, Gil
Calderon, Jose
Calderon, Jose M.
Calderon, Manuela
Calderon, Paula
Camacho, Guillermo
Camacho, Matilde
Campos, Felicita
Campos, Felix
Camuñas, Agustin
Camuñas, Carlos
Camuñas, Jose F.

Camuñas, Julio
Cariño, Juan
Cariño, Luisa
Carmona, Francisco
Carmona, Virtuoso
Carras Carras, Ines
Carras, Altagracia
Carrasco, Berta
Carrasquillo, Alejandro
Carrasquillo, Federico
Carrasquillo, Josefa
Carrasquillo, Maria I.
Carrasquillo, Sebastian
Carrillo, Abigail
Carrillo, Carlos
Carrillo, Espire
Carrillo, Josefina
Carrillo, Juana
Carrillo, Ramon
Carrillo, Raquel
Carrillo, Victor
Carrion, Cecilio (Jr.)
Carrion, Ramona
Carvajal, Celestino
Casanova, Antonio
Casanova, Candelario
Casanova, Gloria M.
Casanova, Jose
Casanova, Josefina
Casanova, Rafael
Casanova, Ramon
Casanova, Rosendo
Casars, Severiano
Casas, Tomas
Castro, Antonio
Castro, Jeronimo
Castro, Jose
Castro, Maria I.
Castro, Pedro
Castro, Rafael
Ceballo, Ramon
Celestino, Pedro
Celia, Providencia
Celis (de), Carlota
Celis Perez, Jose M.
Celis, Anilo
Centeno, Carmen
Centeno, Felicita
Centno, Amelia
Cepeda, Agapito
Cepeda, Julio
Cepeda, Manuel

Cepeda, Maria	Davila, Conchita	Figueroa, Aida	Garcia, Luis
Cerra, Antonio	Davila, Dolores	Figueroa, Amalia	Garcia, Manuel
Cerra, Maria Z.	Davila, Rogelia	Figueroa, Andres	Garcia, Maria M.
Cerro, Joaquin	De Glau, Juana	Figueroa, Aromi	Garcia, Mercedes
Cetat, Alejandro	De Jesus, Antonia	Figueroa, Concha	Garcia, Miguel
Cetut, Julio	De Jesus, Matilde	Figueroa, Dionisio	Garcia, Pedro
Challo, Francisco	De Jesus, Severiano	Figueroa, Dolores	Garcia, Petra
Cidely, Jorge	De Santiago, Santiago	Figueroa, Maria	Garcia, Ramonita
Cifre, Jose Manuel	Del Rosario, Teresa	Figueroa, Pablo	Garcia, Santiago
Cintron, Angel	Delgado, Alejandrina	Figueroa, Rafael	Gautier, Felicita
Cintron, Esperanza	Delgado, Serafin	Flores, Angelina	Gomez, Candida
Cintron, Lola	Delgado, Tomas	Flores, Celestino	Gomez, Carmen Maria
Cintron, Mercedes	Diaz, Amentina	Flores, Daniel	Gomez, Juana
Cintron, Petra	Diaz, Augustino	Flores, Ines	Gomez, Maria
Cintron, Salvador	Diaz, Carlos	Flores, Isaac	Gomez, Miguel
Cintron, Socorro	Diaz, Carolina	Flores, Jose (1)	Gomez, Modesto
Cintron, Teodoro	Diaz, Gloria M.	Flores, Jose (2)	Gomez, Ramon (Jr.)
Coca, Enrique	Diaz, Josefa	Flores, Juan	Gomez, Teresa
Coca, Maria E.	Diaz, Luis R.	Flores, Juan B.	Gomez, Vicente
Colon Morales, Jesus	Diaz, Narciso	Flores, Julio (1)	Gonzalez Matta,
Colon, Flor	Diaz, Petra	Flores, Julio (2)	Francisco
Concepcion, Jose	Diaz, Ramon	Flores, Luis	Gonzalez, Aguda
Contreras, Maria	Diaz, Rosa Maria	Flores, Providencia	Gonzalez, Agustin
Socorro	Diaz, Santiago	Flores, Ramon	Gonzalez, Anita
Cordero, Angelina	Domingo, Alvarez	Flores, Santiago	Gonzalez, Claro
Cordero, Carmelo	Dones, Carmelina	Franco, Anastacia	Gonzalez, Feliz
Cordova, Jorge	Dones, Carmelo	Fuentes, Angeles	Gonzalez, Francisca
Correa, Candida	Dones, Dominga	Fuentes, Francisca	Gonzalez, Luis
Correa, Joaquin	Duchesne, Francisca	Fulladosa, Carmen	Gonzalez, Maria del
Cortes, Esteban	Encarnacion, Gaspar	Gabino, Celia	Carmen
Cortes, Rafael	Enriquez, Carmelo	Ganfan, Enrique	Gonzalez, Severiano
Cotner, Juan	Escalera, Damian	Garay, Maria	Gotay, Pascacio
Cruz, Anastasio	Esteenain, Celestino	Garay, Providencia	Guadalupe, Juan
Cruz, Berta	Escobar, Abel	Garcia A., Sabino	Guadalupe, Marcelo
Cruz, Carlota	Escobar, Ana Maria	Garcia Bird, Federico	Guzman, Carlota
Cruz, Carmen	Escobar, Elisa	Garcia Bird, Luis	Guzman, Carmen
Cruz, Concepcion	Escobar, Mercedes	Garcia Diaz, Julio	Guzman, Carmen M.
Cruz, Crispolo	Escobar, Rafael	Garcia Diaz, Leonor	Guzman, Manuel
Cruz, Eduardo	Escobar, Rosatio	Garcia Diaz, Sebastian	Guzman, Maria Estela
Cruz, Elena	Estela, Anhela	Garcia Diaz, Teresa	Guzman, Pedro (Jr.)
Cruz, Elisa	Estela, Arturo	Garcia Veve, Angel	Guzman, Raul E.
Cruz, Eugenio	Estrella, Andrea	Garcia Veve, Federico	Guzman, Trinidad
Cruz, Eustimio	Farington, Antonio	Garcia Veve, Luis	Haddad, America
Cruz, Faustina	Farrington, Fred	Garcia Veve, Miguel	Haddock, Armando
Cruz, Gregoria	Farrington, Pedro	Garcia, Aleja	Hernandez Rivera,
Cruz, Juan	Felicia, Silvia	Garcia, Angel	Salvador
Cruz, Luz M.	Feliciano, Constanza	Garcia, Aurea	Hernandez,
Cruz, Manuela	Feliciano, Gregorio	Garcia, Carmen	Guadalupe
Cruz, Maria (1)	Feliciano, Juana	Garcia, Dolores	Hita, Vicente
Cruz, Maria (2)	Feliciano, Monserrate	Garcia, Estanislao	Hyland, Mercedes
Cruz, Rafael	Feliz, Epifania	Garcia, Genaro	Ibita, Antonio
Cruz, Trinidad	Fernandez, Angel	Garcia, Ines	Igaravidez, Carmen
Cruzado, Luciano	Fernandez, Fausta	Garcia, Jose	Iglesias, Jose
Cuevas Benitez, Javier	Fernandez, Isabel	Garcia, Juanita	Ilanaza, Pilar

Ilarraza, Merced	Lopez, Carlos	Marcano, Josefina	Melendez, Celestina
Jesus, Lolita	Lopez, Carlota	Marquez, Eugenia	Melendez, Damiana
Jimenez Matta, Juan	Lopez, Carmen M.	Marrero, Margarita	Melendez, Enrique
R.	Lopez, Cruz	Marti, Carmen	Melendez, Evidal
Jimenez, Adolfo	Lopez, Ernesto	Martinez, Anastasio	Melendez, Juan (1)
Jimenez, Alfredo	Lopez, Estevania	Martinez, Carmen (1)	Melendez, Juan (2)
Jimenez, Carlota	Lopez, Fernando	Martinez, Carmen (2)	Melendez, Juana
Jimenez, Carmen	Lopez, Francisco	Martinez, Cruz	Melendez, Leoncio
Jimenez, Josefina	Lopez, Isabel	Martinez, Dolores (1)	Melendez, Luisa
Jimenez, Manuel	Lopez, Joaquin	Martinez, Dolores (2)	Melendez, Manuel
Jimenez, Salvador	Lopez, Jose (1)	Martinez, Elisa	Melendez, Martin
Jimenez, Teresa	Lopez, Jose (2)	Martinez, Fidencio	Melendez, Nadelia
Jimenez, Tomas	Lopez, Juan	Martinez, Flor M.	Melendez, Ramona
Jimenez, Tomasa	Lopez, Julia	Martinez, Francisco	Melendez, Rosario
Julio, Mercedes	Lopez, Julia	Martinez, Jesus	Melendez, Trinidad
Julio, Verminio	Guadalupe	Martinez, Jose	Melendez, Valeriano
Kercado, Delfin	Lopez, Manuel	Martinez, Jose Anonio	Mendez, Angeles
Kercado, Rosalia	Lopez, Maria del	Martinez, Juan	Mendez, Clotilde
King, Ralph	Socorro	Martinez, Juana	Mendez, Eustaquio
Lafont, Avelino (Jr.)	Lopez, Mercedes	Martinez, Julio	Mendez, Jose
Lafont, Eugenio	Lopez, Olimpia	Martinez, Luis	Mendez, Justino
Lafont, Lorenzo	Lopez, Ramon	Martinez, Manuela	Mendez, Nicolas
Larreguera, Celia	Lopez, Regalado	Martinez, Maria	Mercado, Ana
Latorre, Amelia	Lopez, Rita	Martinez, Maria (2)	Mercado, Angelina
Latorre, Angel (Jr.)	Lopez, Santos	Martinez, Maria (3)	Mercado, Aurelio
Latorre, Maria L.	Lopez, Tomasa	Martinez, Maria V.	Mercado, Gloria
Laureana, Ana Luisa	Lopez, Trinidad	Martinez, Mercedes	Mercado, Hipolita
Laureana, Rafaela	Lorenzo, Jose	Martinez, Miguel	Mercado, Isabelo
Laureano, Alicia	Lujan, Jose (Jr.)	Martinez, Oreste	Mercado, Jaime
Laureano, Andres	Madonado, Maria	Martinez, Pilar	Mercado, Joaquina
Lauriona, Francisca	Maduro, Carmen	Martinez, Reyes	Mercado, Matias
Lebron, Carlos	Maduro, Consuelo	Martinez, Roberta	Mercado, Nicolas
Lebron, Juana	Maduro, Matilde	Martiz, Euguenia	Mercado, Ramon
Lebron, Lucia	Maldonado Felicita	Mateo, Francisco	Mesa, Jose (Pepi)
Lebron, Matilde	Maldonado, Abad	Mateo, Maria	Mitchel, Monserrate
Leon, Maria Isabel	Maldonado, Anastasio	Matos, Julio	Mitchell, Eulalio
Llorens, Brunilda	Maldonado, Antonio	Matta, Georgina	Mitchell, Pablo
Llover, Margarita	Maldonado, Carmen	Matta, Jesus F.	Mojer, Francisco
Lopes, Carmen	Maldonado, Celina	Matta, Luis	Mojer, Jose
Lopez C. Esteban	Maldonado, Eduardo	Matta, Nicolas	Mojer, Josefina
Lopez Jube, Esteban	Maldonado, Emilio	Matto, Paula	Molina, Aleja
(2)	Maldonado, Fez	McLane, Kathrine	Molina, Malulo
Lopez Perez,	Maldonado, Flor M.	Medina, Candelario	Molina, Pilar
Crispiniano	Maldonado, Francisco	Medina, Carmen	Molina, Ramon
Lopez Vidal, Jose	Maldonado, Jesus	Medina, Felicita	Montañez, Aurea
Lopez, Agapito	Maldonado, Juan	Medina, Flora	Montañez, Carmen
Lopez, Agustin	Maldonado, Lciano	Medina, Isabel	Monti, Carmen
Lopez, Alfonsa	Maldonado, Manuel	Medina, Juana	Mora, Elisa
Lopez, Amador	Maldonado, Maria A.	Medina, Manuel	Morales, Jesus
Lopez, Angeles	Maldonado, Mercedes	Medina, Maria (1)	Morales, Josefina
Lopez, Angelita	Maldonado, Ramona	Medina, Maria (2)	Morales, Julio
Lopez, Benita	(1)	Melendez, Blasina	Morales, Maximino
Lopez, Bernabel	Maldonado, Ramona	Melendez, Brigida	Morciva, Sixto
Lopez, Candida	(2)	Melendez, Carlota	Morjano, Enrique

Motta, Amparo
Motta, Benigno
Motta, Ramon
Moyano, Alejo
Moyano, Eligis
Moyano, Gracia
Moyano, Jesus (Jr.)
Moyano, Isabel
Moyano, Luis
Moyano, Rafaela
Moyano, Ramona
Moyano, Rosario
Muñoz, America
Muñoz, Anibal
Muñoz, Roberto
Nales, Tecla
Nieves, Jose
Ocaso, Lucia
Ojeda, Domingo
Ojeda, Josefina
Ordoñez Sabater, L.
Ordoñez, Angeles
Ordoñez, Jose
Ordoñez, Maria
Ordoñez, Maria I.
Orellano, Felipe
Orellano, Luis
Orellano, Maria
Orta, Domingo
Ortiz, Asuncion
Monserrate
Ortiz, Candida
Ortiz, J. Elvira
Ortiz, Julian
Ortiz, Mercedes
Ortiz, Nicolas
Ortiz, Tomasita
Ortiz, Victoria
Osorio, Ramon
Pacheco, Benigno
Pacheco, Carmen
Pacheco, Gumersindo
Pacheco, Monserrate
Pacheco, Vicente J.
Pantaleon, Adolfo
Paris, Maria Amalia
Paris, Rosa
Parrilla, Candido
Parrilla, Justo
Pascual Velez, Ignacio
C.
Pascual, Asuncion
Peña, Aida
Peña, Andrea

Peña, Lydia
Peña, Primitiva
Peña, Zoila
Pepin, Carlos Ma.
Pepin, Carmen
Pepin, Margarita (1)
Pepin, Margarita (2)
Perasa, Candida
Pereira Garcia, Genaro
Pereira, Africa
Pereira, Aurora
Pereira, Enrique
Pereira, Francisco
Pereira, Jobo
Peres, Carmelo
Peres, Juana
Perez Alberto,
Margarita
Perez, Angel
Perez, Concepcion
Perez, Cruz
Perez, Emilia
Perez, Juana
Perez, Julio
Perez, Luis
Perez, Manuel
Perez, Monina
Perez, Monse
Perez, Pedro
Perez, Tomasa
Perez, Victor (1)
Perez, Victor (2)
Pesquera, Domingo
Peterson, Consuelo
Piñeiro, Ramon
Piñeiro, Ramona
Piñero, Constanza
Piñero, Gregorio
Pitersont, Carlota
Pizarro, Guadalupe
Pla, Fidencia
Plafont, Jovita
Ponce, Celestino
Ponce, Dolores
Quiñones Matta, Aida
Quiñones Matta, Cesar
Quiñones, Agustin
Quiñones, Carmelina
Quiñones, Clara
Quiñones, Elena
Quiñones, Elisa
Quiñones, Elvira
Quiñones, Fidelina
Quiñones, Flor de M.

Quiñones, Francisco
Quiñones, Gerardo
Quiñones, Jose M.
Quiñones, Jose Ma.
Quiñones, Jovito
Quiñones, Leonor
Quiñones, Manuel (1)
Quiñones, Manuel (2)
Quiñones, Miguel A.
Quiñones, Narciso
Quiñones,
Nepomuceno
Quiñones, Pablo
Quiñones, Ramon (1)
Quiñones, Ramon (2)
Quiñones, Ramona
Quiñones, Teresa
Quiñonez, Josefina
Quintana, Angelina
Ra, Francisco
Ramirez, Ramon
Ramirez, Avelino
Ramirez, Jose
Ramirez, Julia
Ramirez, Maria
Ramirez, Rafael O.
Ramirez, Regino
Ramos, Arcadia
Ramos, Aurelia
Ramos, Bibiana
Ramos, Bienvenida
Ramos, Carlos
Ramos, Carmen
Ramos, Joaquin
Ramos, Josefina
Ramos, Juan
Ramos, Marcolina
Ramos, Maria
Ramos, Nicolas
Ramos, Petronila
Ramos, Rafael
Ramos, Vicente
Rauz, Carmen
Rebollo, Francisco
Rebollo, Jose
Requena, Arturo
Requena, Francisco
Requena, Juan
Requena, Manolo
Resto, Benito
Resto, Susana
Rexach, Emilia
Rexach, Jose
Rexach, Mercedes

Reyes, Ana Angelica
Reyes, Basilio
Reyes, Eduardo
Reyes, Juan
Reyes, Julio
Rios, Avelia
Rios, Carlota
Rios, Faustino
Rios, Rosenda
Rivas, Carmelo
Rivera, Ana
Rivera, Angela (1)
Rivera, Angela (2)
Rivera, Antonia
Rivera, Antonio
Rivera, Aurelia
Rivera, Carmen
Rivera, Domingo
Rivera, Eugenia
Rivera, Felicita
Rivera, Francisco (1)
Rivera, Francisco (2)
Rivera, Gabriel
Rivera, Jose
Rivera, Josefina (1)
Rivera, Josefina (2)
Rivera, Maria B.
Rivera, Martina
Rivera, Obdulio
Rivera, Petra
Rivera, Providencia
Rivera, Pura
Rivera, Rafael
Rivera, Rafael O.
Rivera, Ramon
Rivera, Rita
Robertin, Angel Maria
Robertin, Aurora
Robertin, Carmen
Robertin, Encarnacion
Robertin, Maria L.
Robertin, Zenaida
Roberto, Amalia
Robles, Carmen
Robles, Maria
Robles, Mercedes
Robles, Rafaela
Robles, Tomas
Robles, Zoilo (Jr.)
Rodriguez Alberty,
Miguel
Rodriguez Perez, Jose
Rodriguez, Amparo
Rodriguez, Bernaldina

Rodriguez, Carmen (1)
Rodriguez, Carmen (2)
Rodriguez, Carmen (3)
Rodriguez, Didaka
Rodriguez, Enrique
Rodriguez, Hilario
Rodriguez, Hortencia
Rodriguez, Marcial A.
Rodriguez, Maria
Rodriguez, Milagros
Rodriguez, Santiago
Rodriguez, Tomasa
Rodriguez, Vicente
Roman, Emilio (Jr.)
Roman, Jesus
Roman, Miguel Angel
Romero, Gregoria
Rosa, Amallia
Rosa, Blasina
Rosa, Carmen
Rosa, Celia
Rosa, Epifanio
Rosa, Evangelista
Rosa, Julio (1)
Rosa, Julio (2)
Rosa, Luis
Rosa, Manuel
Rosa, Marcelo
Rosa, Ramona
Rosado, Rafael
Rosario, Abraham
Rosario, Alfonso
Rosario, Epifania
Rosario, Eugenio
Rosario, Ignacio
Rosario, Juana
Rosario, Luisa
Rosario, Manuel
Rosario, Nestor
Rosario, Providencia
Rosario, Saturnina
Rovera, Gregoria
Ruiz, Concepcion
Ruiz, Jose
Sabat, Andrea
Salas, Carlos
Salas, Juan
Salas, Rafael
Saldaña, Carlos
Saldaña, Lucila
Salomon, Lorenzo
Sanchez, Altagracia
Sanchez, Carmen
Sanchez, Carmen G.

Sanchez, Cecilio
Sanchez, Josefina
Sanchez, Marcelo
Sanchez, Monserrate
Sanchez, Tomas
Santana, Carmen
Santiago, Cruz
Santiago, Julio
Santiago, Luz
Santiago, Oscar
Santiago, Rafael
Santos, Maria
Sarraga, Allen
Sarraga, Enrique
Scaca, Maria L.
Sevillano, Manuel
Siaca, Carmen
Siaca, Jesus
Siaca, Manuel
Siaca, Maria C.
Siaca, Miguel
Siaca, Ramon
Siaca, Suno
Silva, Isabel
Silva, Pedro
Simon, Adoldina
Sola, Felix
Soler, Gregorio
Solero, Cruz
Solis, Juan
Sotaz, Rosa
Soto Rivera, Juan
Soto, Agustina
Soto, Candida
Soto, Carmen (1)
Soto, Carmen (2)
Soto, Celestino
Soto, Dolores
Soto, Gabino
Soto, Juan
Soto, Manuela
Soto, Maria Eligia
Soto, Rafael
Soto, Ramon
Soto, Serafin
St. Paul, Alfonso
St. Paul, Elena
St. Paul, Maria I.
Standley, Elita
Tapia, Eusebia
Tapia, Juan
Telleria, Maria
Telleria, Petra
Texidor, Carlos

Texidor, Luis
Thompson, Jose
Tirado, Josefa
Torres, Ana
Torres, Angel
Torres, Clotilde
Torres, Cruz
Torres, Dionisio
Torres, Isabelo
Torres, Juan
Torres, Luis
Torres, Narcisa
Torres, Patricio
Travecier, Maria L.
Tufiño, Amado J.
Uniel, Jesus
Urado, Cruz
Urado, Pola
Vallecillo, Jeronimo
Vargas, Clara
Vasquez, Manuela
Vazquez, Alejandrina
Vazquez, Ana
Vazquez, Angelina
Vazquez, Edelmira
Vazquez, Emilio
Vazquez, Jose
Vazquez, Josefina
Vazquez, Julia
Vazquez, Maria (1)
Vazquez, Maria (2)
Vazquez, Ramon
Vazquez, Ramona
Vazquez, Rosario
Vega, Adolfina
Vega, Maria
Velez, Angelina
Velez, Flor de Maria
Velez, Matias
Velez, Rogelia
Velilla, Antonio
Veve, Angel
Veve, Dolores
Veve, Ines
Veve, Irene
Veve, James
Veve, Josefina
Veve, Juan
Veve, Juan E.
Vidal, Celia M.
Villavuestra, Jose D.
Vizcarrondo, Carmen
Werten, Segunto
Weten, Miguel

Zaccheus, Manuel
Zacchuis, Miguel
Zalduondo, America
Zalduondo, Arturo
Zalduondo, Belen
Zalduondo, Celestina
Zalduondo, Diego
Zalduondo, Josefina
Zalduondo, Juan
Zalduondo, Juan Antonio
Zalduondo, Manuela
Zalduondo, Maria

Hatillo High School

School Children, Hatillo, PR (Telegram)

Almodovar School, Juncos

1st Grade

Cintron, Luis
Collazo, Florentina
Colon, Ramon
Correa, Cruz
Cruz, Filomena
Flores, Francisco
Flores, Justa
Flores, Maria
Fortuño, Rafael
Geigel, Petra
Hernandez, Rosa M.
Jimenez, Evaristo
Jimenez, Luis
Larsen, Emil
Lopez, Jose
Lopez, Ramon
Mendez, Manuela
Morales, Antonio
Moreno, Josefa
Mujica, Dolores
Pagan, Eufigenia
Principe, Carolina
Reyes, Angelica
Rivera, Felipa
Rodriguez, Carmen

Rodriguez, Castulo
Roman, Manuel
Rondon, Augusto
Shroder, Alberto
Torres, Alejandrina
Torres, Solero
Trinidad, Francisco
Urquizu, Anuyerieu
Vazquez, Celestino

2nd Grade

----, Justino
Abiquizu, Maria
Agosto, Andres
Algarin, Manuel
Alicea, Angelica
Alicea, Catalino
Benitez, Jaime
Berrios, Carmen M.
Berrios, Maria J.
Cardona, Estefania
Castrillo, Domingo
Castro, Angelica
Castro, Juan
Castro, Providencia
Cintron, Carmen
Cintron, Leocadia
Cintron, Pura
Collazo, Carmen
Collazo, Elisa Maria
Colon, Blasco
Compte, Gumersinda
Corsino, Juan
Cruz, Ramon
De Jesus, Isabel
Delgado, Armanda
Delgado, Dolores
Delgado, Gaspar
Diaz, Generosa
Diaz, Rafaela
Diaz, Ramon
Donis, Carmelo
Duran, Gala
Eugui, Prudencio
Falero, Ezequiel
Falero, Leonide
Falvio, Mercedes
Flores, Genoveva
Fonseca, Ramon
Garcia, Juan
Garcia, Rafael
Garcia, Severo

Garcia, Telesforo
Gomez, Cecilia
Gomez, Gil (1)
Gomez, Gil (2)
Gomez, Julia
Gonzalez, Agustin
Gonzalez, Angelina
Gonzalez, Bienvenida
Gonzalez, Encarnacion
Gonzalez, Juan
Gonzalez, Leandro
Gonzalez, Leandro
Hernandez, Luis
Herrero, Luis
Jimenez, Filomena
Julia, Luis
Jurado, Leandro
Lamboy, Ramon
Larsen, Adolfo
Lazarribar, Jose
Lopez, Jose
Lopez, Marcelo
Maldonado, Josefa
Maldonado, Rafael
Marcano, Justino
Marrero, Amalio
Martinez, Ramona
Matanzo, Domingo
Matanzo, Juan
Medina, Juan
Melendez, Dolores
Melendez, Maria
Merced, Gregorio
Miranda, Restituta
Molina, Ana O.
Montañez, Julian
Moreno, Marta
Ortiz, Dolores
Pabellon, Claudio
Pabellon, Juan
Pauriel, Arturo
Peña, Carolina
Perales, Jose A.
Pereyo, Adalberto
Piñero, Juana
Principe, Jose
Quiñones, Petra
Quintana, Carmen
Ramos, Demetria
Rexach, Graciela
Reyes, Antero (1)
Reyes, Antero (2)
Reyes, Isabel
Reyes, Pablo

Reyes, Rosa
Rios, Maria
Rivera, Cristina
Rivera, Guadalupe
Robles, Guillermo (1)
Robles, Guillermo (2)
Rodriguez, Pilar
Roman, Tiburcio
Rosario, Juan
Ruibal, Maria
Salabarria, Ramona
Saldaña, Rafael
Santana, Amelia
Santiago, Josefa
Santos, Julio
Sierra, Faustino
Sierra, Ramon
Suarez, Juan
Torres, Francisca
Torres, Pedro
Trinidad, Mercedes
Vazquez, Ramona
Vazquez, Santiago

3rd Grade

Aldrey, Ana L.
Amalbert, Manuel
Amalbi, Catalina
Amalbi, Jose
Aponte, Rafael
Baerga, Rosa M.
Barreras, Benigno
Blanco, Rosa
Caballero, Rafael
Cano, Carmelo
Cardona, Melchor
Carrasquillo,
  Bernardina
Carrasquillo, Felipe
Carrasquillo, Jose
Cobas, Jaime
Colon, Angelo
Corcino, Ana Maria
Corcino, Francisco
Cruz, Ana
Cruz, Andres
Cruz, Carmen
Cruz, Emilia
Cruz, Eneris
Davila, Dolores
De Leon, Juana
Diaz, Manuel

Diaz, Monserrate
Duran, Petra
Estrella, Rafael
Feliciano, Juan
Feliciano, Matilde
Flores, Maximiliana
Garcia, Bersedad
Gomez, Celestina
Gomez, Engracia
Gonzalez, Dolores
Gonzalez, Guillermina
Gonzalez, Isolina
Hernandez, Francisco
Hernandez, Juan
Hernandez, Marcelina
Hernandez, Mercedes
Hernandez, Modesto
Herrero, Maria
Jimenez, Emilia
Jimenez, Victor
Larsen, Lorents
Laureano, Maria
Leon, Candido
Lopez, Antonio
Lopez, Indalecia
Maldonado, Belen
Marrero, Santiago
Martinez, Jose
Martinez, Maximo
Matos, Juana
Molina, Antonio
Molina, Rafael
Morales, Carmen
Moux, Jose
Perea, Juana
Pereda, Ramon
Pereira, Jose
Perez, Antonia
Ramos, Maria
Ramos, Pascual
Rexach, Carmen
  Maria
Rivera, Agustin
Rivera, Eladio
Rivera, Paula
Rivera, Petra
Robles, Eugenia
Robles, Juan
Rodriguez, Carmelo
Rodriguez, Petra
Rodriguez, Ramona
Roman, Claudina
Roman, Miguel
Roman, Otilia

Antonio's Grace

Rosario, Serafin
Ruibal, Carmen
Santiago, Carlos (1)
Santiago, Carlos (2)
Santos, Ramona
Sierra, Jose
Suarez, Julia
Suarez, Maria (1)
Suarez, Maria (2)
Zenon, Jose D.

3rd & 4th Grade

Benitez, Jesus
Bustamante, Amaury
Cantellops, Carmen
Casas, Ana
Cintron, Francisco
Collazo, Fernando
Colon, Lidia
Corsino, Marta
Cortes, Carmen
Diaz, Pedro
Dominguez, Maria
Eugui, Saturnino
Faliro, Tomas
Figueroa, Humberto
Garcia, Julia
Gonzalez, Monserrate
Julia, Francisco
Lamas, Celestino
Larsen, Luz Clara
Maldonado, Julio
Marcano, Casimiro
Matos, Candido
Matos, Jesusa
Mendoza, Ramon
Monero, Josefa
Pagan, Juana
Pereyo, Enrique
Pereyo, Virgilio
Rivera, Julio
Rodriguez, Marcelina
Roman, Luis

4th Grade

Algarin, Jacoba
Algarin, Zenaida
Arzuaga, Carmen
Barreras, Guillermo
Barreras, Rosa

Calenti, Vicente
Carcaño, Cruz
Castro, Providencia
Cintron, Delfin
Collazo, Isabel
Collazo, Maria
Collazo, Monserrat
Daumont, Crisanta
Davila, Gregorio
Febre, Julia
Feltio, Evaristo
Flores, Luisa (1)
Flores, Luisa (2)
Fortuño, Rosa
Fortuño, Teresa
Franquiz, Juana
Gonzalez, Lea
Hernandez, Gertrudis
Jimenez, Juan
Jimenez, Rogelia
Lamas, Jose
Lizarriban, Jesusa
Maldonado, Ignacio
Montañez, Adrian
Mulero, Maria
Pagan, Aguda
Perales, Rosa M.
Piñero, Juana
Principe, Agustin
Principe, Julia
Quiñones, Maria
Quintana, Ana
Rexach, Jose
Reyes, Rafael
Rodriguez, Rosario
Roig, Ramon
Roldan, Dolores
Rufat, Eusebio
Vazquez, Jose
Vazquez, Juana
Vega, Eustaquio
Ydrach, Arturo

5th Grade

Alberio, Leandra
Aldrey, Mercedes
Aponte, Mercedes
Benitez, Alicia
Boria, Elena
Cano, Rafael
Cano, Ramon
Cantellops, Serapia

Cardona, Eladio
Cardona, Higinio
Castro, Jose Ramon
Cobas, Manuel
Cobas, Socorro
Collazo, Domingo
Collazo, Jesus
Collazo, Ramon
Collazo, Rosa
Colon, Josefa
Colon, Julio
Colon, Pedro
Corcino, Pedro
Cruz, Felicita
Daumont, Melba
Davila, Felipa
Davila, Manuel
Delgado, Jose
Diaz, Maria
Duran, Clotilde
Escalona, Carmen
Escribano, Eustaquio
Garcia, Adela
Garcia, Luis
Garcia, Victor
Geigel, Manuel
Gomez, Angela
Gomez, Juana
Gomez, Maria
Gonzalez, Adela
Gonzalez, Dominga
Gonzalez, Francisco
Hernandez, Felicita
Hernandez, Fernando
Hernandez, Rafael
Hernandez, Vicenta
Jimenez, Otilia
Maldonado, Ramon
Martinez, Dolores
Martinez, Herminia
Martinez, Victor
Matanzo, Ramon
Matos, Ramiro
Medina, Pedro
Melendez, Leonor
Merced, Juan
Montañez, Cruz
Mujica, Jenaro
Pagan, Julio
Parrilla, Emilia
Peña, Felicita
Pereda, Laureano
Pereira, Eduardo
Pereira, Erundina

Perez, Petra
Piñero, Preopajita
Portalatin, P.
  Fernando
Quintero, Cruz
Reyes, Clemencia
Reyes, Dolores
Reyes, Octavio
Rivera, Agustina
Rivera, Carmen
Rivera, Ramon
Robles, Francisco
Robles, Jose
Rodriguez, Alejandro
Rodriguez, Celia
Rodriguez, Emilia
Rodriguez, Provi
Roig, Antonio
Saldaña, Antonio
Sanchez, Dolores
Santiago, Franco
Sierra, Rafael
Sierra, Salvador
Torres, Canturia
Zenon, Petra

6th Grade

Aldrey, Oliva
Berrios, Bienvenida
Berrios, Petra
Blanco, Miguel
Camis, Carmelo
Cay, Juana
Cruz, Maria
Davila, Juan R.
Diaz, Rogelio
Duran, Joaquin (Jr.)
Fajardo, Isabel
Feliciano, Leonor
Fortuño, Agustina
Fortuño, Carmen
Garcia, Isabel
Gonzalez y Alberty,
  Fernando
Gonzalez, Adela
Gonzalez, Dolores
Hernandez, Amalia
Hernandez, Isabel
Hernandez, Maria
Julia, Emilia
Lopez Victoria,
  Tomasa

175

Lopez, Maria
Marcano, Francisco
Marcano, Josefa
Merced, Julia
Mujica, Antonia
Muñoz Diaz, Pilar
Pereda, Clemente
Pereda, Ramona
Perez, Paula
Principe Molina, Aurea
Principe, Maria
Principe, Ramona
Quiñones, Monserrate
Rexach Correa, Francisco
Reyes, Manuel
Ricard, Josefina
Rodriguez, Juana
Saldaña, Cruz
Santos, Juan
Silva, Andres
Varona, Ernestina
Vazquez M., Jose

7th Grade

Algarin, Tomasa
Antommattei, Carmen M.
Antommattei, Eva
Barreras, Isabel
Correa, Miguel
Davila, Concepcion
Diaz, Felipe
Dominguez, Juana
Dueño, Rafael
Eugui, Carmen
Falero, Anselmo
Garcia, Juan
Garcia, Modesto F.
Hernandez, Agustin
Hernandez, Lulu
Hernandez, Maria Cristina
Martinez, Carmen
Matos, Mariano
Meaux, Arturo
Mujica, Maria
Pagan, Eulalio
Piñero, Eugenio
Piñero, Ignacio
Principe, Juana

Quiñones, Francisca
Ramos, Justa
Rexach, Agustin
Rivera, Maria
Rodriguez, Asuncion
Smythe, Arthur L.

8th Grade

Baerga, Maria
Benitez, Maria
Calenti, Mercedes
Castro, Santo
Cintron, Elisa
Flecha, Ynes
Gonzalez, Isabel
Gonzalez, Juana
Gonzalez, Julia
Hernandez, Carmen Maria
Hernandez, Pedro
Justo, Dolores
Lopez, Norberta
Medina, Providencia
Mejias, Sara
Mendez, Manuel
Montañez, Francisco M.
Navarro, Antonia
Perez, Eulogia
Reyes, Gabriel (Jr.)
Reyes, Ricardo
Ricard, Ramon
Roda, Jose
Rodriguez, Amparo
Rodriguez, Fredesvinda
Silvestriz, Dolores
Zenon, Matilde
Zenon, Modesta M.

9th Grade

Barreras, Fernando
Berrios, Dolores
Carrion, Mercedes
Cay, Carmen
Cintron, Mercedes
Colon, Amparo
Correa, Providencia I.
Davila, Barbara
Echevarria, Jose

Fernandez, Ramon
Figueroa, Jose
Garcia Fernandez, Jose
Gonzalez, Maria
Hernandez, Trinidad
Jimenez Gonzalez, Jesus
Melendez, Casimira
Morales, Ramon B.
Moux Alverio, Eulalio
Palou, Maria Luisa
Rexach, Gabriel
Reyes, Jose C.
Torres, Joaquina
Vega, Juan

School Students and Teachers, Maricao

Anglero, Genoveva
Anglero, Julio
Aviles, Monserrate
Barnocett, Herminia
Brito, Encarnacion
Brito, Fernanda
Bunet, Virgilio
Cacharros, Salvador
Campos, Julio
Cancel, Candida
Caparros, Herminia
Caparros, Ricarda
Carles, Dolores
Carles, Domingo
Casiano, Aurelio
Casta, Ernesto
Casta, Isabel L.
Chaluisan, Jose
Cordero, Iris
Cordero, Maria
Cordero, Sara
Coronado, Margaret
Enriquez, Rosa Maria
Feliciano, Herminia
Frontera, Francisco
Garcia, Jose
Gonzalez, Carmelo
Gonzalez, Rosa
Hornes, Dalila
Irizarry, Ramon

Liboy, Amelia
Lilia, Ovidio
Marin, Americo
Martinez, Emelina
Martinez, Maria
Massari, J. Andres
Matos, Dolores
McGuire, J. N.
Miro, Antonio
Oms, Francisco
Ortiz, Americo
Ortiz, Angela
Padilla, Augusto
Padilla, Gustavo E.
Pagan, Francisca
Pagan, Monserrate
Pagan, Virginia
Palacios, Catalina
Pietri, Isabel
Pietri, Jose
Plaza, Julia
Pons, Maria Antonieta
Poveymiron, Lorenzo
Quiñones, Gerarda
Quiñones, Maria
Rabassa, Martin
Ramirez, Carlos
Rodriguez, Israel
Rodriguez, Luis
Roman, Juan
Rosello, Jose
Rublan, Emilia
Santoro, Carlos
Santoro, Luisa
Santos, Inocencia
Santos, Soledad
Segarra, Jose
Soler, Antonia
Soler, Gumersinda
Soler, Joaquin
Torres, Juan
Valle, Providencia
Vicenty, Amparo
Villalba, Jose

Central Grammar, San Juan

Agosto, Adrian
Aguilar, Mercedes
Albanese, Santiago

Antonio's Grace

Almeria, Pedro
Amador, Jose
Amato, Miguel
Andrades, Marcelino M.
Arana, Santiago
Arroyo Cruz, Juan
Arroyo, Angela
Arroyo, Antonio
Audinot, Pedro
Ayes, Francisco
Baez, Ignacio
Batlle, Salvador
Beche Berdeguer, Vicente
Benavides, Carmen
Berdeguer, Eduvigis
Berdeguer, Gregorio
Betancourt, Juan
Boada, Pepita
Caballero, Liborio
Cantellops, Rosa
Carazo, Consuelo
Casanova, Mariano
Castell, Jose
Castillo, Providencia
Cespedes, Mercedes
Chico, Concepcion
Colon, Teresa
Cortijo, Jose
Costoso, Benigno
Cruz, Antonio
Cruz, Isabel
Cruz, Merida
Cuevas, Emilio
Cuevas, Enrique
Davila, Carmen
De Felix, Andres
Diaz, Carmen
Diaz, Claridad
Diaz, Lucia
Diaz, Ramon
Dolores Aybar, Carmen
Domenech, Gregorio
Dos Rios, Carmen
Estevens, Socorro
Estevens, Zenaida
Fransqueris, Lidia
Galbany, Concepcion
Gandia, Francisca Margarita
Gaona, Calixto G. (Jr.)
Garcia, Antonio

Garcia, Jose
Garcia, Juan
Garcias, Jesus
Goicoechea y Cotte, Jose Vicente
Goicoechea, Elpidio
Gonzalez, Guillermo
Hernandez, Rafael
Iglesia, Pedro
Infante, Ana M.
Jimenez, Amparo
Jimenez, Jesus
Jimenez, Maria E.
Jimenez, Victor
Lacamba, Dolores
Lameiro, Angelina
Lameiro, Manuela
Lanuza, Carmen Maria
Lassalle, Teresa
Ledesma, Rafael
Lolosa, Petra
Lopez, Dolores D.
Lopez, Maria Luisa
Lopez, Pedro
Lopez, Prada
Loubriel, Julia
Lozada, Mariano
Lugo, Jose A.
Maldonado, Maria
Manzanal, Providencia
Margenat, Carmen M.
Margenat, Paquita
Marin, Victor
Marrero, Agustin
Marrero, Isidro (Jr.)
Marrero, Pura
Martin, Maria
Martinez, Juan
Martinez, Maria
Martinez, Providencia
Martinez, Vicente
Matos, Aminta
Matos, Emma
Mayor, Carmen
Mirabal, Julio
Miranda, Carmen
Miranda, Juan C.
Miro, Carlos
Molinas, Josefina
Montilla, Patria
Moya, Petra
Nistal, Agustin
Noas, Alberto
Noas, Pedro

Ochart, Felix
Oquendo, Rafael
Orriols, Ana L.
Ortiz, Altagracia
Ortiz, Rosa
Pacheco, Carmen
Padro, Paquita
Palma, Candida
Paniagua, Maria L.
Peñalver, Ramon
Perez, Jose
Plard, Agustin
Ponturo, Angel
Power, Julio (Jr.)
Quiñones, Maria Luisa
Quiñones, Miguel
Reyes, Angelina
Richardson, Ella
Rivera, Consuelo
Rivera, Isabel (1)
Rivera, Isabel (2)
Rivera, Juana
Rodriguez, Carmen
Rodriguez, Dolores
Rodriguez, Manuel
Rodriguez, Maria Teresa
Rodriguez, Pedro
Roger, Severiano
Rojas Gorgas, Fredesvindo
Rosa, Angel
Rosa, Viola
Rosado, Eugenio
Rosario, Pedro
Rosario, Virginia
Rossi, Josefina
Rovira, Julio
Ruiz, Jose
Sanchez, Rafael
Santamaria, Veneranda
Santos, M. Ignacia
Serrano, Georgina
Simonpietri, Rafael G.
Sola, Tomasa
Somolino, Isidora
Sosa, Rosario
Sterling, Clara
Suarez, Benita
Suarez, Francisco
Suarez, Ramiro
Suarez, Vicente
Torres, Carmelo

Torres, Carmen
Torres, Carmen M.
Torres, Juan
Trujillo, Nellie
Ubarri, Palmira
Valencia, Julia
Vargas, Julio
Vazquez, Didia L.
Velazquez, Angeles
Velazquez, Josefina
Vera, Eva
Viader, Herminia
Vidal, Aurea
Villa, Fausto
Villanueva, Julia
Ybarra, Candida

Central High School, San Juan

Acosta, Clemencia
Aguayo, Luis Cesar
Alick, Miguel
Allende, Higinio
Alonso, Ramon
Aloy y Delgado, Miguel
Andino, Teofilo
Avis Red, Eleanor
Ayala, Jose
Balasquide, Lorenzo
Barreras, Catalina
Beltran, Antonio
Betancourt, Enrique
Boada, Luis
Bocanegra Lopez, Enriqueta
Bou, Elias
Bravo P., Antonio (Jr.)
Bustamante, Ana
Bustamante, Antonio
Calderon, Rosario
Callander, Isabel
Canales, Eloisa
Canales, Zenaida
Carballo, Carmen
Carmona, Augusto
Castro (de), Gladys
Castro Rivera, Martin
Castro, Eduardo
Castro, Jose

177

Castro, Mercedes
Castro, Pura
Castro, Rafael Ma.
Cerame Cruz, Rafael
Cintron, Leon Carlos
Conde, Pedro
Costa, Isabel M.
Cruz, Antonia
Cruz, Leoncio R.
Cuevas Toro, Esther
Daniell, Carlos (Jr.)
Davis, Dolores
De Jesus, Benigno
Del Valle, William
Diaz, Carmen
Diaz, Salvador
Dubon, Luis E.
Duchesne, Miguel
Escudero, Maria Luisa
Fajardo, Carmen E.
Fernandez, Carlos
Fernandez, Elena
Fernandez, Jose A.
Fernandez, Maria
Ferreiro, Rafael
Figueroa, Gustavo
Figueroa, Victor
Galiñanes, Alejandrina
Garcia Grau, Alfonso
Garcia, Carlota
Giuliani, Jose
Gonzalez, Jose
Gorbea, Gaspar
Gorbea, Luis
Guasb, Arturo P.
Gutierrez, Ana Luisa
Harris, Adolfo
Hernandez Fiol, Jose P.
Hernandez, Juan S.
Hernandez, Nieves
Iglesias, Eugenio
Iriarte, Rafael
Jarque, Olimpia
Laureano, Maria
Lebron, Ramona
Ledee, Francisco
Ledesma, Caralina
Llobet Geigel, Gloria
Llompart, Antonio
Lopez Tizol, Luis
Lopez, Francisco
Lopez, Obdulia
Loyola Castellon,

Jesus
Maldonado, Josefina
Marin, Hortensia
Marquez, Jose
Marquez, Maria
Marrero, Borinquen
Martinez, Angela
Marxuach, Julio
Mascarot, Margarita
Medina Moreno, Feliz
Megwinoff, Alexander
Miro, Rafael (Jr.)
Montilla, Enrique
Moreno, Ana Maria
Muñiz, Emilia
Muriel, Rafael A.
Navarro, G.
Negron, Jose
Negron, Maria Monserrate
Nieves, Rufino
O'Brien, Katherine E.
O'Ferrall, Engracia
Ochoteco, Concepcion
Ortiz, Enrique
Pacheco, Emilia
Padilla, Carmen
Parrilla, Serafina
Pauliver Fernandez, Manuel
Peral, Martin
Perez Diaz, Amparo
Perez Porrata, Rafael
Perez, Alvaro
Perez, Antonio
Perez, Isolina
Perez, Jose A.
Perez, Natividad
Prieto, Rafael
Quiñones, Isaac
Ramirez, Maria Elisa
Ranero, Francisco
Raso, Eufemia
Real Echevarria, Sara
Reyes, Angelina
Rios, Ivana
Rios, Manuel J.
Rivera, Damaso C.
Rivera, Diego Jose
Rivera, Juan S.
Rivera, Luis
Rivera, Nicolas
Rodriguez Delgado, L.
Rodriguez, Antonio

Rodriguez, Luis
Rodriguez, Maria
Roldan, Martin
Roman, Carmen
Roman, Jesus
Roman, Jorge
Roman, Juan B.
Romero, Marcos
Ruiz Foler, Rafael
Ruiz, Vicente
Salas, Guadalupe
Salas, Hermia M.
Santaella, Eugenio
Sarriera y Conde, Manuel
Schwartz, Gustavo
Sevilla, Carmen
Silva Umpierre, Gregoria
Silva, Jose C.
Sinagusa, Ana M.
Sinlug, Enrique F.
Suarez, Amalia
Suarez, Antonio J.
Suarez, Carmen P.
Suarez, Concepcion
Sutcliffe, Olive L.
Taboas, Juan
Temple, Elizabeth Betsy
Toro, Luis
Torres Davila, Jesus
Torres, Rufino (Jr.)
Trigo, Providencia
Trujillo, Lucila
Ubeda, Maria
Umpierre, Angelica
Vargas Ortega, Francisco
Vargas, Cecilia
Vega, Blanca
Vejerano, Eloisa
Ventura, Josefa
Verdejo, Matilde
Vigo, Isabel
Worker, Rafael
Ygaravidez, Candida

Concordia School, Ponce

Acosta, Lucila
Acosta, Maria L.

Acosta, Ulpiano
Alcala, Jose Antonio
Alcala, Maria Luisa
Alcantaro, Ana Maria
Almestico Lebron, Eugenia
Almodovar, Alejandrina
Altenor, Tito
Alvarado y Purcell, Ramon
Alvarado, Rafaela
Alvarez, Andres
Alvarez, Leonor
Alvarez, Rafael
Aranzamendiz, Manuel
Archeval, Pedro
Arroyo Cintron, Eleuterio
Balpais Verdejo, Luis
Bariny y Diaz, Luz Maria
Barnes, Ana
Barrett, Alice
Barrios, Ines Lucia
Basanta, Maria Luisa
Batista, Angel
Batista, Juana
Bausa Villanueva, Tomas
Bauza, Claudio
Bauza, Cristobal
Bauza, Elena
Beauchamps Toribio, Roberto
Benjamin, Cecilia
Berg, Consuelo
Bernardini Serrano, Jose Antonio
Berrios, Carmen
Besosa, Miguel A.
Besosa, Miss (Teacher)
Blackwood, Golda Eugenie
Blanco, Carmen
Blay, Francisco
Bonilla, Pascual
Bono, Carlos J.
Brandi, Pascua Maria
Burgos, Herminio
Burgos, Pedro
Busell, Alberto

178

Caballer, Livia
Cabassa, Alejandro
Cabrera, Nicasia
Caldwell, Edward
Camino, Blanca
 Margarita
Capestrany, Luisa Ines
Capo, Francisco
Cardona, Guillermo
Carreño, Celestina
Carreras, Beatriz
Carreras, Teresa
Casells, Rosita
Castells, Dolores M.
Castillo, Teofila
Castro, Jose
Castro, Juan
Castro, Victor
Cavell, Carlos
Cespedes, Adriana
Cespedes, Eduvigis
Chardon, Enrique
Chardon, Fernando
Chardon, Julio N.
Chavarrez, Juan
Chavarrez, Maria
 Teresa
Cintron, Leoncio
Clavell, Carlos Jaime
Clavell, Herminia
 Maria
Clavell, Miss (Teacher)
Coimbre, Ana
Collazo, Juan
Colon Ventura,
 Lorenzo
Colon, Emma Maria
Colon, Virgilio
 Augusto
Comellas, Maria Luisa
Concepcion Amoro,
 Adela
Concepcion, Roberto
Conde, Jose
Conde, Petra
Conde, Rafael
Contreras, Juan
Contreras, Miguel
Cordero, Antonia
Cordova, Armando
Cornier, Ana Matilde
Cornier, Rosa Emilia
Correa, Maria Luisa
Correa, Pablo

Cortada, Jorge
Costa y Amoro,
 Eugenia
Costa, Joaquin
Costas y Rivera, Carlos
 Juan
Costas, Francisco Jose
Costas, Luz Maria
Cruz, Valentin
Cstas, Maria
Cuberge, Rosa Julia
Cuestas, Felix
Damielser, Luis
Dapena y Quiñones,
 Jose Aurelio
Daroca, Angela Maria
De Jesus, Baldomero
De Ramery, Alberto
De Ramery, Mercedes
Del Valle, Dora
Del Valle, Herminio
Delgado, Federico
Delisa, Juan
Deschamps, Consuelo
 M.
Deschamps, Ella
Deynes, Mercedes
Diaz Colon, Pilar
Diaz, Carmen
Diaz, Catalina
Diaz, Fidel
Diaz, Francisca
Drury, Josephine
Drury, Marion
Echevarria, Francisca
Escobar, Cruz
Espadas, Francisco
Estades, Juan
Exposito Rivera,
 Antonia
Feliciano y Cruz,
 Benigno
Fernandez, Ines
Ferriol, Margarita
Figueroa, Elisa
Figueroa, Ruperto
Fiol Negron, William
Flores, Domingo
Font Ortiz, Alfredo
Foss, Maria Teresa
Fossas, Josefina
Frailes, Miss
 (Teacher)
Garcia, Carmen

Garcia, Carmen M.
Garcia, Joaquin
Garcia, Jose
Garcias, Carmen
 Maria
Garray, Carmelo
Gaston, Vicente
Gautier, Genaro
Gautier, Jose A.
Gelabert Perez,
 Conchita
Gelabert, Ernestina
Gelaberto, Pablo
Geli Collazo, Maria
 Teresa
Germain, Andres
Gomez Mesorana,
 Eugenio
Gomez, Jose A.
Gonzalez, Elena
Gonzalez, Francisco
Gonzalez, Jose
Gonzalez, Jose
 Enrique
Gonzalez, Manuel
Gonzalez, Monserrate
Gonzalez, Pedro
Gordon, Ramon
Gracia, Fernando
Graziani, Melitina
Guanill, Ramon
Gutierrez, Fernando
Gutierrez, Luis
Guzman, Hortensio
Herdman Amill, Isabel
Herdman, Enrique
Hernandez, Francisco
Hernandez, Irma
Hiesada, Victor
Hoheb, Nerida
Holman, Lulu
Jackson, Eduardo
Jackson, Lorenzo
Jackson, Octavio
Jorge, Luz Maria
Jovet, Teodoro
Julia, Agustin
La Torre, Eduardo
Laboy, Antonia
Lago y Lago, Rosa M.
Laino, Jose Antonio
Lamoutte, Aida
Lamoutte, Celia
Landazini y del Toro,

Elisa Ortiz
Lebron, Ms. (Teacher)
Leon Parra, Jose Luis
Leon, Carmen M.
Leon, Gabina
Leon, Maria Mercedes
Leviys, Juan
Lino Aguilo, Miguel
Llorente, Manuel
Loaiza y Panel,
 Francisco
Lopez Rivera, Maximo
Lopez, Manuel R.
Lopez, Rosa Maria
Lucchetti, Miss
 (Teacher)
Malaret, Maria Luisa
Malavet, Isabel
Mandry, Pasto
Manfrediz, Palmira
Mangual, Ana
Mangual, Pedro
Marin, Luz Palmira
Mariota, Angela
Mariota, Marta
Mariotta, Rafael
Martin Porrata,
 Nelson
Martinez, Antonio
Martinez, Elisa
Martinez, Elvira
Martinez, Maria L.
Martinez, Tomas
Martino Fuentes,
 Antonio
Mass., Ramon
Matta, Flora
Maura, Mr. (Teacher)
Mayoral, Carlos F.
Mayoral, Juan
Mayoral, Maximo
Mayoral, William
Medina y Collazo, Jose
Medina, Edualdo
Medina, Isabel
Medina, Ramon
Melendez, Elpidia
Melendez, Pedro
Mendez, Josefa
Mendoza, Irene
Mercado, Encarnacion
Merced, Antonia
Micailk, Rafaela
Mirabal, Digna

Mirailk, Laura M (Teacher)
Miranda, Miguel
Molina, Rafaela
Monagas, Enrique
Monforte, Valentina
Montaner, Antonio
Mora, Josefina
Mora, Pedro
Morales Schuck, Carlos Guillermo
Morales, Genoveva
Morales, Gloria Maria
Morales, Juan
Morales, Margarita
Moreno, Arturo
Muñiz, Socorro
Muñoz, Rafael
Nadal, Ramon
Napoleoni, Maximo
Navajas Espino, Iris
Nazario, Nereida
Negron, Luz Maria
Nigaglioni, Ana Mercedes
Nigaglioni, Carmen
Nisbit, Marcelina
Noriega, Candido
Noriega, Ernesto
Noriega, Pedro
Noriega, Providencia
Ocejo, Maria
Ohrt, Enrique
Olivari, Pedro
Oliver, Jose
Oppenheimer, Isabel
Orellana, Agustin
Orellana, Juan
Orsini, Francisco
Orta, Concepcion
Orta, Maria Isabel
Ortiz de Sandazuri, Alberto
Ortiz, Enrique (1)
Ortiz, Enrique (2)
Ortiz, Fernando
Ortiz, Juan
Ortiz, Rosa Maria
Ortiz, Santiago
Otero, Isabel
Pagan y Torre, Guillermina
Pagan, Leonor
Pardo, Gabriel

Pastor A., Fernando
Pastor Amstrong, Francisco
Pellot, Leocadia
Peña Sanchez, Jose
Peña, Ana Rosa
Perez Gomez, Carlota
Perez Santana, Emilio
Perez, Dolores
Perez, Eloy
Perez, Luis Ramon
Perez, Maria Luisa
Peslon, Francisco
Pierantoni, Maria
Pietri, Petra
Pivacco, Jose
Plana, Antonio
Planas, Alejandrina
Poventud, Joseph
Prieto, Jose A.
Purcell, Manuel R.
Quevedo, Estrella
Quiñones, Celenia
Quiñones, Felita
Ramirez Besosa, Ada
Ramirez, Basilisa
Ramirez, Celina
Ramirez, Estela
Ramos, Gregoria
Ramos, Herminio
Ramos, Ofelia
Renta Mass., Angelita Justina
Renta, Ramona
Reyes, Justina
Riera, Ernestina C.
Rigual Lucca, Raul
Rinaldi, Lucia
Rinaldi, Ramon
Rios, Amalia
Rios, Blas
Rios, Epifania
Rios, Jose
Rios, Julia Dolores
Rios, Maria
Rivas, Rafael
Rivera y Porras, Felix
Rivera, Carmen M.
Rivera, Jose
Rivera, Manuela
Rivera, Maria
Rivera, Maria Rafaela
Rivera, Maximina
Rivera, Pablo

Rivera, Pedro Juan
Rivera, Pedro Juan (2)
Rivera, Ramon G.
Robles, Aurora
Roca, Carmen Maria
Roche, Rosa E.
Rodriguez, Ana
Rodriguez, Anaclio
Rodriguez, Angel
Rodriguez, Angel Juan
Rodriguez, Antonio
Rodriguez, Concepcion
Rodriguez, Emilia
Rodriguez, Fabian
Rodriguez, Facunda
Rodriguez, Faustino
Rodriguez, Francisca
Rodriguez, Francisco
Rodriguez, Guadalupe
Rodriguez, Jaime
Rodriguez, Jose Antonio
Rodriguez, Josefa
Rodriguez, Leonor
Rodriguez, Luis
Rodriguez, Luisa V.
Rodriguez, Manuel Angel
Rodriguez, Miguel Adolfo
Rodriguez, Pastor
Rodriguez, Tirso
Rojas, America F.
Romaguera, Arturo
Romaguera, Jose Mariano
Roque, Arturo
Roque, Carmelo Z.
Roque, Petra Haydee
Rosado, Ignacio
Ruberto, Ana Maria
Rubio, Clarita
Sabater, Inocencia
Sabater, Maria Teresa
Salazar, Angel Luis
Salazar, Manolo
Salinas, Maria Luisa
Sanabria, Anatila
Sanchez, Carmen
Sanchez, Guillermo
Sanchez, Jorge
Sandoval, Emilia Ocasio

Sanjurjo y Ramirez, Dolores Probidencia
Santana Jiaiman, Georgina
Santiago, Eduardo
Santiago, Esteban
Santiago, Isabel
Santiago, Maria
Santiago, Rosa Maria
Santiago, Rosa Maria (2)
Santiago, Sylvia Emelina
Santoni, Guadalupe
Santos, Consuelo
Scipio, Gustavo
Seires Patrix, Encarnacion
Semidei Delucca, Ana Teresa
Seraguea Conde, Francisco
Serbi, Isabelita
Serracante Santiago, Antonio
Serrano y Ramirez, Julio
Serrano, Angela Y.
Serrano, Mercedes
Sierra, Felipe
Silva, Angel
Silva, Jose Maria
Silva, Silvia
Silva, Sylvia W.
Silva, Telma
Skerrat, Ricardo
Solivan, Luis
Somohano, Luz
Soto, Eugenia
Soto, Gloria M.
Soto, Santiago
Subira, Horacio
Subura, Roberto D.
Suro Pico, Joaquin
Suro, Emilia
Tapia, Miss (Teacher)
Toro, Arsenio
Toro, Carmen Rosa
Toro, Monserrate
Torren, Mercedes
Torrens, Florinda
Torrent, Fernando
Torres de Jesus, Hector Raul

Torres, Ana
Torres, Carlos Juan
Torres, Francisco
Torres, Juan Enrique
Torres, Salvador
Torres, Severo
Torruella Fornaris,
  Guillermo
Torruella, Juan N.
  (Jr.)
Torruella, Juan
Torruellas, Carmen
  Maria
Trese, Juana
Trujillo, Tomas
V'ergne, Maria Luisa
Vargas Velazquez,
  Jose
Vargas, Eugenia
Vasquez Alvares
  Miranda, Tomas
Vazquez,
  Buenaventura
Vazquez,
  Hermenejildo
Vazquez, Isabel
Vazquez, Juan
Vazquez, Margaro
Vazquez, Tomas
Vega, Jesus
Velazquez, Luz Maria
Ventura, Felix Manuel
Vergne, Carmen Ana
Vilabrille y Gonzalez,
  Jose Maria
Vilaret, Francisca
Villar, Julia
Villar, Victoria
Villaronga Pasarell,
  Raul
Visot, Eliseo
Vives, Juan
Westerban Sandoval,
  Candida
Wilson, Isabel
Yordan, Eduardo
Yordan, Jaime
Yordan, Jorge
Yordan, Reinaldo
Zayas y Diaz, Petra
Zayas y Zeno,
  Marcelina
Zayas Zeno, Agustin
Zayas, Joaquina

Zehr, Plinio
Zerty, Alfonso

**Band of Mercy,
Ponce**

Letter 1

Esbri y Roberts, Juan
Perez de Guerra, Julia
  G.
Preston, E. G.

Letter 2

Acensio, Manuel
Acevedo, Ernestina
Acevedo, Rosa Maria
Acosta, Eleticia
Acosta, Leonilda
Acosta, Victoria
Albizu, Ana Maria
Albizu, Teresa
Alfonso, Andres
Alfonzo, Pedro
Alicea, Pablo
Almodovar, Ana
Alvarado, America
Alvarado, Arturo
Alvarado, Isabel
Alvarado, Manuel
Alvarez, Luz Maria
Alvarez, Severo
Aponte, Luis
Aponte, Maria
Archeval, Maria
  Rufina
Arroyo, Monserrate
Auffant, Juan
Auffant, Gregoria
Baez, Cristina
Baez, Emilia
Baez, Higinio
Baez, Maximina
Baez, Ramon
Baez, Sixto
Banchs, Eugenio
Banchs, Jaime
Barbosa, Maria L.
Beltran, Carmen
Bernal, Cancio
Bertana, Isabel

Boisjoly, Mariano
Borro, Juan Manuel
Brusa, Maria
Camacho, Adela
Camacho, Maria
Caquia, Maria
Carbia, Rafael
Carreras, Felipa
Cartagena, Antonia
Casiano, Antonia
Castillo, Luis
Castro, Afortunada
Castro, Andre
Castro, Manuel Angel
Castro, Osbaldo
Charloteu, Josefa
Charloteu, Rosa
Cintron, Ezequiel
Cintron, Julio
Cintron, Teodelinda
Collazo, Angela
Collazo, Enrique (1)
Collazo, Enrique (2)
Collazo, Maria
Collazo, Teresa
Colon, Agustin
Colon, Concepcion
Colon, Elisa
Colon, Francisco
Colon, Jacinta
Colon, Jesus
Colon, Josefa
Colon, Julio E.
Colon, Luis
Colon, Pablo
Colon, Victor Manuel
Colon, William
Concepcion, Braulio
Concepcion, Jose
Concepcion, Maria
Conde, Luis Alfredo
Conde, Pablo
Conde, Ynez
Cornelio, Alberto
Cortes, Aniceto
Cortes, Maria
Cruz, Juanito
Cuestas, Enrique
Diaz, Gloria
Dones, Fabiana
Droin, Armando
Dros, Gloria
Droz, Albertina
Duran, Carlos Juan

Echevarria, Felix
Escabi, Pastor
Escale, Vicenta
Feliciano, Ramon
Fernandez, Asuncion
Fernandez, Natividad
Figueroa, Felix
Figueroa, Modesta
Figueroa, Senorra
Font, Rafael
Garcia, Julio
Garcia, Maria Teresa
Garcia, Robertino
Garcia, Ruperto
Geron, Jose Joaquin
Giron, Agustina
Goitia, Rafael
Gomez, Carlos
Gomez, Enrique
Gonzalez, Ana Amalia
Gonzalez, Bernardo
Gonzalez, Carlos T.
Gonzalez, Guadalupe
Gonzalez, Isabel
Gonzalez, Jorge
Gonzalez, Natividad
Gonzalez, Ulpiano
Guillon, Miguel
Hernandez, Carmen
Hernandez, Saturno
Irizarri, Agripina
Jorge, Enrique
Julbes, Ana Maria
Lamonaco, Indalecio
Llanes, Felipe
Llanis, Enrique
Lopez, Carmen
Lopez, Eulalio
Lopez, Homero
Lopez, Ramon
Maldonado, Rosendo
Marquez, Ana Maria
Marquez, Tomas
Martinez, Fermina
Martinez, Jose
Martinez, Justino
Martinez, Maria M.
Martinez, Pedro
Matias, Carmen
Matias, Isabel
Matos, Rafael Antonio
Medina, Francisco
Melendez, Fidel
Melendez, Gregoria

Mendez, Victor
Mercado, Carlina
Mercado, Ulpiano
Milan, Jose Ramon
Milan, Miguel
Monserrat, Alejandro
Morales, Carmen M.
Morales, Feliz
Morales, Francisco
Morales, Nelta
Morales, Nicolasa
Morales, Patria
Morales, Pedro Juan
Moreno, Ana Luisa
Navas, Manuel
Nazario, Maria Luisa
Ocasio, Carmen
Ocasio, Leopoldo
Olivar, Santiago
  Ramona
Oliver, Bandilio
Oliver, Vicenta
Ortiz, Daniel
Ortiz, Emilia
Ortiz, Eugenia
Ortiz, Francisca
Ortiz, Lilia
Ortiz, Rafael
Padilla, Luis A.
Pagan, Luisa
Pagan, Maria
Pauneto, Juan
Pereira, Carlos
Perez, Alfonsa
Perez, Carlos Jose
Perez, Eladio
Perez, Francisca
Perez, Luzpencio
Perez, Olimpia
Perez, Ramon
  Francisco
Pero, Amanda
Pujols, Santiago
Quiñones, Ismael
Quiñones, Jose R.
Quiñones, Margarita
Quintana, Rosa Maria
Quintana, Victor
Quirindongo, Joselito
Rabasa, Evangelia
Ramirez, Luis Meraldo
Ramon, Julio
Ramos, Carlos Juan
Ramos, Mercedes

Rangel, Ana
Rangel, Gregorio
Rangel, Nicomedes
Rangel, Norberto
Rangel, Pedro
Rebollar, Rosalia
Rentas, Juan Pastor
Reyes, Bernardina
Reyes, Gumercindo
Reyes, Marina
Rios, Carmen Maria
Rios, Luz Divina
Rios, Petra
Rivera, Bautista
Rivera, Domingo
Rivera, Francisca
Rivera, Gregorio
Rivera, Herminio
Rivera, Jaime
Rivera, Luisa
Rivera, Mariano
Rivera, Petra
Rivera, Rafaela
Rivera, Ramon
Rivera, Virgilio
Robles, Higinio
Robles, Pedro
Roche, Dolores
Roche, Eladia
Roche, Petra
Rodriguez, Ana Luisa
Rodriguez, Antonio
Rodriguez, Carmen
Rodriguez, Catalina
Rodriguez, Domingo
Rodriguez, Elena
Rodriguez, Emiliano
Rodriguez, Ermelindo
Rodriguez, Euripides
Rodriguez, Genoveva
Rodriguez, Isabel
Rodriguez, Manuel
Rodriguez, Oscar
Rodriguez, Rosa
Rodriguez, Tomasa
Rodriguez, Vicente
Rosado, Carmen
Rosado, Georgina
Rosado, Isidora
Rosado, Juan
Rosado, Petra
Rosado, Rosaura
Rosario, Gabriel
Ruiz, Carlos Manuel

Ruiz, Clotilde (1)
Ruiz, Clotilde (2)
Ruiz, Juanita
Ruiz, Pedro
Sanchez, Antonia
Sanchez, Catalino
Sanchez, Maria Luisa
Sanchez, Rafael
Sandobal, Josefa
Sandoval, Agapita
Santana, Mercedes
Santiago, Agustin
Santiago, Ana Maria
Santiago, Belen
Santiago, Enrique
Santiago, Filomena
Santiago, Paulita
Santiago, Rafael
Santinis, Margarita
Santos, Candida
Serra Colon, Maria
Serra, Maria
Serrano, Maria S.
Sierra, Juan
Sierra, Monserrate
Silen, Rafael
Silere, Jose Americo
Silva, Felipa
Tarascot, Manuel
Tarranto, Carmen
  Maria
Tarrats, Rafael
Texidor, Arturo
Tirado, Antonio
Torres, Aurora
Torres, Carlina
Torres, Joaquin
Torres, Julio (1)
Torres, Julio (2)
Torres, Maria Cristina
Torres, Severo
Torruella, Restituto
Turert, Sixta
Usera, Luis
Vargas, Hipolito
Vargas, Jose
Vargas, Sofia
Vasked, Ester
Vazquez, Elias
Vazquez, Felita
Vazquez, Julia
Vazquez, Pedro
Vazquez, Vicente
Vazquez, Vicente

Velez, Julio
Velez, Miguel
Vidal, Antonio
Vidal, Felicita
Vidal, Tula
Videal, Manuel
Villarin, Elisa
Wys, Rafael
Zengotita, Enrique

Reina School, Ponce

Acevedo, Engracia
Acosta, Jose Antonio
Acosta, Marcelino
Aguayo, Augusto
Alala, Ramon Jesus
Alberto Jose
Alcala y Gimer, Rosa
  Candida
Alcala, Gloria
Alcala, Julia Maria
Alcala, Julio
Alcala, Maria
Algarin, Julia
Alicea, Georgina
Alicea, Victor
Alier, Teresa
Almodovar, Justo
Alomar, Alejandro
Alomar, Roberto
Alvarado, Oscar
Alvarez, Francisco
Alvez, Isabel
Alvira, Jose Antonio
Anes y Westerband,
  Gabriel
Antonio, Miguel
Arce, Frank
Arce, Luis
Archival, Amparo
Archival, Isabel
Arenas, Andres
Arenas, Francisca
Arevalo y Ferrer,
  Josefa
Arias, Ana Rosa
Arias, Jorge
Arias, Maria
Arias, Mercedes
Arroyo, Carmen Maria
Arroyo, Emiliano

Antonio's Grace

Arroyo, Leocadia
Arroyos, Rosario
Asencio, Dolores
Asencio, Francisco
Asencio, Jose M.
Asensio, Roque
Astasio, Gregorio
Auffant, Carlos Luis
Auffant, Josefina
Aviles, Antolina
Ayala, Juanito
Ayala, Santos
Ayala, Vicenta
Bacenet, Luis
Baerga Eduardo, Lidia
Balaguer, Joaquin
Baranta, Luisa
Barnes, Ulpiano
Barros, Francisco
Barros, Jose
Barros, Panchita
Bartolomei, Francisco
Belketui R., Miguel
Bellon, Silvia
Benito, Amelia
Bermudez, Francisco
Berrios, Cesarina
Berrios, Francisco
Bertoliz, Juan
Bocana, Seferino
Bolier, Vicente
Bonelis, Cristobal
Borrero, David
Boscana, Adela O.
Bota, Maria
Braschi, Porfirio
Braulio, Pedro
Braulio, Victor
Builichini, Florencia
Burgos y R., Juana
Burgos, Modesta
Cabrera, Clarita
Cadeno, Alfredo
Cadiz, Julio
Calier, Concepcion
Cambrelen, Isabel
Cambrelen, Alejandro
Cambrelen, Angel
Campos, Carmen
  Josefa
Canals, Geronima
Cancel, Alfredo
Carlo, Porfidia
Carmona, Carlos Juan

Carrion, Monsita
Cartagena, Pedro
Casaduc, Rafael
Casals, Jose Eudaldo
Casanovas, Pedrito
Casiano, Julia
Castillo, Ana Maria
Castillo, Carmen
Castillo, Carmen Ines
Castillo, Dolores
Castillo, Ricardo
Castilloveitia, Felipe
Castro Quesada,
  Horacio
Castro, Lolita
Catariche, Juan
Cedo, Angel
Cepero, Carmen
Cespedes, Samuel
Cespedes, Teofilo
Chardon, Ferdinand
Chardon, Lucia
Chardon, Luis
Cidron, Ventura
Cintron, Gregoria
Colon y Braci,
  Eduardo Luis
Colon, America
Colon, Andres
Colon, Antonia
  Palmira
Colon, Dolores
Colon, Domingo
Colon, Jaime
Colon, Jose
Colon, Panchita
Colon, Patria
Colon, Pilar
Colon, Ramon
Colon, Rodolfo
Colon, Vicente Gomez
Comulada Ortiz,
  Antonio
Conde, Jose
Conde, Jose Luis
Contero, Julio
Coquias, Antonio
Coquias, Emilia
Cordero, Milton
Correa, Julio
Correa, Vicente
Costa, Agustina
Costas, Amelia
Costas, Amelia Iriarte

Cotal, Rosalia
Coto, Maximino
Cruz y Bonilla,
  Monserrate
Cruz, Ana I.
Cruz, Carmen
Cruz, Domingo
Cruz, Juanita
Cruz, Luz Maria
Cruz, Manuela
Cruz, Victoria
Cuevas, Antonia
Cuevas, Francisca
Dadena, Osvaldo
Dahena, Humberto
Dalmau, Sara
Dam, Emilia
Dam, Patria
Danielsen, Helena
Dapena, Carmen
  Maria
Davin, Austin
De Jesus, Carmen
De Jesus, Gabriel
De Jesus, Ramon
De Leon, Juan Jose
De Leon, Maria
Del Rio, Pedro
Del Valle, Carmen
Del Valle, Isabel
Del Valle, Jose
Del Valle, Sebastian
Delgado, Ana
Delgado, Antonio
Delgado, Eladia
Delgado, Ramon
Deynes, Jose Ramon
Diaz, Antonia
Diaz, Enriqueta
Diaz, Julia
Diaz, Julita
Diaz, Justo
Diaz, Paula
Diaz, Rafael
Diaz, Umberto
Druet, Jose
Druet, Ramon
Druet, Victoria
Dueño, Edith A.
Dueño, Eva
Duran, Carmen
Echevarria Gonzalez,
  Antonio
Echevarria, Aurelia

Echevarria, Felicita
Echevarria, Leonor
Echevarria, Pedro
Echevarrias, Modesta
Echevarrias, Patria
Estepa, Domingo
Evans, Francisco
Farinacci, Margarita
Farinacci, Mercedes
Feliciano, Enrique
Feliciano, Jose
Fernandez, Antonio
Fernandez, Esequiela
Fernandez, Gregoria
Fernandez, Sara
Ferraioli, Jose Antonio
Ferraioli, Magdalena
Ferran, Eulalia Maria
Ferrer, Catin
Ferrer, Ibrahim
Ferrer, Jose Miguel
Figueroa, Carmen
Figueroa, Dolores
Figueroa, Maria Luisa
Flores y Ortiz, Felicita
Flores, Jose
Flores, Lucia
Flores, Miguel
Fon, Esteban (1)
Fon, Esteban (2)
Fon, Miguel
Fon, Norberto
Fonfrias, Luisa
Font, Graciela
Fraile, Josefina
Franceschi, Jorge
Franceschi, Modesta
Franceschi, Romana
Franco, Carlos
Frese, Carlos
Frese, Guillermo
Fuente, Elena
Furrell, Radames
Gallardo, Pedro
Gandara, Jose
Gandara, Julio
Gandara, Manuel
Gandara, Toñita
Garcia, Arcadio
Garcia, Epifania
Garcia, Eugenia
Garcia, Florida
Garcia, Isabel
Garcia, Julio

183

Muñoz, Petrona
Muñoz, Sarah
Napoleoni, Anunciada
Napoleoni, Oscar
Napoleoni, Ramiro
Napoleoni, Santia
Navarro, Jose
Navarro, Rafael
Negron, Encarnacion
Negron, Petra
Negron, Santiago
Nieves, Ramon
Nieves, Tomas
Niza, Isabel
Nones, Aurora
Nuñez, Americo
Nuñez, Francisco
Nuñez, Ismael
Ocejo, Rodolfo
Ojeda, Josefina
Oliver, Elsa Maria
Oliver, Tomas
Olivo, Francisco
Olmeda, Jose
Olmo, Nicasio
Oquendo, Pascuala
Orihuela, Zoilo
Orsatelli, Jose
Ortega, Ramon
Ortiz (de), Gertrudis
Ortiz, Andres
Ortiz, Angelina
Ortiz, Benedicta
Ortiz, Eladia
Ortiz, Emilia
Ortiz, Francisco
Ortiz, Hilda
Ortiz, Irene
Ortiz, Jorge
Ortiz, Juan
Ortiz, Manuel
Ortiz, Paula
Ortiz, Victor
Ortiz, Victoria
Orza, Isabel
Otero, Georgina
Padilla Gelabert, Emilia
Padilla, Epifanio
Pagan, Andrea
Pagan, Eduardo
Pagan, Rafael
Pagan, Rossell
Paradi, Luis

Paris, Agustin
Parodi, Jose
Parodi, Nelly
Pastor, Jorge
Pastor, Rosario
Pedevidu, Rafael
Peña, Francisco
Penna, Antonio
Perez, Basilio
Perez, Carmen
Perez, Carmen Dolores
Perez, Emilia
Perez, Enrique
Perez, Fernando
Perez, Gloria
Perez, Jaime Ernesto
Perez, Jesus
Perez, Julio
Perez, Luis
Perez, Manuel
Perez, Moises
Perez, Rafael
Perez, Rita
Perez, Rogelio
Perez, Santiago
Perez, Zenaida
Pericas, Fernando
Pericas, Rosa M.
Pero, Lila
Pietri, Haydee
Pivaco, Concepcion
Plummey, Mercedes
Pola, Juanito
Ponce de Leon, Ramon
Pons, Ana Ines
Pons, Antonia
Porrata, Angeles
Porrata, Armando (1)
Porrata, Armando (2)
Puestas, Guillermo
Quijano, Angelina
Quilichi, Manuel
Quiñones, Amina
Quiñones, Evangelista
Quiñones, Fernando
Quiñones, Juanito
Quiñones, Paquita
Quintana, Gumersindo
Quintana, Modesto
Quirindongo, Maria
Rabainn, Ramona

Ramery, Joosefina
Ramirez Belbru, Inocencia
Ramirez, Joaquin
Ramirez, Josefita
Ramirez, Manolo
Ramirez, Margarita
Ramirez, Petra
Ramos, Ana Rita
Ramos, Pancho
Ramu, Adriana
Regalado, Arturo
Reinaldo Guzman, Umberto
Renaud, Tomas
Renta, Antonia
Renta, Genaro
Renta, Julia
Reyes, Carmen (1)
Reyes, Carmen (2)
Reyes, Luis Ezequiel
Rigual, Irma
Rios, Amneris
Rios, Carmen Maria
Rios, Celina
Rios, Guillermo
Rios, Jose (1)
Rios, Jose (2)
Rios, Mercedes
Rivas, Angel
Rivas, Ramona
Rivera, Adela
Rivera, Ana
Rivera, Andrea
Rivera, Angel
Rivera, Antonio
Rivera, Carlos J.
Rivera, Confesor
Rivera, Emilio
Rivera, Enriqueta
Rivera, Feliz
Rivera, Francisco
Rivera, Gustavo
Rivera, Jacobo
Rivera, Jose
Rivera, Juan (1)
Rivera, Juan (2)
Rivera, Julio
Rivera, Maria
Rivera, Mariana
Rivera, Miguel
Rivera, Pablo
Rivera, Pastor
Rivera, Polito

Rivera, Ramon (1)
Rivera, Ramon (2)
Rivera, Ramon Liborio
Robira, Francisco
Robles y Lugos, Angel
Robles, Candida Rosa
Rodriguez A., Petra Maria
Rodriguez Garcia, Dolores
Rodriguez, Agapito
Rodriguez, Americo
Rodriguez, Antonio
Rodriguez, Carlos (1)
Rodriguez, Carlos (2)
Rodriguez, Carmen Maria
Rodriguez, Dolores
Rodriguez, Erasmo
Rodriguez, Felipe (1)
Rodriguez, Felipe (2)
Rodriguez, Felix
Rodriguez, Gustavo
Rodriguez, Higinio
Rodriguez, Isabel (1)
Rodriguez, Isabel (2)
Rodriguez, Isidro Ramon
Rodriguez, Juan
Rodriguez, Juanita
Rodriguez, Juanito
Rodriguez, Julio
Rodriguez, Luisa
Rodriguez, Manolo
Rodriguez, Manuela
Rodriguez, Maria Cristina
Rodriguez, Nicolas
Rodriguez, Pedro
Rodriguez, Petra (1)
Rodriguez, Petra (2)
Rodriguez, Ramon
Rodriguez, Santiago
Rodriguez, Victoria
Rodriguez, Zoraida
Roig, Gabriel
Roma, America
Roman, Pedro
Roman, Rigoberto
Roman, Victor Manuel
Romero, Gelson
Romero, Ramon
Rosa, Godofreda
Rosado, Catalina

185

Rosaly, Eulalia
Rosaly, Eulalio
Rosaly, Felicidad
Rosaly, Manuel
Rosaly, Patricio
Rosario, Cristobal
Rosario, Emiliano
Rovira, Genoveva
Ruiz Miller, Pedro J.
Ruiz, Antonio
Ruiz, Carlos M.
Ruiz, Concha
Ruiz, Leopoldo
Ruiz, Pablo
Ruiz, Pedro Juan
Sabatel, Antonia
Sabatel, Juan
Sabatel, Maria
  Mercedes
Sabater, Juan
Sacot, Jorge
Salas, Rosa Maria
Salas, Teresina
Salazar, Laura
Salichs, Concha
Salichs, Juan
Salicrup, William
  Henry
Salinas, Aida
Sanchez Fonfria,
  Eloisa
Sanchez, Alfonso
Sanchez, Carlos Luis
Sanchez, Carmen
Sanchez, Digna
Sanchez, Gloria
Sanchez, Justina
Sanchez, Justito
Sanchez, Pablo
Sanchez, Pura Maria
Santaella, Enrique
Santana, Carmen
Santana, Ernesto
Santiago Alfred
Santiago Garcia,
  Aurelio
Santiago Perez,
  Santiago
Santiago Vega, Jose
Santiago, Amador
Santiago, Ana Maria
Santiago, Celia
Santiago, Demencia
Santiago, Genoveva

Santiago, Jose (1)
Santiago, Jose (2)
Santiago, Magdalena
Santiago, Maria Luisa
  (1)
Santiago, Maria Luisa
  (2)
Santiago, Pascuala
Santiago, Pedro
Santiago, Rafael
Santiago, Ramona
Santos Fortier, Hector
Santos, Ines
Santos, Juanito
Santos, Julio Enrique
Sapia, Esther
Sarrio, Panchito
Seda, Antonia
Segarra Micheli, Luis
Segarra, Josefa
Sepulveda, Rosalina A.
Serra, Eulalia
Serra, Jose
Serra, Rafael
Serrano, Manuel
Sierra, Candita
Silva, Adilia
Silva, Ines
Silva, Romualdo
Socorro, Maria
Soldevla, Francisco
Soto, Aristides
Soto, Avelino
Soto, Cruz
Soto, Joaquin
Soto, Justo
Soto, Salvador
Suarez, Angel Morey
Suarez, Cecilia
Suarez, Gregoria
Suarez, Paulino
Suarez, Pedro Juan
Suffront, Eduardo
Suoto, Justo
Tarasco, Rafael
Tarrats, Pedro
Tavarol, Emilio
Tellock, Ana M.
Terry, Mateo
Toledo, Emilio
Tomassini, Tomas
Toro, Ana Luisa
Toro, Angelica
Toro, Carlos Manuel

Toro, Carlos V.
Toro, Fernando Felix
Toro, Francisco
  Manolo
Toro, Gloria
Toro, Ramon
Toro, Rosa Maria
Toro, Ursula
Toro, Victoria
Torrens, Luz M.
Torrent, Manuel
Torres y Rivera,
  Felicita
Torres, Benito
Torres, Eladio L.
Torres, Isabel
Torres, Joaquin
Torres, Juan (1)
Torres, Juan (2)
Torres, Julia Maria
Torres, Luis
Torres, Manuel
Torres, Pedro
Torres, Rafael (1)
Torres, Rafael (2)
Torres, Rosa
Troche, Herminio
Troche, Juana
Urta, Miguel
Vaillant, Carlos (1)
Vaillant, Carlos (2)
Valdivieso, Ana
  Leonor
Valedon, Guillermo
Valenciano, David
Valentin, Gregorio
Valentin, Rosaura
Valle (de), Carmen
Valls, Adelaida
Valls, Gloria Maria
Valpais, Antonio
Varela, Enrique
Varela, Margarita
Vargas, Domingo
Vargas, Serafin R.
Vazquez, Amada
Vazquez, America
Vazquez, Angelica
Vazquez, Carlos
Vazquez, Eugenia
Vazquez, Felipe
Vazquez, Genaro
Vazquez, Juan
Vazquez, Juan Jose

Vazquez, Onelia
Vazquez, Petra
  Antonia
Vazquez, Tulio
Vazquez, Victor
Vega, Maria Teresa
Vega, Rafael
Velazquez PedroLuis
Velazquez, Catalina
Velazquez, Juan
  Bautista
Velez, Rafael
Vellagamba, Antonia
Veves, Isidro
Vidal, Julio E.
Vidaurre, Marcelino
Vidaurre, Maria Luisa
Vidaurre, Providencia
Viera y Toro, Josefa
Viera, Filomena
Vilella, Fernando
Villali, Juanito
Villali, Marcelo
Villaneuve, Pedro
  Enrique
Villarenas, Fernando
  P.
Villlet, Angel
Villodas, Petra
Visot, Eugenio
Vives, Eduardo
Vives, Eufemia
Vives, Humberto Luis
Westerband, Maria
Wilson, Juan
Zalbidea, Ana
Zapata, Tomasa
Zayas, Juan
Zayas, Mercedes
Zayas, Ramona

School Pupils, Ponce

Abasa, Carmen Isabel
Acosta, Juana
Alicea, Catalina
Anglada, Felicita
Aponte, Roberto
Arce, Nicolas
Ascencio, Margarita
Atilano, Dolores
Auffant, Jose R.

186

Antonio's Grace

Ayes, Calzada
Baez, Higinio
Balaguer, Agustin
Bartolomei, Jorge
Bauza, Carmen Rita
Bolaño Overmary,
  Camilo
Bonilla, Margarita
Bonilla, Santiago
Bono, Guillermo
Boscana, Celso O.
Burgos, Ramona
Cabassa, Victor
Cambrel, Marciano
Caolo, Felix
Caolo, Maria Luisa
Carbonell, Rafael
Carmona, Maria M.
Casanovas, Aurea
  Isabel
Casanovas, Candida
  Rosa
Castillo, Amelia
Castillo, Ernesto
Cintron, Isabel M.
Clavell Luccas, Pilar
Collazo, Maximo
Colon, Luis Guillermo
Colon, Mariana
Colon, Teresa Elena
Cordero, Pilar
Costas, Luz Maria
De la Concha, Carlos
  Juan
Del Valle, Jose
Delgado, Josefina
Delgado, Juan
Descartes, Radames
Diaz, Jesus
Duprey, Margarita
Duprey, Silvia
Echevarria, Claria
Ferreira, Jose
Ferrer, Frank
Ferrer, Manuel Angel
Figueroa, Carmen
Figueroa, Francisco
Figueroa, Luis Manuel
Figueroa, Margara
Flores, Ana Maria
Flores, Aurelio
Fortier, Antonio
Garcia, Monserrate
Goico, Mercedes

Goico, Pedro
Gomez, Ernestina
Gonzalez, Carmen
Gonzalez, Felisa
Gonzalez, Jose
Gonzalez, Pascual
Gordis, Carlos Juan
Gorge, Rosa Maria
Gutierrez Franqui,
  Victor
Gutierrez, Victor
Guzman, Romualdo
Hernandez, Carlos
  Manuel
Hernandez, Juan H.
Hernandez, Manuela
Izquierdo, Josefina
Jackson, Miguel A.
Jusino, Gloria
Laboy, Osvaldo
Lamoutte, Ramon
Leon, Genaro
Lopez, Raimundo
Maldonado, Juan
Marias, Marta Maria
Martin, Aurelio
Martinez, Luiz M.
Martinez, Miguel
Martinez, Ramon
Martinez, Sixto
Martino, Alerrio
Mayoral, Ernesto
Medina, Ana Maria
Melendez, Antonio
Melendez, Edelmiro
Melero, Francisca
Menchaca, Mercedes
Mendez, Agustin
  Angel
Mercado, Justino
Mercado, Luis
Molina, Ester
Molinas, Nicolasa
Moreno, Carmen
  Maria
Moret, Clotilde
Moura, Esperanza
Muñoz, Francisco
Muñoz, Josefa
Muñoz, Josefina
Nicolai, Margarita
Nuñez, Aracely
Oliver, Maria Luisa
Ortiz y Dominici,

Vicente
Ortiz, Josefina
Ortiz, Leovigildo
Oscios, Jose
Pagan, Auristela
Pastor, Pedro
Penna, Anita
Perez de Suci,
  Guillermo
Perez, Eugenia
Perez, Maximo
Perez, Rosa
Ponti, Guillermina
Puig, Victor Manuel
Puigsubira y Damas
  M., Margarita
Quilbe, Maria
Quiñones, Rafael
Quintana, Joaquin
Quintero, Victor M.
Ramos, Ricardo
Renta, Josefa
Rios, Francisco
Rivera, Arturo
Rivera, Francisco
Rivera, Juan Fidel
Rivera, Mercedes
Rodriguez, Georgina
Rodriguez, Ismael
Rodriguez, Jobita
Rodriguez, Jose
Rodriguez, Marianel
Rodriguez, Otilia
Romero, Rafael
Romero, Teresa
Rosa, Paz
Rosado Rosa, Sergia
Rosado, Josefina
Rosado, Pedro Juan
Ruig, Zoraida
Salas, Elba Maria
Salas, Ernesto
Salas, Esther
Salichs, Pura
Sanchez, Teresa
  Carlota
Santiago, Donatila
Santiago, Juana
Santiago, Rafael
Santiago, Trinidad
Santiago, Vigermina
Segarra, Eladio
Serrano, Teresa
Soto, Aurelia

Tellechea, Enrique
Toledo, Antonio
Torres, Carlos
Torres, Claudina
Torres, Delta Elena
Torres, Eduardo
Torres, Emilia
Torres, Eugenia
Torres, Felita
Torres, Francisco (1)
Torres, Francisco (2)
Torres, Joaquin
Torres, Jose
Torres, Jose Angel
Torres, Josefa
Torres, Maria Luisa
Torres, Ramona
Ubedes, Honorio
Valentiny, Felicita
Vazquez, Agripina
Vazquez, Luis Jaime
Vega, Dolores Maria
Vegas, Emiliano
Vergne, Amadis
Vila, Providencia
Villaronga, Octavio

School Students, Ponce

Acevedo, Josefa
Acrce Loran, Remigio
Aguirre, Nicolas R.
Alameda, Ramona
Albelo, Antonio
Albors, Ernesto
Alcala, Francisco
Alequin, Augusto R.
Alfonso, Ana
Alfonso, C.
Alomar, Jose A.
Alustiza, Julio
Alvarado, Elisa
Alvarado, Etelvina
Alvarado, Rafael
Alvarez, Carmen
Alvarez, Eduardo (Jr.)
Alvarez, Tomas
Alvarez. Luis
Antinez, Francisco
Aparicio Aparicio, A.

187

Aponte, Juan
Arcilagos, Pedro
Arias, Domingo
Arias, Livia
Arizmendi, Angela
Arjona, Rosaura
Armstrong, Joaquin E. (Jr.)
Armstrong, Tomas
Arroyo, Guillermo
Arroyo, Luis N.
Arroyo, Maria Teresa
Arroyo, Rosa Maria
Arroyo, Tomas
Asencio, Esteban
Astol, Eugenio
Atiles, Dolores
Atiles, Guillermo
Atiles, Paquita
Auffant, Anita
Auffant, Maria
Auffant, Pedro Juan
Aviles, Carmen
Aviles, Carmen Maria
Ayala, Enrique
Ayala, Luis A.
Azorez, Concepcion
Badillo, Evaristo
Baez, Adela
Baez, Agripina
Baez, Felix
Baez, Miguel
Baez, Rosa Maria
Bajandas, Elma Velez
Ballan, Ana J.
Bandas Espada, Jose
Barbosa, Ana Cidela
Barbosa, Jose Vicente
Barnes Colon, Ines
Barnes, America
Barrios, Flerida
Bartolomey, Paula
Basan, Jesus
Bauza, Carmelo
Bauza, Ermelinda
Bauza, Marina
Beitia, Luis
Belfort, Dolores
Bello, Orlando
Beltran, Incocencia
Beltran, Paquita
Beltran, Ricardo J.
Benet, Ramona
Berdeguer, Pura

Divina
Berenguer, Nelia M.
Berlingeri, Maria
Bernal, Juana
Bigas, Jesus
Blaimayar, Juan
Blay, Justa
Bonapart, Carlos F.
Boscana, Carmen A.
Bosch, Joaquin
Bota, Vicente
Bougal, Etervina
Braulio Perez, Carmen
Brignoni, Carlos
Burgos, Antonia
Buscaglia, Rafael
Caballero, Carlos M.
Caballero, Luis
Cabassa, Jose A.
Cabasssa, Antonia
Cabrera, Antonio
Cambretin, Eufemia C.
Campos, Francisco
Campos, Jeronimo
Campos, Jose Miguel
Campos, Maria Mercedes
Campos, Rafael
Canino, Conchita
Cano, Isabel
Carcilagos, Marina
Cardona, Pedro A.
Carrasquillo, Luis
Carrero, Generoso
Carrero, Maria Avelina
Cartagena, Carlos
Casalduc, Felipe A.
Casanova, Francisco
Casiano, Jose
Castaings, Presbitera
Castaings, Carmen
Castaings, Margarita
Castellar, Francisca
Castells, Enrique
Castillo, Elisa
Castillo, Ernesto
Castro, Juan
Castro, Luis
Castro, Luisa
Castro, Victoria
Catala, Julia
Catinchi, Manuel
Catinchi, Pedro J.
Cedo, Rafael

Ceppenkummer, Emma
Cestas, Oscar
Charbonier, Justina
Chardon, Pablo
Christian, Jose L.
Christian, Maria
Cintron, Cruz
Cintron, Dolores
Cintron, Jose A.
Cintron, Luisa
Cintron, Olivero
Cintron, Pedro
Clavell, Luis G.
Clavell, Carlos J.
Clavell, Manuel
Clavell, Roberta
Cocran, Leonor
Coll, Juan L.
Collazo, Adoracion
Colon, Albertina
Colon, Antonio
Colon, Benito
Colon, Carmen Cecilia
Colon, Erasmo
Colon, Fernando Luis
Colon, Gloria M.
Colon, Jose Luis
Colon, Natividad
Colon, Rafael
Colon, Ramiro Luis
Colon, Ulpiano
Colon, Vicenta
Colon, Victorina
Comas, Caridad
Comulada, Carmen M.
Concepcion, Angel
Concepcion, Zamora
Concha, Jose
Conde, Maria Cristina
Conde, Maria Elena
Conesa, Julio M.
Contreras, Elena
Contreras, Tomas
Coppin, Carlos J.
Coquias Muñiz, Carlos
Coquias, Ignacio M.
Coquias, Teresa
Cordero, Carlos
Cordero, Francisco
Cordero, Rosario
Cordova, Estefana
Cordova, Giorgina
Cornier, Maria

Correa, Julia
Correa, Victoria
Cortada, Rafael
Cortes, Felicita
Costa, Petra
Costas, Carlos M.
Costas, Luis Heraclio
Costas, Raul
Cristian, Juana
Cruz, Jacinta
Cruz, Margarita
Cuberge, Juan F.
Cuestas, Vicente
Dalmau, Eloisa
Dapena Layuna, Joaquin
De Jesus, Maria L.
Del Campo, Julio
Del Rio, Carlos
Del Valle, Carlos M.
Del Valle, Eduardo
Del Valle, Maria Teresa
Delgado, Gloria Maria
Delgado, Julia
Descartes, Antonia
Dessus, Luisa
Dessus, Ramona
Devis, Emilio
Deynes, Juanita
Deynes, Paquita
Diana, Constanza
Diaz Brinck, Ursula
Diaz, Antonia
Diaz, Caridad
Diaz, Evangelina
Diaz, Jose
Diaz, Ramona
Diaz, Rosa Maria
Dijol, Maria Cristina
Dion, Ines
Droz, Divina
Droz, Maria M.
Duran, Bienvenido
Duran, Marcelina
Duran, Maria Luisa
Duran, Pedro
Duran, Sarah Ma.
Echevarria, Josefina
Echevarria, Providencia
Esbri, Jose Enrique
Escale, Francisco
Escribano, Luis E.

188

Escribano, Maria Teresa
Espinet, Dolores
Exposito, Manuel I.
Faberlle, Pedro
Falcon, Enrique
Farinacci, Carmen
Farinacci, Pedro J.
Farinacci, Virgenmina
Feliciano Maldonado, Fortunata
Feliciano, Victor
Fernandez, Antonia
Fernandez, Antonio
Fernandez, Aurea Maria
Fernandez, Maria Luisa
Fernandez, Victoria
Ferraiola, Maria
Ferre, Jose A.
Ferrer, Adela
Ferrer, Lucila
Ferrer, Mazimina
Ferrer, Rosa Maria
Ferri, Louis Alberto
Figueroa y Ayala, Roman
Figueroa, Carlos W.
Figueroa, Hortensia
Figueroa, Julio
Foro, Antonio B.
Fortier Mendez, Aida
Fortier, Carmen Maria
Fournier, Guillermina
Fraguada Rivera, Raul
Fraguada, Francisco
Fraile, Luis
Franceschi, Enrique
Franceschi, Mercedes
Franco, Augusto
Franco, Providencia
Freyre, Magdalena
Gallardo, Carlos
Gandia, Isabel M.
Gandia, Maria
Garay, Juan
Garcia, Carmen Maria
Garcia, Dolores
Garcia, Fernando
Garcia, Jose A.
Garcia, Josefa
Garcia, Juan (Jr.)
Garcia, Juan C.

Garcia, Luis
Garcia, Manolo
Garcia, Rafaela
Garcia, Tomasita
Gari, Maria Luisa
Gari, Rosa
Garraton Serbia, Jose
Gaston, Carmen
Gaston, Francisco
Gaudino, Luz Maria
Gautier, Angel
Gautier, Georgina
Gautier, Rafael
Geli Collazo, Concha
Geraldino, Adela
Geraldino, Gustavo
Ghrashan, Pedro
Gines, Laura
Ginestre Bauza, Americo
Ginestre, Aureao
Giol, Maria
Giraldez, Esperanza
Giron, Gloria America
Giron, Manuel
Gispert, Isabel
Gomez y Ruiz de Porras, Cecilia
Gomez y Ruiz de Porras, Rosario
Gomez, Carmen
Gomez, Dolores
Gomez, Jaime N.
Gomez, Juan L.
Gomez, Rodolfo
Gomez, Susana
Gonzalez, Baltasara
Gonzalez, Carlos Juan
Gonzalez, Carmen Elisa
Gonzalez, Conchita
Gonzalez, Eduardo
Gonzalez, Fernando
Gonzalez, Flora
Gonzalez, Jose A.
Gonzalez, Jose J.
Gonzalez, Juan B.
Gonzalez, Maria Cristina
Gonzalez, Modesta
Gonzalez, Ramon
Gonzalez, Rosa Maria
Gonzalez, Tomasa
Gotay, Luisa Maria

Gracia, Tomas
Graciany, Hector
Gual, Francisca
Guerra, Francisca
Guerra, Francisco
Guilves, Herminio
Gutierrez Davila, Belen
Gutierrez, Isidro
Gutierrez, Roman
Gutierrez, Santos
Guzman, Esther
Guzman, Joaquin L.
Guzman, Julia J.
Hansen, Luisa
Hanson, Pugh
Hassant, Aurelio
Henrique, Pastor
Herdman, Clodomiro
Herdman, Juan G.
Hernandez Valera, Josefina
Hernandez, Antonio
Hernandez, Celestino
Hernandez, Domingo
Hernandez, Mercedes
Hernandez, Onelia
Hernandez, Paulita
Hoyos, Guillermo
Hoyos, Jose
Iriarte, Emilia
Irigotti, Carmen
Irizarri, Eleticia
Irizarry, Jose
Jackson, Isaac
Jackson, Maria Teresa
Jaubert, Francisco
Jeissonier, Maria M.
Jeissonier, Maria Teresa
Joubert, Haydee
Joubert, Luis F.
Jusino, Emilio
Jusino, Ubaldino
La Torre, Cruz
La Torre, Lorenza
Laboy, Rufina
Lamoutte, Elias
Lamoutte, Emilia
Lanza, Paquita
Larreguiz, Francisca
Leandry, Jorge
Lebron, Jose
Lebron, Ramon

Leon, Maria Luisa
Lespier, Lillian
Limardo, Miguel
Llorens, Noel
Llorente, Joseffa
Lomas, Ramon
Lonychamps, Luisa
Lopez, Gerardo
Lopez, Olimpio
Luciano, Carmelo E.
Lugo, Eduardo
Lugo, Josefina
Lugo, Marcelino
Machado, Anita
Malaret, Carlos Manuel
Maldonado, Amelia
Maldonado, Candida
Maldonado, Isabel
Maldonado, Jose
Maldonado, Juanita
Marin, Carmen Maria
Mariota, Eduardo
Mariota, Isabel
Mariota, Luz I.
Mariotta, Jose
Marquez, Adela
Marquez, Julio
Marti, Eugenia
Martin P., Enriqueta
Martin, Arsenio
Martin, Rafael
Martines, Josefa
Martinez Zeron, Pilar
Martinez, Angelina
Martinez, Carmen Maria
Martinez, Carmen Rosa
Martinez, Consuelo
Martinez, Domingo
Martinez, Eduardo
Martinez, Gertrudis
Martinez, Guillermo (1)
Martinez, Guillermo (2)
Martinez, Isabel
Martinez, Juan
Martinez, Juan J.
Martinez, Mariana
Martinez, Patria
Martinez, Pedro
Martinez, Rafael

Martinez, Rosaura
Martinez, Zenobia
Mateo, Maria Lucia
Matos, Carlos R.
Mattei, Angela
Mattei, Julio
Mattei, Olimpia
Mattei, Rosa
Mattei, Zenaida
Maura, Fernando
Maura, Susana
Mayoral, Joaquin
Mayoral, Jose A.
Mayoral, Mercedes
Medina, Carlos J.
Medina, Gloria
Medina, Ida Sofia
Medina, Iraida M.
Medina, Juan (1)
Medina, Juan (2)
Melendez Puig, Josefa
Mendez Mercado, Jose
Mendez Mercado,
  Pedro
Mendez, Carlota
Mendez, Rodolfo
Menendez, Candida
Mercado, Arturo
Mercado, Carmen (1)
Mercado, Carmen (2)
Mercado, Carmen
  Maria
Mercado, Carmen
  Matilde
Mercado, Concepcion
Mercado, Fausta
Mercado, Frank
Mercado, Pedro A.
Mercado, Rafael
Merle, Emilio A.
Merle, Modesto
Mesorana, Oscar
Mierks, Matilda
Miguens, America M.
Mirailh, Manuel
Miranda, Emilio
Miranda, Francisco
Miranola, Juana
Mojica, Carlota
Moler, Carmen
Molina, Antonio
Molina, Juan de Dios
Monllor, Carlos E.
Monllor, Herminia

Monsanto, Ana Maria
Montalvo, America
Montalvo, Aoda M.
Morales, Benigno
Morales, Enrique
Morales, Gabriel
Morales, Isabel
Morales, Rufina
Moras B., A. Teresa
Moraza, Gasper
Morel Carvajal,
  Vicente
Moreno, Mercedes
Moret, Matilde
Moullor, Ramon
Moura, Eugenia
Moura, P. Rafael
Munera, Narciso
Munet, Rosa
Muñiz, Carmen
Muñiz, Isabel
Muñiz, Julia
Muñiz, Paco
Muñoz, Jaime
Murcet, Felix
Murillo, Leonor
Muriota, Ines
Napoleon, Juan B.
Napoleones, Tomasa
Napoleonis,
  Guillermina
Nazario, Angela
Nazario, Gregoria
Nazario, Maria
Nazario, Rafael
Negron, Amelia
Negron, Carlos J.
Negron, Jose M.
Negron, Maria Luisa
Net, Ramon
Nicolai, Emeterio
Nicole, Luis Joaquin
Nieves, Gloria M.
Nieves, Juan Ignacio
Noriega, Antonio
Noriega, Jose
Noriega, Teresa
O'Sheah, Adalina
Olivar Amill, Delfina
Oliver, Magdalena
Oliver, Margarita
Oliver, Pedro Jose
Olivieri, Rosario
Olustiza, Toñita

Oppenheimer,
  Fermina A.
Oppenheimer,
  Lutgarda
Oppenhimer, Regino
Orihuela, Jose C.
Orsini, Carmen
Orsini, Pedro Juan
Orta, Dolores
Orta, Palmira
Orta, Toñita M.
Ortiz de Landazuri,
  Maria
Ortiz, Carlos J.
Ortiz, Eugenia
Ortiz, Francisco
Ortiz, Isabel
Ortiz, Josefina
Ortiz, Matilde
Ortiz, Providencia
Ortiz, Rosario
Orvinas, Basilisa
Ossini, Mercedes
Otero, Carmen Maria
Oxios, Luz Maria
Pacheco, Armando
Pacheco, Jose R.
Pacheco, Laura
Padilla, Clotilde
Padilla, Concepcion
Padilla, Cristobal
Padilla, Tomas A.
Padin, Consuelo
Pagan, Amelia
Pagan, Arcadio
Pagan, Carmen Maria
Pagan, Gloria M.
Pagan, Ramon Luis
Pages, Rosa Maria
Palmer, Ramiro V.
Palmira Mictil,
  Carmen
Pani, Elisa
Paoli, Aida
Paoli, Crescencia
Paoli, Felix
Paradis, Conchita
Paradis, Mary
Pardo, Victoria
Parisi, Juan B.
Pariso, Julio
Pastor, Antoñita
Patteine, Carlos M.
  (Jr.)

Peña, Carlos J.
Peña, Isidro R.
Perez Bermudez,
  Antonia
Perez, Adela Maria
Perez, Asela
Perez, Carmen
Perez, Carmen M.
Perez, Carmen Maria
Perez, Guadalupe
Perez, Jorge
Perez, Josefa
Perez, Ramon
Pierluisi, Guillermo
Pino, Primitiva
Piris, Rafael
Ponce de Leon,
  Margarita
Pons, Pablo
Principe, Editta B.
Principe, Maria Luisa
Principe, Oscaldo J.
Puente, Oscar
Puig, Lolita
Puigsubira, Enrique
Puigsubria, Angelina
Puigsubria, Mercedes
Pujol, Miguel (Jr.)
Pujol, Catalina
Purcell, Fecita
Purcell, Juanita
Quero, Hortensia
Quesada, Pedro J.
Quesada, Santiago
Quiñones, Ana Elena
Quiñones, Carmen
Quiñones, Carolina
Quiñones, Clarisa
Quiñones, Maria
  Cristina
Quiñones, Pedro
  Eduvigis
Quintana, Angela
Quintana, Enrique
Quintana, Francisco
Quintana, Josefina
Quintana, Saturnino
Ramirez Quiñones,
  Humberto
Ramirez, Carmen
Ramirez, Fernando
Ramirez, Frank
Ramirez, Jesus
Ramirez, Jorge I.

Ramirez, Laura C.
Ramis, Antonio B.
Ramis, Bartolo
Ramis, Margarita
Ramos de Anaya, Manuel
Ramos, Luisa
Ramos, Maria I.
Ramos, Ramon Maria
Ramu, Luis (Jr.)
Ramu, Luisa
Ramu, Rosa M.
Rangel Lopez, Hilario
Rangel Lopez, Jose Vicente
Rangel, Cayetano
Rangel, Rafael
Rebollar, Manolo
Renaud, America
Renaud, Modesta
Rentas, Ana
Rinaldi, Cecilia
Rios, Alberto
Rios, Aurora
Rios, Esteban
Rios, Ramon
Rios, Tomas
Rivas, Rafael
Rivera Ramos, Leonor
Rivera, Ana
Rivera, Angel
Rivera, Angelica
Rivera, Antonia (1)
Rivera, Antonia (2)
Rivera, Antonia (3)
Rivera, Benigno
Rivera, Candelaria
Rivera, Carmen Maria
Rivera, Esperanza
Rivera, Jose
Rivera, Maria Luisa
Rivera, Providencia
Rivera, Ramon
Rivera, Santiago
Rivera, Teresa
Robles, Paula
Roche, Josefa
Rodas Alvarez, Lila
Rodriguez Mattei, Pepita
Rodriguez Tizol, Antonia
Rodriguez V., Rafael
Rodriguez, Amparo

Rodriguez, Ana
Rodriguez, Ana Josefa
Rodriguez, Antonia
Rodriguez, Arcadio
Rodriguez, Blanca
Rodriguez, Candido
Rodriguez, Conchita
Rodriguez, Consuelo
Rodriguez, Diego
Rodriguez, Dolores Gomez
Rodriguez, Domingo
Rodriguez, Edmundo
Rodriguez, Elvira
Rodriguez, Emilia (1)
Rodriguez, Emilia (2)
Rodriguez, Ernesto
Rodriguez, Esperanza
Rodriguez, Feliciana
Rodriguez, Feliz A.
Rodriguez, Feliz C.
Rodriguez, Florencio
Rodriguez, Genoveba
Rodriguez, Gialda
Rodriguez, Ines
Rodriguez, Jose (1)
Rodriguez, Jose (2)
Rodriguez, Jose Joaquin
Rodriguez, Josefa
Rodriguez, Josefina
Rodriguez, Julia
Rodriguez, Leopoldo
Rodriguez, Lucila
Rodriguez, Maria
Rodriguez, Moserrate
Rodriguez, Octavio
Rodriguez, Policarpia
Rodriguez, Rafael
Rodriguez, Rosa Maria
Rodriguez, Saturnina
Rodriguez, Sergio M.
Rodriguez, Tomasita
Rogers, Erasmo
Roig, Celeste
Romaguera, Antonio
Roman, Juanito
Romero, Antonia
Romero, Ernesto
Romero, Joaquina
Romero, Mercedes
Roque, Honoria
Rosado, Marcial
Rosado, Moserrate

Rosado, Providencia
Rosario, Benigno
Rosich, Clara
Rovera, Rosario
Rubio, Lucia
Rubit, Modesto
Ruiz, Belen
Ruiz, Carmen G.
Ruiz, Juan
Ruiz, Julio
Rullan, Ana Arcelia
Sabater, Jesus
Sabater, Maria I.
Sabater, Petra
Sabater, Vicente
Sacarello, Adelaida
Sacarello, Ovidio
Salano, Maximino
Salas Arce, Carmen Maria
Salas, Candida R.
Salas, Jose A.
Salas, Providencia
Salazar, Jose A.
Salazar, Luisa
Salichs, Juan
Salicks, Elena
Salvatella, America
Sanchez, Candida
Sanchez, Carmen
Sanchez, Eduvigis
Sanchez, Jose
Sanchez, Lorenzo
Sanchez, Maria Antonia
Sandoval, Emilio
Sanjurjo, Josefa
Sanjurjo, Maria Ursula
Santana, Herminia
Santana, Ines
Santiago, Antonia (1)
Santiago, Antonia (2)
Santiago, Antonia (3)
Santiago, Carlos P.
Santiago, Carmen
Santiago, Casimiro
Santiago, Delfin
Santiago, Enrique
Santiago, Estrella M.
Santiago, Gorgina
Santiago, Guadalupe (1)
Santiago, Guadalupe (2)

Santiago, Herminio
Santiago, Isabel
Santiago, Isabel M.
Santiago, Juan
Santiago, Juanita
Santiago, Luis E.
Santiago, Maria Teresa
Santiago, Mercedes (1)
Santiago, Mercedes (2)
Santiago, Pedro (1)
Santiago, Pedro (2)
Santiago, Rafael Rodriguez
Santori, Antonio
Santori, Catalina
Santori, Maria L.
Sapia, Salvador
Schmidt, Concepcion
Schorate, Mario
Seda, Maria T.
Segarra, Felipe
Serra, Palmira
Serrano, Valentin
Shillet, Segurin
Shillet, Sixta
Sierra, Domingo
Silva, Amelia
Silva, Elena
Soler, Julio
Solivan, Carmen
Soltero, Rafael
Soltero, Ramon
Soto, Antonio
Soto, Oscar
Souffront, Emma
Souffront, Luz M.
Suarez, Carmen Maria
Suci, Lucila P.
Suci, Nicolasa
Suro, Jorge
Tarasco, Cecilio
Tarasco, Juan
Tardo, Luisa
Tarrato, Altagracia
Tarrio, Petra
Tedo, Jaime
Teissonnier, Carlos J.
Teissonniere, Luis A.
Thillet, America
Tirado, Marina
Tomasini, Maria
Tormes, Rosa

Torres Andrade, Modesto
Torres Grau, Maria
Torres Ortiz, Mariano
Torres, Amelia
Torres, Antonia
Torres, Carlos Manuel
Torres, Carmen
Torres, Claudio
Torres, Concepcion
Torres, Constanza
Torres, Edusia
Torres, Emilio
Torres, Enrique (1)
Torres, Enrique (2)
Torres, Epifanio
Torres, Eugenio
Torres, Gregorio (1)
Torres, Gregorio (2)
Torres, Isaias
Torres, Luisa
Torres, Margarita
Torres, Maria Teresa
Torres, Maria
Torres, Mercedes
Torres, Oquelinda
Torres, Primitivo
Torres, Quisqueya
Torres, Vicente
Torruella, Ines
Torruella, Jose A.
Torruella, Providencia
Torruellas, Pedro J,
Torruellas, Santiago
Tricoche, Ana J.
Tricoche, Lusila
Tristani, Victoria
Usera, Elpidio
Valdivieso, Fidela
Valdivieso, Rosario
Valladares, Manuel A.
Valle Leandri, Sarah
Valls, Desideria
Valls, Maria Teresa
Valpais, Aniseto
Varela, Maria
Vazquez Rodriguez, Aurelia
Vazquez, America
Vazquez, Armando
Vazquez, Carmen
Vazquez, Demetrio
Vazquez, Domingo
Vazquez, Guadalupe

Vazquez, Jaime L.
Vazquez, Jorge E.
Vazquez, Josefa
Vazquez, Juan
Vazquez, Julio
Vazquez, Lorenzo
Vazquez, Maximino
Vega, Gilberto
Vega, Jose A.
Veglio, Guadalupe
Velazquez, Constanza
Velazquez, Enrique
Velazquez, Maria
Velazquez, Pablo
Velez, Casimira
Velez, Cristina
Velez, Manuela
Vendrell, Jorge
Ventura, Americo
Ventura, Jose Antonio
Ventura, Teresa
Verdejo, Josefina
Vergne, Maria Mercedes
Victor, Luz M.
Vidal, Elisa
Vidal, Francisco
Vidal, Julieta
Vidal, Manuel
Vidal, Petro
Vidart Lopez, Rafael
Vidaurre, Raphael
Vilaro, Juan
Vilella, Marilde
Villafaña, Adolfo
Villafaña, Jaime
Villali, Crispulo
Villali, Josefa
Villamarzo, Eulalia
Villamarzo, Maria
Villamarzo, Modesta
Villamil, Olimpio
Villamil, Pedro Juan
Villaronga, Arturo
Virela, Eduardo
Visot, Luis
Visot, Rafael
Vives, Carmen
Vives, Josefina
Vives, Maria
Vogel, Emma
Wys, Manuel
Zayas, Clotilde
Zayas, Purificacion

School Students, Liga de la Bondad ("Benevolence League"), Ponce

Agostini, Bartolome
Aguirre, Aurora
Alfonso, Agustina
Alfonso, Felix Jaime
Alfonso, Petra
Alicea, Luisa
Alicea, Ramon
Allizu, Fernando
Altrech, Buenvenido
Alustiza, Ramon
Alvarado, Eduardo
Alvarado, Francisca
Archeval, Micaela
Arias, Carmen Luicila
Arizmendi, Modesto
Arjona, Homero
Arjona, Roberto
Armstrong, Aristides
Armstrong, Jose Angel
Arroyo, Angel
Arroyo, Benigna
Artesona, Asuncion
Asencio, Juanita
Astol, Ana Aida
Auffant, Roman
Aviles, Antonio
Badella, Pedro
Badillo, Demetria
Baez, Nerita
Barquet, Jose
Barral, Agustina
Barral, Rosa Maria
Barros, Eugenio
Basanta, Isabel
Bello, Inocencia
Beltran, Maria M.
Bigay, Adelaida
Bigay, Cruz
Bigay, Ramon
Blasini, Emelina
Caballero, Marcelino
Campo, Enrique Juan
Campos, Antonio
Campos, Esther
Capacete, Afortunado

Carret, Maria Mercedes
Castaign, Ramon
Castaing, Antonia
Castaing, Epifania
Castaing, Ezequiel
Castaing, Mercedes
Castell, Zoraida
Castro, Josefa
Castro, Rafael
Catala, Luis
Cedo, Maria Teresa
Chamorro, Maria
Chavier, Luis
Chetrancolo, Celso
Cintron, Guillermo
Cintron, Lorenzo
Collazo, Natividad
Collazo, Rafael
Colon, Adela
Colon, Antonia
Colon, Enrique
Colon, Ernesto
Colon, Jorge
Colon, Josefa
Colon, Manuela
Colon, Maria Cristina
Colon, Miguel
Colon, Pablo
Colon, Ramon
Comulada, Rafael M.
Conde, Vicente
Contreras, Emma
Coppin, Miguel
Cora, Maria Jesus
Cortes, Juan
Cortes, Maria Teresa
Cortes, Paula
Coto, Francisca
Coto, Vicenta
Cruz, Avelino
Cruz, Bartolo
Cruz, Eustacio
Cruz, Fernando
Cruz, Rufina
Dalmau, Marina
Delgado, Guillermo
Delgado, Julio
Deya, Isidora M.
Diaz, Georgina
Diaz, Luis
DiBerse, Esteban
Dones, Jose M.
Dukeron, Genaro

Enrique, Agustin
Enriquez, Antonio
Espinet, Antonia
Esteva, Carlos
Fagot, Carmen M.
Fagot, Emilio
Falcon, Luis
Feliciano, Rafael
Fernandez, Ramon
Ferr, Carlos
Figueroa, Cruz
Figueroa, Luis
Figueroa, Maria
Figueroa, Tiburcio
Freyre, Feliz
Garay, Felix
Garcia, Agustin
Garcia, Daniel
Garcia, German
Garcia, Luis A.
Garcia, Rosa
Garcia, Santiago
Gaston, Angelina
Gelabert, Luis
Geraldine, Carlos
Gomez, Enrique
Gomez, Manuela
Gonzalez, Emiliano
Gonzalez, Isabel
Gonzalez, Rafael
Gonzalez, Teresa
Gordils, Angelica
Gracia, Gregoria
Grau, Manolo
Grau, Maximino
Guerra, Josefina
Guilbe, Luis
Gustavo, Alfaro
Guzman, Pedro
Hardouin, Jorge
Hernandez, Arcadio
Hernandez, Esther
Hernandez, Florencio
Hernandez, Luisa
Herrera, Esperanza
Higuera, Alejandro
Irizarry, Ana Maria
Jesus, Soledad
Julia, Jose (Jr.)
Juratiz, Maria Eugenia
Labarthe, Pedro Juan
Laboy, Lucas
Laga, Eladia
Lago, Francisco

Larriu, Teresa
Lasalde, Marcia
Leadre, Eladia
Lebron, Esther
Lebron, Matilde
Leon, Julio M.
Leon, Miguel Angel
Limardo, Antonio
Llorens, Humberto
Llorens, Luis
Lopez, Ramona
Lorenzi, Jose M.
Lounzi, Luis
Lugo, Irene
Maldonado, Elisa
Maldonado, Luis
Maldonado, Pedro
Marrero, Enrique
Martinez, Armando
Martinez, Atanasio
Martinez, Emerita
Martinez, Juan
Martinez, Julio
Martinez, Manuel
Martinez, Maria
Martinez, Olimpia
Martinez, Pedro
Martinez, Perfecta
Martinez, Rosario
Martinez, Severo
Mayoral, Juan E.
Mendez, Laura
Mercado, Julio
Molina, Ana E.
Molina, Concepcion
Monllor, Ines
Monllor, Margarita
Monllor, Tomas
Morales, Carmen
Morales, Enriqueta
Morales, Julia
Morales, Julio
Moreno, Laura
Munet, Aurora
Munet, Jaime
Muñoz, Feliz
Muñoz, Juanita
Muñoz, Justo P.
Murillo, Rafael
Nazario, Carmen Julia
Negron, Carlos
Negron, Catalina
Nieves, Isabel
Noriega, Crecencia

Noriega, Genaro A.
Nuñez, Guillermo
Nuñez, Lidia
Olivieri, Clementina
Oquendo, Tomasa
Orihuela, Cristobal
Ortiz, Domingo
Ortiz, Fernando
Ortiz, Gracia Maria
Overman, Feliz
Ozores, Antonio
Ozores, Luis
Ozores, Paquita
Ozorez, Enrique
Pabon, Providencia
Pacheco, Fernando
Pacheco, Paquita
Padilla, Magdalena
Pagan, Abigail
Pagan, Epifania
Pagan, Francisco
Pagan, Jose Antonio
Pagan, Petra
Pagan, Ramona
Palacios, Emilia
Palermo, Irene
Palermo, Josefa
Palmer, Josefa
Parsi, Paquita
Pasarell, Rosa Maria
Paydu, Eleuteria
Perez, Francisco (1)
Perez, Francisco (2)
Perez, Maria L.
Perez, Urbano
Perqui, Francisco
Pesqui, Ana
Pow, Carlos J.
Prieto Vila, Benigno
Prieto, Isabel Maria
Principe, Miguel A.
Puertos, Luis A.
Purcell, Petra
Ramirez, Jose Angel
Ramirez, Vicente
Ramis, Andres
Ramos, Ramon
Rangel, Felipe
Rangel, Julio
Rangel, Manuela
Rentas, Amalio
Rios, Dolores
Rios, Jorge
Rios, Josefa

Rivas, Guillermo
Rivas, Leonor
Rivera, Adela
Rivera, Eufemia
Rivera, Filomena
Rivera, Guillermina
Rivera, Mercedes (1)
Rivera, Mercedes (2)
Rivera, Miguel
Rivera, Regina
Rivera, Victoria
Robles, Aida, Maria
Robles, Margarita
Roche, Ana Maria
Roches, Lola
Rodriguez Monserrate
Rodriguez, Alcides
Rodriguez, Carmen
  Maria
Rodriguez,
  Concepcion
Rodriguez, Consuelo
Rodriguez, Eva
Rodriguez, Francisco
  (1)
Rodriguez, Francisco
  (2)
Rodriguez, Gavina
Rodriguez, Gloria
Rodriguez, Jose
Rodriguez, Josefa (1)
Rodriguez, Josefa (2)
Rodriguez, Manuela
  (1)
Rodriguez, Manuela
  (2)
Rodriguez, Marcelina
Rodriguez, Maximina
Rodriguez, Petra
Rodriguez, Petronila
  (1)
Rodriguez, Petronila
  (2)
Rodriguez, Rita
Rodriguez, Rosa
Rodriguez, Tomasita
Rojas, Margarita
Romaguera, Rafael
Roman, Antonia
Roman, Rafael
Rosado, Jaime
Rosado, Juan
Rosado, Sixto
Rosaly, Joaquin

Rosario, Beraro
Rubianes, Andrea
Ruiz, Carlos
Ruiz, Celestino
Ruiz, Francisca
Ruiz, Justo
Ruiz, Maria
Salop, Maria
Sanchez, Eugenia
Sanchez, Manuel
Santiago, Flo
Santiago, Georgina
Santiago, Pablo
Santiago, Panchita
Santiago, Pedro
Santori, Julio
Santos, Isabel
Seda, Cecilio
Serra, Carlota
Serrano, Erasmo
Serrano, Providencia
Serrano, Rosalina
Solis, Santia
Soltero, Rafael
Sotomayor, Pedro A.
Stanley, Adela
Texeira, Petra
Texidor, Luis
Tizol, Luz
Toro, Jose Angel
Torres, Angelina
Torres, Antonio
Torres, Carmen
Torres, Diego
Torres, Eustoquio G.
Torres, Lucas
Torres, Mariana
Torres, Pedro
Torres, Reinaldo, D.
Torruella, Luisa
Tous, Jose
Usera, Ramon
Valencia, Juan
Valentin, Jose A.
Vazquez, Maria Luisa
Vazquez, Pablo
Vazquez, Pedro
Vazquez, Ramon
Vazquez, Rita
Vega, Clara
Vega, Clodomiro
Veitia, Francisco
Velazquez, Andreita
Velez, Jose

Velez, Luis
Velez, Ramon
Ventura, Victoria
Vidal, Mariano R.
Villa, Prudencio
Villafañe, Cresencia
Villamarzo, Francisco
Villamarzo, Manuel
Villanueva, Jose Maria
Villaronga, Mariano
Vives, Pedro Juan

Public School Children, Puerto Rico

Puerto Rico Public
School Children
(Telegram)

School Students, Rincon

Rincon Students and
Mayor (Telegram)

Bancroft School, Rio Grande

1st Grade

Arroyo, Dolores
Ayala, Bonifacia
Benitez, Bernarda
Betancourt, Luis
Calderon, Pedro
Caraballo, Elena
Cardona, Jose
Carrillo, Rafael
Castro, Nicolas
Cepeda, Cristino
Cirino, Julia
Colon, Tomas
Cruz, Bienvenida
Cruz, Erasmo
De Jesus, Emilia
Del Valle, Eduardo

Diaz, Nevada
Estrella, Ramon
Figueroa, Carmelo
Franco, Henry
Franco, Juana
Garcia, Jose Manuel
Gonzalez, Francisca
Hernandez, Pablo
Maysonet, Clemencia
Maysonet, Pedro
Mendez, Carmen
  Maria
Millan, Amparo
Mojica, Julia
Olivo, Domingo
Orta, Carmen
Ortiz, Todora
Padilla, Eriberta
Paz, Herminio
Perez, Pedro
Pizarro, Martin
Ramos, Aejo
Reyes, Mercedes
Rios, Esperanza
Rivera, Ernesto
Roble, Carlos
Rodriguez, Adolfo
Rodriguez, Antonio
Rodriguez, Fortunato
Rodriguez,
  Guadaberta
Rodriguez, Guillermo
Rosario, Jose Maria
Salgado, Dolores
Santiago, Socorro
Siaca, Margarita
Vente, Ramon
Viera, Ramona
Vila, Jose Antonio
Yaraas, Carmen Luz

2nd Grade

Alejandro, Raquel
Arroyo, Ernesto
Baldrich, America
Baldrich, Benigno
Baldrich, Enrique
Baralt, Rafael
Betancourt, Lupe
Burgos, Benigna
Calderon, Alfredo
Calderon, Pilar

Calderon, Porto
Carpes, Emilio
Carrillo, Antonio
Cialles, Ana
Correa, Teodoro
Corsino, Maria J.
Cruz, Clara
De Jesus, Carlos
De Jesus, Juan
De Jesus, Mariana
De Jesus, Pedro
Delgado, Eva Luz
Esther Calderon,
  Maria
Figueroa, Victoria
Flores, Higinio
Fre, Victoria
Fuente, Maria B.
Fuentes, Miguel
Garcia, Antonio
Garcia, Maria M.
Ilarraza, Angela
Mas, Cruz
Medina, Sogia
Mojica, Francisca
Mojica, Mariana
Morales, Federico
Morillo, Maria M.
Orellano, Feliz
Ortiz, Pedro
Osorio, Lorenzo
Osorio, Teresa
Padilla, Martina
Padilla, Ramon
Paz, Santiago
Perez, Flor de Maria
Pizarro, Federico
Quigley, Maria
Ramos, Ana M.
Reyes, Rogelia
Rivera, Adelaida
Rivera, Martin
Rodriguez, Aurora
Rodriguez, Jermina
Rodriguez, Lucila
Rosario, Ramon
Saegaard, Aida
Sanes, Armando
Santos, Fela
Villafañe, Josefa
Vivas, Luis

. . .

Antonio's Grace

3rd Grade

Arroyos, Eloisa
Ayala, Elias
Baldrich, Jose
Benitez, M. Dominga
Benoy, Aurora
Carrillo, Ernesto
Cepeda, Erasmo
De Jesus, Concha
Del Valle, Aradin
Diaz, Adolfo
Diaz, Rafaela
Ferrer, Luisa M.
Figueroa, Eusebia
Franco, Abraham
Franco, Petra
Fuentes, Julio
Garcia, Josefa
Maissonet, Francisco
Mateos, Antonia
Orta, Mario
Otero, Federico
Perez, Julia
Pescador y Lopez, Luis
Pimentel, Manuel
Pimentel, Rosa M.
Quiñones, Amada
Ramirez, Celia
Ramirez, Fernando
Ramos, Antonio
Ramos, Jose
Rivera, Angeles
Rivera, Cayetano
Siaca, Angel
Tejo, Cristina
Tejo, Tomasa

4th Grade

Arroyo, Guillermo
Benoy, Rafael
Calderon, Nicolasa
Calderon, Victoria
Cardona, Dionisio
Ceballos, Melchor
Cepeda, Teodoro
Colon, Alvaro
Correa, Marcos
Correa, Rafael
Cruz, Julio
Delgado, Maria A.

Diaz, Enrique
Diaz, Teodulo
Escobar, Monserrate
Feliciano, Amelia
Fernandez, Pedro
Gautier, Luisa
Gonzalez, Encarnacion
Gonzalez, Gregoria
Guerra, Eugenio
Iglesias, Bienvenido
Jimenez, Ramon
Mas, Juan
Molina, Maria L.
Olivo, Catalina
Orellano, Santiago
Padilla, Juana
Padron, Dolores
Perez, Amelia
Perez, Angel
Perez, Carlos
Perez, Uspicio
Quiñones, Rafael
Quiñonez, Carmen
Ramos, Julio
Reyes, Emilia
Reyes, Valentin
Rodriguez, Jesus
Rodriguez, Julio
Tirado, Flor M.
Viera, Carmen
Viera, Rosa
Villafaña, Maria
Vizcarrondo, Jose A.

5th Grade

Alamo, Fernando
Ayala, Monserrate
Calderon, Ramiro
Carrasquillo, Dolores
Carrasquillo, Saturnino
Carrillo Sanchez, Ramona
Ceballo, Jacinto
Ceballo, Juan
Cepeda, Alberta
Cepeda, Cecilia
Correa, Carmen
Correa, Juan
Crispin, Justina P.
Cruz Gonzalez, Maria
De Jesus, Antonio

De Jesus, Jose
De Jesus, Rodolfo
Diaz, Aracelia
Escobar, Antonio
Fernandez, Gerardo J.
Franco, Pilar
Fuentes, Basilio
Fuentes, Maria
Fuentez, Angelina
Garcia, Concepcion
Gomez, Fermin
Gonzalez, Paula
Gonzalez, Sara Maria
Just, Maria
Mas, Margarita
Maysonet, Ventura
Melendez, Pedro
Millan, Antonio
Moralez, Aureo
Nieves, Esperanza
Orellano, Amparo
Orta, Ramon
Ortiz, Jeronimo
Osorio, Ines
Osorio, Jose M.
Osorio, Nicolas
Parrilla, Peravia
Perfecto, Monserrate
Peterson, Isabel
Ramirez, Isaac
Ramos, Adela
Reyes, Ramon
Rivera, Jose Ramon
Roca, Juan
Rodriguez, Carmen
Rodriguez, Cecilio
Rodriguez, Esteban
Rodriguez, Hortencia
Rodriguez, Jose
Rodriguez, Margarita
Rosario, Joaquina
Rosario, Juan
Santos, Luis
Sedre, Bonifacio
Siaca, Manuel
Villafañe, Amalia
Villafañe, Herminio
Villafañe, Sofia

6th Grade

Andino, Francisco (Jr.)

Benitez Rosario, Tomas
Benoyt, Aurelia
Burgos, Francisco
Calderon Osorio, Evarista
Calderon, Antonia
Castro, Abilia
Correa Matas, Matilde
Correa, Alberto
Correa, Ernestina
Cruz, Maraline
Davila, Basilio
De Jesus, Anselma
De Jesus, Ramon
Del Valle, Edmundo
Escobar, Eusebia
Ferrer, Fernando
Figueroa, Antonio
Fuentes, Julio
Gomez, Luis
Gonzalez, Alvaro (Jr.)
Hernandez de Jesus, Jose
Mas, Carmen
Matos de Santiago, Eloisa
Monge, Carmelo
Morales, Demetrio D.
Orellano, Mercedes
Osorio, Antonio
Osorio, Felipe
Padilla, Ruperto
Padron, Juana
Perez Villamil, Agustin
Quiñones, Alejandro
Quiñonez, Francisco M.
Ramirez, Carmen C.
Ramos, Inocencia
Rivera, Antonio
Rivera, Francisca
Rodriguez Ferrer, Rosario
Rodriguez, Esperanza F.
Rodriguez, Leopoldo P.
Rodriguez, Marcia
Rodriguez, Providencia F.
Rodriguez, Vivina P.
Rosario, Maximo
Santana, Candido

Vahamonde, Arturo S.

7th Grade

Baldrich, Carlos
Calderon, Lino N.
Capblanco, Candida
Carrasquillo, Salvador
Correa, Magdalena
Del Valle, Purificacion
Diaz, Armando
Fuentes, Isaura
Hastings, G. (Teacher)
Maysonet, Aurora
Millardo, Antonio (Jr.)
Morales, Bernarda
Morales, Zenon G.
Orta, Gregoria
Osorio, Josefa
Osorio, Luis F.
Osorio, Manuel
Osorio, Nicolas C.
Osorio, Pablo C.
Padron, Antonio
Paz, Candida
Quiñones, Belen
Quiñones, Luis
Rexach, Rafael (Jr.)
Reyes, Fernando
Rivera, Ernestina
Rivera, Marcelina
Rodriguez, Felicita
Rosario, Josefa
Siaca, Gloria M.
Tirado, Francisca
Vahamonde, Luis S.

8th Grade

Benoy, Salvador
Betancourt, Nicolas
Calderon, Javier
Calderon, Ramon
Carrasquillo, Gonzalo
Carrillo, Gloria C.
Correa, Bienvenido
Diaz, Leoncio
Encarnacion, Eugenia
Escobar, Abigail
Escobar, Alejandrina
Franco, Jose Maria
Garcia, Maria S.

Guerra, Jose Agustin
Lasen, Ramona
Maysonet, Gaspar (Jr.)
Millan, Adamina
Mogicas, Manuel
Orta, Juana
Ortiz, Isabel
Osorio, Celestino
Osorio, Guadalupe
Paz, Francisco C.
Perfecto, Josefina
Pimentel, Rafael
Quiñones, Dolores
Quiñones, Jose
Ramirez, Apolonia
Rivera, Francisco (Jr.)
Rodriguez, Mercedes
Rosa, Ramon
Sanchez Osorio, Inocencia
Sanchez Vahamonde, Maria L.
Sedre, Gregoria
Sola, Mercedes
Vahamonde, Francisco J.

9th Grade

Alejandro, Francisco
Boneta, Blanca, A.
Calderon, Bienvenido
Carrasquillo, Paca
Cuevas, Angel
De Jesus, Julia
De Jesus, Natividad
Dethleffen, Carlos
Garcia, Providencia
Gonzalez, Carolina
Hernandez, Antonia
Iglesias, Eulalio (Professor)
Just, Consolacion
Maysonet, Rosa M.
Mellado, Herminia
Mendez, Generosa D.
Monge, Asuncion
Monge, Luis
Ortiz, Antonio
Parrilla, Pedro
Pimentel, Carmen
Pizarro, Enrique R.

Quidgley, Antonio
Quidgley, Guadalupe
Quiñones, Josefina
Quiñones, Francisco
Rivera, Josefina
Rivera, Nemesio
Rodriguez, Angel
Rodriguez, Hortensia
Rosario, Francisca
Rosario, Laura
Ruiz, Herminio
Snow, Don. W
Sosa, Antonio W.
Velez, Jovita

10th Grade

Baldrich, Gerardo (Jr.)*
Betancourt, Ramon
Correa, Agapito
Cruz, Saturnino
Escobar, Hermogenes*
Ferrer, Osmin*
Garcia, Luis*
Gonzalez, Marcelino*
Osorio, Mariana*
Perez, Jesus M.*
Rodriguez, Ramona*
Suarez, Herminio

_____

* = Also in "Eco Estudiantil"

Eco Estudiantil, Rio Grande

Baldrich, Gerardo (Jr.)
Calderon, Bienvenido
Carrasquillo, Cacu
Cuevas Tirado, Angel
De Jesus Ramirez, Zoraida
De Jesus, Natividad
Dethleffsen, Carlos
Diaz, Generosa
Escobar, Hermojenes
Ferrer, Osmin
Garcia, Providencia

Gonzalez, Carolina
Gonzalez, Marcelino
Iglesias, Eulalio
Just, Consolacion
Maysonet, Rosa
Monge, Asuncion
Monge, Luis
Osorio, Mariana
Parrilla, Pedro
Perez, Jesus M.
Pimentel, Carmen
Pizarro, Enrique
Quiñones, Francisco
Rivera, Josefina
Rodriguez, Hortensia
Rodriguez, Ramona
Rosario, Laura
Sosa, Antonia W.

Escuela Luchetti, San Juan

3rd Grade

Group 1
Acosta, Petrona
Aldrey, Jorge
Balasquide, Antonio
Benitez, Clemencia
Calderon Adelaida
Candelario, Aurelia
Carbia, Ramon
Carbia, Raul
Cepeda, Juana
Cirino, Eusebia
Collazo, Rosa
Cordova, Jose
Cruz, Lina
Diez de Andino, Angel
Dimas, Ramon
Dominguez, Julio
Figuero, Paca
Garcia, Amelia
Gonzalez, Carmen
Guadalupe, Carmen
Guzman, Gilda
Ledesma, Ricardo
Maldonado, Josefina
Matos, Rafael
Mirabal, Salvador
Morales, Carmelo

Antonio's Grace

Morales, Galo
Nadal, Pedro
Naranjo, Isabel
Nin Caparros, Maria
Paoli, Joaquin
Quiñones, Ramon
Quirogas, Francisco
Ramos, Isaac
Richardson, Ernesto
V. S.
Rodriguez, Antonio
Rodriguez, Jose
Roman, Benito
Romero y Torres,
  Hortencia
Rondon, Emelina
Serrano, Marina
Sierra, Guadalupe
Sosa, Sergio
Tejada, Leoncio
Thomas, Eloiza
Torre, Jose Maria
Watlington, Bianca

Group 2
Ward, Nelson
Aquino, Antonio
Calderon, Clemencia
Cotray, Maria
De Jesus, Nieves
Fernandez, Juan
Gual, Consuelo
Llacer, Moserrate
Masdew, Enno
Medina, Roberto
Miranda, Carmen
Padilla, Maria
Padro, Juan
Pereira, Concha
Peterson, Idalia
Quintero, Aureliano
Ramirez, Manuel
Reyes, Francisca
Ricoff, Consuelo
Rivera, Consuelo Ester
Rivera, Mercedes
Rodriguez, Daniela
Rodriguez, Isabel
Rodriguez, Luis
Rodriguez, Milagros
Romero, Cintia
Rosa, Lina
Rosario, Patricio
Rosario, Rosa

Socorro, Francisco
(Jr.)
Suarez, Amado
Tejera, Sabino
Vega, Margot
Viñolo, Cristina

4th Grade

Alegre, Emilia
Armstrong, Julia R.
Ayuso, Pedro
Calderon, Jesus
Cruz, Federico
Davis, Carmen
Faugenet, Gabriela
Fispo, Julio
Franco, Luis
Fuentes, Serafina
Gautier, Jesus
Gonzalez, Enrique
Gonzalez, Gherminia
Iglesias, Carlos A.
Jacobs, William
Lucero, Maria
Mayo, Bernardo
Melendez, Eladio
Mojica, Antonio
Montes, Eloisa
Moreno, Donato
Nieto, Rafael
Olimpia Gimenez,
  Carmen
Ortiz, Francisco
Pantoja, Francisca
Prieto, Maria
Rios, Gregoria
Rivera, Maria A.
Rodriguez, Herminio
Rodriguez, Manuel (1)
Rodriguez, Manuel (2)
Rodriguez, Rafaela
Rubio, Mateo
Shepherd, Adela
Valdes, Carmen
Vasallo, Clemente

5th Grade

Aguilar, Aurea
Alegre, Antonio
Allende, Alberto

Alonso, Providencia
Benitez, Maria
Borges, Clemente
Boyce, Guy S.
Cerra, Luis R.
Clemente, Eugenia
Cortes, Amparo
Faugenet, Leonor
Faugenet, Marcela
Fenlon, Ethel
Figueroa, Florentino
Font, Mercedes
Girona, Teresa
Gonzalez, Orealis
Laham, Matilde
Lord, Helen
Lord, Louise
Mercado, Carmen
Monsanto, P. Juan
Noya Benitez, Julia
  Maria
O'Neill, Arsenio
Otero, Oscar E.
Perez, Margarita
Resard, Alice
Richardson, Milly
Rodriguez Llabres,
  Conchita
Rodriguez, Luis
Rodriguez, Mercedes
Rodriguez,
  Providencia
Roman, Leonides
Rosario, Julio Cesar
Sanchez, Ysabel
Sandoux, Lucas
Santana, Ramona
Shervinton, Nelly
Singleton Boyce, R.
Sosa, Aurora
Vazquez, Francisco
Vidot, Ventura
Villanueva, Josefina
Whatts, Licinia

5th & 6th Grade

Andino, Margarita
Aviles, Maria
Benitez, Margarita
Brisman, Juana
Calderon, Agustin
Calderon, Carmen

Canet, Catalina
Cevallo, Sara
Cruz, Francisca
Cuetara, Jose
Davila, Aida
Diaz, Carlota
Esentel, Rafael
Eyorbea, Mercedes
Ferrer, Russell
Garcia, Carmen
Gonzalez, Carlos
  Alberto
Gonzalez, Rafael
Gual, Carmen
Gutierrez, Eloisa
Gutierrez, Hipolito
Hernandez, Rafael A.
Jacobs, Maria Luisa
Jordan, Oliva
Lopez, Angelina
Lugo Viña, Edward
Marrero, Juan
Martinez, Jose
Marxuach, Enrique
Matilde, Rodriguez
Mora, Mercedes
Muir, Luis
Olivieri, Josefa
Pacheco, Elvira
Ramos, Ramon
Robles, Carmen
Rodriguez, Maria
Rosa, Vicente
Rosario, Catalina
Sandoux, Emilia
Serrano, Francisca
Serrano, Josefa
Thine, Sarah
Torres, Catalina

6th Grade

Achay, Ramon
Aponte, Florencia
Benitez, Gustavo
Calderon, Luis
Casalduc, Jose E.
Cirino, Paulina
Cordova Davila,
  Gilberto
Cuetara, Endosio
Daniel, Virginia
Echazabal, Rafaela

197

Egezcue, Rafael
Escalazan, Dolores
Fenlon, Edith
Filpo, Luis
Fiol, Lina
Font, Providencia
Franceschi, Francisco
Franquez, Concha
Gautier, Ernestina
Girona, Maria E.
Gonzalez, Ricarda
Granado, Federico
Isaac, Eduardo
Kolhoff, V.
Liard, Teresa
Martin, Jose
Martinez, Ramon
Medina, Maria
  Mercedes
Noa, Guillermo
Otero, Carmen
Pacheco, Esperanza
Porrata, Manuel
Portela, Roberto
Quiñones, Obdulia
Ramirez, Orosia
Reyes, J. J.
Rivera, Guadalupe
Rivera, Pedro K.
Rivera, Virginia
Rodriguez, Belen
Salgado, Felipe
Sola, Joaquin
Thine, James
Valdes, Francisco

School Students, Santa Isabel

Alomar, Cecilio
Alomar, Maria
Alomar, Pedro Maria
Alomar, Pedro R.
Alomar, Rafael
Alonzo, Carlos
Alvares, Luis A.
Anes, Gabriel
Anselmi, Carmen
  Lucila
Anselmi, Corina
Anselmi, Rosa Maria

Arce, Rosa Maria
Armada, Agustina
Armada, S. R.
Arroyo, Josefa
Belpre, Margarita
Benjamin, Carolina
Bernal, Aristides
Blanco, Eustaquia
Blanco, Heriberto
Blanco, Jose Modesto
Bones, Epitacia
Burgos, Ana Maria
Burgos, Emilio
Capo, Francisco
Capo, Juliana
Capo, Onelia
Carrasquillo,
  Adalberto
Cintron, Antonia
Colon, Adela
Colon, Adelo
Colon, Catalina
Colon, Epifania
Colon, Epitacia
Colon, Esperanza
Colon, Julio
Colon, Maria Luisa
Colon, Miguel
Colon, Nicolasa
Colon, Rafael
Colon, Robinson
Conde, America
Coto, Virgen
Cruz, Carmen
Cruz, Dolores
Cruz, Esperanza
Cruz, Francisco
Cruz, Manuel
Cruz, Rosa M.
Cruz, Serafin Ismael
De Jesus, Gervacio
De Jesus, Maria Isabel
Diaz, Arturo
Diaz, Eli Samuel
Diaz, Fermina
Diaz, Fernando
Diaz, Francisco
Diaz, Juan
Echevarria, Manuel
Errech, Mario
Fontanes, Arturo
Fontanes, Gloria
Fournier, Ricardo
Gallardo, Julia

Godineaux, Marcelino
Gonzalez, Ramon
Gracia, Domingo
Gracia, Luis
Gracia, Santiago
Huerta, Teresa
Laboy Blanco, Soledad
Laboy, Jorge
Laboy, Juana
Laporte, Francisco
Leandry, Palmira
Malave, Ursula
Marines, Fernando
Marquez, Julia M.
Marquez, Roberto
Martinez, Alfonso
Martinez, Pedro
Mateo, Higinio
Mercado Cedo,
  Mercedes
Mercado, Fernando
Mercado, Isabel M.
Mercado, Magdalena
Miranda, Celedonio
Miranda, Leticia
Monserrate, Angelita
Monserrate, Francisco
  (1)
Monserrate, Francisco
  (2)
Monserrate, Hortensia
Monserrate, Jose A.
Monserrate, Josefita
Monserrate, Juan
  Rafael
Monserrate, Manuel
Monserrate, Soterita
Mora, Patrocinio
Morales, Misterio
Negron, Antonia
Nicot, Ana Matilde
Ortiz, Angelica
Ortiz, Josefa
Ortiz, Julio
Ortiz, Leopoldo
Ortiz, Pedro Juan
Ortiz, Santiago
Paez, Carmen
Picard, Jose
Questell, Rafael
Quiñones, Juan
Ramirez, Flora
Ramirez, Paula
Ramos, Angel

Reyes Rivera, Julio
Reyes, Jaime
Rivera, Andres
Rivera, Aristides
Rivera, Elena
Rivera, Emilio
Rivera, Federico
Rivera, Francisco
Rivera, Guadalupe
Rivera, Ines
Rivera, Jose J.
Rivera, Juan Jose
Rivera, Luis
Rivera, Petronila
Rivera, Rafael
Rivera, Victor
Rivera, Victorio
Roche, Eugenio
Rode, Antonio
Rodriguez, Andrea A.
Rodriguez, Carlina
Rodriguez, Eladia M.
Rodriguez, Enrique
Rodriguez, Eustaquia
Rodriguez, Isabel
Rodriguez, Jose
Rodriguez, Jose
  Dolores
Rodriguez, Julio
Rodriguez, Manuel
Rodriguez, Manuel R.
Rodriguez, Nicolasa
Rodriguez, Primitivo
Rodriguez, Tiburcio
Rodriguez, Zacaria
Rosa, Marciala
Rosado, Saturno
Ruiz, Julia
Sabatell, Etanisla
Sabatell, Julio
Sanchez, Eusebio
Santiago Brito, Jose
Santiago, Adelina
Santiago, Angelina
Santiago, Cristobal
Santiago, Gregorio
Santiago, Heriberto
Santiago, Ismael
Santiago, Jose
Santiago, Juan
Santiago, Pablo
Santos, Parcacio
Santos, Rafael
Seda, Gregorio

Sierra, Ana Livia
Soto, Genaro
Soto, Juan de la C.
Torrens, Guillermina
Torrens, Manuel
Torres, Angel
Torres, Carmen Maria
Torres, Herminia
Torres, Honorena
Torres, Ines M.
Torres, Juan
Torres, Pedro
Valdejuly, Ana
Valencia, Aureo
Vega, Amparo
Vega, Eliseo
Velazquez, Maria
Velez, Andres
Viera, Juana
Villoda, Ramon
Villodas, German
Zambrana, Aida
Zambrana, Anacleto
Zambrana, Francisco
Zambrana, Maria
Zaurjas, Broyoan
Zayas, Josefina M.
Zayas, Monserrate
Zurita, Manuel

Labra School, Santurce

3rd Grade

Group 1
Alicea, Palmira
Almestica, Gualberto
Alvarez, Manuel
Alvarez, Virginia
Amador, Pedro
Andino, Pura
Andreu, Conchita
Anreu, Arturo
Antonetti, Eduardo
Apolinariz, Dolores
Balado, Celia
Balado, Mercedes
Balado, Ramon
Belaval, Jose
Bolivar, Joaquin
Bothwell, Etta

Brennan, Lillian
Canales, Francisco
Carrasquillo, Inocencia
Carrillo, Olegario
Castro, Armando
Castro, Mariano
Catalan, Manuel
Cerate, Natividad
Cristina, Maria
Cruz C., Aurora
Cruz, Brujula
De Jesus, Juan
Delgado, Luis G.
Dones, Alejandrina
Encarnacion, Julian
Fernandez, Enrique
Flores, Alberto
Font, Mila
Fort, Arturo
Fraile, Cayetano
Galindez, Ana
Guillen, Carmen
Jhordsen, Juan
La Costa, Carlos
Landor, Maria
Larregui, Mercedes
Latimer, Tomas
Lee, Waldemar
Limardo, Panchita
Lopez, Alfonso
Lopez, Juana
Lopez, Maria Providencia
Lugo, Pedro
Luyanda, Pedro
Magris, Honoria
Manso, Luisa
Martinez, Gabriel
Molina, Ramon
Morales, Ada
Morales, Emma
Morales, Manuel
Navedo, Catalina
Noriega, Julio
Oller, Gabriel
Ortega, Magdalena
Oviedo, Quintin
Padilla, Amparo
Palau, Julio
Paniagua, Jose
Parrilla, Luis
Perez, Elisa
Perez, Emiliano

Perez, Francisco
Pizarro, Margarita
Prieto, Felicita
Quiñones, Hortensia
Quiñones, Margarita
Quiñones, Modesta
Ramirez, Antonio
Rivera, Luis
Rivera, Mercedes
Rocafort, Miguel A.
Rodriguez, Carmen M.
Rodriguez, Gilberto
Rodriguez, Jose
Rodriguez, Manuel
Rosa, Pablo
Rosado, Valentin
Rosales, Ramon
Rosario, Rosa (Teacher)
Sanchez, Carmen
Sanchez, Emilia
Sanchez, Teresa
Sanchez, Ventura
Santiago, Juana
Valentin, Paca
Vazquez, Francisco
Vazquez, Leonor
Velazquez, Ines
Veve, Maria
William, Esmeralda
Zimmerman, Anne
Zimmerman, John W.

Group 2
Acevedo, Isabel Maria
Acevedo, Margarita
Acevedo, Vidal
Acosta, Jose
Acosta, Pedro
Acuña, Eduardo
Aguilar, Rosendo
Alamo, Jose
Alvarez, Carmen
Amador, Lina
Anido, Maria
Aranzamendiz, Emilio
Aranzamendy, Emilia
Astacio, Cristobalina
Ayala, Fez
Ayala, Julio
Ayala, Ramona
Bauza, Carmen
Beltran, Benito
Berdeguez Diaz, Luis

Berdeguez, Estefania
Berdeguez, Julia
Berdequez, Ana
Betancourt, Modesta
Bithorn, Fernando
Bizoso, Jose
Bizoso, Maria
Boria, Maria Concepcion
Bres, Natividad
Burgos, Susana
Caballero, Josefa
Caballero, Marcelina
Caballero, Maria
Calderon, Maria Victoria
Camacho, Petra
Canales, Agapito
Cantres, Jose Belen
Cardenas, Francisca
Carmoega, Herminia
Carmona, Jose
Carreras, Consuelo
Carreras, Eloisa
Castro, Emilio
Castro, Jose
Castro, Salustiano
Castro, Socorro
Ceballo, Jose
Cepeda, Lucia
Cintron, Gilberto
Clemente, Ambrosia
Clemente, Susana
Collazo, Ana
Colon Gutierrez, Juan
Colon, Ana Carmen
Colon, Catalina
Colon, Erasmo
Colorado, Fernando
Concepcion, Rosa A.
Concepcion, Secundino
Contreras, Antonio (Jr.)
Cordova, Carmen
Correa, Antonia
Correa, Luis
Correa, Rosa
Coto, Isaac
Cruz, Andres
Cruz, Anselmo
Cruz, Carlos Guillermo
Cruz, Carmen Maria
Cruz, Juan

Cruz, Juana
Cruz, Petra
Cruz, Severo
Cubero, Celia
De Castro, David
Decles, Diego
Delgado Lopez, Esperanza
Diaz, Bernardo
Diaz, Delfina
Diaz, Rosa Maria
Dones, Clemencia
Dones, Mario
Ducheny, Rafael
Encarnacion, Isabelino
Enrique, Ondalecio
Esteves, M.
Felse, Petra
Fernandez, Carmen
Fernandez, Generosa
Fernandez, Josefina
Fernandez, Manuela
Fernandez, Virginia
Ferrer, Consuelo
Filemon, Providencia
Flor, Josefina
Flores, Emma
Francis, Julio
Garcia B., Jorge
Garcia Lopez, Carmelita
Garcia, Fernando
Garcia, Juan
Garcia, Justo
Garcia, Susana
Garcias, Nicolas
Gelpi, Carmen
Gomez, Elisa
Gonzalez, Antonia
Gonzalez, Carmen
Gonzalez, Joaquina
Gonzalez, Jose
Gonzalez, Julio
Gonzalez, Manolo
Gonzalez, Nieves
Gonzalez, Rafaela
Gonzalez, Ramon
Gonzalez, Saturnino
Guadalupe, Jose
Guadalupe, Leopoldo
Guasp, Andrea
Hernandez, America
Hernandez, Ana

Hernandez, Ines
Hernandez, Manuela
Hernandez, Natalia
Hernandez, Rafael
Iglesias, Julia J.
Iglesias, Maria H.
Jesus, Silverio
Jimenez, Luisa
Knight, Ernesto
Laedo, Pedro
Lafitte, Ines
Lajara Diaz, Rafael
Lanaussa, Roman
Landron, Francisco
Leavitt, Rosa
Lizardy, Jose
Lopez, Emilio
Lopez, Julio
Lopez, Petra
Lozada, Margarita
Luis, Antonio
Luis, Pedro
Maestre, Francisco
Maldonado, Clotilde
Maldonado, Jose
Manzano, Carmelo
Marceira, Blanca
Marcial, Gumersinda
Margenot, Isabel
Marrero, Manuel
Martinez, Ana
Martinez, Blanca
Martinez, Carmen
Martinez, Carmen Maria
Martinez, Cruz
Martinez, Francisco
Martinez, R.
Martinez, Virginia
Mas, Maria Eugenia
Mascaro y Carmona, Augusto
Mascaro, Jose R.
Matos, Berena
Mayno, Emilio
Medrano, Jose
Melendez, Aurora
Melendez, Mercedes
Melendez, Simon
Mendez, Maria L.
Mendez, Virginia
Mensonet, Americo
Mensonet, M.
Miguel Lema

Miller, Tula
Miro, Milagros
Monges, Alfredo
Monges, Josefina
Monges, Teresa
Montañez, Carmen
Montañez, Francisca
Morales, Alicia
Morales, Candida
Morales, Eusebio
Morales, Luisa
Morales, Ramona
Morales, Santos
Moserrat, Manuel
Moya, Carmen
Moya, Maria
Muro, Miguel
Naranjo, Pedro
Natal, Merida
Nater, Julio
Negron Lopez, Maria
Nieves, Josefa
Nieves, Pablo
Ochart, Carmen
Ochart, Ines
Onofre, Ana Maria
Oquendo, Gabriela
Ortiz, Asuncion
Ortiz, Carmen Pura
Ortiz, Jose
Ortiz, Justino
Ortiz, Lucila
Otero, Ruperta
Pacheco, Aquilina
Pacheco, Claudio
Pacheco, Eduarda
Pagan, Paco
Pagani, Matilde
Paoli, Ramon
Pascual, Gabriela
Pastrana, Juan
Pellissier, Ana Maria
Pereira, Juan
Perez, Alfredo
Perez, Celeste
Perez, Jose (1)
Perez, Jose (2)
Perez, R.
Petersen, Luisa
Pillich, Eucilia
Pizarro, Alejandro
Pla, Mercedes
Pratt, Mary L.
Prieto, Marcelino

Quiara, Enrique
Quiñones, Amparo
Quiñones, Avelina
Quiñones, Sergio
Quintana, Ramon
Ramos, Julia
Ramos, Pablo
Rañales, Baudilia
Rangel, Adolfo
Raso, Juana
Reyes, Carmen
Reyes, Francisco
Reyes, Jose
Ricard, Josefina
Rios, Carmen
Rios, Eduardo
Rivera, Amalia
Rivera, Felipe
Rivera, Maria Luisa
Rivera, Nicolasa
Rivera, Tomasa
Robels, Eloisa
Robles, Antonio
Robles, Luisa
Robles, Matilde
Robles, Rafaela
Rodriguez, Carmin
Rodriguez, Cristina
Rodriguez, Guillerma
Rodriguez, Marina
Rodriguez, Victoriano
Rojas, Efrain
Rolon, Maria Nelfa
Roman, Emilia
Roman, Gloria
Roman, Maria Lina
Roman, Sixta
Rondon, Francisco
Rondon, Teodoro
Ros Robera, Carmen
Rosa, Evarista
Rosa, Matilde
Rosa, Ruperta
Rosado, Enriqueta
Rosado, Isabel
Salcedo, Natividad
Sanchez, Francisca
Santiesteban, Mariano
Santos, Manuel
Sarria, Josefa
Serra Jimenez, F.
Serrano, Maximo
Setty, Dolores
Sierra, Maria

Slira, Isabel
Smith, Eva
Soltero, Carmen Maria
Soto Orlandi, Luz
  Josefina
Soto, Margarita
Souffront, Arturo
Stevens, Hermogenes
Suarez, Encarnacion
Suarez, Tomas
Taull, Luis
Toro, Luis
Torres, Alberta
Torres, Carmen
Torres, Eugenia
Torres, Francisca
Torres, Grandiosa
Torres, Herminio
Torres, Joaquin
Torres, Juana
Torres, Panchita
Trigo, Carmen
Trujillo, Dolores
Tur, Providencia
Valdes, Rafael
Valle, Marcos
Vando, Erasmo
Vega, Armando
Vegas Alicea, Maria
Velazquez, Dolores
Velazquez, Feliz
Velazquez, Ramon
Vera, Carmen Matilde
Viera, Pascual
Villafañe, Adela
Villafañe, Aristides
Villafañe, Julio
Villariny, Nieves I.
Villegas, Dolores
Viner, Antonia
Walters, Philip

4th Grade

Group 1
Arduña, Arturo
Barez, Juan
Benitez Gautier,
  Eugenio
Benitez, Gertrudis
Brennan, Sofia
Calderon Torres, Luis
Canales, Eladio

Castro, Luis
Chaliz, Emilia
Cordova, Abelardo
Cordova, Isabel
Cruz, Enrique
Daniel, Eulalia
Daniel, Pedro
Delgado, Haydee
Elizondo, Ernest
Enrid, Luz
Freyre, Jose
Fuentes, Francisca
Fuentes, Josefina
Garcia, Maria
Guadalupe, Alejandro
Gual, Rosa Maria
Lopez, Placido
Luciano, Pedro
Martinez, Maria
  Dolores
Menendez, Maria
  Luisa
Ortiz, Camelia
Ortiz, Pedro
Ortiz, Vicenta
Pujolo, Lucas
Quiñones, J
Requena, Edelmira
Rios y Rios, Pedro
Rios, Juan
Rios, Margarita
Rivera, Emerita
Rivera, Genoveva
Rodriguez, Isabel
Rodriguez, Jesus
Salle, Antonio
Simompietri, Antonio
  R.
Torres, Adrian
Vachier, Mercedes
Valera, Ana Milagros
Valera, Ernesto
Vidal, Rita

Group 2
Abadia, Isabel
Abella, Maria Socorro
Abella, Venancio
Acevedo, Carlos
Acevedo, Vicenta
Acosta, Jose
Agosto, Antonio
Aguayo, Arturo
Aguilar, Juan

Aguso, Angeles
Albaacete, Lorenzo
Albanese, Angela
Alcaraz, Juan
Alcaraz, Pedro
Alduondo, Julio
Almeria, Ester
Alonso, Isabel
Alonso, Luis
Alvarez, Juan
Amador, Salvador
Amezquita, Ramona
Andino, Lope
Apellaniz, Angeles
Arana, Nicasio
Arce Gomez, Carmen
Arias, Tomas
Arraga, Antonio
Arroyo, Elvira
Arroyo, Joaquina
Arroyo, Juana (1)
Arroyo, Juana (2)
Artau, Virginia
Attiery, Rafael
Bacenet, Victor
Bairan, Jose
Bairan, Pedro
Bairan, Roberto
Barberan, Juan
Barbosa, Jose H.
Barbosa, Rafael
Barreiro, Ana
Barreiro, Jose
Barros, Jose
Bastar, Tirsa Maria
Becerril, Petra
Belpre, Maria
Benitez, Carmen
Benitez, Manuela
Benitez, Maria
  Cristina
Berley, Providencia
Bermudez, Ramon
Bernat, Cecilia
Betancourt, Angela
Bladwell, Hector
Bladwell, Miguel
  Angel
Bonacia, Inocencia
Bonet, Luis
Boneta, Manuel
Bosolet, Rafael
Bouran, Enrique
Burgos, Leopoldo

Burgos, Maria Luisa
Caballero, Concepcion
Caballero, Manuel
Calderon, Alvaro
Calderon, Elisa
Calderon, Jacinto
Calderon, Ramona
Calvente, Juanita
Cantellas, F.
Cantellops, Rita
Carbonell, Luisa
Carreras, Rosa
Carrillo, Fernando
Carrion y Carrion,
  Tomas
Cartazo, Edmundo
Casella, Rafael
Casellas, Miguel A.
Castelao, Damaso
Castillo, Carmen
Castro, Aurea
Cepero, Federico
Cerich Danua,
  Margarita
Charleman, Gerardo
Charleman, Luisa
Charre, Emma
Cintron, Blas
Cintron, Maria
  Vicenta
Cirino, Inocencia
Cirino, Pedro
Claudio, Pedro
Claudio, Santiago
Claudio, Saturnino
Collazo, Jose
Colon Nin, Angeles
Colon, Aurelio
Conde Lemoine,
  Eduardo
Conde, Natalia
Contron, Jose
Corra, Rosario
Corra, Saturnina
Cortijo, Angela
Cortijo, Juana
Cosme, Antonio
Couvertie, Mercedes
Couvertie, Providencia
Cruz, Ana
Cruz, Antonia
Cruz, Augusto
Cruz, Belen
Cruz, Candido

Cruz, Clemencia
Cruz, Jesus
Cruz, Juan
Cruz, Mercedes
Cruz, Rafael (1)
Cruz, Rafael (2)
Cruz, Rosa
Cruz, Rosa Maria
Cucret, Maria
Cuevas, Carmen
Cuevas, Ramon
Cumba, Luis
Daniel, Petra
Davila, Jesus
De Diego, Maria
De Jesus, Guillermo
De la Cruz, Ramona
De la Mata, Isabel
De Thomas, Fermin
Del Pozo, Adela
Del Rosario, C. U.
Del Valle, Gloria
Delaney, Francisco
Delgado, Antonia
Delgado, Felicita
Delgado, Rufina
Diaz, Amalia
Diaz, Ana Maria
Diaz, Antolina
Diaz, Aurora
Diaz, Fausto
Diaz, Gaspar
Diaz, Juan
Diaz, Maria
Diaz, Maria Elena
Diaz, Petronila
Diaz, Pura
Diaz, Quintina
Diaz, Ramon
Diaz, Rosa
Durand, Concepcion
Echevarria, Vicenta
Elias Rosa, Maria
Elvira, Rosa
Enriquez, Juan
Ertrades, Jose
Escalona, Margarita
Escobar, Agustina
Escobar, Amparo
Espada, Concepcion
Espinosa, Carmen
Espinosa, Providencia
Estrada, Francisco
Estrada, Otilia

Estrada, Susana
Esturio, Julia
Esturio, Julieta
Esturio, Vicente
Faura, Juan
Febus, Gloria
Fernandez Torrez,
  Carlos
Fernandez, Carmen
Fernandez, Elena
Fernandez, Jose
Fernandez, Rafaela
Fernandez, Sizta
Ferrer, Cruz
Ferrer, Magdalena
Ferreras, Angel L. (Jr.)
Figueras, Teresa
Figueroa, Angela
Figueroa, Antonio
Figueroa, Maria
Flor, Enrique
Flores, Fidel
Flores, Norberto
Flores, Tomas
Florria, Jose
Fonfria, Emilio R.
Fortuño, Alfredo
Fortuño, Antonio
Franco, Carlota
Franco, Ernesto
Frechel, Manuela
Freiria y Vidal,
  Manolo
Fuentes, Candida
Fuentes, Ignasia
Fuertes, Amparo
Gaecoechea, Georgina
Gaetan, Libertad
Gandia Cordova, Jose
Garcia Cabrera,
  Manuel
Garcia, Candido
Garcia, Carmen Rosa
Garcia, Eduardo
Garcia, Fernando
Garcia, Jose (1)
Garcia, Jose (2)
Garcia, Jose (3)
Garcia, Josefina
Garcia, Juan (1)
Garcia, Juan (2)
Garcia, Luz
Garcia, Manuel
Garcia, Mercedes

Garcia, Nestor L.
Garcia, Victoria
Gautier, F. Hiram
Gearda, Amancia A.
Gearda, Vicia
Geigel, Cesar
Gelpi, Carmen
Gelpi, Jaime
George, Catalina
Ginorio, Maria Teresa
Goicoechea, Lucila
Goicoechea, Rosa
Gomez Ojeda, Paco
Gomez, Genoveva
Gomez, Maria D.
Gomez, Ramon
Gomez, Rosario
Gonzalez, Alfonso
Gonzalez, Alfredo
Gonzalez, Dolores
Gonzalez, Eduardo
Gonzalez, Juana
Gonzalez, Manuel
Gonzalez, Reparada
Granella, Estrella
Grovas, Rafael
Guadalupe, Godofredo
Guadalupe, Rivera
Guillermety, Fernando
Guzman, Julia
Haulon, Franck C.
Haulon, Gisele E.
Henriquez, Carmen
Hernandez, Arturo
Hernandez, Herminio
Hernandez, Juan
Hernandez, Julia
Infant, Dolores
Insemi, Luis
Iriarte, Enrique
Jimenez Reyes,
  Manuel
Jimenez, Carlos
Jimenez, Feliz
Jimenez, Jose
Jimenez, Rafael
Jimenez, Salvador
Jordan, Jorge
Jordan, Magdalena
Jorge, Damian
Justa, Juanita
Kohl, Adolfo Federico
Laboy y Gonzalez,
  Margarita

Labrador, Jose
Labrador, Serafin
Laffitte, Blanca
Lafont, Manuel
Lamar, Esteban
Lanuza, Isabel
Lanuza, Lolita
Lanuza, Ramon
Laracuente, Ana
  Victoria
Larroca, Miguel A.
Larrus, Silvia
Lebron, Bernardo
Lebron, Carlos
Ledesma, Belen
Leocadio, Carlos
Leocadio, Leoncio
Levis, Antonia
Levis, Ismael
Levold, Esther
Llanas, Dolores
Llobet, Carmen
Llobet, Jose R.
Lopez, Ana
Lopez, Arturo
Lopez, Carmen
Lopez, Gerardo
Lopez, Herminia
Lopez, Luis
Loubriel, Lola
Loubriel, Paquito
Loubriel, Rafael
Loubriel, Rosenda
Loubriel, Ulises
Lugo, Maria Teresa
Lugo, Mercedes
Machicote, Carlos
Mahony, Ines
Maldonado, Amparo
Maldonado, Enrique
Maldonado, Rosario
Malpica, Jesus
Manso, Damaso
Manzanal, Carlos
Marcera, Joaquina
Margenat, Isabel
Marin, Carlota
Marin, Lydia
Mark, Ines
Marquez, Edmunds
Marquez, Enrique (1)
Marquez, Enrique (2)
Marquez, Eufemia
Marrero, Maria

Victoria
Martinez M., Luis
Martinez, Altagracia
Martinez, Angel
Martinez, Carmen
  Maria
Martinez, Eduardo
Martinez, Efigenia
Martinez, Isabel
Martinez, Jose
Martinez, Josefina
Martinez, Manuel
Martinez, Paulino
Martinez, Victor
Mas, Alfredo
Matos, Luis Felipe
Mauleon, Carlos M.
Maullon, Jose
Mayor, Belen
Mejia, Emilio
Melendez, Luis
Melendez, Ysidra
Mellado, Rafaela
Mendez, Felicita
Merino, Maria
Micheli, Adolfo
Mirabal, Natividad
Miranda, Celenia
Moczo, Rafael
Molinas, Petra
Monges, Fernando
Montalvo, Francisco
Montañez, Felicita
Montañez, Miguelina
Montenegro, Adelaida
Montenegro, Carmen
Montilla, Rosario
Mora, Carmelo
Mora, Pepita
Morales, Dolores
Morales, Ezequiela
Morales, Juana
Morales, Manuel
Morales, Rafael
Moreno y Goubert,
  Josefina
Moreno, Esteban
Moreno, Inocencio
Moreno, Marina
Moreno, Pedro
Mulinelli, Pedro
Muñoz, Celestino
Muriel, Aniceto
Musa, Rafael

Narvaez, Juan
Navarro, Agueda
Negroni, Isabel Maria
Nieves Bermudez,
  Maria
Nieves Bermudez,
  Maria
Noble, Bartolo
Nogueras, Antonio
Noriega, Enrique
Nuñez, Gustavo
Nuñez, Julio
Nuñez, Miguel
Ohart, Digna
Oivase, Juan
Olivar, Rafael
Oliver, Emilia
Olivo, Jose
Oller, Josefina
Oquendo, Alejandro
Oquendo, Anastasia
Oquendo, Julia
Orriols, Maria
Ortiz, Enrique
Ortiz, Floripes
Ortiz, Manuel
Ortiz, Raul
Otero, William
Owens, Ana Maria
Pacheco, Esteban
Pagan, Francisco
Pagan, Leonor
Pagani, Julio
Palacios, Carmen
Paniagua, Isabel
Paniagua, Josefina
Pankoco, Mercedes
Pares, Gualberto
Pares, Luis
Pares, Rosalia
Paris, Jose (1)
Paris, Jose (2)
Pausa, Maria Teresa
Pedreira, Jose Enrique
Pedreira, Luis A.
Pedreira, Maria Luisa
Pellot, Matilde
Penn, Guillermo
Peral R., Regina
Perez, Antonia
Perez, Antonio
Perez, Candida
Perez, Enrique
Perez, Esperanza

Perez, Gonzalo
Perez, Isabel
Perez, Rafael
Petersen, Elena
Pichardo, Generoso
Pier, Dolores
Pier, Francisco
Pieras, Carmen
Pizarro, Antonia
Pizarro, Justina
Plard, Maria
Plard, Teresa
Plaza, Jeronimo
Ponte, Jose
Pousa, Dolores
Power, Providencia
Prieto, Francisco
Prieto, Francisco C.
Puig, Cayetano
Puras, Jose
Quijano, Fernando
Quiles, Lila
Quiñones, Anita
Quiñones, Belen
Quiñones, Carmen
  Luisa
Quiñones, Cecilio
Quiñones, Fabriciano
Quiñones, Pedro (1)
Quiñones, Pedro (2)
Quiñonez, Concha
Ramirez, Aurelia
Ramos, Jesusa
Ramos, Marcelo
Ramos, Ricarda L.
Rendon Macias,
  Francisco
Requeni, Providencia
Ressif, Justina
Resto Diaz, Andres
Rey, Ana Maria
Rey, Consuelo
Rey, Elvira
Rinaldi, Domingo
Rinaldi, Rita
Rios, Carmen
Rios, Jose
Rivera, Brigida
Rivera, Carlos
Rivera, Carmen
Rivera, Elsa
Rivera, Engracia
Rivera, Eufemia
Rivera, Jesus

Rivera, Josefa
Rivera, M. America
Rivera, Maria Luisa
Rivera, Mariana
Rivera, Miguel A.
Rivera, Otilia
Rivera, Pablo
Rivera, Petra
Robles, Pablo
Rocafort, Angeles
Rocafort, Isabel
Rocafort, Salvador
Rodena, Isabelino
Rodriguez, Alberto
Rodriguez, Angela
Rodriguez, Carmen
Rodriguez, Damaso
Rodriguez, Emilio
Rodriguez, Eugenia
Rodriguez, Francisco
Rodriguez, Jose
Rodriguez, Juan (1)
Rodriguez, Juan (2)
Rodriguez, Lidia
Rodriguez, Manuel
Rodriguez,
  Monserrate
Rodriguez, Ramon
Rodriguez, Ricardo
Rodriguez, Rosa
Roger, Enrique
Roger, Maria Luisa
Roman, Amalia R.
Romero, Leonor
Rooms, Rosa
Roques, Rafael
Rosa, Isabel
Rosa, Jose S.
Rosa, Rafael
Rosario, Jose
Rossello, Julia
Rossi, Isabel
Ruiz, Carlota
Ruvira, Luisa
Saavedra, Luis
Saldaña, Carlos M
Sanchez, Dolores
Sanchez, Ezequiela
Sanchez, Isidro
Sanchez, Jose A.
Santaella, Maria Belen
Santana, Carmen
Santiago, Elpidio
Santiago, Emilio

Santiago, Ernesto
Santiago, Feliz
Santiago, Juan
Santiago, Mercedes
Santiago, Rafael
Santos, Flora
Santos, Joaquin
Santos, Jose
Schomburg, Federico G.
Serra, Juan
Serra, Pilar
Serrano, Aurora
Serrano, Isidro
Serrano, Jose Belen
Serrano, Julio
Serrano, Ramona
Serranos, Vicent
Sevilla, Maria
Sierra Feijou, Saturnino
Sierra, Juana
Sirvent, Angel
Smith, Aida
Sola, Juan
Sola, Paula
Solis, Dionila
Solis, Dolores
Somolino, Valentin
Somoza, Luis
Soriano, Francisca
Soriano, Georgina
Sosa, Guillermo
Sosa, Juan
Soto, Belen
Soto, Josefina
Soto, Manuela
Straun, Belen
Straun, Miguel
Suarez, Jose
Suarez, Maria J.
Tembley, Josefina
Thode, Leopoldo
Tillet, Eduardo
Tirado, Sofia
Torrecillas, Maria
Torres, Angelica
Torres, Cecilio
Torres, Celina
Torres, Elena
Torres, Elisa
Torres, Eva
Torres, Josefa
Torres, Juana

Torres, Rafael
Torres, Rafaela
Torres, Rosaura
Trally, Gloria
Trovas, Maria
Trujillo, Hortensia
Turrull, America
Turull, Carmelina
Udemburg, Felicita
Udemburg, Ruperto
Udemburgh, Santiago
Umpierre, Octavio
Urrutia, Angela
Vaello, Jose
Valderrama, Rafael
Valdivieso, Benigno
Vando, Angel
Vargas, Francisco
Vazquez Prada, Leopoldo
Vazquez, Francisca
Vazquez, Luis
Vazquez, Maria
Velazquez, Guillermo
Velazquez, Remigia
Velazquez, Victor
Velazquez, Victoria
Velez, Alfredo
Velilla, Rafael
Ventura, Jose
Vergara, Pilar
Waymouth, Emilia J.
Waymouth, Ines
Williams, Lucia
Wright, Victor

5th Grade

Acosta, Maria
Alamo, Jesusa
Alchey, Emilio
Aldrich, Maria Luisa
Alsina, Francisca
Altiery, Ricardo
Andino Elvira
Andrades, Miguel
Aquino Rosario, Serafin
Arteaga, Pedro
Astacio, Virginia
Balado, Juanita
Berdeguer, Felipe (Jr.)
Bermudez, Rafaela

Bertran, Francisco
Bithorn, Waldemar (Jr.)
Bizoso, Josefina
Boada Lasanta, Carmen
Bothwell, Jaime H.
Bravo, Esperanza
Burns, Fanny Lydia
Cabello, Trinidad
Campoamor, Antonio
Campoamor, Miguel Angel
Cancel, Juan
Carcador, Eusebia
Cardenas, Carmen
Carreras, Francisco
Carrero Diaz, Carlota
Carrion, Josefina
Castro Rafael
Castro, Eustasia
Castro, Jacinto
Cepeda, Miguel
Chacon, Antolin
Chaliz Perez, Emilia
Cid, Jose
Cirilo, Rosa
Colon, Luis
Concepcion, Ramon
Cortijo, Pedro
Cortines, Francis
Corty, Georgina
Cruz T., Severa
Cruz, Candelaria
Cruz, Juanita
Cruz, Maria
Cruz, Ramon
Davila, Angel
De Armas, Jorge
De Jesus, Dionisio
De Jesus, Jose
De Jesus, Juan
De la Rosa, Osvaldo
Delgado, Carmen
Diaz, Carmen
Diaz, Elidia
Diaz, Enrique
Diaz, Herminia
Diez de Andino, Clara
Domenech, Domingo
Dones, Cecilia
Dualeuz, Felix
Echevarria, Justino
Escalera, Antonio

Escalera, Augusto
Escalera, Trina
Escoda, Rafael
Espejo, Pablo
Espinosa, Luz Maria
Estremera, Ramon
Ferrer, Lorenzo
Figueroa Cuevas, Rafael
Figueroa, Ramon
Fiol, Paca
Flanders, Carlos F.
Flores, Maria
Flores, Monsita
Florit, Pura
Francis, Rafaela
Freyre, Paca
Fuentes, Manolo
Fuentes, Manuel
Galindez, Eugenia
Garcia, Ana Luz
Garcia, Manuela
Garcia, Natalia
Garcia, Petrona
Garcia, Pura J.
Gautier, Salustiano
Gimenez, Jose
Gomez, Adela
Gonzalez, Luis
Gonzalez, Manuel
Gonzalez, Mercedes
Gonzalez, Monserrate
Granado, Mercedes
Guadalupe, Victor Manuel
Guerra, Enriqueta
Guillermety, William
Hansard, Norah
Heredia, Juan
Hernandez, Carmen
Hernandez, Cecilio
Hernandez, Jesus
Hernandez, Jose S.
Hess, Martha K.
Hudo, Jose J.
Huertas, Adelina
Hutchinson, Francis W.
Igaravidez, Laura
Iglesias, Candida
Iglesias, Jose Alfredo
Ildefonso, Manuel
Iriarte, Aida
Irizarry, Hipolito

Jaime, Ramona
Jimenez, Miguel
Jourdan Martys, Daniel
Julia, Julia
Kerador, Cecilio
Kianes, Victor
La Costa, Ricardo
Lamautte, Alice Katie
Lameiro, Ana
Leavitt, Jose
Leavitt, Josefa
Lema, Maria Andrea
Leon, Angel
Leon, Victoria
Lluijans, Celestina
Loisaga, Rosa
Lopez, Andres
Lopez, Armando
Lopez, Aurora
Lopez, Homero
Lopez, Ricardo
Lora, Victoria
Loubriel, Gloria
Marchany, Ramona
Marchany, Rosa
Mark, Margarita
Marrero, Concepcion
Martinez, E. Maria
Martinez, Elena
Martinez, Victoria
Mas, Adriana
Matos, Primitiva
Medrano, Eulalia
Mendez, Eduardo
Menendez, Jose
Merino, Jesusa
Milian, Leonor
Miller, Luis
Mills, Maria
Miranda Rosario, Rafael
Miranda, Jesusa
Modesto, Esperanza
Molinary, Elisa
Montanez, Juan
Morales, Cruz
Morales, Herminia
Morales, Manuel
Navedo, Josefina
Negron, Juana
Negron, Virgilio
Nieves, Cayetano
Noriega, Alicia

Noriega, Jose
Orcasitas, Carmen
Ortiz, Gumersinda A.
Padro, Ana
Pantres, Ana Maria
Parson, Marcos
Pedrosa, Elisa J.
Pellon, Francisca
Peña, Juana
Perea, Palmira
Piña, Luis
Pizarro, Valentina
Prieto, Amelia
Quiñones Flores, Anibal
Quiñones, Juana
Quiñones, Manuel (Jr.)
Quiñonez, Gonzalo
Quirogas, Carmen
Ramirez, Josefina
Ramos, Miguel
Ramos, Milagros
Raso, Maximina
Reina, Carmen M.
Rengel, Luis
Rexach, Jose J.
Reyes, Ezequiel
Rijos, Roman
Rios, Felipe
Rios, Gabriel
Rios, Pedro
Rivera, Clotilde
Rivera, Consuelo
Roberts, Iris
Robles, Julia
Rodriguez, Alberto
Rodriguez, Augusto A.
Rodriguez, Aurea
Rodriguez, Aurora
Rodriguez, Dolores
Rodriguez, Josefina
Rodriguez, Juan
Rodriguez, Julia
Rodriguez, Luisa
Rodriguez, Micaela
Rodriguez, Providencia
Rodriguez, Providencia
Rodriguez, Rosalina
Rodriguez, Victoria
Roldan, Daniela
Roman, Juan

Roque, Soledad
Ruiz, Francis S.
Ruiz, Juan
Ruiz, Rumi
Salcedo, Teresa
Salomon, Georgina
Sanchez, Rita Y.
Santa, Consuelo
Santana, Clarito
Santiago, Eulalio
Santiago, Natividad
Santiago, Susano
Sapia, Josefina
Sapia, Mercedes
Seaton, Modesta
Sevilla, Rafael
Shinery, Glenderline
Sierra, Manuel
Sierra, Teresa
Solas, Jose
Solla, Teresa
Sosa, Josefa
Soto, Amparo
Soto, Josefina
Soto, Pedro
Suarez, Alfredo
Thordseu, Maria E.
Tirado, Elvira
Torres, Emilia
Torres, Jose
Valdes, Francisco
Vargas, Carmen Maria
Vargas, Enedina
Vazquez, Amelia
Vazquez, Tomas
Velazquez, Candido
Vera, Dora
Vergne, Petra E.
Vergus, Carlos
Vilaseca, Isabel
Villanueva, Rafael
Villar Trinidad
Wilson, Catherine
Zapata, Rafael

6th Grade

Abella, Carmen Belen
Adams, Emilio M.
Agostini, German
Agosto, Feliz
Agripina, Milagros
Agudo, Eloy

Aguilar, Berta
Aguilar, Pedro
Aguilar, Ricardo
Albanese, Pablo
Albanese, Teresa
Alcaraz, Mercedes
Alcarez, Carmelo
Alonso, Juan Ramon
Andino, Aurora
Andino, Belen
Andino, Carmen
Andino, Demetria
Andino, Dominga
Andino, Juan
Andino, Julio
Apellaniz, Celia
Appelaniz, Dolores
Arce Gomez, Esperanza
Arenas, Rosa Maria
Arguingoni, Juan
Arias, America
Arias, Ishmael
Arroyo, Concha
Arroyo, Isabel
Artau, Marina
Arteaga, Pura
Ayala, Ramon
Baergas, Eduardo
Bailly, Reyes
Bairan, Mercedes
Balaguer, Enrique
Barasoain, Eduardo
Barberan, Rosalina
Barreiro, Rafael
Barrios, Celia
Barrios, Maria Amparo
Barrios, Pura
Bermudez, Ramon
Betancourt Alberte, Juan
Betancourt, Ana
Betancourt, Juan
Bisot, Carmen
Bladwell, Ramon
Blanco, Tomasa
Boneet, Carmen
Bosolet, Rosario
Cabello, Rafael
Calderon, Juan
Calderon, Ursina
Caliz, Ana Elisa
Campos, Antonio

Camuñas, Manuel (Jr.)
Capelli, Concepcion G.
Capelli, Estrella G.
Carabia, Paca
Carballo, Providencia
Carbia, Enrique
Caro, Antonio
Caro, Rosa
Carrillo, Joaquin
Carrion, Carmen
Cartagena, Elena
Casablanca, Marcolina
Casellas, Jose
Castelao, Domingo
Castells, Mercedes
Castillo, Pedro
Castro, Blasina
Castro, Mario
Castro, Matilde
Cejada, Rafael
Certaine Cruz, Miguel
Cid, Rosa
Civile, Loretta
Clemente, Concepcion
Cobian, J. M.
Colon, Angel F.
Colon, Eduvigis
Colon, Emilio
Colon, Francisco
Colon, Jesus
Colon, Paula
Colon, Ricardo
Colorado, Antonio
Correa, Herminia
Cortijo, Emilia
Costoso, Maria
Cruz Prieto, Vicenta
Cruz, Jose
Cruz, Porfirio
Casanova, Aida
Cuevas, Rosa Maria
Daniels, C.C.
Davila, Francisco
Davila, Gonzalo
De Diego, Pedro (Jr.)
Delgado, Paquita
Diaz, Elisa
Diaz, Matilde
Diaz, Ricardo
Du-Sablou, Pilar
Duchesne, Rafael
Dura, Joaquina
Durand, Mercedes

Durecut, Foyet, Salvadora
Esteves, Maria Teresa
Fabregas, Maria L.
Febus, Maria
Fernandez, Concha
Fernandez, Juana
Ferran, Juana
Figueroa, Ramon
Flores, Natividad
Folch, Francisco
Font, Luis
Font, William A.
Freiria, Evaristo (Jr.)
Froilan, Mercedes
Fuentes, Carmen Navarro
Fuentes, Rafael
Fuertes, Luis
Gaetan, Pura F.
Gambaro, Nieves
Gandia, Francisco
Garcia y Gonzalez, Nicolas
Garcia, Bibiana
Garcia, Guillermo
Garcia, Lorenzo
Garcia, Nicolasa
Garcia, Pilar (1)
Garcia, Pilar (2)
Garza, Angel
Gatell, Jose M.
Gearda, Rina
Gelpi, Jose Enrique
Gomez, Marina
Gomez, Mercedes
Gonzalez Diaz, Antonio
Gonzalez, Leopoldo Luis
Gonzalez, Luis
Gonzalez, Luisa
Gonzalez, Margarita
Gonzalez, Maria Luisa
Gonzalez, Natalia
Gonzalez, R. Jorge
Gonzalez, Rafael
Gonzalez, Rosa
Grasp, Angelica
Guacs, Ramon
Guerra, Asuncion
Guillermety, Fidel Angel
Guzman, Caralina

Guzman, Hortensia
Hernandez Brada, Heraldo Ramon
Hernandez, Ana Maria
Hernandez, Angel
Hernandez, Victor Manuel
Hohl, Angeles
Iriarte, Rosario
Isquierdo, Pedro
Jesurun, Maria Teresa
Jorque, Maria
Knight, Gladys
Labrador, Rafael
Laguna, Carmen
Lajara, Maria
Landor, Providencia
Landron, Blanca Rosa
Ledesma, Maria
Leppe, Alonso
Lervold, Arturo
Llureta, Maria
Lobet, Rita Maria
Lopez Cepero, Jose
Lopez-Cepero, Mariano
Lopez, Eugenio
Lopez, Jesus
Lopez, Providencia
Lopez, Virginia
Loubriel, Jose Ramon
Loubriel, Jose W.
Loubriel, Maria Teresa
Lugo, Adolfina
Lugo, Carmen
Macias Lopez, Arturo
Macias Lopez, Rafael
Madera, Esther Maria
Maldonado, Americo
Marin, Georgina
Marin, Isaura
Marquez, Luis
Martin, Maria C.
Martinez Uriarte, Maria C.
Martinez, Antonio
Martinez, Edelmiro
Martinez, Elmira Aurora
Martinez, Fernando
Martinez, Jose
Martinez, Mercedes
Martinez, Rafael
Matos, Carmen

Matos, Lila
Maymi, Protasio
Mayna, Pacifico
Melendez, Jenara
Mellado, Aurora
Mendez, Josefina
Mendez, Manuel
Mendin, Josefa (Teacher)
Mendin, Matilde
Millman, Alez
Miro, Enrique
Miro, Mercedes
Monagas, Carlos
Monagas, Ulises
Monetes, Candelaria
Montañez, Julia
Morales, Concepcion
Moya, Gabriel
Muñoz, Alfonso
Naranjos, Jacinto
Navarro Fuentes, Isabel
Negron Lopez, Francisca
Neval, Gloria Maria
Noble, Catalina
Nogueras, Providencia
Nuñez, Carmen
Ochoteco, Feliz
Oquendo, Genaro
Ortiz, Adelicia
Ortiz, Herminio
Ortiz, Ricardo
Pacheco, Pilar
Paoli, Concepcion
Paso, Esperanza
Paso, Luis
Pedreira, Bernardino
Pedreira, Julia
Pedreira, Mercedes
Pedrene, Pedro
Pellon, Daniel
Perez Delgado, Ramon
Perez, Angela
Perez, Isabel
Perez, Jacinto
Perez, Lola
Pieras, Luis
Pimentel, Carmen
Pizarro, Maria
Planas, Mercedes
Planas, Pepita
Porrata, Carmen

Porrata, Maria Mercedes
Portalatin, Amelio
Quiñones, Luis
Quiñones, Pepita
Quintero, Carmen
Quiros, Rosario
Ramos Lopez, Juan
Ramos, Carmen
Ramos, Filomena
Real, Juan
Real, Sila
Rechani, Carmen
Rechani, Pura
Rendon, Angela
Rendon, Brigida
Reyes, Belen
Reyes, Emelia
Rijan, Teresa
Ritt, Antonia
Rivera Oyola, Demetrio
Rivera, Aniceto
Rivera, Bienvenido
Rivera, Carmen
Rivera, Jose
Rivera, Justino
Rivera, Rafael (1)
Rivera, Rafael (2)
Rivero, Providencia
Robaine, Max
Robles, Francisca
Rodena, Ramona
Rodriguez Pou, Carmen Maria
Rodriguez, Angel
Rodriguez, Aurora
Rodriguez, Carmen
Rodriguez, Dolores
Rodriguez, Hilda Socorro
Rodriguez, Jose (1)
Rodriguez, Jose (2)
Rodriguez, Jose (3)
Rodriguez, Juan
Rodriguez, Mercedes
Rodriguez, Pepita
Rodriguez, Pilar
Rodriguez, Rosa
Rodriguez, Segunda
Rodriguez, Teresita H.
Roig, Aida
Roman, Maria
Rondon, Isidra

Roque, Julia
Rosa, Carmen
Rosario, Maria
Ross Correa, Gustavo
Rubio, Isabel
Ruiz, Carmen Maria
Ruiz, Eloy
Ruiz Oller, Antonio
Sabat, Eduvigis
Saldaña, Delia
Saldaña, Juana
Santaella, Eduardo
Santamaria, Eladio
Santiago, Florencio
Schomburg, Waldemar
Secola, Celedonio
Seda, Augusto
Serrati, Rafael
Sevilla, Rafael
Sevillano, Isabel
Sierra, Ana M.
Sierra, Jose
Sierra, Paca
Sirvent, Agustin
Soto, Diego J.
Strawn, Julia
Suarez, Andres
Suarez, Margarita
Suarez, Maria Ana
Suarez, Maria T.
Tillet, Adolfo
Tizol, Juan
Toro, Luisa
Toro, Rosa Maria
Torres Crispin, Genaro
Torres, Angeles
Torres, Benito
Torres, Enriqueta
Torres, Guillermo
Torres, Josefina
Torres, Marina
Trigo, Isabel
Trigo, Manuel
Trujillo Guill, Pura
Trujillo, Eulalia
Turrull, Providencia
Ubarri, Alfonso
Uloak, Carmen Dolores
Urdaneta Thaly, Juana
Valdes, Federico
Valle, Celestina

Valle, Maria M.
Velez, Rafael
Venegas, Gilberto
Vere, Oscar
Vergara, Margarita
Verges, Enrique
Vila, Miguel
Villaran, Candido G.
Villariny, Carmen Margarita
Viruet, Jose
Vizcarrondo, Jaime
Wey, Eulalia
Yania, Juan (Jr.)
Yustos, Trinidad

7th Grade

Agenjo, Vicente L.
Agenjo, Elena
Aguayo Santiago, Espiridon
Aldrich, Luis L.
Almiroty, Fernando
Altiery, Francisco
Amador, Rafael
Andino, Francisco
Aponte, Miguelina
Arroyo, Norberto
Balado, Carmen
Ballet, Maximo
Bantres, Felicita
Bas, Conchita
Batista, Ramon
Becerril, Antonio
Beguizo, Eva
Benitez, Jose
Bolivar Pedro
Bolivar, Francisco
Bothuell, Maria
Bothwell, Lyman
Bou, Amparo
Bracho, Isabel
Brown, Edgar
Burns, George
Bustamante, Manuela
Calderon, Monsita
Campesino, Maria
Casco, Jose
Chandri, Pedro
Chavez, Gabriela
Cintron, Luis
Cirino Velilla, Juan

Cirino, Carmen
Clemente Davila, Narciso
Colon, Caren
Colon, Cristina
Cordova, William
Cotto, Alejandro
Cruz, Benito
Cruz, Juan
Davila, Pedro
De Chondins, Concepcion
Delgado, Tula
Diaz, Julio
Diaz, Margarita
Diaz, Santiago
Dominicci, Pedro
Escalera, Agapito
Escalera, Milagros
Escudero, Regina
Estrella, G.
Estrella, Isabel
Fajardo, Felipa M.
Feliu, Juan
Figueroa, Eduardo
Figueroa, Jhakim
Figueroa, Pascasio
Florit, Carmen
Font Pacheco, Ricardo (C. C.)
Font, America
Font, Conchita
Fontanes, Antonio
Franco, Rafael
Fuentes, Juana
Gantres, Isabel
Garcia Correa, Alberto
Garcia, Eduviges
Garcia, Juan
Garcia, Pedro
Geigel, Carmen
Ginorio, Miguel
Gonzalez, Camilo
Gonzalez, Enrique
Gonzalez, Juan Jose
Gonzalez, Providencia
Gonzalez, Teodoro (1)
Gonzalez, Teodoro (2)
Guillan, Mercedes
Guillot, Geronima
Huerta, Evaristo
Hutchinson, Constance
Hutchinson, Harriet

Iglesias, Angel
Iglesias, Emma
Iglesias, Ramon
Jacobs, Ana
Jacobs, Jose E.
Jones, Antonia
Jordan, Angel
Kerchival, McCormick
La Cruz, Amelia
Latimer, C. (Jr.)
Latimer, Mercedes
Loaiza, Gumersinda
Lopez, Juan
Lucero, Rafael
Maiz, Carolina
Marcial, Isabel
Marquez, Mercedes
Marrero, Maria Luisa
Martinez, Carmen
 Luisa
Martinez, Eva
Martinez, Isabel
Marxuach Guisasola,
 Mercedes
Montes, Carmen
Morales Torruella,
 Carlos J.
Nater, Angel
Navarro, Paca
Nieves, Carmen
Nieves, Juan
Ocasio, Maria Luisa
Ocasio, Salvador
Olivero, Enrique
Olmo, Juanita
Oxios, Gregorio
Padilla, Ramona
Padro Naranjo, Jaime
Padro Rourii, Pura
Pagan, Celia
Pardo Encinas, Juana
Parrilla, Gregoria
Perez, Elisa
Perez, Mario
Plau, Conrado
Plaza, Narcisa
Polaco, Rafael
Prieto, Carmen
Pujols, Pedro
Pumarada, Manuel
Quiñones, Matilde
Quiñones, Victor Luis
Quintana, Armando
Ramon, Ramos

Ramos, Candida
Ramos, Damaso
Rassy, Consuelo
Rivera, Gloria Maria
Rivera, Julia
Rivera, Justa
Roche, Amparo
Rodriguez, Ana C.
Rodriguez, Angela
Rodriguez, Asuncion
Rodriguez, Carlota
Rodriguez, Gilda
Rodriguez, Pablo
Rodriguez, Rafael
Rodriguez, Samuel
Rodriguez, Victoria
Rodriguez, Zoraida
Roman, Carlos
Romero, Elidio
Roque, Carmen
Rosa, Jorge
Salas, Milagros
Saldaña, Luis M.
Saldañas, Eduardo L.
Sanchez, Manuel M.
Santana, Dominga
Sierra, Gloria L.
Simounet, Naida
Sindice, Carlos
Suse, Ehsadora
Torres, Juana
Travieso, Manuel
Vachier, Ana
Vassallo Juliaz, E.
Vazquez, Angel
Vazquez, Carmelo
Vazquez, Luis
Velazquez, Gregoria
Velazquez, Rafael
Ventura, Maria
Vergne, Esther
Wilson, John
Wilson, Maria
Wulf, Willie

School Students, Vega Baja

School Children, Vega Baja (Telegram)

High School Ladies, Yauco

Almodovar, Esperanza
Antongiorgi, Lali
Antongiorgi, Nene
Baco Pasarell, Maria
Colon, Petra Maria
Cuprill Rivera, Olive
Cuprill, Leonor M.
Del Toro, Dolores
 Elisa
Diaz, Aurora
Figueroa, Maria
 Teresa
Grau, Goria Elisa
Guzman, Consuelo
Harrington, Ana
Irizarri, Amalia
 Sanabria
Lebron, Maria
 Gregoria
Lucea, Juana Josefa
Miranda, Rosa J.
Negron, Ana Maria
Negroni, Francisca
 Antonia
Negroni, Rosa C.
Nigaglioni, America
Olivieri Grau, Adela
Olivieri Grau, Rosa C.
Perez, Rosa Julia
Pla Aymard, America
Pla Aymard, Pepita
Quiñones, Ursula
Ramirez, Celina
Roura, Francisca L.
Serra, Laura Maria
Silva, Juana Josefa
Tio, Leera Malaret
Torres, Rosa Maria
Torres, Susana
Velez, Benicia
Velez, Esther

IX.

UNIVERSITY STUDENTS

Loyola Medical School Students, Chicago, IL

Alvarez, J.
Bengoa, Jose I.
Berdecia, Ramon B.,
 (Ph.D.)
Caban, Edelmiro J.
Caparros, Jose A.
 (LLB)
Diaz, Rodolfo
Fuentes, Oscar J.
Gotay, Jose B. (Jr.)
Graulau, Louis M.
Hernandez, Jose A.
Hoione, Saha (Jr.)
Lastra, Charriz, J.
Legen, Jorge N.
Mancebo, Juan M.
Mathias, Raymond
Reddis Perez, Dr.
Reyes, Antonio R.
Serra, Jaime
Sosa, Juan C.
Zamadug, Francisco S.

Harvard University Students, Cambridge, MA

Albizu y Campos,
 Pedro
Matienzo, Manuel (I
 Law)
Rivera, Guillermo

. . .

208

209

Lopez, Elena
Lopez, Fidel
Lopez, Ida M.
Lopez, Isabel
Lopez, Jose B.
Lopez, Jose Manuel
Lopez, Lucia
Lopez, Manuel (Jr.)
Lopez, Maria
Lugo Burgos, Juan
Lugo Burgos, Maria
Luna, Luz Maria
Maldonado, Delfin
Maldonado, Juan
Manzano Padro, Aurelia
Manzano, Aurelia L.
Marrero, Carlos I.
Marrero, Carlota
Marrero, Elena
Marrero, Patria
Martinez, Emeterio
Martinez, Erasmo
Melendez, Bienvenida
Melendez, Enrique
Melendez, Florita
Mercado, Maria A.
Millan de Torres, Zoila
Millan Vda. de Burgos, Dolores
Moscoso, Alejandrina M.
Moscoso, Teodoro
Ortiz, Quintin
Pagan, Candido
Pagan, Romualdo
Pascual, Gloria
Pereles, Meliton
Perelez, Emilia
Perelez, Isabel
Perelez, Pedro F.
Perelez, Pedro P.
Perelez, Virginia
Rivera Colon, Rosa Maria
Rivera de Lopez, Nieves
Rivera Gomez, R.
Rivera Rivera, Baldomero
Rivera Vda. de Torres, Carmen
Rivera y Fuentes, Rodolfo

Rivera, Francisca
Rivera, Gloria Mercedes
Rivera, Jesus
Rivera, Josefa
Rivera, Manolo
Rivera, Perfecta
Rivera, Ramon Teodomiro
Rivera, Soledad
Rodriguez del Rosario, R.
Rodriguez Flores, Castulo
Rodriguez Garay, Engracia
Rodriguez, Benigno
Rodriguez, Carlos A.
Rodriguez, Elisa
Rodriguez, Elvira
Rodriguez, Evangelina
Rodriguez, Hotilo
Rodriguez, J. B.
Rodriguez, J. M. (M.D.)
Rodriguez, Julio
Rodriguez, Manuel
Rodriguez, Mateo
Rodriguez, Olimpia
Rodriguez, Providencia
Rodriguez, Sinforosa
Rojas Negron, Angela
Rojas Negron, Concha
Rojas Negron, Elvira
Rojas Negron, Mercedes
Roman Velazquez, Ramon
Rosario, Angelica
Rosario, Manuel
Rosario, Miguel
Rosario, Pablo
Santiago, Santiago
Santini Vda. de Colon, Maseli
Santini, Clemencia
Santini, J. D.
Santini, Jose A.
Santini, Josefa Maria
Santini, Maria Dolores
Santini, Mercedes
Sariego de Rodriguez, Jacinta

Sierra, Auristela
Suarez, Antonio
Todd (de), Celestina R.
Torre, Rita Maria
Torres (de), Placida O.
Torres de Lopez, Lola
Torres, Gregorio
Torres, Hernando
Torres, Manuel
Torres, Modesto
Torres, Rafael
Torres, Ulpiano (I)
Torres, Ulpiano (II)
Umpierre, Arturo
Vazquez, Amalia
Vazquez, Antonio
Vazquez, Clotilde
Vazquez, Floiran
Vazquez, Placida
Vazquez, Sinforosa
Velazquez, Luisa
Villanny, Salvador
Villaron y Hermanos

Bayamon

Damas de Bayamon (Ladies of Bayamon)

Aguayo, Belen
Alum, Elisa
Alum, Leonor
Alum, Lida
Alum, Mariana
Alustiza, Ines
Barreras Rodas, Mercedes
Barreras, Carmen
Barreras, Maria
Bedoña, Petrona
Bochetti, A.
Borrero (de), Mercedes
Burgos, Francisca
Cabrera, Carmen
Cabreras, Julia
Carmona (Vda. de), Maria R.
Carmona, Carmelina
Carmona, Enriqueta

Carmona, Mercedes
Carmona, Rosa Maria
Casas, Rogelia
Cepero de Roque, Dolores
Cerezo, Amanda
Cestero (de), Carmen H.
Cestero (de), Concepcion R.
Cestero Eva
Cestero, Ysolina
Cobian (de), Natalia G.
Coll (de), Maria V.
Coll, Maria
Colon, Carmen R.
Colon, Juana
Cordova, Rosario
Coto, Isabel
Cruz (de), Asuncion
Cruz, Aguda
Cruz, Secundina
Cruz, Soledad
Cumba, Adela R.
Cumba, Antonia
Cumba, Maria
Cumba, Sebastiana
Cumba, Tomasa R.
Davila (de), Carmen N.
Davila, Carmen
Davila, J. V.
Davila, Julia
Davila, Paulina
Davila, Ramona
Davila, Ursula
De Feliu, Angela Balseiro
Del Arroyo de G., Matilde S.
Del Arroyo Vda. de Gutierrez, Maria I.
Del Arroyo, Gracia G.
Descartes, Maria L.
Diaz, Clotilde
Espinosa, Juliana
Espinosa, Maria
Feliu de Feliu, Elena
Feliu de Feliu, Florentina
Feliu y Feliu, Dolores
Feliu y Feliu, Mercedes

Ferno (de), Luz L.
Ferreras, Joaquina
Garcia de Loysele, Ana
Gastanbide, Adriana L.
Gauri, Candida
Gelabert (de), Carmen
Gimenez (de), Eloisa A.
Gimenez (Vda. de), Guadalupe D.
Gimenez, Isabel
Gomez, Silvia
Gonzalez (de), Luisa R.
Gonzalez (de), Maria O.
Gonzalez, Antonia
Gonzalez, Maria
Gonzalez, R.
Gonzalez, Rosa C.
Gregory (de), Concepcion T.
Guijarro (de), Carmen C.
Gulbe (Vda. de), Felicita P.
Gulbe, Maria
Gutierrez del Arroyo (Vda. de), Ysabel M.
Gutierrez del Arroyo, Secundina
Gutierrez, Acacia
Gutierrez, Belen M.
Gutierrez, Carmen
Gutierrez, Georgina
Gutierrez, Mercedes
Hernandez (de), Antonia R.
Higueras, Maria
Jimenez de Bas, Maria Carlota
Jorge, Paca
Jove Descartes, Elsa
Jove, Mercedes
Jove, Rosa Maria
Lampon, Carmen I.
Lampon, Julia
Lampon, Maria
Lavandero, Pablo (Jr.)
Lavandero, Francisca
Lopez (de), Rosa L.
Lopez (de), Tellita I.
Lopez (Vda. de),

Josefa C.
Lopez de Jove, Manuela
Lopez, Blanca Maria
Loubriel, Carmen
Loysele, Ana Matilde
Lugo Vda. de Rosario, Vicenta
Marquez, Juana
Marquez, Luisa
Marquez, Pura
Mas (de), Estela R.
Mas, Julia
Mas, Pura
Matos de Charbomier, Ana Maria
Maymi (de), Florentina H.
Maymi (e), Dominga M.
Maymi, Luisa
Mendizabal, Concepcion
Miller, Emma
Mimiro, Emilia
Mimiro, Rosa
Mitchell, Ramona
Morales, Maria N.
Morales, Sarah Marquez
Negron, Rosario
Nieve, Dionisa
Nieves (de), Maria
Nieves, Aurea C.
Nieves, Carmen Josefa
Nieves, Concha
Nieves, Rosa Maria
Oller (de), Petra M. (1)
Oller, Carmen Maria (1)
Oller, Georgina (1)
Oller, Petra Laura (1)
Oller, Teresa I.
Otero (de), Carmen C.
Otero de Perez, Julia
Pacheco, Benilde
Peña (de), Ines U.
Peña, Julia
Peña, Luz G.
Perez, Maria Jesusa
Perez, Monsita
Perez, Rosa
Pesquera (de), Maria L.

Pesquera Davila, Luisa
Pesquera Davila, Mercedes
Pesquera Davila, Rosa
Pesquera, Amparo
Pesquera, Jesusa
Pesquera, Luisa
Placer (de), Teresa D.
Placer, Rosa
Ponton Carmona, Maria Isabel
Prats, Isabel
Purcell (de), Carmen R
Quiros (Vda. de), Vicenta Perez
Quiros Perez, Rodesinda
Quiros Perez, Teresa
Ramirez de Rosario, Tomasa
Ramirez, (Vda. de), Onofrina
Ramirez, Josefa
Ramirez, Maria
Ramirez, Vicenta
Rengel, Elena
Rijol, Rita
Rivera, Eloisa
Rivera, Georgina
Rivera, Irene
Rivera, Juana
Rodriguez (Vda. de), Carmen F.
Rodriguez de Vela, Dolores
Rodriguez, Enriqueta
Rodriguez, Josefa
Rodriguez, Rosa Maria
Roman, Julia
Roque y Cepero, Dolores
Rosado, Maria R.
Rosales, Manuela
Rosario, Ana Rosa
Rosario, Maria Belen
Salgado Vda. de Maymi, Clemencia
Sanchez (de), L. A.
Sanchez, Angelina
Sanchez, Delfina
Santana de Ferrer, Rita
Santana de Pagan, Juana

Santiago (de), Carmen L.
Santiago, Luisa
Santiago, Maria C.
Santiago, Nicolasa
Sauri, Feliciana
Serrano, Antonia
Serrano, Saturna
Sierra, Lucia
Sierra, Usela
Sifre, Ana N.
Silva (de), Felisabel M.
Silva, Monserrate
Solla, Antonia
Solla, tomasa
Suarez (Vda. de), Rosaura
Tirado, Isabel
Tormos, Rosario
Torres de Tormos, Juana
Torres, O. Jove
Umpierre (de), Maria V.
Umpierre, America
Vaez, Brigida
Vaez, Maria
Vazquez, Epigmenia
Vazquez, Petra
Vela, Carmen Belen
Vela, Maria C.
Vela, Mercedes
Venegas (de), Belen C.
Venegas, Consueleto
Verges, Antonia
Verges, Maria Luisa
Verges(de), Luisa
Viner C., Blanca R.
Viner, Enriqueta M.

Damas de Bayamon (Ladies of Bayamon)

(Telegram)

Jovet, Oriola

...

Damas de Bayamon (Ladies of Bayamon) (Addressing President Wilson)

Acosta (Vda. de), Josefa B.
Acosta de Rivera, Maria Teresa
Acosta de Vela, Guadalupe
Aguayo, Antonia
Aguilar (Vda. de), Antonio C.
Aguilo (de), Concepcion G.
Alamo, Belen
Albizo de Vargas, Ramona
Aldebol, Pura (Srta.)
Alejandro de Esposito, Valeria
Alfaro (de), Mercedes L.
Alisea (de), Carmen A.
Alum, Elisa
Alum, Leonor
Alum, Lida
Alum, Mariana
Alutisia, Antonia
Alutisia, Dolores
Alvarez Aponte, Julia
Alvarez de Cabeza, Manuela
Alvarez, Aurelia
Alvarez, Dolores
Alvarez, Herminia
Alvarez, Julia
Alvarez, Patrocinia
Amador, Angelina
Amador, Juana
Amador, Maria
Aponte de Querol, Agueda
Aponte, Felicita
Ayala, Juana
Baez de Diaz, Carmen
Balseiro de Feliu, Angelina
Balseiro de Milian, Nicolasa

Barbosa (de), Carmen N.
Barbosa (de), Monserrate R.
Barbosa de Cotto, Rita
Barreras, Mercedes
Batalla, Carmen
Batalla, Monserrate
Bernard de Hostos, Marcola
Bibiloni, Manuela
Bonilla, Rosa
Borrero (de), Mercedes
Buron, Celia
Buron Lopez, Celia
Buyosa, Maria
Cabeza, Juana
Cabeza, Angelina
Cabeza, Carmen
Cabeza, Manuela
Cabeza, Maria
Cabrera Gonzalez, M. Cristina
Cabrera Rivera, Crusita
Cabrera Rivera, Herminia
Cabrera Rivera, Maria
Cabrera Rivera, Rosario
Cabrera, Alejandrina
Cabrera, Amelia
Cabrera, Angela
Cabrera, Cristina
Camara, Adela
Camara, Agustina
Camara, Filomena
Camara, Julia
Candelaria, Esperanza
Candia (de), Higinia R.
Canetty de Melendez, Cruz
Carmona (Vda. de), Maria R.
Carmona de Vimer, Enriqueta
Carmona, Clemencia
Carmona, Maria M.
Carmona, Mercedes
Carmona, Monserrate
Carmona, Rosa M.
Carrasco de Garcia,

Maria
Casals, Celestina
Castro, Justina
Castro, Petra (1)
Castro, Petra (2)
Cestero (de), Carmen H.
Cestero Grajirene, Maria
Cestero, Ester
Cestero, Eva
Cestero, Haydie
Cestero, Isolina
Cestero, Mercedes
Charbonner (de), Ana Maria M.
Chaves, Juana
Chevalier Vda. de Laguna, Emilia
Chevere, Generosa
Chiesa (de), Herminia V.
Chiesa, Carmen
Chiesa, Maria Luisa
Chinea (de), Lucia S.
Cobian (de), Natalia G.
Cobian de Sollas, Elisa
Colon (de), Carmen R.
Colon de Natal, Serafina
Colon de Reg., Rosaura
Colon, Ana Maria
Colon, Carmen
Corada (de), Justa Rosa
Corada, Ana Maria
Cordova (Vda. de), Guillermina
Cordova, Rosario
Coto, Trinidad
Cotto Felipa
Cotto Francisca
Cotto, Valentina
Cruz (de), Asuncion S.
Cruz (de), Baldomera
Cruz (de), Cotilde
Cruz (Vda. de), Maria Diaz
Cruz de Hernandez, Aracelis
Cruz de Juan, Maria
Cruz de Sanchez,

Concepcion
Cruz Juan, Juana
Cruz Noble, Rosa
Cruz, Soledad
Cuyar de Otero, Matilde
Davila Vda. de Jimenez, Guadalupe
Davila y Morales, Carmen
Davila y Morales, Paulina
Davila, Catalina
Davila, Guillermina
Davila, Josefa
Davila, Maria
Davila, Mariana
De Llovio (de), Guadalupe D.
De Maymi, Dominga M.
De Viner, Carmen Maria P.
Defontaine, Adela S.
Del Arroyo (de G.), Matilde Y.
Del Arroyo de Alvarez, Belen G.
Del Arroyo, Secundina S.
Delgado, Jesusa
Deliz de Ortiz, Maria
Diaz (de), Romana R.
Diaz Gonzalez, Mercedes
Diaz Vda. de Carrion, J.
Diaz, Antonia
Diaz, Mercedes
Dones, Maria
Duran de Gimenez, Juana
Espinet de Nieves, Eugenia
Espinosa, Juliana
Estrada, Laura
Feliu (Vda. de), Belen M.
Feliu Balseiro, Angela
Feliu de Feliu, Elen
Feliu de Feliu, Florentina
Feliu de Martino, Luisa

Feliu Feliu, Dolores
Feliu Feliu, Mercedes
Feliu, Anita
Feliu, Maria Enna
Ferrer de Torre,
  Basilides
Ferrer de Varela,
  Margarita
Ferrer Vda. de
  Rodriguez, Carmen
Ferrer, Alejandra
Ferrer, Francisca
Figueroa, Vicenta
Figueroa, Victoria
Flores, Maria
Flores, Mercedes
Flores, Petronila
Florit, Carmen
Forteza de Rivera,
  Maria
Fournier (de), Carmen
Fuentes (de), Maria R.
Fuentes Vda. de Tibot,
  Carmen
Garcia (de), Florencia
  D.
Garcia (de), Trinidad
  G.
Garcia de Acosta,
  Carolina
Garcia de Loysele, Ana
Garcia, Carmen
Garcia, Generosa
Garcia, Julia
Gelabert, Carmen E.
Gimenez (de), Eloisa
  A.
Gimenez Davila,
  Amparo
Gimenez, Carmen L.
Gimenez, Isabelita
Gimenez, Nati
Gimenez, Ysabel
Gomez, Celia
Gomez, Faustiana
Gomez, Francisca
Gomez, Josefa
Gonzalez (de), Maria
  O.
Gonzalez, Ana M.
Gonzalez, Antonia
Gonzalez, Carmen
Gonzalez, Maria
Gonzalez, Patria

Gonzalez, Rosa C.
Gracia (de), Bartola L.
Gracia, Antonia
Granela, America G.
Grau, Adelina
Guardarama, Ruperta
Guijarro (de), Carmen
  C.
Guitierrez, Belen
Guitierrez, Giorgina
Guitierrez, Luz Maria
Gulbe (Vda. de),
  Felicita
Guricalday (de),
  Blanca R.
Gutierrez (de), Maria
Gutierrez, Acacia
Gutierrez, Carmen
Gutierrez, Mercedes
Hance, Carmen
Hance, Engracia
Hance, Filomena
Hance, Marta
Hance, Melanie
Heraso, Castula
Hernandez (de),
  Antonia R.
Hernandez de
  Gonzalez, Octavia
Hernandez Montilla,
  Maria Juana
Hernandez,
  Encarnacion
Hernandez, Juana
Hernandez, Nicolasa
Hernandez, Ramona
Higuera Vda. de
  Espinosa, Julia
Higueras (de), Maria
  E.
Higueras, Maria
Hostos de Rivera,
  Teresa
Hostos, Rosalina
Huerta, Candida
Izquierdo (de), Angela
  I.
Izquierdo (De),
  Obdulia R.
Izquierdo de Diaz,
  Josefa
Izquierdo de Dolla,
  Blanca
Izquierdo de Quintero,

Cruz
Izquierdo, Esperanza
Izquierdo, Francisca
Izquierdo, Maria
Izquierdo, Victoria
Izquierdo, Maria Ester
Jimenez de Bas, Maria
  Carlota
Jove Torres, Mercedes
Jove Torres, Oriola
Juan de Juan,
  Policarpa
Juan de Maldonado,
  Maria
Juan Rivera, Ricarda
Julbe, Maria
Julia Santiago, Maria
La Barca, Gloria M.
La Barca, Maria R.
La Barca, Rosa M.
Lampon (de), Candida
  S.
Lampon, Candelaria
Lampon, Carmen
  Odalisca
Lampon, Julia
  Margarita
Lampon, Providencia
Lampon, Rafaela
Lanosa, Providencia
Lebron de Martorani,
  Francisca
Linarez, Cruz Maria
Llano (de), Josefa S.
Llovio, Lucila
Lopez (de), Tellito G.
Lopez Cepero de
  Roque, Dolores
Lopez de Trujillo,
  Trinidad
Lopez, Francisca
Loysele, Ana Matilde
Maldonado, Carmen
Maldonado, Rosa
  Maria
Marcano (Vda. de),
  Heriberta
Marquez (de),
  Eufrosina
Marquez, Trinidad
Marrero, Francisca
Martinez (de),
  Claudina C.
Martinez (de), Maria

C.
Martinez (Vda. de),
  Higinia P.
Martinez de Julia,
  Emilia
Martinez de
  Rodriguez, Carmen
Martinez, Conrado
Martinez, Guillermina
  P.
Martinez, Julia
Martinez, Maria (1)
Martinez, Maria (2)
Martinez, Martina
Martinez, Petronila
Martinez, Ramona
Marvaldi d Reyes,
  Serafina
Mas (de), Estela
  Ramirez
Mas, Isabel
Mas, Merida
Mas, Pura
Maymi, Florentina H.
Maymi, Luisa
Mediavilla (de),
  Asuncion
Mediavilla, Josefina
Mediavilla,
  Monserrate
Mediavilla, Mte.
Mediavilla, Rita (1)
Mediavilla, Rita (2)
Melendez (de) Patrisia
  F.
Melendez de Ducre,
  Carmen
Melendez de Rosa,
  Esequiela
Melendez, Asuncion
Melendez, Mercedes
Menendez, Agustina
Merayes (Vda. de),
  Carmen P,
Mimose, Rosa
Mimoso de Lajara,
  Emilia
Miranda (de),
  Altagracia B.
Mitchell, Ramona
Montero, Modesta
Montilla, Enriqueta
Montilla, Julia
Morales (de), Petra M.

Morales de Davila, Carmen
Morales de Muñoz, Aurelia
Morales, A. Maria
Morales, Francisca
Morales, Juana
Morales, Manuela (1)
Morales, Manuela (2)
Morales, Maria (1)
Morales, Maria (2)
Morales, Obdulia
Morales, Petra
Moratalla, Dolores
Moratalla, Genoveva
Moratalla, Mercedes
Mulers, Engracia
Munich, Encarnacion
Munich, Rita
Muñiz de Torre, Josefa
Muñoz (de), Mercedes A.
Muñoz (Vda. de), Josefa I.
Muñoz de Cordova, Maria
Muñoz de Soler, Josefina
Natal, Regina
Navarro (de), Petra R.
Navas, Rosa
Negron Garcia, Emilia
Negron, Emilia
Negron, Juana
Negron, Maria
Negron, Simona
Nieve de Lavandero, Dionisia
Nieves (de), Maria G.
Nieves (de), Maria Perez
Nieves, Aurea C.
Nieves, Carmen
Nieves, Mercedes
Nieves, Meregilda
Nuñez, Rafaela
Ojeda, Petra
Olivero, Juanita
Oller (de), Petra M. (2)
Oller, Carmen Maria (2)
Oller, Georgina (2)
Oller, Petra Laura (2)

Oquendo, Candelaria
Oquendo, Luisa
Ortega, Monserrate
Ortiz, Nicomedes
Ortiz, Obdulia
Otero (de), Carmen C.
Otero Cuyar, Manuela
Otero Cuyar, Matilde
Otero Cuyar, Mercedes
Otero de Perez, Julia
Otero, Carmelina
Pacheco, Mercedes
Pacheco, Nicomedes
Pacheco, Rafaela
Padro (Vda. de), Dolores F.
Pagan, Elena
Pagan, Isabel
Pagan, Merida
Pagan, Providencia
Pagola, Pepa
Pascual (de), Ysabel G.
Pedrosa, Martina
Pereira, Merida
Pereira, Rosario
Pesquera (de), Julia C.
Pesquera (de), Maria L.
Pesquera (de), Ynes D.
Pesquera Davila, Luisa
Pesquera Davila, Rosa
Pesquera Pascual, Luisa
Pesquera, Amparo
Pesquera, Carmen
Pesquera, Ines
Pesquera, Mercedes
Placer (de), Teresa D.
Placer, Rosa
Pomar (Vda. de), Josefa P.
Ponsa (de), Seculina F.
Portilla (de), Aurora J.
Pumas, Herminia
Quintero (de) Maria T.
Quintero, Manuela
Quiros (Vda. de), Vicenta P.
Quiros Perez, Rodesinda
Quiros Perez, Teresa
Ramires (de), Teresa C.

Ramirez (Vda. de), Onofrina
Ramirez de Mediavilla, Ana Rosa
Ramirez de Rosario, Tomasa
Ramirez, Gloria Josefa
Ramirez, Julia Palmira
Ramirez, Maria
Ramos (de), Felicita
Ramos (de), Maria M.
Ramos (Vda. de), Isabel O.
Ramos de Izquierdo, Ignacia
Ramos, Adriana
Ramos, Dora
Ramos, Luz Maria
Ramos, Margarita
Ramos, Raquel
Ramos, Victoria
Rey Colon, Monserrate
Rey, Antonia
Rey, Josefa
Rey, Maria
Reyes de Rodriguez, Felicita
Reyes, Angela
Reyes, Carmita
Reyes, Hortensia
Reyes, Jenoveba
Reyes, Leonides
Reyes, Mercedes
Reyes, Paula
Reyes, Rosario
Reyes, Cruz
Ribera (de), Rosa B.
Richardson (de), Elena R.
Rijos, Rita
Rivera de Acebedo, Dolores
Rivera de Espinet, Melania
Rivera de Franco, Cruz
Rivera de Gracia, Rosa
Rivera de Ramos, Gregoria
Rivera de Rivera, Asuncion (1)
Rivera de Rivera, Asuncion (2)

Rivera de Torres, Mercedes
Rivera, Amelia
Rivera, Ana M.
Rivera, Angelina
Rivera, Carmen M.
Rivera, Dolores (1)
Rivera, Dolores (2)
Rivera, Eulogia
Rivera, Eva M.
Rivera, Feliciana L.
Rivera, Francisca
Rivera, Josefa
Rivera, Juana
Rivera, Maria (1)
Rivera, Maria (2)
Rivera, Martina
Rivera, Petrona
Rivera, Providencia
Rivera, Pura
Rivera, Ramona
Rivera, Sofia
Rivera, Vandilia
Rodrigues, Consuelo
Rodriguez (de), Estefania A.
Rodriguez (de), Maria P.
Rodriguez (de), Mercedes R.
Rodriguez de Grau, Carmen
Rodriguez de Purcell, Carmen
Rodriguez de Rodriguez, Monserrate
Rodriguez de Rosado, Juana
Rodriguez de Toro, Maria T.
Rodriguez de Vela, Dolores
Rodriguez Vda. de Olmo, Heriberta
Rodriguez, Ana
Rodriguez, Carmen
Rodriguez, Elisa
Rodriguez, Felicita
Rodriguez, Francisca
Rodriguez, Isabel E.
Rodriguez, Josefa
Rodriguez, Juana
Rodriguez, Maria (1)

214

Rodriguez, Maria (2)
Rodriguez, Maria E.
Rodriguez, Maria
  Victoria
Rodriguez, Marta
Rodriguez, Mercedes
Rodriguez, Ramona
  (1)
Rodriguez, Ramona
  (2)
Rodriguez, Rosa
Rodriguez, Rosa Maria
Rodriguez, Ysabel
Rolon (de), Herminia
  G.
Rolon, Aida
Rolon, Angelina
Rolon, Otilia
Roman, Juana
Roman, Julia
Roque de Bosch,
  Carmen
Roque, Juanita
Roque, Lolita
Rosado (de), Hipolita
  F.
Rosado (de),
  Monserrate I.
Rosado Lopes, Adela
Rosado Nieves, Adela
Rosado, Aparicia
Rosado, Carmen
Rosado, Fernanda
Rosado, Julia
Rosado, Leonor
Rosario, Angela
Rosario de Gonzalez,
  Luisa
Rosario, Ana
Rosario, Ana Rosa
Rosario, Victoria
Ruiz, Blacina
Ruiz, Carmen
Salgado (de),
  Concepcion M.
Salgado (de), Ramona
Salgado (de), Ramona
  O.
Salgado Vda. de
  Maymi, Clemencia
Salgado, Teresa
San Miguel, Ercilia
Sanchez (de), L. A.
Sanchez de Wuirall,

Delfina
Sanchez Lopez (Vda.
  de), Concepcion T.
Sanchez, America
Sanchez, Cecilia
Sanchez, Maria
Sanchez, Marina
Santiago (de), Carmen
  L.
Santiago (de), Maria
  M
Santiago Carmen
Santiago, Alicia
Santiago, Altagracia
Santiago, Maria C.
Santos de Cruz, Josefa
Santos de Estrada,
  Maria
Santos, Aurea
Sariego, Flora
Sariego, Maria
Serra, Antonia (Srta.)
Sierra de Lampon,
  Lucia
Sierra de Tirado,
  Ursula
Silva (de), Selisabel
Solla, Tomasa
Sotero de Barbosa,
  Lucia
Soto, Antonia
Soto, Aurelia
Soto, Juana
Soto, Julia
Sotomayor de Vaillat,
  Ramona
Stahl de Robinson,
  Agustina
Suarez (de), Daniela
  D.
Suarez (de), Liboria A.
Suarez (Vda. de),
  Rosaura
Suarez, Ana L.
Suarez, Elena
Suarez, Mercedes
Suarez, Rosa M.
Tibot, Carmen
Tirado, Isabel
Tormos, Carmen
Tormos, Rosario
Torre Muñiz,
  Guillermina
Torre, Rosa Maria

Torres (de), Rosa M.
Torres de Rivera,
  Obdulia
Torres de Rosado,
  Josefa
Torres de Tormos,
  Juana
Torres Tores, Emilia
Torres, Concepcion
Torres, Fidela
Torres, Maria
Torrez de Trinidad,
  Beatriz
Trilla, Pura
Tulbe Poufart, Maria
Umpierre (de), Maria
  V.
Umpierre (de),
  Rosario Y.
Umpierre, America
Umpierre, Carmen
Umpierre, Teresa
Vaillant, Antonia
Valdes, Carmen
Varela de Salgado,
  Julia
Varela, Maria Luisa
Varela, Rafaela (1)
Varela, Rafaela (2)
Varela, Teresa de
  Jesus
Vargas, Julia
Vasques, Catalina
Vasques, Felicita
Vay, Carmen
Vay, Julia
Vazquez, Basilia
Vazquez, Candelaria
Vazquez, Dolores
Vazquez, Epigmenia
Vazquez, Etervina
Vazquez, Juana
Vazquez, Librada
Vazquez, Maria
Vazquez, Petra
Vela Rodriguez,
  Mercedes
Vela, Mary
Velazquez, Angeles
Vengas, Consuelo
Verges (de), Luisa S.
Verges, Antonia
Vicens (de), Petronila
  F.

Vicira, Maria
Vola de G. Del Arroyo,
  Ysabel Maria

Niñas de Bayamon (Girls of Bayamon)

Alvarez, Lolin
Alvarez, Maria
Aponte, Cruz
Arroyo, Ocacia G.
Baez, Emilia
Bas, M. Eiffelina
Camara, Agustina
Camara, Julia
Cestero, Eva
Charbounier, Rosa M.
Colon, Carmen
De Llovio, Antonia
De Llovio, Ernestina
De Llovio, Lucila
Delgado, Blanca R.
Feliu, Angela
Franco, Pura
Fuentes, Concepcion
Fuentes, Ebodia
Fuentes, Josefina
Gimenez, Estafana
Gimenez, Isabel
Gomez, Sylvia
Gonzalez, Ysabel
Guitierrez, Luz Maria
Gutierrez, Carmen
Gutierrez, Georgina
Gutierrez, Mercedes
Laborda, Maria Teresa
Lampon, America
Lampon, Maria
Lampon, Sulima
Marquez, Alicia
Marquez, Lydia
Marquez, Margarita
Martinez, Josefa
Montilla, Julio
Otero, Catalina
Ramos, Adriana
Ramos, Dora
Ramos, Luz Maria
Ramos, Margarita
Ramos, Raquel
Rengel, Elena
Rivera, Maria

Rodriguez, Maria
Rodriguez, Natividad
Roman, Geralda
Sanchez, Ana M.
Sanchez, Mercedes
Sifre, Ana M.
Soto, Julia
Suarez, Ana L.
Suarez, Elena
Suarez, Mercedes
Suarez, Rosa M.
Trilla, Parila
Trilla, Pura
Trillla, Elisa
Umpierre, Elisa
Umpierre, Pura
Vazquez, Dolores
Venegas, Consuelo V.
Verges, Antonia
Verges, Maria L.

Cabo Rojo

Cabo Rojo Mayor
 (Telegram)

Camuy

Aguirre, Manuel J.
Amador, Carmelo
Arrieta, A. L.
Arrieta, B.
Arroyo, Cosme
Arroyo, Juan
Avila, Domingo
Avila, Ramon
Badia, Francisco (Jr.)
Barios, Jose L.
Caban, Manuel
Cagiga, Fructuoso
Caso Soto, Luis
 (Lcdo.)
Crespo, Antonio
Cruz y Vega, Pedro
Cruz, Andres
Cruz, Francisco
Cruz, Hilario
Cruz, Jose
Cruz, Quintin
Cubero, Juan (II)
Cubero, Juan
De Hostos, B.

De Jesus, Felipe
De Jesus, Francisco
De Jesus, Jose
De Jesus, Mateo
Estrella, Antonio
Estrella, Ramon
Firpi, Justicioso
Franqui, Guillermo
Gonzalez, Anivacio
Gonzalez, Antonio
Gonzalez, Dalielo
Gonzalez, Jose D.
Hernandez, Pedro
 (Jr.)
Hernandez, Miguel H.
Hurriño, Adolfo
Jimenez, Adolfo
Jimenez, Andres
Jimenez, Juan
Jimenez, Ramon
Laborde, Osvaldo
Lacomba, Jose R.
Lamourt, Luis
Lapeña, Esteban
Lopez, Cesalio
Lopez, Hilario
Lopez, Juan B.
Martinez, Jesus
Matthews, Jose J.
May, Miguel
Melendez Valero, Jose
Miranda, Alberto
Miranda, J. R.
Miranda, Manuel
Morales Rojas,
 Sinforoso
Morales, Angel
Morales, Juan S. (Dr.)
Nieves, Agustin
Nieves, Jesus
Nolla, Jose
Olivera, Juan A.
Oslan Rios, Jose
Padilla, Baldomero
Paminas, Jose S.
Perez, H. Dario
Pozo, Pedro
Ramos, Nemecio
Rios, Carmelo
Robles, Tomas
Rodriguez, Federico
Roman y Rios, Jose
Roman, Cosme
Roman, Juan

Roman, Lorenzo
Roque, Domingo
Rosario, Eduardo
Santiago, Pedro
Serrano, Manuel
Trigo, Jose B.
Trigo, Valentin
Tripiz, Andres
Valentin, Jose
Vargas, Feliz
Vazquez, Emiliano
Velez Perez, J.
Velez, Santiago

Carolina

Madres de Carolina (Mothers of Carolina)

Acosta (Vda. de), Clara I.
Albandoz (de), Juana C.
Albandoz, Igna
Alonso (Vda. de), F. R.
Arce (de), Italica L.
Aubray, Concepcion
Bas, Aurora
Bernabe de Diaz, Cruz
Betancourt, Flora
Biascoechea (de), D. M.
Biascoechea (de), Juana S.
Biascoechea, Maria
Biascoechea, Sara
Bolorino, Elena
Borrero, Lorenza
Bracero, Clemencia
Bracero, Josefa
Casado, Emilia
Castaño (de), Petra Maria
Castaño (de), Ramona R.
Castro de Martinez, Carmen
Castro Lopez de Rivera, Maria Ana
Castro, Cornelia

Cogley, Josefa
Cogley, Jovita
Colon (de), Carmen C.
Colon de Cuin, Maria
Colon, Manuela A.
Cordero, Jose
Correa de Gimenez, Francisca
Couvertier, Maria
Cruz (de), Eleuteria L.
Cruz de Aponte, Eugenia
Cruz de Gonzalez, Acacia
Cruz Moscoso, Barbarita
Cuin, Providencia
De Castro Lopez, Maria Luisa
Diaz de R. Juanita
Doni F., Carmen
Droz de Bolonio, Leonor
Enseñat (Vda. de), Ceferina
Fernandez (de), Angela H.
Fernandez de Aubray, Amalia
Fernandez, Angela
Fernandez, Dolores
Figueroa, Carmen
Font Guillot, Josefina
Font Guillot, Rosa
Fragoso (de), Encarnacion F.
Frias (de), Isabel F.
Frias (Vda. de), Adela
Frias, Estela
Garcia (de), Matilde
Garcia Piñero, Matilde
Garcia, Micaela
Gari (Vda. de), Angelina, C.
Gari y Cruz, Luisa
Gimenez Correa, Antonia
Gonzalez (Vda. de), Sofia K.
Gonzalez, Balbina
Hecht, Providencia
Heredero (Vda. de), Frasquita
Hernandez (de),

Antonio's Grace

Matilde Hernandez (Vda. de), Teresina J.
Hernandez, Carmen
Hernandez, Maria I.
Hernandez, Sarah
Homar, Catalina
Iturregui (de), Isabel E.
Jimenez (de), Teresa R.
Jimenez de Diaz, Angelina
Jimenez de Gonzalez, Maria
Jimenez Sicardo, Paca
Juarez (de), Emilia H.
Larrononga, Concepcion
Manatu, Teresa
Mangual, Maria Gonzalez (de), Genara
Marin Masson (Vda. de), Carolina
Mezguidor, Catalina
Mezguidor, Margarita
Miranda Vda. de Caballero, Dolores
Ortiz (de), Natividad P.
Ortiz Pastrana, Petra
Ortiz y Marin, Herminia
Palacios (de), Carmen G.
Parson, Leonor
Pastrana, Isabel, H.
Pereira, Mercedes R.
Picorelli, Angela
Quero, Luisa
Ramero, Lucia
Ramos, Elvira
Ramos, Joaquina
Ramos, Marcela
Ribera, Teodosia
Rivera de Rivera, Vicenta
Rivera, Carmen
Rivera, Juanita
Rivera, Maria
Rivero Sicardo, Rosario
Rivero, Mercedes

Rivero, Pura
Rodriguez (de), Angela L.
Rodriguez, Paquita
Ryan, Adela
Ryan, Belen
Ryan, Cruz
Ryan, Josefa
Ryan, Maria
Ryan, Pedro
Sanchez (de), Genoveva C.
Sanchez Carrasquillo, Crista
Sanchez Castaño, Manuelita
Santana (de), Lola A.
Santana Davila, Edelmira
Santana Davila, Mercedes
Schroder (de), Rosa F.
Sicardo, Rosalia
Silbos de Perez, Monserrate
Tizol de Wolkers, Anna
Torres (de), Mercedes
Torres, Carmen M.
Trilla (Vda. de), Amalia A.
Van-Rhyn (de), Maria F.
Vargas (de), Catalina R.
Vargas, Amalia
Vargas, Dolores
Vazquez (de), Luisa P.
Vizcarrondo (de), Lorenza
Vizcarrondo, Catalina
Vizcarrondo, Quintina
Vizcarrondo, Rosenda
Wolkers, Victoria

Ciales

Ciales Citizens

Adorno, Luisa
Alber, Juana
Alonso, Antonia

Alonso, Carmen
Alvares, Rosa M.
Amber, Margarita
Apontes, Carmelita
Arbona, Isabel
Arbona, Maria
Arbona, Rosita
Arce, Aurea
Arce, Dolores
Archilla, Isabel
Armenteros (de), Antonia S.
Arocho, Rosalia
Arroyo, Compsecion (sp) (2)
Arroyo, Concepcion (2)
Arroyo, Maria
Arroyos, Goyita
Aulet Padro, Rosario
Aulet, Dolores
Aulet, Maria
Aulet, Rosario
Ayaela, Aparicia
Bable, Josefa
Barber (de), Eufemina
Barber, Maria L.
Barber, Pilar
Barber, Maria Luisa
Barquero, Emilia
Barreras, Blanca M.
Barreras, Cristina
Basquez, Paulina
Batista, Amelia
Bega, Lunita
Berganzo, Gregoria
Berrio, Engracia
Berrios, Juana
Bilche, Quintina
Blanco (de), Ana P.
Blanco, Blanca
Blanco, Celestina
Blanco, Maria I.
Blanco, Maria L.
Borges, Rosa M.
Burgos, Adelina
Burgos, Basilia
Burgos, Justina
Burgos, Maria R.
Burgos, Ramona
Cabañas, Encarnacion
Cabeza, Maria L.
Cabiya, Esperanza
Cabrera, Maria

Cabrera, Trinidad
Camacho, Juana
Camacho, Rosalia
Campos de Padro, Antonia
Campos, Josefa
Cardona, Camelia
Cardona, Dolores
Cardona, Isabel
Cardona, Josefa
Cardona, Luisa (1)
Cardona, Luisa (2)
Cardona, Maria
Cardona, Mira
Caro, Mercedes
Carrasquillo, Laura
Carrillo, Maria
Carrillo, Virginia
Cartajena, Carmen
Castellano, Antonia
Castellano, Flor Maria
Castellano, Luvelia
Castillo, Escolastica
Chimelis, Angela (1)
Chimelis, Angela (2)
Chimelis, Carmen (1)
Chimelis, Carmen (2)
Cla, Manuela
Clas, Valeria
Claudio, Providencia
Coetes, Adelaida
Colon, Agueda
Colon, Ana Maria
Colon, Antonia
Colon, Belen
Colon, Magdalena
Colon, Manuela
Colon, Pita
Colon, Pitita
Colon, Ricarda
Colon, Rita
Colon, Rosalia
Corda, Francisco
Cordero (de), Carmen R.
Cordero, Carmen
Cordero, Elvira
Cordero, Emilia
Cordero, Providencia
Cordova, Eulalia
Correa de Franceschi, Teresa
Correter, Maria
Corretjer (de), Clorina

217

Corretjer, Ana
Corretjer, Antonia
Corretjer, Carmen
Corretjer, Dolores
Corretjer, Eduvina M.
Corretjer, Elisa
Corretjer, Erminia
Corretjer, Rosa M.
Corretjer, Rosa Maria
Corretjer, Teresa (1)
Corretjer, Teresa (2)
Cortes, Adelaida
Cortes, Dolores
Cortes, Florence I.
Cortes, Isabel
Cortes, Juana
Cortes, Maria
Cortes, Otilia
Cortes, Rafaela
Cortes, Segunda
Cortes, Tomasa
Crespo, Enriqueta
Cruz Rivera, Maria
Cruz, Anastacia
Cruz, Maria (1)
Cruz, Maria (2)
Cruz, Mariana
Cruzado, Amanda
Davila (Vda. de)
  Manuela
Davila, Guillermina
Davila, Mercedes
Davila, Monserrate
De Jesus, Amalia
De Jesus, Clementina
De Jesus, Elisa
De Jesus, Lastenia
De Jesus, Rosa
De Leon Vda. de
  Muñiz, Juana
De los Rios, Emilia
Del Pino Maldonado,
  Juana
Del Pino, Mercedes
Del Rio, Rosa M.
Delgado, Antonia
Delgado, Dolores
Diaz, Amalia
Diaz, Anita
Diaz, Aurora
Diaz, Felicita
Diaz, Georgina
Diaz, Herminia
Diaz, Moncerrate

Diaz, Ramona
Diaz, Rita
Diez de C. Alejandra
Diez, Blanca C.
Dorontis, Ramonita
Duran, Apolinaria
Duran, Cecilia
Duran, Emilia
Duran, Paula
Duran, Rosa
Echavarry, Anastacia
Echavarry, Leonor
Echavarry, Tomasa
Feliz, Francisca
Fernandez, Amparo
Fernandez, Anita
Fernandez,
  Concepcion
Fernandez, Dolores
Fernandez, Emilia
Fernandez, Josefa
Fernandez, Paula
Ferre, Juana
Figueroa, Cristina
Figueroa, Daniela
Figueroa, Elvira
Figueroa, Juana
Figueroa, Maria
Figueroa, Nonverta
Figueroa, Rosario (1)
Figueroa, Rosario (2)
Fixenek (de), Rafaela
  M.
Flotanes, Carmela
Forquer, Laura F.
Ga (de), Hermelinda
Galindez, Juana
Garcia Vda. de Mislan,
  Lola
Garcia, Arcadia
Garcia, Lorenza
Gines, Eufemia
Gomez, Coloma
Gomez, Concepcion
Gomez, Cristina
Gomez, Josefa (1)
Gomez, Josefa (2)
Gomez, Juana
Gonzales, Candida
Gonzales, Celia
Gonzales, Maria
Gonzales, Santo
Gonzalez (de),
  Angelina C.

Gonzalez (de), Eresma
Gonzalez, Altagracia
Gonzalez, Aurea
Gonzalez, Carmen
Gonzalez, Juana (1)
Gonzalez, Juana (2)
Gonzalez, Juaquina
Gonzalez, Julia
Gonzalez, Luisa
Gonzalez, Maria (1)
Gonzalez, Maria (2)
Gonzalez, Purificacion
Gordo, Rosalia
Gracia, Isabel
Gutierrez, Blanca M.
Guzman, Juana
Hernandez (de), Clara
  M.
Hernandez (de), Maria
  P.
Hernandez, Angela
Hernandez, Antonia
  (1)
Hernandez, Antonia
  (2)
Hernandez, Balentina
Hernandez, Cecilia
Hernandez, Dominga
Hernandez, Emelina
Hernandez, Josefa
Hernandez, Juana
Hernandez, Marciala
Hernandez, Maria
Hernandez, Maria D.
Hernandez, Rafaela
Hernandez, Ramona
Hernandez, Rosa (1)
Hernandez, Rosa (2)
Hernandez, Rosa H.
Hernandez, Teresa
Huxench, Teresa
Ituarino, Santia D.
Jimenez, Amalia
Jimenez, Manuela
Lamoso, Filomena
Lanide, Maria del C.
Lasanta, Tomasa
Lasclotas, Rafaela
Leon (de), Josefa
Leon, Antonia
Longo, Clarisa
Lopez (de), Eloisa M.
Lopez (de), Esperanza
  G.

Lopez, Antonia
Lopez, Carmen (1)
Lopez, Carmen (2)
Lopez, Carmen (3)
Lopez, Emilia
Lopez, Flora
Lopez, Joaquina
Lopez, Josefa
Lopez, Juana
Lorenzana, Reyes
Losada, Juana
Maceira, Adelaida
Maceira, Bienbenida
Maceira, Bienvenida
Maceira, Carmen
Maceira, Ramona
Malaret de Berrio,
  Luisa
Maldonado, Basilisa
Maldonado,
  Concepcion
Maldonado, Cruz
Maldonado, Demencia
Maldonado, Ines
Maldonado, Juana
Maldonado, Maria L.
Manzano, Concepcion
Manzano, Luisa
Marrero, Adelina
Marrero, Amelia
Marrero, Angela
Marrero, Carmen
Marrero, Eladia
Marrero, Josefina
Marrero, Juana
Marrero, Tomasa
Martinez, Ana
Martinez, Ana Maria
Martinez, Angela
Martinez, Elisa D.
Martinez, Eulogia (1)
Martinez, Eulogia (2)
Martinez, Fernanda
Martinez, Guillermina
Martinez, Joaquina
Martinez, Mercedes
  (1)
Martinez, Mercedes
  (2)
Mato, Dolores
Mato, Matilde
Mato, Rosa
Matos, Carmen
Mayol (de), Maria P.

Mayol, Maria Ana (1)
Mayol, Maria Ana (2)
Mendez, Eduvijis
Menendez, Aniceta
Micaela, Catalina
Miranda (Vda. de),
  Guadalupe M.
Miranda, Adela
Miranda, Cecilia
Miranda, Dolores
Miranda, Flora
Miranda, Francisca (1)
Miranda, Francisca (2)
Miranda, Germira
Miranda, Luisa
Miranda, Nicomedes
Miranda, Ricarda
Miranda, Virginia (1)
Miranda, Virginia (2)
Mislan, Angela Luisa
Monetes, Paz
Montes, Conchita
Montes, Maria L.
Montes, Rita
Montijo, Adela
Montijo, Matilde
Montijo, Tomasa
Morales, Carmen
Morales, Encarnacion
Morales, Rafaela
Morales, Rosa (1)
Morales, Rosa (2)
Motijo, Adelaida
Muñiz (de), Rosalina
  N.
Muñiz, Rita
Muñoz, Carmen
Nabedo, Joaquina
Nater, Silvana
Navedo, Rafaela
Negron, Cecilia
Negron, Rafaela
Nieves, Zelmira
Noa, Demetria
Nuñez de Rodriguez,
  Maria
Nuñez, Adelia
Nuñez, Carmen
Nuñez, Ramona
Ocacio, Celestina
Ocacio, Fundadora
Ocacio, Rosa
Ocasio, Admirada
Ocasio, Elvira

Ocasio, Emilia
Ocasio, Julia
Olivo, Isabel
Olmo, Aurora
Orama, Angela
Orama, Yemia
Ortega, Antonia
Ortega, Gerturudis
Ortega, Severa
Ortiz (de), Rosa R.
Ortiz, Bernarda
Ortiz, Elena
Ortiz, Hermenegildo
Ortiz, Joaquina
Ortiz, Josefa
Ortiz, Marcolina
Ortiz, Maria (1)
Ortiz, Maria (2)
Otero (de), Rosa O.
Otero, Angela
Otero, Aurea
Otero, Baudelia
Otero, Carmen
Otero, Generosa
Otero, Gregoria
Otero, Gumercinda
Otero, Ines
Otero, Josefa
Otero, Maria
Otero, Quintina
Otero, Rafaela
Otero, Ramona
Pacheco, Antonia B.
Pacheco, Carmen
Pacheco, Gloria B.
Pacheco, Juana
Padilla, Francisca
Padilla, Maria
Padilla, Petra
Padro de Pacheco,
  Gloria
Padro, Asuncion
Padro, Carmen (1)
Padro, Carmen (2)
Padro, Eduvigis
Padro, Elisa
Padro, Herminia
Padro, Margarita
Padro, Maria
Padro, Mercedes
Padro, Noemi
  Moraima
Padro, Rita
Padro, Rosalina

Padro, Rosario
Padro, Susana
Padro, Trinita
Pagan, Carmen (1)
Pagan, Carmen (2)
Pagan, Dolores
Pagan, Guadalupe
Pagan, Josefina
Pagan, Juana
Pagane, Carmela
Pagane, Lola
Pariz, Modesta
Pavon, Juana
Pavon, Pepe
Perales, Marcelina
Perez de Robles, Zoila
Perez, Francisca
Perez, Martina
Perez, Mercedes
Piñeiro, Cruz
Polanco (de), Antonia
  R.
Quiñones, Jovita
Quiñones, Maria
Quintero, Ricardo
Quiros, Carmen
Raices, Carmen
Ramirez (de), Belen I.
Ramos, Angela
Ramos, Candelaria
Ramos, Estaquia
Ramos, Gloria
Ramos, Josefa
Ramos, Julia
Ramos, Regina
Ramos, Rosalina
Ramos, Santo
Rehaniz, Dolores
Resto, Ana Maria
Resto, Carmen
Reventa Vda. de ---,
  Anastacia
Ribiera, Angelina
Rickehoff, Lucila
Rico, Manuela
Rios (de), Mercedes
  M.
Rios, Maria
Rivera (de), Josefa R.
Rivera Aulet, Rafaela
Rivera, Adela
Rivera, Adelina
Rivera, Ana R.
Rivera, Angelica

Rivera, Blanca R.
Rivera, Carmen
Rivera, Carmen M.
Rivera, Castora
Rivera, Catalina
Rivera, Claudia
Rivera, Concepcion (1)
Rivera, Concepcion (2)
Rivera, Concha
Rivera, Cristina (1)
Rivera, Cristina (2)
Rivera, Dolores
Rivera, Emilia
Rivera, Esperanza
Rivera, Guillermina
Rivera, Margarita
Rivera, Maria (1)
Rivera, Maria (2)
Rivera, Ortencia
Rivera, Rafaela
Rivera, Ramona
Rivera, Rosario
Rivera, Tomasa
Robe, Emilia
Roble, Sabina
Robles, Antonia
Robles, Conchita
Robles, Josefina
Robles, Luisa
Robles, Monserrate
Robles, Rafaela
Rodriguez, Adela
Rodriguez, Agustina
Rodriguez, Alicia
Rodriguez, Antonia
Rodriguez, Carmen
Rodriguez, Clausina
Rodriguez, Dolores
Rodriguez, Emilia
Rodriguez, Francisco
Rodriguez, Inocencia
Rodriguez, Isabel
Rodriguez, Maria (1)
Rodriguez, Maria (2)
Rodriguez, Ricarda
Rodriguez, Rita
Rodriguez, Sista
Rodriguez, Solana
Rodriguez, Teresa
Rodriguez, Virginia
Roman, Josefa
Roman, Maria
Roman, Peita
Romero, Elisa

Romero, Vitoriana
Rosa, Antonia
Rosado, Carmen
Rosado, Cecilia
Rosado, Maria (1)
Rosado, Maria (2)
Rosado, Maria (3)
Rosado, Ramona
Rosario, Amelia
Rosario, Barbara
Rosario, Candida
Rosario, Cristina
Rosario, Dolores
Rosario, Emilia
Rosario, Francisca
Rosario, Guadalupe (1)
Rosario, Guadalupe (2)
Rosario, Guadalupe (3)
Rosario, Irene
Rosario, Justa
Rosario, Maria Nicasia
Rosario, Mercedes
Rosario, Milagro
Rosario, Petronila (1)
Rosario, Petronila (2)
Rosario, Primitiva
Rosario, Rosa
Rosario, Rosalia
Rosario, Teodosia
Rosario, Tomasa
Rosario, Ventura
Rozas (de), Brigida R.
Sais (de), Antonia M.
Sais (de), Utalidina
Sais, Aurora
Sais, Carmen
Sais, Coloma
Salgado, Angela
Salgado, Mercedes
San Miguel de Fernandez, Celita
San Miguel, Carmen (1)
San Miguel, Carmen (2)
San Miguel, Jobita
San Miguel, Jose
San Miguel, Julia
San Miguel, Mercedes
San Miguel, Rosario
Sanchez, Adelia

Sanchez, Aide
Sanchez, Alicia
Sanchez, Antonia (1)
Sanchez, Antonia (2)
Sanchez, Benincia
Sanchez, Carmen (1)
Sanchez, Carmen (2)
Sanchez, Carmen (3)
Sanchez, Carmen (4)
Sanchez, Delfina
Sanchez, Dolores
Sanchez, Evarista
Sanchez, Felipa
Sanchez, Flora
Sanchez, Francisca
Sanchez, Inocencia
Sanchez, Joaquina
Sanchez, Josefa
Sanchez, Maria
Sanchez, Mercedes (1)
Sanchez, Mercedes (1)
Sanchez, Miguelina
Sanchez, Paz
Sanchez, Petrona
Sanchez, Ramona (1)
Sanchez, Ramona (2)
Sanchez, Ramona (3)
Sanchez, Ricarda
Sanchez, Rosa
Sanchez, Teresa
Sandoval, Antonia (1)
Sandoval, Antonia (2)
Sandoval, Antonia (3)
Sandoval, Carmen
Santana, Amalia
Santana, Isabel
Santiago (de), Regina B.
Santiago Angela
Santiago Ramona
Santiago, Aurea
Santiago, Blasina
Santiago, Consuelo
Santiago, Juanita
Santiago, Maria
Santiago, Rosalia
Santiago, Victoria
Santigo, Elisa
Santo, Tomasa
Sarras, Ana Luisa
Selva, Rosa M.
Serrano, Maria
Sierra (de), Oliva C.
Sierrra, Olsina Maria

Soler, Maria
Soler, Martina
Soler, Rosa
Sonto (Vda. de), Mercedes
Sto. Domingo de Padro, Rosalia
Tarniela (de), Aminta
Tavarez, Maria
Tirado, Ana M.
Tirado, Antonia
Torres, Felicita
Torres, Isabel
Torres, Rafaela
Torres, Rufina
Tosado, Monserrate
Valderrama, Ana
Valdesa (de), Elisa M.
Vaquez, Josefa
Vasquez, Justina
Vazquez, Barbara
Vazquez, Francisca
Velez (de), Juana A.
Velez (Vda. de), Isabel
Velez, Carmen
Velez, Eulalia
Velez, Isabelita
Velez, Juana
Velez, Maria
Velez, Monserrate
Velez, Pilar
Velez, Ulpiana
Vences, Margot
Viachez, Fen
Vicens, Sostenes A.
Vilches, Maria
Villafaña, Marcelina
Villar, Julia
Vinces, Maria
Virella, Encarnacion

Cidra

Cidra Municipal Council

Santiago Alonso, Praxedes (Secretary)
Zeno, Francisco M. (Mayor)

Cidra Citizens

Almendro, Alfonso
Almendro, Esperanza
Almendro, Jaime
Alonso, Ezequiel
Aponte, Etanisla
Aponte, Francisco
Barrio, Pedro
Barrionuevo, Miguel
Bernart, Angel (1)
Bernart, Angel (2)
Bernart, Antonio
Botet, Pedro
Camuñas, Lorenzo
Candelas, Arturo
Candelas, Jesus Maria
Carrion, Juana
Carrion, Julia
Castrodad, Santiago
Cordero, Gumersindo (Lcdo.)
Cordero, Jose F.
Cortes, Isabel
Cortes, Rosa Elisa
Coto, Gabino
Coto, Juan
Cotto, Concepcion
De Quevedo, Alberto J. (Dr.)
Fernandez, Delfin
Fernandez, Primitivo
Ferrer Garcia, Jose
Ferrer Vazquez, Jose
Ferrer, Arturo
Ferrer, Diego A.
Ferrer, Francisco
Freire, Juan
Gandara, Narciso
Garced de S., Fructuosa
Garced, Arcadio
Garcia, Francisca
Garcia, Francisco
Garcia, Pedro
Garcia, Ramon
Garcia, Ramona
Gelpi, J.
Gonzalez, Hermenegildo
Isega, Cristino
Lopez, Benigno
Lopez, Consuelo

Lopez, Domingo
Lopez, Emilio
Lopez, Joaquin
Lopez, Juan
Lopez, Juana
Lopez, Miguel
Lopez, Octavio
Lopez, Salvador
Manzanarcs, A.
(Lcdo.)
Martinez, Antonio
Martinez, M.D. (Ph.
Gr. C. M.)
Martinez, Vicente
Menendez, Dolores
Mestre, Josefa
Mestre, Luis
Nieves, Basilio
Nieves, Carmen
Nugent, O.
Ortiz, Consuelo
Ortiz, Vicente
Otero, Fecita
Otero, Pedro
Perez, Enrique
Rabelo, Pedro
Ramirez, Francisco
Maria
Ramirez, Jose
Ramos, Domingo
Ramos, Pedro
Ramos, Sista
Reyes, Cristina
Rivera, Carmen
Rivera, Cesareo
Rivera, Eduardo
Rivera, Josefa
Rivera, Maria R.
Rivera, Sofia
Rivera, Tomas (Jr.)
Rivera, Tomas (1)
Rivera, Tomas (2)
Rodriguez Ortiz, M.
(Lcdo.)
Rodriguez, Alfredo
Rodriguez, Eustaquio
Rodriguez, Felix
Rodriguez, Juan
Rodriguez, Petra
Rodriguez, Ramon
Rodriguez, Robustino
Rolon, Juan
Rolon, Manuel
Santiago (de), Elvira

Santiago (de), G.
Santiago (de), Maria
Santiago, Prosedes
(Jr.)
Santini, Luis (Teacher)
Santos, Juan Jose
Santos, Marceliano
Sariego, Asuncion
Sariego, Benigno
Sariego, Fructuosa
Sariego, Maria
Spencer, Hazellon
Suarez, Delfina
Suarez, Julia
Suarez, Providencia
Torres, Aly B.
Torres, Anselmo
Torres, Arcadio
Torres, Tomas
Torres, Valentin
Vazquez Melendez,
Jose
Vazquez, Antonio
Vazquez, Vicente
Velez de Choudens,
Enrique
Vienz Baez, Jacinto
Zabala, Ramon
Zeno (de), Josefa P.

Coamo

Centro de Educacion y Recreo (Educational and Recreation Center), Coamo

Aponte, Clotilde
Baerga, Jose
Bernier, Segundo
Betances, J. G.
C., M.
Caratini, Celestino
Caratini, J. Francisco
Cassarini, Antonio
Cianchini, Rafael
Colon Pico, Carlos
Colon, Nestor C.
Colon, Rufo A.

Colon, Zoilo M.
Colon, Zoilo Maria
(pp)
Cortes, Angel C. (Dr.)
Costa, Agustin
Cot Santiago, Jose
Cot, Pablo
De Pasalacqua, Juan
Emanuell, Gabriel
Emanuelli, Domingo
Emanuelli, Juan
Garcia Davila, Virgilio
Gierbolini, Carlos
Gierbolini, Carlos E.
Gierbolini, Enrique
Gomez, Santiago P.
Hernandez, Erasmo
Huertas, Eduardo
Idrach Duran, Manuel
Luzasoain, Felix
Matos Lopez, Angel
Morera Santiago, J.
Padilla Casla, J.
Passalacqua, Antonio
(1)
Passalacqua, Antonio
(2)
Perez, Justo
Pico, Antonio
Quintana Cajal, A.
Redondo, Lorenzo
Rivera C., Julian
Rivera, Calixto G
Rivera, Celestino
Rivera, D. (Dr.)
Rivera, Diego Ismael
Rivera, Diego R.
Rivera, Jesus
Rivera, Juan
Rivera, Julian R.
Rivera, Manuel A.
Rivera, Manuel J.
Rodriguez Braschi,
Jose
Rodriguez, Celso I.
Rodriguez, Damaso
Rodriguez, Quiterio
Santiago Colon,
Teodoro
Santiago Santiago,
Luis
Santiago, C.
Santiago, Jose Ma.
Santiago, Jose Rafael

Santiago, Jose
Teodoro
Santiago, Juan A.
Santiago, Rafael
Santiago, Virgilio
Santini J., Francisco
A.
Santini, Calixto
Santini, Francisco
Suarez, V. M.
Trujillo, Dr.

Comerio

Comerio Municipal Council (Telegram)

Colon (President)

Damas de Comerio (Ladies of Comerio)

Adorno, Brigida
Agosto, Ilita
Aldebol (de), Tomasa
S.
Alvelo, Agripina
Arana, Rosa
Asuncion, Juana
Balentin, Victoria
Bargas, Josefa
Bazquez, Isabel
Bermudez, Virtudes
Cabrera, Maria A.
Carmona (de),
Heraclia L.
Carmona de Perez,
Sofia
Carmona, Carmen R.
Carmona, Juana
Carmona, Monserrat
Carmona, Ramon R.
Carmona, Teresina
Carrasquillo, Ramona
Colon, Josefa
Colon, Maria (1)
Colon, Maria (2)
Colon, Pia

Colon, Sandalia
Colon, Tibulcia
Cruz, Eleuteria
De la Rosa, Ana
Declet de Hernandez,
Leonor
Del Valle de Umpierre,
Francisca
Del Valle Maria
Del Valle, Delfina
Del Valle, Jesusa
Del Valle, Serafina
Diaaz, Abelina
Diaaz, Carmen
Diaaz, Francisca
Diaaz, Isabel
Diaaz, Juana
Diaaz, Rosario
Diaz Vda. de Ortiz,
Basilisa
Diaz, Baldomera
Diaz, Carmen
Diaz, Delfina
Duran de Montalvo,
Carmen
Ernandez, Juana
Espina de Romero,
Faustina
Estreya, Enriqueta
Falcon, Ramona
Fonseca, Nemesia
Fre, Justina
Gonzalez de Milian,
Juana
Gonzalez, Aleja
Gonzalez, Dolores
Granela, Josefa
Hernandez, Carmen
Hernandez, Esperanza
Hernandez, Juana
Huerta, Juanita
Jimenez, Adolfina A.
Jorge, Rosa
Jorge, Socorro
Lopez, Fecita
Martinez, Rita
Melendez, Carmen
Maria
Melendez, Evangelia
Melendez, Felicita
Melendez, Herminia
Melendez, Isabel
Melendez, Leopoldina
Mendez, Carmen

Milian, Guadalupe
Miranda Declet,
Isaura
Montalvan, Maria
Montalvan, Ramonita
Montalvo (de), Amelia
C.
Montalvo Vda. de
Acosta, Carmen
Montalvo, Celia
Zoraida
Montalvo, Flor de
Maria
Montalvo, Mercedes
Montalvo, Miguelina
Muñoz, Concepcion
Nieves, Agustina
Nieves, Carmen
Ortiz Diaz, Julia
Ortiz, Gloria Maria
Ortiz, Josefa N.
Percia O. de
Rodriguez, Luz
Perez (de), Josefa P.
Perez de Caparras,
Jesusa
Perez, Aurea
Perez, Finita
Perez, Florencia
Perez, Maria
Perez, Parziza
Perez, Santa
Perez, Severa
Perez, Tomas
Ramos, Maria
Reyes, Candelaria
Riberas, Juana
Riberas, Mercedes
Rivera de Bernart,
Dolores
Rivera del Valle,
Ramona
Rivera, Carmen
Rivera, Esquelita
Rivera, Esther Maria
Rivera, Jesusa
Rivera, Josefa
Rivera, Juana
Rivera, Manuela
Rivera, Maria
Rivera, Paziza
Rivera, Rosa
Rivera, Ulpiana
Riveras, Andrea

Rodrigues, Cristina
Rodriguez, Carmen
Rodriguez,
Concepcion
Rodriguez, Juana
Rodriguez, Maria
Rojas (de), Mercedes
M.
Roman, Chule
Roman, Lupe
Roman, Pivicia
Romero, Carmela
Rosa, Juana
Rosa, Maria
Rosario, Maria (1)
Rosario, Maria (2)
Rosario, Tomasa
Salgado, Guadalupe
Santa, Eulogia
Santa, Monce
Santiago de Perez,
Carlota
Santiago, Adela
Santiago, Auria
Santiago, Isaias
Santiago, Juana
Santiago, Maria
Santiago, Matilde
Santiago, Mercedes
Santos, Alcadia
Santos, Bonifacia
Santos, Delfina
Solares (de), Manolita
Texidor, Antonia
Torres de Rodriguez,
Carmen
Torres, Amalia
Torres, Catalina
Torres, Ramona
Umpierre (de),
Hipolita C.
Umpierre, Carmen
Umpierre, Hipolita
Vaez, Fidela
Vazquez, Juana Maria
Vega, Jacinta
Vega, Rosalia
Vermudez, Guadalupe
Vermudez, Juana

. . .

Fajardo

Fajardo Municipal Council

Rola, Carlos M. (Lcdo.)

Fajardo Citizens

Abolafia, Vicente
Acos Veserril, Emilio
Acosta, Eduardo
Acosta, Mercedes
Adorno, Domingo
Agostini de Garcia,
Isabel
Agosto, Isabel
Aguiar de Quiñones,
Ana
Aguiar, Rosario
Albareda, Santiago
Albira, Mariano
Alcencio, Hermogenes
Alcencio, Mireya
Alejandro, Calistra
Alejandro, Paula
Alejandro, Carlota
Alejandro, Marcela
Allala, Francisco
Allala, Ricardo
Allira, Francisca
Almestica, Jose
Aloz, Enrique
Alvares, Juan A.
Alvarez, Juana
Alvarez, Luz M.
Alvarez, Narcisa
Alvarez, Pasquala
Alverto, Monica
Amador, Eladio
Andreu (de), Ramona
Z.
Andreu, Blanca
Andreu, Carmen
Andreu, Cristobal
Andrew, Ana Maria
Anglero, Jose
Aponte, Juan
Arbona Vda. de

Quiñones, Candida
Armaiz (de),
Guillermina G.
Armaiz (Vda. de)
Trinidad
Armaiz, Trinidad
Armestico, Jose
Armestico, Marcelino
Audifre, Dalila
Audifre, Soila
Audifre, Usebio
Avila Antonio
Avila, Catalino
Avila, Josefina
Avila, Juanita
Avila, Nicasio
Ayala Martinez,
Providencia
Ayala, Aurora
Ayala, Concha
Ayala, Feliz
Ayala, Flor
Ayala, Gregorio
Ayala, Juan
Ayala, Juana (1)
Ayala, Juana (2)
Ayala, Maria (1)
Ayala, Maria (2)
Ayala, Maria (3)
Ayala, Quilerio
Ayala, Secundino (1)
Ayala, Secundino (2)
Baez, Ricardo
Bagur de Sifre, Maria
Balentin, Juana
Balentin, Maria
Baralt (de), N. R.
Baralt (Vda. de),
Concepcion
Baralt, Francisco
Baralt, M. F.
Barceiro, Francisca
Barcelo (de), Josefina
B.
Barrio, Santiago
Bas Vda. de Mendez,
Francisca
Basquez, Joaquin
Basquez, Luisa
Bebe Cifre, Joaquin
Becerril, Marta
Begas, Eustaquio
Belaval, Alberto S.
Belaval, Encarnacion

S.
Benabe, Epifanio
Benitez (de), Herminia
S.
Benitez de Cuevas, S.
Benitez de Zaldurado,
Celina
Benitez Sierra, Jose
Benitez, Carmen (1)
Benitez, Carmen (2)
Benitez, Herminia
Benitez, Jacinto
Benitez, Ramona
Bentura, Luis
Benua, Mario
Berel Lopez, Manuel
Bermudez, Nicasia
Bernier, Adela
Berrio, Faustino
Berrios, Jesus
Berrios, Rosa
Bird (Vda. de), Juana
A.
Bird Belma, Jesus
Bird, Lucia
Bird, Maria Isabel
Bisarro, Lino C.
Bizarro Alejandro,
Jose
Bizarro, Hermogenes
Bizarro, Juana
Bizarro, Santiago
Blanco (de), Isabel J.
Blanco, Alberto
Blanco, Pedro
Bloise, America
Borras, Rafael
Brasero, Gervacia
Bravo Vda. de
Guerrero, Salvadora
Brito, Manuel
Brugueras,
Concepcion
Burgos, Mercedes
C. J.
Caballero, Marcia
Calderon, Alejandro
Calderon, Francisco
Calderon, Jesus
Calderon, Justa
Calderon, Manuel
Calderon, Maria
Calderon, Nolvelto
Calderon, Polonio

Caldreron, Etanislaa
Callas, Lorenca
Calmona, Juana
Calmona, Maria
Calzada, Hermogenes
Calzada, Juana
Calzada, Maria
Camacho, Carlos
Camacho, Celestina
Camacho, Guillermo
Camacho, Juana
Camacho, Monserrate
Camacho, Otilio
Camacho, Teodoro
Camargo, Estanislao
Campos, Carmen
Campos, Ysabel
Cancel, David
Canes, Segunda
Caraballo, Juan
Carbajal, Ramon
Carballo, Ramona
Cariño, Juana
Cariño, Maria
Cariño, Obdulia
Carmona Julia
Carmona, Agustin
Carmona, Anselmo
Carmona, Carmela
Carmona, Carmelo
Carmona, Carmen
Carmona, Celestina
Carmona, Diego
Carmona, Guillermina
Carmona, Hortensia
Carmona, Isabel
Carmona, Jose
Carmona, Julian
Carmona, Petra
Carmona, Rosario
Carmona, Santiago
Carmona, Sixto
Carrasco, Angel V. F.
Carrasco, Carmen
Carrasco, Clotilde
Carrasco, Dionisio (1)
Carrasco, Dionisio (2)
Carrasco, Eustaquio
(1)
Carrasco, Eustaquio
(2)
Carrasco, Francisco
Carrasco, Julia
Carrasco, Maria

Carrasco, Ramon
Carrasco, Sebastiana
Carrasquillo, Isidoro
(II)
Carrasquillo Davila,
Josefa
Carrasquillo y
Carruyo, Fela
Carrasquillo y
Carruyo, Teodora
Carrasquillo, Agustin
Carrasquillo,
Guillermo
Carrasquillo, Isidoro
Carrasquillo, Jose
Carrasquillo, Juan
Carrasquillo, Julia
Carrasquillo, Maria (1)
Carrasquillo, Maria
(2)
Carrasquillo, Sinrila
Carrasquillo, Ysabelo
Carrasquilo, Jose
Carreras Vargas,
Francisco
Carreras, Cayetana
Carreras, Concepcion
Carreras, Lorenza
Carrillo, Carmen
Carrillo, Gregorio
Carrillo, Margara
Carrillo, Pepin
Carrion, Arcadia
Carrion, Bartolo
Carrion, Cecilio
Carrion, Laura
Carrion, Manuel (1)
Carrion, Manuel (2)
Carrion, Maria
Carruyo, Carmelo
Carruyo, Jose (1)
Casado, Jose (2)
Casandra, Pascasio
Casanova, Carmen
Casanova, Pedro
Casares, Luisa
Casars, Paula
Casilla, Aquilina
Casilla, Leoncio
Castro, Carmen
Castro, Felix
Castro, Mercedes
Castro, Pepe
Catalan, Marcos

Mercedes
Encarnacion, Modesto
Encarnacion, Sisi
Enrique, Marciala
Escalera de Michel,
Justina
Escalera, Justo
Escobar, Abel
Escobar, Benigno
Escobar, Dominga
Escobar, Elisa
Escobar, Enriqueta
Escobar, Francisco
Escobar, Genata
Escobar, Manuela (1)
Escobar, Manuela (2)
Escobar, Mercedes
Escobar, Merejilda
Escobar, Rosario
Esquilin, Guillerma
Esquilin, Ilina
Estrada, Cristino
Estrada, Juan
Estrada, Manuela
Estrada, Vernardino
Estrada, Ysabel
Estrada. Vicente
Estrella, Faustino
Fajardo, E.
Feliciano Cruz, P.
Feliciano, Amparo
Feliciano, Bacilio
Feliciano, Benigno
Feliciano, Bibicina
Feliciano, Celestina
Feliciano, Dominga
Feliciano, Erminia
Feliciano, Ezequiela
Feliciano, Florentino
Feliciano, Jose
Feliciano, Juan
Feliciano, Juana
Feliciano, Miguelina
Feliciano, Rafael
Felipe, Josefina
Felix, Epifania
Feliz, Manuel
Fernandez, Carmelina
Fernandez, Guillermo
Fernandez, Petra
Fernandez, Teresa
Ferrero (de),
Esperanza C.
Ferrero, Felipe

Ferrero, Manuel
Festald, Carmen
Festald, Susana
Fidela, Alfredo
Figueroa, Aida
Figueroa, Alejo
Figueroa, Amalia
Figueroa, Andres
Figueroa, Antonio
Figueroa, Balentina
Figueroa, Calletana
Figueroa, Carmelina
Figueroa, Carmen (1)
Figueroa, Carmen (2)
Figueroa, Deogracias
Figueroa, Domingo
Figueroa, Emilia
Figueroa, Emilio
Figueroa, Felipa
Figueroa, Flor (1)
Figueroa, Flor (2)
Figueroa, Gabriel
Figueroa, Gemela
Figueroa, Generosa
Figueroa, Georgina
Figueroa, Isaias
Figueroa, Jacinta
Figueroa, Jose I.
Figueroa, Laura
Figueroa, Manuel (1)
Figueroa, Manuel (2)
Figueroa, Monserrate
Figueroa, Patricio
Figueroa, Purificacion
Figueroa, Rafael
Figueroa, Tecla
Flores de Martinez,
Zoraida
Flores Lopez,
Guillermo
Flores, Agapito
Flores, Angel V.
Flores, Antonio
Flores, Arturo
Flores, Brigida
Flores, Carmen Delia
Flores, Celia
Flores, Demencio
Flores, Enrique
Flores, Eulalia
Flores, Eusebio
Flores, Felipe
Flores, Fundador
Flores, Genaro

Flores, Gila
Flores, Guillermo
Flores, Ines
Flores, Juan (1)
Flores, Juan (2)
Flores, Juan (3)
Flores, Julio
Flores, Julio A.
Flores, Luis
Flores, Luisa (1)
Flores, Luisa (2)
Flores, Maria
Flores, Mayo
Flores, Nenita
Flores, Nicolas
Flores, Paula
Flores, Primitiva
Flores, Quintina
Flores, Ramon C.
Flores, Rosa
Fontane, Antonio
Fontane, Arcadia
Fontane, Arturo
Fontane, Laura
Fontane, Soledad
Fontanes, Benita
Forte, Rafael
Forteza (de),
Fernanda B.
Foy, Rene
Franceschi, Francisca
Franceschi, Josefa
Francisco, Juan
French, Constance
Frontane, Carmen
Frontane, Tula
Fuentes (Vda. de),
Pilar
Fuentes Vda. de
Lopez, Manuela
Fuentes, Alcenio
Fuentes, Amparo
Fuentes, Candida
Fuentes, Carlos
Fuentes, Carmen
Fuentes, Concepcion
Fuentes, Demetria
Fuentes, Francisco
Fuentes, Isabel
Fuentes, Jose
Fuentes, Manuel
Fuentes, Paca
Fuentes, Pilar
Fuentes, Rosa

Fuentes, Victor
Fufiño, Casimira
Gabat, Manuel
Gabino, Alejandrina
Gabino, Dolores
Gabino, Federico
Gabino, Inocencia
Gabino, Ramon
Gamboa, Jose
Garcia (de), Adela B.
Garcia (de), Estefana
S.
Garcia (de), Sandalia
P.
Garcia Dante, Manuel
Garcia Davila, Miguel
Garcia de Morales,
Petra
Garcia Ortiz, Juan
Garcia, Agustin
Garcia, Carlos
Garcia, Concepcion
Garcia, Dolores (1)
Garcia, Dolores (2)
Garcia, Eleuteria
Garcia, Eusebio
Garcia, Felix
Garcia, Gudon
Garcia, Jose
Garcia, Jose M.
Garcia, Juan (1)
Garcia, Juan (2)
Garcia, Juana
Garcia, Julio
Garcia, Leonarda
Garcia, Luis
Garcia, Manuel (1)
Garcia, Manuel (2)
Garcia, Manuela
Garcia, Manuela
Garcia, Maria (1)
Garcia, Maria (2)
Garcia, Maria (3)
Garcia, Maria (4)
Garcia, Melida
Garcia, Miguel (1)
Garcia, Miguel (2)
Garcia, Miguel (Jr.)
Garcia, Monserrate
Garcia, Natalio
Garcia, Nicomedes
Garcia, Pedro (1)
Garcia, Pedro (2)
Garcia, Rafael

Garcia, Sebastiana
Garcia, Sinforosa
Garcia, Tomasa
Garcias, Guillermina
Garcias, Luisa
Garcias, Pedro
Gardils, Bandelio (1)
Gardils, Bandelio (2)
Gautier, Pio
Gavino, Antonio
Goaju, Juan
Golero, Jesus
Gomez, Dolores
Gomez, Felipe
Gomez, Francisco
Gomez, Julio
Gomez, Justo
Gomez, Maria
Gomez, Paula
Gomez, Vicente (1)
Gomez, Vicente (2)
Gonzales, Carmen
Gonzales, Dolores
Gonzales, Isabel
Gonzales, Saturnina
Gonzalez, Amparo
Gonzalez, Emilio (1)
Gonzalez, Emilio (2)
Gonzalez, Eulalio
Gonzalez, Felipe
Gonzalez, Flor
Gonzalez, Galita
Gonzalez, Gerardo
Gonzalez, Gilda G.
Gonzalez, Joaquin
Gonzalez, Policarpia
Gonzalez, Ramon
Gonzalez, Trinidad
Gotay, Clotilde
Gotay, Cornelia
Gotay, Francisco
Gotay, Lorenza
Gotay, Maria
Gotay, Ramon
Gracia Pacheco, C.
Guadalupe, Catalino
Guadalupe, Estefania
Guadalupe, Modesta
Guadalupe, Ramon
Guader Lopez,
  Eugenio
Guerra, Juan
Guerrero (de), Maria
  N.

Guerrero Vda. de
  Muñoz, Francisca
Guerrero Vela,
  Francisca
Gutierre, Carmelo
Gutierrez, Cristina
Guzman (de), Isabel
  R.
Guzman (de), Ysabel
  B.
Guzman Lopez, Pedro
Guzman, Cancio
Guzman, Candida R.
Guzman, Idelfonso
Guzman, Inocencio
Guzman, Isabel
Guzman, Juana (1)
Guzman, Juana (2)
Guzman, Julia
Guzman, Manuela
Guzman, Mercedes
Guzman, Orosia
Guzman, Santos
Guzman, Secilo
Guzman, Simplicia
Guzman, Sirila
Hernandez, Antonia
Hernandez, Evaristo
Hernandez, Francisca
  (1)
Hernandez, Francisca
  (2)
Hernandez, Gabina
Hernandez, Josefa
Hernandez, Juana
Hernandez, Rafael (1)
Hernandez, Rafael (2)
Hernandez, Ysidro
Herreras, Luisa
Ilarrasa, Josefa
Ilarrasa, Seferina
Iromi M, Tomasa
Jacchen--, Monserrate
Jimenes, Juan
Jimenez, A.
Jimenez, Alfredo
Jimenez, Angel
Jimenez, Borinquen
Jimenez, Carmen
Jimenez, E.
Jimenez, Isabelo
Jimenez, J. B.
Jimenez, Joaquina
Jimenez, Jose

Jimenez, Leocadia
Jimenez, Luis
Jimenez, Panchita
Jimenez, Rosario
Jimenez, Santiago
Jimenez, Tomas
Jimenez, Victorio
Joilan, Carolina
Joilan, Justo
Juebe, Isabel
Juebe, Manuela
Juebe, Providencia
Julbe, Antonio (1)
Julbe, Antonio (2)
Julbe, Carmen
Julbe, Enrique (1)
Julbe, Enrique (2)
Julbe, Jose
Julbe, Maria Luisa
Julio, Carlos (1)
Julio, Carlos (2)
Julio, Juan
Julio, Luis
Julio, Maria I.
Julio, Rafael
Kercado, Benigno
Lafont de Mendez,
  Angelita
Lafont, Eloisa
Lafont, Julia H.
Lafont, Lorenzo
Lafont, Marta
Lajars, Ramona
Lanuza, Francisco
Lanuza, Manuel
Larosa, Primitivos
Lasvid, Colnelia
Latorre, Adolfo
Latorre, Angel (Jr.)
Latorre, Asuncion
Latorres, Angel M.
Laureano, Rafael
Leal, Jose Rivera
Lebron (de), Adolfa S.
Lebron Soto, Jose
Lebron, Angel
Lebron, Fidelina M.
Lebron, Juana
Lebron, Maria
Ledi, Flor de Maria
Legrand, Carlos
Lima, Placida
Lisiña, Adolfo
Lisiña, Constantino

Lisiña, Mariano
Liuña, Francisco
Ll--, Anselmo
Llorens, H.
Llovel, Rita
Lomba (Vda. de),
  Engracia A.
Lomba Guerrero,
  Pepita
Lomba, Manuela
Lomba, Paquita
Lopez Celis, Maria
  Isabel
Lopez Celis, Mercedes
Lopez Cruz, Isabel
Lopez Cruz, Julia
Lopez Jubes, Manuela
Lopez Rexach, Juan
Lopez, Alejandrina
Lopez, Ana Maria
Lopez, Antonio
Lopez, Bernabe
Lopez, C.
Lopez, Carlota
Lopez, Esperanza
Lopez, Fabiana
Lopez, Fancisca
Lopez, Francisco (1)
Lopez, Francisco (2)
Lopez, Francisco (3)
Lopez, H.
Lopez, Jose A.
Lopez, Jose B.
Lopez, Josefa
Lopez, Josefina
Lopez, Juan (1)
Lopez, Juan (2)
Lopez, Loiza
Lopez, Luis
Lopez, Magdalena
Lopez, Manuel
Lopez, Margarita
Lopez, Maria Ysabel
Lopez, Martin
Lopez, Melida
Lopez, Mercedes
Lopez, Olegario
Lopez, Pilar
Lopez, Praxedes
Lopez, Rosa
Lopez, Rosario
Lugo, J. L.
Luiña, Jose
Luiña, Mariano

Machuca, Cristino
Maduro, Gabriel
Maduro, Georgina
Maduro, Martin
Maduro, Salomon
Magdalena, Maria
Maisone, Jose
Maldonado (de),
  Heriberta Lopez
Maldonado, Aleja
Maldonado, Angelina
Maldonado, Antonio
Maldonado, Camacho
Maldonado, Carmen
  (1)
Maldonado, Carmen
  (2)
Maldonado, Carmen
  (3)
Maldonado, Celia
Maldonado, Cruz
Maldonado, Dolores
Maldonado, Eleuteria
Maldonado, Felipa
Maldonado, Fex
Maldonado, Fidel
Maldonado, Flor
Maldonado, Gabriel
Maldonado, Ignacio
Maldonado, Jasinta
Maldonado, Juan (1)
Maldonado, Juan (2)
Maldonado, Juana (1)
Maldonado, Juana (2)
Maldonado, Juana (3)
Maldonado, Juana (4)
Maldonado, Juana (5)
Maldonado, Leoncia
Maldonado, Lorenzo
  (1)
Maldonado, Lorenzo
  (2)
Maldonado, Manuel
Maldonado, Manuela
Maldonado, Maria (1)
Maldonado, Maria (2)
Maldonado, Modesto
Maldonado,
  Monserrate
Maldonado, Nicanol
Maldonado, Nicolasa
  (1)
Maldonado, Nicolasa
  (2)

Maldonado, Palmira
Maldonado, Pedro
Maldonado, Petra
Maldonado, Ramon
Maldonado, Rosa
Maldonado, Silverio
Maldonado, Tomas
Maldonado, Tomasa
Maldonado, Ursula
Maldonado, Victor
Maldonado, Virginia
Malloral, Evangelista
Mangual, Gumersindo
Marcano Julia
Marcano, Claudino
Marcano, Jose
Marcano, Nicolas
Marchese, Carmelina
Marquez, Eduvijes
Marquez, Juan (1)
Marquez, Juan (2)
Marquez, Paula
Marquez, Rosa
Marrero de Celis, Ynes
Marrero, Balbasara
Marrero, Teresa R.
Martin, Carmen
Martin, Jose
Martin, Matilde
Martin, Rosa Maria
Martinez (de),
  Josefina G.
Martinez Gallardo,
  Jose
Martinez Pineda,
  Josefa
Martinez, Alfredo A.
Martinez, Antonio
Martinez, Antonio P.
Martinez, Benigno
Martinez, Carlos R.
Martinez, Carlota
Martinez, Carmen
Martinez, Carolina
Martinez, Cecilia
Martinez, E.
Martinez, Eduvijes
Martinez, Epifanio
Martinez, Eugenio
Martinez, Eusebia
Martinez, Felicita
Martinez, Felipe
Martinez, Florencia
Martinez, Francisca

Martinez, Francisco
Martinez, Gilberto
Martinez, Hilario (1)
Martinez, Hilario (2)
Martinez, Hipolita
Martinez, Ines
Martinez, Jesus
Martinez, Joaquin
Martinez, Jose C.
Martinez, Juan (1)
Martinez, Juan (2)
Martinez, Juana
Martinez, Juandio
Martinez, Leonardo
Martinez, Luis (1)
Martinez, Luis (2)
Martinez, Luz Maria
Martinez, Manuel (1)
Martinez, Manuel (2)
Martinez, Manuela
Martinez, Maria Luisa
Martinez, Meraldo
Martinez, Mercedes
Martinez, Miguel
Martinez, Nicasio (Jr.)
Martinez, Petra
Martinez, Providencia
Martinez, Rafael
Martinez, Ramon
Martinez, Rodrigo
Marudo, Providencia
Mas (de), Critina M.
Mata, Juliana
Mateo, Carmen
Mateo, Elisa
Mateo, Francisca
Mateo, Rafael
Mateo, Santiago
Mateo, Virginia
Mateu, Rafael
Matos (de), Antolina
Matos, Afonso
Matta (de), Georgina
  B.
Matta Vda. de Cerra,
  Concepcion
Matta, Carmelo
Matta, Elisa
Matta, Elvira
Matta, Jose (Jr.)
Matta, Josefa
Matta, Juana
Matta, Manuel
Matta, Manuela

Matta, Maria (1)
Matta, Maria (2)
Matta, Pragede
Matta, Santiago
Mayer, Francisco
Medina, Angel
Medina, Armando
Medina, Asiclo
Medina, Bernabe
Medina, Edubijis
Medina, Eleuterio
Medina, Eustaquio
Medina, Juan
Medina, M. B.
Medina, Magdalena
Medina, Manuel B.
Medina, Ramon
Medina, Ricardo
Medina, Rita
Medina, Salustiana
Medina, Susana
Medina, Vicente
Melendez Vargas,
  Miguelina
Melendez, Angel
Melendez, Antonio
Melendez, Balentin
Melendez, Carlos
Melendez, Catalina
Melendez, Emilio
Melendez, Francisca
Melendez, Francisco
  (1)
Melendez, Francisco
  (2)
Melendez, Jesusa
Melendez, Jose E.
Melendez, Juana (1)
Melendez, Juana (2)
Melendez, Leoncia
Melendez, Roman
Melendez, Rufino
Melendez, Simplicio
Melendez, Ysabel
Melon de Vazquez,
  Hortensia
Menaz, Domingo
Mendes, Esperanza
Mendez, Abigail
Mendez, Anita
Mendez, Artruro
Mendez, Carmen
Mendez, Eduardo
Mendez, Elisa

Mendez, Esther
Mendez, Felipe
Mendez, Isaia
Mendez, Luis
Mendez, Maria
Mendez, Rafaela
Mendez, Rosario
Mendez, Shara
Mendoza, Ana
Mendoza, Benito
Mendoza, Castula
Mendoza, Otilio
Menendez, Candelaria
Mercado (de), Julia
Mercado (Vda. de)
  Carmen R.
Mercado, Carmen
Mercado, Eugenio
Mercado, Faustino
Mercado, Francisco
  (II)
Mercado, Francisco (1)
Mercado, Francisco (2)
Mercado, Francisco (3)
Mercado, Irene
Mercado, Juan
Mercado, Julian
Mercado, Maria (1)
Mercado, Maria (2)
Mercado, Miguel
Mercado, Petrona
Mercado, Ramon
Mercado, Teresa
Micha, Esteban
Micha, Monserrate
Michel, Ynes
Millan, Carlina
Mitchell, Alejandrino
Mojer, Moncerrate
Mojica, Eugenia
Molina Calderon,
  Angel
Molina Calderon,
  Francisca
Molina, Calmelo
Molina, J. R.
Molina, Pablo
Molina, Ramona
Molina, Rufo
Molino, Carmen
Mondriguez, Romana
Monet, Antonio
Monet, Evangelita
Monet, Juan (1)

Monet, Juan (2)
Monet, Mercedes
Monet, Pregorio
Monet, Rosendo
Monet, Saba
Monjes, Felicita
Monjes, Gabina
Monl, Rufina
Montanez, Jose
Montañez, Juan
Montanez, Julio
Montañez, Leoncio
Montes, Juliana
Montes, Magdalena
Montes, Victoria
Moore, John
Mora Vaamonde, B. G.
  (Dr.)
Morales (de), Carmen
  C.
Morales (de), Justina
  R.
Morales (de), Ramona
Morales (Vda. de),
  Angela R.
Morales, Alejandrina
Morales, Andrea
Morales, Ceferino
Morales, Cristina
Morales, Estelvina
Morales, Felipe
Morales, Francisco
Morales, Jose
Morales, Juan
Morales, Juana
Morales, Justina
Morales, Manuel
Morales, Maria
Morales, Pedro
Morales, Petra (1)
Morales, Petra (2)
Moreira, Felicita
Moreira, Lorenzo
Morel, Cecilio
Morena, Cosme
Morera de Garcia,
  Mariana
Morfi (de),
  Alejandrina
Morfi, Carmen
Morfi, Joaquin
Morfi, Pedro
Morfi, Vicente
Morfis, Dolores

Morfis, Julio
Moriarty Cetut, Luisa
Morjano, Ines
Morphy, Jose D.
Moyano Providencia
Moyano, Lola
Moyano, Rafael
Moyano, Ramon
Moyano, Rosario
Moyer Navan, Miguel
Moyer, Miguel
Mulero, Esteban
Müller (Vda. de),
  Joaquina
Müller, Alicia
Müller, Fanny S.
Muñoz Belava, Maria
Muñoz, Cardona
  Amparo
Muñoz, Concepcion
Muñoz, Dolores
Muñoz, J. B.
Muñoz, J. E.
Muñoz, Ysabel
Nata, Picolasa
Navargas, Maria
Navarro, Maria
Navidad, E.
Negron, Pedro
Nieves, Antonio
Nieves, Juana
Nieves, Providencia
Noble (Vda. de),
  Cesarea J.
Noble, Amparo
Noble, Elvira
Noble, Evangelina
Ojeda, Domingo
Ojeda, Jeremias
Ojeda, Maria
Olivero, Alquimides
Olivero, Ramona
Olmeda, Vicente
Oltiz, Rosendo
Oquendo, Carmen H.
Oquendo, Isabelo
Ordoñez de Lopez,
  Maria Luisa
Ordoñez, L.
Ordoñez, Maria Luisa
Ortiz, Florentino C.
Ortiz Soto, Amparo
Ortiz y Quiñones,
  Dolores

Ortiz, Agapito
Ortiz, Alfonso
Ortiz, Angel
Ortiz, Balbina
Ortiz, Carmen
Ortiz, Ernesto
Ortiz, Estevania
Ortiz, Eulojo
Ortiz, Feliz
Ortiz, Francisco
Ortiz, Jacinta
Ortiz, Juana
Ortiz, Luis
Ortiz, Maria
Ortiz, Petra (1)
Ortiz, Petra (2)
Ortiz, Providencia
Ortiz, Rosa
Ortiz, Rufina
Ortiz, Sila
Ortiz, Tomaso
Osorio de Madonado,
  Carmen
Osorio Vda. de
  Martinez, Eugenia
Osorio, Carmen
Osorio, Jacinta
Osorio, Jose Ma.
Osorio, Juan
Osorio, Juana
Osorio, Julia
Osorio, Maria Luisa
Osorio, Mauricio
Osorio, Nieves
Otero (de), Mercedes
  O.
Otero Salgado, Elisa
Otero Salgado,
  Paquita
Otero Salgado, Rosa
Otero, Francisco
Otero, Marcial
Otero, Vicente
Ozorio, Maria
Ozorio, Carmela
Ozorio, Lala
Pacheco Gomez, Luis
Pacheco, Agueda
Pacheco, Alfonzo
Pacheco, Atanacio
Pacheco, Dolores
Pacheco, Isabel (1)
Pacheco, Isabel (2)
Pacheco, J. B. (1)

Pacheco, Jose M.
Pacheco, Juan
Pacheco, Juana
Pacheco, Julia
Pacheco, Julio
Pacheco, Margarita
Pacheco, Maria
Pacheco, Nicolasa
Padilla, Juana (1)
Padilla, Juana (2)
Padron, Enrique G.
Padron, Jose
Padron, Julia
Padron, Monica
Padron, Rosendo
Padron, Rosendo (Jr.)
Pagan, Castula
Pagan, Leocadia
Pagan, Margarita
Pantaleon, Adolfo
Parilla, Juana
Paris, Narciso
Paris, Teresa R.
Parquez, Barbara
Parquez, Miguel
Parrilla, Antera
Parrilla, Arsenio
Parrilla, Candido
Parrilla, Eusebio
Parrilla, Lola
Parrilla, Manuel
Parrilla, Pascacio
Parrilla, Valentin
Parrondo (de), Luisa D.
Parrondo, Amelia
Parrondo, Jose
Parrondo, Manuel
Parrondo, Maria Luisa
Pastor de Martinez, Elisa
Pastrana, Antonio
Peña, Antonio
Peña, Gregorio
Pena, Luis
Penedo, Carlos
Penedo, Constanza
Penedo, J.
Penedo, Jose
Penedo, Maria I.
Penedo, Pura
Pepin de Lopez, Matilde
Pereida, Ramon

Pereira Davila, Jovito
Pereira, Antonia
Perejra, Arturo
Pereira, Carmen
Pereira, Pedro
Pereira, Rafael
Pereira, Rosario
Pereira, Zoilo
Peres, Martina
Perez (de), Juana S.
Perez (de), Monserrate C.
Perez (Vda. de), Paquita
Perez Bernal, Juan
Perez Selles, Francisco
Perez, Carmen
Perez, Eladia
Perez, Escolastica
Perez, Evaristo
Perez, Manuel
Perez, Manuela
Perez, Nicolas
Perez, Pedro (1)
Perez, Pedro (2)
Perez, Pepe
Perez, Placida
Perez, Ricarda
Perez, Santiago (1)
Perez, Santiago (2)
Perez, Valerio
Pineda Vda. de M., Dolores
Piñeiro, Agapita
Piñeiro, Agapito
Piñeiro, Gabriela
Piñeiro, Manuel
Piñeiro, Ramon
Piñero (de), Estefania G.
Piñero, Guillermo
Piñero, Juan J.
Piñero, Rosario
Polu, Fernando
Pomada, Maria
Ponce Franco, Catalina
Ponce, Angelina
Ponce, Josefa
Pont, Leonicia
Ponz Benase, Juan
Portane, Zoila
Portela, Marcelino
Prado, Antonio

Prado, Carmen
Prado, Joaquina
Prado, Norverto
Prado, Petra
Prieto, Cristina
Prisco & Vizcarrondo DDL (Business)
Quiles, Esequiel
Quiñones Aguiar, Carlos
Quiñones Pacheco, Ramon M.
Quiñones, Carmelina
Quiñones, Carmen
Quiñones, Clemencia
Quiñones, Cristino
Quiñones, Elena
Quiñones, Flor de Maria
Quiñones, Francisca
Quiñones, Herminia
Quiñones, Jacinto
Quiñones, Jesus
Quiñones, Jose
Quiñones, Jose M.
Quiñones, Juan
Quiñones, Julia
Quiñones, Justina
Quiñones, Manuel
Quiñones, Paca
Quiñones, Rafael
Quiñones, Ramon
Quiñones, Reparada
Quiñones, Teresa
Quiñones, Ysabel
Quiñonez, Valentina
Ramirez, Florencio
Ramirez, Julia
Ramirez, Julio
Ramirez, Maria
Ramon, Marcela
Ramos de Jesus, Ricarda
Ramos Ramona
Ramos, Abad
Ramos, Aleja
Ramos, Ana
Ramos, Angelina
Ramos, Aurelia
Ramos, Carmen (1)
Ramos, Carmen (2)
Ramos, Demetrio
Ramos, Emilia
Ramos, Galletana

Ramos, Genaro
Ramos, Hipolita
Ramos, Jose
Ramos, Josefa
Ramos, Juan (1)
Ramos, Juan (2)
Ramos, Juan (3)
Ramos, Juana
Ramos, Julia
Ramos, Justa
Ramos, Luis
Ramos, Marcela
Ramos, Marcola
Ramos, Martin
Ramos, Paula
Ramos, Rafael (1)
Ramos, Rafael (2)
Ramos, Ricarda
Ramos, Tomasita
Rebollo, Claudio
Rebollo, Jose
Regulado, Pedro
Relles, Domicinda
Rendon, Estefania
Rengel, Ana
Rengel, Rafaela
Resach, Francisco
Resach, Linencia
Resach, Mercedes
Resach, Modesto
Resach, Onsiclo
Rexach, Andres
Rexach, Concepcion
Rexach, Domingo
Rexach, Epifania
Rexach, Isabel
Rexach, Juana
Rexach, Manuel
Reyes Gomez, Juan
Reyes, Daniel
Reyes, Estebania
Reyes, Juana (1)
Reyes, Juana (2)
Ribera, Cirino
Ribera, Epifania
Ribera, Natalio
Rieño, Adolfo F.
Rincon (de), Mercedes A.
Rincon, Felisa
Rios, Ana
Rios, Barbara
Rios, Jose
Rios, Juan (1)

Rios, Juan (2)
Rios, Juana
Rios, Julia
Rios, Olegario
Rivas, Juan
Rivera, Amalia
Rivera, Aniceta
Rivera, Antonia J.
Rivera, Bernardo
Rivera, Carmen
Rivera, Catalina
Rivera, Conchita
Rivera, Conrada
Rivera, Cruz
Rivera, Emeterio
Rivera, Emilio
Rivera, Enrique G.
Rivera, Eugenia
Rivera, Francisca
Rivera, Guillermo
Rivera, Herminio
Rivera, Isidoro
Rivera, Jacinta
Rivera, Jesus
Rivera, Jose
Rivera, Jose Ma.
Rivera, Josefa
Rivera, Josefina
Rivera, Juan (1)
Rivera, Juan (2)
Rivera, Juana
Rivera, Julian
Rivera, Julio
Rivera, Justo
Rivera, Lidova
Rivera, Lorenzo
Rivera, Luis
Rivera, Manuel
Rivera, Maria
Rivera, Modesto
Rivera, Nolberta
Rivera, Nolberto
Rivera, Patricia
Rivera, Paula
Rivera, Pedro
Rivera, Pepe C.
Rivera, Primitivo
Rivera, Quintin
Rivera, Rosalia
Rivera, Sinforoso
Rivera, Teresa
Rivera, Ulises
Rivera, Ynocencia
Rivera, Ysidoro

Riveras, Martina
Robertin (de), Maria
A.
Robertin, Agustina
Robertin, Angel Maria
Roberto, Hilario
Roberto, Victoriana
Robles, Anselma
Robles, Francisca
Robles, Geronimo
Robles, Hipolito
Robles, Jose H.
Robles, Maria
Rodriguez (de), Maria
Y.
Rodriguez (de),
Veneranda
Rodriguez Alberty, R.
Rodriguez de Olmeda,
Eulalia
Rodriguez, Adela
Rodriguez, Agustin
Rodriguez, Albina
Rodriguez, Asuncion
Rodriguez, Blas
Rodriguez, Carmen
Rodriguez, Claudio
Rodriguez, Diego
Rodriguez, Epifania
Rodriguez, Eugenio R.
Rodriguez, Eulalia
Rodriguez,
Fernandina
Rodriguez, Flor
Rodriguez, Gonzalo
Rodriguez, Isabel
Rodriguez, Jesus
Rodriguez, Jose
Rodriguez, Jose Ines
Rodriguez, Juan
Rodriguez, Juana (1)
Rodriguez, Juana (2)
Rodriguez, Julia
Rodriguez, Julio (1)
Rodriguez, Julio (2)
Rodriguez, Leandro
Rodriguez, Leonor
Rodriguez, Lola (1)
Rodriguez, Lola (2)
Rodriguez, Manuel
Rodriguez, Manuela
Rodriguez, Maria
Rodriguez, Modesta
Rodriguez,

Monserrate
Rodriguez, Pablo (1)
Rodriguez, Pablo (2)
Rodriguez, Santiago
Rodriguez, Severiano
Rodriguez, Tomas
Rodriguez, Vicente
Rodriguez, Vitoria
Roman, Cosme
Roman, German
Roman, Manuel
Romero, Juan
Romero, Juana P.
Romero, Magdalena
Rosa, Angel
Rosa, Antonio
Rosa, Jose Ma.
Rosa, Lorenzo
Rosa, Margarita
Rosa, Pedro (1)
Rosa, Pedro (2)
Rosado, Arcadia
Rosado, Demesia
Rosado, Manolina
Rosado, Maria
Rosado, Monserrate
Rosado, Natividad
Rosado, Victoria
Rosales, Andres
Rosario, Celestina
Rosario, Cirila
Rosario, Eleuterio
Rosario, Fernando
Rosario, Jacoba
Rosario, Jose Maria
Rosario, Juan (1)
Rosario, Juan (2)
Rosario, Maria (1)
Rosario, Maria (2)
Rosario, Olegario
Rosario, Valentina
Rota, Leticia
Ruiz Maria
Ruiz, Andres
Ruiz, Felipe
Ruiz, Fermina
Ruiz, Francisco
Ruiz, Gregoria
Ruiz, Manuel
Ruiz, Ricardo
Ruiz, Roman
Ruiz, Senobia
Ruiz, Tomasa
Sabat, Evangelista

Sabat, Manolin
Sabat, Regalada
Sabina Martinez,
Carmen
Salao, Fenancio
Salazar, Jose Ma.
Saldaña (Vda. de),
Monsita R.
Salgado, Jose
Salgado, M. R.
Sampayo, Isabel
Sampayo, Jose
Sampayo, Juan
Sampayo, Rodolfo
San--, Juan
Sanaga, Antonio
Sanagas, Arturo
Sanche, Maria
Sanchez (Vda. de),
Maria P.
Sanchez Carrasquillo,
Angel
Sanchez, Anita
Sanchez, Antonio
Sanchez, Carmen
Sanchez, Celestino
Sanchez, Demetrio
Sanchez, Escolastica
Sanchez, Ignacio
Sanchez, Isabel (1)
Sanchez, Isabel (2)
Sanchez, Jacinta
Sanchez, Juan (1)
Sanchez, Juan (2)
Sanchez, Julia
Sanchez, Lucia
Sanchez, Max
Sanchez, Maximina
Sanchez, Modesto
Sanchez, Teodora (1)
Sanchez, Teodora (2)
Sanchez, Tomas
Sanchez, Victoria
Saniel, Barbara
Saniel, Carola A.
Saniel, Juan
Saniel, Juan M.
Santa, Maria
Santana, Carmen
Santana, Jesusa
Santana, Josefa
Santana, Pedro
Santana, Ramona
Santiago (de), Antonia

Santiago (de), Maria
Santiago (de), Monserrate
Santiago (de), Nan
Santiago, Agustina L.
Santiago, Albelto
Santiago, Angela
Santiago, Anselmo
Santiago, Antonia
Santiago, Erivelto
Santiago, Fabia
Santiago, Gregorio
Santiago, Isabelo
Santiago, Joaquin (1)
Santiago, Joaquin (2)
Santiago, Jose E.
Santiago, Josefa
Santiago, Juan (1)
Santiago, Juan (2)
Santiago, Juanito
Santiago, Manolo
Santiago, Marcelo
Santiago, Maria
Santiago, Monserrate
Santiago, Obdulia
Santiago, Pedro
Santiago, Providencia (1)
Santiago, Providencia (2)
Santiago, Rafaela
Santiago, Ramon (1)
Santiago, Ramon (2)
Santiago, Ricardo
Santiago, Sino
Santiago, Tiburcio
Santos, Domingo
Santos, Felipe
Santos, Victor
Sarraga, Alejandrina
Sarraga, Belen
Seigel Gonzalez, N.
Selles, Carolina
Sepeda, Agapito
Sepeda, Gumercinda
Sepeda, Santos
Serupo, Serapio
Sevillano, Carmen
Sevillano, Rafael
Siaca (de), Dolores Q.
Siaca Pacheco, M.
Siaca Soto, Manuel
Siaca, Arturo
Siaca, Benito

Siaca, Dolores
Siaca, Juan
Sifre, Armando J.
Silva Gutierres, Candida
Silva Hilarza, Elias
Silva Martinez, Agustin
Silva Perez, Juan
Silva Torres, Candida
Silva Torres, Froilan
Silva Torres, Ramon
Silva, Dominga
Silva, Enrique
Silva, Fortunato
Silva, Julia
Silva, Maria L.
Silva, Ramona
Silva, Ricarda
Silver, Lorenza
Siment, Elvira M.
Simons, Alejandrina
Sintron, Santiago
Sintron, Serafin
Sirva, Jose
Sobrino de Lomba, Josefa
Solero, Laura
Solero, Nieve
Soto (de), Argentina R.
Soto (Vda. de) Soto, Monserrate
Soto de Mayor, Maria
Soto de Siaca, Carmen
Soto, Antonia
Soto, Bernardino
Soto, Carmen
Soto, Delfin
Soto, Fela
Soto, Manuel
Soto, Miguel (1)
Soto, Miguel (2)
Soto, Petra
Soto Rosa
Suarez, Elvira
Suarez, Emilio
Suarez, Feliz
Suarez, Luisa
Suarez, Saturnina
Susarre, Juana
Tapia, Carmen
Tapia, Concepcion
Tapia, Cruz

Tapia, Felix
Tapia, Francisco
Tapia, Inocencio
Tapia, Irene
Tapia, Jose
Tapia, Josefina
Tapia, Julio
Tapia, Natividad
Telemaco, Monserrate
Texidor (de), Carlota
Texidor, Herminia
Texidor, Luis
Thomas, Emilio
Tirado, Epifanio
Tirado, Josefa
Tirado, Maria
Torcador, Sandalio
Torrens, Benjamin
Torrens, Elena
Torrens, Mercedes
Torres Colina, Gregoria
Torres Vasquez, Juan
Torres, Angela
Torres, Avelina
Torres, Calmela
Torres, Catalina
Torres, Cruz
Torres, Dominga
Torres, Eriverto
Torres, Francisco
Torres, Modesta (1)
Torres, Modesta (2)
Torres, Ramona
Torres, Santiago
Torres, Trinidad
Torres, Vicenta
Trebiño, Bandila
Trebiño, Manuela
Treviño, Adolfo
Treviño, Joaquin
Treviño, Rafael
Tufiño, Blas
Tufiño, Juan
Tufiño, Ramona
Tufiño, Rosenda
Tufiño, Vicenta
Ufrai, Pascual
Urbistondo (Vda. de), Elvira
Vadiez, Marcelino
Valentin, Josefa
Valero, Calista
Valle, Dolores

Vallecillo, Enrique
Vamonde, Manuela
Vanterpool, Alfredo
Vargas Paula
Vargas, Adela
Vargas, Carmen
Vargas, Francisco
Vargas, Isabel
Vargas, Jose
Vargas, Juan
Vargas, Julia
Vargas, Justa
Vargas, Manuela
Vasquez, Antonio
Vasquez, Pulido
Vazques, Ambrosio
Vazquez de Herrera, Carlota
Vazquez Fernandez, Juana
Vazquez, A.
Vazquez, Alejandro
Vazquez, Andres
Vazquez, Andres
Vazquez, Angela
Vazquez, Emilia
Vazquez, Esperanza
Vazquez, Esteban
Vazquez, Isabel
Vazquez, Julio
Vazquez, Lorenza
Vazquez, Lucila
Vazquez, Manuela
Vazquez, Miguel
Vazquez, Nicolas
Vazquez, Perfecto
Vazquez, Rafael
Vazquez, Rosa
Vazquez, Sara
Vazquez, Tiburcio
Vega, Antonio
Vega, Beatriz
Vega, Miguel
Vega, Rafaela
Vegas, Dolores
Vela de Martinez, Etelvina D.
Velasco, Isaura
Velasco, Pilar
Velazquez, Clota
Velazquez, Isac
Velazquez, Valdomera
Velez de Pascual, Josefa

Velez, Angel
Velez, Damiana
Velez, Juan F.
Velez, Leonol
Velez, Tomas
Velilla de Zalduondo, Sofia
Velilla, Angel
Velilla, Carmen
Velilla, Dolores
Velilla, Teresa
Vellamura, Agapito
Ventura, Candida
Vera Carrillo, Santiago
Veve de Matta, Carmen
Veve Galchiando, Arturo
Veve, J. (Jr.)
Veve, Juan (M.D.)
Veve, M. A. (Mrs.)
Veve, Nemesio
Veve, R.
Vicente, Rafaela
Vidal Planell, Jose
Vidal, Carmen
Vidal, Lola
Viera, Juana
Viera, Ricardo
Villafaña, Martin
Villanueva, Julia
Villanueva, Natalio
Villaveitia, Adela
Vinuesa, Rita
Vlasco de la Rosa, Juana
Walker, Amada
Walta, Juana
Westen, Emilia
Westen, Nefel
Westen, Ramon
Williams, Angela
Williams, Luisa
Wilson, Thomas
Winthrop, K.
Wiston, Zenon
Wittman, Modesta
Ygnasio, Jose
Yriarte, Elisa
Zalduondo Veves, Javier
Zalduondo, Luis
Zalduondo, Luz
Zalduondo, R.

Zalduondo, Rafael
Zepeda, Manuel
Zepeda, Santiago

Hatillo

Hatillo Mayor
(Telegram)

Humacao

Humacao Mayor
(Telegram)

Isabela

Isabela Citizens

Abreu (de), Juana
Abreu Diaz, Ana
Abreu Diaz, Antonia
Abreu Diaz, Marina
Abreu Diaz, Rafaela
Abreu, Luis
Alarcon, Fulgencio
Aldarondo, Domingo
Alers, Marina
Aviles, Delfina
Aviles, Gabriel
Ayorva (de), Juana
Banuchi (de), Vitoria D.
Banuchi (Vda. de) Eladia
Banuchi, Enrique
Banuchi, F. R.
Banuchi, Ramiro
Banuchi, Sebastian
Battistini, Teofilo H.
Brown Luevin, A. (Dr.)
Cabra (Vda. de), Teresa F.
Calero, Ernesto
Cardenas, Rogelio
Cardona (de), Generosa I.
Cardona Piquet, J.
Cardona, Sergio
Carval, Danilo
Castro (de), Carmen A.

Castro Leon, Genaro
Chaves (de), Amelia E.
Chaves (de), Maria R.
Chaves del Valle Isabel
Chaves del Valle, Agustin
Chaves del Valle, Pilar
Chaves Estrada, Pilar
Chaves, Belen
Chaves, Carmen Maria
Chaves, Dominica
Concepcion, Zenon
Cruz Valle, B. V.
Cruz, Jose
Cruz, Ventura
De la Cruz, Julio
De la Rosa (Vda. de), Herminia
De la Rosa, Blanca
De la Rosa, Eduvigis
De la Rosa, Laura
De la Rosa, Maria
De Vern, Miguel
Del Castillo, Avelino
Del Valle, Blanca
Del Valle, Maria Teresa
Delgado de Gles, Modesta
Deliz, Pedro
Domenech (de), Teresa E.
Domenech, Fernando
Estrada (de), Dolores F.
Estrada de Quevedo, Dolores
Estrada, Eloy
Estrada, Juanita
Fernandez Morales, R.
Ferrer de Domenech, Nieves
Garcia (de), Pilar R.
Garcia, Hersilia
Garcia, Lino
Garcia, Ricardo
Geigel (de), Josefa R.
Geigel (de), Prudencia P.
Geigel Paredes, Antonio
Geigel Paredes, Vicente
Geigel, Estrella

Geigel, Patria
Girald Cruz, Adrian
Girald, Gerardo
Girald, Guillermo
Gonzales, Leopoldo
Gonzalez Badillo, Ramon
Gonzalez de Polanco, Ysabel
Gonzalez, Diego G.
Gonzalez, Eugenio
Gonzalez, Gerardo
Gonzalez, Jose D.
Gonzalez, Julio
Gonzalez, Pepita
Guffain (de), Milagros M.
Guffain (Vda. de), Clara
Guffain, Clara
Gutierrez Ramon
Gutierrez, Bienvenido
Hernandez (de), Juana
Hernandez (Vda. de), Paulina
Hernandez, Domingo
Hernandez, J. R.
Hernandez, Luis Felipe
Hernandez, Pepe
Hernaz (de), Carmen A.
Jimenez Soto, R.
Jones, Ramon
Jordan, Martin
Lameler, Alfredo
Lameler, Beatriz
Lausell, Alfonso
Lopez, Tomas A.
Mendez (de), Juana G.
Mendoza, Antonio
Mendoza, Francisco
Mercado, Alonso
Mercado, Sotero
Miranda, Americo
Miranda, Orosio
Mirayes (de), Juana S.
Monclona, Juan
Monclova (de), Ysabel H.
Montalvo, Eulogio
Otero de Bravo, Pilar
Pagan (de), Belen

Antonio's Grace

Paredes, Candelario
Pino, Francisco
Polanco, Santiago
Quevedo (de),
  Magdalena A.
Quevedo (de), Teresa
Quevedo (Vda. de),
  Ramona
Quevedo Arroyos,
  Gloria
Quevedo y Gonzalez,
  Rosa
Quevedo, Esther
Quevedo, Fl. L.
Quevedo, Luz
Quevedo, Maria
Quevedo, Raquel
Quiñones (de),
  Carmen H.
Quiñones Calero, A. F.
Quiñones, Arturo
Rafols (de), Rosa A.
Ramirez (de), Rosa B.
Ramos, Felipe
Raviela, Demetrio
Rios, Clodomiro
Rivero (de), Juana C.
Rivero (de), Maria O
Rodriguez de Estrada,
  Luisa
Rodriguez, Casimiro
Rodriguez, Felipe (1)
Rodriguez, Felipe (2)
Rodriguez, Ramon
Rosa (de), Joaquina L.
Rosa (de), Manuela S.
Rosado, Silverio
Ruiz, Emilio
Ruiz, Teresa
Ruiz, Ysabel
Santiago, Luciano
Selles (de), Juanita R.
Selles, Encarnacion
Silva, Placido
Suarez (de), Eladia B.
Suarez, Alberto
Suarez, Augusto
Suffain, C. R.
Tamalos, Francisco
Ubiñas (de), Sofia H.
Urrutia, Rodolfo
Van Derdys, Paulina
Varela, Ana
Vargas, Jose A.

Velez, Ortiz, Jose M.
Velez, Pedro
Vendrell, Eugenio
Venegas (de),
  Altagracia
Venegas, Paquita
Zengoitita (de), Maria
  Luisa

Juncos

Juncos Mayor

Barreras, Jose

Juncos Citizens

Ainalbert, Jose M.
Algarin, Carmelo
Alvares, Leoncia
Alvarez, Leopoldo
Arzuaga Aponte, A.
Arzuaga Torres,
  Antonio
Arzuaga, Jose G.
Atils, Ramon
Barrera, J. (Jr.)
Barreras, Jose
  ("Alcalde Municipal")
  (Municipal Mayor)
Berrios, Jesus (Jr.)
Betances, Alfredo
Bojano, Galletano
Caballero, Jose
Cano, Antonio A.
Cantellor, Bartolome
Carrasquillo, Juan
Carrion, Segundo
Casas, Sandalio
Castro, Carlos
Cay, Antonio
Cintron, Jose G.
Colon, Ramon
Corcino, Juan
Corens, Fernando
Cortes, J. M.
Cortes, Rafael
Costa, Inocencio
Cruz, Juan Maria
Cruz, Manuel J.
Cruz, Severo
Dat ---, Jose

Davila, Felipe
Delfans, Antonio
Delfans, Jose
Delfans, Juan
Diaz Diaz, Francisco
Diaz, Rafael
Diaz, Rogelio
Elosegin, Ernesto
Falala, F.
Falero, Serafin
Fariña, Clemente
Fernandez y Lanza, C.
Fernandez, Ceferino
  (Jr.)
Fernandez, Jose
Fernandez, R.
Figueroa, Justino
Fizol, Franco R.
Flores, Ventura
Fonseca, Jesus
Fortuño, A.
Garcia, John
Garcia, Saturnino
Gomez, Antonio
Gonzalez, Fernando
  (Dr.)
Gorsino, Francisco
Guzman, Fernando
Harcam, Antonio
Hernandez, Jose
Hernandez, Jose M.
Hernandez, Juan
Hernandez, Zenon
Lanboy, Evangelio
Lopez, Genaro
Lopez, Nicolas
Lopez, Peña,
  Francisco
Lopez, Ramon
Maldonado, Jose
Marquez, Juan R.
Marrero Torres,
  Eugenio
Marrero, Felix
Marrero, Fernando
Martinez, Eulogio
Martinez, Gregorio
Martinez, Jose J.
Martinez, M.
Martinez, Rafael
Medina, Pedro
Mejias, Luis J.
Mendez, Jose
Mendez, Lucas

Miranda, A.
Miranda, Juan A.
Miranda, Lino R.
Molina, A. G.
Montañes, Gregorio
Morales, Jose
Morales, Jose Miguel
Morales, Ramon B.
Morales, Vicente
Mujica del Rosario, A.
Ocasio, Perfecto
Palva Azpunsa, Pedro
  S.
Peña, Arturo
Pereira, Jose Maria
Piñero (Jr.), Fulgencio
  (Lcdo.)
Principe, Tomas
Quiñones, Pedro
Ramirez, Agapito
Ramos, Joaquin
Reyes, Francisco
Ricasol, Modesto
Rivera, Manuel J.
Rivera, Rafael
Rodriguez, C.
Roig Bayonet, F.
Roldan, Juan
Roldan, Pablo
Rosario, Fiburcio
Sanchez, Carlos
Sanchez, Manuel
Santiago Rosario,
  Pedro
Santiago, Jose A.
Santiago, Nicolas
Sierra, Fernando
Sierra, Modesto
Silva Lopez, Pedro
Silva, Alejandro
Silvestriz, Salvador
Sino, Joaquin
Suarez, Gil
Torres Rodriguez,
  Pedro
Torres, Cayetano
Torres, Victor
Trinidad, Francisco
Varona, Carlos A.
Varona, Narciso
Vazquez, Jose
Vazquez, Rafael
Vazquez, Rufo
Vazquez, Ynes

233

Virella, Nemecio
Zayas, Pascual
Zeno, Justo C.

Lajas

Lajas Municipal Council

Morales, Jose A.
Ramirez Ortiz, Jose (Mayor)

Lajas Citizens

Abidez, Alicia
Avila, Margarita V.
Aviles de Roura, Gumersinda
Baez, Emilia
Biaggi (Vda. de), Anita Cruz
Biaggi, Irene
Biascochea, Carmen
Buenahora, Gloria B.
Buenahora, Inosensia
Calder, Emma
Calder, Virginia
Camacho, Carmen
Camacho, Maria
Camacho, Otilia
Cancel (de), Nicolasa A.
Cancel, Engracia
Coll (de), Isabel B.
Cordero, Amelia
Crespo, Magdalena
Davila, Juanita
De Santiago, Emelina
De Tio, Beatriz F.
Diaz, Paquita
Espinosa, Angela
Feliu (de), Maria I.
Feliu, Elvina
Feliu, Isabel
Figueroa (de), Rosaura, O.
Figueroa, Maria
Figueroa, Monserrate
Flores, Norberta
Frank (de), Julia P.
Frank de Irizarry,

Rosa Julia
Fur, Ana
Garrastagil, Monserrate
Ines (de), Geesje
Irizarry (de), Teresa C.
Irizarry Toro, Josefina
Irizarry, Adolfina
Irizarry, Amparo
Irizarry, Antonia
Irizarry, Carmen Ma.
Irizarry, Laura
Irizarry, Maria C.
Irizarry, Miguelina
Linarez, Micaela
Lluch, Cialo
Lopes, Virginia
Lopez, Carmen
Lugo de Garces, Felicita
Lugo Y., Indra
Lugo Y., Josefa
Lugo, Candelaria
Lugo, Carmen (1)
Lugo, Carmen (2)
Lugo, Maria A.
Lugo, Maria M.
Lugo, Rosalia
Martinez, Josefa
Martinez, Monserrate
Mercado de Velez, Rosario
Mercado, Ofelia
Mercado, Sixta
Milan, Rafaela
Milan, Rosalia
Morales (de), Catalina O.
Morales (de), Isolina
Morales Ortiz, Margarita
Morales, Augusta
Morales, Aurora
Morales, Celsa
Morales, Concepcion
Morales, Delia
Morales, Eustaquio
Morales, Providencia
Morales, Rosario
Muñoz, Guadalupe
Navea de Noriega, Amparo
Ortiz (de), Carmen R.
Ortiz (de), Fidelina B.

Ortiz (Vda. de), Emilia R.
Ortiz, Eloina
Ortiz, Emelina
Ortiz, Lola
Ortiz, Manuela
Ortiz, Merela
Ortiz, Rosa Aminka
Ortiz, Teresa
Pagan, Ana P.
Pagan, Carmen
Pagan, Isaura
Pagan, Juanita
Pagan, Manuela
Pagan, Vidalina
Paganacci, Rosalina
Pancorbo, Mercedes
Pardo, Adolfina
Perez de Pabon, Carmen
Perez, Carmen Luisa
Pierz, Ramona
Puig (de), Rosario G.
Puig, Maria de R.
Quijano, Dolores
Quiñones, Teresa
Quiñones, Ursula
Rivera, Leonor
Rodriguez, Amelia
Rodriguez, Clotilde
Rodriguez, Monserrate
Rodriguez, Ramona
Rosa, Luisa
Rosario, Carmen
Roura, Flordeliana
Ruiz, Consuelo
Santana, Maria
Seda, Dolores
Suarez, Elena
Tiradera, Cecilia
Tomey, Antonia
Toro, Cruz
Tradera, Victoria
Urizarry, Coleman
Urrutia, Candida
Urrutia, Lucila
Vazquez, Leonor
Velez, Dolores
Velez, Rafaela
Vila, Josefina
Yrizarry y Losada, Maria
Zambrana, Basilisa

Zambrana, Matilde

Lares

Students, Lares (Telegram)

Loiza

Loiza Citizens

Adorno, Micaela
Aguayo, Antonio
Alonso, E.
Alonso, Julio
Alvarez Garcia, Jesus
Alvarez, Miguel
Alvarez, Miguel C.
Aquino, Cecilia
Arana, Luis
Aubray, Jose (Dr.)
Benitez, Julio
Betancourt, Isaura
Betancourt, Jose
Betancourt, Pilar
Betancourt, Rita
Bonilla, Dolores
Bonilla, Francisco
Bonilla, Pablo (1)
Bonilla, Pablo (2)
Bracenet, Justino
Budet (Vda. de), Belen
Budet de Mangual, Caridad
Bunbury, H.M.E.
Calderon, Juan Ramon
Calzada de Budet, Maria
Calzada, Candita
Calzada, Catalina C.
Calzada, Elivera
Calzada, Francisco
Calzada, Teresa
Calzada, Teresa C.
Carrion, Diana
Carrion, Jose Ma.
Carrion, Pastor
Castro, Enrique
Castro, Jose
Castro, Juan

Colon --, J.
Cordero (Vda. de), Maria
Correa, Amelia
Correa, Cristina
Correa, Jesus Ma.
Correa, Merida
Correa, Panchita
Correa, Rosendo
Cruz Fermin
Cruz, Simolicio
Cruz, Vicent
Cullen, Pablo
De Leon, Felipe
Del Valle, Luis
Diaz (de), Francisca C.
Diaz, Ana
Diaz, E. (Lcdo.)
Diaz, Gregoria
Diaz, Jose
Diaz, Maria
Duchesne, Luis E.
Elicrir, Jose
Encarnacion, Cruz
Encarnacion, Eugenio
Encarnacion, Juana
Encarnacion, Monserrate
Esquilin, Anastacio
Ferminoca, Ceferino
Fernandez (Vda. de), Carmen
Fernandez, Ceferino
Fernandez, Maria
Figueroa, Trinidad
Flores, A.
Flores, Sergio
Franco, Anastasio
Franco, Hermenegildo
Franco, Patricio
Franco, Simplicio
Fuentes, Candido
Gambaro (de), Rosa R. (P. M.)
Gambaro, Carlos
Gambaro, Felicita
Gambaro, Ramona
Garcia, Asuncion
Garcia, Emiliano
Garcia, Juan
Garcia, Rafael
Gonzalez, Nemecia
Hernandez, Luis
Hernandez, Maria E.

Isurrini, E. (Lcdo.)
Juana, Anita
Lopez, Amparo
Mangual, Saturnino
Martinez, Enrique
Martinez, Lorenzo
Matos, Jose
May, William S.
Mendez Sanchez, Alejandro
Mendez, Rafael
Menendez, Marcelina
Mojica, Rafael
Mundo (de), Antonia B.
Mundo, Cruz
Ocasio, Maximo
Olivera, Angel
Orta, Justina
Ortiz Pacheco, Virginia
Ortiz, Ines
Ortiz, Rita
Osorio, Belen
Osorio, Julian
Osorio, Sancho
Otro, Juan C.
Pacheco Vda. de Ortiz, Erasma
Palacios (de), Carmelina G.
Palacios, Jose G.
Pastrana, Guillermo
Pastrana, Julio
Prados, Angelina
Queipo, Antonio
Quiñones, Juana
Reyes Olmos, F.
Rios, Jose Maria
Riu Diaz, Jose
Rivera, Esteban
Rodriguez, Josefa M.
Rodriguez, Luis
Rodriguez, Prospero
Salaman, Juan
Sanchez (de), Carmen C.
Sanchez (Vda. de), Delfina
Sanchez, Antonio J.
Sanchez, Antonio K.
Sanchez, Benedicta
Sanchez, Carmen
Sanchez, Valentina

Santiago, Ramona
Santos, Leopoldina
Sarria del Uveda, Felipe
Serrano, Jacoba
Sierra, Josefa
Sierra, Ramona
Sosa, Celeste
Sosa, Maria
Suarez (de), Sofia Amor
Suarez, Cecilio
Suarez, Jose
Suarez, Marcial
Trenche, Emilio
Trinidad, Antonia
Vazquez, Fermin
Vazquez, Petra
Villalobos (de), Obdulia C.
Villalobos, Antonio
Villalobos, Carmen
Villalobos, Jose
Villalobos, Luis
Villarini, Damas
Wolker, Celina

Mayaguez

Damas de Mayaguez (Mayaguez Ladies) (Telegram)

Morovis

Ladies & Gentlemen of Morovis (Telegram)
Morovis Municipal Council (Telegram)

Naguabo

Naguabo Municipal Council

Gallardo, Arturo (Jr.) (Mayor)
Rivera, Esteban (Pres.)

Patillas

Patillas Municipal Council and Citizens

Acosta Tio, Joaquin
Agostini, Domingo
Alvarez, Julia
Arias, Luis
Arroyos, Santiago P.
Baerga, L.
Bernaerniere, Felix
Bernier, Julian
Bernier, Santos
Bone, Zenon
Borras, Jose E.
Borras, Victor
Camacho, Roman
Capelli, Antonio (Lcdo.)
Caraballo, Joaquin
Carmindy, Jose D.
Cavian, Carlos
Cepera, E.
Cintron, Ramon
Cofresi, Domingo
Cokran, Hipolito
Cora, Bautista
Corona, Agustin
Cruz, Aurelio
De Jesus, Luis
Del Campo, Cristobal
Del Cerro, Pedro
Delgado, Miguel
Diaz, Facundo
Diaz, Fulgencio
Diaz, Gonzalo A.
Diaz, Jose R.
Diaz, Ramon
Echevarria, Francisco
Feliciano, Alfonso
Fernandez, P.
Figueroa Eusebio
Font Torres, Enusti
Forcellida, Jose
Fuenari, J.
Garcia, Eugenio
Gaya, B.
Gely, Jose
Gely, Miguel
Gonzalez, Arturo

Gonzalez, Luis
Guifford, Jules (Rev.)
  (Catholic Priest)
Guzman Cubano,
  Arturo
Huete, Jose
Igo, Euclides
Ildefonso, Bonifacio
Ildefonso, Celedonio
Ildefonso, Jesus
Janer, Feliciano (Dr.)
  (M.D.)
Lanadebel, Tomas
Latallade, Juan
Lebron, Ambrosio
Lebron, C.
Lebron, Candelario
Lebron, Emilio
Lebron, Laureano
Lebron, Manuel
Lebron, Ramon
  (Municipal Judge)
Lehrig, Encarnacion
Librau, Domingo
Lopez, Enrique
Lopez, Jose
Lopez, Tomas
Lugo, Antonio
Marquez, Jesus M.
Mauras, Jose
Maurat, Teodoro
Morales, Evaristo
Morales, Jose M.
  (Rev.) (Methodist
  Minister)
Morales, Manuel
Olmeda, Juan
Ortiz, Francisco
Pared, Nicolas
Piñeiro, Jose
Planas, Jose
Planas, Severo O.
Quiñonez, Jose
Ramirez, Diego
Ricarvet, Rafael
Ricci, Alberto (Mayor)
Rivera, Decenol
Rivera, Manuel
Rivera, Miguel
Rivera, Nicomedes
Rivera, Roque
Rivera, Wenceslao
Rodriguez (de), Ana
Rodriguez, Angel

Rodriguez, Fernando
Rodriguez, Jose
  Ramon (Lcdo.)
Rodriguez, Pedro
Roman, Genaro
Ruiz, Secadio
Sanchez, Cleto
Santiago, Eulelio
Sicar, Carlos
Sierra, Sergio
Solis, Pablo
Soto, Florencio
Soto, Ivan
Stella, Mateo
Tañon, Huntino
Torres Aponte, Jose
Torres, Juan
Valles, Miguel
Vargas, Jose
Vazquez Ortiz, Jose
Vega, Juan L.
Veigne, Carlos
Velazquez, Arturo
Villamil, J. C.
  (Secretary, Municipal
  Council)
Villarini, Ismael
Villariny, Jorge A.

Peñuelas

Peñuelas Municipal Council

Balasguide, Gabino
  (Mayor)
Nazario y Nazario,
  Felipe (Secretary)

Ponce

Ponce Mayor

Salazar, Felipe
  (Deputy Mayor)

. . .

Ponce Citizens

Aguileras, D.
Alvarez, Mateo
Andino, Jose
Aviles, P.
Barroas, Jose
Berenguell, Fa.
Bermudez, Antonio
Bermudez, Juan
Brita, Zoilo
Campos, Juan
Caquias, F.
Cara, Juan
Caraballo, W.
Certa, Rogelio
Costas, Luis
Cristian, Antonio
Cuebas, H.
Diaz, Pablo
Diaz, Santos
Fernando, Pedro J.
Galve, Derrick
Garcia, Calixto
Garcia, Leoncio
Garcia, Paco
Guilve, Juan
Guitre, S.
Jesus, Pablo
Lopez, Antonio
Maldonado, C.
Maldonado, J.
Maldonado, Tomas
Manguals, Jose
Martin, J.
Martinez, E.
Martinez, Feliz
Medina, J.
Melendez, G.
Mora, M.
Morel, Jose
Olan, H.
Ortiz, Domingo
Ortiz, Ramon
Pacho, Atanacio
Pacho, Luciano
Perez, Victor
Pio, Francisco
Pio, Juan
Polanco, Cantalicio
Quiles, Eduardo
Quiñones, D.
Quiros, Zoilo

Ramirez, Vicente
Ramos, Jorge
Raspaldo, Francisco
Rigual, E.
Rivera, Mariano
Rodriguez, Toribio
Rosado, Marcos
Rosas, Gregorio
Sanchez, Francisco
Sanchez, Ramon
Santiago, A.
Santiago, Agustin
Santiago, Basilio
Santiago, Ricardo
Sepulveda, Watalio
Tomas, Sanchez
Toro, Juan
Torres, Ramon
Valeon, Luis
Vargas, E.
Vargas, Simon
Vazquez J.
Vazquez, Dionicio
Vazquez, W.
Vega, E.
Vega, Miguel
Velez, Amadeo
Velez, Escolastico

Rincon

Rincon Students and
  Mayor (Telegram)

Rio Piedras

Rio Piedras Municipal Council

President, Municipal
Council, Rio Piedras
(Telegram)

Salinas

Salinas Citizens

Acosta, Pedro

Alvarez (de), Martina S.
Alvarez, Amelia
Alvarez, Crucita
Alvarez, Evaristo
Alvarez, Jose
Alvarez, Julia
Alvarez, Luis
Amuralli, Gedein
Amy, Cesar
Antonle, Marcelin
Arce, Jose M.
Arroyo, Guillermo
Atilano, Guillermo
Caballero, Belen A.
Caballero, Celso
Castillo (Vda. de), Javiera A.
Castillo, Juan E.
Castillo, Petronila M. (Teacher)
Castro, Jose
Cianchini, Luisa (Teacher)
Cintron, Isaura (Acting Principal)
Colon, Victor
Constantino, D.
Cordova, J.
Cruz, Jose Maria
Cruz, Luis
Cruz, R.
D., C.
Diaz, Gaston
Diaz, Luis M.
Espada, Dionisio
Garcia, G.
Garcia, Sutero C.
Gines, J.
Gines, R.
Gines, V.
Gonzales, Pedro
Gonzalez, C.
Gonzalez, C.
Gonzalez, J. M.
Izquierdo, Francisco
Jeri, Miguel
Jordan, Zoilo
Lecola, Francisca
Lind, Pedro
Lopez, Lucas
Luchese, Angelina
Menendez, B.
Mercado, Arturo

Miranda, Epifanio
Monserrate, Hipolito
Monserrate, J.
Monserrate, Jesus
Morerg (de), Maria C.
Morerg, Leopoldo
Ortiz, Angelito
Ortiz, Jesus
Ortiz, Ricardo
Padilla, E. O.
Paniagua, Providencia
Paravisim, J.
Perez, C.
Pizarro, Rogue
Platet, Alfredo
Platet, Eduardo
Po, Arturo
Pomales, Luis
Rami, Jacobo
Ramos, Luis
Rivera, Arturo
Rodriguez, Antonio
Rodriguez, Francisco
Sanchez, Jose G.
Santiago, Maximo
Secada (Vda. de), Monserrate B.
Secada, Francisco
Secola, J. A.
Soto, Eduardo
Torres, Eugenio
V., Ramon
Vargas, Epifanio
Vazquez, Jose E.
Vazquez, Mario R.
Vazquez, Regis
Velez, Jose

San Juan

Municipal Council, San Juan

Todd, Roberto H. (Mayor)

San Juan Citizens

Andino, Julian R.
Barbosa, --
Barbosa, Francisco J.

Cepeda, Julio
Esturio, Jose I.
Jimenez, Jose Patricio
Olivo, Juan (Jr.)
Perez, Emilo
Sola, Jose

San Juan Signatures Collected by "Ladies of Puerto Rico"

---, Gonzalo B.
---, J.
(Migdalia)
Abadia, Esperanza
Abalia, Ramon
Abarca, A.
Abarca, Juan
Abelazzi, Bernardo
Abiles colon, Jose
Aboy de Cintron, Encarnacion
Aboy Longpre, R.
Abramonde, Luis Francisco
Abrau, E.
Abril, Mariano
Acebedo, Pepita
Acevedo, Juan
Acevedo, Nicacio
Acosta Calderon, Carmen
Acosta de Palacios, Eva
Acosta Trijo, J.
Acosta, Andres
Acosta, Antonio
Acosta, Clemencia
Acosta, Gino
Acosta, Jose A.
Acosta, Jose F.
Acosta, Jose I.
Acosta, Juanito
Acosta, Maria
Acosta, Maria Luisa
Acosta, Serafin
Acosta, Soledad
Acuña (de), Camen B.
Acuña (de), Dolores A.
Acuña (de), May

Adamo (de), Maria I.
Adan, Mariana
Adorno, Araceli
Adorno, Carmen
Adorno, Margarita
Adorno, Maria
Adorno, Micaela
Adorno, Monserrate
Affigne, Carmelo
Agostini de Baena, Emilia
Agosto Pastora
Agosto, Julio
Agosto, Manuel
Agosto, Rafaela
Agosto, Ramon
Agosto, Rufino
Agrait, Maria Teresa
Aguallo, Ramon
Aguayo, Gil
Agudo, Antonio
Agudo, O.
Agueda, Rafael
Aguiar, Antonio
Aguiar, Feliciano
Aguiar, Manuel R.
Aguiar, Maria
Aguiar, Maria L.
Aguilar, Catalina
Aguirre, Jose
Agusty, Joaquin
Alarcon, Rafael
Albaca, Mariana
Albacete (Vda. de), Angeles F.
Albarado, Sabina
Albert, Antonia
Alberto Vda. de Vega, Vicenta
Albesegin, Manuel
Alcaraz, Antonia
Alcaraz, Juanita
Alcaraz, Mercedes
Alda (de), M. L.
Aldany, Rafael
Aldea Sigles, Jose
Aldea, Ernesta
Aldea, Jose
Alegria, Angela
Alejandro Pinto, Ignacio
Aleman, Ernesto
Aleman, Herminio
Aleman, Rufina

Alfonso, Manuel
Alfonzo Gonzalez, Lola
Alfonzo Vda. de
  Garcia, Carola
Alfonzo, A.
Alfonzo, Alfonso
Algain, Monserrate
Alguacil, Luis
Alica, Jose
Alicaro, Jorge A.
Alicea, Angela
Alicea, Blas
Alicea, Carmen
Alicea, Dolores
Alicea, Jose
Alicea, Olegario
Alicea, Petra
Alicea, Ramona
Allala, Epifanio
Allala, Marcela
Almadeo, J.
Almanzan, Maria
Almanzar, Rosa
Almanzar, Rosalia
Almeida Otilio G.
Almeida, Alexander
Almiraty, Nicolas
Almiroty, Maria
Almodovar, Teresa
Alonso, Benito
Alonso, Celestino
Alonso, Jose Maria
Alonso, Juan M.
Alonso, Julia
Alonso, M. (1)
Alonso, M. (2)
Alonso, Maria
Alonso, Victor
Alonzo, M.
Alonzo, Miguel
Alribiades, Josefa
Alvarado, Emilio
Alvarado, Francisco
Alvares Peña, Julian
Alvares, Jose
Alvarez (Bautista)
Alvarez (de), Teresa
  M.
Alvarez (Vda. de), H.
  M.
Alvarez Colon, Aurelio
Alvarez Rojas, Jose
Alvarez Santos, H.
Alvarez Torres, Belen

Alvarez Valdes (de),
  Julia C.
Alvarez Valdes, Dr.
Alvarez, Adelaida
Alvarez, Adolfo
Alvarez, Alberto
Alvarez, Antonio
Alvarez, Aurora
Alvarez, Beatriz
Alvarez, Candido
Alvarez, Celso
Alvarez, F. J.
Alvarez, Generoso
Alvarez, Juan F.
Alvarez, Luis
Alvarez, M.
Alvarez, Maria
Alvarez, R.
Alvarez, Ramon
Alvarez, Ysaac
Alvarez, Ysabel
Alvaro, Eladio
Alvelo, Maria
Alvelo, Nicomedes
Amable Abreu,
  Dominicano
Amado, Maria
Amado, Rafael
Amador (de), Luisa A.
Amador Arias, Maria
  F.
Amador Rivas, Luisa
Amador, Angeles
Amador, Araceli
Amador, Eloisa
Amador, Enriqueta
Amador, Galadora
Amador, Manuela
Amador, Maria de los
  Angeles
Amador, Ricarda
Amador, Trefina
Amalbit, Rafael
Amato, Dolores
Amato, J. M.
Amato, Joaquina
Ambrosiani de
  Montilla, Angeles
Amols, Juan
Amy (de), Monserra
  M.
Anastea (de), Catalina
  C.
Andino Akuar, J. D.

Andino de Jarer,
  Asuncion
Andino, Ana Maria
Andino, Angel
Andino, Antonio
Andino, Belen
Andino, Bernardo
Andino, Carmen
Andino, Edelmira
Andino, Francisco M.
Andino, Juan
Andino, Luis
Andino, P. F.
Andino, R.
Andino, W. Victor
Andrade, Eugenio
Andrade, Felicidad
Andrade, Juliana
Andrade, Lucas
Andrade, Marcelino
Andrade, Marcelino
  M.
Andrade, Nicasio
Andrade, Placido
Andrade, Rosalia
Andrades Laredo,
  Ercira
Andrades, Claudio
Andrades, Felix
Andrades, Hernando
Andrades, Juan
Andrades, Luciano
Andrades, Martin
Andrades, Monserrate
Andrades, Ruino
Andrades, Rumaidra
Andrades, Saturnino
Andradez, Bernabe
Andradez, Cruz
Andradez, Josefina
Andradez, Juana
Andradez, Luis
Andradez, Nabrana
Andrez, Ana Mari
Anduce, Jorge
Andujar, Manuel G.
Andujar, Ysabel
Anei, Ramon
Angulo, Angel
Angulo, Antonio
Angulo, Francisco
Annoria, Antonio
Añol, Eulogia
Antolin, Clotilde

Anton Hernandez,
  Carlos
Antonetti (de),
  Josefina M.
Antonetti, Margot
Antonetti, Salvador
Antonetti, Vicente
Antongiorgi, Antonia
  L.
Antonio, Felipe
Antonsanti, Frank
Antonsanti, Rosalina
  B.
Aparicio, C. S.
Aparicio, Francisco S.
Apellaniz (de), Luisa
  G.
Apellaniz, Ana
Aponte Pico, Jose
Aponte, Agripina
Aponte, Eduardo
Aponte, Felix
Aponte, Felix L.
Aponte, Francisco
Aponte, Jose Ivan
Aponte, Josefa
Aponte, Julian
Aponte, Maximo
Aponte, Paco
Aponte, Pepe
Aponte, Rosina
Aponte, Saturnino R.
Aque, Alonso
Aquenza (Vda. de),
  Maria B.
Aquino, Juan
Arabit, Jose
Aracie, Providencia
Aragon, Jose
Arana, Angel L.
Arana, Gonzalo
Arana, Luis
Aranda, Margarita
Aranjo, Emilia
Aranzamendi Vda. de
  Asencio, Carmen
Araujo (de), Dolores
Araujo, Juan
Araujo, Mercedes
Araujo, Pedro
Arbelo, Atilano
Arbelo, Dolores
Arbelo, J. Jesus
Arburua, F.

Arce del Freije, Blanca
Arce Marrero, Celia
Ardin, Antonia
Arena, Juan
Arena, Luis F.
Arenas, Angelina
Ariaga, Georgina
Arias, C.
Arias, Carmen
Arida, David
Aristud, Julio
Aristud, Pedro
Arnagas, Tomasa
Arragone, Consuelo
Arreche, Edo
Arribi, Paco
Arroyo (de), Primitiva M.
Arroyo de Santiago
Arroyo Martinez, Juan
Arroyo Pagan, Manuel
Arroyo Weynes, Jose
Arroyo Zeppenfeldt, Nicolas
Arroyo, Amador
Arroyo, Ana Joaquina
Arroyo, Catalino
Arroyo, Claudio
Arroyo, Dolores
Arroyo, Gregoria
Arroyo, Jose (1)
Arroyo, Jose (2)
Arroyo, Jose (3)
Arroyo, Jose C.
Arroyo, Julian
Arroyo, Lupercio
Arroyo, Miguel
Arroyo, Oliva
Arroyo, Ricardo
Arroyo, Victoria
Arruz, Juan
Arruza (de), Zoraida P.
Artau, Antonio
Artau, Damian
Artau, Gustavo
Arte, Juan R.
Arteaga, Juan E.
Arteaga, Vicente
Arvelo, Juana
Arzuaga de Gomez Brioso, Ana
Arzuaga, Carmen
Arzuaga, G.
Asencio Alo. Torres,

Javier
Asencio, Ana Maria
Asencio, Eloisa
Asencio, Maria
Asensio, Besee
Asensio, Eduardo
Asise, Tomasa
Asisi, Matilde
Asknaz, Tom
Astasia, Victoria
Atiles Par, Ysabel
Atiles, Belen
Aubar, Amalia
Audinot, Juan (Jr.)
Audinot, Juan
Audinot, Pedro
Audinot, Rafael
Aufonso (Vda. de), Esperanza P.
Ausa, Ramon
Austian, Maria
Aviles, Adolfo
Aviles, Emilio
Aviles, Jesus (1)
Aviles, Jesus (2)
Aviles, Jesus (3)
Aviles, Justina
Aviles, Vicente
Ayala Rivera, Cruz
Ayala, Anastacio
Ayala, Fernanda
Ayala, Isolina
Ayala, Juana
Ayala, Ramon
Ayala, Tomas
Ayala, Victor (1)
Ayala, Victor (2)
Aybar (Vda. de), Cruz
Aybar, Andres
Aybar, Dolores
Aybar, Luciana
Azores, Eduardo
B., Jose Antonio
B., S.
Babilonia de Albas, Lavinia
Badia, Miguel
Badiena, Eugenio
Badiena, M.
Badillo, Pilar
Baena, Pedro
Baesta (de), Maria B.
Baez (Vda. de), Dolores A.

Baez De G., Carmen
Baez Rodriguez, Rafael
Baez, Agustina
Baez, Alberto
Baez, Carmen
Baez, Jose
Baez, Rosendo
Baez, Ynocencia
Balaguer, Dolores
Balaguer, Francisca
Balaguer, Jose A.
Balalral (de), Sarah M.
Balbina, Eulalio
Baldorioty (de), Rosa G.
Baldorioty Vega, A.
Baldorioty, Julia
Ball (de), Amalia G.
Ball, Carlo
Ball, Victor R,
Ballester, Isabel
Ballesteros, Eduardo
Balseiro (de), Dolores B.
Balseiro (de), Lola R.
Balseiro Gomez, Rafael M.
Balseiro, Carmen
Balseiro, Rafael (1)
Balseiro, Rafael (2)
Bamagero, Carlos
Bandera Vda. de Rodriguez, Carmen
Banicke, Florence
Baquero (de), Isabel G.
Baquero, Bienvenida
Baragaia, J.
Baragaño, Rafael
Barange, Jose
Barbara, Jose
Barbe, Carolina
Barbosa, Carmen
Barbosa, Francisco J.
Barbosa, Leoncio A.
Barbosa, Luis
Barbosa, Luis J.
Barbosa, Manuel
Barbosa, Paula
Barbosa, Pedro J.
Barbosa, Sofia
Barcelo, Jaime
Barcelo, Jose

Barcener, Lorenza
Barclay, Martin L. H.
Barentzen, Hubert
Baron, Jose
Barranco Dominicana, Lidia
Barraza, Maria
Barreiro, Tomas E.
Barrera, Carmen
Barreras (de), Francisca B.
Barreras, Manuel A.
Barrero, Juana
Barreto, Rosa
Barriere Bermudez, Maria J.
Barriere de Suarez, Dolores
Barriga Acevedo, Alfredo
Barrintas, Emiliano
Barrios, Belen A.
Barrios, J.
Barrios, Jose (Jr.)
Barrios, Mato
Barrios, Mercedes C.
Barros, Justo
Bartoli, Dorotea
Barton, Guillermo H.
Bas (de), Elvira C.
Bas (de), Herminia C.
Bas, Sixto E.
Basalto, Carmen
Bastal, Isabel
Bastidas, Maria
Batalle, Miguel
Batista (de), Lola P.
Batista, P. R.
Bauta, Juana
Bautista, Juan
Bauza, Bernardo
Bayonet Diaz, Juanita
Bayonet Diaz, Rosario
Beamut Llanos, Eloisa
Beamut Llanos, Maria R.
Becerra, Francisco
Becerril (de), Maria L.
Becerril, Joaquin
Becker, Georgina
Beige, Harry B. (Esq.)
Beiro, Luis R.
Bel de Rosario, Maria
Belaner, Jose

Belaner, R.
Bellber, Rafael
Bellber (de), Dolores A.
Bellber, Arminta
Bellber, Blanca
Bellber, Gloria
Bellber, M.
Belpre Nogueras, Elisa
Belpre, Eugenio
Belpre, Felipe
Belpre, Isidoro
Belpre, Pedro
Beltran, Gloria
Beltran, Ignacio
Beltran, Joaquin
Beltran, Juan
Beltran, Juana
Beltran, Martin
Beltran, Paulino
Benavente, Lola
Benero, Fidel
Benet, Rafael
Benites, Juana
Benitez (de), Ana M.
Benitez (de), Carmina C.
Benitez (de), Josefa G.
Benitez Gomez, Margarita
Benitez Gomez, Jose
Benitez Gomez, Maria
Benitez Gomez, Pepiña (1)
Benitez Gomez, Pepiña (2)
Benitez, Clementina
Benitez, Eduardo
Benitez, Enrique
Benitez, Gloria
Benitez, Juan
Benitez, Juana
Benitez, Lucas (1)
Benitez, Lucas (2)
Benitez, Luisa
Benitez, Margot
Benitez, Sara
Bennett, M.
Benny, Jose
Bentine, Isidoro
Bentura Freyre, Enrique
Berdejo, Candida
Berly Vda. de Bonilla,

Juana
Bermudez (de), Juana A.
Bermudez Collazo, Felipe
Bermudez, Candida
Bermudez, Frances
Bermudez, Francisco
Bermudez, Isabel
Bermudez, Luisa
Bermudez, Marina
Bernier, Octavio R.
Berrio, Jose
Berrios (de), Tula I.
Berrios, Angel Luis
Berrios, Antonio
Berrios, Delfina
Berrios, Francisco
Berrios, Geronimo
Berrios, Isabel
Berrios, Jacinta
Berrios, Jose
Berrios, Juan (1)
Berrios, Juan (2)
Berrios, Juana
Berrios, L. M.
Berrios, Lao
Berrios, Luciana
Berrios, Oscar
Berrios, Ramon
Berrios, Rita
Berrios, Rosa
Berrios, Vidal
Berrrios, Evaristo
Bertran Fernandez, Gloria M.
Bertran, Felix
Besosa (de), Leticia Q.
Besosa, Ascension
Besosa, Julian
Besosa, Ramona
Betances, Fermin P.
Betancourt, Alfonsa
Betancourt, Celsa
Betancourt, Elisa
Betancourt, Encarnacion
Betancourt, Enrique
Betancourt, Francisco
Betancourt, Ignacio
Betancourt, Jose
Betancourt, Josefa
Betancourt, Juana (1)
Betancourt, Juana (2)

Betancourt, Juana (3)
Betancourt, Margarita
Betancourt, Rosa
Betancourt, Saturnino
Betancourt, Violeta
Betancourt, Zoilo
Bey, Rita
Biascoechea (de), Dolores
Biasgoechea (Vda. de), Eduvina
Bibas (Vda. de)
Bibas, Belen
Billegas, Angela
Billegas, Modesto
Biosca Gonzalez, Juan
Bioy, Emilio (Lcdo.)
Bithorn (de), Maria S.
Bizno, Manuel
Bizoso, Manuel (Jr.)
Bizoso, Rafaela
Blamobias, G.
Blanco (de), Maria F.
Blanco (de), Teofila
Blanco (de), Teresa L. C.
Blanco Fernandez, Josefina
Blanco Morales, Maria
Blanco Morales, Pura
Blanco Perez, Mercedes
Blanco y Morales, Luz
Blanco, Felipe M.
Blanco, Gumersindo
Blanco, I.
Blanco, Luis
Blanco, M.
Blanco, Maria (1)
Blanco, Maria (2)
Blanco, Roman
Blanco, Ysabel
Blandilla, Ruesa
Blandino (de), Salvadora I.
Blas, Gumercindo
Boada Perez, Jesus
Boada, Amparo
Boada, Belen
Boada, Rafaela
Bobe, Isabel
Boeras, Sergio
Boglio y Javaviz, Ana
Boison, Jose

Bonacia, Angela
Bonacia, Eugenia
Bonet (de), Ulpiana V.
Bonet, Roberto
Boneta, E.
Boneta, Fernando P.
Bonets, Isabel M.
Bonhom, Ceferino
Bonilla de Aumerich, Luisa
Bonilla de Esbri, Josefa
Bonilla de Vazquez, Angelina
Bonilla, Beatriz
Bonilla, Joaquin
Bonilla, Magdalena
Bonilla, Mercedes
Bonit, Ignacio
Börch, Emma F.
Bordey, Salbador
Borges, Felipe
Boria, Felipe
Borras Vda. de Bas, Antonia
Borras, Asuncion
Borras, Ismael
Borras, Juan
Borut, Juan
Borzi, Alejandro (Jr.)
Borzo (de), Amneris L.
Borzo, Elisa E.
Boscana, Teresa
Bosch Colas, Antonio
Bosch Colas, Carmen
Bosch Colas, Eduardo
Bosch Colas, Esperanza
Bosch Colas, Pilar
Bosch de Hernandez, Carmen
Bosch, Eduardo
Bosch, Enrique
Bosch, L. S.
Bosch, Wenceslao
Bou, Alfredo V.
Bou, Salvador
Bouret, J. P. (II) (Ch. O. Lind.)
Bouret, J. P.
Bozzo Romañat, Laura
Brachs (de), R.
Brachs, Maria
Bras, P. J. (Jr.)

240

Bravo, Benito
Brioso (de G.), Pilar M.
Brisasier, Madame
Britton, Laura S.
Brown, Rafael
Brozo, Guillermo
Barrios, Antonia
Brumbleck de Fernandez, Josefina
Bruno de Cañellos, Cecilia
Bruno de Coste, (Mrs.)
Bruno de Lopez, Enriqueta
Bruno de Luzunaris, Julia
Buenhome, Eusebia
Bugella, Dolores
Bulthong Agudo y Gliome, John
Bultron, Damiane
Burgos Pizarro, Julio
Burgos, Luis B.
Bustelo (de), Josefa L. (1)
Bustelo (de), Josefa L. (2)
C., J.
C., Leocadia
Caballero, Carolina
Caballero, Delfin
Caballero, Matilde
Caballero, P. (Jr.)
Caballero, T.
Caballero, Ynes
Caban (de), Dolores R.
Caban Rodriguez, C.
Caban, Pablo (Lcdo.)
Caban, Pedro
Cabello, Antonino
Cabello, Florencio
Cabello, Jesus
Cabello, Trinidad
Cabral Baez, Pablo (1)
Cabral Baez, Pablo (2)
Cabrense, Martin
Cabrera Jesus J.
Cabrera, America C.
Cabrera, Antonia
Cabrera, Armando
Cabrera, Asuncion
Cabrera, Domingo
Cabrera, Fela

Cabrera, Flores P.
Cabrera, Julio
Cabrera, Justa
Cabrera, Leneu
Cabrera, Manuela
Cabrera, Pedro
Cabrera, Rafael
Cachon Calvo, Claudino
Cadierno, J.
Cadierno, Jose R.
Cadierno, M.
Caezas, Genara
Cafio, Carmen
Cajias, Amparo C.
Cala de Flores, Delfin
Calderin, Modesto
Calderon (de), Elisa A.
Calderon (de), Mercedes C.
Calderon Acosta, M.
Calderon Rosa, Regino
Calderon, A.
Calderon, Angela, S.
Calderon, Anita
Calderon, Brijido
Calderon, Damina
Calderon, Dolores
Calderon, Guillerma C.
Calderon, J. R.
Calderon, Jesus P.
Calderon, Jose G.
Calderon, Juanita
Calderon, Mercedes
Calderon, Nicolas
Calderon, Pablo
Calderon, Rita
Calderon, Ursina
Caldreron Rivas, Francisca
Calero, Guadalupe
Calicruo, Eduardo R.
Callot, Juan N.
Camacho, Dolores
Camacho, Eduviges
Camacho, M.
Camacho, Pedro
Camara de Paniagua, Aida
Caminero (de), Maria Josefa R.
Campesino, Evaristo
Campoamor, Miguel

Campos, Joaquin
Camuñas, Consuelo
Camuñas, Engracia
Cana Castro, J.
Cañada, Francisca
Cañada, Juana
Canales (de), Guarina
Canales Encarnacion, Nicomedes
Canales, Gerardo
Canales. B.
Cañamagne, Antonio
Cancel, Angel
Cancel, Jesus
Cancel, Julio
Cancel, Librado
Cancel, Rafael
Candelaria, Epifamia
Candelario, Carmen
Candina de Sagastibelza, Paulina
Candina, Clara
Candon, Elise
Caneja, Morero F.
Cañellas, Miguel
Canino Gonzalez, Juan
Cannoni, Adela
Cano Lucero, Silvia
Caño, Emilio
Cano, F.
Cantellops (de), Rosa
Cantellops, B.
Cantellops, H.
Cantellops, Paquita
Cantero, J.
Cantero, Petra
Caparrez, Maria
Caparros (de), Demetria
Caparros, F.
Caparros Rivera, Maria
Capellaniz, E. W.
Capestrany (Vda. de), Enriqueta
Capestrany, L. A.
Carabia, Juana
Carambot, Jose
Caravaca, Macelino
Carazo Perez, Jose
Carazo, Ricardo
Carballo, Juanita
Carbia (de), Antonia M.

Carbia, Enrique
Carbonell, Francisca
Carbonell, Mercedes
Carbonell, Pilar
Carcel, Carmen
Carcel, Romualdo
Carcel, Simeon
Cardena, Jesus
Cardenas, Francisca
Carderaro, Consuelo C.
Cardona, Nicomedes
Cardona, Victoriano
Cargas, Jose A.
Carlos, Sergio
Carmenero, Severa
Carmoega, Elvira
Carmona, Carmelo
Carmona, Francisco
Carnell, Guadalupe
Caro, Belen
Carpuitro, Deogracias
Carraballo, Francisca
Carraballo, Maria
Carrasquillo, Emma
Carrasquillo, Irene
Carrera, Almanyor
Carrera, Claro
Carrera, J. A.
Carreras Valle, Josefa
Carreras, Ramon
Carreras, Belen (1)
Carreras, Belen (2)
Carreras, Benito
Carreras, Benito J.
Carreras, Carlota
Carreras, Carolina
Carreras, Celso
Carreras, Damasa
Carreras, Dolores
Carreras, Francisco
Carreras, G.
Carreras, Genoveva
Carreras, Geronimo (1)
Carreras, Geronimo (2)
Carreras, J.
Carreras, J. (Jr.)
Carreras, Jose
Carreras, Jose D.
Carreras, Jose E.
Carreras, Jose G.
Carreras, Juan

Carreras, Juana
Carreras, Lola
Carreras, Luis (1)
Carreras, Luis (2)
Carreras, Maria
Carreras, Rafael
Carreras, Rodrigo
Carreras, Rosa
Carreras, Santiago
Carreras, Zacarias
Carrero (de), A. M.
Carrero, Javier
Carretty, Carmelo
Carretty, Jaime
Carretty, Ramon
Carril, Benito
Carrillo, Genara
Carrillo, Jose Felix
Carriño, Gregoria
Carrion, Annie
Carrion, Belen
Carrion, Clemencia
Carrion, D. R.
Carrion, Eduardo
Carrion, Isabel
Carrion, L. Hernan
Carrion, Ramon
Cartija, Hipolita
Caruzo, M.
Carvajal, Manuel
Caryue, Jose
Casa, Angela
Casa, Concepcion
Casalduc de Aviles,
  Delia
Casalduc, Carmen (1)
Casalduc, Carmen (2)
Casalduc, Luis
Casals, Jose
Casanova, Alejandrina
Casas de Villamil, Fela
Casas Vda. de
  Marquez, Carmen
Casas, Carmen
Casellas, A.
Casellas, Amalia
Casellas, Juan L.
Casellas, Juana
Casenave, Jose Maria
Caser, Josefa
Casigne, Benina
Cassals, R.
Cassenios, S.
Castañer de Pons,

Rosa Maria
Castaños (de),
  Gregoria C.
Castazas, Josefina
Castelao, Victoria
Castillo
Castillo, Carmen
Castillo, Fernando
Castillo, Juana L.
Castillo, Nicolas
Castor, Magdalena
Castro (de), Emilia
Castro (de), Maria F.
Castro (de), Mercedes
  M
Castro (de), Y. R.
Castro de Alcaraz,
  Barbara
Castro, Angel M.
Castro, Blasina
Castro, Carmen P.
Castro, Cecilio
Castro, Concepcion
Castro, Cruz (Jr.)
Castro, German
Castro, Jesus
Castro, Jose
Castro, Jose Mercedes
Castro, Luis (1)
Castro, Luis (2)
Castro, Manuel
Castro, Manuel E.
Castro, Marcela
Castro, Marcola
Castro, Marino
Castro, Paulino E.
Castro, Rafael
Castro, Ramon (1)
Castro, Ramon (2)
Castros, Angela
Catala de Varas,
  Magdalena
Catala, Jose
Cataldo, Maria
Catauro, M.
Catraz, Lorenzo
Caubet (de),
  Guillermina G.
Caubet, Damian
Ceba, Petra
Cebrin, Joaquin
Cegarra, Ezequiel
Cela, Antonio
Cela, Matilde

Cepeda, Carmen
Cepeda, Juan
Cepeda, Julio
Cepeda, Leonardo
Cepero, Amparo
Cepero, Hermenegilda
Cepero, India
Cepero, Lopez R.
Cepero, Monserrate
Cepero, Vicente
Cerecedo
Cerecedo Hermanos &
  Co. (seal)
Cerida, Nicolas
Cermeño, Concepcion
  C.
Cermeños, Julio
Cerrera, Francisca
Cespede de Roman,
  Clemencia
Cestero (Vda. de), Ana
  O.
Cestero Mangual,
  Encarnita
Cestero Mangual,
  Teresa
Cestero Mangual,
  Teresita
Cestero, Elisa
Cestero, Ferdinand R.
Cestero, Jorge A.
Ceynal, N.
Chabert, Oscar
Chacon (de), D. L.
Charbonoriz, Belen
Chardon, Camila
Chardon, Herminia
Charless, Jaime
Chateau, Emile
Chavonies, Antonia
Cheiches, Miguel
Chela, Josefina
Chevere Sanchez,
  Ramon
Chico, Francisco
Chior, Fidel
Ciales, Maria
Cid (de), Julia P
Cid, Edmundo
Cid, Jose
Cid, Julia
Cid, Martha
Cifredo, Ana Luisa
Cifredo, Dolores

Cintron (de), Julia F.
Cintron, Gilberto
Cintron Vda. de
  Bermudez, Ysaura
Cintron, Aggeo
Cintron, Ana Maria
Cintron, Andres
Cintron, Blas
Cintron, Jose (1)
Cintron, Jose (2)
Cintron, Jose N.
Cintron, Leoncio
Cintron, Rafael
Cintron, Vidal R.
Cintron, Ygnacio L.
Cirilo, Juana
Cirilo, Pedro
Cisneros, Rosendo
Classen, Rosa
Classen, Tomasa
Claudio
Claudio Pereira,
  Carmen
Claudio Pereira, Lucila
Claudio Pereira, Maria
Claudio, Armando
Claudio, Emilio
Claudio, Esteban
Claudio, Felipe
Claudio, Guillermo
Claudio, Ines
Claudio, Juan
Claudio, Pablo
Claudio, Pedro
Claudio, Venancio
Clavijo, Juan
Clavijo, Maria
Clavijo, Tonicio
Clemente, Angela T.
Clemente, Damasa
Clemente, Guillermo
Clemente, Manuel
Clystan, R.
Coastas, Elvira
Cobian, Rosendo
Cobian, Sergio
Coda de Suarez,
  Silveria
Coda Oomy, Celia
Cofriegas, Fernan
Cohen, Rafael
Colas de Bosch, Juana
Colas V., Concepcion
Colas Vda R.

Izquierdo, Ana	Conde de Guia,	Correa, Carolina	Cruz Niebe, Lila
Colas Vda. de Colaz,	Mercedes	Correa, Ceferino	Cruz Pagan, Basilio
Carmen	Conde, Amelia	Correa, Evaristo	Cruz T., Severa
Collacio Garcia,	Conde, Jose Maria	Correa, Fernando	Cruz Vda. de Arias,
Ramon	Conde, Sofia	Correa, Hipolito	Balbina
Collazo, Manuel	Conlon, Nidulio A.	Correa, Juan	Cruz, Altagracia
Colon (de), Paula G.	Conofre, Praxedes	Correa, Juana	Cruz, Andres
Colon Delgado, Oscar	Constanza, Rosa	Correa, P. J.	Cruz, Antonia (1)
Colon Lizardi, Julio	Contreras, Felicita	Correa, Polonia	Cruz, Antonia (2)
Colon Lopez, Joaquin	Contreras, Gabina	Correa, Telesfora	Cruz, Berta
Colon Marquez,	Coon, Clota	Correa, Valentina	Cruz, Braulio
Ovidio	Corbella (Vda. de),	Cortada, Ramona	Cruz, Carlos M.
Colon, Fuentes	Margarita	Cortes de S., Santos	Cruz, Carmen (1)
Colon Nin, Angeles	Corbella, Juan	Cortes Martinez, Juan	Cruz, Carmen (2)
Colon Nin, Isabel (1)	Cordero (de), Marilde	Cortes, Avilio	Cruz, Carmen (3)
Colon Nin, Isabel (2)	B.	Cortes, Carlos	Cruz, Constantino
Colon Vazquez,	Cordero (Vda. de),	Cortes, Flora	Cruz, Delfin
Serafin	Gaetana	Cortes, Maria	Cruz, Diego
Colon, Alejandro	Cordero, Dolores	Cortijo, Alfonso	Cruz, Dionisio
Colon, C.	Cordero, Felipe R. (D.	Cortijo, Eladio	Cruz, Emilia
Colon, Carmen	D. S.)	Cortijo, Esteban	Cruz, Encarnacion
Colon, Catalina	Cordero, Gorbina	Cortijo, Jesus	Cruz, Felix
Colon, Cristobal	Cordero, Hector	Cosini (de), Amada	Cruz, Francisca
Colon, Dionicia	Cordero, Horacio	Cosini, Eugenio	Cruz, Gaspar
Colon, Elvira	Cordero, Horacito	Cosini, Euripides	Cruz, Isabel
Colon, Enrique S.	Cordero, Josefa	Cosini, Jose	Cruz, Jose R.
Colon, Eufemia	Cordero, Juana	Cosme A.,	Cruz, Juan (1)
Colon, Faustino	Cordero, Maria	Encarnacion	Cruz, Juan (2)
Colon, Felix	Cordero, Maria del	Costa, Anibal B.	Cruz, Juan (3)
Colon, Gregorio	Pilar	Costa, Dolores	Cruz, Julian
Colon, Isidora	Cordero, Matildita	Costa, Francisca	Cruz, Lola
Colon, J. M.	Cordero, Miguel	Costas, Manuel	Cruz, Luis
Colon, Joaquina	Cordero, Paquito	Coste Bruno, Thelma	Cruz, Manuel
Colon, Jose D.	Cordero, Rafael	Costoso, J.	Cruz, Merida
Colon, Josefa	Cordero, Ramon	Coto, Balentina	Cruz, Obdulia
Colon, Juan	Cordero, Ramon	Coto, Serafin	Cruz, Pedro (1)
Colon, Juanita	Cordoba, Pedro	Cotto, Tomasa	Cruz, Pedro (2)
Colon, Julio	Cordova (de), Carmen	Cottos, Augusto	Cruz, Pedro (3)
Colon, Lidia	B.	Couvertie, M.	Cruz, Pedro G.
Colon, Lope	Cordova (de), Patria	Cranser, Herminia	Cruz, Petra
Colon, Maria	Cordova de Garcia,	Crespo, Manuela	Cruz, Porfirio
Colon, Olimpia	Josefina	Crispin, Julia	Cruz, Ricardo
Colon, P.	Cordova Rios, S.	Crosas de Saldaña,	Cruz, Rosalia
Colon, Ramon	Cordova, Jose A.	Maria	Cruz, Rosario
Colon, Regina	Cordova, Lolita	Crozas (Vda. de),	Cruz, Ruperto
Colon, Rios, Maria	Cordovez, Juan S.	Carmen G.	Cruz, Sergio
Colon, Santiago	Corgaya, Agustin	Cruz (de), Asuncion	Cuadrado, Concepcion
Colony, Victorio	Corninego, Angel	Cruz (de), Maria	Cubero, Gregorio
Comez, Isabel	Corral, J.	Cruz Cepero, Andres	Cubero, Nemesio
Concepcion, Carmen	Corras, Rafael	Cruz de Hernandez,	Cuchi, Flora
Concepcion, Justo	Correa (de),	Dolores	Cuchnez, Leopolda
Conde (de), Teresa F.	Monserrate N.	Cruz Duperon, Rosa	Cudas Padilla, Jose
Conde (Vda. de),	Correa de Gonzalez,	Cruz Gonzalez, Maria	Cuebas, Antonio
Fabriana	Angeles	Cruz Jimenez, Manuel	Cuebas, Catalina

Cuesta, Modesto
Cuetara (de), Juana R.
Cuetara, Eudosio
Cuetara, Manuel
Cuetara, Miguel
Cueto de Gonzalez
Padin, Francisca
Cueto, Ana M.
Cuevas Pulido, Juan (1)
Cuevas Pulido, Juan (2)
Cuevas Torrecillas, Jesus
Cuevas, Enrique
Cuevas, J.
Cuevas, Jose (Jr.)
Cuevas, Juan A.
Cuevas, Manuel
Cuevas, Maria
Cuevas, Raul
Cuevas, Rosa
Cuijar, Luis C.
Cumba, Jose
Cumba, Lorenzo
Curbelo (de), Francisca O.
Curbelo, Guillermo (Dr.)
Curet Lago, Pedro
Dabubon, Angeles
Dalmany Cancel, S.
Dalmau Florez, E.
Daloni, Ramon
Daniel, Eduvigis (1)
Daniel, Eduvigis (2)
Danus, Carlota
Dapena, Rafael R.
Dardio Diaz, Carmen
Darraga, Dionisio
Daubin, Ramon L.
Davila (de), Esperanza G.
Davila (de), Leonor R.
Davila (de), Manuela A.
Davila de Vega, Maria
Davila Salicrup, Fernando
Davila Salicrup, Luis Alberto
Davila Salicrup, Maria Luisa
Davila y Nater,

Mercedes
Davila, Agustin
Davila, Agustina
Davila, Alberto
Davila, Antonia
Davila, Antonio (1)
Davila, Antonio (2)
Davila, Asencion
Davila, Bev.
Davila, Carmen
Davila, Enrique (1)
Davila, Enrique (2)
Davila, Felix
Davila, Feliz
Davila, Hipolito
Davila, Jesus
Davila, Josefa
Davila, Juan (1)
Davila, Juan (2)
Davila, Juana (1)
Davila, Juana (2)
Davila, Luis
Davila, Luis Alberto
Davila, Luz E. (1)
Davila, Luz E. (2)
Davila, Manuel
Davila, Margarita (1)
Davila, Margarita (2)
Davila, Maria Luisa
Davila, Mariana (1)
Davila, Mariana (2)
Davila, Mariano
Davila, Natividad
Davila, Nicolasa
Davila, Pepilla
Davila, Rosario (1)
Davila, Rosario (2)
Davila, Segunda
Davila, Serafin
Davila, Tomas
Davila, Virgilio (1)
Davila, Virgilio (2)
Davis de Jimera, Cruz
De A. Vda. de Lama, Carmen
De Albornoz, Manuel (1)
De Albornoz, Manuel (2)
De Aldrey, Elena
De Aldrey, Rosenda M
De Andino, Miguel M.
De Arrura, Juan
De Arteaga, Francisco

M.
De Diego, Georgina B. (1)
De Diego, Georgina B. (2)
De Diego, Jose (Speaker of the House of Representatives, Puerto Rico)
De Elzaburn, Luisa
De Elzaburn, Mercedes C.
De Espino de Martinez, Carmen
De Gesurun, Lolita
De Guzman Santos, Juan (Lcdo.)
De Hostos, B. de A. V.
De Hostos, Luisa Amelia
De Hostos, Maria A.
De Jesus Aponte, Maria
De Jesus Vega, F.
De Jesus, Avelino
De Jesus, J.
De Jesus, Luis
De Jesus, Pablo
De Jesus, Ramon
De Jesus, Ramona
De Jesus, Salvador
De Juan, C.
De Juan, Fernando
De la Camara, Rosa
De la Cruz Perez, Esteban
De la Cruz, Ramona
De la Mata, Ramon
De la Paz, Isabel
De la R. de Cabrera, Lolita
De la Riviera, G. G.
De la Roca de San Antonio, Maria
De la Roca, Josefa
De la Rosa de Roig, Natividad
De la Rosa, Estela Nieves
De la Rosa, Manuel (Jr.)
De la Vega Nevares, Manuel

De Lara, Auristela
De Leon, Miguel
De Leon, Rosa
De Lora, Jose J.
De Navedo, Belen
De Navedo, Rosa
De Quevedo de Paniagua, Maria G.
De Quixano, Luis
De Roca, Mercedes
De Ruiz, Andrea M.
De Sabat, Carmen
De Sanquirico y Ayesa, Luis
De Santiago, Santiago
De Soto Gras, Antonia I.
De Susman Soto, Jose (Dr.)
De Toro, Florentina G.
De Vidal, Carmen P.
De Villamil, Julio
DeCaro, Frederick
Decheneux, Rita
Del Balle, Pastora
Del Busto, Joaquin
Del Busto, Rosario
Del Campo, Santos
Del Cristo, Pablo
Del Foro y Cuebas, Fernando
Del Manzano, Obdulia
Del Moral, Mariano
Del Morel, Adolfo
Del Olmo, Carmen
Del Pino, Carmen
Del Pino, Maria
Del Toro Cordova, Eva
Del Toro Cordova, Moncerrate
Del Toro Cordova, Pura
Del Valle (de), Belen G.
Del Valle (de), Maria B.
Del Valle (de), Maria L.
Del Valle Atiles, Juanita
Del Valle Atiles, P. (M.D.)
Del Valle Buso, Aida
Del Valle de Castañer,

Rosa
Del Valle Goenaga, Mercedes
Del Valle, Concepcion
Del Valle, Elias
Del Valle, Felipe
Del Valle, Jose
Del Valle, Lola
Del Valle, M. V.
Del Valle, P. (Mrs.)
Del Valle, Polisa
Del Valle, Salvador
Delanoy, Amelio
Delgado (de), Gertrudis I.
Delgado (de), Juana A
Delgado Ayala, Rafael
Delgado de Pilato, Ramona
Delgado Garcia, Pedro
Delgado Pla, Eusebio
Delgado y Colon, Ana
Delgado, Altagracia
Delgado, Amalia
Delgado, Angela
Delgado, Aurora
Delgado, Elena
Delgado, Emilio J.
Delgado, Filomena
Delgado, Gollita
Delgado, Gumersindo
Delgado, Isidoro D.
Delgado, L.R.
Delgado, Lorenza
Delgado, Pepita
Delgado, R. H.
Delgado, Ramon
Delgado, Regina Ada
Delgado, Sandalio
Delgado, Ysabel
Delpin (de), Sabina A.
Denacia, Proda
Denton, C.
Denton, Carmen
Denton, Ceferina
Denton, H.
Denton, Rupert R.
Desorden, Amadeo
Desorden, Domingo
Desorden, Maria Luisa
Despian Balseiro, B. B.
Desuden, Maria (1)
Desuden, Maria (2)
Dias, Facia

Diaz (Vda. de), Salustiana E.
Diaz Baldorioty, Virgilio
Diaz Ball, R.
Diaz de Contreras, Maria I.
Diaz de Cordova, Mercedes
Diaz de Delgado, Rita
Diaz de Gonzalez, Maria
Diaz de Llobet, Paula
Diaz de Miro, Dolores
Diaz de Rodriguez, Genara
Diaz Desorden, Guane
Diaz Loado, Jose
Diaz Marcilias, Alfonso
Diaz Marcilias, Enrique
Diaz Marcilias, German
Diaz Marcilias, Jose
Diaz Marrero, Jose
Diaz Miro, Jose
Diaz Travieso, Juan
Diaz, A.
Diaz, Alejandrina
Diaz, Alejandrina D.
Diaz, Angelina (1)
Diaz, Angelina (2)
Diaz, Antolina
Diaz, Armando
Diaz, Asuncion
Diaz, Balbina
Diaz, Benigno
Diaz, Benito N.
Diaz, Blanca
Diaz, Buenaventura
Diaz, Carlos
Diaz, Carmen
Diaz, Cornelia
Diaz, Dolores
Diaz, Edelmira
Diaz, Elias
Diaz, Emilio
Diaz, Eusebio
Diaz, Felipe (1)
Diaz, Felipe (2)
Diaz, Francisco
Diaz, Gaspar
Diaz, Georgina

Diaz, Heriberto
Diaz, Ines
Diaz, Jose
Diaz, Josefina
Diaz, Juan (1)
Diaz, Juan (2)
Diaz, Juan (3)
Diaz, Juan (4)
Diaz, Juana (1)
Diaz, Juana (2)
Diaz, Julio
Diaz, Leoncia
Diaz, Maria (1)
Diaz, Maria (2)
Diaz, Maria (3)
Diaz, Maria (4)
Diaz, Maria (5)
Diaz, Maria (6)
Diaz, Maria C.
Diaz, Mercedes
Diaz, Pablo (1)
Diaz, Pablo (2)
Diaz, Rafael
Diaz, Ramon (1)
Diaz, Ramon (2)
Diaz, Ramon (3)
Diaz, Ramona
Diaz, Roberto
Diaz, Rosenda
Diaz, Sebastian
Diaz, Sergio
Diaz, Silveria
Diaz, Tomas
Diaz, William
Dib, Antonio
Dibe, Marcela
Dibe, Maria
Dieffer, Jose
Diego Matos, Maximiliano
Diez de Andino y Cordova, Dolores
Dionisio, M. G.
Dixon (de), Elena C.
Dolores de la Granja, F.
Dolores, Domingo
Dominguez (de), Sara I.
Dominguez de C., Maria
Dominguez Lopez, Juan
Dominguez Vda. de

Sulsona, Luisa
Dominguez, D.
Dominguez, E.
Dominguez, Jorge
Dominguez, Jose (1)
Dominguez, Jose (2)
Dominguez, Luisa
Dominguez, P.
Dones, Ramon
Dordal, Luis Ramon
Doria, Pedro
Dorna, Manuel
Dorrios, R.
Droz, Asuncion
Duaden, Gaoyou
Ducheny, Carmen
Ducheny, Jose (Jr.)
Ducheny, Jose
Ducheny, Maria
Ducheny, Rosita
Duchesne, Aria
Duchesne, Juan
Duchesny, Carmen
Ducret de Vazquez, Eustacia
Ducret, Carmen
Ducret, Maria
Dugela Briffle, Eduardo
Duperrg, Carmen
Duprey, F.
Duran, Antonia
Duran, Dolores
Duran, Jose
Duran, Ysabel
Durand, Juan
Durecut, Isabel
E., Manuel
Ebia, Luisa
Echavarria, Panchita
Echeliu, Juan Alberto
Echevarria (de) Dolores C.
Echevarria, Andres
Echevarria, Emilia
Echevarria, Gerardo
Echevarria, Juan
Echevarria, Juio
Echevarria, Luis
Echevarria, M.
Echevarria, Maria
Egozcue, Concha
Egozcue, Elisa
Egozcue, Elviera

Ferreiro, Jose
Ferreiro, Luisa
Ferreiro, Providencia
Ferrer (de), Maria C.
Ferrer de Carballeiro, Julio
Ferrer de Davila, Juana
Ferrer Hernandez, Marcelina
Ferrer Vda. de Ojeda, Carmen
Ferrer, Acela
Ferrer, Agustin
Ferrer, Andres
Ferrer, Angela
Ferrer, Armanda
Ferrer, F.
Ferrer, Isaias Gabriel
Ferrer, Jaime
Ferrer, Mar
Ferrer, Maria
Ferrer, Pablo
Ferrer, Paulino
Ferreras (de), Josefa
Ferreras, Carmen
Ferreras, M.
Figosa, Dolores
Figuera, Amparo
Figueredo, S. Fernando
Figueroa (de) Dominicana, Maxima
Figueroa Berrios, Jose
Figueroa de Rosa, Tomasa
Figueroa, Amalia
Figueroa, Angel
Figueroa, Antonio (1)
Figueroa, Antonio (2)
Figueroa, Beatriz
Figueroa, Belen
Figueroa, Carmelo
Figueroa, Carmen
Figueroa, Eugenia
Figueroa, Guada
Figueroa, Juan
Figueroa, Manuel Sierra
Figueroa, Margarita
Figueroa, Maria
Figueroa, Micaela
Figueroa, Ocaulu R.

Figueroa, Pedro
Figueroa, Vicenta
Figueroa, Vicente
Figueroa, Victor
Fiol, Eugenio
Flehe, Elian
Flehe, Joaquin
Fleites, J.
Flenge, Jose
Fleuranjes, Rodolfo
Flor de Maria
Floreras, Herminia
Flores (de), Amparo M.
Flores Larrosal, Manuel
Flores R., Jose
Flores Roberts, Jose
Flores, Abelardo
Flores, Adelaida
Flores, Ageda
Flores, Bartola
Flores, Belen
Flores, Carmen (1)
Flores, Carmen (2)
Flores, Carmen (3)
Flores, Enrique
Flores, Jose
Flores, Jose Ramon
Flores, Leonardo
Flores, Maria (1)
Flores, Maria (2)
Flores, Paula
Flores, Teresa
Flores, Victor
Florido Reventos, Francisco
Florido, Jose A.
Florit (de), Belen G.
Florit, Elisa
Florit, Francisco
Florit, Hector
Florit, Pedro
Flower, Joney
Fonfria, Blanca R.
Fonfria, Jose
Fonseca, Eduvijes
Fonseca, Emilia
Fonseca, Joaquina
Fonseca, Maria
Font (de), Concepcion G.
Font (de), Cristina S.
Font (de), Mercedes A.

Font Pacheco, Feliz
Font y Guillen, Eliseo (Dr.)
Font, Carmen
Font, Eliseo (Jr.)
Font, Eugenio
Font, Francisco
Font, Jose (1)
Font, Jose (2)
Font, Juan
Font, Luis
Font, Manuel (1)
Font, Manuel (2)
Font, Manuela
Font, Maria A.
Font, Maria Antonieta
Font, Maria L.
Font, Maria Luisa
Font, Pascual (1)
Font, Pascual (2)
Font, Rita
Font, T.
Fontanez, Celestina
Forba, M.
Forsas (de), Consuelo L. C.
Fort, Marian
Fortes, Antonio
Fortuño (de), Sofia L.
Fortuño, Juan B.
Fossas, Ramon
Fournier (De), Isabel G.
Fournier (de), Ofelia L.
Fournier, Elisa M.
Fournier, James
Fournier, Pepita
Fournier, Rosario
Foyas, Julia
Fracio, Maxima
Francisco R.
Franco de Gonzalez, Rosa
Franco Valdes, Lola
Franco, Cruz
Franco, Emilio
Franco, J. M.
Franco, Joaquin
Franco, Juan
Franco, Nicolas
Franco, Vicente
Franqueri, Ignacio
Fransico, Catalina

Fransico, Emilio
Fransico, Maria
Fransico, Miguel
Frasinetty, Plasida
Frasqueri (de), Candida C.
Frasqueri (Vda. de), Josefa G.
Frasqueri, Maria Teresa
Frasquery, Luis
Freiria (Vda. de), Juanita
Freiria, E.
Freiria, Francisca
Freirias, Jesus
Freirias, Ramon
Freirias, Teodoro
Freytes, Ines
Frias, J.
Frias, Maria L.
Frias, S.
Friol (Vda. de), Lina C.
Frise (Vda. de), Eloisa
Fuente, Crisanta
Fuente, Edelmira
Fuente, Manolo
Fuente, Marco
Fuentes de Audinot, Hipolita
Fuentes de Suarez, Serafina
Fuentes, Edicto
Fuentes, Jose A.
Fuentes, Lino
Fuentes, Magsimina
Fuentes, Rafael
Fuentes, Rosa C.
Fuerte, E.
Fuerte, Victoria
Fuertes, Faustino (Jr.)
Fuertes, Higinia
Fuertes, M.
Fuertes, M. (Mrs.)
Fuertes, Manuel
Fuertes, Mariano (D.D.S.)
Fuertes, Restituto
Fulladosa (de), Adelina A.
Fur, Dulcelina
Furniz, Josefina C.
Furniz, Luisa
Gaetan, Eladia

Gaetan, Elena
Gainain, Jose
Galarse, Peter
Galarza, Jose
Galey, Georg
Galiñanez, M.
Gallardo, C.
Gallardo, Elisa
Gallardo, J.
Gallardo, Juan R.
Gallardo, Rita
Galva, Juan
Gamaya, Violet
Gambara, America
Gambara, Carmen
Gambara, Ramona
Gambaro, America
Gambaro, Carmelita
Gambaro, Carmen
Gambaro, Leonor
Gambaro, Ramona
Gamboa Eduardo
Gamez, Jesus
Gamez, Julio
Gamez, Ramon
Gandia (de), Elisa F.
Gandia, Carmen C.
Gandia, Francisco
Gandia, G. A. (hijo)
Gandiel, Lorenzo
Gar, L.
Garabio, Carmen
Garabio, Paquita
Garabis, Franco
Garat Jimenez,
  Herminia
Garata, Jose Luis
Garay, Encarnacion
Garay, Ines
Garay, Juana
Garay, Valentina
Garcia (de), E.
Garcia (de), Elisa M.
Garcia (de), Elvira B.
Garcia (de), Felicita A.
Garcia (de), Gertrudis
  G.
Garcia (de), Maria (1)
Garcia (de), Maria (2)
Garcia (de), Maria
  Luisa C.
Garcia (Vda. de),
  Felicita R.
Garcia (Vda. de),

Jacoba F.
Garcia Casuela (de),
  Laura Y.
Garcia Cintron, Jose
Garcia de Muñoz,
  Providencia
Garcia de Quevedo de
  Herrera, Maria
Garcia de Quevedo y
  Robert, Herminia
Garcia de Quevedo,
  Maria
Garcia G., Carmen
Garcia Gaona, Ciro
  Cesar
Garcia Gonzalez,
  Eduardo
Garcia Mauricio, Paca
Garcia Navedo, Maria
Garcia Orra, Jose
Garcia Orse, Isabel
Garcia Perez, Jose
Garcia Ramirez, Isaac
Garcia Rodriguez,
  Amalia
Garcia Rodriguez,
  Jose
Garcia Rodriguez,
  Porfirio
Garcia y Garcia,
  Balbino
Garcia, Adelaida
Garcia, Agapito
Garcia, Amalia
Garcia, Amparo
Garcia, Angel
Garcia, Angeles
Garcia, Antonia (1)
Garcia, Antonia (2)
Garcia, Antonio (1)
Garcia, Antonio (2)
Garcia, Antonio (3)
Garcia, Antonio
  Manuel
Garcia, Aura
Garcia, Aurea
Garcia, B.
Garcia, Beatriz
Garcia, Consuelo
Garcia, Dolores (1)
Garcia, Dolores (2)
Garcia, Dolores (3)
Garcia, Eulalia
Garcia, Feliciano

Garcia, Felix
Garcia, Fernando
Garcia, Florencia
Garcia, Francisco
Garcia, Gabriel (1)
Garcia, Gabriel (2)
Garcia, Gloria
Garcia, Gonzalo
Garcia, Graciela
Garcia, Grecus
Garcia, Jacinta
Garcia, Joaquin (1)
Garcia, Joaquin (2)
Garcia, Jose (1)
Garcia, Jose (2)
Garcia, Jose (3)
Garcia, Juan (1)
Garcia, Juan (2)
Garcia, Juan (3)
Garcia, Juanita
Garcia, Juanita L.
Garcia, Julia
Garcia, Lidia
Garcia, Lorenza
Garcia, Macxcimina
Garcia, Maria (1)
Garcia, Maria (2)
Garcia, Maximina
Garcia, Mercedes
Garcia, Narciso
Garcia, Paula
Garcia, Peora
Garcia, Pepita
Garcia, Porfirio
Garcia, Providencia
Garcia, Rafael
Garcia, Rafaela L.
Garcia, Rafaelita
Garcia, Ramon (1)
Garcia, Ramon (2)
Garcia, Ramon (3)
Garcia, Ramon A.
Garcia, Ramon Julio
Garcia, Rosario
Garcia, Rosita
Garcia, Salvador
Garcia, Sandalio
Garcia, Teresa
Garcia, Vector
Garcias (de), Carmen
  M.
Garcias, Agapito
Garcias, Jose
Garcias, Manuel

Garcias, Ysabel
Garcoliaga, Cesareo
Gardia, Rafael
Gareza (de), Julia H.
Garibaldi, Natividad
Garmendia Ybañez,
  Graziella
Garmendia Ybañez,
  Luisa M.
Garmendia, Oscar
Garza, Domingo
Gatell Rodriguez,
  Palmira (M.D.)
Gatett Vda. de Borel,
  Rita
Gaudier, Fernando
Gautan, Cruz
Gauthier (de), Rosa G.
Gauthier (Vda. de),
  Braulia M.
Gauthier, Felipe
Gauthier, Gloria
Gauthier, Rodulfo
Gautier de Sanchez,
  Carmen
Gautier Vda. de
  Lindegren, Rafaela
Gautier, Pascasio M.
Gaviño, Dolores
Gaviño, Gloria
Gaviño, Teresa
Geigel (de), Micaela B.
Geigel de Escalona,
  Carmen
Geigel Rivas, Eduardo
Geigel, Carmen
Geigel, Fernando J.
Geigel, Jose Eduardo
Geigel, Maria
Geigel, Providencia
Gelada de Perez,
  Francisca
Gelpi, Angel
Genaro, Maria
Genaro, Pedro
Genaro, Sista
Gerdomo, Dolores
Ghoyco, Pedro
Giaca, Carmen
Gigel, A. L.
Gigel, Teresa
Gil Ortiz, Aurelio
Gil, Alfredo
Gil, Ana Maria

Gil, Bacilia
Gil, C.
Gil, Josefina
Gil, Mercedes
Gilaber, Carmen
Gill, William P.
Gimenez Aguayo,
  Carmen
Gimenez Torres,
  Segundo
Gimenez Triaño, S.
Gimenez, Francisca
Gimenez, Jose L.
Gimenez, Jose Patricio
Gimenez, Juan
Gimenez, Marcelino
Gimenez, Mercedes
Gimenez, Pedro
Gimenez, Ramon
Gimenez, Rosario
Gimenez, Salvador
Gines, Pedro
Giorgetti (de), Aurea
Girardi, Dolores
Girardiz, Pilar
Girona, Mariana
Giuliani de Dobal,
  Victorina
Giusti, Carmen Maria
Giusty, Ramon L.
Glandio, Micaela
Glanirll, Charles
Gliome, O.
Glureta, Isaac
Goag, Rafael
Goble (de), Maria
Goenaga (de), Esteban
  A.
Gofe (de), Angela G.
Gofe, Cristobal
Goicoechea, J. (Jr.)
Goitia, J.
Gomes, Cebera
Gomez (de), Antonia
  E.
Gomez (de), Nicolasa
Gomez (Vda. de),
  Evarista B.
Gomez (Vda. de),
  Luisa L.
Gomez (Vda. de),
  Valentina L.
Gomez Brioso, J. (M.
  D.)

Gomez de la Roca,
  Jose
Gomez de Marchan,
  Sra.
Gomez e Hijos
  (Comerciante)
Gomez Gonzalez,
  Maria
Gomez, Antonio
Gomez, Carmen
Gomez, Eduardo
Gomez, Francisco
Gomez, Genaro
Gomez, Juan J. (1)
Gomez, Juan J. (2)
Gomez, Justina
Gomez, M.
Gomez, Pablo F.
Gomez, Prudencio
Gomez, Rafael (1)
Gomez, Rafael (2)
Gomez, Rafael (3)
Gomez, Rosa
Gomez, Rosita N.
Gonzales, Belen A.
Gonzales, Enrique
Gonzales, Placido
Gonzales, Rafaela
Gonzalez de Laboy,
  Maria L.
Gonzalez (de),
  Adelaida M.
Gonzalez (de), Amelia
  M.
Gonzalez (de), Ana O.
Gonzalez (de),
  Angelina M.
Gonzalez (de), Blanca
  M. L.
Gonzalez (de), Elena I.
Gonzalez (de), Irene C.
Gonzalez (de), Luisa
  C.
Gonzalez (de), Maria
  C.
Gonzalez Bonilla,
  Isidoro
Gonzalez Carcel,
  Antonio
Gonzalez Correa,
  Pedro
Gonzalez Davila,
  Regina
Gonzalez Forruet,

Julio
Gonzalez Gonrs, J. (1)
Gonzalez Gonrs, J. (2)
Gonzalez Martinez,
  Alberto
Gonzalez Martinez,
  Antonio
Gonzalez Martinez,
  Elena
Gonzalez Martinez,
  Jose
Gonzalez Martinez,
  Manuel
Gonzalez Martinez,
  Maria
Gonzalez Martinez,
  Monserrate
Gonzalez Mendez,
  Antonio
Gonzalez Nieves,
  Josefina
Gonzalez Padin
  Company
Gonzalez Padin,
  Anselmo
Gonzalez Padin, Jose
Gonzalez Padro, A.
  (Jr.)
Gonzalez Quiñones,
  Manuel
Gonzalez Ramirez,
  Carmen
Gonzalez Sierra, J.
Gonzalez Ternoull, A.
Gonzalez, Abelardo
Gonzalez, Adela
Gonzalez, Adolfo
Gonzalez, Alberto
Gonzalez, Alfonsa
Gonzalez, Alfonso (1)
Gonzalez, Alfonso (2)
Gonzalez, Alfredo (3)
Gonzalez, Amparo
Gonzalez, Ana Ines
Gonzalez, Ana Ynes
Gonzalez, Andres
Gonzalez, Angel
Gonzalez, Angelina
Gonzalez, Antonia
Gonzalez, Antonio (1)
Gonzalez, Antonio (2)
Gonzalez, Arturo
Gonzalez, Asuncion (1)
Gonzalez, Asuncion

(2)
Gonzalez, Aurea
Gonzalez, Aurora
Gonzalez, B.
Gonzalez, Belen
Gonzalez, C. M.
Gonzalez, Carmen (1)
Gonzalez, Carmen (2)
Gonzalez, Carmen (3)
Gonzalez, Carmen (4)
Gonzalez, Carmen (5)
Gonzalez, Clemente
Gonzalez, Concepcion
Gonzalez, Concha
Gonzalez, Conrado
Gonzalez, Dolores
Gonzalez, Elisa
Gonzalez, Emilia
Gonzalez, Encarnacion
Gonzalez, Enrique (1)
Gonzalez, Enrique (2)
Gonzalez, Esteban
Gonzalez, Estevania
Gonzalez, Francisca
Gonzalez, Francisco
  (1)
Gonzalez, Francisco
  (2)
Gonzalez, G. M.
Gonzalez, Gregorio
Gonzalez, Isaac
Gonzalez, Isabel
Gonzalez, J.
Gonzalez, Jacinta
Gonzalez, Jacoba
Gonzalez, Jesus A.
Gonzalez, Joaquina
Gonzalez, Jose (1)
Gonzalez, Jose (2)
Gonzalez, Jose (3)
Gonzalez, Jose (4)
Gonzalez, Jose (5)
Gonzalez, Jose (6)
Gonzalez, Jose (7)
Gonzalez, Josefa
Gonzalez, Juan (1)
Gonzalez, Juan (2)
Gonzalez, Juan (3)
Gonzalez, Juan S.
Gonzalez, Juana
Gonzalez, Justo
Gonzalez, Laura Y.
Gonzalez, Leopoldo F.
Gonzalez, Lorenzo

Hernandez, Ana Maria
Hernandez, Angela
Hernandez, Angelina
Hernandez, Antonina G.
Hernandez, Antonio (1)
Hernandez, Antonio (2)
Hernandez, Avelino
Hernandez, Benita
Hernandez, Carmela
Hernandez, Celia
Hernandez, Dolores
Hernandez, Eduvigis
Hernandez, Eduvijes
Hernandez, Euclides
Hernandez, Felicita
Hernandez, Flora
Hernandez, Francisco
Hernandez, Gabina
Hernandez, Gavino
Hernandez, Glafila
Hernandez, Gregoria
Hernandez, Jesus (1)
Hernandez, Jesus (2)
Hernandez, Jesus Maria
Hernandez, Jose (1)
Hernandez, Jose (2)
Hernandez, Jose (3)
Hernandez, Jose (4)
Hernandez, Jose A.
Hernandez, Juan (1)
Hernandez, Juan (2)
Hernandez, Julia
Hernandez, Laura
Hernandez, Manuel (1)
Hernandez, Manuel (2)
Hernandez, Manuela
Hernandez, Maria (1)
Hernandez, Maria (2)
Hernandez, Maria A.
Hernandez, Maria de los A.
Hernandez, Martin
Hernandez, Monserrate
Hernandez, Pedro
Hernandez, Pio
Hernandez, R.
Hernandez, Rafael
Hernandez, Ramon (1)
Hernandez, Ramon (2)

Hernandez, Soledad
Hernandez, Tomasa
Hernandez, Victoria
Herrera (de), Maria F.
Herrera Geigel, Anibal J.
Herrera, Concepcion
Herrera, Ignacio
Herrera, Julio
Herrerias, Bruno
Herrero, Jose H.
Hidalgo, Dolores, D.
Highwood, Andres S.
Hogg (de), Mercedes T.
Hohill, J. A.
Houston, Eduardo
Hudo, Miguel
Huerta, Anselma
Huerta, Josefa
Hueso, Miguel
Hurtado, Francisca
Ibiguero, A.
Ichazo, A.
Iderseu, August
Igaravidez
Igaravidez, Antonio
Igaravidez, Laura
Iglesia (Vda. de), Rosario R.
Iglesias Rodriguez, Carlos
Iglesias, Anastasio
Iglesias, P.
Infante, Ana M.
Infante, Esperanza
Infante, Maria L.
Iriarte (de), Candita Maria
Iriarte (de), Margarita E.
Iriarte, E.
Iriarte, Francisco
Iriarte, Isabel
Iriarte, Rosa
Irilla L., Jesus
Irizarry Daniel, Jose
Irizarry, Antonio
Irizarry, Hipolito (1)
Irizarry, Hipolito (2)
Irizarry, Mariano
Irrivald, D.
Irvine-Rivera, Edith M.

Isabel, Maria
Iturondo, Dionisia
Iturregui, Jorge
Iturregui, N.
Izquierdo, Rafaela
Jacchim (de), Maria M
Janer, Angel
Jerez, Maria
Jesus (de), Luisa
Jesus (de), Maria
Jesus, Jesus
Jesus, Maria Dolores
Jimenez (Vda. de), Carolina
Jimenez Couvertier, Carmen
Jimenez O'Neill, M.
Jimenez, Amparo
Jimenez, Angel
Jimenez, Austina
Jimenez, Carlos
Jimenez, E.
Jimenez, Emilia
Jimenez, Felipe
Jimenez, J.
Jimenez, Jesus
Jimenez, Lorenzo
Jimenez, Mercedes
Jimenez, Rita
Jimenez, Tiburcio
Jimenez, Victoria
Jira de Ramos, Julia
Jivertier, Luis
Joglar, Domingo
Jones, Anita (Dra.)
Jones, Guillermo
Jordan Ochoteco, Mercedes
Jordan Vda. de Capetillo, Apolonia
Jordan, Irene
Jordan, Juan
Jorge, Maria
Jose, Alias
Jose, Antonio
Jose, Juana
Jose, Matilde
Jose, Simon
Jose, Susana
Juan (de), Carlota M.
Juan, Manuel
Juanien de Gonzalez, Rosario
Julia (de), Petra G.

Julia, Ada
Julia, Alicia
Julia, Julio
Julia, Rafael
Julia, Ramon
Jumet, Federico
Jumet, Ramon G.
Junceda, Laureano
Jürgenson, Lelia Anna
Justicia, Andres
Justicia, Maria
Kearney (Vda. de), Eulogia N.
Kearney, Josefina M.
Kichrhan, Rosa
Kohl (Vda. de), Juana A.
Kohl, Adolfina M.
Kuenghi, Jamers
Kuilan, Clementina
Kuinlam, Luisa
Kupfer (de), Elena B.
La Rosa Vda. de Garcia, Concepcion
Labiosa, Ramon
Laborde, A. L.
Laboy, Juana
Laboy, Luis
Lacomba, Fernando (1)
Lacomba, Fernando (2)
Lacomba, J. R.
Lacomba, Mercedes
Lafont, Marta
Laguna Torres, Carmen
Laguna, Ernesto
Laguna, Jollete
Laguna, Margarita
Laguna, Pedro
Laguna, Santiago
Laistos, Kaal
Lajara, Carmen Ysabel
Lajara, Concha
Lalvina, Juan
Lama, Ana Rita
Lamar Rodriguez, Rafael
Lamar, Celestino
Lamecino Juncos, Jose
Lamla, Jose L.
Lamoutte, Sara

Lamper de Segura, Marta
Lanausse, Maria
Lanchean Vda. de Garcia, Amalia
Landau (Vda. de), Nicolasa M.
Landau, Antonio
Landez, Trinidad
Landrau, Eva
Landron Perez, Luis
Landron, Candido
Lanuza, Isabel
Lanuza, Lolita
Lanuza, Ramon
Lanza, Piedad
Lanza, Silfredo
Lanzo, Antonio
Lanzo, Cornelio
Lanzo, Lorenzo
Lanzo, Socorro (1)
Lanzo, Socorro (2)
Lara de Gallardo, Belen
Lara, Pedro
Laragoza, Francisca
Lasala L., Josefa
Lasalde, Feliz
Lasanta, Ysabel
Lassalle, Beatriz
Lassalle, Carlos
Lassalle, Concepcion
Lassalle, Erasmo
Lassalle, Felipe
Lassalle, Providencia (1)
Lassalle, Providencia (2)
Latimer (de), R. F.
Latimer, G. B.
Latimer, Rosario
Latorre, Natalio
Launo (de), Fruitoso
Lauriano, Maria
Lausell Badillo, Aguedo
Laveigne, Flora
Laveigne, Marie
Lavligne, Paul
Laza, Isabel
Lazaga, Antonio
Lazaro (de), Maria I.
Lazaro Garcia, Jose Manuel

Lazaro Garcia, Luis Fernando
Lazaro Garcia, Maria del Carmen
Leavitt (de), Teofila S.
Leavitt, J.
Lebron, Antonia
Lebron, Candita
Lebron, Jesus
Lebron, Juanito
Lebron, Petrona
Lecompte, Rosenda
Lecompte, Teresa
Ledesma, Fernando J.
Ledesma, Jose
Ledesma, Luis
Ledesma, Mercedes
Leguinz, M.
LeHardy, L. P.
Lema, Petra
Lema, S.
Len, Eloisa
Leoir, Julio
Leon, Angel
Leon, Damaso
Leon, Elvira
Leon, Emerejilda
Leon, Flores
Leon, Juan
Leon, Julio
Leon, Margarita
Leon, Pastor
Leon, Rafael
Leon, S.
Leppenfeldt, Antonia
Leppenfeldt, Julio
Lereza, Antonio
Lergue, Teresa
Leviz, Cecilia
Levy, Francisco
Licaro, Tomas A.
Lindergren y Gautier, Emily
Ling, Petra
Liresa, Antonio
List, R. G.
List, R. G. (Mrs.)
List, Rudolph G.
Lizardi, Ascension
Lizol, Maria
Llabies (de), Haydee M.
Llabres, Roman
Llado (de), Maria B.

Llado, Jose
Llang Erpia, E.
Llanillo, Jose
Llanillo, Juana
Llanillo, Pedro
Llanillo, Rafaela
Llanos Vda. de Gonzalez, Lina
Llanos, Concepcion
Llanos, Concepcion F.
Llanos, Emilia
Llata, B.
Llauri (de), Carmen F.
Lleguis, Inocencio
Llera, Ysabel
Llinas, M.
Llobet (de), Matilde P.
Llobet Diaz, Providencia
Llobet Geigel, Carmen
Llobet Geigel, Juana
Llobet, Ana Maria
Llobet, Josefina
Llobet, Juana
Llobet, Natividad
Llobet, Rita
Llompard Noa, Julio V.
Llorenti, Eustilo
Lloves, Belen
Lobet Passapera, Josefina
Loira (de), Gloria E.
Loira, Maria
Lomba, Andres
Lopez (de), Matilde N.
Lopez (de), Piedad
Lopez (de), Providencia P.
Lopez Alvarez, Andres A.
Lopez Antongiorgio, Rafael
Lopez Bruno, Josefa
Lopez Campos, Tomas
Lopez Castro, Leonor
Lopez Cepero (de), Carmen B.
Lopez Cepero, H.
Lopez Cepero, Mariana F.
Lopez Cruz, Maria
Lopez de Jesus, Rosa
Lopez de la Rosa, Jose

Lopez de Victoria de Reus, Maria
Lopez de Victoria, Jacobina
Lopez de Victoria, Margot
Lopez Felemond, Julio
Lopez Gaztambide, J.
Lopez Landrau, Angel
Lopez Lopez Miguel
Lopez Muscez, Isabelita
Lopez Noa, Clara
Lopez Nussa, Victor R.
Lopez Ramos, Concepcion
Lopez Salas, Emilio
Lopez Soto, Jose
Lopez Vda. de Casals, Josefa
Lopez, Adela
Lopez, Adolfo
Lopez, Albertina
Lopez, Amparo
Lopez, Ana
Lopez, Andrea
Lopez, Andres
Lopez, Antonio (1)
Lopez, Antonio (2)
Lopez, Armando (Jr.)
Lopez, Arturo
Lopez, Carlota
Lopez, Carmen
Lopez, Carruto
Lopez, Dolores
Lopez, Emilia
Lopez, Esteban
Lopez, Francisco R.
Lopez, Geraldo
Lopez, Grata
Lopez, Gustavo
Lopez, Isabel (1)
Lopez, Isabel (2)
Lopez, Jacinta
Lopez, Jacinta
Lopez, Joaquin (1)
Lopez, Joaquin (2)
Lopez, Jose (1)
Lopez, Jose (2)
Lopez, Jose (3)
Lopez, Juan
Lopez, Mamerto
Lopez, Manuela
Lopez, Marcial

Lopez, Maria (1)
Lopez, Maria (2)
Lopez, Maria Dora
Lopez, Martin
Lopez, Matilde
Lopez, Paula
Lopez, Pedro
Lopez, Petra
Lopez, Puro
Lopez, R. H.
Lopez, Rafael
Lopez, Ramon
Lopez, Remedios
Lopez, Ricarda
Lopez, Rita
Lopez, Rodrigo (1)
Lopez, Rodrigo (2)
Lopez, Sixto
Lopez, Soledad
Lopez, Tomas (1)
Lopez, Tomas (2)
Lopez, Tomas (3)
Lopez, Wenceslao
Lopez, Ygnacio L.
Lopez, Ynes
Lopez, Ysabel
Lora, Jose
Lora, Pilar
Lorenzi, Sampiero
Lorenzo (de),
  Providencia F.
Lorenzo, Pedro
Lores (de), R. Blanco
Losada, Carmen
Loubriel (de), Julia M
Loubriel (de), Micaela
  C.
Loubriel Cueto,
  Providencia
Loubriel, Belen
Loubriel, Bernalda
Loubriel, Caridad I.
Loubriel, Josefina (1)
Loubriel, Josefina (2)
Loubriel, Juan
Loubriel, Julia
Loubriel, Maria
Loubriel, U.
Loundoy, G. M.
Louzan, Antonio
Lovena, Aquilino
Lozando, Sinforosa
Lozano de Garcia,
  Josefa

Lozano, Alma
Lozano, Carmelo
Lozano, Victor
Lucchetti (de),
  Madeleine
Lucchetti, Louise
Lucero, Gregoria
Lugo-Viña (de W.),
  Grace
Lugo-Viña, Jose
  (M.A.)
Lugo, Amelia
Lugo, Euripiades
Lugo, Fernando
Lugo, Luis
Lugo, U. M.
Luiggi, Felix
Luiña, Malgor
Luiña, Manuel
Luisa Yeter, Maria
Lujanes, Alfonso
Lumbana, Cebastian
Luyanda, Aurora
Luyando Ayala, Fidel
Luzunaris de Roca,
  Araceli
Luzunaris, Julio
Luzunaris, Maximino
M., Alejandro
M., Gilberto
M., Luis
Machicote, Emilia
Madero, Francisco
Maduro (de), Carmen
  N.
Maien, Pedro
Malabte., Ernesto
Maldenieth, Sam.
Maldonado Porrata,
  Herminio
Maldonado, Carolina
Maldonado, Eufemia
Maldonado, Francisco
Maldonado, Maria
Maldonado, Maria E.
Maldonado, Martina
Maldonado, P.
Maldonado, Paula
Maldonado, Segundo
Maldonado, Zoila
Malea, Amparo
Malpica (de), Carolina
  S.
Malpica, Abelardo

Mandia de Blanche,
  Addia
Mandia y Martinez,
  Belen
Mandia, Belen (1)
Mandia, Belen (2)
Mandres, Natolio
Mangual de Cestero,
  Teresita
Mangual, Florentino
Mangual, Nicolas
Manogorez, -
Manzano, Enriqueta
Manzano, F. A.
Manzano, Juana
Manzano, Luis
Manzano, Mercedes
Manzano, Pedro
Manzano, Rafael
Marcano (de), Maria
  R.
Marcano, Domingo
Marcano, Eusebia
Marceora, Tecla
Marchan, Antonio
Marcial Santiago,
  Juana
Marcial, Juana
Marcial, Manuel
Marcial, Robustiano
Mardones, Leoncio
Margarida (de),
  Matilde U.
Margarida Hudo, R.
Margarida, Rosalia
Margary Cruz, Rafael
Margenat Marrero,
  Alfredo
Margnaty, Melchor
Mariana (de), Celia C.
Mariana, Oscar
Mariana, Ricardo E.
  (1)
Mariana, Ricardo E.
  (2)
Mariani, Angel O.
Marich, Gabino
Marien de la Fuente,
  Elisa
Marien, Carmen
Mariere, Emilia
Marin (de), Rafaela
Marin (Vda. de)
Marin (Vda. de)

Marin de Andino,
  Angela
Marin Marien, J.
Marin, Angelita
Marin, Augusto
Marin, M.
Marin, Ramon
Marin, Sebastian
Marin, Zoilo
Marina, Jose
Marino, Victor M.
Marisonave,
  Humberto N. (Lcdo.)
Mark, Antonio
Mark, Margarita
Marly Veray, A. (Dr.)
Maroscuru, Pablo
Marque, Ramon
Marques, Ana
Marques, Andres
Marques, Brigida
Marquez (Vda. de),
  Antonia P.
Marquez Nater, Rafael
Marquez, Andrea
Marquez, Carmen
Marquez, Cornelia
Marquez, Estebania
Marquez, Galletano
Marquez, Gloria
Marquez, Josefa
Marquez, Modesta
Marquez, Pedro
Marrero (de), Dolores
  C.
Marrero (de), Maria P.
Marrero, A. (Jr.)
Marrero, Agustin (Jr.)
Marrero Melendez,
  Juan
Marrero, Agustin
Marrero, Amalia
Marrero, Andres
Marrero, Beatriz R.
Marrero, Carmelo
Marrero, Felix
Marrero, Fernando
Marrero, Francisca
Marrero, Graciano
Marrero, Jose A.
Marrero, Jose H.
Marrero, Lolita
Marrero, Manuel (1)
Marrero, Manuel (2)

253

Marrero, Maurisio
Marrero, Miguel
Marrero, Providencia
Marrero, Rafael
Marrero, Santiago
Marsariz, Juan
Martell, Generoso
Marti (de), Maria E.
Marti de Bulbena,
  Mercedes
Marti de Colon, Pilar
Marti, Casimiro
Martin Sojo, Diego
Martin Vega, A.
Martin, Frank
Martin, Maria
Martines, Cristina
Martines, Rosario
Martinez (de),
  Mercedes J.
Martinez (Vda. de), A.
  R.
Martinez (Vda. de),
  Josefina
Martinez (Vda. de),
  Victoria
Martinez Acosta, C.
Martinez Campos,
  Ramon
Martinez Carrion
  Maduro, Luis
Martinez de Gonzalez,
  Josefa
Martinez de Gonzalez,
  Juana
Martinez de Mandia,
  Mercedes
Martinez Dios,
  Ceferino
Martinez H., Rafaela
Martinez Jordanes,
  Jesus
Martinez Llovin, J.
Martinez Martinez, R
Martinez Naranjos,
  Rafael
Martinez Pagan, Jose
Martinez Pereña,
  Jesus
Martinez Suarez, Jose
Martinez Vargas,
  Camilo (1)
Martinez Vargas,
  Camilo (2)

Martinez-Alvarez,
  Maria
Martinez, Adela
Martinez, Alejandrina
Martinez, Ana
Martinez, Ana Maria
Martinez, Angela (1)
Martinez, Angela (2)
Martinez, Anita
Martinez, Antonio
Martinez, Asuncion
Martinez, Bartolome
Martinez, Carlina
Martinez, Carlos
Martinez, Carmelo
Martinez, Carmelo R.
Martinez, Ceferino
Martinez, Concepcion
Martinez, Constanza
Martinez, Consuelo
Martinez, Dolores
Martinez, Eduardo
Martinez, Emiliano
Martinez, Emilio
Martinez, Enrique
Martinez, Ernesto
Martinez, Eugenio
Martinez, Eusebio
Martinez, Felipe R.
Martinez, Felix
Martinez, Felix M.
Martinez, Francisca (1)
Martinez, Francisca (2)
Martinez, Francisco (1)
Martinez, Francisco (2)
Martinez, Gavina
Martinez, Genard
Martinez, J. M.
Martinez, Jesus
Martinez, Joaquin
Martinez, Joaquina
Martinez, Jose (1)
Martinez, Jose (2)
Martinez, Jose (3)
Martinez, Jose (4)
Martinez, Jose C.
Martinez, Jose D.
Martinez, Josefa
Martinez, Juan (1)
Martinez, Juan (2)
Martinez, Julia
Martinez, Luis (1)
Martinez, Luis (2)
Martinez, Luis (3)

Martinez, M.
Martinez, M. R.
Martinez, Manuel
Martinez, Marcela
Martinez, Marcolina
Martinez, Maria (1)
Martinez, Maria (2)
Martinez, Maria (3)
Martinez, Mario
Martinez, Mercedes
  (1)
Martinez, Mercedes
  (2)
Martinez, Paula
Martinez, Pepin
Martinez, Pepita
Martinez, Perfecta
Martinez, Pilar
Martinez, Ramon
Martinez, Ramon A.
Martinez, Ricarda
Martinez, Rosa
Martinez, Santos
Martinez, Secundino
Martinez, Teresa
Martinez, Ulises A.
Martinez, Valentin
Martino, Josefina (1)
Martino, Josefina (2)
Martorell (de), Rosa
  Blanca G.
Martorell (Vda. de),
  Angela P.
Martorell de Ojeda, A.
Martorell Vda. de
  Urrutia, Eduarda
Martorell, Amparo
Martorell, Celestina
Martorell, Josefa
Martos, Antonio
Marvez, Erasmo
Marvez, Rosa M.
Marxuach, Ana
Marxuach, Jaime
Marxuach, Rafael
Marzan, Secundina
Mas y Perez, Jose
Mas, Jose (Jr.)
Mas, Jose
Mascaro, Candida
Mascaro, Pilar
Mass, Herminio
Matango, F.
Matango, Rafaela F.

Matanzo (de), Rafaela
Matanzo, Rafaelita
Matas, Primitiba
Matheu, Dominga
Matos, Eladio
Matos, Jacinto
Matteu, Joaquin
Maui, Enrique
Maurano, Jose P.
Mauret (de), Semiare
Mayer Boggs, Laura
Maymi, Asela
Maymi, J. Lino
Mayo, Palmira
Mayol, Juana (1)
Mayol, Juana (2)
Mayoral, Angel M.
Mayoral, Antonio
Maysonet, Eriberto
Maysonet, Eugenio A.
Mediavilla (de), Ana
  R.
Mediavilla (de),
  Morayma M.
Mediavilla Linaje,
  Jose
Mediavilla Mercy,
  Jose
Mediavilla, Antonio (1)
Mediavilla, Antonio (2)
Mediavilla, Carmen
Mediavilla, Jesus
Mediavilla, Maria
Mediavilla, Panchita
Medina, Carmen N.
Medina, Felipa
Medina, Mateo
Medina, Rosario
Medina, Telesforo
Medraño, Benito
Megivinoff (de), Maria
  G.
Megrand, Francisco
Mejes, R. O.
Mejia (de), Catalina
  M.
Mejia, P. C.
Melendez y Laboy
  (de), Sue
Melendez, Agustin (1)
Melendez, Agustin (2)
Melendez, Amparo
Melendez, Desposori
Melendez, Francisco

Melendez, Gumercindo
Melendez, Jacinto
Melendez, Juan
Melendez, Marcelina
Melendez, Maria (1)
Melendez, Maria (2)
Melendez, Mario
Melendez, Miguelina
Melendez, Narcisa
Melendez, Rafaela
Melero, Arturo J.
Melon, Enrique
Meltz (de), Juana A.
Meltz, Jose
Mendez Garcia, Waldo
Mendez Suarez, David
Mendez, Angel
Mendez, Antonio (1)
Mendez, Antonio (2)
Mendez, Carmen Maria
Mendez, Eduardo
Mendez, Eleuterio
Mendez, Feliciano
Mendez, Jasinto
Mendez, Jose
Mendez, Jose Maria
Mendez, Leonardo
Mendez, Manuel (1)
Mendez, Manuel (2)
Mendez, Maria Luisa
Mendez, Pablo
Mendez, Santiago
Mendez, Vicente
Mendia (Vda. de), Rosa M.
Mendia, M.
Mendia, Marina
Mendin Pereira, Jose
Mendin, Jose (M.D.)
Mendin, Josefa (1)
Mendin, Josefa (2)
Mendin, Julia
Mendin, Luz (1)
Mendin, Luz (2)
Mendin, Matilde
Mendizabal, Guadalupe
Mendoza Jaime, Jesus
Mendoza, Diego
Mendoza, Jose
Mendoza, Rodolfo
Menendez (de),

Herminia S. Menendez
Colimenaro, Ramona
Menendez, Juana Maria
Menendez, Rafael
Menendez, Ysabelo
Menia (de), Carmen P.
Mensonet, Rafael
Mercader, Patricio
Mercado, Francisco
Mercado, Genara
Mercado, Juan S.
Mercado, Oliva
Merced, Flor
Merced, Manuel
Mercedes Kohl, Ana
Merecian, Pedro
Merino, Carlos
Merino, Jose
Merio, Jose A.
Merle y Cabrera, Tomas
Mesa, Luis
Messa Torres, Francisco
Mestre (de), Isabel B.
Meteo, Dominga
Micheli, Luis
Micher, Josefina
Miguel, Carmen
Milan, Andres
Millan Corra, Manuel
Milland (de), Concepcion O.
Miller, A.
Millmon, Lilliam
Mills, F.
Mills, Lusia (Mrs.)
Mira Ramos, Ramon
Mirabal, Carlos
Mirabar, Francisca
Miranda (de), Mercedes
Miranda (Vda. de), Mercedes A.
Miranda, Aniceto (1)
Miranda, Aniseto (2)
Miranda, Aniseto (3)
Miranda, Antonio
Miranda, Antonio P.
Miranda, Camilo
Miranda, Emilio
Miranda, Gloria

Miranda, Jesusa
Miranda, Jose
Miranda, Jose P.
Miranda, Juan (1)
Miranda, Juan (2)
Miranda, Julio
Miranda, Justa
Miranda, Manuel
Miranda, Pilar
Miranda, Ramon (1)
Miranda, Ramon (2)
Miro (de), Angela C.
Miro (de), Rosario P.
Miro, Angelina
Miro, Antonio
Miro, Carlos
Miro, Carolina
Miro, Clara B.
Miro, Jose
Miro, M. E.
Miro, Rafael
Miron, Carlos
Mirra, Modesta
Mistal, Eduardo
Miyares, Enrique
Moceno, Francisco
Mocyol Baniel, Pedro
Moguis, Siril
Mojica (Vda. de), Hipolita M.
Mojica Rivera, Carmen
Mojica, Americo
Mojica, Emilio
Mojica, Jose A.
Mojica, Juana
Mokdol, Gerardo
Moledo P., Modesto
Molina (de), Ana C.
Molina (de), Encarnacion G.
Molina (Vda. de), Milagros
Molina Ceiseiro, Leopoldo
Molina de Brown, Antonia
Molina de Rolon, Francisca
Molina de Soto, Providencia
Molina de T., Alejandrina
Molina, Conrada

Molina, Evarista
Molina, J. M.
Molina, Jose (1)
Molina, Jose (2)
Molina, Petrona
Molina, Tito A.
Molinary, Elisa
Monagas, Juan A.
Monagas, Rafael H.
Monclova, Jose Lara
Monge, Belen
Monje, Salvador
Monroig (de), Consuelo F.
Monroig, Antonio
Monsanto, Juana
Montalvo, Eladio
Montañez, Anastacia
Montañez, Aurelio
Montañez, Damiana
Montañez, Eulalia
Montañez, Filomeno
Montañez, Inocencio
Montañez, Paula
Montañez, Trinidad
Montañez, Victor
Monte, Jose
Montes y Sterling, Diego
Montes, Angel
Montes, Narcisa
Montes, R.
Monteserin, Petra
Monteserin, Primitiva
Montijo (de), Belen R.
Montilla de Carbia, Matilde
Montilla, Antonia
Monts de Oca, Angel
Monts, Inocencia
Moor, Santiago
Mora (Vda. de), Hortensia P.
Mora, Juana
Moragon, Pablo
Morales Vda. de Blanco, Ana
Morales Vda. de Sanchez, Ana
Morales Zamo, Domingo
Morales, Alejandrina
Morales, Angel
Morales, Antonia

Morales, Demetrio
Morales, Domingo
Morales, Felipe
Morales, Jesus
Morales, Jose E. (Jr.)
Morales, Jose P.
Morales, L. E.
Morales, Luis
Morales, Luis N.
Morales, M. E.
Morales, Maria
Morales, Maria Nicomede
Morales, Mercedes
Morales, Paca
Morales, Providencia M.
Morales, Rosario
Morales, Victor Manuel
Moralez Muñoz, Eduardo
Moralez, Angela
Moras, J.
Moraza, Ramon
Morazo, Benito Jose (Lcdo.) (Attorney and Delegate to House of Representatives)
Morel, Alejandrina
Morell Gerena, Meliton
Moreno, Epifanio
Moreno, Fabriciana
Moreno, Ines
Moreno, Isabel
Moreno, Juana
Moreno, Julian
Moreno, Pedro
Morera, Juan
Morey, Francisca
Morillo Vda. de Ilarraza, Micaela
Moris, Emilio
Mouraller, Fidel
Mouzo, Josefa
Moya, Antonio
Mozon de Gil, Secundina
Mucano, Rosario G.
Muganda (de), Maria H.
Muir, Belen M.
Mujica, Felix

Mulero, Luis
Mulet, Antonia
Mulet, Cecilia O.
Mulet, Isabel
Mulet, J. A.
Mulet, M. L.
Mulet, Rosario
Muñiz, Juan
Muñoz (de), Inocencia R.
Muñoz Colon, L.
Muñoz de Negron, Carmen
Muñoz Garcia, R.
Muñoz Morales (de), Maria R.
Muñoz Souffront, Salvador
Muñoz Vda. de Aybar, Carmen
Muñoz Vda. de Garcia de Quevedo, Lola
Muñoz Vda. de Orcasitas, Mercedes
Muñoz, Angel
Muñoz, Antonio
Muñoz, Flora
Muñoz, Jesus
Muñoz, Manuel
Muñoz, Merchor
Muñoz, Sinensia
Muriel Abad, Jose
Muriel, Petra
Murillo Samper, Abel
Murillo, Mercedes
Muro, Rafael
Murrier, Leopoldo
Musa, A.
Musa, Agustina
Musa, J.
Muyer, Cristina
N., Jose
Nabarro, Julia
Nadal, Hilaria
Nadal, Jose
Nadal, Mercedes
Naranjo (de), Concepcion D.
Naranjo, Isabel
Naranjo, Jacinto
Naranjo, Josefina
Naranjo, Juan
Naranjo, Pascual
Naranjo, Rafael

Narganes, F.
Narvaez, Alejo
Narvaez, Carmen
Narvaez, Crucita
Narvaez, Cruz
Narvaez, Juan
Narvaez, Juanito
Narvaez, Manuel
Natar, Jose
Nater (Vda. de), Ynes N.
Nater Carreras, Jose
Nater de Brull, Ricarda
Nater Girona, Carmen
Nater Girona, Josefa
Nater Nadal, Francisco
Nater, Lolita
Nava, Jose
Navarro Rosa
Navarro, G.
Navarro, G. C.
Navarro, Susana
Navas, Emilio
Navas, Lupercio
Naveda, Angel J.
Navedo de Garcia, Ines
Navedo, Inesita
Naves, Francisco
Navoa, Jacinto
Nazario de Martinez, Amelinda
Negron Flores, R.
Negron Mattei, F.
Negron Muñoz, M. D.
Negron Muñoz, Mercedes
Negron, Amparo
Negron, Antonio
Negron, Brigida
Negron, Esteban
Negron, Evarista
Negron, Francisco
Negron, Gregoria
Negron, Jose J.
Negron, Josefina
Negron, Manuel
Negron, Mercedes
Negron, Pasita
Negron, Pedro
Neist, J. O.
Nerafi, Aureliano

Neral (de), Saturnina A.
Neral, Gloria Maria
Nicolas, Ambrosio
Nicolau de Puig, Maria
Nicolay, Francisca
Nidot, Alberto
Niebe, Eladia
Niebe, Eseciel
Niebe, Georgina
Nieto Vda. de Pagan, Rosalia
Nieve, Pedro J.
Nieves de Gonzalez, Generosa
Nieves T., Antonio
Nieves Vda G., Oliva
Nieves, Angel
Nieves, Fidela
Nieves, Generoso
Nieves, Isidro
Nieves, Jose
Nieves, Manuel
Nieves, Marcelino
Nieves, Maria
Nieves, Pedro
Nieves, Rosalia
Niguerco, J.
Nin (de), Joaquina F.
Nin de Toro, Milagros
Nin, J. C.
Nistal, Manuel
Noa, Georgio
Noa, Jorge
Noa, Lorenzo (Jr.)
Noble, J. B.
Noble, M. J.
Noell, Josefa
Norrit, Dolores
Novoa, Alfonso
Noya, Josefa
Noyas, Emilio J.
Nuñez Farias, Alberto
Nuñez Perez, Emilia
Nuñez, Arturo
Nuñez, Miguel
Nuñez, Rafael
Nusa, Demetria
O'Neill, Fermin
O'Neill, Jose
O'Neill, Nicolas
Ober de Montella, Juan
Obregon, Victoria

Ocacio, Inginia
Ocacio, Sabino
Ocaña, Martin
Ocasio, Cecilia
Ocasio, Juan
Ocasio, Maria
Ochoa, Manuel
Ochoteco (de),
 Trinidad M.
Ochoteco de Veige,
 Maria L.
Ochoteco Maldonado,
 Trinidad
Ochoteco, F.
Ochoteco, Feliz
Ochoteco, Ines
Ochoteco, Isabel
Odiocraz, E.
Odiol, Antonio
Offeral, Carlota
Offeral, Rafael
Offeral, Rosa
Offeral, Severio
Ojeda Ferrer, Belen (1)
Ojeda Ferrer, Belen
 (2)
Ojeda, Aniceto
Ojeda, Carmen
Ojeda, Jose
Ojeda, Lolita
Ojeda, Luis
Olazagasty, Dominga
Olivera Suarez, A.
Olivera, Manuel
Olivero Calderon,
 Antonio
Olivero, Pedro
Olivo, Asuncion
Olivo, Cruz
Olivo, Europa Ysabel
Olivo, Juan (Jr.)
Ollangure, Ana Luisa
Oller Vda. de Matos,
 Ana
Oller, Jose
Olmedo, Gregoria
Oomy (de), Georgina
 L.
Oomy, Armando
Oomy, Arsenio
Oquendo, Balentin
Oquendo, Carlota
Oquendo, Carmen
Oquendo, Felicita

Oquendo, Fernando
Oquendo, Gregorio
Oquendo, Leonor
Oquendo, Maria
Oquendo, Providencia
Oquendo, Saturnino
Orcasitas de Torres,
 Josefa
Orcasitas (de), Maria
 S.
Orcasitas, C.
Orillano, Alejandrina
Orlandi, Josefina
Orrach, Monserrate
Orta y Orta, Evaristo
Ortega, Domingo
Ortega, Eloy
Ortega, Martin
Ortega, Ramon
Ortega, Teodoro
Ortega, Zoilo
Ortiz (de), Juana
Ortiz (de), Ysabel G.
Ortiz de Torres, Otilio
Ortiz de Zarate,
 Carmen
Ortiz Flatt, Salvador
Ortiz Ginorio, E.
Ortiz Llanger, Jose
Ortiz Ortiz, Ramon
Ortiz Rivera, Jesus
Ortiz Rivera, Juan
Ortiz Vda. de Furiarty,
 Ana
Ortiz y Renta, A. H.
Ortiz, Acisclo
Ortiz, Angel
Ortiz, Antonio
Ortiz, Concha
Ortiz, Domitila
Ortiz, Gerardo
Ortiz, Gregorio
Ortiz, Jose
Ortiz, Jose M.
Ortiz, Marcela
Ortiz, Margarita
Ortiz, Maria Luisa
Ortiz, Mercedes
Ortiz, Monserrate
Ortiz, Nicolasa
Ortiz, Patria
Ortiz, Petra
Ortiz, R. Melendez
Ortiz, Ramon

Ortiz, Sabina
Ortiz, Serafin
Ortiz, Ulises
Ortiz, Valentina
Ortiz, Visitacion C.
Osores, Javier
Osorio Osorio, Juan
Osorio Reyes,
 Filomena
Osorio Trigo, Julian
Osorio, Angel
Osorio, Bentura
Osorio, Felipe
Osorio, Lola
Osorio, Luz Maria
Osorio, Pedro
Osorio, Providencia
Osorio, Rafael
Osorio, Regina
Osorio, Urbano
Otero, Benito
Otero, Catalina
Otero, Francisco
Otero, Guadalupe
Otero, Hortencia
Otero, Isabel
Otero, Ramon
Ozta, Jesus
Ozta, Julia
P. Blas, M.
P., D.
Paalacios, Juan
Pabon, Genara
Pabon, Jose Maria
Pacheco Mangara,
 Emma
Pacheco Vda. de
 Subira, M.C.
Pacheco y Vega, Luisa
Pacheco, Adela
Pacheco, Domingo
Pacheco, Eulalia
Pacheco, Jesus
Pacheco, Ricardo
Pacheco, Saturnina
Padial, M.
Padilla de Jimenez,
 Callita
Padilla, Jorge Juan
Padilla, Justo
Padilla, Monserrate
Padilla, Rafael
Padin, Lola
Padin, Ramon

Padre Nueva Paz
 (Director of "La
 Verdad" newspaper)
Padro Faj., J.
Padro, Palo
Padron, Jose
Pagan F., Luis
Pagan, Aracelis
Pagan, Dominga
Pagan, Herminia
Pagan, Jose
Pagan, Juan
Pagan, Juana
Pagan, Laura
Pagan, Luis J.
Pagan, Manuel
Pagan, Maria M.
Pagan, Pedro
Pagan, Placido
Pagan, Rafael
Pagan, Rosa
Palacio y Salazar,
 Rafael
Palacio, Jose
Palacio, Luisa
Palacios Appellaniz,
 Rafael
Palacios, Rafael
Palacios, Ricardo
Palermo, Gabriel
Pallas, Sergio
Palleka, Manuel
Palma, Maria
Palomo, Carmen
Pamela, Jaime
Paniagua (de), C. M.
Paniagua (de), Luisa
 M.
Paniagua (Vda. de),
 Petra
Paniagua de Aliaga,
 Abigail
Paniagua Molina,
 Blanca
Paniagua Molina,
 Gloria
Paniagua, Alfonso
Paniagua, Angelo
Paniagua, Antonio (1)
Paniagua, Antonio (2)
Paniagua, Bartolome
Paniagua, Blanca
Paniagua, Isabel
Paniagua, Luisa

Paniagua, Marina
Paniagua, Mercedes (1)
Paniagua, Mercedes (2)
Paniagua, Natalia
Paniagua, Pedro
Paniagua, R.
Paniagua, Tomas
Paniagua, Tomasa
Pantoja, Concepcion
Pantoja, Conrado (1)
Pantoja, Conrado (2)
Pantojas, Elcadio
Paonessa, Rafael
Paradis, Perfecto
Paradis, R.
Paredes, Manuel
Paredes, Teofilo
Pares, Maria
Pareta, Nicomedes
Pares, Pedro (Jr.)
Paris de Pillich, Eugenia
Paris, Juan Ruiz
Paris, Luisa
Paris, Victoria
Parrillo, Vacilio
Pasapera, Franco
Pasarell, Maria Amelia
Pasarell, N.
Pasarell, Orvill
Pascual (de), Cecilia E. G.
Pascual (de), Prudencia I.
Pascual Ilarraza, Jesus
Pascual Pedro
Passalacqua, Luis Felipe
Pastrana Rodriguez, Jose (1)
Pastrana Rodriguez, Jose (2)
Pastrana, Maria
Patiño (de), Lorenza L.
Patiño Vda. de Valls, Colia
Patron, Pedro
Pavon, Domingo
Paz, Francisco
Pearl (de), Jesusa M.
Pedero, Jose S.

Pedero, Simon
Pedrero, Agapito
Pellon (de), Eldemira F.
Pellon, Daniel
Peña (de), Aida Y.
Peña Reyes, Miguel
Peña, Eulalio
Peña, Gregoria
Pena, Jose
Peña, Juana
Peña, Manuel
Peñagaricano (de), Teresa R.
Peñas, Luisa
Peñaze, Ramon
Penedo Rios, Rosariot
Penedo, Pepita
Pepin, Joaquin
Pereira (de), Cruz A.
Pereira de Alvarez, Consuelo
Pereira, Concepcion
Pereira, Flora
Perelez, Genaro
Pereyo, Elisa
Perez (de), Cristina R.
Perez Casaldu, Eduardo
Perez de Marce, Gregoria
Perez Dominguez, Manuel
Perez Lopez, Joaquina
Perez Porrata, Rafael
Perez Santiago, Ramon
Perez Vda. de Salgado, Braulia
Perez Viegue, Tomas
Perez, Abino
Perez, Adelaida
Perez, Albasciala
Perez, Alejandrina
Perez, Altagra
Perez, Amansio
Perez, Amparo
Perez, Andres
Perez, Angela
Perez, Angeles (1)
Perez, Angeles (2)
Perez, Antonio (1)
Perez, Antonio (2)
Perez, Antonio (3)

Perez, Arturo
Perez, Asuncion
Perez, Aurora
Perez, Avelino
Perez, Belen
Perez, Carlota
Perez, Carmen (1)
Perez, Carmen (2)
Perez, Carmen (3)
Perez, Cruz
Perez, Dolores
Perez, Dominga
Perez, Domingo (1)
Perez, Domingo (2)
Perez, Domingo (3)
Perez, Elvira
Perez, Emilio (1)
Perez, Emilio (2)
Perez, Escolastica
Perez, Esteban
Perez, Esther
Perez, Eulaliz
Perez, Faustino (1)
Perez, Faustino (2)
Perez, Faustino (3)
Perez, Felix
Perez, Fermin
Perez, Francisco (1)
Perez, Francisco (2)
Perez, Gabriel
Perez, Graciano
Perez, J. M.
Perez, Joaquina
Perez, Jose Antonio
Perez, Juan
Perez, Juana (1)
Perez, Juana (2)
Perez, Juana (3)
Perez, Juanita
Perez, Julia (1)
Perez, Julia (2)
Perez, Julia (3)
Perez, Julio (1)
Perez, Julio (2)
Perez, Luis (1)
Perez, Luis (2)
Perez, Manuel
Perez, Maria
Perez, Maria Jose
Perez, Narciso
Perez, Pedro
Perez, Pedro
Perez, Pio
Perez, Rafael

Perez, Rafaela
Perez, Ramon (1)
Perez, Ramon (2)
Perez, Regina
Perez, Rita
Perez, Salvador
Perez, Salvio
Perez, Victoriano
Perfecto, Maria
Pesante Rigual, Jose
Pesante, Bibiana
Pesquera (de), Dolores C.
Petersen, Devin
Pheerremont, Rosa
Pherremonth, Cecilia
Picornel, Marita
Pier, Margarita
Pietri, Raul
Pildando, Antonio
Pildando, Carmelo
Pillich, Callo
Pillich, Catalina
Pimentel, Emilia
Piña (de), Norberta F.
Piña, Cosme
Piña, Lino
Piñas, Salvadora
Piñeiro Diaz, Antonio
Piñeiro Rivera, Eugenio
Piñeiro, Concepcion
Piñeiro, Jose
Piñeiro, Ramon
Piñeiro, Rogelio
Pinela Vda. de Puig, Angela
Pinela, Adelaida
Pinela, Carmen
Piñero Rodriguez, Nicolas
Piñero, Francisca (1)
Piñero, Francisca (2)
Piñero, J. D.
Piñero, Jose
Pino, Enrique
Pino, Fidel
Pinos, F. G.
Pirello, Angel
Pirrilla Gomez, Nicolas
Piszzini, Maria
Pitarque, Severina H.
Piza Vivas, Miguel

Pizarro, Angel (1)
Pizarro, Angel (2)
Pizarro, Catalino
Pizarro, Eustaquio
Pizarro, Jose (1)
Pizarro, Jose (2)
Pla y Vila, Angel
Pla, Agustin (Jr.)
Pla, Maria
Plas, Ramon A.
Plaza, Carmen
Plaza, Enriqueta
Plaza, Maria J.
Po de Cuetaro,
   Armando
Polinary, R.
Pomales, Amalia
Pomares, Eustaquio
Pons, E. F.
Pons, Maria
Ponte, Isabel
Porras (de), Ines Ruiz
Porrata (Vda. de), Ana
Porrata Doria de
   Ferrary, Martina
Porrata, Ana Maria
Porrata, Maria
   Dolores
Portela Loubriel,
   Ricardo
Portela, Fausto
Portela, Jose
Portela, Josefa
Portela, Maria
Portela, Rogelio
Portella, Ofelio F.
Portilla (de), Virginia
Portilla, Virginia
Portela, Monserrate
Portela, P.
Poventu y Fizol, Jose
   M.
Power Anguilo,
   Carmen
Power, J.
Power, Jorge J.
Power, Julio
Prado, Juana
Prah, Salvador
Prats de Rios,
   Mercedes
Prats, Alfonso
Prats, Araceli
Prez, Jose

Prieto (de), Mercedes
   O.
Prieto, Amelia
Prieto, Cesarea
Puchades, Paco
Puidallezo (de), Josefa
   C.
Puig Doller, Antonio
Puig Munet, J.
Puig, Angelina
Puig, Carmen
Puig, Cristobal
Puig, Maria Luisa
Puig, Pablo
Pujals Santana,
   Joaquin (Semper)
   (Heraldo Español)
Pujals, Juan
Pujols, Rosa Lina
Pulliza, Eloy
Pulzoniz, Filomena
Purcell, Luis M.
Queipo, Maria
Quero, Maria
   Eustaquia
Quesada, Carmen
Quevedo Baez (de),
   Eloisa P.
Quevedo Baez, M.
   (Dr.)
Quevedo Pacheco,
   Joaquin (P.J.)
Quevedo Serrano,
   Manuel
Quevedo Suarez, Julio
Quevedo, Domingo
Quijana, Luis
Quijano Vda. de
   Lozano, Manuela
Quijano, Cruz
Quijano, Petra
Quile, Ceferina
Quiles, Macario
Quiles, Manuela
Quiñones (de),
   Enriqueta R.
Quiñones (de), Maria
   F.
Quiñones de Gil,
   Maria
Quiñones Porrata,
   Pedro
Quiñones Quiñones,
   Andres

Quiñones, Braulio
Quiñones, Candida
Quiñones, Claudio
Quiñones, Domingo
Quiñones, Eulalia
Quiñones, Francisco
Quiñones, Francisco
   P.
Quiñones, Gloria
Quiñones, Honorio
Quiñones, Idelfonsa
Quiñones, J. M. (Jr.)
Quiñones, Jesus
Quiñones, Josefa
Quiñones, Juan M.
Quiñones, Julio
Quiñones, Lola
Quiñones, Luis F.
Quiñones, M. D.
Quiñones, Marcelino
Quiñones, Maria
Quiñones, Olimpia
Quiñones, Pedro
Quiñones, Ramirez,
   Ernesto
Quiñones, Ramon
Quiñones, Rosalia
Quiñones, Sensepio
Quiñones, Teofilo
Quiñones, Vda. de E.,
   Maria de la Cruz
Quiñonez I, Julio
Quiñonez Vda. de
   Ybañez, Gregoria
Quiñonez, Analuisa
Quiñonez, Dominga
Quiñonez, Geronimo
Quiñonez, Josefa
Quiñonez, Juana
Quiñonez, Luis
Quiñonez, Martin
Quiñonez, Rosario
Quintana, Angel
Quintana, Emilio
Quintana, Maria
Quiros, Albertina
Quiros, Maria
Quiros, Victor M.
Quixano (Vda. de),
   Angeles D.
Quixano, Angeles
R., Francisco
R., Salvador
Rabel, Gregoria

Rabelo, Ines
Racco Torrecillas,
   Vicente
Rada de Tarazona,
   Salvadora
Rahola, Julia E.
Raida, E.
Raiel, Gregoria
Rainyer de Bolina,
   Fela
Raiza de Vera, Maria
   Ana
Raldiris, Luis M.
Ramallou, Juan
Rambolla, Pedro
Ramires, Pascuala
Ramires, Sotero
Ramirez Vda. de
   Zaragoza, Marcolina
Ramirez (de), Maria
Ramirez Brau,
   Enrique
Ramirez de Arellano
   (de), Carmen R.
Ramirez de Escudero,
   G.
Ramirez Torres,
   Antonio
Ramirez, Celso
Ramirez, Concepcion
Ramirez, Dolores
Ramirez, Eugenio
Ramirez, Francisco
Ramirez, Gabina
Ramirez, Guarionex
Ramirez, Isabel
Ramirez, Joaquin
Ramirez, Jose
Ramirez, Jose Antonio
Ramirez, Jose G.
Ramirez, Josefa
Ramirez, Juan (1)
Ramirez, Juan (2)
Ramirez, Leonor R.
Ramirez, Leopoldo
Ramirez, Maximiliano
Ramirez, Mercedes
Ramirez, Rafael (1)
Ramirez, Rafael (2)
Ramirez, Rafael (3)
Ramirez, Roberto
Ramirez, Rosa
Ramirez, S.
Ramirez, Sarah

Ramirez, Selina
Ramirez, Tomasa R.
Ramirez, Ysabel
Ramirez, Ynes
Ramon, A.
Ramon, Andres
Ramon, Armando
Ramon, Blanca Rosa
Ramon, J.
Ramon, Joaquin
Ramon, Juan (1)
Ramon, Juan (2)
Ramos (de), Maria R.
Ramos (de), Ricarda
L.
Ramos (Vda. de),
Mercedes G.
Ramos Cousain, J.
Ramos de Anaya, J.
(Jr.)
Ramos Gonzalez, A.
Ramos Perez, Tomas
Ramos, Anita
Ramos, Antonia (1)
Ramos, Antonia (2)
Ramos, Benita
Ramos, Carlos
Ramos, Carmen
Ramos, Casta
Ramos, Celia
Ramos, Dolores
Ramos, Emelia
Ramos, Emilio
Ramos, F.
Ramos, Felipe
Ramos, Francisca
Ramos, Gracia
Ramos, Guillermo
Ramos, Isabel
Ramos, Isabel Maria
Ramos, Jose (1)
Ramos, Jose (2)
Ramos, Josefa
Ramos, Leopoldo
Ramos, Manuel (1)
Ramos, Manuel (2)
Ramos, Maria
Ramos, Mercedes
Ramos, Nicolas
Ramos, Pablo
Ramos, Pedro
Ramos, Petra
Ramos, Providencia
Ramos, Ramon (1)

Ramos, Ramon (2)
Ramos, Romulo
Ramos, Rosario
Ramos, Rosenda
Rancano, Aquilino
Ranero, Georgina
Raso, Eufemia
Raso, Maxima
Rauschenplat, Celeste
Rauschenplat, Iraida
Rayer (de), Josefa R.
Ready Armstrong,
Juana
Real, Emilio
Real, Francisco
Real, Matias
Real, R.
Real, Romualdo
Reas, Carmen C.
Rechany Rodrigo, J.
M.
Redea y Nazario,
Manuel
Redondo (de), Maria
Lopez
Redondo, Gregorio
Reglero, R.
Regnero, Luis
Rego, Menolo
Rego, Vicente
Reichard, C. B.
Reichard, Maria
Reina, Juana
Reinosa, Maria
Rengel (de), Belen D.
Rengel (de), Georgina
Ll.
Rengel de Cabrera,
Maria
Rengel, Belen
Rengel, Carmen
Rengel, Isabel
Rengel, Luis
Rengel, Maria
Rengel, R. V.
Requena, Acacia
Requena, Edelmora
Requena, Eugenia
Requena, Juan
Requena, Maria
Requena, Mercedes
Requena, Rosa Luisa
Requena, Rosario
Requena de Alicea,

Antonia
Ressy, Ramon
Ressy, Rafaela
Reveron, Balbino
Revilla, Juan A.
Rexach de Ruiz,
Carmen
Rexach, Amparo
Rexach, Luis
Rexach, Sofia
Rey Cangas, Eugenio
Rey Cangas, Juanita
Rey de Jordan,
Candida
Rey, A.
Rey, Manuel
Reyes (de), Margarita
Reyes (de), Modesta
R.
Reyes (de), Nieves O.
Reyes (Vda. de), Juana
R.
Reyes Ayendez,
Estevan
Reyes Chieanes,
Eugenio
Reyes de Alvaro,
Rosario
Reyes Rivera, Rosa
Reyes Ruiz, Belen
Reyes Ruiz, Julia C.
Reyes, Arcadio
Reyes, Carmen
Reyes, Carmen M.
Reyes, Emilio
Reyes, Encarnacion
Reyes, Enrique
Reyes, Francisco
Reyes, J. P.
Reyes, Juana
Reyes, Julia (1)
Reyes, Julia (2)
Reyes, Julio
Reyes, Lucas
Reyes, Maria
Reyes, Pura
Reyes, Reynaldo
Reyes, Soyla
Reyne (de), Amelia F.
Reynosa Flores, Pedro
Rezquena, Dolores
Ribas, Carmen
Ribera, Antonio
Ribera, Juan

Ribera, Nemesis
Ribero, Maria
Riboh, Antonio
Ricard, Enrique A.
Richardson, E. V.
Rieckehoff (de), Ana S.
Rieckehoff, Adolfo
(C.E.)
Riera (de), Teresa G.
Riera, Eulogio
Rifas, Ana Maria
Rigio, Fermin
Ringel, Emilio (Lcdo.)
Rios (de), Ramona M.
Rios Ocaña, Domingo
Rios Ocaña, Guillermo
Rios Serpa, Juan
Rios, Gumersindo
Rios, Jose (1)
Rios, Jose (2)
Rios, Jose (3)
Rios, Maria
Rios, Maria L.
Rios, Prov.
Rios, Quintin
Rios, Rafael
Rios, Rosario
Ripor, Pablo
Riso, Juan
Rivas, Felicita
Rivas, Jose
Rivas, Manuel
Rivas, Manuel C.
Rivas, Nicolas
Rivera (de), Eduviges
J.
Rivera (de), Maria A.
Rivera (de), Ramona
C.
Rivera Baldonez,
Manuel
Rivera C.
Rivera Dalmau, Rafael
Rivera de Casals,
Cecilia
Rivera de Castro,
Maria
Rivera de Gelpi, G.
Rivera de Quiñones,
Leonor
Rivera Martinez,
Arcadio
Rivera Martinez, P.
Rivera Nader, Juan

Rivera Santiago, Juan
Rivera Santo, E.
Rivera, --
Rivera, Adolfo
Rivera, Alejandrina
Rivera, Amalio (1)
Rivera, Amalio (2)
Rivera, Angel
Rivera, Angela (1)
Rivera, Angela (2)
Rivera, Angela (3)
Rivera, Antero
Rivera, Antonio
Rivera, Artura
Rivera, Belen S.
Rivera, Carlota
Rivera, Carmelo
Rivera, Carmen (1)
Rivera, Carmen (2)
Rivera, Carmen G.
Rivera, Catalino
Rivera, Ceferino
Rivera, Celestino
Rivera, Celia
Rivera, Cosme
Rivera, Cristobal
Rivera, Cruz (1)
Rivera, Cruz (2)
Rivera, Diosconvide
Rivera, Dolores
Rivera, Emiliano
Rivera, Estefania
Rivera, Felix
Rivera, Francisca
Rivera, Francisco (1)
Rivera, Francisco (2)
Rivera, Francisco (3)
Rivera, Georgina
Rivera, Gertrudis
Rivera, Gregorio
Rivera, H. R.
Rivera, Higinia
Rivera, Isaac
Rivera, Isabelino
Rivera, Jaime
Rivera, Jorge
Rivera, Jose
Rivera, Jose M.
Rivera, Josefa (1)
Rivera, Josefa (2)
Rivera, Juan
Rivera, Juanita
Rivera, Julia (1)
Rivera, Julia (2)

Rivera, Julio
Rivera, Justino
Rivera, Luis (1)
Rivera, Luis (2)
Rivera, Luisa D.
Rivera, Manuela
Rivera, Margarita
Rivera, Maria (1)
Rivera, Maria (2)
Rivera, Maria (3)
Rivera, Maria (4)
Rivera, Maria Luisa
Rivera, Martina
Rivera, Miguel
Rivera, N.
Rivera, Norberta
Rivera, Octavio
Rivera, Paula
Rivera, Paulina
Rivera, Pedro (1)
Rivera, Pedro (2)
Rivera, Pedro (3)
Rivera, Rafael (1)
Rivera, Rafael (2)
Rivera, Rafael (3)
Rivera, Ramiro
Rivera, Ramona
Rivera, Ricarda
Rivera, Rita
Rivera, Rodulfo
Rivera, Rosa (1)
Rivera, Rosa (2)
Rivera, Salome
Rivera, Severo
Rivera, Tomasa
Rivera, Victoriana
Rivera, Zenaida
Riveras, Fruto
Riveras, Julio
Riveras, Maria
Riviera, Francisco
Robaina, Leoncio
Robas de Andreu,
  Paca
Roberto, Emma
Roble, Agustina
Robles, Anastasio
Robles, Carmen
Robles, Francisca
Robles, Manuel de
  Jesus
Roblez, Ramon
Roca de Roca, Juanita
Roca, Jose

Roca, Jose R.
Roca, Pepita
Rocafort Rosich, Jose
Rocafort, J.
Rocca (Vda. de),
  Martina C.
Rodena, Rafaela
Rodenas, Dolores
Rodrigues, Maria
Rodriguez (de),
  Carolina S.
Rodriguez (de), Maria
  C.
Rodriguez (de), Maria
  F.
Rodriguez (de), Maria
  Luisa P.
Rodriguez (de), Maria
  P.
Rodriguez (Vda. de),
  Esperanza
Rodriguez (Vda. de),
  Josefa
Rodriguez (Vda. de),
  Nieves B.
Rodriguez Aloy, J.
Rodriguez Arias, Jose
Rodriguez Castells,
  Americo
Rodriguez Cepero,
  Mariana
Rodriguez Cintron,
  Juan
Rodriguez Cruz, Diosa
Rodriguez de Cid,
  Juana M.
Rodriguez de Gracia,
  J. A.
Rodriguez de Jimenez,
  Aurea
Rodriguez de Velez,
  Agueda
Rodriguez Gonzalez,
  R.
Rodriguez Hidalgo,
  Jose
Rodriguez Jimenez,
  Jose
Rodriguez, Ricardo
  (Jr.)
Rodriguez Lopez, Julia
Rodriguez Martinez,
  Jose (C. de C.)
Rodriguez Puig, S.

Rodriguez R.,
  Francisco
Rodriguez Sanjurjo, J.
Rodriguez Suarez,
  Emiliano
Rodriguez Varela,
  Antonio
Rodriguez Vda. de
  Garcia, Carmen
Rodriguez Vera,
  Pepita
Rodriguez Vincenty,
  Cruz
Rodriguez y Compañía
  (Business)
Rodriguez Zaboada,
  Jose
Rodriguez, Adela
Rodriguez, Alejandro
Rodriguez, Alternio
Rodriguez, Amelia
Rodriguez, Ana M.
Rodriguez, Ana Maria
Rodriguez, Angel
Rodriguez, Antonio (1)
Rodriguez, Antonio (2)
Rodriguez, Aristides
Rodriguez, Arturo (1)
Rodriguez, Arturo (2)
Rodriguez, Aurora
Rodriguez, Blanca N.
Rodriguez, Carlos E.
Rodriguez, Carlos P.
Rodriguez, Carlota
Rodriguez, Carmen (1)
Rodriguez, Carmen (2)
Rodriguez, Carmen M.
Rodriguez, Castula
Rodriguez, Clotilde (1)
Rodriguez, Clotilde (2)
Rodriguez, Consuelo
Rodriguez, Cristina
Rodriguez, Dionisia
Rodriguez, Dominga
Rodriguez, Domingo
Rodriguez, Eduardo
Rodriguez, Elena
Rodriguez, Eloy
Rodriguez, Engracia
Rodriguez, Esperanza
Rodriguez, Esteban F.
Rodriguez, Felipe (1)
Rodriguez, Felipe (2)
Rodriguez, Feliz

Rodriguez, Felo
Rodriguez, Fermin
Rodriguez, Fernando
Rodriguez, Fidel
Rodriguez, Fortunato
Rodriguez, Francisca
Rodriguez, Francisco (1)
Rodriguez, Francisco (2)
Rodriguez, Francisco (3)
Rodriguez, Georgina
Rodriguez, Gregorio
Rodriguez, Guillermo
Rodriguez, Hipolito
Rodriguez, Inocencio
Rodriguez, Isabel
Rodriguez, Isidro (1)
Rodriguez, Isidro (2)
Rodriguez, Jesus
Rodriguez, Jose (1)
Rodriguez, Jose (2)
Rodriguez, Jose (3)
Rodriguez, Jose (4)
Rodriguez, Jose (5)
Rodriguez, Josefa
Rodriguez, Josefina
Rodriguez, Juan
Rodriguez, Juana (1)
Rodriguez, Juana (2)
Rodriguez, Juana (3)
Rodriguez, Juanita
Rodriguez, Julio
Rodriguez, Leocadia
Rodriguez, Leocadio
Rodriguez, Leoncio
Rodriguez, Leonor
Rodriguez, Leopoldo
Rodriguez, Lorenzo
Rodriguez, Luis G.
Rodriguez, Luis V.
Rodriguez, M.
Rodriguez, Manuel (1)
Rodriguez, Manuel (2)
Rodriguez, Manuel G.
Rodriguez, Manuela
Rodriguez, Maria (1)
Rodriguez, Maria (2)
Rodriguez, Maria (3)
Rodriguez, Maria (4)
Rodriguez, Maria Ana
Rodriguez, Mariano
Rodriguez, Mario

Rodriguez, Micaela
Rodriguez, Miguel (1)
Rodriguez, Miguel (2)
Rodriguez, Modesto (1)
Rodriguez, Modesto (2)
Rodriguez, Modesto C.
Rodriguez, Monsita
Rodriguez, Pedro M.
Rodriguez, Perfecto
Rodriguez, Pola
Rodriguez, Providencia (1)
Rodriguez, Providencia (2)
Rodriguez, Pura
Rodriguez, Rafael
Rodriguez, Rafaela
Rodriguez, Ramon (1)
Rodriguez, Ramon (2)
Rodriguez, Ramon (3)
Rodriguez, Ramon (4)
Rodriguez, Ricarda
Rodriguez, Ricardo (1)
Rodriguez, Ricardo (2)
Rodriguez, Romana
Rodriguez, Rosalia
Rodriguez, Rufino
Rodriguez, Sebastian
Rodriguez, Segundo
Rodriguez, Silverio
Rodriguez, Simplicio (1)
Rodriguez, Simplicio (2)
Rodriguez, Valentin
Rodriguez, Viola M.
Rodriguez, William
Rodriguez, Zenon
Roger (de), Rosario N.
Roger, Rafael
Roger, Rosario
Rojas de Mesa, Amparo
Rojas, Carmelo
Rojas, Emilia
Rojas, Francisco G.
Rojas, Jose
Rojas, Julio
Rojas, Manuel
Rojas, Petra
Rojas, Rafael
Roldan, Serafin

Rolon de Agosto, Juana
Rolon, Catalina
Rolon, Dionisio
Rolon, Juan
Rolon, Ramon
Roma, Francisco
Roman Pereira, Candida
Roman Pereira, Isabel
Roman Pereira, Jesus (1)
Roman Pereira, Jesus (2)
Roman Pereira, Rafael
Roman Pereira, Victor
Roman Rivera, Dolores
Roman Sosa, E.
Roman, Amparo
Roman, Anita
Roman, Bibiano
Roman, Brigida
Roman, Candida
Roman, Dolores
Roman, Eusebio
Roman, Gloria Maria
Roman, Guillermo
Roman, Jose
Roman, Juan
Roman, Julia
Roman, Marta
Roman, Moserrate
Roman, Rufo
Roman, Sixta
Romero (Vda. de), A. S.
Romero de Dorna, J. M.
Romero Vda. de Garabio, Julia
Romero, Antonio
Romero, Carmen
Romero, Carmen L.
Romero, Catalino
Romero, D. (Jr.)
Romero, Gabriel
Romero, Jose A.
Romero, Juan
Romero, Manuel
Romero, Petronila
Romeu, Rafael
Romf, Manuel F.
Rondon, Antonio

Rondon, Engracia
Rondon, Francisco
Rondon, Isidra
Rondon, Isidro
Rondon, Jose
Rondon, Manuel
Rondon, Marco
Rondon, Maria
Roque (de), Josefa G.
Roque, Arturo C.
Ros, Eligio
Ros, Santiago
Rosa de Villega, Leocadia
Rosa, Angel (1)
Rosa, Angel (2)
Rosa, Aurea
Rosa, Caralino
Rosa, Evervina
Rosa, J.
Rosa, Jesus
Rosa, Jose
Rosa, Pablo
Rosa, Pepito
Rosa, Ramon R.
Rosado de Nieves, Franco
Rosado de Villafañe, Juana
Rosado Villafañe, Francisco
Rosado, Antonio
Rosado, Carmen
Rosado, Felicita
Rosado, Fermin
Rosado, Joaquin
Rosado, Jose
Rosado, Juan (1)
Rosado, Juan (2)
Rosado, Panchita
Rosado, Rafael
Rosado, Regalada
Rosado, Roffo
Rosario Bel, Regina
Rosario Martinez, Luis
Rosario Ramos, J.
Rosario, Carmen
Rosario, Cornelia
Rosario, Cornelio
Rosario, Domingo
Rosario, Gabino
Rosario, Guadalupe
Rosario, Guillermo
Rosario, J. E.

Rosario, Jesus
Rosario, Jose
Rosario, Juan Jose
Rosario, Juana
Rosario, Luis
Rosario, Manolo
Rosario, Marcos
Rosario, Maria
Rosario, Matea
Rosario, Pedro
Rosario, Tula
Rosas, Providencia
Rosello, Candelario
Rosenfeld, Felix
Rossello (de), Carmen O.
Rossello (de), Filomena
Rossello, Antonio
Rossello, Carmen M.
Rossello, J.
Rossello, Rosa M.
Rossi, Iacobina
Roura de Cardi, Rusa
Roura, Margarita L.
Rouse, C.
Rovellat (de), Guadalupe R.
Rovira (de) Maria L.
Rovira, Cristina
Rubert C., Emo.
Rubert, Juana
Rubi, Rafaela
Rubin, Salbador
Rubio, Elisa
Rugito, Leonor
Ruiz Arnau (de), C. C.
Ruiz Cifre, Fernando
Ruiz de la Rosa, Miguel
Ruiz de Rosenfeld, Rosa Blanca
Ruiz Estasen, Gloria
Ruiz Manzano, Lorenzo
Ruiz Martinez, Dano
Ruiz Perez, Jose
Ruiz Perez, Juan
Ruiz Rexach, Josefina
Ruiz Soler (de), Ana
Ruiz Soler, J.
Ruiz, Benito C.
Ruiz, Carmen
Ruiz, Cristina

Ruiz, Elias
Ruiz, Emilia
Ruiz, Federico
Ruiz, Gregorio M.
Ruiz, Jose
Ruiz, Justino
Ruiz, Magdalena
Ruiz, Manuela
Ruiz, Margarita (1)
Ruiz, Margarita (2)
Ruiz, Maria E.
Ruiz, Mercedes
Ruiz, Pedro
Ruiz, Rafael
Ruiz, Raimunda
Rullan, P. Daniel ("Sup. en los PP Franciscanos")
Rus, Rafael
Ruzades, Benito
S. Z., Pablo
Sabat de Mendin, Martina
Sabat, Encarnacion
Sabater de Villamil, Jose
Sabater, Teresa
Sachew, C.
Sagastibelza, G.
Saino, Maria
Salamanca, Georgina
Salas (de), H.
Salas B., S.
Salas, Amado
Salas, Domingo
Salas, J.
Salas, Luis
Salas, Manuel A.
Salas, Maria
Salaza, Felix
Salazar (de), Aurora
Salcedo, Juan
Salcedo, Natividad
Salcedo, Teresa
Saldaña (de), Georgina C.
Saldaña Crosas, Anita
Saldaña de Goenaga, Josefina
Saldaña Torres, Rafael
Saldaña, B.
Saldaña, Francisca
Saldaña, Josefina
Saldaña, Maria Luisa

Saldaña, Petronina
Saldaña, Sixto
Sales de Borras, Marcola
Salgado Gonzalez, Jesus
Salgado Marquez, Carmen
Salgado Perez, Ricardo
Salgado, Antonia
Salgado, Ricardo
Salgado, Rufina
Salguero (de), Pilar L.
Salguero, Jose H.
Salicrup de Davila, Josefa
Salierujo, L. J.
Salotr (de), Ramona
Salva de Andreu, Concepcion
Salva, Juan
Salvador, Fortunato
Salvatella, Cristina
Salvatella, J. G.
Samaleu (Vda. de), Josefa I.
Sampher de Segura, Marta
San Antonio, Anibal
San Antonio, Baldomero
San Antonio, Maria de la Luz
San Juan, Arturo
Sanabria, Andreo
Sanabria, Mercedes
Sancenon, Tomasa
Sanches, Antonio
Sanches, Augusto
Sanches, Rafael
Sanches, Santos
Sanchez (de), Maria U. (Commissioned to collect signatures)
Sanchez Borges, Jose
Sanchez Cabrera, Rafael
Sanchez Morales (de), Maria A.
Sanchez Morales, F.
Sanchez Morales, S.
Sanchez Salazar, P.
Sanchez, A.

Sanchez, Adela
Sanchez, Adela
Sanchez, Antonia
Sanchez, Antonio
Sanchez, Artemia
Sanchez, Balbina
Sanchez, Candida
Sanchez, Emilio
Sanchez, Enriqueta
Sanchez, Felipa
Sanchez, Filomena
Sanchez, Francisco (1)
Sanchez, Francisco (2)
Sanchez, Georgina
Sanchez, H,
Sanchez, Jesus
Sanchez, Jose
Sanchez, Jose A.
Sanchez, Josefina
Sanchez, Luciano
Sanchez, Luis
Sanchez, Maria
Sanchez, Pedro (1)
Sanchez, Pedro (2)
Sanchez, R.
Sanchez, Rafael
Sanchez, Ramon (1)
Sanchez, Ramon (2)
Sanchez, Ramon (3)
Sanchez, Ramon Benito
Sanchez, Sebastiana
Sanchez, Tomas
Sanchez, Valentina
Sancto, Etanilao
Sandi, Placido
Sandoval, Gaspar
Sanjurjo, Juana
Sanllut, Benita
Sanse, Sinforosa
Santaella, Emilio
Santamaria, Pablo
Santana Nater, Francisco
Santana, Angelina
Santana, Elisa
Santana, Inocencia
Santana, Jose G.
Santana, Jose I. (Jr.)
Santana, Juan
Santana, Maria
Santana, Pepita
Santana, Rosa
Santi, Anselmo

Santiago (de), Mercedes E.
Santiago Andujar, Simplicio
Santiago M., Artemia
Santiago, Andres
Santiago, Antonio
Santiago, Aurelia
Santiago, Catalino
Santiago, Elviro
Santiago, Feliz
Santiago, Gonzalo
Santiago, Ignacia
Santiago, Isabel
Santiago, Jose
Santiago, Jose Pl.
Santiago, Luisa (1)
Santiago, Luisa (2)
Santiago, Maria (1)
Santiago, Maria (2)
Santiago, Maria (3)
Santiago, Modesto
Santiago, Monica
Santiago, Pablo
Santiago, Pelegin
Santiago, Ramona
Santiago, Rosendo C.
Santiago, Toribio
Santiesteban, Margarita
Santisteban, Cesareo
Santisteban, Jose
Santisteban, Millan
Santoni, Amanda
Santoni, Ines
Santos Alcaya, Luis
Santos Gandia, Maria
Santos, A. B. R.
Santos, Altagracia
Santos, Armanda
Santos, Emilia
Santos, Francisco J.
Santos, Hilario
Santos, Jose
Santos, Luis
Santos, Margarita
Santos, Maria (1)
Santos, Matia (2)
Santos, Mercedes
Santos, Pedro
Santos, Rafaela
Santos, Raimunda
Santos, Remigia
Santos, Santiago

Santos, Santo
Santos, Venceslada
Sardos, Joaquina
Sarmiento, Amalia
Sarmiento, Antonio
Sarmiento, B. P.
Sarmiento, Maria
Sarraga, Maria Teresa
Sastre, Epifanio
Sato, Guiyermo
Sauri, Antonio
Savino, M.
Schettini (Vda. de), Elena P.
Schettunf, Rada
Schlüter (de), Elena C.
Schlüter (de), Margarita B.
Schlüter, Luisa Elena
Schomburg (de), Dolores L.
Schomburg, Ar.
Schröder, Enrique J.
Se--, Arturo
Seaton, Henry
Sedano, Dolores F.
Segarra, Lucia
Segnet Figueroa, Josefina
Segñet, Carmen
Segñet, Encarnacion
Segui Mercado, Tula
Segui, Generosa
Segundo, Ceferino
Segura de Fraile, Belen
Segura, Gabriel (Jr.)
Segura, Antonio
Segura, Catalina
Segura, Gabriel (1)
Segura, Gabriel (2)
Segura, Gonzalo
Segura, Rafael
Seijo (de), Isabel P.
Selles, Aquilina
Seoane Arranguis, Luis
Seoane, Antonia
Sepia, Ramon
Sepulbedas, Jose R.
Serbia, Celina
Serra, Francisco
Serra, Marcelino
Serra, O. O.

Serralina, Emilia
Serralta, Manuel
Serrano Carrion, Manuel
Serrano, Adrian
Serrano, Balsina
Serrano, Carmen
Serrano, Cruz
Serrano, Isidro
Serrano, Jose
Serrano, Juan
Servero, Juan
Setty Riveras, Segundo
Severo, L. Luisa
Sevilla, Feliciano
Sevillano, Juan P.
Sevillano, Ysabel
Seyban, M.
Shine (Vda. de), Juanita B.
Siaca Pacheco (de), Carmen G.
Siaca Pacheco, Maria Providencia
Sicardo, Alicia
Sicardo, Ana Maria
Sicardo, Juan
Sicardo, Lola
Sicardo, Rosa
Sierra (de), Angela C.
Sierra B., Enriqueta
Sierra B., Saturnino
Sierra, Clotilde
Sierra, Concepcion
Sierra, Conrado
Sierra, Gertrudis
Sierra, Higinio
Sierra, Jose I.
Sierra, Manuel
Sierra, Pedro
Sierra, Saturnino
Sierrabastra, Arturo
Sifeli, Jose
Sifre (de), Belen D.
Sifre (de), Eulalia L.
Sifre Lajora, Rafael
Sifre, Belen
Silva (de), Aralis U.
Silva de Ballesteros, Felicia
Silva de Font, Lucila
Silva de Zayas, Maria
Silva, Alejandrina

Silva, Carmen
Silva, Carolina
Silva, Celia E.
Silva, Claudio
Silva, Concepcion
Silva, Eliodoro
Silva, Jose C.
Silva, Pepiña
Silvero, Celestino
Sippitt, W.O.
Sirron, Jose S.
Slenson, E.
Slenson, R.
Slenson, W.
Smith, Andres
Snare, Luis
Sobrinos de Portella
Sojo (de), Maria P.
Sojo, Catalina
Sola, Jose
Sola, Juan
Solano, Roman
Solar, Enriqueta
Soldevila, Ismael
Soler (de), Matilde M.
Soler de Diaz, Maria
Soler Lacroix, Francisco
Soler Vda. de G. de Quevedo, Ynes
Soler, Carlos M.
Soler, Clotilde
Solis, Julio
Sollee, Gregorio
Solomon, A.
Solomon, Alfredo (1)
Solomon, Alfredo (2)
Solomon, Guillermino
Solomon, Isabel
Solomon, Rosario
Solomon, Stella
Soltero, Mariano
Soriano, Carmen
Sosa (de), Carmen B.
Sosa, Carmen
Sosa, Daniel
Sosa, Eloisa
Sosa, Tomasa
Sostre, Nicolas
Sotelo de Cordero, Petronila
Sotero, Andres
Soto (Vda. de), Paca
Soto de Guzman,

Antonio's Grace

Carmen
Soto Giker, N.
Soto, Herminia
Soto, Isabela
Soto, Jose A.
Soto, Jose C.
Soto, Juan B.
Soto, Maria
Soto, Maria Elena
Soto, Maria V.
Soto, Rafael
Sotomayor, Gregoria
Sotomayor, Juan M.
Sotomayor, Juana
Sotomayor, Justo
Sotomayor, Lesone
Sotomayor, Ramon
Sotos, Jorge
Souffront, Arturo
Souxa Gez, J. L.
Souza, Antonio
Souza, Victoria
Spear, Jose C.
Spech, Pedro
Steffens, Dora
Sterling, Aurelio
Sterling, Teodosio
Suares, Filomena
Suares, Maria
  Magdalena
Suarez (de), Maria
Suarez (Vda. de),
  Mercedes F.
Suarez Anturrany, C.
Suarez Carrion, Emilio
Suarez Maldonado,
  Carmen
Suarez, A.
Suarez, Benito
Suarez, Felix
Suarez, Francisco
Suarez, Gil
Suarez, Jose (1)
Suarez, Jose (2)
Suarez, Manolo
Suarez, Manuel
Suarez, Maria (1)
Suarez, Maria (2)
Suarez, Maria (3)
Suarez, Maria Ana
Suarez, Rodriguez E.
Suarez, Teresa
Sulsona, Estela
Sulsona, Herminio

Sunbario, Abraham
Surilla Reyes, Jose
Tabernas, Angela
Tabernas, Asuncion
Tachey, N.
Tapia, Jose
Tarazona, Ana
Tavarez de Storer,
  Elisa
Teijeiro (de), Celina F.
Teijeiro, Julio
Teijeiro, Luis
Teijeiro, Rafael
Tejada, Teresa
Tejares, Ceferino
Terran, A.
Texidor (de), Nicolasa
  G.
Texidor, Jacinto
Thompson, Jose
Timothee (de),
  Rosario A.
Timothee, Carlos E.
Timothee, Pedro C.
Timothee, Rafael
Tingle, O.
Tirado, Aguedo
Tirado, Alberto
Tirado, Filo
Tirado, Maria
Tirado, Paulino
Tirado, Serafina
Tirador, Teresa
Tiya de Garcia, Lula
Tizol, Ana
Tizol, Asuncion
Tizol, Carmen
Tizol, Felipa
Tizol, Manuela
Tizol, Sra.
Toderi (de),
  Guadalupe F.
Tofe (de), Donnina D.
Tofe Gomez, Eduviges
Tomas, Enrique
Tomas, Lucia
Tomas, Marcos
Toraño, S.
Tormos (de),
  Concepcion B.
Toro (de), M. N.
Toro (de), Matilde G.
Toro (de), Olimpa
Toro Santiago, I.

Toro, Francisco
Toro, Julia
Toro, Manuela
Toro, Rafael
Torre Ruiz, Micaela
Torrecillas de Cuevas,
  Amelia
Torrecillas, America
Torrecillas, Maria
Torres (de), Carlota R.
Torres (de), Felicita A.
Torres (Vda. de),
  Genoveva G.
Torres Bargas, Josefa
Torres de Martinez,
  Maria L.
Torres Lopez, Jose
Torres Monge,
  Ernesto
Torres Rique, Julia
Torres Rodriguez,
  Juan
Torres Vda. de
  Cabrera, Teresa
Torres y Rodriguez,
  Antonia
Torres, Amparo
Torres, Anastacio
Torres, Andres
Torres, Antonia
Torres, Antonio
Torres, Carlos (1)
Torres, Carlos (2)
Torres, Carmen
Torres, Domingo
Torres, Francisco (1)
Torres, Francisco (2)
Torres, Geronimo
Torres, Hilarita
Torres, Ines
Torres, Isabel
Torres, Jesus (1)
Torres, Jesus (2)
Torres, Joaquin
Torres, Jose (1)
Torres, Jose (2)
Torres, Jose V.
Torres, Juan (1)
Torres, Juan (2)
Torres, Juan V.
Torres, Juana (1)
Torres, Juana (2)
Torres, Juanita
Torres, Julia C.

Torres, Leonalda
Torres, Manuel
Torres, Maria (1)
Torres, Maria (2)
Torres, Mercedes
Torres, Miguel A.
Torres, Paco
Torres, Pedro A.
Torres, Providencia
Torres, Rafael
Torres, Rafaela
Torres, Ramon
Torres, Rosamaria
Torres, Teresa
Torres, Victoria
Torrest Garcia, Mayra
Torrez, Jesuz
Toste Ero, Carlos
Toste, Isabel
Tozores, Manuel
Tralga, Calista
Trapaga (de), Emma
  C.
Trapaga (Vda. de),
  Juana I.
Trapaga de Loubriel,
  Sofia
Trapaga, Luisa
Trapaga, Manuela
Travieso (de), Elisa F.
Travieso, Luis F.
Travieso, Lydia Maria
Travieso, Maria
  Mercedes
Travieso, Sara Luisa
Trento, Susana
Triana, R. (Jr.)
Trias, Carmen
Trigo, F.
Trigo, Maria
Trigo, Paula
Trigo, Providencia
Trilla Quiñones,
  Josefa
Tristany, Ursula
Troche, Bartolo
Trujillo Gual, Heraclio
Trujillo Nuñez,
  Matilde
Trujillo, A.
Trujillo, Araceli
Trujillo, Dionicio
Trujillo, Elisa
Trujillo, Francisca

265

Ventura, Euridio
Vera Riera, Isabel
Vera, Jose
Vera, Miguel
Vergara, Isabel
Verges, Eduvigis
Verges, Eleuteria
Verges, Maria
Verlales, Gumersindo
Veve Colon, Luis
Veve, Rafael
Veve, Santiago
Viaeler Hernandez, Lola
Vias, Catalina
Vicente, Adela
Vicente, Angelina
Vicente, Carmen
Vicente, Melina
Vicents, Crisina
Vidal (de), Asuncion M.
Vidal (de), Juana R.
Vidal de Freiria, Amparo
Vidal, Aurea
Vidal, E.
Vidal, Guillermo
Vidal, Joaquin
Vidal, Maria
Vidal, Miguel
Vidal, Secundino
Vidott, Domingo
Viera, Bernarda
Viera, Felix
Viera, Feliz
Viera, Juana
Vige, Luis
Vila, Angel
Vila, Berta
Vila, Luis
Viladesan, J.
Vilalta, Juan
Vilar Gimenez, Pedro
Vilar, Rafaela
Vilar, Ramona
Vilaseca, Leo
Villa, Juan
Villafana, Emeteria
Villafañe y Rosado, Jose
Villafañe, Antonio
Villafañe, Cruz
Villafañe, Dionicia

Villafañe, Eliseo
Villafañe, Juan Maria
Villafañe, Maria
Villalba, Santiago
Villalta de J. E., Altagracia
Villamil, D.
Villamil, Eustaquio (1)
Villamil, Eustaquio (2)
Villamil, Joaquin
Villamil, Rita
Villanueva Vda. de Aymerich, Providencia
Villanueva, Ceferina
Villanueva, Crispin (1)
Villanueva, Crispin (2)
Villanueva, Everisto
Villanueva, Gregoria
Villanueva, Teresita
Villanueva, Victoriana
Villar, Paulino
Villarini, Juanita
Villariny (de), Josefa L.
Villariny, Angel E.
Villariny, Maria
Villavega, Jose (Der.)
Villaverde (de), Rosa G.
Villega, Carmen
Villegas, Genaro
Villegas, Juana
Villodas (Vda. de), Matilde L. N.
Villodas Lugo-Viña, Andrea
Villodas Lugo-Viña, Caridad
Viña, Pilar
Viñals, Concepcion L.
Viñas Rivera, Ramona
Viñas, F.
Viñas, J.
Viner, Antonia
Vista, Octavio
Vivas, J.
Vizcarrondo, Alfonso
Vizcarrondo, Aurora
Vizcarrondo, Barbarita
Vizcarrondo, Elena
Vizcarrondo, Juanito
Vizcarrondo, Luis
Vizcarrondo, Paulino

Vizcarrondo, Ursula
Von del Valle, Guillermo
Vrader, Jose Blanco
Vricet, Juan
Walderrama, Natalio
Walters, Justo
Warren (de), Angela S.
Wheat, A.
White, Cora
White, Ed.
Woodrow, S. M. (Mrs.)
Woods (de), Amelia P.
Woods, E.
Woods, Juanito
Ybañez Vda. de Garmendia, Amalia
Ybañez Vda. de Nadal, Magdalena
Ybañez, Tomasa
Yeco. P.
Yeguirva, Juan
Yetir, Inocencio
Ygaravides, Jose
Ygaravidez Freytes, Eufrasia
Ygaravidez, Fr.
Ygaravidez, Octavia
Yglesias, Julio
Yglesias, Maria
Yglesias, Mario
Yglesias, Ramon
Yiter, Madison
Ysturiz, Maria
Yuclan, Serafin
Yzaguirre, Eduardo
Zabala, Alfredo
Zaldirondo, Benito
Zanes, Ernesto
Zanso, Jose (1)
Zanso, Jose (2)
Zanso, Rosa
Zapata, Dolores
Zapater, Jose
Zapater, Valero
Zar, Florencia
Zaragoza, Clara
Zaragoza, Emilia
Zayas, Bernalda
Zayas, Rosa
Zeno, Carlos
Zorrilla, Feliz

. . .

San Sebastian

Damas de San Sebastian (Ladies of San Sebastian)

Alonso de Ferrer, Julia
Ballester, Ricarda
Cardona, Generosa
Cardona, Julia
Crespo, America
Crespo, Estrella
Cuevas, Juana
De Victoria, Adela L.
Del Toro, Maria A.
Feliciano, Justina
Gonzalez, Eulalia
Gonzalez, Josefina
Gonzalez, Maria
Guzman de Torres, Paula
Jimenez, America
Jimenez, Diega
Jimenez, Julia D.
Laborde de Perez, Franca
Mendez, Eladia
Mercado, Ana
Mercado, Angela
Montano, Dolores
Morales de Cardona, Herminia
Nieve Feliciano, Maria
Perez de Nieves, Pepita
Perez de Vera, Maria L.
Polidura, Amelia
Polidura, Paca
Quiñonez, Julia
Rodriguez, Hermenejilda
Roman de Santiago, Josefa
Rosa, Virginia
Rubio, Josefa
Sanchez de S., Damasa
Sanchez, Eugenia
Sotomayor de L., Bentura
Torres de Polidura, Juana

Torres de Rosa, Francisca
Torres, Leonor
Torres, Rita

San Sebastian/ Patillas Citizens

Amy Ramu, Enrique (Substitute President)
Diaz, Felix
Gaya, M.
Merle, Jose G.
Picon, Francisco (President)
Ricci, Alberto
Rios, Alberto
Rivera, Jose G.
Stella, Luciano
Villariny, Juan C.

Santa Isabel

Santa Isabel Municipal Council

Fontanes, Heriberto B. (Secretary)
Rodriguez, Manuel Nestor (Mayor)

Santa Isabel Citizens

Alarotta Lianza, Rosita
Alonso, Awilda
Alvalle, Manuel
Alvarez Burgos, Gino
Alvarez, Maria
Alvarez, Matea
Andrades, Aquilina
Anis, Mauricio
Anselmi (de), Carmen R.
Aponte, Pedro Tomas
Arcelay, Carmen Maria
Arroyo, Antonio

Arroyo, Nicolas
Battini, Eugenia
Belpre (de), Carmen P.
Belpre, Epifania
Belpre, Gloria Dolores
Belpre, Leoncio
Benjamin, Hortensia
Benjamin, Josefa
Bernal de Homs, Maria
Bernal, Dolores
Bernal, Herminia
Blaimayard, Jaime
Blanco, Fortunato
Blanco, Juan J.
Blanco, Maria Jesus
Blanco, Palmira
Cabinero, Consuelo
Canevaro, A.
Canevaro, Julio
Cintron, Alejandro
Clara, Tomas
Colon Espada, Agustini
Colon, Braulio
Colon, Carmen
Colon, Ezequiela
Coma, Pedro (J.M.)
Cordero Lopez, Francisco
Cordero, Victor
Coto, Agapito
Cruz Perez, Manuel
Cruz, Cosme
Cruz, Damaso
Cruz, Felipe
Cruz, Luis
De Carlo, Rosa B.
De la Rosa, Livia B.
Delfin, Estevan
Deliz, Ramon
Diaz, Adelaida
Diaz, Florentina
Espada, Federico
Esteves, Saturnina
Florinzano, Juan
Franceschi, Thomas
Gonzalez, Magdalena
Gonzalez, Manuel
Guzman, F. S.
Ildefonso, Jose Maria
Laboy, Aquilino
Lantanes, Heriberto J.
Marty, Bibiano

Matta, Candida D.
Mercado, Enrique
Miranda, Celedonio
Monserrate (de), Maria R.
Monserrate, Angel
Monserrate, Manuel M.
Moredo Vda. de Rivera, Guadalupe
Moredo, Baudilia
Moreno, Vidal
Moro, Manuel
Ortiz, Juana
Pacheco y Robert, Rafael
Perez Elias, Juan
Perez Elias, Ramon
Perez Elias, Vicente
Perez, Jose J.
Perez, Manuel
Ramos Perez, Juan
Rivera (de), Valentina R.
Rivera, Adriano
Rivera, Alejandrina
Rivera, Consuelo
Rivera, Isabel
Rivera, Jose Santiago
Rivera, Milagros
Rivera, Monserrate
Riveras, Julio
Rodriguez (de), Juana R.
Rodriguez, Juanito
Rodriguez, Manuel Nestor
Rodriguez, Manuel R.
Roman Fontanez, Anselmo
Romero, Rafael
Rosado, Saturno
Sanchez, Aniceto
Santiago (de), Elena M.
Santiago, Andrea
Santiago, Francisca
Santiago, Maria
Santiago, Ramon
Santiago, Victoria
Sapi, Heliodora
Sierra (de), Ricarda S.
Sierra, Analibia
Sierra, Celia

Sierra, Margot
Sierra, Martin
Sierra, Ricarda
Suarez, Mercedes O.
Tejeras, Juan
Torres (Vda. de), Rosalia
Torres, Angel B.
Torres, Pedro
Torres, Reyes
Valdejuly, Juan
Vega, Luis
Zambrana, Ernesto
Zambrana, Esperanza
Zayas, Delfina
Zurita, Antonio

Toa Alta

Toa Alta Mayor

Velilla, Manuel

Toa Alta Citizens

Alfaro, Domitila
Archilla, Lidia
Archilla, Luz Ester
Archilla, Matilde
Burgos, Agustina
Cabrera de Miranda, Lucila
Cabrera, Francisca
Cabrera, Manuela
Cabrera, Mercedes
Cabrera, Providencia
Calranes, Rita
Cintron, Ana
Cintron, Sandra
Colon (de), Isabel J.
Cosme, Flora
De Jimenez, Josefina M.
Del Valle Vda. de Lopes, Rudesonda
Diaz (de), Mercedes
Diaz, Adelina
Diaz, Maria
Ducret, Georgina
Ducret, Luisa
Fernandez, Maria Lina
Ferrer de O., Carlota

Galvarin, Calista
Garcia, Mercedes
Garciandia, Pura
Genen, Eloisa
Gonzalez Nieves, Ramona
Guardiola, Candelaria
Jordan, Carmen
Lopez (de), Matilde C.
Lopez, Angela
Marrero, Francisca
Marrero, Rita
Martin, Carmen
Martin, Emilia
Martinez, Cornelia
Martinez, Maria J.
Matos, Herminia
Mayol, Catalina
Monclova (de), Dolores O.
Morales, Benilde
Morales, Carmen
Morales, Carola
Morales, Elisa
Morales, Maria Esther
Morales, Mercedes
Morales, Providencia
Nevarez, Maria
Nevarez, Rafaela
Nieves, Angelita
Nieves, Dominga
Nieves, Maria
Nieves, Tomasa Maria
Ortega, Marcelina
Otero, Carmen
Perez (de), Amparo N.
Perez Correa, Agustina
Perez de Colon, Saturna
Perez de Limo, Carmen
Perez Hernandez, Emilia
Perez Rios, Agustina
Perez-Claudio, Isolina
Perez-Guerra (de), Isolina N.
Perez, Emilia
Perez, Felisa
Perez, Josefa
Perez, Manuela
Perez, Maria
Perez, Nicomedes
Pesante (de),

Mercedes
Quintero, Angela
Quintero, Candelaria
Ramirez de Vick, Ana L.
Rios Perez, Agripina
Roca Luisa
Rodriguez, Adela
Rodriguez, Evarista
Romero, Josefa
Rosarios, Josefina
Rosendo, Rosario
Salgado, Carmen
Salgado, Isabel
Salgado, Milagros
Santiago, Mercedes
Silva, Josefa
Sotelo de Nieves, Ceferina
Valentin, Josefa
Vazquez, Carmen
Velilla, Josefa
Villafaña, Manuela

Trujillo Alto

Trujillo Alto Mayor

Valcarcel, Andres (Mayor)

Trujillo Alto Citizens

Adorno, Carmela
Adorno, Eusebia
Adorno, Felicita
Adorno, Florentino
Adorno, Ignacio
Adorno, Mariano
Adorno, Narcisa
Adorno, Segunda
Betancourt, Nazaria
Caraballo, Cayetano
Caraballo, Elisa
Caraballo, Juana
Castro, Genaro
Cruz Olmo, Justo
Cruz, Justo
Cruz, Vicente
Diaz de Diaz, Rosario

Diaz de Garcia, Eugenia
Diaz Monge, Domingo
Diaz Monge, Jose
Diaz, Lorenzo
Diaz, Valentin
Diaz, Ventura
Gonzalez, Alberto
Gonzalez, Emilio
Hernandez de Diaz, Carmen
Ildefonso, Hipolita
Jumillo de Viera, Catalina
Marquez, Pedro
Martinez, Alfonsa
Martinez, Leonor
Martinez, Pascasia
Morales, Lucia
Ocasio, Esteban
Olmo, Gavina
Ortiz, Ricardo
Pacheco de Diaz, Inocencia
Pacheco de Diaz, Romana
Pacheco de Martinez, Leonor
Pacheco, Eleuterio
Pacheco, Lorena
Pacheco, Maria
Quilino, Emiliana
Quilino, Maria
Rivera, Juana (1)
Rivera, Juana (2)
Rivera, Pedrona
Rodriguez de Diaz, Felipa
Sandoval, Felicita
Viera, Narcisa
Viera, Pedro

Vieques

Vieques Municipal Council

Blurdez, Juan A. (Secretary)
Bonnet, Luis Amedee (Mayor)

Marin, Miguel
Martinez, Alfonso
McFarline, Jose (Substitute President)
Robles, Juan Francisco
Villafañe, Rafael

Yauco

Yauco Municipal Council

Antommattei, J. (Mayor)
Franceschi, Andres (Councilmember)
Mejia, Rafael (Councilmember)
Olivari M., Pedro (Councilmember)
Olivera, Crispulo (Councilmember)
Troche, Manuel (Secretary)
Vicario, Manuel (President)
Villeneuve, Santiago (Councilmember)

Ladies of Yauco

Agostini, Julia
Agostini, Maria E.
Amill (de), Luisa R.
Amill (de), Lulu G.
Anglada, Cariucu M.
Anziani, Maria A.
Barletta (de), Endosina
Bartolome, Dolores
Benavente de Ramirez, Amparo
Borras, Josefa
Brigantti (de), Carmen N.
Brigantti (de), Rosa L.
Brigantti, Sabbina
Castañer (de), Rosario M.
Commins, Araceli

Cros, Maria
Cueto, Malin
Cuto (Vda. de),
  Antonia M.
De Jesus, M. Higinia
Diaz, Delfina
Feliciano, Virginia
Figueroa, Rogelia
Franceschi (de), Elena
  F.
Francheschi (de), Rosa
  R.
Fuentes (de), Adelaida
Fuentes (de), Hanita
  R.
Grillasca (de),
  Concepcion
Harrington, Ana
Hernandez y Diaz,
  Justa
Irizarry, Eulalia
Lacroix, Hortensia

Lacroix, Teresa
Llinas (de),
  Magdalena M.
Lluci Vda. de Carli,
  Amelia
Maldonado, Maria C.
Marianis Garcia,
  Lolita
Medina, Dolores
Medina, Juanita
Mejia, Rosa E.
Melendes, Mayila
Melendez, Damasa
Mercado, Juana
Milan, Ester L.
Molini, Ana Laura
Morales, Josefina
Morales, Nereida
Morsomma Gutierrez,
  M.
Negroni, Cesaria C.
Nidert (de), Pura L.

Nigaglioni, America
Nigaglioni, Angelina
Nigaglioni, Hercilia
Nigaglioni, Josefina
Nigaglioni, Magdalena
Olivari (de), C. P.
Olivari de Martinez,
  Malin
Oliveras, Angelina
Olivieri, Elois
Olivieri, Felicita
Ortiz, Justa
Picaiso, Amelia
Pieraldi y Pieraldi,
  Ursula
Pieraldi, Maria
  Antonia
Pieraldi, Mercedes
Pieraldi, Ursula
Pietri, Nuncia
Pla de Olivari, Bianca
Pla, America

Quiñones, Palmira
Rexach de Paz, Maria
  Esther
Rodriguez, Ana L.
Rodriguez, Angela
Rodriguez, Teresa
Ruiz de Molina,
  Monserrate
Santoni, Adela
Serra, Laura Maria
Silva, Juana Josefa
Siurano, Otilia
Solis (Vds de), Balbina
Torre, Eugenia
Velez, Esther
Vicens, Anita
Vivaldi (de), Antonia
  B.

.

Index

About the Author

Yasmin Tirado-Chiodini is an attorney and family historian. She is a former U.S. Space Shuttle engineer and adjunct professor of legal ethics and negotiations for the Executive M.B.A. program at Rollins College, Crummer Graduate School of Business in Winter Park, Florida. She is the author of *Antonio's Will* (Book 1 of The Antonio's Series), a historical novel telling the story of injustice of the first Hispanic executed in the electric chair in the United States, and the nonfiction companion book, *Antonio's Grace* (Book 2). She has also authored the nonfiction book *Does Your Compass Work? A Legal Guide for Florida Businesses*. She practices business law, is a speaker, blogger, and frequently publishes in various media. She lives in Florida with her husband, daughter and their rescued Labradors.

For more information:

Visit the author's website and join her Advanced Reader Group at:
http://www.Tirado-Chiodini.com

Visit her books' websites at:
http://www.AntoniosWill.com
http://www.AntoniosGrace.com
http://www.DoesYourCompassWork.com

Follow her on Facebook at:
http://www.facebook.com/Yasmin.Tirado.Chiodini.Author

Subscribe to her blog at: *https://TiradoChiodini.wordpress.com*

Contact her directly via e-mail at: *Yasmin@Tirado-Chiodini.com*

Reader's Notes

www.ingramcontent.com/pod-product-compliance
Lightning Source LLC
Chambersburg PA
CBHW030913090426
42737CB00007B/176